DAVID MARTYN LLOYD-JONES

The Fight of Faith
1939–1981

DAVID MARTYN
LLOYD-JONES

The Fight of Faith 1939–1981

Iain H. Murray

THE BANNER OF TRUTH TRUST

THE BANNER OF TRUTH TRUST
3 Murrayfield Road, Edinburgh EH12 6EL
PO Box 621, Carlisle, Pennsylvania 17013, USA

*

© Iain H. Murray 1990
First published 1990
Reprinted 1990
ISBN 0 85151 564 9

*

Typeset in 10 on 12pt Linotron Sabon
at The Spartan Press Ltd, Lymington, Hants
Printed in Great Britain by
Dotesios Printers Limited, Trowbridge
and bound by
Hunter & Foulis Limited, Edinburgh

FOR THE ONCOMING GENERATIONS
WHO WILL PREACH
THE GLORIOUS GOSPEL OF CHRIST.

Contents

Contents

Abbreviations

Romans, vols 1–8	The full titles for these volumes by D. M. Lloyd-Jones are given on p. 801. It should be noted that the volume numbers do not correspond to the chapter divisions of these Epistles.
Ephesians, vols. 1–8	

Sermon on the Mount, vols. 1 and 2   *Studies in the Sermon on the Mount*, D. M. Lloyd-Jones (London: IVF), 1959, 1960

Preaching   *Preaching and Preachers*, D. M. Lloyd-Jones (London: Hodder & Stoughton), 1971

Puritans   *The Puritans: Their Origins and Successors: Addresses Delivered at the Puritan and Westminster Conferences, 1959–1978*, D. M. Lloyd-Jones (Edinburgh: Banner of Truth Trust), 1987

Knowing the Times   *Knowing the Times: Addresses Delivered on Various Occasions, 1942–1977*, D. M. Lloyd-Jones (Edinburgh: Banner of Truth Trust), 1989

WR   *Westminster Record* (published monthly at Westminster Chapel)

vol. 1   *David Martyn Lloyd-Jones: The First Forty Years 1899–1939*, Iain H. Murray (Edinburgh: Banner of Truth Trust), 1982

Illustrations

Biographical Table

As Martyn Lloyd-Jones was born at the very end of the last century (Dec 20, 1899) his age virtually coincided with the years of the twentieth century.

1939	Sept. 3	Second World War begins the day before ML-J was to be formally inducted as co-pastor of Westminster Chapel.
	Dec.	Reunited with family at the new home at Haslemere.
		First book of sermons, *Why Does God Allow War?*
1940–41		Westminster Chapel struggling to survive the effects of evacuation and bombing.
1941	July 7–10	Policy Conference of IVF leaders at Kingham Hill School.
		A Ministers' Fraternal begins at Westminster Chapel.
1942	May 5	'Bible Witness Rally', St Andrew's Hall, Glasgow.
1943	Aug.	Retirement of Dr Campbell Morgan from Westminster Chapel.
	Nov.	Removal from Haslemere to Colebrooke Ave., Ealing.
1944	June 18	Destruction of Guards Chapel, Westminster.
1945	Jan. 15	Formal opening of the Evangelical Library in London.
	July	Removal to Mount Park Crescent, Ealing.
1946	Sept.	Visits Sweden.

1947	*July–Sept.*	Third visit to North America. Chairs first Conference of International Fellowship of Evangelical Students in Boston.
	Oct. 5	Starts Philippians series.
1948	*July–Aug.*	On the Continent.
	Oct. 3	Starts 1 John series.
	Nov. 30	First public lecture for the Evangelical Library, 'Isaac Watts and Hymnody in Worship'.
1949	*Summer*	'A real turning point'.
	Sept.	First Inter-Varsity Conference in Wales (Borth). School of Theology and Second General Committee of IFES at Cambridge.
1950	*Oct. 1*	Starts Sermon on the Mount series.
	Dec.	First 'Puritan Conference' at Westminster Chapel.
1952	*Apr. 27*	Starts John 17 series. At Swanwick for IVF and at Darmstadt, Germany, for IFES.
1953	*March*	Attacked in the *British Weekly* on the publication of his IVF address, 'Maintaining the Evangelical Faith Today'.
	Summer	Monti-Locarno, Switzerland, IFES.
1954	*Spring*	The Billy Graham Greater London Crusade.
	Oct. 3	Starts Ephesians series.
1955		Conferences of the Evangelical Movement of Wales.
	Oct. 7	Starts Romans series Friday nights.
1956	*July–Sept.*	United States, first visit to West Coast. IFES at Glen Orchard, Ontario.
1957		The Banner of Truth Trust founded.
	Aug.	On the Continent, L'Abri, Rome, etc.
1958	*May 10*	Opening of the new London Bible College building.
	Aug.	South Africa.
1959		*Studies in the Sermon on the Mount*, vol 1 (first major volume of expository sermons). Sermons on Revival at Westminster Chapel.

 ## Biographical Table

1959	*Aug.*	Paris, IFES.
	Sept.	21st Anniversary at Westminster Chapel.
1961	*Aug.*	In Greece.
	Oct. 24	Albert Hall Commemoration of the 350th anniversary of the Authorised Version.
1962		Tercentenary of Great Ejection of 1662.
	Oct. 7	Starts series on the Gospel of John.
1963	*June 11*	'Consider Your Ways', a crucial address to the Westminster Fellowship.
	July	Fifth visit to North America.
1964	*Aug.*	Outer Hebrides.
1965		Removal to Creffield Road, Ealing.
1966	*July–Aug.*	In Finland and Denmark.
	Oct. 18	'Evangelical Unity' appeal at the Evangelical Alliance Assembly of Evangelicals, London.
1967	*Feb.*	First issue of *The Evangelical Times*.
	April	Keele Congress; Anglican evangelicals announce a new policy.
		Westminster Chapel joins the British Evangelical Council and the FIEC.
	July–Aug.	Sixth visit to North America.
	Nov. 1	'Luther and His Message for Today', address at first major conference of the BEC.
	Nov. 15	Aberfan services on the first anniversary of the disaster.
1968	*March 1*	Illness suddenly closes his ministry at Westminster Chapel with his 372nd and last exposition of Romans.
	May 29	Decision to retire announced to deacons.
1969	*March 30*	'How to Safeguard the Future', last address at IVF Swanwick.
		Last visit to the United States, lectures on 'Preaching'.
1970	*May*	The publication of *Growing into Union: Proposals for Forming a United Church in England* ends the Puritan Conference.

1970 May   *Romans, Atonement and Justification*, publication of the first volume of the major series.

1971   Last visit to Continent and addresses for IFES, 'What is an Evangelical?'.
      Dec.   Westminster Conference replaces the Puritan Conference.

1972   *God's Way of Reconciliation*, first of the volumes in the Ephesians series.

1977 Feb. 6   At Sandfields, Aberavon, on the fiftieth anniversary of the start of his ministry.

1977 Oct. 6   Inaugural address for the London Theological Seminary.

1978 June   Last annual visit to the Conference of Welsh Evangelical Ministers at Bala.

1980 May–June   Last services in Scotland, Wales and England.

1981 March 1   St David's Day, dies at Ealing.

Introduction

In the course of preparing this second volume on the life of David
Martyn Lloyd-Jones I have sometimes recalled two rather conflicting statements on the subject of biographies. In the view of
C. H. Spurgeon too many biographies are as weighty as tombstones
and as effective in burying their subjects from the attention of
posterity. Biographers would be more useful, he thought, if they
practised a greater economy of words. Since Spurgeon's day a
different style and length of religious biography has come into vogue
but Dr Lloyd-Jones, while also intolerant of the tedious, thought that
the pendulum had now swung too far the other way. It was his view
that if a biography was worth writing at all then it should contain a
full record, with ample materials from which the reader could arrive
at his own assessments. A biography trimmed down so that it is little
more than the impressions and conclusions of its author was not at
all to his taste.

I did not deliberately set out to uphold the second of these views. A
two-volume biography was not my original intention, still less a
second volume of this size. If length was not an asset in Spurgeon's
time it is certainly less so today. In a real sense I am surprised myself
at the outcome and must therefore give the reader some explanation
of why it happened.

While Dr Lloyd-Jones spent the greater part of his life as the
minister of a congregation, he lived in more than one world at once.
For almost all the years covered by this volume there was little
happening of an important Christian character with which he was
not in some way related. The decline of the English Free Churches,
the waning of the era of evangelical agencies and missionary
societies, the rise of the ecumenical movement, the new attention to
the Third World (as in the work of the International Fellowship of
Evangelical Students), the heyday of Crusade evangelism in the

fifties, the recovery of Calvinistic belief and then the very different movement for charismatic renewal – in all these things and much else the minister of Westminster Chapel was no mere onlooker. But although these years are now past history, it is remarkable how little evangelical literature the Christian Church currently possesses on them, literature which might show why things have happened as they have. That being so, and as Dr Lloyd-Jones' life and work cannot be understood without the larger context, I have felt compelled to include some spiritual history of his times.

A further reason for the size of this second volume lies in the nature of the resource material which I have had at my disposal. The narrative covered by Volume 1 lay outside my experience, but for the larger part of the years covered by these pages I had collected many personal notes of events and conversations. These were augmented in numerous discussions with Dr Lloyd-Jones towards the close of his life, when he approved the preparation of this biography and went over what he considered to be the salient points of his life and thought with me. We talked chiefly of things contained in this second volume and it has been a most important help to me that at vital points of interpretation I have been able to turn to his own words either in notes or on the transcripts of our discussions which were tape-recorded. There has thus been much material of a first-hand character upon which I could draw. While I have not sought to produce an uncritical life – an exercise of which he would not have approved – I have tried to give the reader, as closely as possible, and often in his own words, his thinking on the issues which arose.

My resource material also grew to be far larger than originally anticipated for another reason. Friends and correspondents have generously supplied me with a large amount of information, most of which has again related to the second half of Dr Lloyd-Jones' life. A biographer could not wish for more help than I have received. It has been a tangible reminder to me of the depth of affection in which the subject of these pages was held by so many people around the world. I have obviously had to be selective in the use of this material but if I have erred on the side of recording more rather than less, it has been in part because of the thought that writers on Dr Lloyd-Jones in future years will naturally find it harder to gather information from those who knew him. His immediate contemporaries are already almost gone, together with some others whose words I have been able to use in these pages. If future biographers prefer to be more selective they will at least find fuller information here upon which they can draw.

I do not, however, mean it to be thought that I consider my supply of information to have been exhaustive. That is far from being the case. My informants have tended to be the circle of friends already known to me and that circle is by no means co-extensive with the whole circle of those who knew Dr Lloyd-Jones well. For this reason, I would add, it would be a mistake for anyone to suppose that this volume can provide some kind of guide to the names of all those who stood closest to him. Often I may quote one source rather than another because it was the best one available to me.

I cannot attempt to name all those to whom I am greatly indebted for their help. A full record would contain scores if not hundreds of names. But I must mention a few to whom special thanks are due. They include Dr Douglas Johnson, Geoffrey T. Thomas and Dorothy Thompson (formerly archivist at Westminster Chapel) who were among the first to encourage me. Indispensable assistance has been given by Dafydd Ifans of the National Library of Wales, Aberystwyth, who has expended much time and care in tracing everything of significance that has appeared by or on Dr Lloyd-Jones in Welsh and in providing me with English translations. The Reverend Kenneth W. H. Howard likewise gave major assistance in the loan of his valuable notebooks as did Dr Philip Edgcumbe Hughes in providing copies of Dr Lloyd-Jones' correspondence with him through more than thirty years. I am grateful to the deacons of Westminster Chapel for their church records and particularly to three of Dr Lloyd-Jones' one-time helpers in that diaconate, Geoffrey Kirkby, M. J. Micklewright and John P. Raynar. The Reverend Edwin E. King, one of my successors as Assistant to Dr Lloyd-Jones, has provided me with stimulating thought and aid, and I have had important assistance from the records of the Evangelical Library, London, and the UCCF, Leicester.

At all stages this volume has benefited from the close scrutiny of my wife and, when it was finally approaching completion, a careful reading by four ministerial colleagues, Maxwell Bonner, Paul E. G. Cook, Sinclair Ferguson and Graham Harrison, enabled me to make a number of changes and improvements.

The support given to me by Mrs Bethan Lloyd-Jones and by her daughters, Lady Catherwood and Mrs Ann Desmond, belongs to an altogether different order and without it this biography would have been immeasurably different and poorer. Their friendship and hospitality will always remain among the happiest memories of the years spent in the preparation of the two volumes. Dr Lloyd-Jones' papers, sermon notes and family correspondence (usually requiring translation by Mrs Lloyd-Jones from the original Welsh into English)[1] have been essential sources for supplementary information and the family has allowed me a great privilege in the unlimited access which I have had to them. These Lloyd-Jones manuscripts will probably ultimately be housed in the National Library of Wales at Aberystwyth.

I must also thank fellow trustees of the Banner of Truth Trust and all my colleagues in its work for their customary whole-hearted co-operation. Behind the scenes they have so often relieved me of responsibilities so that I could have more time to give to this book, most of which has been written in Australia.

Before coming to a final comment on the way in which this book grew I must mention several other matters. It was not an easy decision to know how to designate the subject of these pages. Martyn Lloyd-Jones was by no means alone in British church history in being given the title 'the Doctor' as an expression of both affection and esteem, though he was probably the first eminent preacher to owe that title to a medical training. In his earlier years in Wales people spoke of him, or addressed him, as 'Doctor Martyn'. Then the title without the name subsequently became near universal in evangelical circles. This usage will understandably never be taken on by those who did not know 'the Doctor' and who belong to a different age. I have therefore made no attempt to perpetuate that once popular abbreviation in these pages. Frequently I simply adopt his initials shortened to 'ML-J'. For many Christians this will be as quickly recognizable as the letters 'CHS' were for Charles Haddon Spurgeon.

My other passing comment has to do with accuracy. Many times in writing these pages I have had occasion to remember the ease with which errors can become a part of history. Such is human fallibility that the fact that a person 'remembers' such-and-such an event or statement is no sufficient proof that the information is dependable.

[1] On pp. 781–84 I have included a letter from Dr Lloyd-Jones to his wife, written in 1937, which was not available when Volume 1 was prepared. This letter could be read at the outset for its spirit gives an immediate insight into their life-long relationship.

Introduction

In all matters of significance I have therefore sought to rely upon information recorded at the time or at least recalled by two people independently. In Dr Lloyd-Jones' case, I should add, I scarcely encountered an instance where further research proved his memory to be wrong. His power of recall was phenomenal. This is not to say that he remembered everything but, if questioned on something in his distant past, he seemed to know instantly whether the information was in his grasp or not. Usually it was.

On the point of accuracy it is perhaps necessary to remind the reader that not all that appears in print with reference to eminent men can be assumed to be factual. Many erroneous statements about Dr Lloyd-Jones are already in written circulation. That he was 'bombed out of his home in London', 'preached through Isaiah in three years', was present at the Berlin Congress of 1966 as 'an unpublicized observer' are but a few examples from different publications. Among misstatements of a more serious kind, pride of place must belong to the writer who confidently says of ML-J that 'he was clearly out of sympathy with evangelism'.[1] This list could very easily be extended and the fact provides good reason for caution in believing all that we hear or read.

There is one final reason to which I must turn in explaining why these pages could not be shorter. Martyn Lloyd-Jones might have been an eminent physician or barrister or politician. He had the natural gifts for all these spheres. Instead he was called to the Christian ministry and the greatest thing in his life ceased to be anything that belonged to him by nature, it was rather the truth in which he believed, to which he adhered and for which his whole life became the most earnest advocacy. Detached from that truth his career might still possess interest but, in his judgment, it would have been a thing of very small and passing significance: 'For all flesh is as grass, and all the glory of man as the flower of grass. The grass withereth, and the flower thereof falleth away: But the word of the Lord endureth for ever . . .' (1 Peter 1:24–25). In this perspective the praise of men and the verdict of history are of no account. The one thing that matters is the judgment of God which will be finally expressed for believers in terms of standards that are eternal.

Fundamental then to ML-J's whole thinking was the conviction that life cannot be divorced from the Bible and its teaching. Given the

[1]Quoted in *Martyn Lloyd-Jones, Preacher*, John Peters, 1986, p. 131.

number of titles by Dr Lloyd-Jones now in print, it might be
supposed that his general theological position is well enough
understood and in need of little mention in a biography. But no true
biography of him could be written on that assumption, for the man
cannot be understood apart from his message. There is also reason to
believe that his spiritual vision is not yet well understood. Doctrines,
he would often say, cannot be separated and atomised. But that is
precisely what has tended to happen among some who, since his
death, have concentrated upon certain particulars and details in his
thinking rather than first looking at the whole. I have sought to bring
forward the whole. I have not been concerned to defend his views in
all details; he would not have expected me to do so. The important
thing is the big message in its God-centredness, in its features which
put him in the succession of Calvin, the Puritans, Whitefield, the
Calvinistic Methodists and Spurgeon. This is the faith which the
church and the world needs today and will ever need as long as time
shall last.[1]

I close with Dr Lloyd-Jones' own words in prayer, after an
occasion we had met to discuss this biography and not long before
his death. After words of thankfulness to God for His grace and great
salvation, the prayer concluded:

And now, O Lord, with grateful hearts, we commit and commend
ourselves and our conversation and consultation to Thee. Thou knowest
all about us and that our desire is to glorify Thy name. Lord, if this
whole idea and project does not do that we are not interested in it, we
are not concerned about it. We are afraid of any merely carnal interest.
And so we pray, dear Lord, to guard us and to shield us and to so
overrule everything that it will be a profit to many godly men and
women in different parts of the world . . .

Iain H. Murray
Sydney, Australia
July 18, 1989

[1]A Lloyd-Jones Memorial Fund to assist students for the ministry to attend
the London Theological Seminary was opened after his death and remains in
need of support. This may be sent direct to the Principal, the Rev. Hywel R.
Jones, London Theological Seminary, 13 Wickliffe Avenue, Finchley, London,
N3 3EL.

PART ONE

A DECADE OF SURPRISES, 1939–49

In 1926 Martyn Lloyd-Jones left his promising London career in medicine for the pulpit of Bethlehem Forward Movement Mission at Sandfields, Aberavon. His hope, shared by his wife Bethan, was for a life of evangelism in the South Wales which they loved. Through the next twelve years their expectations were more than fulfilled. Then, instead of an anticipated move to the Calvinistic Methodist College of his denomination at Bala, North Wales, he found himself back in London and alongside the aged Dr Campbell Morgan at Westminster Chapel, close to Buckingham Palace.

Here, in 1939, Dr Lloyd-Jones was constrained to accept a call to be co-pastor and so, following their summer holidays that year in Wales, he planned that, with their two children, Elizabeth (11) and Ann (3), they would settle in a permanent home of their own in London. But the brief summer of 1939 was to change their lives as well as those of countless others. War and an aerial attack in London seemed suddenly inevitable and, with the capital hastily evacuating her mothers and children, he left the family in Llanelli and returned alone to take up his duties on the first Sunday of September. For the time being his home would continue to be that of his mother and brother at 12 Vincent Square, Westminster. Before him lay years of a very different nature from anything he could have anticipated.

I

War

The dawn of Monday, September 4, heralded 'a perfect day' in the late summer of 1939, and yet, long before that hour, London's inhabitants were reminded that it was the second day of World War II. Martyn Lloyd-Jones, whose mother and brother Vincent were both away from 12 Vincent Square, the family home in Westminster, had promised that he would not stay there alone. Instead he spent the weekend at the Regent Palace Hotel where, from 2.30 am to 3.15 am on that same morning, he found himself for the first time in an air-raid shelter. 'It was a strange experience to wake suddenly to the sound of air-raid warnings,' he wrote to Bethan. 'There was not the slightest trace of panic among the people. The arrangements in the hotel are really excellent. The shelter is two storeys below the ground floor. There are dozens of wardens and preparations against every kind of emergency . . . I had some difficulty in going back to sleep again.'

In the day which followed there was little time to admire the weather. Dr Lloyd-Jones had plans in motion to purchase a house in London and these had now to be stopped. There had to be discussions with Dr Campbell Morgan at the nearby St Ermin's Hotel over what should be determined regarding services for the following Sunday. The previous day there had been confusion during the morning service. Dr Morgan, accompanied by his colleague, had been in the pulpit only some thirty minutes when an air-raid warning had halted the service. But the police had allowed no one to go out into the street, leaving the people to wait uncertainly until an all-clear sounded. The evening service was cancelled, partly because it was heard that buses and trains were to be used for evacuating children. The discussion of the two ministers on September 4 resulted in a determination to announce services for 11 am and 6 pm on September 10. Not all ministers in London were of the same opinion. In a phone call, ML–J's old friend Eliseus Howells (also removed from Wales to London) voiced his doubts whether there should be any services at all – especially for the Welsh community, many of whom had left the city.

Apart from such conversations, there was practical work to be done to prepare 12 Vincent Square for war-time conditions. 'We have spent most of the time today,' Martyn wrote to Bethan, 'in putting "sticking paper" on the windows to save them from blast, breakages and splinters. Sticky and very tiring work!' Despite the facilities at the Regent Palace Hotel (and all for '10/– bed and breakfast, and use of bath'), Dr Lloyd-Jones returned to sleep at Vincent Square, his mother and brother also coming back after the weekend. The houses in the Square overlooked a garden in which an air-raid shelter – actually a trench – had already been dug. 'About my quarters,' he wrote Bethan on September 5, 'quite seriously I am of the opinion that these shelters are safer than anywhere else, because there is no risk of fire, or explosions or collapsing buildings – no pieces of glass, splinters, etc. The time given as warning is more than sufficient . . . You need not worry about my not going into the trenches. I shall do so invariably.' He went on to express his belief in the probable ineffectiveness of any air attacks: 'I wish you could see the balloon barrage over the whole of Westminster . . . The news of the German air-raids on Poland confirm what was found in the Spanish war, that the defence has advanced very much more than the attacking power recently.'

Whether this was true or not, the next day he was faithful to his promise, as he reports in another of the daily letters to his wife:

This morning I awoke at 6.45 am. I had been feeling rather tired, so I set the alarm clock on from 7.00 to 7.30. That very moment I heard police whistles. I had no idea what they meant, but as they increased in volume, I jumped out of bed to see, and realised that it was a warning, and, with that, the sirens started up. I awoke Vin and mother and in a few minutes we were crossing the road and into the shelters. There is an opening in the fencing [round the Square] almost exactly opposite us in No. 12. We were there till 8.55. You will have heard the news on the wireless – still nothing in London as yet. The shelters are really good. I wear trousers, waistcoat and jacket over my pyjamas and put the socks in my pocket and put them on in the shelters. I also took my heavy overcoat – the old one – as well. Vin had neither waist-coat nor overcoat!

The truth was that London was in a state of confusion and unreality. The air-raid sirens, heard since Sunday morning, were not 'false alarms', they were simply trial runs for the 'Air Raid Precautions' (ARP). A million-and-a-half people had left Britain's cities, urged by the government which, privately, feared as many as one million casualties from aerial bombing in the first two months of the war. Gas masks were issued to all although, as Dr Lloyd-Jones found when he called at the City Hall in Charing Cross Road, there were none yet available for children aged two to five: 'They are being made. When available I will send one on,' he reported to Bethan. To eleven-year-old Elizabeth he wrote:

You would be greatly surprised if you could see all the various changes in London these days. *All* lights are out at night, including the street lamps. And there is no light to be seen in any house anywhere. As I was walking along to the hotel on Monday night a taxi-man shouted out to me for help. He was in that little street by Carey Mansions quite lost and what he wanted to know was the way to Horseferry Rd. The Londoners are not used to darkness in the way that people brought up in the country are.

As days passed, Germany continued to show no interest in an onslaught upon western Europe. It seemed possible that once Poland was conquered, the Reich would offer terms which France and Britain might accept. Certainly France, which had 106 Divisions on the Maginot Line faced by only 23 German Divisions, was not about to launch any offensive to save Poland. 'I feel tolerably certain that the war will not last a year,' wrote ML-J, anticipating by many weeks 'a general feeling' which was to be widespread in Westminster the following month. With London so quiet it was difficult to believe anything else. Vividly remembering, as he did, the summer of 1914, he commented to Bethan: 'The difference, in London, between this war and the last is incredible. The best thing ever done was to pass the Conscription Bill. There are none of the recruiting meetings and the silly excitement of the last, and there are very few soldiers to be seen around.'

It was scarcely surprising, therefore, that with the expectation of an early, intensive attack from Germany proving false, there was a general bewilderment over the real state of affairs. After a brief visit to see the family in Wales on September 15, Martyn wrote to Bethan, 'I don't think I ever felt so miserable at leaving you'. On his return journey to London he had observed the movement of evacuees back to the cities which was already occurring: 'There were dozens of women and children on the train yesterday, some very little children like Ann. I understand them perfectly, but still feel that they are very unwise.'

The confusion in the national position was matched by a large element of uncertainty in Dr Lloyd-Jones' own mind. For one thing, given his qualifications, there seemed to be a real possibility that he might be called upon for medical duties in the national interest. On September 4 he was expecting 'something might come to me here from the BMA regarding medical services'. On this subject he wrote to Bethan on September 18:

It seems that everything is in great confusion in the world of doctors. The consultants are all out in the base hospitals – with nothing to do! The agreement they made was that they would leave their private practices at once and be paid £800 per annum in these hospitals. All this was in expectation of terrible air-raids on London beginning immediately. In view of this, it is no wonder that people like Douglas Johnson and myself have heard nothing from the BMA.

Dr Douglas Johnson we have already noticed briefly as the man who first won ML-J's hesitant interest in the larger work of the Inter-Varsity Fellowship – first at Swanwick,[1] and, more recently, in the successful international conference at Cambridge held in the summer of 1939. Although now only thirty-five years of age Johnson had already led the IVF as its General Secretary for fifteen years (since 1934 in a full-time capacity). At the persistent urging of Professor Rendle Short – one of the movement's first Presidents – he had relinquished his hopes of serving as a medical missionary in Southern Rhodesia in order to give his life to a calling which was to be far more international than he could then have realized.

With the advent of war these two ex-medicals, only five years apart in age, were brought more closely together. It was not simply that ML-J, elected annual President of the IVF in April 1939, now had an official advisory role in the student work, but rather that the two men had a natural affinity – despite the nationality difference ('DJ is so *English*,' quipped an American, 'that he even carries his gloves to church on Sunday!'). Both were omnivorous readers and

[1]See vol. 1, pp. 295–97.

born conversationalists. The exchange of views over books was to form part of their life-long friendship. In the autumn of 1939 they would meet over tea at the large table in the basement dining room at Vincent Square, when Mrs Lloyd-Jones Sr was the hostess.

With the IVF's simple office at 39 Bedford Square closed and helpers scattered (some as chaplains in the Forces), the continuance of the work needed firm leadership and the commitment of ML-J gave needed strength. Also, it must be said, it gave Douglas Johnson occasional problems. ML-J's address on 'Sanctification' at Cambridge, for example, was so different in emphasis from the prevailing view, that when the publication of all the Cambridge addresses was put in hand by the IVF, some were anxious to safeguard the publishers against negative repercussions. To a note from Johnson on this subject, Lloyd-Jones replied with tongue in cheek on September 9, 1939:

I think I told you a year ago that there was the danger of my being a liability to you and the IVF. Clearly I was a true prophet.

I see no objection at all to your suggestion that a note be put in as a general introduction to the whole report. It seems quite gratuitous even to do that but it might help certain people. Rendle Short's second suggestion I will not accept as I think it would be wrong to single out my address in that way to apologize for it as if I were the heretic!

At the same time I do not want IVF to suffer. If you prefer, leave out my address altogether. I will print it as a pamphlet and get Lamont and Bouma and Grosheide to write words of commendation! Oh yes, and also Sebestyen![1]

The last suggestion was not, of course, a serious one as 'DJ' (Dr Johnson's popular nickname) would know. But it was humour at the General Secretary's expense. Here were IVF publications advisers hesitating over an issue upon which the four international leaders present at Cambridge were all united.

Some weeks were to pass before it was clear that ML-J and Johnson would not be called up for military service. By that time Dr Lloyd-Jones' mind was concentrating on the entirely unexpected problem to be faced at Westminster Chapel. Although the congrega-

[1]The four leaders named were from Scotland, the USA, the Netherlands and Hungary, respectively.

tion in the years immediately preceding the Second World War was not as large as that which Campbell Morgan had known in earlier days, it was well able to support two ministers. On Sunday morning September 3, 1939, the numbers had been much as usual but thereafter, with the evacuation and petrol rationing, there was bound to be a change. The autumn evenings were also already bringing a shortening of daylight hours, and, as the long, high windows of the chapel could not be 'blacked out' to comply with the restrictions now imposed on buildings used at night, the future of the services on Sunday and Friday evenings was in doubt. A Friday evening Bible School was held for the last time on September 15, with about 500 present, and thereafter it was switched to 2.30 pm on Saturdays. Similarly, a final Sunday evening service was held at 6 pm on September 17 and thereafter an afternoon service appointed for 2.30 pm. With numbers strong on the evening of the 17th, when Dr Lloyd-Jones preached, he was obviously doubtful about the change. In the letter to Bethan, already quoted, written the next day he says:

There was a really good congregation last night – many more than poor Hutton used to get at his best. The number of men present had struck everybody, and many felt that we should hold on to the 6.0 service for a while, and then back to 5.0, etc., etc., if it became necessary.

The probability of difficult days ahead at the Chapel was, however, rightly foreseen by Dr Morgan. The older minister had no pension and at seventy-five still depended for income upon the work of preaching which he loved. Westminster, where he also lived at St Ermin's Hotel two blocks away from the Chapel, was the centre of his life. But in the early days of the war Morgan did not see how his ministry could continue. In another letter to his wife Martyn reported:

Blackie phoned today to say that CM is very depressed, feeling that he ought to go – that there is no need of him at Westminster now.[1] But then they have nothing to live on. I had told him, on Saturday, that I would go if the church could not support us both. What he tells Blackie about that is that it is he who ought to go and leave the younger man in charge. But you will see his difficulty. I cannot allow him to suffer, and I am

[1]Margery Blackie, a distinguished physician and general practitioner, was a member at Westminster Chapel and a close friend of the Morgans.

determined, should it be necessary, that I will go for the time being. But perhaps we shall find congregations better than we think, and the problem may not arise.

On the third Sunday of the war the loose collections came to £35. 'Quite good,' ML-J commented, 'and yet, in view of the expenses on the place, not nearly enough'. At an emergency meeting of the deacons on October 1, four senior men were appointed to review the entire financial position. The Chapel had only £48 left in its 'reserve fund' and the treasurer had had to borrow £100 from another fund in order to meet expenses to the end of September. Dr Lloyd-Jones wrote to Bethan the next day: 'I shall be very glad when the position at Westminster is made clear one way or another . . . I understand that there would be very strong opposition to my leaving. We must exercise patience and live from day to day.' At the next deacons' meeting, on October 22, it was reported that when Dr Lloyd-Jones was invited to become joint minister the estimated receipts for the six weeks following were £4,227, whereas now the receipts in the first six weeks of war were £2,686 – a decrease of £1,541. In the words of the Deacons' Minutes, 'The problem was how to decrease our expenditure to the extent of £1,541'. It was decided that, except for terminating one of the Chapel cleaners, all other staff could be retained provided salaries were cut. Thus Dr Morgan's salary was reduced by £300 to £800, Dr Lloyd-Jones' by £200 to £500 and those of Mr A. E. Marsh (Church Secretary) and Sister Dora (Deaconess) were halved to the figure of £150.

Dr Lloyd-Jones was perfectly satisfied. Reporting the meeting to Bethan, he said, 'In view of this, I will, of course, go on, and we shall have to consider various possibilities for you three'. The family, as we shall note later, was to return from Wales in December.

The problems of autumn 1939 were to prove small indeed compared with what was to follow. During this initial period of the 'phoney war' the reasons for Hitler's inactivity in the West were not rightly understood. Repeating newspaper reports, Martyn wrote to Bethan that autumn: 'Many are prophesying that there will not be any air-raids. It seems that London's defences are beyond our comprehension.'

The illusion was soon to be dispelled. In April, 1940 with the East secured behind him, Hitler launched his forces into Norway and Denmark. A month later it was France's turn. The last British troops were out of Dunkirk on June 3 and the Germans entered Paris on June 14. Upon the fall of France, Hitler expected Britain's surrender as a natural consequence and then a 'thousand-year Reich'. But Britain, in which the only fully-equipped division of troops was Canadian, stood fast. 'The Battle of Britain' for the control of the air over southeast England began in August and, although not won by the Germans, they were still able on September 7, 1940 to begin day and night bombing on London in earnest. At that same date across the English Channel forty German divisions were ready to invade on a front extending from Folkestone to Bognor, an action which was postponed 'until further notice' on September 17. That month, with his colleague on holiday and preaching in Wales, Campbell Morgan was alone in the Westminster pulpit. Extracts from his diary give some idea of what was happening in London one year after the outbreak of war:

Sept. 1 [Sunday] At 11 started service at Westminster when warning sounded. Closed and came home. All clear by 11.30. Went back and found a number of people so continued service and preached. Lunch at 12.30. Started to rest and again a warning at 2. All clear at 2.30, so finished the rest. Tea at 4. At 6 o'clock took service – a good attendance.
Sept. 2–6 Two or three air-raid warnings every day and night.
Sept. 7 A daytime raid. They came pretty near. At night the heaviest attack so far on London and coming pretty near us.
Sept. 8 [Sunday] Got things in order for possible service. It being National Day of Prayer, at 11 o'clock I gave a brief address and we had prayer. Whole service lasted 45 minutes. Warning at 12.30. All clear at 1.30. Preached again at 6. Warning at 8 so down to the lounge.
Sept. 15 [Sunday] Preached in Westminster at 11. As I was uttering the last sentence warning went at 11.52. All clear 12.55. Another warning at 2.12. All clear at 3.20. At 6 to Westminster but very few and no service. Warnings all night.[1]

The era of mere ARP practices and of 'false-alarms' already seemed to lie in the distant past. On Wednesday, September 25, came the further entry in Dr Morgan's diary: 'Went to look at church after incendiary bomb hit it last night. A sad sight.'
Since 1938 the two colleagues at Westminster had been alternating every month in the services which they took, one man taking the morning service for four or five weeks and the other the second

[1] Quoted in *A Man of the Word, G. Campbell Morgan*, Jill Morgan, Pickering and Inglis, 1951, p. 309.

service. When Lloyd-Jones returned on October 6, 1940, it was to commence a month of morning services. But some, and probably Morgan himself, clearly felt that it was too dangerous to continue services at Westminster. The damage from the incendiary bomb on September 25 had not been serious, yet it was enough to lead Morgan to change the venue for morning worship on September 29 to the Livingstone Hall, the headquarters of the London Missionary Society in nearby Victoria. At Westminster Chapel there were no air-raid shelters at hand for the congregation when alarms occurred during services, neither could anything adequate be provided upon the premises. After two October Sunday mornings in the Chapel a transfer to Livingstone Hall was arranged to take effect at once. Meanwhile Morgan had held no afternoon service on September 29, nor throughout October 1940. He had already dropped his weekly Bible School at the end of June.

As though a witness to the uncertainties of this dark hour, for the next three months the long-kept Vestry Register at Westminster Chapel, in which the preacher noted his text every Sunday, lay unused and no record of what either man preached has survived. Something of what was being discussed by the two preachers in private, however, is known. Morgan, who had lived to see spiritual and national conditions undreamed of when he had gone to his first pastoral charge in Staffordshire in the far-off summer of 1889, had moments when he feared that the end of the work at Westminster was near. Humanly speaking that was a real possibility, with the old congregation scattered and the very survival of the building in serious doubt. For fifty-seven nights in succession, an average of two hundred German bombers were over London every night. Churchill later wrote, 'At this time we saw no end but the demolition of the whole Metropolis'. Before the end of October, 1940 the Bishop of London was to state that in his diocese alone 32 churches had been destroyed, and 47 seriously damaged. What hope had Westminster Chapel, standing as it did so close to Buckingham Palace and other primary targets for German bombing? Morgan and Lloyd-Jones usually met weekly and the old veteran did not hide his dismay over the situation into which his friend had been brought. It was not so much that Morgan was concerned for himself. 'Although I confess it is not easy,' he wrote, 'I am constantly hearing in my own soul the words: "In nothing be anxious, but in everything by prayer and supplication with thanksgiving, let your requests be made known unto God".' But he did fear that Lloyd-Jones might be left without work and without a pastorate. Already his colleague was facing numbers considerably less than those to which he had been accustomed on Sundays in Wales. Recalling the effect of the War on the size of the congregation, ML-J was to say in later years: 'Almost immediately our congregation went down to about 300 as most people who could get out of London did so . . . Finally only 100 to 200 were left of Campbell Morgan's great congregation.'

In October, 1940 Dr Morgan temporarily left all the work to his colleague by cancelling his own afternoon services. He wanted there to be no question of his friend leaving, so long as there was any congregation at all. No one could have been more magnanimous. Perhaps not everyone realized this at the time. Several years later when Dr Lloyd-Jones was about to address a group of professional men, his chairman (another doctor) employed his 'chairman's remarks' to pass on his 'knowledge' of how things had stood during the joint ministry at Westminster. Dr Lloyd-Jones, he declared, had experienced a most difficult time because Campbell Morgan wanted to monopolize the pulpit and had given him little opportunity to preach. Not for the first or the last time Dr Lloyd-Jones had to correct his chairman. The actual situation, he informed the gathering, was the opposite to what they had just been told. 'The old man had to be encouraged by me and so reluctant was he that there were occasions when he would try to withdraw from his turn to preach even when we were preparing to leave the minister's vestry for the pulpit.' 'Dr Morgan,' Lloyd-Jones was also to say on another occasion, 'was a very kind and very generous man'.

In the deacons' meetings held in October, 1940 something of the strain behind the scenes was revealed. In a meeting on October 13 there was some comment on the different practice of the two ministers with regard to air-raids. The records note: 'It was pointed out that at present Dr Morgan closes the service at once [if warning sounds] whereas Dr Lloyd-Jones continues at any rate until the more imminent danger.' After discussion, the general but not unanimous opinion was that 'the service should be closed when warning was given'. More delicate than this, however, was a matter contained in a letter written to Morgan by Lloyd-Jones respecting the termination of the second service on a Sunday. Lloyd-Jones, who was chairing the deacons' meeting of October 13 in Morgan's absence, clearly wanted the two services maintained – in part, probably, for Morgan's own sake.

This issue was too important to be long postponed. Another deacons' meeting was held on October 20 with Morgan presiding and Lloyd-Jones present. At this meeting it was noted: 'The matter relating to the question raised by Dr Lloyd-Jones in his letter to Dr Campbell Morgan was further considered. It was unanimously agreed: That the present ministerial arrangement be continued, with the resumption of a second service commencing in November, if such can be arranged [at Livingstone Hall] and to review the general position again early in December.' So Lloyd-Jones took an afternoon service on November 3 and continued it through two successive months to December 29, 1940.

As a church meeting on November 10, 1940 had revealed, there were a number who did not approve the move to Livingstone Hall. A senior member of the church, Mr J. B. Gotts, wanted to know, 'Why are we having services at Livingstone Hall? Would it be possible for Dr Lloyd-Jones to amplify the statement he recently made from the pulpit at Westminster regarding the holding of services in Livingstone Hall?' Perhaps as a result of this discussion the Vestry Register for the first Sunday of 1941 contains the note, 'Returned to Church' although not until the next Sunday was the more than three months' silence broken and a record of the preachers' texts resumed. Possibly because of the sickness of his colleague, Lloyd-Jones preached at both services throughout January 1941. For January 12 his text for one service, as recorded in the Vestry Register, was Habakkuk 3:17–18, 'Although the fig tree shall not blossom, neither shall fruit be in the vines; the labour of the olive shall fail, and the fields shall yield no meat; the flock shall be cut off from the fold, and there shall be no herd in the stalls: Yet I will rejoice in the Lord, I will joy in the God of my salvation.'

It was a text singularly appropriate for the ministers as well as for the people. Lloyd-Jones presided at a deacons' meeting on January 26, 1941, Morgan being 'absent with a chill'. The Church Treasurer, Mr J. Ryley,[1] was also absent but he sent in a statement which was read by his friend, Mr A. W. Caiger. Despite all economies and cuts in salaries already agreed, he reported that the year 1940 had ended with an overdraft of £150.6s.0d. Further, the weekly offerings through the winter had been averaging little more than £10 and the position was worsening! Reading Ryley's state-

[1] A member since 1905, he died in 1943, when he was succeeded by Caiger.

ment, Caiger said: 'I think we should begin by telling our Ministers that we see no prospect of paying them their present stipends after the end of March, possibly February. How to keep the Church going at all is a problem . . .'

While granting the reality of the difficulties, it cannot be said that the diaconate at this date appear as men with strong spiritual priorities. Concern was expressed that the Bible School should be restarted in order that the funds which were being lost from that source might be made up. Finally, it was agreed to continue the ministers' allocations until the end of March when the position would be reviewed. At the next recorded meeting of the diaconate on April 6, 1941, Messrs Ryley and Caiger proposed that henceforth both ministers' salaries be terminated and that they both be paid simply on a supply basis of £10 a service – thus reducing weekly expenditure upon the ministry to £20 per week, or £30 when Dr Morgan resumed his Bible School on May 2. It was also proposed that money be saved by ending the tradition of inviting a visiting preacher in the summer period (John Hutton had preached for four weeks in August, 1940). Instead the two ministers should alternately take double duties during the holiday months. Such were the extremities to which the deacons now believed themselves to be driven and they unanimously adopted the above proposals.

The spiritual deficiency in the diaconate reflected the long-standing weakness of the whole congregation. The large pre-war attendance had disguised the extent to which lower standards prevailed. There was a definite liberal element in the membership and particularly in that of the 'Institute' which constituted a kind of church within the church.[1] Speaking of his reception at the Chapel, Dr Lloyd-Jones once said: 'They were very kind to me but I felt a great lack of spiritual understanding and spiritual fellowship. There was no prayer meeting at all and no spiritual meeting'. With Dr Morgan's ready acquiescence, ML-J introduced a Monday evening 'Fellowship' meeting in the autumn of 1939 with the intention of encouraging spiritual conversation and discussion. Mr and Mrs L. G. Covell were among the 'smallish company' which gathered in the Church Parlour week by week for this purpose and, forty years later, they remembered these meetings as 'oases of spiritual enrichment in the early months of the "phoney" war'. Mr Covell writes:

[1]On the Institute and conditions at the Chapel when Morgan resumed his ministry there in the 1930's see vol 1, p. 362–363.

It was the Doctor's custom to invite questions, and amongst the many topics raised and dealt with so adequately and convincingly I remember one of outstanding interest. It was the problem of a Christian minister in dealing with the communion service and individual communicants. What about persons who should not, on moral grounds, be qualified to participate? The Doctor drew on his experience. At his former pastorate in South Wales he had known the great majority of his people and had refused the elements to a person who he knew was living adulterously.

There was also some discussion that same evening on the difficulty over the right administration of the Lord's Supper in a congregation such as Westminster Chapel's where the people were drawn from a wide area and might often be unknown both to the minister and to one another.

With the advent of serious bombing in September 1940, the Monday Fellowship meeting had to be abandoned for the time being. From that date onwards the destruction of London continued. By March 1941 a number of London's most historic churches had gone. They included St Andrew, Holborn where George Whitefield once preached; Austin Friars, a Reformed church of immigrants from the reign of Edward VI; St Magnus-the-Martyr, the burial place of Miles Coverdale the Bible translator; John Newton's St Mary Woolnoth and St Andrew-by-the-Wardrobe, scene of the ministry of William Romaine. Among more modern buildings, St Columba's (Pont Street), Spurgeon's Tabernacle and the City Temple shared in the devastation. An observer, writing on 'London Churches in the Blitz' in the *British Weekly* for April 24, 1941, reported: 'The first building visited, The City Temple, was the completest ruin I ever saw . . . Among the rubbish where I stood were pieces of a tablet commemorating the founding of the church in 1640 by Thomas Goodwin, the Puritan.' At the Congregational Union Assembly the following month, it was reported of the denomination that 'no fewer than 260 churches have been damaged more or less seriously.' At one of their weekly conversations in St Ermin's Hotel, Morgan, reflecting on what was happening, exclaimed to his colleague, 'I have brought you here, and this is what I have brought you to! We are almost certain to be bombed completely to the ground'.

Dr Lloyd-Jones did not share that fear. There were some occasions in his life when he had strong presentiments about the future. These impressions, it should be said, were not always correct, neither did he ever make them a rule for others, but explain it as we will, in the worst of the Blitz he believed that Westminster Chapel would be preserved. In this respect the weekend of Sunday May 11, 1941, was to be for him one of the most memorable of the war. Between 11.30 the previous evening and 5.37 on the Sunday morning some 507 planes of the Luftwaffe made a supreme effort to shatter London. A raid in March had caused 750 civilian deaths in the metropolis but this May weekend was to claim 1,436 victims and before dawn on the Sunday 2,200 fires were reported, with as much as 700 acres ablaze at one time. Around Westminster Chapel many buildings were hit, including the Houses of Parliament, Westminster Abbey and Westminster School. When dawn came many streets were blocked by fallen buildings or by fire-fighting equipment.

It was not Dr Lloyd-Jones' turn to preach until the evening[1] and consequently he had gone the previous day to Oxford where he had an engagement to preach in the Chapel of Mansfield College on the Sunday morning. Lloyd-Jones recalled his experience that weekend as follows:

I was staying with the then Principal of Mansfield, Dr Nathaniel Micklem. We had gone to bed on the Saturday night, and the next thing I remember is that I was awakened in the morning by Dr Micklem who had brought me up a cup of tea. As he handed me the cup of tea he said, 'Look here, I am going to announce this morning in the service that you will be preaching at night as well as in the morning'. I said, 'But you mustn't do that, I am preaching at Westminster Chapel tonight'. 'My dear man,' he said, 'you will not be preaching in Westminster Chapel tonight.' 'Why not?' I replied. He said, 'There is no Westminster Chapel'. I said, 'What do you mean?' 'Well,' he said, 'there has been a terrible raid last night, the worst we have ever had. I have heard on the wireless that the whole of Westminster is practically flattened, so why not preach here tonight?' I said, 'Listen to this. I am telling you that Westminster Chapel has not been demolished, and that I shall be preaching in it tonight'. He was amazed at this, and especially at my certainty.

So I did not allow him to make the announcement that I would be preaching at night also. I preached in the morning and after lunch got my train to London. I remember that approaching Paddington I could see fires burning in places on both sides of the line. I got out of the train and found a great queue of people waiting for taxis. At last I got one. 'Where for, sir?' said the taximan. I said, 'I want a chapel called Westminster

[1]An early evening service at 6 pm had been restored on April 6, 1941.

Chapel, halfway along Buckingham Gate, Westminster'. 'I'm afraid, sir,' he said, 'you cannot get into Buckingham Gate'. 'Why not?' 'Oh, terrible bombing last night,' he said, 'everything flattened.' I said, 'Look here, you get down in the direction of Victoria and I will guide you'. I had decided to bring him along Palace Street and then to turn in here into Castle Lane. While all this was going on he was telling me about what he had seen; but I was still absolutely certain that I would be preaching in this chapel. I will never forget it. We came round the corner from Palace Street into Castle Lane. I looked, and here was this old building standing as if there had not been a raid at all. I believe I am right in saying that two window-panes on the left side from the pulpit were cracked; and that was all that had happened. I preached here and took the service as usual.[1]

Severe difficulties continued throughout 1941. On October 8 Morgan could write, 'London is going through a tremendous ordeal. I have not been in bed for six weeks. Down in the lounge we do get some sleep during the night at intervals, and so we are keeping up . . . The chapel has been hit three times.' Without fire-fighters constantly on the premises it would undoubtedly have been burned out. As it was the congregation had to return for a time to Livingstone Hall. Nor had the financial situation improved. On October 26, 1941, a letter from Mr Ryley, who was unwell, was read to the diaconate once more emphasizing the seriousness of the position and proposing that the ministers should appeal for higher giving. One of the ministers, at least, is unlikely to have acceded. Dr Lloyd-Jones was never known to appeal for money in the churches which he served.

No records exist of how many who attended Westminster Chapel lost their lives in the blitz. One unusual case, however, has been recalled by Mrs Lloyd-Jones. From the first days of the war, two sisters, the Misses Spain, were among the most faithful attenders at all services. 'They always sat together in the middle block, near the front – hardly elderly, late middle age perhaps – always pleasant and courteous, but we knew very little about their background, except

[1]*Westminster Chapel* (1865–1965), Centenary Address, 1965, reprinted in *Knowing the Times*, pp. 222–45. The air-bombardment diminished after this date as Hitler moved planes to the East for his attack on Russia – an action which, with the entrance of the United States into the war at the end of the year, secured his final defeat. As one Editor wrote in 1941: 'Hitler is regarded as a sort of superman. But we have had supermen before. History has a way of dealing with them catastrophically.'

that their father had been a business man, and that both he and their mother were dead.' One Sunday they were present as usual though the church was then meeting in the Livingstone Hall. Dr Lloyd-Jones was preaching that day on 'the wedding garment' and on the danger of being found without 'the wedding garment'. Mrs Lloyd-Jones continues:

At the end of the service, the elder Miss Spain came to speak to him. She had come to thank the Doctor for the sermon – a thing she had not done before – and during the conversation she told him that they had one other sister in an important government post down on the South Coast. Apart from this, they had no family, near or far. Drawn to talk because of Martyn's interest, she told him that this third sister was feeling lonely and was coming up to London that very evening to stay for a few days with them. As she was leaving, she turned back and half shyly said: 'Doctor, I am so glad I have on that wedding garment, thank you', then went out to join her sister.

That night a bomb fell on their house and all three sisters were killed outright. The members of Westminster Chapel were their family at the burial.

The Doctor always felt, after his conversation with Miss Spain that night, that it was of the Lord's mercy that they had been taken together, theirs was such a close relationship. We might have thought it strange that the third sister had come up from the South Coast to join them on that particular night. But, knowing that the Lord is not only 'rich and merciful' but also 'very kind', we will not call it strange.

What was strange was that had Miss Spain not had that conversation with the Doctor on that Sunday night, no one would have known what had happened to the third Miss Spain and, except for her employers, not even of her existence! The authorities were grateful for the few facts which the church could give them.

ML-J's notes in actual size of a sermon preached on November 23, 1941 (see p. 34). In all they came to three sheets written on five sides which he would have with him in the pulpit.

'A MESSAGE FROM OUR PRESIDENT FOR 1940'

... (1)   The present war has revealed the utter failure of all human systems to deal with the problem of mankind ...

(2)   Never was the biblical view of man and of sin so evidently and clearly right as to-day. The radical evil in human nature is manifesting itself on a world scale. Never again can it be said, or should it be said, that man inherently and naturally desires the right, and the best, and is ready to accept it if it be but offered to him.

(3)   The uncertainty of life in these days makes people more ready to listen to the Gospel. The most 'blasé' person is uncomfortable at the thought of death, though he may try to hide the fact.

Here then lies our opportunity.

We must not abuse it by simply turning to those who do not know Christ and saying, "I told you so." Events in the world will truly prove we were right. But what matters is not that we shall be right, but that others may be put right.

We can seize the opportunity in many ways, but there are two special ways which we must always remember.

The first is our general life and conduct. There should be about us a calmness, a poise of spirit and general control of our lives which should differentiate us Christians from all others. Whatever the conditions, and however trying, we should show that we have hidden resources of which the world knows nothing. The way in which many of the first Christians faced death was the means of converting many to Christ and earned the encomium – 'these Christians die well'.

The other way is the right use of conversation and of social intercourse. Almost every conversation to-day turns upon the strangeness of life and the uncertainty of the future. No more perfect opening for the Gospel is conceivable.

God grant that we all may be worthy of our high calling!

ML-J

The above is part of a letter sent by the Inter-Varsity Fellowship to all past members of the University Evangelical Unions whose addresses could be located. It was a first move to establish a link between graduates and the success of the idea was to lead to the creation of a Graduates Fellowship with their own magazine.

2

The Message for the Hour

The outbreak of World War II stunned into silence the numerous contributors to the religious press who, until so recently, had been discussing the apparent failure of the Church. And a new uncertainty was equally evident among preachers. Those who had long used the pulpit as a platform for the giving of political advice to governments temporarily lost their message. C. E. M. Joad, the philosopher, might continue to advocate pacifism but no preacher, confronted with a congregation experiencing the realities of war, appeared willing to do so. Even Leslie Weatherhead, one of London's most popular liberal preachers, confessed: 'Our minds go round and round until we can think no more . . . My pacifism would have been a refusal to think . . . I tore up my "peace pledge" avowal. I began to think again.'[1]

In most cases, it would have to be said that the rethinking was not of any fundamental kind. The dominating influence upon the pulpit of the pre-war years was the supposed well-being and happiness of the hearers. Preachers were aware of what kind of sermon the people wanted and commonly they attempted to supply it. Once the initial shock of war was passed, this same attitude continued to assert itself. Less was heard, to be sure, about 'the essential goodness' of human nature, yet man remained the main subject and, particularly, how he could be heroic, serene and happy despite the war. The old pre-war theme was again to the fore in March, 1941 when Weatherhead provided two articles for the *British Weekly* on why 'the Church has lost its grip on the people'. Representing prevalent views – and views to become yet more prevalent – Weatherhead argued that churches were empty partly because of the Church herself, partly because of the preaching and partly through the failure of ministers to give

[1] *Thinking Aloud in War-time*, 1940, pp. 11–12, 22.

[21]

David Martyn Lloyd-Jones: Volume Two

youth what it wanted. Many churches, he believed, were 'a travesty of that living, vital, radiant, passionate, heroic, beautiful thing that Jesus meant by religion'. Let the example of Christ be presented and followed and a 'new age' would dawn! In the weeks following Weatherhead's articles numerous correspondents followed up the same theme with proposals of all manner of similar remedies.

The same month that Dr Weatherhead's articles appeared, Dr Lloyd-Jones was in Edinburgh delivering three addresses at the Free Church College on 'The Tragedy of Modern Man'. The standpoint of the two men could hardly have been further apart. The 'tragedy', according to the visitor to Scotland, had to be stated in these terms:

First and foremost we are face to face with the fact of the wrath of God . . . God has decided and ordered and arranged that a life of forgetfulness of Him, and of antagonism to Him, shall not be successful and happy. Cursing falls upon such a way of life. The facts of life, the story of history, proclaim the wrath of God against all ungodliness and unrighteousness. That is our first problem. We have sinned against God . . .

It is as the idea of judgment and the wrath of God have fallen into the background that our churches have become increasingly empty. The idea has gained currency that the love of God somehow covers everything, and that it matters very little what we may do, because the love of God will put everything right at the end. The more the Church has accommodated her message to suit the palate of the people the greater has been the decline in attendance at places of worship.

These convictions drew considerable attention, first in the Edinburgh press and then in their subsequent publication as a book under the title *The Plight of Man and the Power of God*.[1] We must, however, pause to view them in the whole context of the burden of Dr Lloyd-Jones' preaching in the early years of the war. Basically the events of 1939 brought no change to his message. As we have already seen, he considered the preacher's one business in the pulpit was to bring the Word of God to the people. His fundamental criticism of most contemporary preaching was that it did not *start* with the Bible; it only made use of Scripture to present a philosophy of religion which was not the Christian gospel at all. Rejecting the authority of Scripture, these preachers never seriously attempted to find *biblical*

[1]London, 1942.

[22]

reasons for the war which was raging. Instinctively they seemed to know that any such reasons would undermine their whole philosophy. Lloyd-Jones, on the other hand, held that it is the Bible which gives an understanding adequate for every crisis, 'It is the Bible alone that explains the genesis and the origin of this present war'.

In September, 1939, Dr Lloyd-Jones was taking the evening services at Westminster. Taken by surprise, with everyone else, at the beginning of the month, he had no time to plan a series on a consecutive theme. One of his first impressions – which formed the basis of a sermon for Sunday evening, September 17 – was that the war would soon test the real spiritual position of all church-goers. The new situation was therefore, in his view, a call to self-examination. As usual, the message was preached to himself first. Speaking on a personal note, he wrote to Bethan: 'This is a real test of our beliefs and of our faith. Without a doubt, we have – all of us – been slack for various reasons, and the first call upon us is to repentance'. His text for that Sunday (September 17), as he also tells Bethan the next day, was Acts 16:25, 'And at midnight Paul and Silas prayed, and sang praises unto God: and the prisoners heard them'. 'I preached on Paul and Silas singing in the prison – the contrast between the two Christians and the other prisoners. I was given freedom in preaching, and I felt that there was unction on the message.'[1]

In the same letter, Dr Lloyd-Jones also told his wife something of the direction which his thoughts were taking on the future course of his pulpit ministry: 'I feel that there is a tremendous opportunity for preaching. At the moment what is wanted is the comforting note to help people over the shock. But, following that, the need will be for the prophetic note to awaken the people.'

The comforting note was still prominent as he took up a series for the five Sunday mornings in October. A 'general theodicy' – a justification of the ways of God – was how he described to Bethan the theme of the series. The first of these sermons was intended to deal with the tendency of people to complain about their unanswered prayers. 'Many ask,' he said in his introduction, 'why it is that God

[1]In *The Baptist Times*, Nov. 17, 1966, under the title, 'The Sermons They Most Remember', R. G. Pritchard described how all that were in Westminster Chapel that September evening in 1939 'were to hear a sermon which they could never forget'. 'Referring to the "midnight" in which we as a people found ourselves,' says this hearer, Dr Lloyd-Jones 'urged his hearers to pray as never before.'

did not hearken unto the prayers that have been offered since the crisis of September, 1938?' Having further stated the question, he showed the answer from his text, 1 Timothy 2:8, 'I will therefore that men pray everywhere, lifting up holy hands, without wrath and doubting'. 'There is nothing which is so utterly contrary to the whole teaching of the Bible as the assumption that anyone, and at any time, without any conditions whatsoever, may approach God in prayer . . . Man, by sin, has forfeited his right to approach God, and, indeed, were he left to himself he never would approach God.'

From a further two texts from the New Testament, and two from the Old, he developed the theme, 'Why Does God Allow War?'. He argued that not only were wrong answers being given to the question but that the whole approach to the subject was commonly wrong. The Church was unprepared to face the unexpected because:

Precise thinking, and definition, and dogma have been at a serious discount. The whole emphasis has been placed upon religion as a power which can do things for us and which can make us happy. The emotional and feeling side of religion has been over-emphasized at the expense of the intellectual. Far too often people have thought of the Christian religion merely as something which gives a constant series of miraculous deliverances from all sorts and kinds of ills. The slogans of which we have heard so much testify to this. The phrases most frequently used have been 'Try religion' or 'Try prayer', and the impression has often been given that we have but to ask God for whatever we may chance to need and we shall be satisfied . . . We have been so intent upon ourselves and our moods and feelings and inward states, that when we are confronted by an external problem that nevertheless affects us profoundly, we do not know how to think or where to begin.

War, said the preacher, was not to be viewed as the interruption of personal convenience and of the enjoyments of life. Something far more serious was involved. War is divine judgment upon the very lives which men pursue; it is permitted 'in order that men may see through it, more clearly than they have ever done before, what sin really is' and thus be led back to God.

We are the work of His hands, indeed we are to God what the clay is to the potter. Do you doubt it? Well, let me ask you certain questions. What control have you really over your life? You had no control over the beginning and you will have no control over the end. We have no idea as to how long we shall be here. Our lives are altogether in God's hands. We cannot control health and sickness, accidents and disease. We know not what a day may bring forth. Who could have foretold the present state of affairs? Men have failed to prevent it. We are the creatures of time, and entirely subject to forces over which we have no control. We are quite helpless. As our Lord put it, we cannot 'add one cubit to our stature'. And yet we venture to try to measure God. How monstrous! . . . You cannot understand? You are tempted to question, and to argue, and to query? The reply to you is, in the words of St Paul, 'Nay but, O man, who art thou that repliest against God! Shall the thing formed say to Him that formed it, why hast thou made me thus?' 'But that,' you may say, 'is not fair argument. It is rather a prohibition of argument, and the exertion of an unfair authority.' To which I reply, that we were never meant to argue with God, and that we should never have started from the assumption that it was to be a discussion between two equal disputants. God is in heaven, and we are upon earth. God is holy, and we are sinful. God knows all things, and sees the end from the beginning . . . God needs no defence, for He is on the Throne. He is the Judge of all the earth. His Kingdom is without end. Cease to question and to argue! Bow down before Him! Worship Him! Get into the right attitude yourself, and you will begin to understand His actions.

The advent of war, he argued again, ought not to have been a surprise:

Under the blessing of peace since the last war, men and women, in constantly increasing numbers, have forsaken God and religion and have settled down to a life which is essentially materialistic and sinful. Thinking that the last war was indeed 'the war to end war,' with a false sense of security, buttressed also by insurance schemes and various other provisions to safeguard themselves against the possible dangers that still remained, men and women in this and in every other country gave themselves to a life of pleasure-seeking, accompanied by spiritual and mental indolence. This became evident not only in the decline in religion, but still more markedly in the appalling decline in morals; and indeed, finally, even in a decline in a political and social sense. It led to the decadence on which the rulers of Germany banked, and on which they based their calculations. Then came a crisis in September, 1938. Men and women crowded to places of worship and prayed for peace. Afterwards they assembled to thank God for peace. But was it because they had decided to use peace for the one and only true purpose, namely, to 'live a quiet and peaceable life in all godliness and honesty'? Was it in order that they might walk 'in the fear of the Lord and in the comfort of the Holy Ghost'? The facts speak for themselves. Thus I ask the questions: Had we a right to peace? Do we deserve peace? Were we justified in asking God to preserve peace and to grant peace? What if war has come because we were not fit for peace, because we did not deserve peace; because we by our disobedience and godlessness and sinfulness had so utterly abused the blessings of peace? Have we a right to expect God to preserve a state of peace merely to allow men and women to continue a life that is an insult to His holy Name?

These five sermons from October, 1939 were immediately published and were the preacher's first book.[1] At this period most of the contents of the *Westminster Record*, published monthly, were supplied by Morgan. In 1940 only three occasional sermons of ML-J's were printed in the *Record*. But between 1941 and 1943 three series of his sermons were printed in the Chapel's monthly magazine. The first series (following the deacons' decision that they could afford no visiting summer preachers in 1941) was preached by Dr Lloyd-Jones on the five Sunday mornings of August of that year. They consisted of an exposition of Peter's imprisonment, recorded in Acts 12, with the general theme 'The Persecution of the Church'. The second series, first preached at Westminster in February, 1940, on Romans 1:18–22 were the addresses ('The Tragedy of Modern Man') repeated in Edinburgh the following year to which we have already referred. The third series which came into print was 'Paul's Order of the Day', five sermons preached from 1 Corinthians 16:13–14 in August, 1942.

These sermons, and the few other occasional sermons published in the *Westminster Record*, give a very clear idea of how he applied the Word of God to the need of the hour. The following were his main emphases:

First, it is necessary to understand that the power of evil, whether represented by Herod (Acts 12) or by Hitler, is supremely directed against God and his Church. And this evil power is of the same nature in individuals as it is in nations. The anti-God spirit is common to all men by nature. It is the spirit of arrogance and pride and leads to self-glorification – man choosing for himself what he likes and what he wants. The essence of sin is the worship of man. 'The man who ceases to believe in God tries to deify himself.'

[1] *Why Does God Allow War?*, Hodder and Stoughton, Dec., 1939. A second printing was called for in the following month.

Secondly, Christianity is not a solution for the problems of man's bodily and temporal needs. Man has necessities far more urgent than the avoidance of physical calamities and material losses. The non-Christian's overriding concern about the physical and the material is due to his failure to understand the needs of the soul. 'We are very agitated in physical calamity but is the Church fully alive and awake to the problems of the *souls* of men? We are concerned about men going to war. I wonder if we are equally concerned about the souls of men going to perdition? It is a tragedy for men to lose their lives in warfare, I admit, but is it not a greater tragedy for them to lose their souls?'

This theme was developed in a sermon on Matthew 10:28, 'But fear not them which kill the body, but are not able to kill the soul; but rather fear him which is able to destroy both soul and body in hell':

Our Lord never promises or prophesies easy things. He ever prepares His followers for the worst. Nothing is further removed from our Lord's method than the giving of some vague general comfort and encouragement designed merely to ease and to pacify them for the time being . . .

Realize what man can do to you. Realize what God can do . . . He offers pardon and forgiveness, a new life, and a fatherly care which knows no bounds or limits . . . These are the things that really matter in this life, and they are the things that will alone matter in eternity. And with regard to these things we can defy any and every enemy. These are things that bombs cannot smash, that tanks cannot crush. These are things beyond the range of the most powerful gun . . . No man can touch your soul and no man can kill your soul . . .

Thirdly, when Lloyd-Jones spoke of the power of evil being manifested against the Church he was not thinking in any nationalistic sense. He never equated Church with his own country. 'The Church, according to the New Testament, is not so much international as supernational'. The condition of the Church in Europe, and in Germany, ought to be of equal concern to true Christians. And everywhere the true spiritual battle was similar, 'The Christian Church has been passing through dark waters, the enemy has been proud and arrogant, not only in Germany, but in our own land, with its materialism and rationalism'.

Undoubtedly the Christians from the Continent whom he had met at Cambridge in August, 1939 enlarged his own consciousness of the unity of the Church. He had been moved, for instance, to hear the

testimony of the widow of a German Moravian bishop who told him
'that the universal testimony of all the Christians in Germany who
had suffered untold hardships on account of their faith was, in her
experience, that they would have missed none of these things, that
indeed they thanked God for them'. Affliction had led to spiritual
blessing.

As the war slowly closed all doors in Europe, he also knew that the
ministry at Westminster Chapel was being remembered by the
Church there. A brief note from a Christian in Norway, cut open by
'Censor 1296', shortly before that country fell to the Germans in
1940, contained the words: 'Just a line to show you I think of you
and all your work. I will never forget all your kindness and sympathy
last summer . . . I am glad and grateful there *is* the one great fellowship of love, nobody and nothing can disturb it. We realize more and
more the blessings of knowing people who are on "the way" with us,
as you said that Sunday I first saw and heard you at Westminster
Chapel. Though we are suffering, we are well and know Jeremiah
29:11.'

Fourthly, Dr Lloyd-Jones preached that much needed to be said
about the things men least wanted to hear, namely, the nature of sin
and God's view of sin. Beginning one sermon on this subject he
anticipated an objection:

I can imagine someone saying, Surely you are not going to spend your
time in discussing a purely negative subject like this? Why not deal with
something positive? Surely you are not going to be ensnared by that
which was so characteristic of the Puritans? Surely, says this critic,
instead of spending your time describing and dissecting something
which is ugly, and black, and foul, it would be much better if you spent
your time in telling us about the beauty of Jesus, or the love of God . . .

What are we to say by way of reply to such objections? First, I would
point out that such an attitude denotes an entirely false view of
preaching. What is really implicit in that criticism is this, that preaching
should always give men what they desire rather than what they need.
There is the feeling that men have a right to demand certain things of the
messengers of God. That is a popular view of preaching, and I have no
doubt that it accounts very largely for the state of the world to-day.

Again, in his opening sermon in *The Plight of Man and the Power
of God* he described the failure of the pulpit to deal with the real
problem of man during the First World War as 'one of the saddest

chapters in the history of the Christian Church'. 'If we are anxious to help and to speak the redeeming word, we must first of all probe the wound and reveal the trouble. That cannot be done without giving rise to pain and perhaps also to offence.'

As mentioned earlier, articles by Leslie Weatherhead in the *British Weekly* in 1941 gave rise to much correspondence. When it had died down there was one further letter from a British missionary in Morija, Basutoland. Setting aside Dr Weatherhead's proposals, Mary Burton wrote:

No, the thing which has emptied churches is lack of need of God. A man conscious of the sin of his soul seeks God and does not wait to be attracted by church stunts. But the knowledge of good and evil has been lost in a welter of words . . . What must be rediscovered is God's attitude to sin.

This was precisely Dr Lloyd-Jones' conviction. Far from preaching that more morality was the need of the hour, he demonstrated – and especially in the sermons on Romans 1 – that morality *follows* a true relationship with God, just as unrighteousness follows ungodliness. There is therefore no hope for man in himself. He must be brought back to God and this is exactly the purpose of the Christian gospel. This, then, was his first and supreme emphasis. The gospel is 'the power of God unto salvation'. Sin will not have the last word for the living God is in control.

Thus in a third sermon on Peter's deliverance in Acts 12, he preached the principle that God acts in history. The gospel is the message of God coming in when nothing else can change man's condition. Referring to the words of Acts 12:7, 'Behold . . . a light shined in the prison,' he says: 'The whole message of this verse is just this, that it matters not what your situation may be, however dark, however black, however tight your bonds, however imprisoned and fettered you may be, if God wills your deliverance, it can be done, it will be done . . . Prison cells, and wards, and chains and iron gates – they are nothing to the God who made the world, and sustains everything by His power.'

This is not to say, as he shows in a fourth sermon on Acts 12, that God always works by the miraculous, but in all situations God is in command and, if He does not deliver from death, He will give His people 'a composure and a calmness which the world at its very worst can never destroy'.

In these, and other sermons, his call to Christians was to *think* aright about God. That must come first. Not even prayer is to be put before it: 'We talk far too much about our faith, and about our prayers. If we only concentrated upon the power of God.' His concern was that his hearers should not simply derive comfort from passages of Scripture but that they should think *theologically*. This point is constantly to the fore. In his sermons on 'Paul's Order of the Day' he demonstrates that Christian resolution is a very different thing from what the world calls 'courage', it arises rather from *knowing* 'the faith'. Speaking from the words, 'Watch ye, stand fast in the faith, quit you like men, be strong' (1 Cor. 16:13), he said:

We stand fast in this faith by reminding ourselves of it constantly, by reading and thinking about it, by meditating concerning it. This is something for which I would plead at the present time. We must return to a consideration of the terms of the faith. That is specifically necessary, perhaps, for those of us who are Evangelicals. I plead, in other words, for a revival of the study of theology . . . It is not enough to cultivate the devotional life.

It is essential to 'stand fast in the faith' when we are assailed by doubt. And it is essential as against feelings. If we trust to our feelings, and to our moods, the time will come when we shall be feeling miserable. We shall wake up in the morning feeling tired and lethargic, and the question will come to us, Why go on with it? I do not feel like going on with it. There is only one answer when you feel like that. It is the faith, the truth – it is our only means of happiness. It is essential also as against the facts of life. There come 'the slings and arrows of outrageous fortune', illness comes, disappointment comes, difficult circumstances arise, a world war takes place, our profession is lost, our business is gone, sorrow knocks at the door of your home, and someone dearer than life is taken away, death comes, either in battle, or on the sea, or in the air, or quietly in a room. How can I face the facts of life? There is but one way. 'Stand fast in the faith.' It has envisaged all these things. It has provided for them all; it covers them all. It is faith for life. It is faith for death. It is the faith for all eternity. 'Stand fast in the faith'.

*　　　　*　　　　*

The congregation which heard Dr Lloyd-Jones at Westminster was comparatively small and transient. As already noted, most of the pre-war congregation had been quickly scattered and a new congregation had yet to be gathered. But from the number of his hearers in those years enough testimonies survive to give some impression of the impact of this preaching.

Dorothy Thompson, for example, was an Ulster girl of Presbyterian background who came to London three years before the war to work for the Inland Revenue Department. Already a Christian, she had tried to find a spiritual home in several churches, including Westminster Chapel when Dr Morgan was there alone. 'My memory of those services,' she wrote forty years later, 'is that they were essentially beautiful in character, times of worship certainly, but there was little to grip and hold me spiritually. Then one Sunday in 1940 I went along to the Chapel and heard Dr Lloyd-Jones preach. I cannot recall the contents of his sermon but the effect was dynamic. I felt it was indeed God's Word of truth being proclaimed in the power of the Holy Spirit and decided there and then to join the fellowship at Westminster Chapel.'

Geoffrey Thomas, who lived in Chelsea, was already a member of the church at this date and was one of the over-night 'fire-watchers' in the building during some of the worst months early in 1941. But he recalls being more awe-struck by some of the preaching than by the bombing. On one hot Sunday evening in the late summer of 1940 one memorable sermon ended with a call to repentance, based upon the 'woes' pronounced upon Chorazin and Bethsaida and the words 'for if the mighty works which were done in you had been done in Tyre and Sidon, they would have repented long ago in sackcloth and ashes' (Matt. 11:21). 'He gave no soft comfort, there was no alternative to repentance except "woe" . . . "Look at people in the air-raid shelters, with bombs falling! What are they doing? Are they prepared to meet God? No, they are singing 'Roll out the Barrel' and 'On with the Dance'. Woe to London!"'

A number who heard him were young people who did not survive the war. Carl Johan Bruhn was a young Dane who with his British bride, Anne, was driving over forty miles to sit under Dr Lloyd-Jones' preaching when war broke out. Although not yet qualified in medicine, it was only after Dr Lloyd-Jones' strong advice that he desisted from offering to serve for the Red Cross in Finland's terrible struggle against Russia. When Dr Lloyd-Jones preached from Romans 8:28 (the last of his short series on 'Why Does God Allow War') it was Carl Bruhn who came to the vestry to ask for the exact Scripture references which he had quoted at the conclusion of the sermon and especially where he could find the words, 'My grace is sufficient for thee'. The next year, there was no detaining Bruhn – now qualified – from the struggle in Europe. He offered and was accepted for service with the Resistance Forces in his own country, now overrun. Taken by the RAF to be dropped by parachute into Denmark in December, 1941, weather conditions proved too bad for the jump. A second run was made on December 28; about midnight, with his plane over its correct position, Bruhn said farewell to the flight crew and leaped into the night. His parachute never opened.

On January 22, 1942, in a four-page letter to Anne Bruhn, Dr Lloyd-Jones wrote:

I cannot tell you how shocked I was to hear the news of the passing of your dear husband from Commander Hollingworth this morning on the telephone.

And yet, at a time like this, it is something which happens constantly. At once I thought of your last letter to me in which you stated that you had a sense of foreboding . . .

We feel for you more than we can tell you. But it is good to know that you will not mourn as 'those without hope'. It is at such a time as this that one realizes the full value of the Christian faith. Were this life and this world all, how terrible would be the outlook. More than that 'God giveth grace' and you will not be left to yourself . . .

I have not heard the details of what happened, but I am certain that calmly and deliberately he sacrificed his life for freedom, truth and honour against the hateful tyranny of Nazism . . .

Probably you feel that all you had planned and looked forward to has suddenly gone, but however hard it is, you will believe won't you that God knows best and 'all things work together for good to those that love God'.

Speaking many years later of this time, Dr Anne Bruhn (or Connan, for she frequently used her British maiden name), wrote, 'I began attending Westminster almost as soon as Dr Lloyd-Jones came there and was then a very immature groping Christian'. One of the first effects of his ministry which she found was a new urge to explore the Scriptures for herself. 'He so exalted the Lord Christ, and never obtruded himself, that he created a real thirst in me for the living God – but never left me with a feeling of self satisfaction, neither so deflated as to be near despair.'

Perhaps the most remarkable providence at this period was related to the new faces which were now gradually replacing the many pre-war hearers. The newcomers were not Londoners but frequently service men and women. Some were Europeans escaped from the Continent and now serving with the Allies, others were from distant parts of the Commonwealth and, later, from the United States. In this way his ministry became international in a sense which no one anticipated. Campbell Morgan's fears lest he had brought his colleague to the wrong place at the wrong time were unfounded.

An unknown number of these overseas visitors were converted at Westminster Chapel. Deliberately, Dr Lloyd-Jones employed no methods to register such conversions. 'I believed the message and that God would honour my efforts,' he said many years later. That was enough. But although he did not see the tabulation of results as part of his work there were not infrequently cases which came to light:

I remember how during the depths of the Second World War when everything was about as discouraging as it could be – bombing had scattered our congregation and so on – and I was facing great discouragement. I suddenly received a letter from the Dutch East Indies, now known as Indonesia. It was from a Dutch soldier who wrote saying that his conscience had been pricking him and, at last, had driven him to write to tell me what had happened to him eighteen months before. He explained how he had come to England with the Dutch Free Army and while stationed in London had attended our services for some time. While doing so he had been convinced of the fact that he had never been a Christian at all though he had thought he was. He had then passed through a dark period of conviction of sin and hopelessness, but, eventually, he had seen the Truth and had been rejoicing in it ever since.

Another Dutch attender at Westminster Chapel at this period was a member of the premier aristocratic family of his country, an aide-de-camp to Queen Wilhelmina, and serving with the Dutch Government in exile. His father was President of Queen's Council through-out the war and, with other members of the Dutch Government, lived at St James' Court (a large block of apartments) next door to the Chapel. Forty years later this former aide-de-camp was to write to an English friend of his memories of Sundays at Westminster: 'How impressive were those sermons! I have heard many excellent preachers but none of them could equal Lloyd-Jones in his grasp that

[33]

so united many passages of the Scriptures. Alas, nobody here of the people I see ever heard of Dr Martyn Lloyd-Jones and those who were in London during the war are no more.' The writer, who was the Dutch Ambassador in Moscow after the war, closed his letter with the Russian Christian greeting, 'The Lord has arisen!'.

A number of young Christians in the services who came to Westminster Chapel gained a benefit from the ministry which was to become a permanent influence in their future Christian service. One of several such men was Robert S. Miller, who left home in New Zealand in January, 1941, and reached Chatham, Kent, the following May for officer-training in the Royal Naval Volunteer Reserve. He wrote in his diary for Sunday, May 25: 'I went into London to hear Dr Martyn Lloyd-Jones at Westminster Chapel. He gave a very fine message, and I had the pleasure of meeting him after the service.' His next opportunity to be at the Chapel was on October 4, 1941, when he was accompanied by Des Wardell, another New Zealander: 'On Sunday morning we went to Westminster Chapel and heard Dr Martyn Lloyd-Jones who was again excellent. His message was *apropos* of the times. He spoke for 35 minutes and there was rapt attention all the time.'

As Miller and Wardell left the service they were welcomed by a Mrs Dagmar André, who also enquired if the two 'sailor boys' with New Zealand shoulder flashes possessed New Testaments. Mrs André was a Swedish lady who turned her comfortable flat on Park Lane into a 'home away from home' for many servicemen and women. The two New Zealanders went there for the first time that day.

On Sunday, November 23, 1941, Miller was again in London and his diary reads:

After dinner at the N.Z. Forces' Club, I went across to Westminster Chapel at 3 p.m. to hear Dr Lloyd-Jones. I am becoming quite well known there now and was shown to a seat right down the front. Again we had 'Eternal Light', which seems to be one of the Doctor's favourites, for he often quotes it. He preached on four words from the story of Lot: 'Escape to the mountain'; and stressed the fact that the Gospel message *begins with a warning*. It was a most impressive and convincing sermon. He absolutely trounces all the wishful thinkers, modern critics and their ilk.

By this date Miller was finishing his officer training at HMS King Alfred, Hove, on the South Coast. It so happened that Mrs André owned a holiday home in that vicinity which had been enjoyed by missionaries until war-time restrictions on travel to the English Channel curtailed its use. This house she now gladly made available to the officer-cadets at HMS King Alfred and when Miller, with twelve other sub-lieutenants graduated in January, 1942, Mrs André came down from London for the occasion, accompanied by ML-J. The New Zealander recorded:

Mrs André threw a party for the benefit of our friends, at which eleven of the boys were present. We had a great dinner party, then games, followed by a splendid, straight-forward simple Gospel message by Dr Martyn Lloyd-Jones, who was the guest of the evening, and made the trip from London especially for the purpose. Much of his address was testimony – why he left medicine for the Ministry. Our chaps were definitely impressed, particularly two Australians. It was grand also to have a good personal talk with the Doctor. He is a great man and a great preacher; and withal so humble, human and helpful.

That January night in Hove, shortly before Miller left the United Kingdom, was long to be remembered by him. And there was one incident, recalled in later years, which did not gain a mention in his diary at the time: 'One of the games that evening, between the meal and the message, involved the transfer, without hands, of a match-box cover, from one's own nose to that of another! Being of even height, I found myself "matched" with the worthy Doctor!'

Although Robert Miller's personal link with Martyn Lloyd-Jones was thus comparatively brief, it was to have an enduring impact upon his own life and future ministry as a Presbyterian preacher and professor of church history in New Zealand and Australia.

I believe that it was God who arranged that the main path of my life would cross the path of the one who agreed, and yielded at last, to be my wife. On January 8, 1927, we started walking together along the 'way that leads to life'.

ML-J,
on Radio 4 (Wales), 21 April, 1971

Let us in our married relationships show how Christ binds together two persons in holy love . . . let us so live in this relationship that people of the world looking at us shall say, 'Would to God we could live like that; would to God we were as happy as they are . . .'.

ML-J,
1948 (*The Life of Joy*, a Commentary on
Philippians 1 and 2, p. 207, 1989)

3

Inside the Family

From the time of the Lloyd-Joneses' arrival in London in 1938 they had lived at 12 Vincent Square until it was clear that they were meant to stay in England. Then, as already noted, on the very eve of buying their own house war had been declared. The first months of the war brought the longest separation of Martyn from Bethan to occur during their married lives.

From the end of August 1939 Mrs Lloyd-Jones, Elizabeth and Ann stayed with the Pearces in Llanelli – the family with whom they had first stayed for the memorable Christmas of 1929.[1] The house was large enough for them to live separately and to look after themselves independently. In Bethan's own words: 'It was kind enough of our hosts to give us house-room, without adding another family to their load of domestic work. So, I "did" for us to the last detail'. (The lack of such freedom for most evacuee mothers and children was a factor in the decision which soon brought them back to the cities.) Dr Lloyd-Jones had only one major concern about the household arrangement at Llanelli and it was one which was to amuse them in later years. Hitherto, as in most middle-class families, their home had never been run without a maid. Even while staying in Vincent Square, Theresa, their Welsh maid, had been with them. Suddenly the Second World War ended this household pattern forever. 'What worried Martyn,' his wife tells us, 'was that I was not used to it. In those incredibly far away days, I had never been without some domestic help with household chores, and he thought that the cleaning and working and washing and care of the girls would find me wilting! Actually, of course, it was nothing but a gentle introduction to the change that the war was going to make in ordinary domestic life and living. It never worried me.'

[1]See vol. 1, p. 194.

The letters from ML-J at Vincent Square to Llanelli reveal how troubled he was at Bethan having to do such things as lighting fires in the morning. Expressing his objections, he reluctantly admits in a letter of September 16, 1939, 'I have thought and thought again, but I cannot see any better arrangement than the present one'. 'Don't kill yourself with work, and get enough sleep,' is a characteristic exhortation. On another occasion, after a visit to the family, he expressed his pleasure that, despite so much to do, Bethan had been able to speak at a local 'Sisterhood' meeting. His reasoning, however, made her smile:

If I did not remember to say a word about your talk in the Sisterhood yesterday, I did remember to pray for you in the train. I'm sure you were doing the right thing and I'm sure you would greatly help the women. But quite apart from that, even, I want you to do this, if only to use your mind. That is one of the things that grieves me when I think of you with so much to do that you do not have time to read.

Their financial situation at this time also gave him added concern lest Bethan's necessary economies should be too stringent. Although he shares with her the likely difficulties ahead at Westminster – 'Gotts told me that the collections are down £1500 [i.e. *per annum*] on an average!' – he is insistent: 'There is no need for you to cut back on expense at all. Take care to prepare and to eat proper meals . . .'. 'Don't worry about the cost of Elizabeth's books . . . she has got to have them.' In later years when he so often helped struggling pastors with gifts for their families, they little realized that he and Mrs Lloyd-Jones had known what it was to experience that same problem.

Dr Lloyd-Jones' capacity for sympathy with others is an aspect of his character which often appears in his letters to Bethan. It comes out in comments on many people, from Campbell-Morgan and Bethan's parents, to their former maid, Theresa, who had become seriously ill: 'I am truly sorry for Theresa, I have thought much about her and remembered her in prayer all day.' In an address to fellow doctors he once said, 'I seriously question whether anyone has a right to be practising clinical medicine who has no real concern for persons and for people'. He possessed that quality in large measure.

It was not Dr Lloyd-Jones' habit to speak of personal affairs and even those close to him in the troubled autumn of 1939 supposed that he divided his time between London at the weekends, and

Llanelli mid-week. They were wrong. The truth was that his mid-week preaching engagements – which he had once supposed might ease on his leaving Wales – continued to take him to many different places. Certainly Llanelli was where he wished to be, but calls to preach were not to be refused on account of war or his family, and so visits to South Wales could only be occasional. Letters, however, were constant, and while his week-day engagements away from Westminster Chapel were similar, he never failed to tell Bethan what they were:

I had a somewhat busy day yesterday, as I had to prepare two new addresses – one for the ministers, who belong to the London Baptist Association, with whom I am to be on Tuesday morning, and the other for Rheinallt's induction meeting.[1] I felt that the two addresses had to be quite different. I shall address the ministers on The Ministry *Today*, but Rheinallt on the unchangeable nature of the ministry . . .

Concerning another week he writes:

I am preaching in a Mission with the Congregationalists in the Old Kent Road on Monday afternoon and, of course, there is the Fellowship on Monday night. Then on Wednesday I am due to preach in Richmond Hill, Bournemouth for Dr John Short, who followed Dr J. D. Jones, preaching afternoon and evening. I shall have to stay there overnight, I'm afraid. That is all I am doing this week . . .

The war, however, caused a few mid-week meetings to be cancelled. Even so, in the period September–November, 1939 his engagements away from Westminster included visits to such places as Worthing, Whitchurch, Carmarthen, Brighton, Croydon, Fulham, Cambridge, Nuneaton, Aldershot, Manchester, Holywell, Rhyl, Cardiff and Haslemere. The visit to the last-named proved to be of particular significance. Haslemere is a small country town high in the Weald of Surrey. Gerald Golden, a surgeon who lived there, had invited Dr Lloyd-Jones to preach in a local cinema on two consecutive evenings towards the end of October. By this date, as ML-J had been travelling in quiet areas of Southern England, the idea had already occurred to him of their renting a house near enough to

[1] Rheinallt Nantlais Williams, later to be the Principal of the Theological College at Aberystwyth.

London for him to be able to travel into Westminster by train. Both Worthing and Brighton were tempting; he did not know how vulnerable both coastal resorts were soon to become in their situation on the English Channel. Haslemere, however, deep in the country and half-way between the South Coast and London, had not occurred to him prior to his visit. By early November 1939 he was still considering housing possibilities in various places in Surrey and Sussex, though now of the opinion that 'Haslemere is the best idea'. Meanwhile the Goldens were looking in their neighbourhood, and on November 9, 'almost too excited to write', Martyn passes on to Bethan a letter from Dorothy Golden which describes a 'find' which she and her husband could recommend. It was a new semi-detached house available on a rental. In Mrs Golden's words, 'clean and marvellously healthy, with a lovely view at the back, and the living rooms get all the sun'. Dr Lloyd-Jones speedily went to see it, and after letters and phone calls to Bethan they decided to take it. The disadvantage was its smallness, it would not be large enough to take all their furniture and his books which were still in storage in Cardiff. But on the situation he shared Dorothy Golden's enthusiasm: 'It is very beautiful,' he wrote to Bethan, 'standing about 500–600 feet above sea level. Pine trees all over the place and lovely walks . . . It is a hundred times better than Brighton.' It could be leased for the duration of the war and at a rental of only £150 per year, 'whereas rates and rent for one year at Kensington would have been £210'. The house was taken and because it had no name or number Dr Lloyd-Jones had to find a name quickly for its identification in the legal agreement awaiting signature. 'The Haven' was his choice and it was to be their home for the four years from December 1939 to November 1943.

Before we leave the period when Mrs Lloyd-Jones and the girls were at Llanelli, there remains one thing more to be said about the letters between husband and wife. There is an argument which recurs in their letters (the only argument, as Philip Henry used to say, permitted between a husband and wife), namely, who loved the other the most. Bethan's side of the 'argument' has not survived, but it would not have been easy for her to be the winner! Dr Lloyd-Jones was always indignant about the view he sometimes heard in evangelical circles that any two Christians should be able to marry one another. On the contrary, he believed that couples needed both to 'fall in love' and to stay in love. The following gives a glimpse of the happiness of his relationship to 'the dearest girl in the world':

I see time passing terribly slowly, and the absence of your company is overpowering. There are dozens of things that arise from what I notice, or from what I am thinking or reading, that I would like to talk about with you. But you are not here . . .

I was thinking much about you on my travels yesterday. I was passing through Harrow and that brought back innumerable memories of the days when I used to make my way down to see you, and of our trips out to Rickmansworth, etc. I remember the inner excitement as we approached Harrow station and as I thought about you. But that was not to be compared with what I felt yesterday as I thought about you. With every passing year I realize more and more that I am the luckiest man in all the world . . . No lover ever longed for his beloved as much as your poor husband longs for you.

At the end of November 1939 he was due to preach in Cardiff (not far from Llanelli) and he was anxious to make arrangements to meet Bethan there, although the next week they were all to remove together to the new home in Haslemere. The following letter is so characteristic that it is given in full:

12 Vincent Square
November 27, 1939

My dear Bethan,

A word in a very great hurry, to give you 'instructions' for tomorrow.

I was glad to have your letter this morning and to know that you had really enjoyed yourselves Saturday and yesterday.

We had amazingly good congregations yesterday, considering the weather. I preached a new sermon on Acts 3 – the point being: 'expecting to receive something of them' – wrong attitude to the church and her Gospel.

Vin returned last night having found everything all right in Hereford. I have been at it all day doing this and that – talking to Douglas Johnson, preparing a manuscript for Marsh for the *Westminster Record*, and so on. Of course the Fellowship is at 6.30. Now, about tomorrow. Here are the 'instructions': You'll arrive probably on Platform 2. If you find, on asking! – that my train is *not* yet in, walk down the steps to the subway and walk up the steps to Platform 3 – the one on which I shall arrive. If you are told that the train is going to be late, go and sit by the fire in the waiting-room. When the train arrives stand on the platform, *between* the two stairs that lead to the subway. I shall make for that point. If I am in first, I shall stand between the two stairways leading to the subway, on platform 2. So, have a look there first. We cannot miss each other. There is no danger of our missing each other – if you were in a haystack I'd find you. My only anxiety is that someone else will be trying to get hold of you too! Remember that Cardiff is a very cold place. Put plenty of warm clothes on and eat plenty of breakfast. How to wait till tomorrow I don't know?

Till then all my love to you my dear love, and to the two girls and my affectionate regards to all there.

Ever yours, Martyn.

❊   ❊   ❊

Although it might hardly seem so from his itinerary, Dr Lloyd-Jones was still at this date struggling with the health problems which were noted at the conclusion of his ministry at Aberavon.[1] He had not yet been able to throw off the general feeling of exhaustion which he came to experience in his late thirties and this had given him sufficient concern to put himself under his old chief, Lord Horder, in 1939. ML-J's own experience in treating ministers and clergy when he was practising medicine had led him to consider them all 'a pack of neurotics'. Given the state of his own health, he had to revise that view and to confess, 'There are tensions in the ministry – the very nature of the work tends to produce them'.

Not naturally inclined to much exercise, Dr Lloyd-Jones made a special effort at this period. There were frequent references to it in his letters to Bethan while she was still at Llanelli. 'The post is here at about 8.10 every morning, so I read your letter before going out for my walk every day.' 'I walked for 45 minutes before breakfast this morning.' 'Nowadays I am walking for 40 minutes before breakfast, and again in the afternoon for the same length of time. It must surely be beneficial.'

When the family was together again under one roof there was still need of occasional letters to Bethan. With war-time conditions too uncertain to be able to depend upon the railway on Sunday mornings, and not possessing a car, ML-J usually went up to London from Haslemere on Saturday evenings. Sometimes, depending on the location of his mid-week engagements, he was not home again until the following Thursday. Wherever he was he rang Bethan every day and often sent a short letter. From these letters it is clear that his health was a continuing concern to them both.

In a note to his wife from Vincent Square at the conclusion of

[1]Vol. 1, pp. 331 and 337.

Sunday, February 11, 1940, Martyn reported: 'The catarrh was quite bad as I preached and, after some 30 minutes, I felt that my voice was going. This meant that I could do no more than give a synopsis of the two last points. CM had not noticed that anything was wrong.' The following night he travelled overnight by train for engagements at Newcastle.

Two weeks later, after the Sunday morning service at the Chapel, he wrote:

Just a word to let you know that I feel much better today. I decided in the train last night that my 'gout' was the trouble, after all, and having made the right diagnosis, I began to get better. I am now quite sure that I never had the influenza at all!

I got through the service with no difficulty at all – Vincent says he never heard so much resonance in my voice. It was quite a good service, too, and yet I feel that this is the weakest of the four sermons.

I am now off to Paddington Chapel . . .[1]

Apart from his general run-down condition it was his voice which was giving him the greatest problem at this time. The trouble was the result of a long-established bad habit, for, instead of the use of correct voice production in public speaking, he had depended on the physical energy of youth. As that energy came to fail him he faced persistent problems. There were several references to it in the letters of 1939 to Bethan. 'I don't feel tired, but I had to be careful with my voice last night.' 'I'm sure you were thinking of me in the services yesterday. Well, I got through both without losing my voice, but I had to be very careful.'

His deliverance from a misuse of his voice in preaching owed much to a lady by the name of Miss Hicks who had helped many other public speakers, including Lloyd George. Bethan Lloyd-Jones speaks of her 'genius in voice production', and writes the following about her visits to Haslemere:

[1]i.e. to take an evening service. Thus, while sharing the Sunday services at Westminster with Dr Morgan, he frequently took another service elsewhere in London. At Sunday lunch-time, and in the afternoon, he took the opportunity to meet various members of the congregation. In one Sunday letter to Bethan, written in his vestry at Westminster, he says: 'Mr and Mrs Ryley and I had lunch with Lady Hearn who lives in a flat in Buckingham Gate – a good and fine woman. Then I joined a group of young people who meet here on Sunday afternoon for Christian fellowship.'

Miss Hicks deserves notice. She was of the same general shape and outline as Queen Victoria, with equal authoritative determination and gimlet eye. I cannot remember how Martyn got in touch with her. She came and stayed at a small hotel and spent two or three hours every day correcting Martyn's faulty voice production – giving him various exercises, etc. She was to be remembered with gratitude for she certainly knew her job. To the very end if he had any throat trouble or if he were tired, I would hear him go through the exercises and the trouble would soon be gone.

With regard to the measures needed for the recovery of ML-J's health in 1940, there was some difference of opinion among his medical advisers. In Horder's view he was still doing far too much and many of his commitments needed cancelling. But in a letter to Bethan from Vincent Square on April 1, 1940, Martyn reported another opinion:

As for myself, as I told you on the phone, I have been feeling very tired all day. I did not sleep too well last night for some reason. The sermon on Matthew 11:28–30, went very well. I don't think I have ever been wiser or more sensible in my preaching, as far as the use of my voice goes – no, never before. (Many people had noticed this). If only I had not shouted somewhat more than was necessary at about 7.0 it would have been perfect. I do believe that I have mastered the principles in this matter.

The exhaustion came on at about the same time, about 5.30. I felt better at this end than at the beginning. As I told you, Dr B— is wonderfully optimistic – 'It's a real gift' was his phrase. 'We can cure it absolutely.' He was not at all willing for me to cancel all my engagements. 'I want you to stick to the mid-week engagements away from home,' he said. 'Can you help me in the meantime,' said I. 'Certainly!' The diagnosis is 'sympathetic nervous system dysfunction, due to over-exertion.' As you know, I agree entirely with this.

I have slept for half-an-hour now and feel better. I am just off to the Fellowship. I'll send you a line from Birmingham D.V. I am disappointed that I cannot reach home on Thursday, but it cannot be helped.

While Bethan – herself a doctor – hesitated over the soundness of this advice, Thomas Horder attempted to enforce his judgment as the following letter from Martyn to his mother of April 11, 1940, reveals:

I have been out for a walk today and feel all the better for it. I propose to walk now every day. It is a pity that it still remains coldish though today is nice. I do not think that I can promise to go to Stanley White's place on Sunday night. I think that Horder should have written to you rather than to the deacons of Westminster Chapel about my condition! I must reserve every ounce of energy I have and not use it except when absolutely essential. My trouble has been that I have lived on my nervous energy.

One can be sure that ML-J was not prepared to allow his health to be discussed at deacons' meetings. 'He persuaded us all,' says Bethan, 'that to do only one service on Sunday was enough of a rest. But, of course, it never came to that – well, hardly ever.'

Dr Lloyd-Jones' own poor health in 1940 was over-shadowed early in that year by the more serious illness of his friend, Douglas Johnson, who, after prolonged over-work, suffered a coronary occlusion. In the course of a letter to Mrs Johnson of January 19, 1940, ML-J wrote:

I am so glad to hear that he is somewhat better.

I feel I must tell you that every time I pray for him (and I do so twice daily) I have a very definite and unmistakable consciousness of the fact of his complete and entire recovery.

That kind of thing, as he will know, is not common with me. I report it because it is so very definite.

Unable to meet, the two men corresponded as well as speaking on the phone. In a letter to DJ on May 8 ML-J writes: 'It is good to hear of your continued progress. I am also improving daily – with Miss Hicks still in attendance!'

ML-J's own slow improvement he attributed – for the present, at least – to the greater opportunities for physical exercise afforded by the situation at Haslemere. Besides afternoon walks with his girls when school was over, the garden of the newly-built house which they were renting was in need of attention. It consisted merely of rough earth, with much builder's rubble still lying about. And there was another reason, in addition to his health, for addressing himself to the garden. Gerald Golden recalls: 'This was a time of great national stress, and everyone was deeply committed to helping the war effort in some way or other. In a small country town the most obvious way for many was food production, and the vegetable garden was a "must". Martyn was not slow to accept the challenge, though his competence in this direction was limited. I remember his

laboriously planting out cabbage plants, but they did not prosper. I
don't think he ever had much satisfaction from his garden labours.
Though he took the work seriously he always looked ill at ease and
gently amused.'

In the early summer of 1941 Bethan was ill with pneumonia and
for convalescence she went, with Ann, to her parents who had
evacuated from the London suburb of Harrow to the peace of
Newcastle Emlyn in West Wales. Martyn and Elizabeth remained at
Haslemere and from a letter to Bethan of June 18 it is evident that
gardening was still in full swing:

I'm glad you had a better journey than I did and that you arrived safely. I
hope above all things that you are having the same wonderful weather as
we are – it is marvellous, if anything too hot.

I have earthed the potatoes, all but two rows. I have also given the peas
some kind of support – with some string running from one to another. I
believe that will be enough to hold them until I can get some better
stakes. The cabbage and lettuce have taken well. I am afraid that one of
the marrow plants has died. I give them water every night. The carrots
and beetroot are looking very well, and there are flowers on the broad
beans. So you see that I am fairly diligent! I go to the garden every night
at about 6.15 for a couple of hours.

Oh, yes, Mr Oberheim lent me a spanner and I was able to correct the
fault in the two hot taps. You can see that, between one thing and
another, you have a really useful husband!

The days pass very slowly, but if you come back strong, well, I am
willing to wait in patience.

You know that I am preaching in the More Street Baptist Church
tomorrow evening at 7 o'clock. I mean to go up [to London] with the 2
o'clock train to meet Sangster[1] and to have tea with him. The meeting in
Mrs André's Mission is on Saturday afternoon.[2] I shall go up with the 11
o'clock train, have lunch with her and then she will take me in her car.

Tell Ann I greatly miss the 'little gardener'.

According to ML-J's later memories, his achievements at gardening came to a head one Good Friday (probably in 1942). While he

[1]W. E. Sangster, the Methodist minister of Westminster Central Hall, close to
Westminster Chapel.
[2]Mrs André looked after a mission hall on the docks in the East End of London
(similar to the Poplar mission where he had preached once or twice before
leaving Medicine). In another letter he describes her as 'a really good woman'.

was up at Westminster preaching on that particular day Bethan accepted the offer of a load of manure which was dumped in the road at the front of the house. It had all to be removed to the back, by wheelbarrow, and over rough ground as there was no pathway around the house. The result of this 'splendid' Saturday exercise was that, after preaching at Westminster on the Sunday, he had to spend three days in bed to recover! Amusing though the incident was, it had its important side because it helped him to reach a final conclusion about himself. He was not meant for physical exercise. He would later say that it took him a number of years to recognize this. By way of explanation he distinguished sharply between 'nervous' and physical energy. In his opinion, he possessed much of the former and little of the latter. 'Any physical exertion always exhausts me.' The after effect of physical labour was to lower his blood pressure and, thus, far from being a stimulus, it was actually debilitating: 'I had to stop. I couldn't do my work if I didn't. I have no physical energy at all, if I expend it I cannot read or think.' But in situations demanding 'nervous energy' (such as public speaking), he could say, 'I have seen physically strong men almost fainting when I was fine'.

This was one of the few personal things about which Dr Lloyd-Jones did speak in ministers' meetings because he was convinced that 'great damage' could be done to some men by the theory that a vigorous athletic life is always the best way to promote health. He regarded all such generalizations as wrong:

I am an opponent of universal set rules for all. Nothing is more important than that a man should get to know himself. I include in that that he should get to know himself physically as well as temperamentally and in other respects. I say this because there are those who would prescribe a programme for a preacher and minister; they tell him when to get up in the morning, what to do before breakfast, and what to do later and so on. They do not hesitate to draw up systems and programmes and to advocate these, and indeed almost to suggest that, if a man does not follow such a programme, he is a sinner and a failure. I have always been an opponent of such ideas and for this reason, that we are all different, and that you cannot lay down a programme of this nature for everybody.

We live in the body, and our bodies differ from case to case. We also have different temperaments and natures, so you cannot lay down universal rules . . .

Some of us are slow starters in the morning; others wake up fresh and brimful of energy in the morning, like a dog on the leash, waiting to go to work. We do not determine this; it is something constitutional. It depends on many factors, partly, if not chiefly, on blood pressure and such matters as your nervous constitution, the balance of your ductless glands, etc. All these factors come in. I argue therefore that our first business is to get to know ourselves. Get to know how you, with your particular constitution, work. Get to know when you are at your best and how to handle yourself.[1]

These words came from personal experience as well as from medical knowledge. It was in large measure his better understanding of himself which led to the improvement in his health in these years. He passed out of a tendency to depression (which he regarded as common in the early-forties age group) and, in Bethan's words, 'steadily regained his old tireless elasticity'. Those who only saw him so amazingly active at a later period would have found it hard to believe that he had ever passed through such a problem with respect to his health.

*　　　　*　　　　*

The War had brought a change to the family routine on Sundays. When they had first moved to England, and were staying at Vincent Square near Westminster Chapel, they were all in church, with Ann being introduced to public worship from her infancy as Elizabeth had been. There was a crèche for babies and infants but ML-J expected all children to be present with their parents for a whole service just as soon as they could be quiet. Of course, there were occasional mishaps, as the Lloyd-Joneses themselves experienced. Once when Elizabeth was very small, on observing her father bow his head to pray as he led the service, she exclaimed audibly, 'He has gone sleepy byes!'

With the move to Haslemere, it was virtually impossible for Bethan and the children to be at Westminster on Sundays and so the local Congregational church became their place of worship until November 1943. Another Sunday event which these new circumstances ended was the afternoon walk. While still at Vincent Square either Bethan or Martyn would take the girls on a short walk to St

---

[1]*Preaching*, pp. 167–8.

James' Park. Ann was still a toddler. When the duty was in Bethan's hands it usually ended with the weary infant being carried home and both mother and child exhausted. But the conclusion was different when her father was in charge. On hearing the plea to be carried he would respond cheerfully, 'Oh, I *am* sorry, are you tired? All right you shall carry my umbrella then.' This never failed both to bring him back fresh and Ann happy, trailing the umbrella behind her. 'He was devoted to the girls,' writes Mrs Lloyd-Jones, 'and however busy and hard pressed he was would always have time for them. He would also, it seemed, be as defensive as he dared, on their behalf, when mother was "laying down the law"!'

Speaking of her husband's view of the Lord's Day, as it affects the family, Mrs Lloyd-Jones has also written:

Martyn regarded Sunday as a gift to Christians from the Lord – for one day in seven they were released from 'the daily round and common task' and could give every waking minute to the things of God and of the spirit. Therefore he believed that chores should be cut down to the minimum but one ought not to be like the orthodox Jew who gets his neighbours to come in and light the fire on a Sabbath morning. Such legalistic Sabbatarianism is born of the spirit of fear. Be reasonable – leave all that can be left till Monday. Don't spend your Sunday afternoons writing letters. If you have no church duties, spend it reading the Bible and books helpful to the spiritual life.

He was never strict or rigid with the children! They came to Church (where they soon learnt to sit still) and Sunday School, and then, as long as they did not play noisy games to disturb other people, they could do what they liked. It was left to me to suggest that dolls were suitable, as they were their children, and had to be washed and dressed – and taken to Sunday School! M's dictum always was: 'Don't expect Christian behaviour from non-Christians [e.g. the children before conversion], you are being cruel in taking from them innocent natural things they can enjoy, before they know anything of spiritual joys – it leaves them with nothing, and that is unkind.' All he asked was that Sunday should be seen to be 'different', by our example.

On the practical level, two areas of life affected by the austerities of war-time were those of food and clothing. These were the years of queues and scarcities, of ration cards and clothing coupons. With respect to clothing ML-J was unconcerned for it was a subject about which, in his wife's words, 'he had no interest'. That is not to say he was indifferent to the question of what he wore, on the contrary he believed that a minister of the gospel should always dress appropriately to his office, not in terms of a clerical collar (which he never wore) but in general appearance. He was invariably dressed in dark grey, with ties to match and a stiff white collar. Such things as coloured shirts or socks he never owned. The one item of his dress which tended to draw attention was his heavy dark overcoat, not on account of its appearance, but rather because of its use which frequently mystified people. Whenever he was preaching, regardless of the weather, the overcoat and, usually, a mackintosh, would be with him. After perspiring freely in the pulpit he would invariably don the coat before leaving the pulpit and then add the mackintosh as he left the building! Westminster Chapel provided the one variation in this procedure, for he could there go straight from the pulpit to the electric radiant fire which would be on in the vestry awaiting his return. In later years, when on visits to the States, there was another exception which could be still more bewildering to an onlooker. If the weather was overpoweringly hot he might leave a service with his coat over his arm and *then* put it on as he went into the hotel or wherever his hosts were taking him to lunch or supper. Having been caught once by the coolness of the air-conditioning common in public buildings, he never suffered again!

The Second World War was a time for simplicity and plainness in food and, by and large, this corresponded with a change in ML-J's own taste. 'As a young man,' Bethan Lloyd-Jones says, 'he liked what we think of as "stodge" – steak and kidney suet puddings – apple puddings, syrup puddings, apple tarts, apple charlottes, etc., etc., but they all, every one of them, got phased out as he learnt that they were not all that good to preach on! That was the standard, and all he did and all he ate had eventually to conform to that, so the plain and simple fare took over and light sponges would take the place of the suet offerings! Pastry was *out*, but to the end of his days he loved custard (boiled!) or a sweet white sauce with a nut of butter in it, and chocolate biscuits (indeed any form of chocolate) were first favourites.'

On the question of alcohol, his views were closer to contemporary evangelicalism than to the older nonconformists. To quote his wife again:

He would never say that to take an alcoholic drink was a sin, though he would expect Christians to abstain from indulging because its *misuse* in these days has become a national sin and a very real moral problem. In other words, abstain for the good of the 'weaker brother'. In addition to this he would often say, you never know that you may not yourself *be* the weaker brother. We never kept alcoholic drinks in the house, nor offered them to anyone – indeed, I still have, untouched, the small flask of whiskey and a bottle of brandy which my father gave us when we were married, insisting that we should keep some in the house in case of emergencies!

*   *   *

What had been true of ML-J's experience in his childhood was to remain true all his days, 'Our family life,' he could say, 'was extremely happy'. Home was his highest earthly blessing and to miss it – *hiraeth* – was the worst of all natural afflictions. On that level nothing ever exceeded the pain he had known in having to leave home for school in Tregaron at the age of eleven and later years only deepened his conviction about the rightness of that feeling. Few who knew him only as a public figure would anticipate the side of his character which the following narrative reveals:

I shall never forget myself travelling in a train back from Plymouth to London once. We arrived at Newton Abbot and a woman with two small girls came into the compartment where I was sitting. It was obvious that the children were returning to a boarding school after the holidays. After placing the girls in their seats the mother got out and stood on the platform until the train started. As the carriage began to move slowly away the smaller of the two little girls kept on looking after her mother longingly with tears filling her eyes. And then the elder sister told her sharply – and she was as near to tears herself – 'Don't look at her you fool!' I am not ashamed to say that I lifted the book which I was reading to hide my face and I cried with the little girls. I was back in my lodgings at Tregaron once again, and it took me a great deal of time to recompose myself. I believe that I shall never totally recover from this until I reach the country where we shall meet never to part anymore.[1]

When Dr Lloyd-Jones' preaching engagements often took him

[1]From the Reminiscences of his early life, given on Radio 4 (Wales) April 21, 1971, and published in Welsh in *Y Llwybrau Gynt*, ed. Alun Oldfield-Davies, vol. 2, Llandysul, 1972. Apart from the few extracts in these pages, the whole of the autobiography can be found (in translation) in volume 1.

away from Bethan and home he would usually ring her at night and, if his absence was for more than 48 hours, often write to her as well. Characteristic of the newsy letters which he wrote on these occasions is one from Hertford College, Oxford, on February 4, 1941, while he was taking part in a mission to the University:

I was disappointed that I failed to phone last night. I was kept in Jesus College till 9.50. I got on to the phone as soon as I got back, but was told '2 hours delay'. I put the call in tonight before leaving for the meeting so hope to get through about 10.0 – we'll see. I sent the telegram to let you know I was all right.

The meeting in St Mary's on Sunday night went very well. I had not a moment of trouble with the acoustics, and I felt that the congregation listened well. The text was Luke 12:54–57, the place was full.

I dined with the dons in 'Jesus' before the meeting with some 20 of the boys. The discussion was exceptionally good, and I believe that the Chaplain received great benefit.

I went to listen to Prof. O. C. Quick lecturing at 10.0 this morning. He was very good, but, to tell the truth, I felt that I had dealt with the matter in a much deeper way in the Brotherhood at Sandfields!

Today I am due to have lunch with Dr and Mrs Micklem in Mansfield. I am to be in Ena's old college[1] at tea time and speaking tonight at 8.15 in the Sheldonian Theatre.

There is nothing special on Thursday but meetings in different colleges. On Friday I am due to have breakfast with William Riddle's son – a second edition of his father. Then I will go with him to a lecture given by C. S. Lewis (author of the book on *The Problem of Pain*) and I am to have lunch with Lewis,[2] dinner that night with John Marsh, the chaplain at Mansfield, speaking to the medicals at tea-time and a meeting at Christ Church at 9.15 pm.

It is very cold here. Ann's hot water bottle has been a blessing and I have had an extra rug on the bed. The snow has cleared and today is a better day.

---

[1] St Hugh's, where his sister-in-law Ena had attended.
[2] Lewis is said to have valued ML-J's appreciation and encouragement when the early edition of his *Pilgrim's Regress* was not selling well. Vincent Lloyd-Jones and Lewis knew each other well, being contemporaries at Oxford. ML-J met the author again and they had a long conversation when they both found themselves on the same boat to Ireland in 1953. On that later occasion, to the question, 'When are you going to write another book?', Lewis replied, 'When I understand the meaning of prayer'.

That's my news, and I feel all right. I hope it's not too cold with you – mind you keep warm. I hope to phone tonight.

✻   ✻   ✻

For summer holidays in war-time the conditions naturally curtailed travel. It made little difference for Martyn and Bethan as they had no higher preference than Wales which was easily reached by train. The first stop each year was usually at Sunnyside, Bethan's parents' home at Newcastle Emlyn where they could enjoy quiet and restful days. As usual on vacation, ML-J would read in the mornings. His main authors continued to be B. B. Warfield, J. C. Ryle and Charles Hodge but he was also at this date appreciating the Anglican, E. A. Litton and enjoying Henry W. Clark's *History of English Nonconformity* ('I was reading a lot of history at that time'). 'We spent many afternoons,' writes Bethan, 'visiting Martyn's relatives in the farms all around. Martyn loved the farming "ambience" (for want of a better word) and was never bored. We would go here and there for a day or two when mother had company.'

From Newcastle Emlyn they would commonly move on to Aberystwyth and to the home of Professor Morris Jones, 'Jasper House', which was lent to them on many occasions. Sometimes as in earlier years there were also August visits to Nantstalwyn sheep farm in mid-Wales, near the source of the Towy river. Speaking of times at Jasper House, Bethan Lloyd-Jones writes: 'The girls loved Aberystwyth. Our Sundays there were typical of Martyn when he was not preaching – 10 a.m. Welsh service. 11 a.m., slope out with the last hymn and go to the English. 2:00 p.m., about a mile up the hill out from Aberystwyth, a Welsh service. Home for tea. Evening, 6:00 or 6:30, wherever there was a preacher he was anxious to hear. He loved it all. He loved to hear preaching – he did not often have the chance.'

Wales never failed to refresh ML-J even though soon there were some things he would begin to miss. No words of his can give a better impression of the mark which his childhood among Welsh farms had left upon him than the following, spoken many years later, with which we conclude this chapter:

For me, there is no animal that beats a horse for grace and pomp. If someone should ask me, 'What sound would you like to hear again?' I should ask to hear the sound of a Shire stallion of about eighteen hands in height, newly shod for a show, walking accompanied by a man along a hard street and breaking, now and again, into a half trot and then walking orderly, regularly and graciously. Let the psychologists make what they like of the fact, but that sound had the same effect on me as listening to the music of Mozart. The thought of it still gives me a thrill, but unfortunately I have not heard the sound for years. If someone else were to ask me, 'What would you like to see?', I should answer at once, 'To see a number of hackneys in harness competing for a prize in one of the main shows.' Who can describe the dignity of these beautiful creatures with their heads and tails in the air, raising their four feet high and then striking the front ones forward? If seeing something of the sort is not undeniable proof of the being of God, then one must be a blind sinner. A man with all his cleverness cannot produce anything like it. Some years ago I was persuaded one evening to go to the White City to watch the jumping at a horse show which was being held there. I was enjoying myself quite well, but quite unexpectedly for me, a parade of harness horses was announced as the next item on the programme. And the best horses came in and paraded before us. I might as well admit that I was floored completely, and that the tears were pouring down my cheeks, to use one of the old Llangeitho sayings 'my heart was churning inside me'. What are hunters, cattle, sheep and pigs to compare with a sight like this? I hardly ever visit agricultural shows because the absence of horses, especially hackneys, is such a grief to me. I had much rather live on memories.[1]

[1]From his Reminiscences of his early life.

*In the religious world of Britain today Dr Lloyd-Jones occup-
ies quite a unique place.*

DONALD MACLEAN
Calvin Forum, April 1941, p. 198

*We had a good congregation again yesterday morning at
Westminster. And again in the afternoon. I am staying tonight
in Liverpool. I go on from there to Manchester for the
mid-day service tomorrow, then on to Grimsby on Wednesday. On Thursday night at Spalding, Stanley White is to be the
chairman. It is his home church.*

ML-J
To his mother, Oct. 26, 1942
(This itinerary is typical of the weeks when he was away from
home).

4

A Leader in Britain

In the England of the late 1930's and the 1940's there was a vacuum in the leadership of the nonconformist denominations. An old guard was passing, leaving the outward life of the Free Churches much as they had been in Victorian times, but within there was the consciousness of a loss of influence and direction. Theological liberalism had promised, fifty years earlier, that a Christianity in which the supernaturalism of the biblical records was muted or discarded would win the acceptance of the modern man. The spiritual weakness of the church was an eloquent commentary on that promise. Among the able voices of a younger generation in the religious scene of London there was no voice offering a new approach to the situation. Sometimes it was those altogether outside the church who made the most acute observations. Dr C. E. M. Joad, made famous by his part in the BBC's weekly 'Brains Trust' programme, wrote in 1940: 'We have abolished the fear of God and instead we live in constant fear of man. We have done away with the idea of a hell in the future and we have succeeded in turning our lives in this world into a living hell.'

The outlook of liberal Christianity had been that man was sound at heart, competent to achieve 'the greatest good for the greatest number' and, given 'Christian education', he would surely succeed. Now, however, many doubted that assumption. Even Aldous Huxley, the well-known agnostic, had been compelled to confess: 'Is the universe possessed of value and meaning? I took for granted that there was no meaning. I had motives for not wanting the world to have a meaning. Most ignorance is invincible ignorance – we don't know because we don't want to know.'

One notable figure to abandon liberalism by 1939 was

D. R. Davies whose book *On to Orthodoxy*, published that year, received widespread attention. *The Christian World*, still one of the foremost of Nonconformist weeklies, gave its 'Book Page' to Dr Lloyd-Jones for a major review of Davies' work. The choice of reviewer, in a paper hardly renowned for its orthodoxy, was significant. Dr Lloyd-Jones wrote:

The utter futility of all that has so often passed as gospel during the past hundred years is made terribly and tragically clear. Surely this is what is needed above all else at the present time. And especially, first and foremost, in the Churches. That complacent optimistic view of man and his nature that has so long controlled and directed thought and preaching must be given up, and must be replaced by the tragic view which is taught everywhere in the Bible.

Given this changing climate of opinion, there was a degree of readiness for a different message. We noted that in 1938 Dr Lloyd-Jones had been heralded by a spokesman for the National Free Church Council as 'the modern Moody', but there was now a consciousness that he was more than that. Dr J. D. Jones, the father figure of that Council, had already seen it when he urged Campbell Morgan to get him to Westminster. Here was a leader in a different mould. What made his biblical certainty the more remarkable was that, as everyone knew, he came from a background of science and medicine. It was virtually an axiom of modern thought that no one could be a scientist and a believer in an authoritative Bible at one and the same time. Science was supposed to have rendered impossible the claim of Scripture to be the Word of God. This was the supposition which, once embraced, had reduced whole generations of preachers to uncertainty. For years on end, clear teaching upon many parts of Scripture was never to be heard in many congregations. A preacher who might have been a consultant in Harley Street treating every verse of the Bible as the Word of God, including the Genesis account of creation, was akin to a Copernican revolution.

From the outset of Dr Lloyd-Jones' permanent settlement in London in September, 1939 it is clear that a number of his ministerial peers expected him to take a leading role in his new church connexions. This was not only true of the Congregational Union but of all the Free Churches. Almost immediately he was

A Leader in Britain

called upon by the London Baptist Association, as earlier noted; the London Presbyterians already knew him and Methodist churches and missions throughout the country now extended preaching invitations. All these denominations commonly worked together through the Free Church Federal Council and the Secretary of the Council, the Rev. S. W. Hughes, was one of Dr Lloyd-Jones' warmest supporters. In the suburbs of London and throughout England and Wales many local Free Church Councils, linked to the National Council, convened special mid-week services.[1] It was due to Hughes and other leaders of the National Council that Dr Lloyd-Jones very rapidly had calls to preach on such occasions in many places. One of the first of these engagements had been at Newcastle in 1938 and he was very often to be found at that same location in subsequent years. It was while preaching at the annual convention of the Newcastle and District Free Church Council that an incident occurred which was reported in the national press under the heading, '"Fiery" Speech'. 'Dr Lloyd-Jones was preaching in Brunswick Chapel,' the reports read, 'when a box of matches in a pocket of his waistcoat burst into flames. With the help of the Rev. H. T. Donaldson he extinguished the "outbreak", and although the garment was damaged he continued his address.'[2]

Dr Lloyd-Jones was early introduced also to the private London meetings of the Council leaders. Referring to this he wrote to Bethan on October 9, 1939:

I was in a meeting with the Free Church Council this morning in S. W. Hughes's Council Chamber. There were about 40 present – all of them leaders such as Sidney Berry, Dr Garvie, Dr Scott Lidgett, James Reid, Belden, Weatherhead, Sangster, etc. etc. It was almost exclusively a political discussion and a great deal of misunderstanding and disagreement. Some wanting peace immediately and others wanting to get rid of Hitlerism. Interesting enough. I never said one word – neither did Reid, Sangster and many others.

Tomorrow morning I have to meet the London Congregational

[1]In 1914 there had been 1,000 such local councils. By 1956 there were only 400 as the ecumenical movement and the British Council of Churches gradually diminished their importance.
[2]The trouble was not in fact caused by matches but by tablets ignited by the friction of his contact with the pulpit!

[59]

Union in Whitefield's Tabernacle, in order to be received! A purely formal occasion, it seems.[1]

Resulting from this contact, Dr Lloyd-Jones was asked by W. E. Sangster, the minister of Westminster Methodist Central Hall, to share in their May 24, 1941 commemoration of the date associated with the conversion of John Wesley. Leslie Weatherhead was to preach an afternoon sermon. At an evening rally, Ernest Brown, Minister of Health in the Government, and Dr Alan Don, Anglican Chaplain to the Speaker of the House of Commons, were to share the speaking with Dr Lloyd-Jones. Finally the day was to conclude with a service in the open-air 'intended to be reminiscent of Wesley'. These spokesmen on Wesley were not of one view upon questions of history let alone upon theology.

Sangster introduced the newcomer as 'a Congregational neighbour', a point playfully taken up by Lloyd-Jones in his opening remarks. ML-J explained that in reality he was a Welsh Calvinistic Methodist − 'the earliest of the Methodist movements' − and that he was there as the representative of George Whitefield, who scarcely had his rightful place in such celebrations. He believed that Whitefield − a name which many of the Central Hall attenders probably heard for the first time − was the outstanding evangelist of the eighteenth-century revival. His tribute to John Wesley, whose biography was 'one of the best things he had read in his life', was equally warm. On Sunday evenings, in his first days in the ministry, he told the gathering, he had worked through that 'incomparable document', Wesley's *Journals*.

The touch of humour, the surprise and the charm of his opening remarks ensured that there was no offence even for those present who could scarcely agree with his sentiments. It was upon the spiritual issues to which he next turned that opinions were more deeply divided. Two months before this date Leslie Weatherhead had written the articles in the *British Weekly* in which he offered his own explanation of the reasons why the Church was losing its influence. Dr Lloyd-Jones (a regular reader of that journal) waited

---

[1]The *British Weekly* deemed it sufficiently important to include a photograph of ML-J being welcomed. ML-J appears to have been present as a visitor at the executive committee of the Council for in its issue of April 18, 1940, *The Christian World* announced that the committee 'welcomed a distinguished new member to its fellowship − Dr D. Martyn Lloyd-Jones'.

until the Central Hall commemoration to give both John Wesley's remedy and his own. According to the *British Weekly*'s summary of what he had to say:

Dr Lloyd-Jones saw the need today of preaching that led to conversion, an opinion evoking marked approval from the audience. Methodists must think more carefully over the discrimination between the 'once born' and the 'twice born'. Attendance at worship or even official service did not necessarily mean that 'something had come to a man that had an inward reality and power in his life'. Decision may not mean conversion. The tragedy of the pulpit was that ministers were not preaching a 'converting Gospel'.

The Wesley commemoration closed with a practical reminder that something had indeed changed since the days of Wesley. Few more than a hundred joined an open-air service to brave a brief half-hour in the rain before making their way homewards.

The younger generation of Free Church ministers (and a number of the older) were certainly not in favour of any return to the old message. Weatherhead and Soper were united in the conviction that it was 'stern' views of God which were the supreme reason for the alienation of the people from Christianity and they were ready to blame 'bibliolatry' for the existence of such 'wrong' ideas of God. When, a little earlier, H. Tydeman Chilvers, the retired pastor of Spurgeon's Tabernacle (and a man who appreciated Spurgeon's doctrinal emphases) wrote in the *British Weekly* on 'The Revival of Calvinism', a shocked elder statesman of Congregationalism, Dr A. E. Garvie, responded, 'A return to Calvinism would be reaction not progress . . . Are we to cast away the gains of the progressive theology of the last half century?'

Other senior Free Churchmen, however, were far less confident that the Christian scene revealed 'progress'. Confessing that he too did not want 'the extreme Calvinistic dogmas', Dr J. D. Jones also affirmed, 'We should be all the better for some of the Calvinistic iron in our blood . . . For the past fifty years we have allowed the Gospel of the greatness of God to fall into the background.' Significantly it was Jones – 'the unmitred bishop of Congregationalism' – along with some other leaders of the Free Church Federal Council who aimed at preparing the new minister at Westminster Chapel for leadership in the days to come.

[61]

J. D. Jones had retired from Richmond Hill Congregational Church, Bournemouth in 1938 to Brynbanon, a beautiful house in the Welsh hills near Bala, from whence he kept in close touch with Nonconformist affairs. In 1941 at the age of seventy-six he suffered something like a seizure. When, after a final visit to London in February, 1942, it was apparent that he might not recover, he sent a message to ML-J, through Dr Vernon Lewis, expressing a great desire to see him. Faced with the urgency of this unexpected request, Dr Lloyd-Jones made the journey to Bala where the former 'Archbishop of Nonconformity' pleaded with him to recognize his duty and to lead the Free Churches in the years ahead. He was the man destined for it! Mindful of what he already knew of conditions in the English Free Churches, Lloyd-Jones protested that he could not do it because he was an evangelical. 'Oh, just give them some political sops occasionally,' JD retorted, 'and they will follow you.' From church affairs the conversation at length turned to more personal things as Dr Lloyd-Jones recalls that evening at Brynbanon:

It was for me a crucial night. I will never forget it. He asked me point blank whether he was going to get well and although he had been a very strong man I had to say, honestly, 'I am afraid not'. He began to weep and said, 'It's all right. I really don't want to leave this' – pointing out of the window to the beautiful scenery – 'but it's all right, I believe what I've been trying to preach', placing his hand upon his heart. When I went to bed I could not sleep because I was faced with this question. 'What if somebody said to you what you have told him, that you have got to die quite soon? Where would you stand? How would you feel?' This was the subject which kept me awake and confirmed me in my decision that I could not do what he was asking me. I also had to face death ultimately; I had to render an account unto God.

J. D. Jones died on April 19, 1942 and ML-J was often to look back on that last meeting as one of the most crucial events in his life.[1] With his congregation so depleted by war-time conditions, there was force in the dying man's plea that he should pursue the wider

[1] Arthur Porritt in *J. D. Jones of Bournemouth*, 1942, p. 150, simply notes that 'Dr Martyn Lloyd-Jones of Westminster Chapel journeyed specially to Brynbanon, on Mrs Jones's appeal, to break the news to him that he could not get better', evidently unaware of the wider issues discussed.

leadership. But the seriousness of death, as he saw it afresh that night, far superseded all questions of earthly positions and he knew with certainty that the compromise proposed to him was impossible. He could not lead the Free Churches, nor did it much concern him, for of what worth was it in comparison with the issues of eternity.

Such decisions as the above which, on the face of it, appeared to limit his larger usefulness were a necessary ingredient in what was to be his true calling. Preaching 'as a dying man to dying men' is not a commitment arrived at in the pulpit. It requires the preacher himself first to live in the consciousness of the nearness of eternity and while such living may involve costly renunciations it is ever an essential element in true preaching.

By 1942 Dr Lloyd-Jones' leadership as an evangelical preacher was being seen in Scotland where his acceptance was entirely unrelated to any denominational status. In March 1941 as already mentioned, he had accepted an invitation from Dr Donald Maclean, Professor of Church History at the Free Church of Scotland College, Edinburgh, to speak on 'The Tragedy of Modern Man'. In this, ML-J's first engagement under Free Church of Scotland auspices, his hosts considerably underestimated the degree of public interest. Previously, when visiting reformed scholars (such as William Childs Robinson and Auguste Lecerf) had been invited to give public lectures at the College, the meetings had been held in the afternoon, in the limited accommodation of the Presbytery Hall (within the College building on the Mound). The assumption was that the hearers would largely be limited to students, for theological lecturers do not normally draw crowds. But in this instance the College miscalculated. On successive afternoons the Presbytery Hall was packed to capacity, with others sitting in adjacent rooms and corridors for as far as his voice could be expected to carry. In addition to Free Church of Scotland men there were also some from the Church of Scotland whose theological hall (New College) stands close by on the Mound. Each morning *The Scotsman* gave a synopsis of the addresses on Romans 1:18–22 and in a lengthy report in *The Monthly Record* Professor Alexander Ross wrote:

No one who has heard Dr Lloyd-Jones speak will doubt for a moment that in preaching he has found his real life-work, and no one who has listened to him will fail to recognize that in him God has given to His Church a singularly gifted preacher with an authentic message, indeed, with *the* message which the modern world most desperately needs . . . At the close of this final Lecture Professor Maclean proposed a vote of thanks to the lecturer. He paid a glowing tribute to the eloquent exposition which Dr Lloyd-Jones had given of the Reformed evangelical theology, and alluded to the sacrifice Dr Lloyd-Jones had made when he entered upon the work of the ministry. In reply, Dr Lloyd-Jones said this: 'I gave up nothing; I received everything, I count it the highest honour that God can confer on any man, to call him to be a herald of the Gospel.'

All the preachers who listened to him received, let us hope, a new incentive and a mightier stimulus to proclaim the only Gospel that is 'the power of God unto salvation to every one that believeth'.[1]

There were to be long-term consequences from this visit. As the words of Ross indicate, the Scots Free Churchmen were mightily encouraged, while for Dr Lloyd-Jones himself the experience opened a large, new circle of friendships. Hitherto he had met a few of the denomination's leaders – including one of their much-esteemed elders, Professor Duncan McCallum Blair, formerly Professor of Anatomy in King's College, London, and by now Regius Professor of Anatomy in Glasgow – but at this time he came to know others well in this 'week of rich fellowship in the great city of John Knox'. Outstanding for ML-J were the times spent daily with Principal John MacLeod after lunch in his study at the Free Church College. Lloyd-Jones was enthralled with the aged preacher's knowledge and love of the great periods of revival when experimental religion characterized the Scottish Church. He was later to speak of John MacLeod as 'one of the godliest men' he had ever met. No less prized were the evening hours in the home of his host, Dr Maclean, who lived with his widowed daughter Mrs Una MacLeod. Here, nightly, Maclean gathered a company of like-minded ministerial brethren to meet his guest and to talk together on the cause of the gospel. Some were Free Church men, as, for example, G. N. M. Collins (minister of Free St Columba, Edinburgh) who became a life-long friend of Dr Lloyd-Jones; others were from different denominations. Later that month, on March 24, 1941, Maclean wrote to ML-J:

[1] *The Monthly Record of the Free Church of Scotland*, April, 1941.

It is impossible for me to put in words how much I enjoyed your fellowship during a week that will remain a landmark in my life, and in the life of the College. The memory of it will continue a quickening and stimulating force in the years that may yet be mine. My joy lies not only in the privilege of having you under our roof, but in the hope of the success of your God-appointed task to re-awaken the consciences of a slumbering people to the great verities of our faith. From every point of view the Lectures were a success, and I am certain that not a few of each day's audience will thank God for the messenger and his message . . .

You go on with your great work. As an old campaigner in the battle for Truth, I give you my blessing and the assurance of experience that God is mightier than the floods whose tumbling and confused noise may at times test the faith and confidence of God's own people. As we say in Scotland: 'More power to your elbow' . . .

Now, my dear Dr Lloyd-Jones what more need I say, except that the heart's warmth cannot flow through black-ink.

Close ties with the Free Church of Scotland were to endure for the remainder of Dr Lloyd-Jones' life.

It was in the following year, shortly after the death of J. D. Jones, that the extent of the Welsh preacher's acceptance in Scotland received its fullest confirmation in a 'Bible Witness Rally' held in the great St Andrew's Hall, Glasgow, on Tuesday, May 5, 1942. While the newspapers gave one account of the meeting, Dr Lloyd-Jones was to remember it as an occasion when he was unusually conscious of the special help of God. Glasgow's veteran religious reporter, Alexander Gammie, wrote in the *Evening Citizen* for May 9:

In all my experience of religious gatherings in Glasgow I have seen nothing more remarkable than the Bible Witness Rally held this week.

On Tuesday evening the longest queues in the city were not at cinemas or other places of entertainment, but all round St Andrew's Hall were queues of people eager to secure admission to this great Rally. After the hall had been packed in every corner it was estimated that over 1,000 people had to be turned away. Nor was it wholly, or even largely, a crowd of 'greybeards hoary'. The proportion of younger people impressed every observer.

What was the purpose which attracted such a throng? Its aim was defined as being 'to proclaim belief that the Bible is the Word of God, and to recall the nation to the prayerful reading and study of it'. It was not only one of the largest gatherings of the kind ever seen in Glasgow, but it was one of the most mixed. Never, perhaps, had there assembled under one roof at one time so many representatives of so many different creeds. The atmosphere was not ecclesiastical but evangelical. Almost every branch of the Church was represented, along with the Salvation Army, the Christian Brethren, and the many undenominational and independent missions and agencies in which Glasgow is so prolific. It raised the question as to what might not be accomplished were it possible to marshal for action all these evangelical forces in the city.

The speaking was worthy of so great an occasion. Professor D. M. Blair, as chairman, struck the right keynote. Professor Daniel Lamont, in speaking on the Authority of the Bible, was at once academic and evangelical, as is his wont, with that inflexion of tones in his voice which made him known as the silver-tongued Moderator. Professor A. Rendle Short of Bristol, eminent surgeon as he is, made ruthless and skilful use of his knife in dealing with some aspects of modern science. And with a rare intimacy of knowledge, he revealed some aspects of the Bible.

Then came the Rev. Dr D. Martyn Lloyd-Jones, the former Harley St. physician, who is now colleague-minister with Dr Campbell Morgan in Westminster Chapel, London, and he brought the meeting to a triumphant and impressive climax. To him had been allotted the task of speaking on 'The Bible and Today', and right nobly did he use the opportunity. His address was as gripping and powerful as it was popular in appeal. As an oratorical *tour de force* it would have roused a political audience to tumultuous enthusiasm. He held his hearers in thrall as he made point after point, and altogether the impression he produced was profound.

The preacher himself remembered other things from this Tuesday night in 1942. The previous day, after leaving London in the morning, he had preached in Sunderland (in the North-East of England) the same night. He did not normally begin a weekly preaching itinerary on a Monday and, not surprisingly, after liberty in preaching in Sunderland, Tuesday found him tired as he started what ought to have been a straightforward train journey to Glasgow. Instead the day became a proof of how war-time conditions could turn railway time-tables into chaos. The train, with no refreshment car, which should have arrived in Glasgow at lunchtime, eventually pulled in at 4 o'clock in the afternoon, by which hour he had a migrainous headache. Professor Duncan Blair was at hand to greet him at the station but as there was insufficient time to go to Blair's home before the evening meeting a visit to a nearby hotel had to suffice. Large areas of Glasgow had suffered severely from the bombing and such was the current petrol shortage that the two men had to walk the distance to St Andrew's Hall.

In normal circumstances the sight of the crowded building would probably have roused Dr Lloyd-Jones, but weary and with his headache persisting, he had a long wait until three speakers before him had finished reading their carefully prepared speeches. Two were professors of medicine (Blair and Rendle Short) and the third, Daniel Lamont, a professor of divinity. As the hour drew near to 9 o'clock, with signs of inattention among at least some in the vast congregation, and with the knowledge that all he had in his pocket was a slip of paper with some main headings, the youngest man on the platform felt depressed and inadequate for the occasion. It was only Professor Blair's words of introduction – having an effect which was not intended – which finally stirred him. Noting that all the previous speakers were professors, Blair said of the final speaker, 'This man might have been a professor of medicine and we hope he will be a professor of theology'. It was not the words themselves that aroused Lloyd-Jones but the train of thought which they occasioned. As he got up from his seat to walk some ten paces to the rostrum, 1 Corinthians 15:10 came to him with such force that it gave him the fuel which he needed for his unprepared opening remarks:

Mr Chairman, Ladies and Gentlemen,
Realizing as I do that there is a limit to the absorbing capacity even of a Scottish brain, I want to assure you that I am not going to keep you unduly late. Indeed, I feel that after the excellent things to which we have been privileged to listen together, my standing before you at all is almost an intrusion, and yet, having been invited and having come such a distance, I feel it to be my duty to say a few words to you on this theme which has been allotted to me.

I cannot refrain from saying that I feel a peculiar pleasure once more in visiting your great country. What you may be to-day in Scotland I am not quite sure, but I always still think of you in terms of the Covenanters, and I think of Scotland very largely as still being the Land of the Book.

At the same time, I am very proud this evening that I have been given the privilege of sharing this platform with three such distinguished speakers. As you have been told, I am not a professor. There are some who say that I have ceased to be a physician. And I fear that the majority of my brethren refuse to regard me as a theologian. But like another who once lived on the face of this earth, I can say positively that 'I am what I am by the grace of God'. And it is in that capacity and in that way that I stand before you and speak to you this evening.

To this point the vast audience at once visibly responded and as he went on to take up his theme he was given such a liberty of speech that the evening was to remain one of the most memorable in his life. As he ended his address his final words were actually drowned in an outburst of approval from the people – hardly a normal response to preaching in Presbyterian Scotland! In many successive years there was no part of the United Kingdom where Lloyd-Jones' preaching was more warmly welcomed than in Glasgow.

*   *   *

Just as Scottish response to Dr Lloyd-Jones showed that he was to be much more than a denominational statesman, so did the theological leadership which he was now giving in the Inter-Varsity Fellowship in England. Elected president in 1939, the war-time conditions gave excuse to retain him in that capacity, it was hoped, for the duration of the war. In the event, he held it for three years, finally insisting in 1942 that he should not be regarded as a 'serial president'. Douglas Johnson speaks of the 'outstanding' presidential addresses which he gave in these years at the students' annual Easter Conferences. In the years 1941–42 these five-day conferences were held in Trinity College, Cambridge. Here in 1941 the presidential address was on 'Christian Leadership'. The next year it was virtually an evangelistic sermon, with the raising of Jairus' daughter as its theme. On both these occasions the students were surprised to see present the Master of Trinity, G. M. Trevelyan, in cap and gown, accompanied in 1942 by another Trinity man, Professor G. D. Broad, the eminent Cambridge philosopher. After the address on the raising of Jairus' daughter Trevelyan made his way to the speaker and, removing his cap, said with considerable emotion, 'Sir, it has been given to you to speak with great power'. Broad, less impressed, was later to tell a student, 'If the Master hears that man much more he is going to be converted'.

Much other speaking for ML-J both in these IVF conferences and in those of the Theological Students' Fellowship was now inevitable. The latter was a younger branch of the IVF and at this period its annual conference was often at the same venue and overlapping with the general conference. The theme for the 1940 TSF Conference was 'Soundness and its Limits'; with ML-J down to speak on 'The Biblical Doctrine of the Fall'. In the 1941 general conference he shared the leadership of four informal sessions with Duncan Blair when the topics for discussion included 'What *is* "Preaching the Word"?' and 'How Should We Combat the Spirit of the Age?' The title for the 1942 Conference at Trinity was 'The Word of God to Rebellious Man' and in another discussion session led by Lloyd-Jones the title put down on the programme was, 'How Shall We Confront the New Secularism?'. It is noteworthy that the influence of the medical men was strong in all these conferences; the 'chiefs', Blair and Rendle Short, were there in 1940–41, and Blair again in 1942. Douglas Johnson, holding his usual place in the background, was also always present. The 'informal meetings' or 'discussions' were invariably led by the medical men, introducing the students to the Socratic method of questioning to which they had become accustomed in student days. In handling this form of instruction and debate ML-J was the only minister who could match the two 'chiefs'. There was no experience in the normal ministerial training which resembled the grilling which a medical professor's students were put through on ward rounds and sometimes it was the other conference speakers (as well as the students) who were shaken by the interrogation involved in this method. After the 1940 Conference, at which ML-J could not be present, he had written to Douglas Johnson: 'The account of the Conference was most interesting. Blair seems to have behaved in truly giant fashion. I fear that poor Warner and Aldis could never stand up to him'.[1]

The effect of Dr Lloyd-Jones' leadership in the IVF was quite as important in private as it was in public. Not only in the Fellowship's Advisory Committee (made up of senior evangelical leaders) but in almost constant contact with Douglas Johnson, there was much discussion which would bear fruit through the years in the lives of thousands. No General Secretary ever led a work from such an unobserved position as Johnson and only his closest friends knew what he was doing. 'He is,' wrote ML-J in a personal letter to a friend,

[1]Letter dated 24 April, 1940. Canon S. M. Warner and the Rev. W. H. Aldis were other speakers at this Conference.

'in many ways, the most important person in evangelical circles these days'.[1] The two men were ideally complementary to one another, one a public spokesman and leader, the other a born administrator and organizer behind the scenes; ML-J strong in general principles and insight, DJ careful and exact in all matters of detail. In his judgments of issues and of people ('his Welsh intuition was deadly accurate'), ML-J often saved DJ much time, while the latter equally saved his friend's time in a whole variety of ways from proof-reading and book-hunting to reports on contacts and situations important to the evangelical cause. In a sense it resembled a medical partnership. Each talked in terms which the other understood including the 'My Dear Dr Lloyd-Jones' and 'My Dear Dr Johnson' with which their letters to each other generally began. (Dr Lloyd-Jones allowed himself the variation, 'My Dear Sir', or, if he meant to warn Johnson of some missile about to be delivered, 'My Very Dear Sir'!) The relationship was certainly not all serious. Summing up the way he saw their friendship, DJ was to say in later years, 'If I were able to help him at all then it was as part jester, part confidant, part arguer, part fighter alongside him and part devotee of the apostolic line of Christianity'. Or, in an analogy suited to those war years, 'It was like crusaders in a war, with ML-J as Alexander or Montgomery and I as Chief of Staff (to get the administration done)'.[2]

One of the most important examples of the work of the two doctors was the private conference at Kingham Hill School, near Oxford, in which they shared with others to plan for the future. Held from 7–10 July, 1941, the host was the Rev. G. T. Manley (Vicar of St Luke's, Hampstead) and others present included F. F. Bruce (lecturer in classics at Leeds University), Donald Maclean (Edinburgh), W. J. Martin (Rankin Lecturer in Semitic Languages, Liverpool University), Alan Stibbs (Vice-Principal of Oak Hill Theological College, at this time evacuated to Kingham) and J. Stafford Wright (Principal of the BCMS College, Bristol).

---

[1] To Philip E. Hughes, March 2, 1942. For other high assessments of the influence of Douglas Johnson see *Lord of the Years: Sixty Years of Student Witness: The Story of the Inter-Varsity Fellowship, Universities and Colleges Christian Fellowship, 1928–1988*, Geraint Fielder, IVP, 1988, pp. 62–63.
[2] Dr Gaius Davies writes: 'It is my belief that the close association between two medical men who had left the prospects of glittering prizes for the work of God's kingdom will feature largely in a true and proper account of Christian work in the middle of the 20th century'. *Martyn Lloyd-Jones: Chosen by God*, ed. Christopher Catherwood, 1986, p. 65.

The stated objective of this Conference was the revival of evangelical theology, a need underlined during the previous twenty years by the almost complete absence of good commentaries and doctrinal works from evangelical authors. All present were sympathetic with this objective although there were some differences with respect to priorities. Manley was disturbed 'that so few conservative evangelicals had recently been appointed as Bishops, Headmasters or members of the staffs of the Theological Colleges'. Maclean saw the need for more doctrinal precision within their own ranks and advocated that future endeavours for biblical theology should be linked with an acceptance of the Reformed Confessions (e.g. the 39 Articles and the Westminster Confession). To Lloyd-Jones was given the task of delivering the first of the main addresses and, proceeding on the principle that correct diagnosis should precede any proposal of cures, he spoke on 'The Causes of Present Weakness'. The analysis of the existing situation which he gave was certainly too threatening to evangelical unity to have been published. As he explained in his introduction, it was impossible to give a meaningful diagnosis without being controversial and provocative. In the first place he covered eight 'General Causes' of weakness, which are given here in much abridged form from DJ's notes:

1. Weakness exists in the entire Church, though for different reasons. The liberal section substitutes philosophy for theology. It teaches philosophical theology and, because this outlook is anthropocentric, true theology is lost. If one's whole interest is in *man*, and his viewpoint, then you cannot have *theology*. [This he qualified by reference to the orientation newly introduced by the neo-orthodox Karl Barth and Emil Brunner.]
2. There is a general evangelical tendency to assume that one cannot maintain a strong evangelistic front and at the same time excel in biblical scholarship.
3. To answer liberals there is the need for highly trained persons of the academic type. In the case of the opponents of theology in our own ranks we need practical and persuasive men of understanding who can demonstrate the need for accuracy and clear-sightedness in the very fields of evangelistic endeavour, which is their professed priority.
4. Up to 90%, or more, of our own people do not seem to be concerned about the true doctrinal position and basis for the activities of the church. Less than 10% can really help us, but at least these are aware of the lack, though only a very small percentage of them seem to be

really clear about what is wrong. For the majority – even amongst those who proclaim their steadfast Evangelicalism – experience and subjectivity (in various forms) have been substituted in the pulpit for truly effective exposition of Scripture. A fundamental biblical theology and an effective application of the Word of God is often lacking where it is most to be expected.

5. *Some* distinction, however, needs to be made to allow for various parts of the country. For example Scotland has retained more of the older art of biblical exposition and theological interest than the South, as, also, have Wales and Northern Ireland.

6. Greatly daring, I venture to comment on certain aspects of *English* Evangelicals. They frequently pay fulsome lip-service to their evangelical forefathers, such as the Wesleys, Charles Simeon at Cambridge, William Wilberforce and the men of the late 18th and early 19th centuries. But I ask, do they realize what these men were really like in their actual views? They certainly were much more convinced 'churchmen' than many of their successors, but they were also better scholars and more painstaking in expounding a text in its context. These earlier men would be amazed at the average of spiritual food offered weekly from the pulpit!

But not only has biblical theology and accurate exegesis been neglected, it is often regarded as 'too heavy' or as dangerous. The average Englishman, of course, suspects intellectual ability and abominates anything like cleverness. So there has resulted (a) lack of any system in doctrinal matters and resistance to logic; (b) little attempt at 'preaching' (in its truest meaning) the result being a short address or talk, even if it can be called that; and (c) neglect of accurate exegesis and exposition.

7. A fear of 'intellectualism' has produced a negative and evasive reaction towards Anglo- and Roman Catholicism on the one side and to theological liberalism on the other. At present evangelicals encourage ordinands to start preparing to become teachers in the church, and then suggest that they should not go into theology too deeply!

8. In general in church history there has been a periodicity, and an alternation between what we might call 'Pietism' and 'Puritanism'. The Puritanism of Tudor and Caroline times was followed by the arid intellectualism of the late 17th century, then to be corrected by the 'Pietism' of the 18th century. Something similar has taken place in the 19th and 20th centuries.

Lloyd-Jones then proceeded to particular causes of weakness:

1. The enduring influence of movements in the early nineteenth century (particularly noticeable in Edward Irving's Catholic Apostolic

Church and among the Brethren) which emphasized the imminence of the Second Advent or the availability of gifts of prophecy in a manner which lessened the need for scholarship. A rich and accurate knowledge of Scripture was essential unless the Early Church's charismatic gift of prophecy, in the form of new knowledge, was restored as Irving believed was happening in his time. Certainly a wrong type of preparation for an imminent Second Coming and a misapplication of the promise of the Holy Spirit's guidance left a legacy which militated against scholarship in the service of biblical theology.

2. A later nineteenth-century movement, connected with the arrival of Moody and Sankey, had the same effect. The Moody missions did immense spiritual good but it was necessary to be frank about the new direction which was given to 'evangelism' as a whole. It must be said (on clear evidence) that Moody brought in a new type of evangelism and it did in fact tend to divorce the Gospel message as presented in Scripture from evangelical theology. Today an appeal to come to Christ is often given completely out of its context and in virtual isolation. After Moody the image of an 'evangelist' became that of a layman. He was not ordained, for that would be too learned. He was 'with it', he made jokes and he was clever in illustration. The people soon came to think of him as a specialist, who was expert in the techniques of evangelism – for evangelistic *methods* had by now become more important than the truth. It would be too dull and ineffective to have someone (skilled in doing it) to speak or preach the truth and then leave the results to God!

   Another danger arising from what critics at the time called 'Moodyism' is that lay leaders arose in the church who came to have too great an influence throughout their denominations generally and the 'checks and balances' of due order in the local and national churches were disturbed. Leadership fell into the hands of personalities (sometimes aristocrats or plutocrats) who were not theologically trained and who tended to dismiss the need for doctrinal accuracy as 'hair-splitting'. Too often the idiosyncrasies, and sometimes the oddities, of these lay evangelists and supporting personalities became, and were expected to become, the viewpoint of the churches they influenced.

3. The Keswick 'higher-life' movement had also contributed to a reduction of interest in biblical theology and deeper scholarship. No Christian in his right mind will desire anything other than true holiness and righteousness in the church of God. But Keswick had isolated *one* doctrine, holiness, and altered it by the false simplicity contained in the slogan, 'Give up, let go and let God'. If you want to be holy and righteous, we are told, the intellect is dangerous and it is

[73]

thought generally unlikely that a good theologian is likely to be a
holy person . . . The apostles, who wrote 'stir up your minds',
'strive', 'fight the good fight of faith', and many such things, would be
surprised to hear what some people now can say about 'the higher
life' . . . You asked me to *diagnose* the reasons for the present
weakness and I am doing it . . . If you teach that sanctification
consists of 'letting go' and letting the Holy Spirit *do all the work*, then
don't blame me if you have no scholars!

In defence of their general lack of interest in biblical doctrine as a
whole, Lloyd-Jones went on to say that evangelicals were far too
ready to profess, 'Well, I'm a *Bible-man*. I believe in simple Bible-
study'. They do not face the need to interpret all facets of truth in
harmony with the fundamental general teaching of Scripture. A
return to evangelical theology, he concluded, means a return to the
Bible and scholarship.

This address, delivered it must be remembered in private, provides
one of the clearest indications of ML-J's own approach to the
contemporary religious scene. There was indeed a basic unity in
interdenominational evangelicalism but in its existing condition it
provided no strong alternative to the general church scene. It
assumed that it was concentrating on the essentials, namely evangelism and holiness, yet it was in those very areas that it revealed its
superficiality.

Further addresses at Kingham Hill dealt largely with particular
proposals for future action. These included plans for more literature,
the establishment of a Centre for Biblical Research, Summer
Vacation Schools for Study, and the organization of funds to assist
students. During discussion it was noted that many promising
evangelical scholars were lost to the cause through the influence of
University supervisors who were liberals or advanced modernists.
Would it not then be possible, asked a younger member of the
Conference, to set up a new interdenominational theological college,
with a wholly conservative staff? This, in turn, could go on to
develop a postgraduate department, taking higher degrees either in
the University city where it was established, or an external Ph.D. of
London University.

This latter proposal alarmed several of the senior men. The main-
line denominations would simply ignore such a college and it would
lead to a new denomination just as Westminster Theological
Seminary in Philadelphia had recently led to a new denomination.

The alternative was to give extra-curricular help to evangelical theological students and to encourage them to attain to standards of scholarship that would bring about a revolutionary change in the theological departments of universities. Urging this viewpoint, W. J. Martin of Liverpool University explained: 'None of the experts or leading figures paid much or any attention to work from the average theological college or lesser academic centres. Hence, it is essential that the work of evangelicals should be good enough for their work to compare with that of the best authorities and to get included in the right journals and larger publications. If we wish to challenge or modify the work of those in university chairs, then they must be met at their own standards.'

In the midst of enthusiastic support for this proposal to raise up evangelical specialists in biblical studies, Dr Lloyd-Jones intervened before the end of the Conference. He feared that they were aiming to supply a corrective which would bring new dangers. He was not against teams of evangelicals facing problems at the highest levels. By God's grace, and given a right call, steps should be taken by some in this direction at the close of the war. But if the end result was the creation of 'specialists' something would be seriously wrong. Having himself worked 'at university levels' in the research department of St Bartholomew's Hospital, he fully appreciated and endorsed Dr Martin's plea for standards. But in his experience, he went on to say, there was danger in ultra-specialization. As expertise increases over an ever-narrowing field, the perspective which sees the proportions in the whole case is easily lost sight of. 'General physicians' and 'general practitioners' were what the church chiefly needed. Let specialists do their work, but if the end result was that elements of Old and New Testament theology were not co-ordinated into the whole of truly systematic biblical theology, there would be no true benefit.

At Kingham Hill, Lloyd-Jones was among men highly competent in their own fields and, in some instances, his seniors in years. In the unpublished reports it is, however, his contributions which stand out both in their spiritual insight and in their grasp of general principles. They help us to understand the significance of his unrecorded and on-going contribution to the organization which was doing more than any other to shape the thinking of coming generations of university students.

The many-sidedness of his leadership in IVF is also noteworthy.

His part at Kingham was distinctly theological, with lessons analysed from history which would have brought credit to any professor of church history. But in much of the time which he gave to the student world at this period he was doing the work of an evangelist and he was in repeated demand to take a leading part in university missions.

We have already mentioned the Oxford mission of 1940 from which he had to withdraw on account of illness and another in February 1941, organized by a number of Oxford societies, when he preached on 'What is Wrong with us?' and 'How God is Found'. The other speakers on the latter occasion were William Temple (then Archbishop of York) and the Rev. St John B. Groser, well known for his pastoral work in the East End of London. Then in February, 1943 he took a main part in a mission to the same University organized by the evangelical union (OICCU), the other speakers being the Rev. E. W. Mowll (the Provost of Bradford) and Capt. B. Godfrey Buxton. His first engagement in this mission was to speak to about 30 medical students in Balliol. His main mission addresses were sermons from Jeremiah 6:14–16. The Rev. E. Noel T. Sandford, a student at that period, remembers how several conversions were recorded in the term before the Mission and 'at least ten' while it was taking place. Dr Lloyd-Jones, he recalls, 'would come to the lectern, take a very small Bible out of his pocket, read out the verse he had chosen, probably close the book again, and then launch into a closely argued and entirely coherent address without a note to guide him . . . He would speak for upwards of half an hour, though it never seemed long.'

ML-J's preaching at Oxford demonstrated his conviction that while specialists had some part to play in the defence of the Faith, the Faith itself advances in the world as it is proclaimed in its own terms, regardless of the supposed attainments or abilities of its hearers. He had no special apologetics designed for undergraduates – a fact which sometimes surprised both students and fellow-missioners. Of an incident in the 1941 mission in Oxford, he once said:

It fell to my lot to preach on the Sunday night, the first service of the mission, in the famous pulpit of John Henry Newman – afterwards Cardinal Newman – in St Mary's Church, where he preached while he was still in the Church of England. It was, of course, chiefly a congregation of students. I preached to them as I would have preached anywhere else. It had been arranged, and announced, that if people had any questions to put to me, an opportunity would be given to them if they retired to another building at the back of the church after the service had ended. So the vicar and I went along expecting just a few people. But we found the place packed out. The vicar took the chair and asked if there were any questions. Immediately a bright young man sitting in the front row got up and said that he had a question to put; and he proceeded to put it with all the grace and polish characteristic of a union debater. He paid the preacher some compliments and said that he had much enjoyed the sermon; but there was one great difficulty and perplexity left in his mind as the result of the sermon. He really could not see but that that sermon might not equally well have been delivered to a congregation of farm labourers or anyone else. He then immediately sat down. The entire company roared with laughter. The chairman turned to me for my reply. I rose and gave what must always be the reply to such an attitude. I said that I was most interested in the question, but really could not see the questioner's difficulty; because, I confessed freely, that though I might be a heretic, I had to admit that until that moment I had regarded undergraduates and indeed graduates of Oxford University as being just ordinary common human clay and miserable sinners like everybody else, and held the view that their needs were precisely the same as those of the agricultural labourer or anyone else. I had preached as I had done quite deliberately! This again provoked a good deal of laughter and even cheering; but the point was that they appreciated what I was saying, and gave me a most attentive hearing from there on. There is no greater fallacy than to think that you need a gospel for special types of people.[1]

In accordance with the last statement ML-J did not view himself primarily as an evangelist to students. All kinds of evangelistic enterprises sought his support and there can have been few evangelistic campaigns of any size being conducted in Britain at this date without his being either invited or consulted. His was the first name announced in connection with a five month campaign planned in Glasgow in 1943–44. 'The full list of speakers is not yet complete,' reported the Glasgow press, 'but an invitation to take part has been accepted by Dr Martyn Lloyd-Jones who has become one of the most powerful evangelical forces of our time'. Similarly, when English evangelical leaders met at the Bonnington Hotel, London, about the same date, 'to consider the launching of a nation-wide campaign' it was Dr Lloyd-Jones who was asked to give the main address.

[1] *Preaching*, pp. 129–30.

We shall note in chapter 16 ML-J's reasons for being critical of the prevalent type of organized evangelism. But he was glad to accept these invitations and he used the opportunity in both places to urge Christians to recognize that they were in danger of missing the *first* need of the hour. At the inaugural Glasgow meeting, instead of giving a ringing call for more mass evangelism, he spoke on the words, 'This kind can come forth by nothing but by prayer and fasting' (Mark 9:29). 'Before we rush into activities,' he told the audience in the St Andrew's Hall on October 4, 1943, 'let us make certain that we know the nature of the problem that confronts us . . . Is this Evangelistic Campaign going to be enough? You will probably get results, but I say, if you stop at that, you will fail . . . Go on with your campaign, but do not stop at that. "This kind can come forth by nothing but prayer and fasting." In other words it seems to me that the call to every one of us is not to help in general with this great organized campaign; it is to consecrate and dedicate ourselves specifically to the task of praying for that spiritual revival which God alone can send. The trouble with us, I am afraid, is that we have not sufficiently diagnosed the situation. We are still confident in our methods. It seems to me there is no hope until we shall have so realised the nature of the problem that we are driven to our knees, to wait upon God.'[1]

At the Bonnington Hotel Conference in London he elaborated his reservations still further:

Whereas we are all agreed about the fundamental truths of the Gospel, the vital question is, What is the particular emphasis that is needed to-day? For myself I have no hesitation at all in answering that question. The sooner we realize that the evangelism of fifty to eighty years ago is no longer adequate to meet the present conditions the better it will be. Yet we still cling to those methods, and we act upon certain assumptions which we are not entitled to act upon. The fundamental position with which we are confronted is that there is almost a complete ignoring and forgetfulness of God . . .

I am one of those who still believe that the key to the present situation is the individual local church. It is possible for a revival, if we are waiting and praying for it, to start at any moment. Before we think about

---

[1] *Glasgow Evangelistic Campaign, October, 1943 – February, 1944, Report of Inaugural Meeting*, pp. 18–19. The campaign proceeded in more than twenty centres, ML-J only spoke at Kelvinside Church in the same week as the inaugural meeting.

planning and organizing in order to reach the outsider, let us concentrate upon our own churches. Are our own churches alive? Are our people real Christians? Are they such that in their contacts with others they are likely to win them for Christ and to awaken in their hearts a desire for spiritual things? That would be my own word to you to-day; that instead of spreading outward, we should concentrate inward and deepen and deepen and deepen our own spiritual life, until men here and there get to the place where God can use them as leaders of the great awakening which will spread through the churches and through the land.[1]

Later pages will show that no subjects were to exercise Lloyd-Jones more as a leader in Britain than those of evangelism and revival. His call for a major change in emphasis in contemporary evangelicalism was never to be widely received yet there were to be some who did understand and in that process the three new agencies which will be considered in the next chapter played a vital part.

[1] 'Notes' of this address were printed in *The Christian Herald*, Feb. 11, 1943.

I say once more, as I so often say in these annual meetings, that it is a simple fact to say that I personally could not have done the little that I have been enabled to do were it not for the help which I have had so constantly throughout the years from this particular Library . . . It has been a thrilling and remarkable piece of history as far as I am concerned. I will never forget my sense of joy and of rejoicing when, with my friend I visited Beddington thirty years ago. It was a bitterly cold day and whatever some of you may think of the heating here I can assure you that this is luxury and warmth by contrast to what obtained there. But I remember very well my feelings. They were certainly reminiscent of those of Cortez 'when with eagle eye he gazed on the Pacific'. I felt very much the same . . .

ML-J,
Report of the Annual Meeting of the Evangelical Library, 1965.

5

New Agencies

One of the most significant things in Dr Lloyd-Jones' early period at Westminster Chapel was the establishment of three new agencies in London which were to have far flung influence. In all three he was closely involved and two were to remain under his leadership until the end of his life.

The most improbable and romantic of these new institutions was The Evangelical Library. Although the name and site in London were only determined in 1943, the beginnings of this work may be dated to the conversion of a certain Geoffrey Williams forty years earlier. On a stormy day in 1903, 'at the request of a school girl', Williams went to a service at Galeed Chapel, Brighton, a Strict Baptist congregation of Gospel Standard persuasion. There, as a seventeen-year-old youth, he heard the gospel preached by Pastor J. K. Popham and discovered, in his own words, 'I was a sinner needing a Saviour'. Not without a struggle he came to peace with God and began to long 'for grace and wisdom to render unto my dear Saviour some measure of service in the salvation of souls'. Through Popham's ministry Williams was directed to some of the great spiritual classics of Christian literature. They included *Pilgrim's Progress*, Rutherford's *Letters* and Brainerd's *Journal*. Puritan authors, and John Owen in particular, were frequently urged upon his hearers by the pastor of Galeed. Inspired by a love for the 'free-grace' teaching in such books, Williams began to collect their works, yet without seeing any connection between them and his prayer to be of usefulness in the cause of Christ. 'For a time I could not see that I was fitted for any worthwhile contribution which could help in the extension of His kingdom.' By the 1920's, however, he was lending some of his books to Christian friends and, seeing the help which they proved to be, he felt an 'irresistible urge' to provide 'a widespread loan library fitted to enable people everywhere to borrow books true to Scripture, calculated to bring sinners to the foot of the Cross and to establish Christians in our most holy faith'.

Borrowers slowly increased and by zealous hunting in many quarters Geoffrey Williams' books multiplied. Old second-hand volumes of spiritual worth were then comparatively plentiful, as well as little valued. Convinced of their long-term importance, Williams became like Joseph in Egypt, laying up stores for famine years which were ahead. By 1928 the library had outgrown his house and garage at Beddington, Surrey, and had to be moved to a small building in Wordsworth Road, Beddington. It amounted to some 20,000 volumes in the tradition of orthodox Christianity but, in the owner's words, 'specializing in the more rare works of the Puritans and the Scottish covenanting authors as well as in the great eighteenth-century revivals'.

To Geoffrey Williams' great disappointment the 1930's saw little or no increase in the readers and borrowers of his books. The Beddington location was inaccessible – twelve miles south of London – and the many antique books, shelved amidst portraits of equally ancient divines, had an appearance of quaintness and irrelevance in modern times. Williams' concern was that the library should be 'a living force', not a curiosity for occasional visitors, and yet humanly speaking there was no prospect that it would be anything other than a museum. He was already past fifty years of age and facing what seemed to be an impasse. With this situation much on his mind and prominent in his prayers, he called one day in 1938 at John Phillips' chemist's shop in Great Portland Street, London, to make a small purchase. The owner – who served him – happened to be a member of Charing Cross Calvinistic Methodist Chapel and the two men soon found that they had things in common. In the words of Williams: 'I was attracted by his Welsh accent and getting into conversation I opened my heart to him in regard to the difficulty I faced. He at once exclaimed, "Why you must meet Dr Martyn Lloyd-Jones. His interest will be aroused and he will suggest a way out. I will tell him about your project".'

Williams came to view the day when he visited Phillips' shop as a turning point in his life. Hitherto almost all his Christian contacts had been among the Strict Baptists and for him the minister of Westminster Chapel was literally a figure 'out of the unknown'. Phillips fulfilled his word and, not long after, Dr Lloyd-Jones with his friend Eliseus Howells made a visit to Beddington. The result was the following letter:

12 Vincent Square,
Westminster.
S.W.1.
4.1.1939

Dear Mr Geoffrey Williams,

I write to congratulate you on the wonderful fruits of your labours known as the Beddington Free Grace Library. You will recall that I visited the Library with my friend the Rev. Eliseus Howells the other afternoon.

He and others had already sung its praises, so I came expecting much. Having arrived, and having spent some two and a half hours inspecting the contents, I felt that I was in the precise position of the Queen of Sheba on the occasion of her visit to Solomon.

The collection is remarkable and indeed unique.

As far as I am aware, there is, and can be, no such collection of books anywhere. For anyone who is at all interested in true Protestantism, and especially in its revival in the eighteenth century, the Beddington Free Grace Library is a sheer delight.

I have but one criticism to offer, and that is with regard to the location of the Library. It should be somewhere in the heart of London within easy reach and access.

As you know, I am prepared to do what I can, not only to make the existence of the Library known, but also to help in more practical ways to bring its treasures within easy reach of all who are interested.

I pray God's continued blessing upon all your self-sacrificing efforts in this great work.

Yours very sincerely
D. Martyn Lloyd-Jones

When the outbreak of the Second World War occurred later that year it seemed that any removal of the Beddington Free Grace Library would have to be postponed indefinitely. Such a prospect was more than Geoffrey Williams, with his hopes now raised, could accept. He pressed Dr Lloyd-Jones with reminders of the need, until the latter turned to Douglas Johnson for aid. Early in 1941 Johnson made his own reconnaissance of the Library and soon observed that its site, close to Croydon aerodrome and to factories, made it uncomfortably exposed to enemy bombing. Like ML-J he was impressed with the books but advised Williams that the collection needed to be located in a country area and that he should look for a suitable farmhouse! Although his host would not hear of such a suggestion, Dr Johnson's homeward journey that night confirmed him in its correctness. He recalls:

[83]

I got half caught in a late enemy raid after saying 'Goodbye' to Mr Williams. The train was blacked out – no lights inside and going slow to avoid sparks from the live rails. I can remember well the darkness of the carriage and how the train stopped as the heavy drone of aircraft was right overhead, then the great swish of the bomb's coming, passing over us, before the 'thud' and almighty explosion – carriage windows breaking and the springs of the train shaking like a boat in a rough sea! . . . On a Sunday, some weeks later, about twenty German planes passed over our house and, swooping, laid stick after stick of bombs on the factories 200 yards from the Library.

It may have been of this latter event that Geoffrey Williams wrote in a letter of May 8, 1941, published in *The Calvin Forum*, Grand Rapids, under the Editor's heading, 'In London Under Fire': 'The Library still stands unscathed through the protection of Providence . . . My home in Beddington Gardens has been bombed, but we ourselves and the books in my home escaped.'[1]

Undeterred, Geoffrey Williams continued to pursue Dr Lloyd-Jones by way of Dr Johnson, even managing to enthuse the latter to visit the neglected library of the late Henry Atherton at Grove Chapel, Camberwell, in the hope of adding its resources to his own. The project was unsuccessful and once more the slow evening journey home had to be made in an air raid. By October, 1942 the General Secretary of the IVF, with a thousand other commitments, had carried the Library project as far forward as he could, raising a little 'working money' – for there were no funds – and advising Williams on a small 'acting committee' to plan for removal into London and to secure Dr Lloyd-Jones as President 'post war or when the situation has been cleared up'.[2] This provisional committee of four met at the Kingsley Hotel on December 15, 1942, to discuss an agenda which read: 'Consideration of value of Library to Christendom (and especially to the Evangelical School of thought) and what steps can be taken to: (a) Secure it, free of all claims, for the Church of God (b) Centralize it (c) Finance the running of it as an active organization'.

Still there was no way forward. The Rev. E. J. Poole-Connor was the only man on the committee possessed of some influence, yet he had no means of awakening public interest in the bringing of a 'Puritan'

[1] *The Calvin Forum*, May 8, 1941, p.251.
[2] So Johnson informed ML-J in a letter of October 6, 1942, and with characteristic humour added that he had also advised Williams that Eliseus Howells, 'the arch Druid', should take the chair in the acting committee.

library to London. Williams was ready for a sum as low as £500 to pass over his great collection into the hands of a Trust but as he had liabilities to repay he could not lower that figure. Then there was the whole problem of the removal of 25,000 books, weighing 15 tons, to a central London location. Williams came to the conclusion that nothing would be accomplished until Dr Lloyd-Jones threw in his weight. As the latter was to say: 'Mr Williams proved to be a man neither easy to daunt nor willing to brook delay; and practised as he was in the use of the telephone, he pressed his suit with unabated zeal and, I had almost said, cried daily to me, with something of the importunity of the man in the parable.'

A disinclination towards involvement in a committee and in the leadership of a Library was not Dr Lloyd-Jones' only reason for holding back. Through all his life he was cautious about any public identification with ministries which might not be compatible with his own. Certainly he admired Mr Williams' choice of books and he meant what he had said in 1939 about making the Library known. But to be 'President' of the Library, as others wanted him to be, would involve him more closely and there were aspects of Mr Williams' restricted Strict Baptist background which worried him. The older man – 15 years his senior – clearly needed coaching and guidance at many points. There would be an on-going work of shepherding needed. So ML-J hesitated. He believed in the potential of the Library and valued Geoffrey Williams' evident zeal and prayerfulness for the revival of the Church. These were the considerations which finally prevailed and in 1943 he committed himself to what was to prove a life work. He was in the chair at two meetings of an enlarged committee held in his vestry at Westminster Chapel, on June 15 and 28, when a trust deed was settled, the name 'The Evangelical Library' unanimously agreed and a statement was put on record of their 'utter dependence on the Holy Spirit for the success of the undertaking'. It was further agreed that the Library be housed at 55 Gloucester Road, Kensington, at a rent of £70 per annum.

There is no record of the reason why it took a further 20 months before the Gloucester Road premises were finally opened in January 1945. Clearly there were further difficulties, including the second blitz which London suffered in 1944. Paying tribute at a later date to E. J. Poole-Connor, Dr Lloyd-Jones was to say, 'I am quite certain that were it not for his enthusiasm, and his unfailing optimism, we might very well have floundered at this point'.

Those who gathered for the formal opening of The Evangelical Library at 3 pm on Monday, January 15, 1945 heard an address by Dr Lloyd-Jones on its origins, character and future prospects. A reporter for *The Times* agreed that there was promise of a work of 'far-reaching importance'.[1] The *British Weekly* (Jan. 25, 1945) announced the opening under the heading, 'Discovering a Library', and its correspondent supported the sentiment of the chairman's address – 'It was no ordinary enterprise, a statement with which his hearers agreed, for on entering they had found books in several rooms, with passages and landings also lined with books, books everywhere, indeed . . . Great institutions, when vitalized by the experience and sagacity of some devoted individual, have had such an origin as this Evangelical Library.'

Dr Lloyd-Jones' hope that he would be able to help Geoffrey Williams – the honorary Librarian – as well as the Library itself was fully realized. Far from being resistant to counsel in those areas where his limitations had troubled the younger man, Williams became increasingly appreciative; writing in the 1970's he said:

It is impossible to exaggerate the profound effects of Dr Lloyd-Jones' influence upon my thinking and indeed my very life . . . He taught me to eschew the extreme elements of the thinking in the body of Christians in which I was cradled from my conversion, and yet left me tenaciously adhering to the vital basic teaching for which that body is distinguished, standing like an immovable bulwark for the truth when liberalism and error of every kind threatened the very life of the churches. Again the Doctor delivered me from the tendency to suspect the reality of those professed Christians born again amongst other communions. He reinforced and extended my belief that fellow Christians may often be wrong *in the head* and yet right in matters essential to salvation *in the heart*.[2]

*   *   *

The second new agency which came into existence in the early years of the war was the group of ministers who were later to be known as 'The Westminster Fellowship'. This seems to have begun in 1941 as a

---

[1] Feb. 4, 1945.
[2] From an unpublished 'tribute to my greatest living friend on earth' written for the author.

quarterly Tuesday morning meeting at Westminster Chapel intended for pastors and men in positions of Christian leadership. It was a private meeting, with attendance only by invitation. The inspiration for it came from ministerial contacts made through Inter-Varsity, aided by the usual encouragement from Douglas Johnson who knew of the similar gathering which ML-J had led at Aberavon. Initial attendance was small (no more than a dozen) but it was augmented somewhat by an occurrence early in 1942. The Rev. Alan Stibbs, Vice Principal of the evangelical Anglican Oak Hill College in North London, was at this time leading a small IVF study group in central London, and it had reached a point of some difficulty with respect to the doctrine of original sin. Two papers on the subject had been presented at one meeting, the first followed the popular and superficial view current among evangelicals and the second, given by Philip Edgcumbe Hughes (a London curate) had argued for a more biblical and reformed position. Stibbs needed help and sending both papers to ML-J asked if he could speak and lead a discussion on the subject at their next meeting, January 27, 1942. After this meeting, which took place at Tottenham Court Road, the Rev. Godfrey Robinson wrote on behalf of the group, 'I would like you to know how much we appreciated your coming . . . You probably gathered from the discussion how really interested we were'.

Hughes had been wanting to meet Dr Lloyd-Jones since first hearing him at the Albert Hall in 1935, when 'the intense firmness of his features and the earnest eloquence with which he spoke' had arrested him. From this time in January, 1942 the two became life-long friends. To a letter from Hughes, Lloyd-Jones replied on February 3, 1942:

I had never heard of your name until I received your paper from Mr Alan Stibbs . . . The character of your exposition appealed to me tremendously. For years I have bemoaned the fact that as evangelicals we lack scholars and writers. I have been looking out for men constantly . . . A number of us, including Rev. Alan Stibbs have started a new fellowship of evangelical ministers and clergy. I have suggested that all of you who meet with Mr Stibbs be invited. The next meeting is on March 10, at 10.30 a.m. If you come to that we shall have a long talk afterwards.

Hughes, Robinson and others, were thus added to the Westminster group of which Stibbs became the Secretary. In October, 1942 the men met at the new hours of 1.30 to 4.15 p.m. and for many years this remained the established time for the quarterly fraternal. In form the meetings differed from what they became in later years. The afternoon was divided into two, with a fifteen-minute break in between. In the first session opportunity was given for everyone present (upwards of a dozen men) to speak from personal experience of recent blessings or difficulties in their work – a procedure which led someone to dub the fraternal 'The Confession' (a name which stuck for a few years). The smallness of the numbers attending required a room rather than a hall for the venue and the only one suitable on the premises of Westminster Chapel was the downstairs 'parlour' where the light of the sun never reached the ever-shut windows and where the air soon grew heavy. ML-J was not in agreement with Spurgeon's dictum that the next most important thing to grace is oxygen and remained unperturbed when 'The black hole of Calcutta' became another nickname for the fraternal.

It is clear from the form which the first session took that Dr Lloyd-Jones did not envisage the gathering as a place for listening to addresses. He wanted it to be a 'fellowship'. The experimental and practical issues were to be prominent, and at the same time he sought that men should learn, through discussion, how basic biblical theology points to the solution of almost all problems in the life of the church. Alan Stibbs, in a circular to members dated November, 1942, spoke of the success of this plan. Some members, however, had queries. A. J. Vereker, the energetic Secretary of The Crusaders' Union, wrote to Dr Lloyd-Jones:

I wonder would you allow me to make a suggestion or two with regard to your most helpful quarterly Ministers' meeting.

I thoroughly enjoyed having this fellowship, which I believe is most useful. I am afraid however that I can never stay for the whole time, unless you change the hour of meeting, which is hardly possible . . . 5 o'clock would suit me best, when I could stay on to 7.0.

If we must meet at 1.30 p.m. may I suggest that instead of each member giving his experience, which takes a good hour, that only five or six produce a problem and then more time could be given to the solution. Should you think it essential that every man should have a say during the first half of the meeting then why not have the discussion immediately after each personal problem is stated?

I feel rather strongly about this because last Tuesday there were four or five most important points raised in the first hour and I had to leave without hearing the discussion on any one of them . . .

May I take this opportunity of thanking you for the help you are giving to so many on these occasions.

The time of meeting certainly curtailed the number of laymen in positions of Christian leadership who could attend but in ML-J's view this was not a handicap to the meeting. Other gatherings existed for them, whereas pastors had experiences which they needed to discuss together. In later years it was stipulated that membership in the 'Fellowship' was for those in the work of the ministry. Students did not attend.

A. J. Vereker, a nephew of Lord Gort, was one of the foremost of the men who led the inter-denominational evangelical organizations. In this capacity he was secretary of a Joint Committee of the four major youth organizations (Inter-Varsity Fellowship, the Children's Special Service Mission and Scripture Union, the Crusaders and the Girl Crusaders), made up of two or three representatives from each, which met periodically. From the outset he sought to introduce Dr Lloyd-Jones' influence into the work of The Crusaders' Union.

It was to a conference of leaders of The Crusaders' Union at Sion College that Dr Lloyd-Jones gave his first major comment in England on modern evangelism in February, 1942. It was published by the Union as a booklet with the title *The Presentation of the Gospel.*

This statement on evangelism was as clearly different from prevailing evangelical views as his address on 'Sanctification' had been at Cambridge in 1939. The presentation was balanced, analytical and compelling. By way of introduction he indicated that there were two positions to be avoided – first, that of men whose belief is 'perfectly orthodox' yet whose work is utterly barren and, secondly, that of those who seem to get 'phenomenal results' without concerning themselves over-much how they are obtained: 'They take a campaign, or preach a sermon and, as a result, there are numbers of decisions for Christ, or what are called "conversions": but they are not permanent; they are merely of a temporary or passing nature.' He then went on to indicate the two main ways in which the subject of the presentation of the gospel should be studied.

The first is to study the Bible itself, with special reference to the Acts of the Apostles, and the Epistles of the New Testament. That must always be put first . . . We must go back to our textbook.

The second method is a supplementary one and is to make a study of the history of the Christian Church subsequent to the New Testament times. We can concentrate specially on the history of revivals and the great spiritual awakenings; and we can read also the biographies of men who have been greatly honoured by God in the past in their presentation of the Gospel. But here we must notice a principle of the greatest importance. When I say that it is a good thing to go back and read the history of the past, and the biographies of great men whom God has used in the past, I hope that we are all clear in our minds that we need to go back beyond the last seventy years. I find so many good evangelicals who seem to be of the opinion that there was no real evangelistic work until about 1870. There are those who seem to think that evangelistic work in Great Britain was unknown until Moody came to this country. While we thank God for the glorious work of the last seventy years, I do plead with you to make a thorough study of the history of the Church in the past. Go back to the eighteenth century. Go back to the time of the Puritans; and even further back still, to the Protestant Reformation. And go back even beyond that . . . Go right back to the time of the Early Fathers . . .

There followed what he called 'five foundation principles', which were:

1. The supreme object of this work is to glorify God . . . The first object of preaching the Gospel is not to save souls . . . Nothing else, however good in itself, or however noble, must be allowed to usurp that first place.
2. The only power that can really do this work is that of the Holy Spirit . . .
3. The one and only medium through which the Holy Spirit works is the Word of God . . . The medium which is used by the Holy Spirit is the truth.
4. The true urge to evangelization must come from apprehending these principles and, therefore, of a zeal for the honour and glory of God, and a love for the souls of men.
5. There is a constant danger of error, and of heresy, even amongst the most sincere, and also the danger of a false zeal and the employment of unscriptural methods.

All this constituted the first half of Dr Lloyd-Jones' address. The second half concentrated on a vigorous application of the principles to the contemporary evangelistic scene. It may be doubted whether such an address had been given in England for a long time.

The principles underlying *The Presentation of the Gospel* threw light on the nature of the preaching at Westminster Chapel, but its controversial implications did nothing to lessen Vereker's appreciation for ML-J's ministry. The two men continued in regular contact and Vereker did all he could to see Lloyd-Jones' influence extended in all the main evangelical youth organizations. In November 1943, writing to ML-J as secretary of the Joint Committee, he asked him to speak to 'all the members of our four Committees', and explained, 'We think it would do us good if we were to hear some frank criticism of the work of these Societies from one who has not grown up amongst us, but at the same time is interested in us – and you are the man.' Both CSSM and IVF were to reprint *The Presentation of the Gospel*.[1]

*　　*　　*

It was also Vereker who was in large measure responsible for the third new agency with which ML-J became closely connected at this period. From about 1933 Vereker had repeatedly urged the idea of a college in London which would give biblical instruction to Christian workers. Slowly various parties became interested. Among the Anglicans were the Revs. W. H. Aldis (home director of the China Inland Mission and chairman of the Keswick Convention) and H. A. Evan Hopkins. The Christian Brethren were represented by Montague Goodman and J. W. Laing. Campbell Morgan threw in his weight and – need it be said – so did Douglas Johnson. The four men present at an exploratory discussion in May 1939 were Vereker, Johnson, W. H. Aldis and G. T. Manley (who 'was not enthusiastic'). Some progress was made, only to be stopped – like the Evangelical Library project – by the advent of war. But unwilling to let matters rest, in the latter part of 1941 and when the blitz was at its worst, Johnson and Vereker, joined only by H. A. Evan Hopkins, met again. At the Drift Bridge Hotel, Tattenham Corner, 'they talked and prayed, and there they resolved to resume the self-imposed labours which had been laid down in 1939'. Johnson and Vereker both lived on Epsom Downs and besides often travelling in and out of London together by train, the two men shared the same air-raid

---

[1] It was also reprinted in Wellington by the Crusader Movement of New Zealand. The full text of this address is currently available in *Knowing the Times*, pp. 1–13.

shelter together at DJ's home after both their families had been evacuated. Far from distracting them, their mutual work and plans were only advanced by the closer fellowship. 'We used to draft letters,' says Johnson, 'to the tune of the guns and the crash of the bombs in the distance and sometimes near.'

Neither man had any doubt as to who should be Principal of the new evangelical college, plans for which were well in hand by 1942. 'Almost from the beginning,' writes the historian of the London Bible College, 'it had been hoped that Dr D. Martyn Lloyd-Jones would serve as Principal of the proposed college.'¹ In the early summer of 1942 the invitation was put to him. He declined but promised to give whatever assistance he could. For the committee W. H. Aldis replied on June 26, 1942:

Thank you for your letter of June 16. The Committee met yesterday afternoon, but the number present was small.

I read your letter and we all desire to express our great regret that so far as you have any light at the present time your answer to the suggestion I made to you in regard to the Principalship of the Bible College is in the negative. I am thankful to know we shall still have your prayerful fellowship in this matter, and we have suggested a few alternative dates for the next meeting of the Committee, about which Mr Evan Hopkins will be communicating with you.

Thereafter, in the next crucial few years, Dr Lloyd-Jones worked with the committee and became Vice-Chairman of the College Council in 1943. No alternative Principal was proposed, but the name of Dr W. Graham Scroggie was put forward to be 'Director-of-Studies' for the duration of the war. Lloyd-Jones supported this suggestion. But in view of opposition anticipated from the Brethren element in the College sponsors, Evan Hopkins (Secretary of the Committee) wrote to ML-J to say that it would be 'a great help' if he would propose Scroggie's name in person at the General Council meeting on March 1 [1943].²

Dr Lloyd-Jones, with the opportunity to influence the future emphasis of the London Bible College, was hard put to it to come up with the name of any lecturer holding his own theology. The one

¹*London Bible College, The First Twenty-Five Years*, H. H. Rowdon, 1968, p. 27.
²Letter of Feb 16, 1943.

name for the Faculty which he did propose to the Council was that of Ernest F. Kevan, born in 1903 and serving in the Metropolitan Association of Strict Baptist Churches. Kevan had been pastor of Zion Baptist Church, New Cross, in South London since 1934. The Association to which the New Cross church belonged was a traditionally Calvinistic grouping, although now mixed with influences from a broader evangelicalism. But the Strict Baptists, as a whole, retained enough Calvinistic doctrine to prevent their being popular in the main current of evangelical life, nor did they have many preachers from other denominations in their pulpits. They regarded Dr Lloyd-Jones, however, with equanimity and in the war years he became a welcome preacher at annual chapel anniversaries and other special occasions. It was in this way that he had first met Ernest Kevan and discovered his love for Puritan authors.

Kevan joined the Westminster Fellowship, and was added to the Evangelical Library Committee in June 1943. When he was asked during the same summer to consider the post of part-time tutor at the new college he no doubt knew who was behind the proposal. At any rate, he wrote ML-J to ask for a discussion with him on the matter in late August 1943. Another letter of October 7 carried the same request:

My Dear Dr Lloyd-Jones,
   As you will remember, we are meeting next Tuesday first for 'The Confession' and then for the Library Committee.
   Am I trespassing on your time if I ask whether you can spare me the lunch hour on Tuesday? Could we meet at 12.15 p.m. somewhere and have lunch together while we talk? I want to ask you one or two things about the London Bible College.[1]
   Would you be so kind as to drop me a line suggesting an hour and a place where we might meet, if it is possible for you to arrange this?

Following these discussions with ML-J, Ernest Kevan accepted the part-time post and, with others, subsequently commenced to supervise correspondence courses and to give evening lectures. The administrative and secretarial work of these early stages did not appeal to Dr Scroggie, and his release from the original arrangement soon brought Kevan into a leading role. By the time the College was

[1]Published records show that Kevan was not formally invited to teach part-time until January 1944 but, clearly, there were earlier discussions.

settled at 19 Marylebone Road, London in 1946, with sixteen full-time students, he was the Principal – a role in which he was to continue for nearly twenty years.

Dr Lloyd-Jones had thus done much to see the College established and, as we shall note later, the College's close links with Westminster Chapel were to be a means of far-reaching influence. The affection with which 'the Doctor' was viewed by the early LBC staff can be judged by a letter from Francis Hare, on behalf of the College, written November 20, 1946:

Thank you very much indeed for your gift to the College. We do appreciate both this and all your many kindnesses to us, and I only hope that all of us here may play our part in fulfilling the vision which God gave to yourself and the others who were concerned in the founding of the London Bible College.

I do hope that you will always keep an eye on its course and progress, as those of us here are always apt to get too close to see clearly.

*   *   *

While the three evangelical institutions outlined above possessed no formal connection with one another, the involvement of the same personnel secured cordial relationships and mutual support. The overlap in the leadership in the Westminster Fellowship, the Evangelical Library and the London Bible College added significantly to the strength of their early years. No one except ML-J and Johnson was initially involved in all three, but Vereker, Poole-Connor, Howells and Stibbs were involved in two and, after 1943, Kevan (introduced to the Library Committee by Johnson and ML-J) belonged to the three. While other individuals participated in one of the individual agencies, it was the partnership of this 'team', in which the natural leader was ML-J, which contributed the major overall influence. That these three agencies should have become established in central London simultaneously was undesigned and how much each was to mean to the others only later years would show.

If ML-J contributed largely to these institutions, he also benefitted personally and not least in the formation of new friendships. Two names in particular deserve mention here. E. J. Poole-Connor was a man past the age normally associated with new ventures when ML-J came to know him through the Library project in 1942. Born in

London in 1872, he was already seventy years of age but his enthusiasm, already mentioned, was unbounded. He was even the principal 'carpenter' in the supply of shelves for the Library.

Reared in the Calvinistic Independent tradition, Poole-Connor had become a pastor in the Baptist Union where he found his position, as one close to the convictions of C. H. Spurgeon, increasingly isolated. After he left the Union, his last charge was to be that of Talbot Tabernacle, London, interrupted mainly by service as Secretary of the North Africa Mission. Dismayed by the non-existent or very loose connections between independent evangelical congregations and by the decline of biblical Christianity in England, Poole-Connor had initiated 'The Fellowship of Undenominational and Unattached Churches and Missions' in 1922.[1] Between Lloyd-Jones and Poole-Connor there gradually developed a deepening bond of mutual esteem and affection.

A second close and enduring friendship dating from this period was that between Dr Lloyd-Jones and Fred Mitchell. Mitchell came to London in January 1943 to succeed W. H. Aldis as Home Director of the China Inland Mission. Hitherto a chemist and Methodist lay-preacher in his native Yorkshire, it was the first time that a man who had not served overseas was called to this influential position. He was soon to be widely known in all evangelical circles as one who loved the Bible and believed in prayer. In 1948 he was also to be the successor to Aldis as Chairman of the Keswick Convention. For his first nine months in London Mitchell understudied Aldis and this brought him into immediate contact with the Council of the London Bible College and, accordingly, with Dr Lloyd-Jones. Representing though they did two different branches of Methodism – Calvinistic and Wesleyan Arminian – the two men were quickly drawn to each other. ML-J liked the individuality revealed in Mitchell's north-country personality. As he was later to say: 'Fred Mitchell came into evangelical circles at the right time, as a breath of fresh air. He came from the provinces – which is a very good thing for those of us in London! As a Yorkshire man he came without labels, without prejudices.' More especially he valued the fact that Mitchell had none of that 'boisterousness and easy confidence' which was too common in evangelical circles. Both men were natural leaders; both had similar temperaments, combining a gentle graciousness with

[1]The name was subsequently changed to 'The Fellowship of Independent Evangelical Churches', more commonly known as the FIEC.

firmness; and both belonged to that school of spirituality which believes that men of God should be God-fearing men.

Mitchell became an earnest supporter of Dr Lloyd-Jones' ministry. After hearing a lecture by ML-J in October 1943 he wrote to thank him and to say, 'I only wish I were near enough to be a member with you there!'. Prayer for Westminster Chapel became a regular part of his life and through their friendship ML-J was to be drawn more fully into the work of the China Inland Mission, speaking repeatedly at their public meetings, addressing their missionaries on furlough at the headquarters in the London suburb of Newington Green, and becoming a member of the CIM Council in October 1945. As a Council member he took seriously the role which was to require several hours in most months over the next ten years.[1]

Dr Lloyd-Jones had a considerable aversion to committees as thieves of time. The Westminster Fellowship operated without any committee. The Council of the London Bible College to which he belonged seems to have left regular meetings to the Executive Committee. His constant attendance and chairmanship of the Evangelical Library Committee has to be explained in terms of his singular commitment to that work and, similarly, his frequent presence at the CIM headquarters is a testimony both to his attachment to that missionary agency and to Fred Mitchell himself.

London in the 1940's was perhaps still the hub of the world's evangelical agencies and missionary societies. With the majority of these ML-J was now in contact, receiving endless invitations to speak at their annual meetings or to join their advisory councils. That he came to occupy such a position of influence at the centre of an evangelicalism about which he had considerable misgivings is an indication both of his greatness and of his catholicity. He was fitted both to bring men together and to hold them together. The degree of harmony in the evangelical leadership is a marked feature of this period and he contributed largely to it. This needs to be remembered when we come later to look at the circumstances which strained some relationships and made Dr Lloyd-Jones' leadership less acceptable to evangelicalism as a whole.

---

[1]Thereafter the pressure of other duties made this degree of commitment impossible. His resignation from the Council was minuted on June 18, 1959.

CONVERT'S LIBRARY

LONDON HOME FOR 20,000 RELIGIOUS BOOKS

From the smallest beginnings in a semi-rural area in Surrey there has been built up through the inspiration and mainly through the personal efforts of one man a remarkable library of 20,000 volumes, which has now been housed in London and which promises to be of great influence and far-reaching importance.

Its founder is Mr. Geoffrey Williams, of Wallington, who, after his conversion, studied especially the doctrines which emphasize free grace, and collected a large number of books dealing with this aspect of faith. From the substantial nucleus thus established he sought to expand the project with the possible building-up of branches throughout the kingdom and, indeed, throughout the world. Friends to whom he outlined his plans agreed to help and to pool their resources and the collection of new and ancient books grew rapidly.

Now it has been found a temporary, central home—until a special building can be provided for it—in rooms at 55, Gloucester Road, South Kensington, and Mr. Williams is acting as honorary librarian and organizing secretary under a small committee of trustees.

Dr. D. Martyn Lloyd-Jones, one of the trustees, explained that the library will provide for the theologian, the scholar engaged in historical research, and the divinity student preparing for examination. Its wide field, he said, covered a collection of volumes of the seventeenth and eighteenth centuries which were probably without parallel; exhaustive studies of the history of revivals; and a fine collection of rare manuscripts.

The library will be open daily—except Sundays—for inspection free of charge; it can be used for the purposes of reference by non-subscribers at the rate of 1s. a visit; and for a minimum annual subscription of 7s. 6d. members may borrow books (by post or otherwise) and use the library for reference and research. It is hoped also that the library will afford a background for an authoritative information bureau.

Mr. S. E. Denning, one of the joint honorary treasurers, pointed out the need for financial help if the undertaking is to be extended.

The Times, *February 4, 1945*

345 St Ermin's
Westminster, S.W.1
July, 18, 1943

TO THE CHURCH OF GOD AT WESTMINSTER

My Dear People,
 I have to place in your hands my resignation, to take effect at the end of August.
 It is not an easy thing for me to do . . . On John Wesley's monument in the Abbey the words are found, 'God buries His workmen, but carries on His work'. Westminster will go on. There have been hours in which I have been somewhat anxious about its future. I am no longer so, for in my colleague, Dr Martyn Lloyd-Jones we have been led by God to a man whose whole ministry is strictly biblical, and who is in himself loyal to the fundamentals of our Faith.
 And so with all confidence, I employ the words of Paul addressed to the elders in Ephesus, as recorded in Acts 20:32, 'And now I commend you to God and to the word of his grace, which is able to build you up, and to give you an inheritance among all them that are sanctified'.
 With sincere affection,
 I am, Faithfully yours,
 G. Campbell Morgan

6

Westminster Chapel, 1943–44

On a July Sunday in 1943 Dr Campbell Morgan announced his resignation from the pastoral charge at Westminster. He was in his eightieth year and the fact was that the man who had once preached twelve times a week now found the burden of one regular sermon every Sunday too much for his failing powers. Twice before Morgan had offered his resignation only to be met by the appeal of Dr Lloyd-Jones and the church officers that he should continue. But in 1943 it was clear that his public work – first begun at Westminster in 1904 – was done. His letters to his family indicate that the decision was made easier by the certainty of his colleague's loyalty to the Word of God. 'Preaching is not what it used to be,' he wrote to one of his sons a year earlier. 'I have now just to work my way through my notes and not trust to the inspiration of the moment for anything . . . However, I mean to keep on as long as I can and am able. I am greatly comforted and helped by my colleague . . . He is a remarkable preacher and a delightful personality.' To another correspondent Morgan says of his successor, 'I cannot tell you with what pleasure I listen to him . . . It is mighty preaching, most appropriate for these days'.

At a church meeting on July 25, 1943, Morgan's resignation, to take effect from the end of August, was accepted. At that meeting his old friend, Mr A. E. Marsh (whom Morgan had called back from Princeton Theological Seminary in 1907 to be his Assistant and Church Secretary) summarized something of his labours. Between 1886 and 1942 Dr Morgan had travelled 812,014 miles by rail and sea and preached 23,690 times – an average of 'one and one fifth of a sermon each day in the 57 years'. The latter figure did not include 401 lectures!

On the last Sunday in August, when Dr Morgan entered the pulpit of the church he loved for the last time as its minister, he brought nearly twenty-four years of service to Westminster to a close as he preached from the words of Deuteronomy 1:6, 'Ye have dwelt long enough in this mount'.

The transition from the joint ministry at Westminster to that of ML-J continuing alone was not, in fact, as smooth as the appearance might suggest. There were influential members of the congregation from pre-War years, including men in the leadership of the diaconate, who were by no means enamoured with the prospect of hearing nothing but Dr Lloyd-Jones. Hitherto they had tended to suffer the new preaching while expressing their undisguised preference for Dr Morgan. Some members even chose to attend only when the older man was preaching, and one of these, mistaking the arrangements for a particular Sunday, was overheard at Sunday lunch in the Grosvenor Hotel to say with indignation, 'I went to Westminster to hear Dr Morgan but it was that Calvinist'. The same attitude was strongly represented in the diaconate itself. One of its most forceful men even took exception to ML-J's customary benediction that the presence of the triune God might abide throughout the remainder of this 'our short, uncertain earthly life and pilgrimage and' – 'and before we are carried out dead to the mortuary' he would interject under his breath! Others lacked his animus yet remained uncommitted. The biographer of Dr Margery Blackie, for example, tells us, 'When Margery first knew Dr Lloyd-Jones, and listened to his sermons, she did not take kindly to him . . . She was even somewhat prejudiced against him.'[1]

Another member of Westminster, Mrs Norah Rowe, throws some light on this. She had joined the Chapel as a young woman about 1927 and also the 'Institute', 'which was quite liberal in its teaching'. 'Congregationalism,' she recalled, 'was, of course, very modernistic.' She owed her conversion to Campbell Morgan's preaching on a summer visit, yet, though the pulpit was stronger after his second settlement in 1932, there was a major spiritual weakness in the congregation. Mrs Rowe became a missionary with the China Inland Mission and remembers how shocked two of her colleagues were at the 'atmosphere' when they were asked to speak at the 'Institute' in 1938. When Dr Morgan resigned in 1943 it was her belief that, behind the scenes, 'the liberal element tried to get Dr Lloyd-Jones out'.

I never spoke to ML-J on this point but a document from the time seems to confirm it. Although Morgan's letter of resignation was dated July 18 he had actually given that resignation verbally to the

[1] *Champion of Homoeopathy, The Life of Margery Blackie*, Constance Babington Smith, 1986, p. 76.

deacons on May 30. The deacons then proceeded to meet – alone! – on June 16, after which they wrote to ML-J 'to ascertain,' in the words of their letter of June 17, 'your views as to the position arising from Dr Morgan's resignation, as it affects your Ministerial office as Dr Morgan's colleague'. The same letter expressed their 'intention to hold another session as soon as we have further information as is required from Dr Morgan and yourself'. The implication seemed to be that as it had been a collegiate ministry ML-J's appointment might terminate along with that of Campbell Morgan. No record survives, but we can assume that ML-J dealt firmly with this ploy.

Commenting on this period, Mrs Lloyd-Jones has written:

Of course there were those who did not want him, he was far too evangelical for them – he even made them 'feel like sinners!'. I know I just watched and waited, and saw how, in nearly every case, he – or his gospel – won them and many who had been less than inviting became his firmest friends.

One of the latter was Margery Blackie. Yet unsupportive men remained on the diaconate for some years to come and by the time that they were finally gone the custom of paying ML-J a comparatively poor salary had become so habitual that it was never properly adjusted. Dr Morgan's pre-War salary at Westminster had been £1,100. The deacons determined on a figure of £800 for ML-J from October 1, 1943, and ten years were to pass before this was increased by £300![1]

One of the first men at Westminster with whom ML-J came to have a close affinity was Mr A. G. Secrett, a builder in Ealing, who joined the church from a Strict Baptist background in the dark months of 1941. He was to become, in later years, one of ML-J's most trusted deacons. How much the understanding support of this one individual meant to ML-J is revealed in a letter he wrote to Secrett on April 19, 1943:

[1] As recorded earlier, the deacons took the desperate measure in 1941 of reducing both ministers' stipends to £10 for each service taken. How long this arrangement continued is not recorded in the Westminster Chapel archives, nor do details appear of any change after 1953. One American preacher who visited Britain in the late 1940's somehow heard the unpublicized figure which ML-J received as his salary and immediately deduced that he could not possibly be the outstanding preacher that he was reputed to be!

I have told you before of what you have meant to me as regards my ministry at Westminster. You can never know what it means to have someone who is in such sympathy with the message and from every standpoint. Coming as I did from a warm-hearted community where I was surrounded by men and women whose main and supreme interest in life was the Gospel and who delighted in discussing it, and the problems which it raises, more than anything else, I felt terribly lonely at Westminster for the whole of the first year. Indeed I could scarcely believe that it was actually possible for a church to be so spiritually cold.

*   *   *

According to the report of one London newspaper at the time of Dr Morgan's resignation, while the two ministers had shared the preaching since 1938, Lloyd-Jones was already undertaking the pastoral and administrative work. Nonetheless, the sole responsibility for all future services meant a considerable addition to his work load. If his health and voice had not much improved since 1940 it would have been impossible both to lead Westminster single-handed and to maintain his itinerant ministry throughout the British Isles. For many it was in that latter role that he was best known. 'Wherever he goes,' reported the *British Weekly* of November 18, 1943, 'in England or Scotland, but especially beyond the Tweed, he is recognized as a powerful evangelist.'

From October 3, 1943, his first Sunday back home after a family holiday in Wales, ML-J seems to have established a pattern for his two services which he would continue. One sermon would usually be more directly evangelistic and the other designed primarily as instruction for those already Christians. It was a reflection of his priorities that the evangelistic emphasis was pursued in the morning congregations, which were larger at this date than the number attending the second service in the afternoon. Thus for the morning of October 3 he took 1 Corinthians 2:2 which he introduced with the words, 'There is no more perfect statement to be found anywhere of the function of the ministry and of the church than in these words'. In the afternoon of the same day, for the smaller congregation meeting at 3.30 pm, he began his first extended expository series, giving the first of what were to be 25 sermons on the First Epistle of Peter. As the idea of a series by him was new to the congregation he considered some explanation to be necessary: 'I propose,' he told the people, 'to consider the message of this epistle in a series of consecutive studies. While, therefore, there will be of necessity a connection between them each one will be a separate sermon and message and complete in and of itself.'

On the day before this first Sunday as sole minister ML-J had written to his mother who was now spending much of her time in Wales:

Somehow or other we have been extremely busy ever since we returned. The black-out material has arrived and I helped Bethan to cut it out. It took a long time.

And of course I have more preparation work to do for Westminster now. We four are all well here. There was great excitement because the house was advertised as 'for sale'. Several came to view it on Tuesday and Wednesday.[1]

The explanation regarding the house is that with the heavy bombing apparently over in London, and the war moving slowly towards the victory of the Allies, Dr Lloyd-Jones had decided to move back to the capital and end the incessant train journeys to Haslemere. Mr Secrett, from his knowledge as a builder, had been able to guide them to a suitable house available on a rental in West London.

On the Monday following the second Sunday in October ML-J, who had been in Scotland the previous week, wrote again to his mother:

I had a good trip to Glasgow . . . I unfortunately caught a bit of a cold on the return journey but it has not bothered me much. Indeed I was less tired after the two services yesterday at Westminster than I have often been after one service only.

By the way, the attendances there and the collections have been good both Sundays – well ahead of last year. CM looks very well but he was complaining yesterday that his right leg is almost becoming useless . . .

Our visit to Ealing last Wednesday was very satisfactory. Secrett has done the house really beautifully.

To this new home, 2 Colebrooke Avenue, Ealing, the family moved in November, 1943 and the remainder of their possessions

[1]As the Lloyd-Joneses had given notice of their intention to terminate their lease of 'the Haven' at Haslemere the owners had put the house on the market.

(which had been stored in Cardiff since 1938) were at last brought up to London.

If the new work-load was not a burden to Dr Lloyd-Jones, other factors certainly pressed him hard. One was the problem of establishing a true church fellowship in the congregation at Westminster. Traditionally it had been regarded by many as a preaching centre where people were strangers to one another. The total absence of a church prayer meeting, as already mentioned, was indication enough that a strong spiritual bond was missing from amongst the people. Compared with Sandfields the weakness was unmistakable. And not unrelated was the fact that there were few in the regular membership who understood the distinctive nature of his preaching although, as already seen, some understood it sufficiently to dislike it.

In five sermons on Acts 2:42, preached on Sunday mornings in October and November, 1943, Lloyd-Jones set before the people what he believed to be the biblical pattern for the life of the church. The place of prayer was fundamental. A writer in the *British Weekly* commented on this series at some length under the eye-catching but misleading heading, 'Free Church Minister Discusses Liturgy':

What truth was there, the preacher asked, in the fathers' description of the prayer meeting as a thermometer and as the 'power-house of the church'? The apostolic Church was undoubtedly a praying Church. Could there be anything sadder than the decline of the prayer meeting during the past 25–30 years. Prayer kept the first community fervent in spirit and hot in its evangelism. Church history showed a close relation between prayer meetings and revival . . .

And the form of prayer in the apostolic gatherings, the preacher insisted was that of the fresh utterance of the spirit, spontaneous and powerful. Dr Lloyd-Jones deprecated the increasing tendency in Nonconformity towards liturgy, with read or recited prayers. In Anglican and Nonconformist Churches alike the emphasis was falling upon the 'beauty' of prayer, when it ought to be upon the power of prayer. A story clinched this point. Dr Lloyd-Jones had recently shared the platform with an Anglican clergyman who said that his community believed more in worship than did the Free Churches. Dr Lloyd-Jones pointed out that he was confusing liturgy and worship . . .

A central London church must acutely feel war conditions. Members are in the provinces and the younger men and women in the Services. The evening service has had to be brought to 3.30 not only because of the difficulty of blacking out a large building, but also because it is felt not to be right to expect worshippers to come long distances on dark nights. What of post-war? Dr Lloyd-Jones believes that a living church is far better than a preaching station, and he is understood to be fostering that kind of development. With the minister's reasoned appeal and urgent evangelism, Westminster Chapel may be expected to be a great spiritual centre again when the lights come back.[1]

With Campbell Morgan's ready agreement, Dr Lloyd-Jones had started a church prayer meeting in 1942. When the longer light of summer permitted an evening service at 6 pm, the prayer meeting preceded the service at 5.15 pm, otherwise it was held at 10.15 on Sunday mornings prior to public worship at 11 am. While present at these meetings ML-J took no vocal part apart from a brief concluding prayer; he always asked some other man to commence with a short reading of Scripture and prayer. Open prayer and intercession followed with a succession of men and women praying in turn.

For over six months after his sole pastorate commenced Dr Lloyd-Jones left Campbell Morgan's long-standing 'Bible School' in abeyance. Then, instead of resuming that meeting, traditionally convened on a Friday evening, he re-established in its place the 'Fellowship and Discussion' which had met on Monday evenings in 1939–40. That he gave preference to this type of meeting over a more formal service, was an indication of his conviction that every church must have a meeting in which there can be general participation. This Friday evening meeting was to continue unchanged until 1952 and we shall return to it later.

*   *   *

Equally significant, perhaps, with regard to the work at Westminster was what Dr Lloyd-Jones refrained from doing with regard to any re-organization of congregational life as people began to drift back to London. The Sunday School was resumed in 1943 but otherwise all the pre-war institutions such as the Women's League, the Institute (with activities ranging from table tennis and gymnastics to an annual Eisteddfod of singing and elocution), the Boys Brigade, the Girl Crusaders, and even the Church Choir, were to disappear

[1]The writer was T. Graham and the date November 18, 1943.

permanently. There was to be no separate youth organization (an informal gathering of younger people on Sunday afternoons hardly meriting such a designation). Nothing was said about the omissions but they were noted and particularly so by some of the 'old guard' who were long accustomed to regard such things as essentials for numerical success. In a building capable of holding 2,000, and with an actual regular congregation at this date of less than a quarter of that figure, people might be forgiven for a certain pre-occupation with numbers. Some of Dr Lloyd-Jones' friends were themselves not without doubts whether the primitive simplicity of church life in Calvinistic Methodism could succeed in London. Dr Johnson later confessed, 'when I saw that he was (without choir, musical entertainment and any external aids) set to *preach* the Chapel full, I wondered if he could – with his away preaching in the week – sustain the load'.

In Dr Lloyd-Jones' mind, however, questions of numbers and of church organizations, were very secondary to something else. A letter to Philip Hughes at this period gives us such thoughts as he would only reveal to those close to him. Hughes, it needs to be said, risking the continued hazard of U-Boats in the Atlantic, had left England for Christian work in South Africa.

> The Haven
> Chatsworth Avenue
> Haslemere
> Surrey
> April 26th, 1943

My Dear Philip,
The arrival of your airograph bringing the information that you had at last reached the end of your journey in safety rejoiced all our hearts.

Needless to say we have thought of you constantly since you left. Certain ugly reports came through on the wireless of ships sunk etc. and we thought of you. And yet I was certain throughout that you were all right. Then when your letter from New York arrived we were comforted. Reading between the lines we gather that you had had some strange experiences. Some day we must hear the full report.

Your journey to South Africa has certainly been a most extraordinary one. I am sure that you have been a great source of strength and comfort to many of your fellow passengers.

When this reaches you you will be more settled in your work. And we must henceforth pray for you in that connection. It is not necessary that I should say that we have missed you very much and that I am still not fully reconciled in mind to your departure. However, I have great faith in your judgment and in your ability to judge the guidance you have received correctly.

There is not much for me to report to you. It has been a singularly fruitless winter as far as I am concerned. At any rate from the standpoint of writing. As regards the work at Westminster Chapel I am glad to say that I have experienced great freedom and our congregation there has been visibly and steadily improving and growing.

But I long for greater and bigger things – I long to see people being broken down in large numbers. I know that finally the trouble is in myself.

When I read the New Testament and think of the things that have been experienced by God's people in the past I feel ashamed. It is all there for us in all its wealth and fulness and yet my life seems so weak and poor and barren. I have undergone considerable searching of spirit along that very line during the past few months. I praise God for the fact that I have had a clearer view than ever before of my own unworthiness and utter inadequacy. But still I rely over-much on myself. How foolish does sin makes us. What utter fools we are.

As I say, from the standpoint of writing it has been a poor winter. Actually there has been nothing of any great value published. Should anything appear from time to time I shall not fail to let you know.

You will be glad to know that that fellowship of ministers and clergy which meets at Westminster continues to thrive. Our last meeting, held a fortnight ago, was particularly good and we all felt much helped. It seemed clear that God was dealing with us all along the same lines – creating a longing within us for greater spiritual power in our work and personal experiences.

I attended the last meeting of the Biblical Research Committee of the IVF. The question arose of finding suitable men for writing commentaries on the various books of the NT. I mentioned your name and it was received very warmly and especially by Mr Bruce the chairman. He however felt that you were essentially a dogmatic theology man and I tend to agree. He will be writing to you asking for contributions to the Bible Dictionary which they contemplate producing.

By the way, you will have heard of the passing of Dr Maclean to his eternal reward. He was a fine man and I grieve to think that I shall not have the pleasure of meeting him again on earth. But *The Evangelical Quarterly* will continue as of old the new editor being Prof. Burleigh (former assistant) and Mr F. F. Bruce. I hope you will continue to send articles to them . . .

We shall look forward much to hearing of your routine and your new surroundings and work and your ideas in general. You will let me

know if your ideas of a work on The Holy Trinity develop. We all join
in warmest regards indeed in our love to you.
Yours very sincerely,
D. M. Lloyd-Jones

Those who saw Dr Lloyd-Jones only in the pulpit were often
surprised on their first meeting with him in private. He was
eminently approachable and the first impression which Christians
had was not of his gifts but of his spirituality. Geoffrey T. Thomas,
recalling the pastoral help which he often received from ML-J, has
written:

There was nothing forbidding and no hint of condescension in the great
preacher. One felt in his presence that he was a man who obeyed his oft-
quoted injunction 'Take time to be holy'. Thus his bearing was one of
benign calmness and kindly gravity and on one occasion on calling at his
house at Ealing I thought he had come straight from the presence of God.
Indeed at my very first interview with him as a pastor I felt, as he shewed
me to the bus on the way home, a sense of calm by being in his presence.
This was in 1944. Some 15 years later when writing an article on the bicentenary of the birth of Wilberforce I was interested to note his words
after an interview with the saintly John Newton, 'I felt in Mr Newton's
presence a great sense of calm'.

By 1943–44 the number of men and women from the Armed
Forces present at Westminster had markedly increased. Arthur
Gunn, arriving from the Far East (where he had served as a
missionary with the China Inland Mission) to train with Bomber
Command, was at once impressed by the number of people in
uniform at Westminster Chapel. For as long as possible Gunn was to
travel in from East Anglia and be present every Sunday morning.
Other future Church of Scotland ministers to visit Westminster
included James Philip, J. D. Douglas and Tom Allan. Douglas's first
visit on leave from the Air Force was memorable. His directions to
the Chapel only took him as far as St James' Park Underground
Station, where (although only a few minutes walk away) he was at a
loss which way to turn. Approaching a man for directions, he was
surprised when the stranger responded by asking who had told him
of Westminster Chapel. It was Dr Lloyd-Jones who had himself just
arrived on the Underground from Ealing!

One of the service-women attending the Chapel at this period was Joan Turner who belonged to the WAAF. As a young Christian from a country village in Norfolk, she was drafted to London to attend a course early in 1943. In her lodgings on Ebury Bridge she was musing one Saturday afternoon as to where to go to church the next day, when Wilfred Petty, a family friend, arrived with the solution to her question. He had come to show her the route to the church where he wanted her to be the next morning. As they neared the end of their walk and took the final turn which would lead into Buckingham Gate, her enthusiastic elderly companion asked her to note that it was 'Wilfred Street', which could readily be remembered as it bore his own name! Thereafter, wherever Joan was stationed in the Home Counties, she would reach 'the Chapel' on Sundays if at all possible. She writes:

The day came when I was posted to London – how excited I was – I could not have been posted anywhere better! I would be able to go to Westminster Chapel regularly. I was billeted in a block of luxury flats overlooking Regents Park and was within walking distance.

More often than not I was able to attend all services and came to know many more folk. Misses Trotter and Nicholson were two very kind friends – they invited me to their little flat in Buckingham Palace Rd – there on a Sunday afternoon we would sit and chat and talk on the things of God with other service-women – then enjoy home-made cakes and tea – a real treat in those days!

United States service men and women were also present by this date. One such person was Mary-Carson Kuschke, in London with a unit of the American Women's Army Corps, and in her letters home a particularly graphic impression of Sundays at Westminster Chapel has been preserved. Mary-Carson arrived in London in November, 1943, with advice from her Presbyterian mother to attend the ministry of Graham Scroggie who was known to her through speaking engagements in the States. But after attending Dr Scroggie's congregation (The Metropolitan Tabernacle), and certain others, she was still unsettled as to a permanent church connection. At that particular time her brother, Arthur Kuschke, wrote to recommend Westminster Chapel. Her mother had heard Campbell-Morgan in the States but did not know anything of his successor. Sunday, January 8, 1944, saw Mary-Carson at Westminster for the first time. Excerpts from her subsequent letters read as follows:

Jan. 12   Received Arthur's letter about Dr Lloyd-Jones so went to his church last Sunday. He preached an excellent sermon, I talked with him afterwards, and he knows all about Dr Machen and Westminster Seminary and he heartily approves. Delighted to have me, hopes I will come often, etc. The people seem very friendly, and altogether it's a delightful situation.

Jan. 18   Last Sunday I went to hear Dr Lloyd-Jones again and heard another very good sermon. He's giving a series on the Epistle to the Hebrews. Dr Campbell Morgan came in during the first hymn and went out during the last hymn. He's a nice-looking old man with snow white hair and a vandyke beard, and he's very feeble. It seems he was still preaching until about four or five months ago.

Jan. 20   Think I shall definitely abandon Dr Scroggie in favor of Dr Lloyd-Jones, whom I quite thoroughly like.

Feb. 2   I shall perhaps go to hear Dr Scroggie again sometime, but I'm so much pleased with Dr Lloyd-Jones that I hate to miss him if I'm in town.

   . . . Last Sunday I went to the morning service, and again in the afternoon. They have a three-thirty service rather than an evening one because of the blackout. I don't think there is Sunday School for any but the children. However there is a small group of young people (about my age, or some older) who meet at six o'clock for a short talk and discussion. I went last week and enjoyed it thoroughly. They don't go home after the afternoon service, but gather in the church kitchen for tea, sandwiches and cake – supplied by the group. Then we wash our dishes and move into the church parlor for the meeting. There are about ten in the group. They seem very nice, and quite delighted to have me. One of them gave a short talk on Nehemiah and prayer, and then we discussed. The regular church services are very well attended – much better than any other church I've attended around here.

Feb. 10   Communion service in the morning. They hold it after the (regular) service so that those who don't want to stay may leave. The congregation is getting to know me, and a lady by the name of Miss Dean has invited me to share her pew.

April 9   It is Easter Sunday evening, and today I have heard two excellent sermons from Dr Lloyd-Jones. The first on the subject, 'Why is it incredible to you that God should raise the dead?', and the second 'What the fact of the resurrection means to us'. What did you think of the sermon I sent you? Today also I took the box of chocolates to the supper group. They were most appreciative, and asked me especially to thank you for them.

April 19   Dr Lloyd-Jones has started a Friday night discussion group, which I attended last week and enjoyed a great deal. They couldn't have picked a worse night for me, as Friday is the night we all stay in and scrub the billets for Saturday morning inspection. But the meeting starts at 6:30 and lasts only a little over an hour, so if I skip supper and go straight from the office I can make it on time and still be back to do my share of the work. The meeting opens with a hymn, scripture reading and prayer, and then Dr Lloyd-Jones calls for a question. Anyone may pose any question he wishes (on Christian faith or practice) and from there on it's open discussion, with Dr Lloyd-Jones acting as 'parliamentarian'. There were about seventy-five people there last week, including a doctor, two lawyers, and almost all of the 'Sunday supper' group. You would quite like this church, I'm sure. Wish you could visit it with me some Sunday. I have discovered that Dr Lloyd-Jones is a physician . . .

April 30 Went to the Friday night discussion group again this week. They were considering the problem of what should be done to increase church attendance – although I don't know why, as Westminster Chapel is usually quite well filled. In the course of the evening I ventured a few opinions on the strength of which several people came over and shook my hand – and two sisters named Hewitt invited me out to their home with some of the young people for one day next week.

The discussion of that April Friday evening in 1944, and Mary-Carson's contribution to it, merited more space than was given to it in the above letter sent home to Pennsylvania. The question proposed was 'How can we again fill the galleries?' and the course of the discussion which ensued soon revealed that there were a number who had more sympathy with what Westminster had been in former days and who doubted whether the plain services now established, with forty-five minute (or longer) sermons and not even an organ voluntary, would ever bring back the numbers which once crowded the building. In later years Mary-Carson saw more fully the significance of the differences expressed that evening and recalled:

The question was admitted for discussion, and members of the group began making suggestions along the lines of more music, livelier music, special musical numbers, shorter sermons, sermons not so deep, more variety in the services, etc. I was listening to all this with mounting consternation, and when, in response to the idea that the church members could help fill the galleries by inviting others to the services, someone said that such invited visitors would not return a second time if they did not enjoy the service, I was finally constrained to raise my hand and request the floor. I do not recall my exact words, but I presented myself as one who had come among them as a stranger, had come a second time, liked everything that I saw and heard, and was obviously continuing to come. I said that for my part, no changes whatsoever were needed to keep me coming. Dr L-J smilingly thanked me for 'the first kind words I've heard this evening!'. He then rose and asked the group what they would say if he told them he knew a way to ensure that every seat in the Chapel would be filled on the following Lord's Day. He assured them that he did, in fact, know how this could be accomplished. 'Tell us, tell us!', they said, and 'Let's do it!'. 'It's very simple', he said. 'Simply put a notice in the Saturday edition of *The Times* that I shall appear in the pulpit the next day wearing a bathing costume!'. This was followed, of course, by a period of shocked silence. He then went on to expound the biblical basis for proper worship, using as counterpoint the error, then just beginning to be prevalent, of introducing various forms of entertainment into the worship service as a means of enticing people to attend.

The next news of Westminster in a letter home read:

May 15   Sunday morning I slept late, had a piece of bread and jam from our private larder, and walked to church. Usually I go by bus, but it's a nice walk. Part of it is through a park, and right past Buckingham Palace. Excellent sermon on the text 'Be strong in the Lord, put on the whole armor of God'. A little different emphasis than I've heard before. A soldier must be *both* strong and well-equipped. A strong man, unarmed, cannot fight effectively; nor can we expect victory if our troops, although well-equipped, are physically weak. Thus the Christian needs not only spiritual strength but also the proper weapons for spiritual warfare.
  I was invited to Sunday dinner by friends from the discussion group. We had a true English dinner of roast beef and Yorkshire pudding. I stayed with them until time for the afternoon meeting, then tea and the evening service.

A complete military censorship meant that nothing relating to the war was included in Miss Kuschke's letters. In May, 1944 the Allied armada about to cross the English Channel was in the final stages of preparation for the surprise landings in Normandy which came on June 4. The numbers in uniform in the church services declined as comrades joined the forces – over one and a half million – who were in France by the end of July. One representative of this number, Lieutenant E. A. Steele of the United States Navy, anticipating his removal, wrote to Dr Lloyd-Jones on April 11, 1944:

I cannot leave here without letting you know how much your preaching has meant to me. Your unusual ability to apply God's Word to our daily problems in such a practical manner has been very helpful. You have added considerably to my personal Christian knowledge and to my understanding of the will of God as set forth in His word. I do not know how soon I may be leaving, or if I shall ever be back, so it seemed advisable to tell you this now rather than put it off until some later date.

It has been said by many, and I believe advisedly, that you are one of England's foremost biblical scholars and its outstanding evangelical preacher. What a marvelous tribute that is. I do not hesitate to pass this on to you, because we know that the credit belongs to Jesus Christ alone. 'For without me ye can do nothing'.

I do pray God that the value and scope of your witness may continue to grow under the power and guidance of the Holy Spirit. How the world does need teaching such as yours. What a wealth of meaning in your oft-repeated prayer: 'Oh God save the people; have mercy on the world'. In one of your recent afternoon services you pointed out the majesty of the apostle Peter's words: 'But the God of all grace, who hath called us unto His eternal glory by Christ Jesus, after that ye have suffered a while, make you perfect, stablish, strengthen, settle you'. What a wonderful message to a suffering people, lost in a world 'blacked-out' with sin. I would that there were hundreds and thousands like you, forcefully and clearly proclaiming the word of God and the message of salvation through Jesus Christ to all the world. Unfortunately, there are all too few. 'The harvest truly is plenteous but the labourers are few'.

If it is possible, I would like to be put on the permanent mailing list for your *Westminster Record*. It will serve as a constant reminder through the coming years of all that your preaching and your Church meant to me during the time I spent here in England.

There is little more that I can add. I do pray that those who love our Lord may through the guidance and power of the Holy Spirit live full lives of service for Him. We know that if we will humbly consecrate all that we have to Him and to His service, that He will use us all according to His divine purpose.

'Blessed are they that hear the word of God, and keep it. Thanks be to God, which giveth us the victory through our Lord Jesus Christ'.

Unknown to the people of London at the time of the D-Day landings, they were themselves about to face a new and final peril. On June 12, 1944, the first pilotless planes (the V1) were launched by the Germans on London from bases in north-west France. Although these 'flying bombs', each carrying a ton of explosives, were soon disdainfully called doodle-bugs on account of their flying slowly and low, they caused 10,000 casualties within their first week of operation. In addition to the actual danger the psychological factor was considerable in a population which thought it had seen the end of heavy bombing. Thousands heard the menacing sound of their flight – 'A terrific noise like an express train with a curious hidden undertone' – never knowing when the noise was about to cut out and the rocket descend. On the night of June 15 fifty of these flying bombs exploded in the London area.

To all appearances the morning service at Westminster on June 18, 1944 was going to be much the same as any other wartime service. But at 11.20 a.m., when Dr Lloyd-Jones had not long begun the long prayer, the unmistakable rumbling of a V1 could be heard approaching. 'I went on praying,' he said afterwards, 'until the noise was so great that I could not hear myself speak'. Many who were present that day have unforgettable memories of what followed. Derrick Fenne,[1] based in London with 21st Army Group and shortly to join the troops already in France, has written:

The engine cut out almost overhead and after the silence, when the Dr faltered – a tremendous bang! The chapel structure cracked audibly under the effect of the blast and bits of ceiling and dust fell from the roof.

It had actually landed only a few hundred yards away on the Guards Chapel at Wellington Barracks where a service commenced at 10.30 and was still in progress. Over sixty people, many of them serving officers, were killed and 300 were injured. A nurse from the Westminster Hospital had intended being at the Guards Chapel but was late getting off duty on account of the number of casualties from the previous night's air-raid. As Westminster Chapel was slightly nearer Molly Pickard went in there and was one of the congregation at 11.20 a.m. She recalls:

As the impact of the doodle bug was heard, the entire congregation rose to its feet. After the most brief pause the Dr continued his prayer, as though nothing had happened, and we all sat down again. It was only after he had finished talking to God that anything regarding the incident was said to the congregation.

[1]Derrick Fenne met Joan Turner, mentioned above, at this period. They were married by ML-J in 1948.

All that ML-J said was to advise any who were nervous to move to seats under one of the galleries, and Mr Marsh for the first and last time in sixty years at Westminster ascended the pulpit with a duster to remove the fallen dust from the desk and preacher before the sermon. Only the window above the front porch of the Chapel was blown in by the blast. When the service was over many had to walk past the scene of devastation at Wellington Barracks where the rear part of the bomb's fuselage was lying in the road.

The whole congregation that day had been steadied by one man's prayer. Some, no doubt, saw his presence of mind as gifted crowd-control but the fact is that his prayer was of the usual length and he prayed as one who believed that a Christian has a right to be at peace in any situation. Forty years later, writing in *The New Gazette* of St George's Hospital Medical School, Dr George Newbold related how he had been in Westminster Chapel the morning that the crowded Guards Chapel had received a direct hit: 'The preacher on that occasion was the Rev. Dr Martyn Lloyd-Jones, a distinguished physician as well as a theologian, whose calm demeanour through-out was especially noteworthy. After the close of the service, and returning to the hospital, casualties began to arrive, so that the surgical teams were occupied non-stop until well past midnight.'[1]

Duties had prevented Mary-Carson Kuschke from being at church on that eighteenth of June. On July 2 she was back, riding there on her bicycle and hearing 'a very fine sermon from the Book of Jude in which it became evident that Dr Lloyd-Jones is an amillennialist'. The following Friday she was also free but discovered there was no meeting. Censorship prevented her giving the reason in her letter home the next day, 'Our Friday evening meetings have been temporarily discontinued, due to the necessity of making different arrangements about a place to meet'. For most of the congregation it was not until the Sunday morning of July 9 that they discovered that the Chapel had suffered the worst damage of the war. 'Arriving at the Chapel,' writes Derrick Fenne, 'I found the building damaged and debris lying everywhere. A bomb had fallen on the flats opposite the

[1]'Forty Years On', *The New Gazette*, vol. 5, Autumn 1983. At the National Club, to which a number of army officers belonged, one high-ranking officer said to Major Human over lunch on that same Sunday: 'Were you at Westminster Chapel today? I have seen many things in the trenches in France but I have never seen anything more remarkable than the way that man went on with his prayer as though nothing had happened.'

Chapel in Castle Street. A notice outside indicated that the service would be held in Livingstone Hall.' The bomb had blown half the roof off and shattered all the windows on the side of the building nearest to Buckingham Palace, moving the wall itself an inch and a half out of position. Some main joists in the roof were also damaged but remarkably the interior of the building was undamaged.

In terms of aerial attack this was one of the most dangerous periods of the war for all who lived in London and from that aspect the move from Haslemere in November, 1943 had certainly been premature. Elizabeth and Ann slept nightly in the Morrison shelter in the living room at Colebrooke Avenue, joined by their parents when warnings sounded. To get all the family under this slender cover was something of a squeeze and it occasioned the comment, 'Keep your feet in or else we shall be de-feeted!'.

Eight thousand flying bombs were launched against London between June and August, 1944, although by the latter date the majority were being destroyed by the RAF en route. Writing to his mother in Wales on Sunday, July 23, ML-J reported:

Thursday night was a bad night for us – the most continuously rowdy we have had. Friday was certainly the worst day so far – it went on practically without stop all day.

At a quarter to twelve mid-day I was speaking to Shrimpton on the telephone when there was a terrible crash obviously near. I really do not know how our windows stayed in. It fell in Uxbridge Rd as the enclosed paper explains. You know the shops well, of course, especially the little Boots Chemist's Shop. Elizabeth and I went to have a look round at 4.0 p.m. and it was still burning. There is not a window left anywhere below the West Ealing Station and several of the shop windows are out in our shopping centre at the bottom of the Avenue.

Yesterday was better and so was last night except that one seemed very near us in the night. We have had several about this afternoon and have heard several explosions.

A week later, as he wrote to his mother again on Sunday from the National Club, conditions were much the same:

Last night was a very rowdy night again with the P-planes going over and bursting . . . Yes! the manager of the Boots shop was killed. But Mr Jones of Jones and Knight is all right. It seems that a bomb dropped in High St., Kensington on Friday, doing much damage.

This was his last Sunday in London before a six week summer break with his family in Wales. By July 31, 1944, flying bombs had killed 4,735 people, and about 17,000 houses were totally destroyed. In the weeks that followed the bases from which the V1's had been launched were overrun by the Allies. The family's return to London in September co-incided with the commencement of the last and most irresistible of the German weapons, the V2. This new rocket was fired from the greater range of 200 miles and reached a height of fifty miles before dropping at a speed of about 4,000 miles an hour without warning on its target area. The potential of this missile was not at first commonly realized. Martyn wrote of them to his mother on September 18: 'Nobody seems to take them very seriously here and most people think they are coming from Holland so they shall soon come to an end.'[1]

Dr Lloyd-Jones had hoped that Westminster Chapel could be sufficiently repaired to be in use again by the end of July. He had strong feelings on the merits and deficiencies of particular buildings and disliked the Livingstone Hall but they were still meeting there in September.

As Mary-Carson Kuschke told her parents:

Sept 19   In the morning M went with me to hear Dr Lloyd-Jones who preached an excellent sermon on a verse which I can't quote exactly, but you know it – to the effect that sufferings of this present time are not worthy to be compared with the glory that lies ahead. After the service we were talking briefly with Dr Campbell Morgan. I had been wanting to speak to him but somehow never before had the right opportunity. He said that he knows Wilkes-Barre well and has been there many times.

Sept 24   Cycled in the rain to my church, which is still meeting in a borrowed hall. Dr Lloyd-Jones preached on Romans 5:3, 4, 5 – a continuation of last week's message. He said that we should glory in tribulation, not in and of itself, but because tribulation transforms our doctrine into *experience*, our *faith* into *assured knowledge*. Wish you could hear him sometime.

One of these services at the Livingstone Hall at this period so impressed one visitor that he wrote of the experience nearly twenty years later in a Glasgow newspaper. Tom Allan first heard Lloyd-

---

[1]In the first two months of their use 456 people died from the new rockets but their launching sites were pushed back by the Allied advance in Europe.

Jones in Glasgow in 1938 when, he says, his interest in religion was 'immature, speculative and secondhand'. Although he was to forget the preacher's face – which he saw only at a distance – he never forgot the text and burden of the sermon. After speaking of that first hearing of ML-J, Allan continues:

Six years later, in 1944, I was stationed in London with the RAF. My religion – in so far as it had ever been a personal thing – had long since gone by the board. I needed help, and I needed it badly.

I remember going one Sunday morning to the Caxton Hall in Westminster – where Martyn Lloyd-Jones's congregation was worshipping. They had been bombed out of their own church a few weeks before.

I wanted to hear Lloyd-Jones, for in my pursuit of some kind of peace in the midst of breakdown, I had listened to so many other voices.

There was a thin congregation. A small man in a collar and tie walked almost apologetically to the platform and called the people to worship. I remember thinking that Lloyd-Jones must be ill and that his place was being taken by one of his office-bearers.

This illusion was not dispelled during the first part of the service, though I was impressed by the quiet reverence of the man's prayers and his reading of the Bible.

Ultimately he announced his text and began his sermon in the same quiet voice. Then a curious thing happened. For the next 40 minutes I became completely unconscious of everything except the word that this man was speaking – not his *words* mark you, but something behind them and in them and through them.

I didn't realize it then, but I had been in the presence of the mystery of preaching, when a man is lost in the message he proclaims.

The essence of Lloyd-Jones's message to our time is vivid and unmistakable – the only hope for man in this world or in the world to come is to abandon his illusions and come as a helpless child to God.[1]

After 14 weeks in the Livingstone Hall (Allan's reference to 'the Caxton Hall' was a slip of memory) services were resumed in Westminster on October 1, 1944. Before the end of the day Mary-Carson took time to write home:

Friday evening I went around to the church to help get it ready for the 'reopening'. They had asked for volunteers to dust hymn books, etc.,

[1] 'The real secret of a great preacher' in the *Evening Citizen*, Nov 18, 1961.

and since I now consider myself a member of the congregation in good standing, I volunteered. My particular job turned out to be polishing the brass railing around the pulpit. After we finished, one of the English girls and I stopped off for fish-and-chips before calling it a night. And today we met in the church building for the first time in several months. Communion following the morning service.

In the evening as I walked to church a British soldier wandered along and wanted to take me 'to the pictures' – so I took him to church instead. He was quite interested and said he might come again next week.

Despite the continuing disturbance of bombing, Dr Lloyd-Jones' October was as full of engagements as ever. During the first week the Ministers' fraternal met on Tuesday, he preached at Uxbridge on Wednesday, resumed the Fellowship and Discussion meeting at Westminster on Friday and preached on Saturday afternoon at South Woodford in East London.

The next week he was further afield, as he reported to his mother on its conclusion:

I had a very good week in South Wales and specially at Merthyr. We had anything up to 1,000 people in the afternoon and at night there were at least 1,700 people. I thought that both services were the best I had had for a long time, both the Welsh and the English. And that in spite of the fact that we had been disturbed twice on Monday night by warnings at 12.20 am and 4.40 am. Then I had to get up at 7.0 am. On top of all my train was so late arriving at Cardiff that there was no time for lunch. I just had a snack and a cup of tea on the station and went on . . . On Wednesday we had a real hurricane and torrential rain. The congregation at Abertillery were marvellous in spite of that and I enjoyed myself there as I always do.

The train back yesterday was very crowded. I travelled first class and paid the 7/4 excess. It was well worth it. I found all well here. They had had no warnings at all on Tuesday night. Last night during the night there were three warnings but we heard no plane or bombs.

The next day, Saturday, October 14, Dr Lloyd-Jones had no engagements apart from sermon preparation and so it proved an opportunity to have a guest at home. It was Mary-Carson Kuschke's first personal meeting with the family and it was the special news in her next letter to Pennsylvania.

Oct. 20   Last Saturday I had dinner and spent the evening with the Lloyd-Jones family at their home in Ealing – a London suburb. I enjoyed them *thoroughly*. There are two daughters, Elizabeth, aged 17, and Ann, about six or seven. Ann and I held a lengthy discussion on the works of Beatrix Potter. Elizabeth expects to enter Oxford next year – is extremely bright and very nice. In the course of the conversation it came out that I had 'connections' in Carmarthen and had been there last spring. Dr Lloyd-Jones is well acquainted with Carmarthen, and knows the Daniel Johns family. And when I told them that my grandmother's name was Llewellyn and that she came from South Wales, why they practically took me in as a member of the family! Dr Lloyd-Jones knew about the Orthodox Presbyterian Church, and was very much interested in any new information I could give him; he's a great admirer of Dr Van Til; he subscribes to the *Westminster Theological Journal*, and wants me to let him have my copies of the *Presbyterian Guardian* after I've read them. They had family prayers in the evening while I was there – just as we do.

At the beginning of the following week ML-J was in Keighley, Yorkshire, staying with the Yorkshire MP, Ivor Thomas and sharing a meeting with Donald Soper. On Wednesday he preached twice in the suburbs of London and again on the Saturday afternoon. The following Monday (October 23) he wrote to his mother:

Between everything, I am having an exceptionally busy time. We had a good day again yesterday. The morning congregations are really good these days but the evenings are poor. I am given to understand that the 6.0 pm is not taking well anywhere. We may consider changing it and having it at a slightly earlier hour.

The Friday night discussion meeting was started again at the beginning of this month and is also going quite well, considering the black-out. There were about 60 people there last Friday.

On the whole we are having a quiet time as regards bombing. The flying bombs never seem to get anywhere near here and the warnings only last about 1/4 hour. But at 1.30 am on Saturday morning there was a terrific explosion from one of these rocket bombs. It shook the house and we knew it was not very far away . . . Their noise is terrible and, unlike the [earlier] flying bombs they make deep craters and do not spread so much.

I am just off now to Manchester. I shall stay tonight with the Rev. and Mrs D. L. Rees. I preach in Manchester at 12.45 pm tomorrow, then I go on to Rhyl where I am due to preach Tuesday and Wednesday evenings. Back home on Thursday in time for Elizabeth's birthday tea, D.V.

Let us know your needs

Our fondest love to you, my dear Mama . . .

The remainder of the year 1944 was similarly occupied. Mary-Carson knew nothing of her minister's visits elsewhere (for it was always his practice to say nothing of them to the congregation) but her reports home continued to give news of the Chapel, the sermons and the new friends she was meeting. That circle was widened on December 10 when after the evening discussion group she joined with seven others in the home of Dr Margery Blackie, 'Supper was delicious, conversation was good, and there was a blazing fire in the grate'. After nearly a year of hearing this different preaching she expresses the opinion: 'His sermons get better and better. I've never heard such preaching! Sometime, somehow you must hear him – and meet him.'

For the same correspondent Christmas Day, the last Monday of 1944, came as a fitting end to a memorable year far from home. The day was beautiful and clear with the ground white with frost. There was the usual 11 am service at Westminster after which she joined the Doctor and Mr Emlyn Davies, the organist, in the minister's vestry for a thermos of hot coffee before they left together for Ealing. The coffee was too hot to drink, but with no time to spare if they were to catch the next train, the preacher gave his surprised American guest a swift lesson in how to drink out of a saucer held in both hands! This accomplished, they caught the train and Mary-Carson found the immediate Lloyd-Jones family augmented by Mrs Lloyd-Jones Sr, Mrs Emlyn Davies and Geoffrey Thomas (quoted earlier in this chapter). Describing the day in her letter home, she wrote:

Their diningroom was nicely decorated for the season and we had a fine dinner of *goose* – with all the trimmings – followed by two hot Christmas puddings. They put 'prizes' in their puddings, as we do in wedding cakes, and I drew a duck and a thrupenny bit, which I shall bring home with me as souvenirs of the occasion. I took along my two-pound box of chocolates and they were all delighted – said it was the best they had eaten since pre-war days. After dinner we talked a while, listened to the King's speech, and then started to play games. We played all sorts of games, some old, some new, and everybody played – from seven year old Ann to her grandmother and everybody in-between. We all laughed uproariously and had a marvellous time. I taught them how to play 'Spoof' – with clothes pins in the middle of the table. Do you remember it? They loved it and we played two full games, which takes some little time. It ended up with Dr Lloyd-Jones and me scrambling for the last clothes pin.

For supper we had cold goose, vegetables, assorted cakes and tea. Ann came in dressed in a Santa Claus suit and gave us all little presents from her pack. After supper we sang, around the piano. Carols first and then Welsh hymn tunes. I wish our hymn books at home had more of the Welsh music in them – it's really beautiful.

I had an over-night pass, as we all knew it would be too late for me to get back to town, and was staying with the Davies because they had an extra room. So Mr and Mrs Davies and I left at about midnight. It was about a fifteen minutes walk to their home, and a beautiful night. Moon shining through a light fog, heavy frost on the trees and shrubbery, coating every twig – as we have so often seen it in the Poconos. Had an early breakfast with them the next morning, and got back into town in time to report for duty. And so endeth the story of my Christmas – a very happy one, thanks to some very fine people.

Mary-Carson Kuschke was posted back to the United States in February 1945.

On one occasion, twenty years later, when ML-J was preaching on 'fellowship' and 'the communion of saints' as a mark of the church, he commented on the 'very wonderful' illustration of its reality which he had seen during the Second World War. As a large part of the congregation knew little of the war years at Westminster he continued:

There were troops, you remember, in this country; they came from Canada, from America, from Holland, from Norway – they came from almost every part of the world. Here they were for a while in London and they would come to the service and at the end of the service they would come to see me. I had never seen them before but I knew them and they knew me. We had never spoken before but you recognize a brother, you know at once, you belong together immediately. It does not matter what the colour is, you are speaking the same language, you are brethren![1]

[1] Sermon on Acts 2:41–47, March 14, 1965.

One of the highlights of the Assembly was the evening service with Dr. Martyn Lloyd-Jones of Westminster Chapel, London, as preacher. There was a great attendance and the preacher was at his best – which is saying a great deal. His text was Paul's affirmation, 'I am debtor both to the Greeks and to the barbarians, both to the wise and to the unwise'.

It was a masterly sermon – both in its exposition and its practical message. Dr. Lloyd-Jones began quietly, but soon he was like a man possessed by a mighty theme. He became impassioned and at times dramatic, though I believe quite unconsciously so. I never heard him preach with greater abandon. He said to me later in the evening that Scots listeners make a man preach. But some preachers make people listen. Many ministers were busy taking notes of the sermon, but still more gave themselves up to catching something of the inspiration and glow of the preacher. The clock in the church stopped just as Dr. Lloyd-Jones began his sermon, but one hearer said to me next day that for him, in any case, time stood still and he could have listened long enough.

'Churchman' reporting on the first evening
of the Assembly of Scottish Congregationalists in Edinburgh, April 30, 1945.
Evening Citizen, May 5, 1945.

7

The Year 1945

Although Dr Lloyd-Jones had retired from the presidency of the Inter-Varsity Fellowship in 1942, the time which he gave to student work was to increase. In particular he had become virtually the permanent speaker and host at the four day Conference of the Theological Students' Fellowship which met annually in January. In Douglas Johnson's opinion he was indispensable for these occasions, not least because of his leadership of the discussion sessions which had now become an established part of the Conferences. Following the 1944 Conference, in the course of a letter to ML-J, written on January 13, Johnson reported:

Those students with whom we were in contact at the Conference, and from whom we have heard subsequently, were very definite in their expressions of appreciation for your part in the programme, including those who did not show up too well in the discussion! We have the impression that it is at last dawning on the minds of the theologues – and this change for the better is very clearly marked in the case of some of the graduates – that the discussion method and dialectic are probably unequalled as teaching procedures. The graduates gave us many expressions of appreciation this time. We are very much hoping that as they get used to the grinds of what we might call our school of thought (*the* school of thought) they will gradually spread good reports in the various University and theological centres.

The Theological Students' Conference of 1945 received more than usual publicity. In a lengthy notice the Church of England's old newspaper recorded:

The leaders of the IVF and organizers of the Conference held at Cambridge from January 1–4 affirm that it was the best for years past. The intellectual and the spiritual were refreshingly blended. The

[125]

Conference owed more than can be said to the deep spirituality and
discerning skill with which the host, Dr D. Martyn Lloyd-Jones, guided
the discussions, and to the brilliance of his searching addresses on 'The
Place of Preaching in the Church To-day' and 'Preaching the Reformed
Faith To-day'. The latter particularly was a massive and prophetic
contribution.[1]

But the most spoken of event at this Conference was a 'discussion'
which had not been part of the programme. The other main speaker
was D. R. Davies, whose book *On to Orthodoxy* had been
published by Hodder and Stoughton at ML-J's instigation in 1939.[2]
The former Marxist was now vicar of a South London parish and
was regarded by some evangelicals as 'a prophet for the times'. This
was not a view shared by ML-J for, as he had pointed out in
reviewing Davies in 1939, his return to orthodoxy was incomplete at
certain vital points, including the doctrine of Scripture. Concerned
over what others did not recognize as missing in Davies, Lloyd-Jones
proceeded to ask his fellow Welshman some questions following his
addresses on 'The Church and Civilization'. This ignited an exchange which was to go on for some one-and-a-half hours. In the
words of *The Record*'s correspondent, 'The audience were amazed,
and delighted, by the first class informal debate which at one point
ensued between the chairman, Dr Martyn Lloyd-Jones and the
speaker'.

The substance of their debate was over the presentation of the
Christian message in the modern context. Davies was arguing that if
intellectual humanists and socialists such as Harold Laski were to be
converted they had to be met on their own ground by men able to
discuss politics and social affairs. ML-J recalls:

I was saying it was the exact opposite. I pointed out how D. L. Moody
had appealed to the aristocracy in this country – the common people up
to a point, but noticeably to the aristocrats – and how John Wesley was
more successful among miners than he was in Oxford. My argument
was that Davies was quite wrong psychologically and that Harold Laski
was more likely to be converted by a Salvation Army speaker than by
D. R. Davies. Psychologically people do not like to be proved that they
are wrong, and more than that, generally, if people become Christians,

[1] *The Record*, Jan 19, 1945, p. 32.
[2] *In Search of Myself, Autobiography of D. R. Davies*, London, 1961, p. 198.

they capitulate completely. In their conversion there is an emotional element rather than an intellectual one: in other words, they stop 'reasoning' and surrender and abandon themselves to Christ.

Davies, Lloyd-Jones believed, while using biblical ideas, was not truly dependent upon revelation and the activity of the Holy Spirit. His weakness remained what it had been when he wrote *On to Orthodoxy*. At the end of his lengthy review of the book in *The Christian World* ML-J had said: 'Mr Davies suggests that the modern preacher knows too little about modern man and his problems. I would suggest that the trouble rather is our ignorance of the power of God, especially in our own lives.'

D. R. Davies never spoke again for the IVF. In his autobiography he pays tribute to ML-J while retaining his assumption that an uncritical acceptance of Scripture indicates a limited power of thought. Speaking of the period when he was emerging from his disillusion with rationalism, Davies writes:

I felt now greatly the need for worship . . . Occasionally I went to Westminster Chapel to hear Dr Martyn Lloyd-Jones, whose influence on me defies analysis. He was not a thinker; he had no background of theological culture; he had no literary gift. Yet he held me. Something in the man spoke to the deeps in me.[1]

Dr Lloyd-Jones' work in the opening months of 1945 followed its normal course. His mid-week itinerant preaching included visits to Wales in January, Yorkshire in February and Somerset and Wiltshire in March. There were the usual public meetings in London (in support of evangelical agencies or suburban churches), committee meetings of the Evangelical Library and the Free Church Council, and Westminster Fraternals in January and March.

Dominating all other interests in the public mind was the approaching end to the War in Europe with the Allied Forces now poised to enter Germany itself. The prospects for the post-War world were already being widely discussed in the press and on the radio. While against what is normally understood as 'topical preaching', ML-J believed in making full use of current moods to drive home the teaching of Scripture. In October and November, 1944 he had preached nine sermons from Ephesians on 'God's Plan for World

---

[1] *In Search of Myself*, p. 194.

Unity' and when the BBC in Wales asked him to give a further series of radio addresses he took for his subject 'Religion Today and Tomorrow'. The third and last of these was recorded on February 23, 1945. It did not supply the customary comfort given by religious broadcasters:

All our fears for the future of the Church and religion, our feeling of hopelessness as we see the world falling deeper into sin and vanity, our inclination towards multiplying arrangements, committees and movements, stem from the same thing, namely our lack of faith in the workings of the Holy Spirit.

If the Church in Wales would go back to the lessons of the eighteenth century, then, he believed, she would see that the first step to recovery is not to bring down the standard of church membership, but to raise it up.

We must re-grasp the idea of church membership as being the membership of the body of Christ and as the biggest honour which can come man's way in this world. Through discipline, we must lay great acclaim on membership of the society and we must re-emphasize the truth that God gives the Holy Spirit only to those who obey him. The need is not for widening the appeal, but to proclaim that strait is the gate, and narrow is the way, which leadeth unto life. This means possibly that many will shy away from the churches and will leave them; and from the point of view of statistics and accounts and collections everything looks hopeless, and those who try to keep the churches alive are afraid. But be sure of this, that the Lord's word will be verified: 'Whosoever will try to keep his life will lose it, and whosoever will lose his life for my sake will receive it.'[1]

One of Dr Lloyd-Jones' rare long letters, written to his friend Philip Hughes in South Africa, belongs to this period:

> 2 Colebrooke Avenue
> Ealing
> London W13
> March 13, 1945

My Dear Philip,
    My one consolation as I now write to you is that I warned you before you left that I am a truly bad correspondent! The fact is that I

[1] *Knowing the Times*, p. 30. He had given three addresses (in Welsh) on the Welsh Home Service in 1943 (see vol. 1, p. 314), and another on 'John Calvin' in 1944, published in *Knowing the Times*, pp. 32–37.

am doing too much between my work at Westminster and my travelling about the country. And then I have to do all my correspondence myself and for some reason or other I find writing tires me very much physically. It was my firm intention last summer, when my journeyings slackened, to write to you. But just at that time the flying bombs began and our days and nights were so disorganised that I barely managed to keep my essential work going. However, there is no real excuse and I am profoundly sorry.

First and foremost I want to congratulate you and your good lady on your marriage. It is not too late to do so for there is always a freshness and newness about truly spiritual wedlock . . .

We moved from Haslemere here a year last November. I had become very tired of all the travelling and when Dr Campbell Morgan gave up at the end of August 1943 and I took sole charge at Westminster it really became essential that I should be somewhere in London. We were led in a most remarkable manner to this house. Our landlord is a fine Christian man and we have a happy home here. Elizabeth and Ann go to a High School which is but six minutes walk away. By the way you will be glad to hear that Elizabeth did extremely well in her school certificate and matric a year last December. She is now working for the Higher and hopes to go to Oxford sometime. Her chief interest is English literature.

I am glad to say that the work at Westminster is encouraging at the moment. Our congregations are rising slowly and we have had conversions.

A discussion meeting which I hold on Friday evenings produces over a 100 people regularly and seems to attract thoughtful young people.

I can say quite honestly that I have never enjoyed preaching as much. The word and its message grips me more and more and the joy of preparation has never been so great. I am conscious also of freedom in speaking and of authority. And yet I feel that these are but days of sowing. I long for revival comparable to that of the 18th century. More and more am I convinced that there, and there alone, lies our hope. I believe that the people at the back of the 'Faith for the Times Campaign' are beginning to see that now. But they so enjoy organising activities and meetings!

I have given three talks in Welsh recently on the wireless on 'Religion Today and Tomorrow' and in them I have been at pains to stress the need for revival. I enjoyed analysing and trying to answer the current issues that characterise the present phase – Barthianism, ecumenicity, sacerdotalism, Religion and Life weeks, factory meetings etc. etc.

Oh! how I long to know exactly what Paul means in 1 Corinthians

2:1–5, and to experience it in my ministry. I have become tired of all else and when I read of Whitefield I feel that I have never really preached in my life.

But that is enough about myself and about our affairs, except perhaps a word about books and reading. I do not know that anything of very great value has appeared since you left.

Easily the best thing I have read is a book on the Apocalypse by an American. It is *More than Conquerors* by W. Hendriksen, published by Baker's Book Store, Grand Rapids, Michigan. He is a professor at the Calvin Seminary and often reviews books in *The Calvin Forum*. I take it that you know the *Forum* and receive it regularly.

This book on 'Revelation' is first rate and will appeal to you immensely. It is easily the most satisfying thing I have ever read on the subject. You must read it.

Recently I was asked to read the MS of a book on prophecy called 'The Kingdom of the Messiah' by an old Baptist minister called John Thomas who died last year. It is a devastating analysis of the dispensationalism of the Scofield Bible and again a first rate bit of work. There are many difficulties in the way but I am going to print and I shall let you know if we succeed . . .

I find the *Westminster Theological Journal* of the Westminster Seminary, Philadelphia, is very good always. It is published twice yearly. I have not seen sufficient copies of the new *Theology Today*, edited by Dr John A. Mackay, the President of Princeton Theological Seminary to speak of it as yet . . .

By the way the IVF have opened a place at Cambridge called Tyndale House for biblical and theological research. There is to be a resident librarian. Douglas Johnson said to me the other day, 'Of course the man who would be simply perfect there is Philip Hughes'. I entirely agree. Of all the young men I have met in all my contacts with evangelicals you are not only the only one who can write but you are the only one who has a theological mind. And above all, it is all so perfectly balanced and controlled by your over-ruling devotion to our Lord and your passion to serve Him.

Although I have been so poor as a correspondent I can say truthfully that never a day passes but that I pray for you and my longing to see you grows constantly . . .

We are now looking forward to the end of the year and to all the strange possibilities of the days of peace. What do they hold for us? There are, alas! no signs whatever of any spiritual understanding of the significance of the times in this country.

I often feel that we may yet see what we long for, starting in Germany and Russia among those who have passed through the purifying fires of persecution.

From the above, and from earlier statements, it is apparent that ML-J was not among those who were confident of a return to religion in a post-war Britain. Ivor Thomas MP, for example, writing in *Time and Tide* for April 21, 1945, professed that he could already see features of a 'religious revival which is quietly fermenting in our midst'. He instanced the interest in the writings of such authors as C. S. Lewis and J. Middleton Murry, the broadcast plays of Dorothy Sayers 'jerking the minds of hundreds of thousands into thinking about the Christian religion', and what he judged to be 'the success of the Religion and Life meetings all over the country'. Yet although Thomas' viewpoint was so different from that of Dr Lloyd-Jones, the latter was the only preacher whom he mentions. Following the reference to Sayers he wrote:

But I should be the last person to decry what the clergy are doing, and among them I would specially mention as a sign of the times the Rev. Martyn Lloyd-Jones, who abandoned a flourishing practice in Harley Street to enter a Free Church pulpit because he discerned that the real malady lay not in men's bodies but in their minds and wills; and when he preaches it is as though the Prophet Elijah had descended to earth in his fiery chariot.[1]

In April 1945 the one question in every mind was when the war in Europe would end. British armies were into Germany in the north, American further south, and Russian in the east. Yet even on April 23 (two days before American and Russian forces linked up) Churchill warned against assuming that 'Victory Day' was on the verge of reality. Nonetheless, with Berlin surrounded, ML-J had reservations about being away from Westminster for a long standing engagement in Scotland on Sunday, April 29 because it had been announced that there would be a service of thanksgiving at the Chapel on the morning immediately following a German surrender. His Sunday commitment was for his friend the Rev. G. N. M. Collins of Free St Columba's, Edinburgh, whose church was celebrating the centenary of the opening of its building. He did go north and preached what Collins was to remember as 'the finest sermon I ever heard from him'. The text was 'Enter ye in at the strait

[1]The reference to Elijah suggests that the Westminster MP had recently been at Westminster Chapel for ML-J had preached four Sunday morning sermons on Elijah at Mt. Carmel (1 Kings 17:18–24) in February 1945.

gate . . .' (Matt 7:13). At the end of the service only two of the three ministers with ML-J in the pulpit returned at once to the vestry. Looking back from the vestry door to see what had happened to the third (Alexander Ross), Collins saw him remain like a man in a trance and then, very slowly, move to join them as he muttered under his breath, 'Wonderful, wonderful'.

ML-J had been asked to preach the next day at the opening service of the annual Assembly of the Congregational Union of Scotland. Collins, who accompanied him, was quietly amused at an exchange which occurred in the vestry prior to this service. The Union's Secretary, anxious that proceedings to follow the service should not be unduly delayed, said to the visiting preacher, 'You like a little more time than usual – you could take about fifteen or twenty minutes'. To which he received the disconcerting reply, 'Oh that is of no use to me!'.

The next day, Tuesday, May 1 at 3.30 p.m., Hitler killed himself in the bunker of the Chancellery in Berlin and Lloyd-Jones determined to return at once to London, cancelling an engagement in Newcastle on the Wednesday. In fact, a further week was to pass before London went jubilant with the news of Germany's unconditional surrender and celebrated 'Victory Day in Europe' on May 8. That same day, when King George VI wrote in his diary, 'We look back with thankfulness to God that our tribulation is over', and Parliament laid aside its business to 'attend at the Church of St Margaret, Westminster, to give humble and reverent thanks to Almighty God for our deliverance,' ML-J lunched with Donald Coggan to confer together on the future. Coggan, a vice-president of CICCU in 1930 and a subsequent leader in the IVF, had recently returned from Canada to be Principal of the London College of Divinity.

When the thanksgiving service was held the next morning in Westminster Chapel one figure particularly was missed. Campbell Morgan, who first preached in that building in the far off summer of 1902 and who had been with the church through the worst of two World Wars, would be there no more. Jill Morgan, his daughter-in-law, recalling that memorable week, has written:

Winter yielded to Spring, and VE Day came on the eighth day of May. The moon shone down upon the scars of London, but the terror of pilotless planes and rocket bombs was over. The weary, the aged, and the young could sleep unmolested and waken to see flowers appearing in the ruins. Another chapter in history was closed.

The man lying on the couch in St Ermins was waiting. Each day he grew weaker but there was no anxiety in his heart. He had walked too long beside the Shepherd to doubt His love and wisdom now. Through the window the tower of Westminster Chapel could be seen standing against the sky. The work would go on; the Word would be proclaimed to the generations to come.[1]

Morgan died on May 16 and for many who assembled for a memorial service at Westminster Chapel on May 28 his passing was akin to the passing of a whole era. Certainly the men, and the one woman, who shared that service with Dr Lloyd-Jones – W. H. Aldis, John A. Hutton, Mildred Cable, Charles Brown, Sidney M. Berry and S. W. Hughes – were people whose work was done in the broad evangelicalism which had survived for fifty years after its influence was strongest in the Victorian era. They were themselves older representatives of a tradition which was passing and of which Morgan was, in a sense, the last great preacher.

In terms of that tradition Lloyd-Jones was certainly not Morgan's successor, but in his generous praise of his former colleague at the memorial service there was little more than the briefest hint of that fact. 'We differed theologically, but we never discussed that; we believed in the same final authority of this Book. If one of us was a little bit Calvinistic in his preaching, the other was always Calvinistic in his praying! So we never quarrelled at all, and we just said nothing more about it.'

The only failure which ML-J recalled in his relationship with Dr Morgan was one in which he would have had the sympathy of his hearers, 'I tried to persuade him to write the story of his life, or his memoirs, but he would not do it'. Morgan was more than a great preacher, 'He became an institution . . . He seems to me to have occupied in the religious life of London the same place as Sir Henry Wood in the musical life of London.' Of his personal characteristics ML-J spoke of his 'bigness', his boundless energy, his individuality, his humility and the powerful intelligence which 'persisted until almost the last moment of his life'. Speaking further of his intelligence he allowed himself to give the following personal reference:

[1]*A Man of the Word*, op. cit, pp. 318–19.

I called to see him on the last day of his life; it was somewhere round about half-past twelve, and he was obviously dying. I tried to be natural, and to speak as I always spoke to him, and I left with the impression that I had not revealed in any way my feeling that that was to be our last meeting here on earth. However, a short time afterwards he was visited by his doctor, and he said to her, 'I am dying'. 'What makes you think that?' she asked. 'I saw it in Lloyd-Jones' face.' He was dying, life was ebbing away; but with that flashing eye and that keen intelligence of his, he was watching me, and he diagnosed my feelings alright.[1]

*　　　　*　　　　*

It was usually a rush to get away for summer holidays but especially so in 1945 for with 2 Colebrooke Avenue, Ealing, being sold by its owner, it was necessary to move house in July. The selling price of £2,500 was beyond ML-J's resources. Mr A. G. Secrett had been able to come up with another property which could be rented by the church, and this – 39 Mount Park Crescent – now became the new home. A comfortable Edwardian house on three floors, it was situated on a quiet road and yet only a few minutes walk from Ealing Broadway station. Here, in the fifteenth house in which ML-J had lived, he was to stay longer than in any other.

After a month of upheaval the Lloyd-Joneses were at last ready to leave for Jasper House, Aberystwyth, on Monday, July 30, though (with Elizabeth already away in North Wales and unable to help with last minute arrangements) the effort to reach the train in time was considerable. Among ML-J's final duties was the need to take the household cat to the care of an 'Animal Defence' home. 'I expect when the people saw her,' Mrs Lloyd-Jones wrote to Elizabeth, 'they wondered why on earth we were so anxious to keep her! . . . You really cannot imagine the rush of getting away, it was terrific. The telephone kept going every minute. Dada did all the sandwiches for the journey! We got to Paddington [station] about twenty to nine, rather fearing our chances for a seat, only to find that Auntie Kit was already established in her corner, with Aunties Janie, Dilys, Mary and Lizzie and a Miss Daniels holding the fort for us! It was a far better journey than last year, though I couldn't sleep till we got into a cooler train at Carmarthen.'

Writing to his mother (then at Port Talbot) the next day, ML-J reported:

[1] *W R, Memorial Number to Dr G Campbell Morgan*, July, 1945, p. 62.

It was my intention to write to you yesterday but I literally failed to find a moment. For some reason or other we had the greatest rush of our lives and had to leave in the end without a meal!

Sunday was an excellent day at Westminster – two remarkably fine congregations and collections. I finished my series of four sermons on the prodigal son at night. By the way, Caiger as treasurer on Thursday night informed the Church meeting that the collections during the past month had reached a higher total than they had done for 15 years.

The holiday at Aberystwyth followed its usual course except that Ann, being without Elizabeth for the first time, seems to have had somewhat more of her father's time, playing golf with him most mornings and evenings, despite the poor weather. There were outings to such beauty spots as the Devil's Bridge, agricultural shows to visit and the opportunity to go to the Eisteddfod at Ysbyty Ystwyth. As ever there was a stream of relatives and friends to see them, including a whole Sunday School outing party from Bethel Chapel at Newcastle Emlyn. They arrived in pouring rain and so stayed indoors for most of this annual visit to the sea-side!

The relaxation for ML-J did not seem to be spoiled by the fact that he was preaching every weekend – at Llandudno (two Sundays), Hoylake, Llanidloes and Haverfordwest. For the only occasion in his life, he even broke into his holidays and returned to Westminster for a special service following President Truman's announcement of the Japanese surrender on August 14.[1] Writing to his mother on August 12 he explained:

I felt that we ought to have a thanksgiving service at Westminster when the official end of the war was declared. I, therefore, got in touch with Marsh on Saturday and got him to announce that a service would be held on the VJ night by me. We listened to the 11.0 p.m. news on Tuesday and as it was clear that the end was at hand, we stayed up and heard the 11.50 p.m. which told us that Attlee would speak at 12.0 mid-night.

The result was that I left here on the 10.0 a.m. on Wednesday. The journey was one of the most crowded that I have ever known in my life. We got to Paddington by 6.10 and Dr Blackie was there to meet me with her car.

There was quite a good congregation present and I was glad that I had gone up. I caught the 9.25 p.m. back and had quite a good journey with a fair amount of sleep, arriving here at 9.30 a.m. yesterday morning. I feel none the worse for it all.

[1] A new era of world history had dawned on August 6 when the Allies used an atomic bomb on Hiroshima.

There was no time, of course, to see people at Westminster or to get any news. But my impression was that there was nothing like the same excitement as over VE day.

We are having an excellent holiday here. It is certainly the best weather we have ever had at Aberystwyth.

The following week, with Elizabeth now back from camp, they all left Aberystwyth for Newcastle Emlyn and then, on September 3 went to Combe Down, Bath where they were to enjoy a further holiday. This visit was the result of a letter which ML-J had received the previous year from R. G. Tucker, the pastor of Union Chapel, Combe Down, expressing sympathy over the flying bomb disaster which had destroyed the Guards Chapel. Dr Lloyd-Jones was so taken with the tone of Tucker's letter that he had readily agreed to preach in his little church in March 1945. The two men at once formed a life-long friendship and so ML-J returned in September to introduce his family to the Tuckers and to a beautiful part of England.

The Tuckers' son, Paul, was still living at home, with no idea that in later years he would be a minister in London contemporary with Dr Lloyd-Jones. In those later years the Lloyd-Joneses' visit to his home in September 1945 was to be recalled by him as 'an unforgettable holiday':

I was emerging from my teens. Petrol was rationed but available for private motoring. Father instructed me to drive Dr Lloyd-Jones wherever he wished to go. Ann was about 8 and Elizabeth a young teenager. I met Dr at Bath station for the first time. I had seen him at Corsham but not spoken to him. The thing that impressed me was his eyes. I forget their colour, they seemed luminous – he was so transparently humble and grateful to be met at the station as if I were doing him some great favour. Several things stand out about the eight days which followed.

For one thing, there was the Dr's humanity. He and my father joked a lot about all sorts of things. Father could tell West Country yarns that had their own brand of humour – not bawdy but earthy. Dr's shoulders would heave with laughter. I remember one of Dr's jokes about a Welsh preacher who relied on the elders in the 'big seat' to encourage him with their 'Amens', 'Diolchs' etc. One morning there was silence, no response whatever. The minister found the first quarter of an hour of his sermon hard going. Then a brother shouted 'hallelujah' as the preacher began to get liberty. The minister paused and, leaning over the pulpit, remarked, 'Now that dawn has come, one cockerel has begun to crow'.

During the holiday we spent a day at Weston-super-Mare, Burrington Combe (shades of Toplady) and Cheddar Gorge. At Weston Ann wanted to go on the pier. One of the most attractive features to her was the big dipper. 'Let's go on it' said Ann. Imagine my surprise when Dr without hesitation got in the front seat with Ann. I shared the back seat either with Mrs. L-J or Elizabeth. It was a hair-raising ride but Dr appeared thoroughly to enjoy it. I tried to visualise the sedate Westminster congregation and their great preacher on a pier roller-coaster. While the Lloyd-Jones were with us Elizabeth received news via 'phone that she had passed examinations. She wheeled around several times on her heel and said 'Oh Dad, Dad, I've passed'. Dr looked at us with an indulgent smile and said, 'You must forgive her; she has been under great strain for several weeks'.

I was also impressed with his capacity for work. Though on holiday he had lots of letters to answer. These were personally handled. Most were invitations to preach. Every day Dr worked away at letters. He read a weighty tome by Van Til with incredible speed. I was in the same room and struggling with *The Two Humanities* (D. R. Davies). Noting my interests, he spoke to me about the ministry and said that if I was called to be a minister he would advise me as follows: 'Don't waste time reading Barth and Brunner. You will get nothing from them to aid you with preaching. Read Pink[1].' At that date, when Pink's writings had a limited circulation, I was thus introduced to *Studies in the Scriptures* long before Pink became the almost 'cult' figure that he is today. I was very grateful for Dr's advice. He also advised me to study 1 Corinthians, chapters 1 to 3, saying, 'I am convinced that no chapters are more important to preach from at this time'. Dr told me something interesting about Davies' *On to Orthodoxy*. When showing Dr the original MS he had said, 'I am thinking of calling it *Back to Orthodoxy*'. 'No,' the Dr replied, 'that gives the impression of a retrograde step. Call the book *On to Orthodoxy*.'

It was during the holiday that Dr prepared the second edition of his book *The Plight of Man and the Power of God*, first published in 1942. I 'helped' Dr by checking the first edition content as he read rapidly the paragraphs of the proofs for the second edition.

The following Christmas Paul Tucker was surprised to receive a gift of *The Plight of Man and the Power of God* inscribed to 'my dear friend' by the author. It was, however, typical of the encouragement

[1] ML-J read A. W. Pink's monthly *Studies in the Scriptures* from about 1942 until it concluded with the author's death ten years later.

which ML-J gave to young men. Commenting on his large-heartedness, Paul Tucker also says how much it meant when, on his marriage a few years later, his wife and he received a letter from ML-J and a gift of £5: 'It was a lot of money then. Part of our honeymoon was taken up with deciphering the handwriting of the Dr.'

Two letters from ML-J to his mother during the holiday at Combe Down, which ended on September 11, are largely taken up with news of the outings which they had enjoyed:

On Wednesday we were motored to Weston-super-Mare and had an excellent time. Ann was thrilled by the donkeys that trotted and galloped. The Aberystwyth ones only walk. I also rowed her and Elizabeth in a boat and she enjoyed the amusements on the Pier . . .

I was greatly impressed by Wells, Cheddar and Glastonbury. Of all the sights I feel that the Cheddar caves impressed me most of all. Nothing can excel nature. We climbed up to the top of Glastonbury Tor. The view of the country around in every direction is simply wonderful.

I much enjoyed my visit to Swansea on Sunday.[1] We had large congregations, especially at night when it was packed out. Three people fainted during the service owing to the heat . . .

We are all very well. Bethan looks particularly well and says she is ready for work!

As ML-J returned to London in September 1945 there was one particular matter concerning the work at Westminster which had needed thought. With the war over there were those who now expected him to resume Westminster Chapel's once famous institution, the Friday night 'Bible School'. At the Memorial Service to Campbell Morgan in May Dr Charles Brown, speaking of the Bible School, had gone as far as saying, 'Nothing like it had been known in London before' and, turning to Dr Lloyd-Jones, had advised, 'I do not know, Sir, whether you intend to carry on here now in that way, but there are people here, there and everywhere who owed Campbell Morgan their souls through the influence of that Bible School'.

Lloyd-Jones probably caused a surprise by deciding against what amounted to an additional service on Friday evenings. Numbers might have been drawn from other churches for a meeting that

[1]He had crossed back into Wales for Sunday, September 9, at Argyle Chapel, Swansea.

evening (as had happened in Morgan's time) but he was convinced that the needs of those already at the Chapel were being better served by the Discussion meeting which was now well established on Friday evenings. As well as its teaching value, the meeting had a unifying influence as people heard others speaking of spiritual experience and common concerns. Some who never spoke wrote to ML-J and these letters also underlined the importance of this unusual type of meeting.

One lady began a letter, 'When I left our Discussion meeting last Friday evening, I knew I ought to thank you for the help I had received, but passed you without doing so'. Such letters were not always from Christians. After one such meeting in 1944 a man wrote to him asking for further help and explaining: 'I am not going Christ's way and it seems to me there comes a time when the logic of the Gospel has to be admitted but there remains fear of God. Fear of handing over to him, fear of what Christianity is going to mean in your life, fear of what you'll have to do – in fact it's a case of fear of living and fear of dying.'

Another factor may have entered into ML-J's decision not to revive the Friday Bible School. He could not move the Discussion meeting to another night of the week without limiting his frequent mid-week travelling away from London, and to have replaced the Discussion with another service would have significantly added to pressure on his time. The Discussions, being spontaneous, virtually required no preparation on his part, whereas he never entered a pulpit without careful preparation.

Conscious of the wider need, ML-J would not consider the alternative of curtailing his preaching elsewhere. Between September and December 1945, excluding engagements in the greater London area, he was to preach in Cardiff, Swansea, Carmarthen, Merthyr Tydfil, Taunton, Swindon, Worthing, Liverpool, Holywell, Bedford, Glasgow, Walsall, Rochester, Pontypool and Penarth. These services were almost invariably evangelistic. They were continued without any declaration of 'results' for, unlike the prevailing evangelism, ML-J never allowed repentance and faith to be confused with a call for a visible 'decision' on the part of his hearers.

At Westminster he frequently reminded his hearers that he was available in the vestry and would be privileged to speak further with anyone. But he believed that God deals directly with individuals and sometimes the most heartening news came from individuals whom he had never met, such as a Westminster hearer who wrote to him on October 21, 1945:

London SW

Dear Sir,

This is probably my last Sunday in London as I am expecting to move permanently away. I have had the privilege of hearing most of your morning sermons since last December, and I can do no more than thank you for them. I have attended Divine service in many places and heard many preachers over the past 50 years (including your predecessor) but nobody has preached the Gospel so consistently and with such absolute truth and conviction as you do – or so it seems to me.

If I had spent hours in trying to tell you of my own particular problems and needs at the present moment and had you designed the whole of this morning's service for my special benefit, not a verse or a petition or a word would have needed to be altered. *Perhaps* the very reason for the difficulties that have kept me in London this week was to enable me to be present at Westminster this morning.

In the name of God, Sir, I thank you for your interpretation of his message.

Another letter, written thirty years later, gives the testimony of a young woman who was a rising star in the world of ballet when she visited Westminster Chapel a few years after the War, finding the interior filled with scaffolding as its ceiling was still being repaired:

How great is our heavenly Father that I should ever have entered Westminster Chapel and peeped through scaffolding to hear a man preaching on Esther and Mordecai. I sat in that back seat for months. I didn't want to speak to anyone in case I should lose the things I had just heard. The Lord God moved me tremendously and gave me a glimpse of His glory. I was never the same again. I couldn't stay in the ballet, and have never really been able to understand people who do stay in the theatre.

I remember very well when we were in the USA in 1947 that I had to leave my wife and younger daughter in Boston on a Monday night to travel all night and the following morning and afternoon in a train to speak at a conference. I was to alight from the train in a station in Indiana, and there friends were to meet me in a car. As it happened these friends mistook the time of arrival with the result that I found myself in a small station in the middle of the country with no-one there – not visibly at least – but myself. The rain was pouring down and black clouds above had the threat of thunder – and I was at once back in Tregaron and feeling exactly the same as I had done on numerous occasions in the lodgings on Monday evenings. Believe me or not, but I stared at the time-table on the wall to see if there was a convenient train back to Boston! Fortunately there wasn't one – or I fear that I would have turned my back on the conference.

ML-J

when speaking of the *hiraeth* of his school-days in his Reminiscences of his early life.

8

Overseas Visits, 1946–48

Dr Lloyd-Jones did not speak at the annual IVF students conference held at Regent's Park College, Oxford, in March, 1946, but on Thursday, March 28 he came up from London for a committee meeting which was immediately to follow. After the 1939 international students' conference at Cambridge a make-shift international conference committee, of which he was a member, had held occasional meetings. It was only now, however, that the International Conference Executive of 1939, augmented by a number of observers, could assemble for two days at Regent's Park College. Nineteen men were present and their discussion centered upon international student relationships of the future. Prior to World War II the British IVF had pioneered national student movements in Canada, Australia, New Zealand, Switzerland, France and Holland. There were also links formed with evangelical student bodies already existing in other European countries.

Much had happened since the pre-war years. In 1939 the various European groups, not wanting any organizational connection, regarded a triennial international conference as a sufficient expression of their overall unity. But the isolation and repression which marked the five years of German occupation had brought a change of attitude in several countries. Norwegians, Danes and Dutch were now eager for much closer ties with others, and it was from them that a proposal had come for the commencement of an International Fellowship of Students. While the British IVF had no resources to finance a larger work, a consideration relevant to the new proposal was the existence of an American Inter-Varsity Christian Fellowship, officially founded in 1941. North America offered a large potential for the expansion of student work and its two leaders, C. Stacey Woods and John Bolten, had come to the international committee meeting at Oxford to promise their aid.

Stacey Woods was a thirty-six-year-old Australian. Anticipating ordination in the diocese of Sydney, he had gone to North America in the early 1930's to complete his training. Instead he became caught up in a lifetime ministry of student work. Having become General Secretary of the IVCF of Canada in 1934, it was Woods who carried the work into the USA where one of his early supporters was John Bolten. Bolten was a business man and a financier who had been driven out of his native Nürnberg, Germany in the late 1920's to become a multi-millionaire in the land of his adoption. But Europe remained close to his heart, and in the two-day committee meeting in Oxford his plea for far greater concern for the work of God in his defeated homeland was well received. 'Spontaneously,' Douglas Johnson recalls, 'time was given to prayer that God would raise up his student witnesses in that fallen nation.'[1]   March 28, 1946 at Regent's Park College was the occasion of ML-J's first meeting with Woods and Bolten, and it proved to be the beginning of a life-long connection. The two visitors from North America had brought an invitation from the joint IVCF's of Canada and the USA that the next meeting of the International Conference Executive should be held at Harvard (Boston), Massachusetts, in August 1947. Following serious discussion, it was agreed both that the invitation be accepted and that a proposal be sent to all the co-operating movements that the pre-war link by means of conferences should now be extended by the formation of an International Fellowship of Evangelical Students.

After one day at the Regent's Park College meeting Lloyd-Jones had to return to London and he was not present when a draft constitution for the proposed IFES was drawn up on the Saturday morning for approval at Boston. The constitution made it clear that the organization was to amount to nothing more than a loose fellowship. ML-J no doubt heard the conclusion from Woods, whom he met again the following week, as well as from Douglas Johnson. The two men from North America were also at Westminster for a Sunday service and Bolten (who was a member of Dr Harold J. Ockenga's congregation of Park Street, Boston) determined that the Welshman must preach in their city when he came to the Harvard Conference in 1947.

[1] *The Growth of a Work of God*, C. Stacey Woods, 1978, p. 138. Woods adds, 'It would seem that this was the initial spiritual impulse that resulted in the founding of the Student Mission in Deutschland'.

In the meantime ML-J had another overseas trip to undertake arising out of his IVF contacts. Scandinavian leaders had always been ready for co-operation with the British IVF, although somewhat puzzled over what to them appeared as the fragmented inter-denominationalism of English evangelicalism. (Student work in Norway and Sweden was closely related to the Lutheran state Churches). No fewer than four of the six members of the International Conference Executive Committee, which continued from the 1939 Conference, were Scandinavians and it was Nils Dahlberg of Sweden who chaired the meetings at Regent's Park College. Eager for closer ties, some of these men invited ML-J to Norway in September 1946 and he readily accepted.

When September came he was holidaying as usual with the family in Wales. Leaving them in Newcastle Emlyn, he journeyed to north-east England and embarked on the 'Bretagne' to cross the North Sea from Newcastle on September 7. Even before boarding ship he was to discover that, in the conditions following the war, international travel was not as straightforward as he had known it in earlier years. The authorities at embarkation deprived him of all his money, except for the legally permitted £5 (promising its restoration on his return!). Further, due to some confusion in his travel arrangements, the boat was not going, as he had expected, to Bergen (from whence he had expected to enjoy a scenic railway journey) but direct to Oslo. His hosts in the Norwegian capital, sharing in this confusion, consequently did not know his time of arrival. Nonetheless, as he writes home, it was a good journey and after the austerities of war-time rationing, which was still in force in Britain, matters of cuisine received more than normal comment:

> Indremisjonshotellet, Oslo
> September 9, 1946

My dear Bethan,

I hope you got the cable, to say that I had arrived safely, before this. I hope, too, that the letter I sent from Newcastle on Saturday arrived safely.

Well, here I am in a strange country indeed, and feeling further away from home than ever I did before. I believe it is the language that is chiefly responsible for this. It seems a very, very long time since I said goodbye to you in Carmarthen. The presence of Mrs. D. O. Evans made me think of 1937 when I went to America from Waterloo. Strange how she happens to be present when I go overseas without you.

Now for some kind of account of the journey. As I told you in my letter from Newcastle, I had a very comfortable train journey. The boat was marvellous in every way. I had a very nice cabin to myself with one of the best beds I have ever had. As far as food goes, I have never seen so much, nor such a variety, since before the war. It was unbelievable. We had fried fish for supper on Saturday night and then we all had to go to a large central table to help ourselves to whatsoever we fancied – every kind of fish, boiled ham, spam, sardines, cold meats, salads of all kinds, several varieties of cheese, as well as any amount of sweets and fruits. As I say, it was very difficult to believe that such a thing was possible.

We reached the open sea very soon so there was nothing of any interest to be seen. I went to the prow of the ship to do my usual exercises and felt they were beneficial.[1] I went to bed at 9.30 and slept really well all night, only waking once, till 8.30 yesterday morning. The sea was calm and smooth. All day yesterday I sat reading out on deck. I ate every meal with no difficulty. I felt a wave of nausea every now and then, but eating gave me complete relief every time. The truth is that the sea was so calm that nobody could have been sick – though I did hear that one or two had been seasick on Sat. night. Many also complained of extreme drowsiness and a complete lack of desire for food. There was an R.C. priest on board. He came to speak to me on Saturday night and again yesterday afternoon. He was a thoroughly nice young man, brought up in the Anglican Church. We had very interesting conversations. He maintained that he *did not* look upon me as a lost soul. He said I was in the unseen church and so in the Body of Christ, though I was not receiving the privileges that belong to the one who is a member of the visible Church. After dinner last night he invited me to join a very interesting company to discuss these things peacefully. There were: a girl from Norway, a girl from London, a girl from Scotland, an older woman from Ireland, a professor of mathematics from Poland, the Roman Catholic and me. We had a happy enough time. After leaving the company, I asked the priest about the different people – were they Catholics, etc. – and I discovered that the Irish lady was a sister to Richard O'Sullivan.[2] When I told her who I was, she said that she knew Vincent well, had met him many times with her brother!

We saw land for the first time at 5.30 p.m. yesterday – the eastern

---

[1] As a remedy for sea-sickness he recommended that at the outset of a voyage a passenger should stand for five minutes as near to the prow of the vessel as possible and, with knees slightly bent and body relaxed, look only at the horizon, from left to right in an arc of 180°.
[2] A friend of his brother, Vincent.

part of Norway to the south of Stavanger. After that we followed the coast line for the rest of the voyage. Norway is a very mountainous country. Now we saw the start of several of the fjords.

I told you in Saturday's letter that D. J. had made a mistake and that I was on a boat that was coming here direct, without going to Bergen. I slept well last night too. I got up at 6.50 a.m. in order to see the Oslo fjord. It is very beautiful – rocks coming down to the water, and trees – pines – everywhere on the rocks. There are also many islands – again tree-covered rocks. It was like a kind of fairy-land. Some Norwegians pointed out the most interesting spots to us. The entrance to Oslo harbour is really beautiful. I saw the house where Quisling lived during the war. It was strange to think of the Germans sailing up this quiet sea on that awful morning in April 1940. When I landed there was no one to meet me, of course, because of D. J's mistake about the boat. The girl from Norway, the one who was in the company last night, saw my difficulty and came to me. She and her mother and father took me in a taxi to their house, and then on to this hotel where I am staying. The mountains here rise steeply from the sea, and these people lived some 1600 ft. above sea level. There are pines everywhere, and everything is very beautiful. After reaching the hotel and getting hold of a telephone, I managed to contact the friends who were supposed to be meeting me. They were surprised to hear my voice. They came to me at once, and I have been with them all day. This hotel is very comfortable – a Christian hotel. Its name means: 'Internal or Home Missions Hotel'.

Well, that is all to date. It has poured with rain all day. Yesterday was very fine, without a drop of rain.

I am to address the students in the University tomorrow night – open meeting. Conferences with Hallesby[1] and other individuals on Wednesday, meeting for the Students Union on Thursday night. Those are my chief commitments so it will not be too heavy for me.

Only one thing detracts – that is that you are not here with me. I feel exactly as I did in America in 1937. It is not right for me to be travelling by myself like this. I hope to write a word again on Wednesday, with an account of my doings. I believe that letters take about a week to arrive, as a rule. So I am sending this by air mail, hoping you will get it on Thursday at latest.

I hope all is well with the three of you. My thoughts are ever with you.

All my love to you, my dearest girl, and once more leave you to share out with Elizabeth and Ann.

[1]Professor O. Hallesby, a foremost figure in student work whom ML-J had first met at Cambridge in 1939.

My love, too, to all there.[1] I don't remember ever before having had such a happy time together.

Once more, my dearest love,

ever yours, Martyn.

There was only the opportunity for one more letter before he returned to London on September 16 and, once again, we give it in full.

Oslo
Sept. 11th, 1946

My dear Bethan,

Since this is my last chance to get a letter that is at all likely to get to you before we see each other on Monday, I am writing a hurried word before going to meet Prof. Hallesby. I hope that the letter I posted on Monday has arrived.

Let me give a further account of things. On Monday night we were in the home of one of these men – Hereide. Elizabeth heard him speaking in a meeting in Bloomsbury Chapel. He is a thoroughly nice chap, with a nice wife and three children – 5, 3 and 6 months.

The food here is very different from ours. They eat their fish and ham and bacon raw – uncooked! They also drink milk and sour milk with nearly every meal. We all had a very happy time together. The housing shortage is worse than with us. The government – socialist – and almost communist – allow, on average, one room per person. As a result Mr & Mrs Hereide and the three children have to sleep in one room. Yesterday I went 100 miles by car to meet Dr Lindly – a medical doctor and an exceptionally good man. It was a glorious run and took us three hours. For most of the way we journeyed along the shores of the largest lake in the country. As for the scenery, it reminded me forcibly of parts of Ontario. The soil is very poor, with the underlying rock to be seen everywhere. What makes the scenery beautiful is the pine forestry. It was a glorious day. I should say that the houses are wooden houses here too – everything is very like Canada. This is a poor country, and the farming primitive. I saw much harvesting done with scythes and hay-cutting machines. It was unusual to see a binder. The cattle are very like ours, but the horses very inferior. We had a marvellous dinner in Mrs Hereide's home. Her father is a manufacturer who also runs a farm. Here's the menu for your interest – soup with

[1] At Newcastle Emlyn.

hard-boiled egg in it! Pork chop, potatoes, cabbage – with caraway seed sprinkled on it – gravy, etc. Stewed red currants and cream *ad lib*. Coffee with cream.

I forgot all the rules[1] and enjoyed everything. I have no time to write of Dr Lindly now. It took us three hours to get back. I slept for half an hour, and after a light supper we went to the meeting. There were at least 500 people present – the hall full to overflowing. I felt I was given some measure of freedom in speaking. It was obvious that everybody could understand me and that there was no need of an interpreter. The listening – or attention – was incredibly good, and many came at the end to speak to me.

I was not over-tired in spite of everything, and I slept really well. I asked them to call me at eight. They did so on the telephone and this was the conversation:- The phone rang, then The Porter: 'The clock is eight'. Me: 'Thank you'. Porter: 'Please'.

Well, that is all now, and indeed all that could reach you before Monday.

All my love to you, dear Bethan, and to E. and A. Affectionate regards to all there.

Ever yours, Martyn.

ML-J commenced his four-day journey home with a twelve hour train journey from Oslo to Bergen on Friday, September 13 and revelled in the scenery as the train climbed to 3,662 feet above sea level amidst snow covered mountains. The North Sea crossing on Saturday and Sunday was less pleasant and it is not easy to understand how he still retained his faith in the exercises for the prevention of sea sickness! It was so rough that even five days later he could write to his mother: 'I still feel a little giddy and light headed . . . I have never seen such waves before'. Nonetheless his memory of his first visit to Norway was to be one of immense enjoyment, and there can be no doubt that it fulfilled the hopes of those who had invited him.

The next visit overseas was for the conference to establish the International Fellowship of Evangelical Students at Boston, August 18–23, 1947. This engagement was to be combined with a number of others and accordingly the family (excepting Elizabeth who was to visit Europe) sailed on the 'Empress of Canada' from Liverpool on Wednesday, July 16. A letter to his mother, 'in thick mist' as they were approaching Quebec on Tuesday, July 22, gave all the

[1] i.e. his self-imposed diet.

news of the trip. With Northern Ireland providing a last sight of Europe on the previous Thursday, they had enjoyed a calm voyage all the way across, sighting Newfoundland to the south and Labrador to the north on the previous day. Meetings with various passengers were described, ranging from the assistant purser (whose helpfulness merited the comment, 'Again I have proved what a real advantage it is to be a Welshman') to the lady who, on hearing that Bethan's husband was minister of Westminster Chapel, asked, 'But where is Dr Lloyd-Jones now then?' No one enjoyed the new acquaintances – old and young – which the ship provided more than Ann, 'She seems to know everybody and to be friendly with everyone.' After a 6.30 a.m. breakfast on Wednesday, July 23, and with tears from the ten-year-old member of the family (who was to be 'shipsick' for a few days), they landed in Montreal and reached Toronto by train by 6.25 p.m. the same day. The remaining three days of the week were to be almost the only free time for ML-J until the return voyage. Thursday and Friday were spent shopping, after which he was to report to his mother: 'There seems to be plenty of most things . . . Toronto is much as it was 15 years ago. I found my way about quite easily without having to make any enquiries at all.' On the Friday he also contacted a school friend from Llangeitho days, Dai Crymbychan, an estate agent in Toronto whom he had not met for over 30 years. Dai was full of enthusiasm at the unexpected re-union and insisted on taking them to Niagara on the Saturday. 'They had a lot of reminiscences,' Bethan Lloyd-Jones wrote home, 'and it delighted Ann to learn of some of Dad's naughtiness at school.'

The next day, July 27, amidst a terrible thunder-storm and torrential rain, ML-J took the first of three Sundays at Knox Church, preaching from 2 Corinthians 4:17–18 and Luke 12:54–57. The intervening weeks between the next two weekends were spent at two holiday Conferences, the first being the Canadian Keswick, 130 miles north of Toronto on one of Ontario's million lakes, and the second in a similar but more primitive venue at the Canadian IVF 'Campus in the Woods'. Writing to Mr and Mrs Secrett of the first of these Conferences, and then of the Toronto services in general, Bethan Lloyd-Jones said:

Martyn spoke in one meeting a day and I think enjoyed speaking. It was significant that all those who spoke to him said the same thing, namely that they had never heard anything like it before and hoped that he would say the same things in the States . . . Knox Church is aesthetically most beautiful and must have cost many fortunes. I believe it is evangelical *in intention* but it does seem to me that evangelicals are so sorely lacking in knowledge and theology that they have very little discernment . . . But M. certainly has a receptive and appreciative audience here and many old friends of 1932 – some who have come testifying of conversion then and going on well.[1]

On Monday, August 11, the Lloyd-Joneses left Toronto for Wheaton College (near Chicago) where Carl F. H. Henry had asked ML-J to give the first series of Jonathan Blanchard Lectures on a subject related to apologetics. The result was five addresses subsequently published as *Truth Unchanged, Unchanging*. In essence they were an explanation of his whole approach to evangelism: the modern secular scene requires no new apologetic because man's condition in sin is the same as it has always been; only the Bible can explain that condition and only the gospel provides a remedy radical enough for the problem.

One relaxation in the heat wave which overtook them at Wheaton was an outing to the farm of some Welsh relatives in Illinois. After writing to his mother with news of the relatives, ML-J had to add something on his special interest: 'They certainly have some wonderful ponies. Unfortunately it was too hot for us to see any of them in motion'.

The night of Friday, August 15, 1947 saw them on the long train journey to Boston where he was to take the first of three Sundays in Park Street Church the same weekend. The following Monday saw the opening, at 11 a.m., of the much anticipated Conference for the formation of the IFES. The twenty-five delegates met in Phillip Brooks House, Harvard, and were housed for the week in the historic 'Yard' of the College which the New England Puritans had founded in 1642. Nils Dahlberg had resigned as chairman of the International Committee the previous year. At the request of Dahlberg ML-J was acting as chairman until, with the plans for the IFES finally approved, he was elected chairman under the new constitution.

[1] At the door of Knox Church a beautifully dressed old lady, described to him as one of the wealthiest ladies in Canada, said to him after his first Sunday morning service there: 'I understand that you preach to Christians in the mornings and to sinners in the evenings. Believe me, I shall be here every evening from now on!' She was true to her word.

The settling of the new constitution was not, however, a mere formality. In the words of Stacey Woods, 'This was a meeting of outstanding leaders'.[1] They included such figures as Herbert J. Taylor, president of Club Aluminium Company and a past president of Rotary International, Judge John Reid of the International Court of Justice at The Hague (heading the Canadian delegation) and Howard Mowll, Archbishop of Sydney. But precisely at this point there lay a difficulty. A keystone of British policy for the IVF was that it was to be a *student led* Fellowship, the participating Christian Unions not being under the direction of the General Secretary (Douglas Johnson) or any full-time staff. But when the British delegation got to Boston, with student representatives from Oxford and Cambridge, it found that no other student representatives were present at all. Further, it was clear that the Canadian and American IVCF's were being run as corporations under the control of boards of business men and financiers. Certainly they were corporations existing as a mission to students, but they were scarcely student organizations. Given this North American influence, and the general absence of students, it meant that the decisions for an International Fellowship of *Students* were being made by others on behalf of the students.

This situation led to the keenest debate of the week. Speaking of the Harvard Conference, Stacey Woods has written:

This was a difficult meeting in many ways. The weather was intolerably hot and humid. We represented a diverse group of people in terms of nationality, culture and ecclesiastical conviction and affiliation. There were the Lutherans from Scandinavia – with some tension still existing between Sweden and the other Scandinavian countries due to happenings in World War II. There were also the Continentals with tensions between German and French and Swiss. There was the perhaps unconscious but real desire of the British Inter-Varsity to impose its philosophy of student Christian work, with student leadership as the keystone.[2]

For a successful outcome Woods gives special credit to ML-J: 'With consummate skill and unimaginable patience, Dr Lloyd-Jones

---

[1] *The Growth of a Work of God*, p. 139.
[2] This, and a subsequent quotation, are from a letter to the author, March 19, 1981. Woods appreciated the importance of student initiative but did not think it could work at national or international level. See his *The Growth of a Work of God*, p. 60 ff, where he also observes, 'American Christianity had for too long been conditioned by American business ideology and practice'.

chaired this Conference until a constitution was hammered out and an international movement was formed.'

This is not, however, the whole story. The fact is that Douglas Johnson and the English student representatives were far from happy at ML-J's handling of the issue of student participation. When DJ moved an amendment that in any full delegation of three represent-atives to an International Conference *one* should be a student – a seemingly very modest proposal – he found himself being ruled 'out of order' by the chairman. ML-J favoured the North American idea of firm senior control, which he supported with the apostolic precept, 'Not a novice . . .' (1 Tim. 3:6). It was generally ML-J's friends who had the hardest time debating against him and Douglas Johnson was no exception. Even in the face of the chairman's injunction to 'sit down', he persisted with, 'Well, it is ironic that the *British* should have to come to Boston to argue "No taxation without representation" and to try to get some kind of democracy!'. This brought Judge Reid to the side of the lone Englishman (the students not daring to venture into the fray!) and the amendment was eventually passed.

In the evenings it had been arranged that ML-J would speak to the delegates and on these meetings Johnson (who was probably chiefly responsible for their existence on the programme) had no reserva-tions: 'Dr Lloyd-Jones' conference addresses in the evenings proved a great inspiration to the members of the Committee.'[1] By the time that the gathering closed on Saturday morning, with the prayer of Psalm 90:16, 17, 'Let thy work appear unto thy servants, and thy glory unto their children . . .', a unity was forged which, in the next quarter century, was to make the International Fellowship of Evangelical Students the strongest student movement in the world.

At Boston, Stacey Woods took over from Douglas Johnson (the previous organizer of the international work) as General Secretary of the IFES, a role which he was to combine, initially, with his position as joint-General Secretary to the Canadian and USA movements. The regard which the two men had for each other, despite some differences ('Dr Johnson,' said Woods, is so 'essentially insular and English beyond imagination!'), was to underpin the whole work. 'No small admiration must be accorded to the working capacity and stamina of Stacey Woods,' wrote DJ at a later date,[2] while Woods

---

[1] *A brief history of the IFES*, ed. Douglas Johnson, 1964, p. 76.
[2] *Contending for the Faith: A History of the Evangelical Movement in the Universities and Colleges*, IVP, 1979, p. 272.

was to speak of the Englishman's more than 'forty unselfish years' devoted to the growth and maturity of Inter-Varsity.[1] It was also to be of major significance in the growth of IFES that both these men regarded ML-J as the natural leader and backed him as Chairman of the Executive Committee through the formative years which followed 1947. Woods writes:

During the first ten years of the International Fellowship of Evangelical Students, Dr Martyn Lloyd-Jones put his stamp upon the movement. He gave us backbone, conviction, a refusal to compromise, a willingness to stand alone against the World Council of Churches and the World Student Christian Federation if necessary.

It is hard to tell how far ML-J himself sensed the future importance of the IFES at this time of its formal commencement at Boston. With two more Sundays at Park Street Church,[2] and a first visit to Winona Lake Bible Conference, Indiana, in between, he can scarcely have had time to reflect. Writing to his mother from Winona Lake on August 27, 1947 he says:

I have certainly never worked so hard in my life and the heat has been terrific. But I am glad to say that I feel very well in spite of it all.

So much has happened since I last wrote that it is impossible to know where to begin . . . The two Sundays so far at Boston have been most happy and we have had what they describe as exceptionally large congregations. The students' conference[3] went well. It was very strenuous as I had to be chairman of practically every meeting. We started at 9.0 a.m. each day and went on until about 9.30 at night. So far what I have enjoyed most has been our trip to Plymouth to see where the Pilgrim Fathers landed. I thought it was most moving. We went also to see the place near Concord where the American War of Independence began.

---

[1] *Op. cit.*, p. 137.
[2] His evening sermons from Park Street were broadcast and this led to his receiving a number of letters. One who wrote was a member of a group, 'generally disinterested in sermons', who had listened and wished 'to hear more of this high type of discourse'. Another letter of gratitude was from a member of Les Missionnaires Oblats De Marie Immaculee. A newspaper reporting these Boston services said, 'The crowds taxed the capacity of one of the largest churches in that city, and it was necessary to arrange for over-flow meetings'.
[3] The remainder of the party from Britain would have smiled at this description of the Harvard meetings!

I travelled out here alone on Monday, leaving Boston at 7.50 p.m., and reached here yesterday afternoon at 5.0 p.m. I have already spoken twice . . . I hope to return to Boston on Friday and arrive there Saturday.

But his work was still not concluded. Leaving Boston on Monday, September 1, there was a break in New York for a few days and he found the city 'as fascinating as ever'. Here they met Mary-Carson Kuschke again and also the Rev. and Mrs Cynolwyn Pugh. Then, leaving Bethan and Ann in New York, he took the long train journey to Ottawa for his final Sunday and other meetings (arranged by Judge John Reid). An over-night train finally brought him back to New York, where they all embarked on the 'Mauretania' for England on September 12.

*　　　　*　　　　*

For many years after 1947 the international student work was to be an important part of Lloyd-Jones' wider ministry. It was this ministry which took him to the Continent in 1948, for the first European Conference of the IFES was to meet at Vennes, Lausanne, Switzerland, from August 7–15. Leaving Elizabeth and Ann with friends in East Anglia, he crossed the English Channel with Bethan on July 26, landed at the Hook of Holland and took the train to Amsterdam. There they were warmly met by friends whom they had come to know in London. For the next two days Bethan enjoyed a holiday with their hosts while ML-J was largely occupied with attendance at a Calvinistic Congress. It was only a few weeks later that representatives of a hundred churches were to assemble in the same city for the historic formation of the World Council of Churches over which he had serious misgivings. He was not without misgivings, however, about the Calvinistic Congress. After hearing the first lecture in the church where they were meeting, he was about to leave for the scheduled coffee break when he was informed that there was no need to do so. Coffee was to be brought in, said his neighbour, lighting a cigar as he spoke. Others took out pipes and soon the place was as smoky as a saloon. ML-J was disturbed by the feeling that truth was being handled with a detachment which is foreign to the spirit of the New Testament. The whole Congress alerted him to a danger which he had not previously met, 'It was a warning to me of an intellectual Calvinism'.

[155]

The Congress having finished by the Thursday morning, there followed a full day of sight-seeing with the help of a stranger who had greeted ML-J in the street. The man – a lawyer at The Hague – turned out to be someone who had frequently been at Westminster Chapel. The kindness of Dutch hospitality and the attractiveness of Amsterdam ('a beautiful old town built on a series of semi circular canals') made the Netherlands memorable for them.

Friday, July 30, 1948 was spent in the train for Paris. They were full of interest at the changing scenery but Mrs Lloyd-Jones believed that she had never been so dirty or so hot! The French capital, where they stayed with friends at 80 Avenue Mozart until the following Tuesday, soon made up for the journey: 'I think,' said Bethan, 'it is the loveliest city I have ever seen'. Saturday was spent at Versailles ('like Hampton Court only more so and more of it') and Sunday morning found them as worshippers in the Church of Scotland congregation. That afternoon Mrs Lloyd-Jones wrote to Elizabeth and Ann:

Sunday afternoon in Paris and so hot that Dada has given in and gone to sleep and I am gaining some comfort from writing this on a marble table. It is so hot that all windows are shut and curtains drawn in order to keep out the heat until sundown. We went this morning to a Scottish Presbyterian Church but were not well rewarded in the visiting minister. I don't know how Dada endured it . . . I don't know what we are to do this evening as there are no English services in the evening seemingly.

At 7.45 a.m. on Tuesday, August 3 they left Paris for Lausanne where they arrived at 8 o'clock in the evening with Bethan still recovering from the new experience of hurtling down the Swiss side of the Alps pulled by an electric train after that had changed from a steam one at the Vallorbe tunnel. They were guests of René Pache, Principal of the Emmaus Bible School, and as the Conference did not begin until the Saturday there were days free for sight-seeing. Wednesday found them in Geneva, in the company of Stacey Woods and John Bolten (appointed treasurer of IFES at Boston the previous year). Mrs Lloyd-Jones reported to her daughters:

We saw Calvin's house and the cathedral where he preached for about 28 years. They show the chair where he sat to speak. Then we went to see the [Reformers'] Memorial and had a cup of coffee in a cafe near by in the open air – under a great orange umbrella, the sparrows hopping hopefully all around, cheekier even than the London ones. Then we went for a look at the town – the lovely wide streets of the modern part – and the indescribably coloured Rhone rushing out of the lake . . . Now it began to pour, so we sheltered from the worst of it and then went shop crawling – a fascinating pastime here. I wish I could bring home even 1% of the lovely things. I am trying to persuade Dada to buy a suit – hitherto unsuccessfully!

The next day, sight-seeing took them to the ancient Chateau de Chillon at the entrance of the Rhone valley – making the journey there by train and returning by boat on Lake Geneva. At the castle Bethan survived a climb of 120 steps into the tower only to suffer a fall on mud in the dungeons which ruined a valued pair of nylon stockings!

For the Conference which began on the Saturday students had come from more than eight different countries and two Oxford students had even bicycled from England. Most of the IFES leaders were also present. Other speakers included Harold J. Ockenga of Boston (who arrived on the following Monday after preaching at Westminster Chapel) and Professor Kis from Budapest. Writing to the girls at home, on Monday, August 9, Mrs L-J reported:

The Conference is now in full swing. There are 300–400 students here, over 40 Germans. The meetings have to be in three languages. Yesterday morning Dada was preaching – sentence by sentence – while he was being translated into French and German simultaneously – the French in the hall where we were and the German through a microphone into the adjoining hall. The countries take it in turn to be in the outer hall – we, the English-speaking, were there last night. The French students in one hut said that they were able to follow Dada very well like that because he had a logical mind. But I don't like the method. Pache does the interpreting really well, even unconsciously imitates Dada's tones and gestures . . .
Douglas J. and Stacey W. are here, there, and everywhere. Stacey as Chaplinesque as ever.

The large numbers present at this Conference at a time of widespread financial shortage in Europe was in part related to there being no fixed charge. All that was required of participants, as indicated in the printed programme, was 'a Bible, note-book, sleeping bag or sheet and blankets'. It was another instance where ML-J's dietary rules were inappropriate and the family correspondent reported: 'We eat the oddest messes imaginable here, but I must say I enjoy it all. Any complaints from Dada about food from here on and I shall remind him of what he ate in camp!' Mrs Lloyd-Jones' letters continue:

Tuesday, August 10

I thought Dada's meeting last night was very good, 'Why I believe the Cross is the only way of salvation'. He piled up Scripture evidence with a great and convincing body of truth. Bolten told him that two Germans were converted in that meeting. There is no one more appreciative of Dada's ministry than Mr Bolten.

Raymond Johnston, one of the English students present, treasured his notes of that address more than thirty years later. From the conclusion of the preacher's address on the cross he wrote down:

The great problem is the holy nature of God; sin must be punished with death. Reverently we ask, how can God pardon man? Christ crucified is the answer. It is primarily a transaction between God the Father and God the Son – *God* has acted . . . Only at the cross can I see the enormity of sin, revolt against God. It shows me how helpless I am, the cross shows the futility of all human effort . . . The answer to the power of sin is also through the cross. By seeing the cross in the Holy Scriptures, through the Holy Spirit, I come to hate sin, to understand the nature of sin. And I come to realise that I am not my own and that I have no right to myself.

After preaching of this kind it is not surprising that the question of assurance of salvation arose in the Conference and that much time was given to discussing it.

It is impossible to avoid the impression that this first European Conference of the IFES gave an impulse to minds and hearts which was to bear fruit in churches and mission fields across the world. But even after the summer of 1948 no one yet imagined the extent to which the international influence of ML-J's ministry would grow. The students who met under the preaching of the cross at Vennes were the forerunners of a multitude still in the future.

We seem to be opposing everything and thus we receive criticisms from all sides . . . For myself as long as I am charged by certain people with being nothing but a Pentecostalist and on the other hand with being an intellectual, a man who is always preaching doctrine, as long as the two criticisms come I am very happy, but if one or the other should ever cease, then is the time to be careful and to begin to examine the very foundations. The position of the Scripture as I am trying to show you is one which is facing two extremes. The Spirit is essential, experience is vital, truth and definition and doctrine and dogma are equally vital and essential, and our whole position is one which proclaims this, that experience which is not based solidly upon truth and doctrine is dangerous.

ML-J
preaching from 1 John on June 12, 1949

It has ever been my view, on my understanding of the New Testament, that the work of evangelism is to be done regularly by the local church and not by sporadic efforts and campaigns. More and more as modern influences tend to disintegrate and disrupt the recognised and divinely ordered units in life, such as the family and the home, shall we need to stress the unique value and importance of the church and church life as the vital unit in the spiritual realm. The glory of life in the church is that it is corporate without violating individual personality as is done by crowds and mass meetings and movements.

As we face the future we are more determined than ever 'not to know any thing save Jesus Christ, and him crucified', and, eschewing all worldly and carnal methods and devices, to rely upon the power of the Holy Spirit.

ML-J
in his annual letter to the members of Westminster Chapel,
Jan 1, 1947

9

The Rebuilding of a Congregation

It might seem obvious that Dr Lloyd-Jones, once called to London, would remain there for the rest of his pastoral ministry. At the end of World War II he had seen Westminster Chapel through seven of its most difficult years and was now aged forty-five. But it was far from obvious to the preacher himself that his work there was to continue and in later life he was to say that had he been offered the Superintendency of the Forward Movement of the Welsh Presbyterian Church in 1947 (as many anticipated he would be) he believed he would have taken it. The truth is that he was not consciously settled in a life work at Westminster Chapel in 1945. To the factors which contributed to his uncertainty we must now turn.

Though not at the top of his concerns, there was in the first place the influence of his enduring attachment to Wales. To his old friend, E. T. Rees of Aberavon, he could write in 1943, 'Your letter filled me with a great *hiraeth*[1] for those great days at Sandfields'. At other times he would speak of the cloud of homesickness which he felt on returning to Westminster after summer holidays in Wales and of how he would console the Chapel organist, Mr E. Emlyn Davies, who suffered from the same problems. 'I knew exactly what he felt,' ML-J was to say on Davies' death in 1951, 'and he was one of the few people who could sympathise with me when I felt the same.' Dr Lloyd-Jones also knew how his friends in Wales had not been entirely enthusiastic about his becoming pastor at Westminster in 1943 following the associate ministry with Morgan. As one of them had written from Ton Pentre, Glamorgan: 'I had always hoped that you would some day return to your native land and to the *Hen Gorff*[2] where your presence is very much needed.'

[1] *Hiraeth* – longing, nostalgia, grief for one's home and familiar surroundings when one is far from them.
[2] *Hen Gorff* – literally 'the old body', a colloquial and affectionate way of referring to the Calvinistic Methodist Connexion.

A broader consideration against the permanency of this settlement in London lay in his consciousness that the climate of opinion amongst the leadership of the Free Churches in England — the Churches for which J. D. Jones and others hoped he would be a powerful spokesman — was alien to him. He still spoke alongside men whose theology was far different from his own, but the difference was unmistakable and he knew that it was not going to be reduced. Nor was it merely over one or two subjects. Beginning with a different standpoint his thinking never seemed to be in agreement with his peers in their plans for the future of Nonconformity. All except ML-J, for example, believed that priority should be given to finding a new unity between Churches. But in the opinion of the minister of Westminster Chapel:

Spiritual power is not something which belongs to the world of mathematics, and so if we united all the denominations and added all the powers which each has together, even that would not create spiritual life. The burial of many bodies in the same cemetery does not lead to resurrection. Life is more important than unity.[1]

At the annual meetings of the Congregational Union in May 1944 ML-J was asked to give an address on evangelism — a practical subject upon which he could, perhaps, be expected to speak for the denomination. Instead of simply giving a plea for more evangelism, however, Dr Lloyd-Jones offered reasons for the existing ineffectiveness. As reported by *The Christian World*, he said:

The churches had lost their evangelistic power because the authority of the Bible had been undermined and because some fifty years ago Nonconformity had become too politically minded. He discussed the right and wrong motives for evangelism. The crux of the whole matter was the message to be delivered: we had stressed the social aspect for the past fifty years, and men had increasingly turned their backs on us. It was not the wooing note which was needed but the note of judgment. We must convict men of sin and make them feel that they were under the condemnation of God. There were many in the Assembly who did not agree with Dr Lloyd-Jones' diagnosis of the position and who could not accept all his theology . . .[2]

[1]'Religion Today and Tomorrow', three addresses on BBC Wales, given in 1945. See *Knowing the Times*, 1989, p. 24.
[2]*The Christian World*, May 18, 1944. It was one of the last of ML-J's public addresses which Campbell Morgan heard and, as he told the speaker at the bottom of the pulpit steps afterwards, it was 'the greatest thing you have ever done'.

A division between him and the English Free Church leadership was only a matter of time. This did not concern him nearly as much as the likelihood of disagreement with fellow evangelicals. What he had said to evangelicals on evangelism in 1943 and at other times had not been heeded and the hope of reaching an increasingly irreligious society by means of 'campaigns' remained a main feature of the evangelicalism of the post-war years. ML-J was closer to this type of evangelism which believed in sin and conversion than he was to the broader denominational type which thought more of winning people 'back to the churches'. Yet, to his regret, he found himself increasingly unable to co-operate. It was not that he did not make the attempt, as can be illustrated by his relationship with Tom B. Rees who had suddenly become the best known of non-ministerial evangelists. Rees founded a conference centre for young people at Hildenborough, Kent in 1945, and later that year began a 'This is the Victory' campaign in the Albert Hall, London. ML-J shared a meeting with him in Glasgow in November 1945, organised by the St Andrew's Halls Campaign Committee, and also took part in one of Rees' own meetings in the Albert Hall. But he came away from the Albert Hall meeting with a troubled spirit, convicted that he had accepted the invitation out of expediency and that he could not do it again. While thankful for the gospel which Rees preached, he believed that in the deliberately light-hearted atmosphere of these meetings, and in other things, the truth that methods as well as message need to be biblical was not being practised. 'Much time was spent in singing choruses,' he wrote on April 17, 1946 to Philip Hughes. 'There is a levity and carnality about such efforts which I simply cannot reconcile with the New Testament.' His basic unease with English evangelicalism was its failure to see its need for true spiritual power. As he said to Hughes in the same letter: 'The general state of the people in London and in the country is one of apathy and deadness . . . Nothing but an unusual manifestation of God's power through the Holy Spirit can possibly meet the present need. I pray daily for revival and try to exhort my people to do the same.'

It was clear to ML-J that if he remained in England he would be constantly faced with the problem of trying to help the evangelical agencies while maintaining a conscientious adherence to the distinctive principles which he believed needed to be honoured. This was the reason which had entered largely into his declining the Principalship of the London Bible College in 1942. The broader evangelical ethos which the College was intended to represent was not his own and he knew that acceptance of the post 'would only lead to trouble'.

More pressing than all these concerns was the state of Westminster Chapel itself. He had experienced one major readjustment in the unexpected situation brought about by the War and now he was faced with another. For, just as the 1939 congregation had been broken up, so the smaller congregation of about 500 in 1945 had been faced with another change by the coming of peace. The many uniformed figures in the pews were scattered by demobilisation and soon became a thing of the past. 'People began to return to London,' ML-J said of this time, 'but we lost the vast majority of our membership; the pre-war remnant that remained was middle-aged and elderly.'

Virtually a new congregation was in need of being built up. This was a problem which went much deeper than a question of numbers. Some who had joined the church in recent years were beginning to share their minister's vision for what a church should be, but this was not the case with the majority of the pre-war remnant who still looked back to the 'great years' when the building was crowded. They could see no difference between a successful preaching centre where people did not know one another and a spiritual, united fellowship. At the same time, this low view of the local church was often coupled to a strong denominational attachment, as ML-J found when he proposed the withdrawal of the congregation from the Congregational Union at a church meeting in 1947. The vocal protest from this party within the membership was one of the factors which led him not to press his initial resolution for disaffiliation from the Union.[1]

Further, as there had been no election of deacons throughout the War years, this same attitude was strongly represented in the diaconate. The men who had queried whether their Associate Minister intended to remain in 1943 were still in the key positions. Mr M. J. Micklewright, one of the first of the new deacons appointed after the War, has recorded an episode which reveals what the atmosphere in the diaconate could sometimes be like as he first knew it. At one meeting chaired by ML-J, a request was received from a

[1]Instead, at a further church meeting on October 16, 1947 it was agreed that the church would remain in the Union, but it would withdraw its delegates from the annual Assembly and implement a new policy of allocating money to be given within the denomination to individual evangelical congregations.

former member of the Chapel who had become the minister of a suburban church. This church was in need of a communion table and its minister recalled that ever since a new table had been given as a memorial to Dr Jowett at Westminster Chapel the older one had ceased to be required. He therefore approached the deacons to enquire if they had any further need of the table which had been displaced.

One of the oldest of us, who was given to rather picturesque phraseology, said, 'Why don't you give them that monstrosity that stands on the platform?'
There were a number present whose service on the Diaconate went back a long way and immediately a storm broke! One said, 'That table is a memorial to Dr Jowett'. Another indicated very pointedly that that fact was in no way of interest to him, Dr Campbell Morgan's ministry was far to be preferred to Dr Jowett's! Back and forth went such remarks until the original speaker mildly observed, 'I am not saying anything against Dr Jowett, I only mean that that table is aesthetically bad'.
All was immediately calm once more.
During the discussion Dr Lloyd-Jones had sat silent at the head of the table. He then spoke and pointed out how easily a strong or explosive expression can lead to such heated and useless exchanges.

These, then, were the reasons why, in the period immediately following the War Lloyd-Jones was not convinced that he was intended to stay at Westminster. It was a question with which he had to struggle, for, while the invitation to lead the Forward Movement never came, there were enquiries from churches in Canada, the United States and Scotland concerning his availability to receive a call. The outcome, as we know, was his persuasion that he was intended to remain in a situation which he would not have chosen for himself. When, in later years, younger ministers would hear him exhort them to see difficulties and challenges as God-given opportunities they little knew the extent to which he was speaking from experience.
I turn now to the manner in which ML-J faced the work of rebuilding. It is worth noting that he did nothing to uproot church officers who had clearly little sympathy with his ministry. He wanted to win them to the truth. His conviction was that everything depended upon God using His Word as it was preached week by

week. He was also persuaded that too often Christians had no grasp of truth as *a system* because of the type of preaching to which they had been chiefly accustomed. 'The great trouble of our time is the lack of theological preaching,' he told the students at Spurgeon's College when he spoke there in January 1948. While preaching 'should be essentially exposition', with the text and context governing the form of the sermon, 'theology will safeguard a correct exposition; it will save us from becoming fanciful'. Before concluding that address he anticipated the question likely to be put to him, 'Will people listen to this kind of preaching?'. To which he replied:

They have more or less given up listening to the other kind! The low level of the life of the church today is due to the lack of doctrinal preaching. This is a question never to be asked: we have a commission to preach; a commission to God; not the call to satisfy the popular palate. 'Preach the Word.' Our one concern should be to preach the truth.

But while the pew is not to control the pulpit, the preacher is always to consider the state and capacity of his hearers and ML-J at this period was only gradually introducing them to consecutive expository preaching. His early series were usually no more than four sermons long. Gradually the length increased. At the beginning of October 1946 he began a series of sermons on 2 Peter which continued until the end of March 1947, and on Sunday evenings, from October 27, 1946, a series of six evangelistic sermons on John 3, to be followed by another six on Isaiah 35:1–8. Many sermons at this date, however, were not in an expository series at all.

It would appear that there was a marked evidence of the Holy Spirit's work in the congregation in the second half of the year 1946. In his letter to Hughes of April 17, 1946, from which we have already quoted, ML-J could speak of 'seeing occasional conversions'. At the end of that year, however, in his annual letter to members, dated January 1, 1947, he could say: 'The steady increase in the size of the congregation both morning and evening has been noticeable . . . above all else we rejoice in the fact that God has been pleased to bless the preaching of the word to the conversion of many souls.'[1] Even so, the numbers attending in 1946 were insufficient to fill the ground

[1] From this time onwards ML-J wrote a letter to all members at the beginning of every year.

floor of the auditorium, with the two galleries above entirely empty. It seems to have been after a morning series of sermons on Philippians beginning in October 1947 (37 sermons to July 1948) that there were stronger signs of the way in which sustained expository preaching could build the congregation. At any rate in May 1948 it became necessary to re-open the lower gallery. The fact that this re-opening occurred for the evening services some weeks before the morning ones may indicate that the evangelistic preaching – now switched to the second service – was slightly ahead in drawing in visitors and outsiders.

Alongside the work of the pulpit Dr Lloyd-Jones pursued his conviction that changes were needed if the congregation was to be more than a collection of individuals. He gave new emphasis to the meetings for church members, slowly increasing their number, and whereas they had once been short, formal meetings, he introduced the practice of having a missionary speaker to give an address after matters of church business were concluded. At an informal 'At Home', preceding the first church meeting after the summer vacation, he and Mrs Lloyd-Jones sought to meet everyone personally, and on January 1 of each year he wrote a letter exclusively for members in which he spoke more personally of the work at the Chapel. In this annual letter the corporate nature of the fellowship in which they shared was often underlined.

In the establishment of a closer unity ML-J gave great importance to the Friday meeting 'For Fellowship and Discussion' of which we have already spoken. More needs to be said, however, of this meeting and of the part which it came to play in strengthening a common vision within the congregation.

Some two hundred people were attending the Friday discussion by the autumn of 1947 and, in many cases, they were to become spiritual leaders either in the congregation or in other places in the years ahead. The form of the meeting has already been described. Anyone was free to propose a question of a practical and spiritual nature. ML-J wanted questions arising out of the personal circumstances and problems which Christians encounter in their lives; the merely theoretical was not allowed. His objective was to bring people to apply the teaching of Scripture and to see that 'it is failure to understand doctrine that causes failure in practice'.[1] So, if a

---

[1] On this point see *Ephesians*, vol. 5, pp. 19–22.

question was accepted as the subject for the evening, he made no attempt to answer it himself immediately. Rather he aimed to stimulate a discussion in which the people themselves would think their way to the relevant biblical principles and to their correct application.

The kind of questions raised and discussed were as follows: How do we know the will of God? How do we distinguish between an intellectual assent to Scripture and true faith? Should a Christian covet experience or power? Has God a plan for our lives? Does physical tiredness or bodily illness excuse sin and failure? How do we deal with a person who has suffered a calamity in their life? What is the least knowledge we can expect in a new convert?

The discussion might often begin with ML-J asking for Scripture references appropriate to the question. If a speaker thought that one or two texts proved that the right answer to the question was perfectly simple he might well suffer an interrogation from ML-J which would leave him convicted that his solution was premature. The strength of this interrogation might depend upon ML-J's assessment of the self-confidence of the person concerned, his intention being to deepen the level of consideration and to bring other speakers to their feet. A new and nervous contributor would never get the rough treatment which tended to be reserved for some of the young men in whom the chairman had a special interest. John Waite (a future College Principal) recalls how he and Fred Catherwood (a future son-in-law of ML-J and a future Member of the European Parliament) were 'often shot down in flames'! Sometimes a critical cross-questioning was only to test the strength of a speaker's convictions (with whom ML-J actually agreed); or he would temporarily allow speakers to pursue a wrong track so that ultimately the whole gathering could understand more clearly the reason why it was wrong. Frequently the main question could not be answered until other preliminary questions were also dealt with and so one theme might extend over several weeks. Even so, there were conclusions (towards which ML-J had been judiciously steering and directing the discussion) reached every week. It was in the latter part of the evening that he usually said more and at times became involved in a more protracted debate with one or two individuals who were not willing to be carried to the conclusion to which they suspected they were being led. The cut and thrust of such exchanges with the chairman was often the highlight of the meetings and although occasionally humorous the atmosphere was far from being one of entertainment. His final summing up was generally impressive and heart-searching and the intense attention given to it was akin to the spirit in the Chapel at the conclusion of a Sunday service.

Some examples will make the nature of this meeting clearer. On Friday, October 10, 1947, a lady raised the question why she should be so unsuccessful in personal evangelism and spoke of her failure to help her brother to whom she had explained the way of salvation by letters on many occasions. This raised so much initial comment that time had gone before the discussion could begin to take shape. As a concluding lesson ML-J urged the necessity of thinking in an orderly manner in dealing with any problem. The proper starting point on this subject, he said, was not the person to whom witness was being given but the person seeking to witness. On the next Friday, therefore, discussion began at that point and centered on the question whether an individual needs special gifts in order to engage in personal evangelism or should it belong to any and every Christian? The conclusion reached was that, while some are more gifted in this work than others, yet it does belong to all. Did this mean, then, that personal evangelism is the test as to whether a person is a Christian at all? The meeting of October 24, 1947, took up this question and decided, as ML-J reported in a letter to Elizabeth (who was studying at Oxford in the years 1946–49) that 'the answer is No, not *the* test but a very important test'. The next stage, on October 31, was to discuss why Christians find personal work difficult and ML-J pressed for speakers to give reasons from their own experience. One man then said that his reticence to speak to non-Christians was because he was more conscious of his own unworthiness than he was of the worthiness of Christ. Geoff Kirkby, who wrote a summary of some of the discussions afterwards, noted the general surprise of the meeting at these words and the chairman's response which was, 'Do you mean to say that a person can be more conscious of his own unworthiness than of the worthiness of Christ *and* still be a Christian?' 'I am afraid I should have withered under that challenge,' Kirkby wrote. But the man held his ground and, as ML-J reported to Elizabeth, it led to 'a valuable and searching meeting'. ML-J's letter to his daughter continued:

Our conclusion was that such a person is a Christian although a badly taught Christian and a very defective Christian, but still a Christian. I said that there are always two things present in the Christian, (1) A sense of personal unworthiness, (2) A sense of the worthiness of Christ. Both are essential. The absence of either means that we are not Christians. But in practice it is the relative position of the two in conscious experience that determines what we do . . .

The Christian with a high consciousness of Christ's worthiness still knows his unworthiness but his usefulness is not thereby hindered.

We concluded that the glib, light-hearted type of Christian is as defective as the opposite type that always seems depressed and scarcely ventures to claim that he is a Christian at all.

On the following Fridays hindrances to personal witnessing continued to be the theme, with particular thought being given to the question whether such witnessing was something which one should 'force' oneself to do. This led to a discussion on motivation in which ML-J introduced the subject of self-examination as he 'interrogated' a speaker:

ML-J   In other words, you agree that you would favour the idea of self-examination in this matter?
Speaker   Well, I am not altogether in favour of introspection . . .
ML-J   Ah, wait a minute! I didn't say introspection, I said self-examination. Now are you quite clear on the difference?

As a hesitation followed this question ML-J went on to explain that introspection is a self-centred state of mind and habit, whereas self-examination is a procedure by which a person considers his life in relation to God and His Word. Specific texts were then discussed. ML-J's main point over motivation was that to force oneself to do something as a duty, without a true inner inclination, can readily lead to a deep-seated problem being left unresolved – like a defective car he once knew which would go for a time when the engine was tapped hard in a certain place while the basic trouble remained uncorrected.

This subject of self-examination was so new to many present that it was continued for three weeks. Some had long held the view that it was a bad and unhealthy thing to ask oneself such questions as, 'Do I really believe on the Son of God?' 'Was the subject related to 2 Peter

1:10, "Give diligence to make your calling and election sure"?' one person asked. On the latter question ML-J could get no one to offer a comment so he queried, 'Can I say this, that there is *some* little contribution that I can make to my own salvation?'. 'Not too certain a response,' Kirkby noted, 'but the Doctor seemed to gain the general impression that his statement was not altogether approved. He thereupon made it perfectly clear that if we are of the opinion that we can do even a *little* bit towards our own salvation then we are undermining the whole foundation of the gospel message. Salvation is of grace and by faith . . .'.

Only on December 12, 1947 did the discussion come round to the question, put by ML-J, 'In preparing to speak to someone what are you trying to do?' Was there a general method to be recommended? Response was slow in coming. 'You would try to make them conscious of sin,' suggested one speaker. 'But how?' he was asked, 'Would you begin the conversation by asking a person "What is your view of sin?"' 'No, lead up to it by speaking of the general state of the world today,' someone else proposed.

Others began to draw on what they supposed were the lessons of their own experience. One said that at a gospel meeting he had received Christ 'as a friend' and that only later did he become aware of his sin and 'accept Christ as his Saviour'. A lady agreed: 'I believed in Christ and His good news and it was only afterwards that I accepted Him as my Saviour.' When asked what she regarded as 'the good news' she promptly replied, 'The Second Coming and the knowledge that He will put the world right'.

ML-J allowed all this to proceed before bringing the subject round to the true nature of conversion and of how it differed from experiences which were only psychological. It can be seen from the above paragraph that people in all sorts of differing stages of understanding were attending the meeting.

The thing that especially impressed Geoff Kirkby about the discussions was the logical character of ML-J's mind and how he brought others to see that the scriptural teaching is itself logical. 'It is very noticeable,' Kirkby observed after one Friday evening, 'how the Doctor will not be sidetracked. Someone might go to considerable pains to express a certain idea and the Doctor would dismiss it with a brief recognition, where necessary endorsing the truth of the statement but still waiting for another thought on the lines on which he was thinking, in logical sequence.'

For several weeks in the early months of 1948 the discussions ranged over many aspects of the question, 'To what extent can a person be carnal and still be a Christian?' (cf Rom 8:6 and 1 Cor 3:1). This prompted many subsidiary questions such as, 'How is carnality to be assessed?' and, 'What is the difference between the false asceticism condemned in 1 Timothy 4 and Colossians 2 and true Christian discipline?'. On the latter point the conclusion was that false asceticism regards the body as evil, whereas the Christian believes in using it rightly.[1] This led to three weeks on the subject of the Christian and recreation, the length of the discussions being a direct result of the strict code of behaviour of a 'pietistic' kind which was then common in evangelicalism. For example, there was the idea that, with the exception of business, 'we should not give our minds to anything except what is distinctly and specifically Christian'. 'The fallacy there,' as ML-J wrote to Elizabeth afterwards, 'is that all things are from God and glorify Him. That is how I would justify your studying English, etc.' In a further letter to his daughter of March 2, 1948, he said:

The Friday night meetings these days are difficult to report though of an excellent quality. The main point last time was to try to decide when we cross the line between the legitimate use of things that are not directly and immediately spiritual and their abuse. In the conversation I asked the question, 'Is it right for a Christian to become enthusiastic about these things?'. This led to a fine discussion. My own reply on the whole was that the Christian should enjoy these things but that there should always be an element of detachment in his enjoyment. He must not be taken up by them and moved to such an extent that they control him instead of his controlling them. He must certainly never become excited about them.

Two weeks later the subject was 'the problem of conduct' – a problem, in ML-J's view, because evangelicalism tended to give young Christians a list of taboos and a ready-made position which they were expected to accept. His criticism of this, as summarised by another note-taker was as follows:

While younger Christians should follow the example of older Christians (1 Cor 11:1) they must be taught to examine things *for themselves* and to

[1]See *Ephesians*, vol. 5, p. 132.

'prove all things'. If this is not done, when a practice is assailed, it will collapse. We must not give a ready-made Christian position. If we do, what will happen to the young Christian when he encounters something not 'on the list'? If the guidance we give becomes dictation, it is no longer guidance, and that does despite to the Holy Spirit and to the man's own personality.

Is it right to advise a young Christian against a thing though he does not see it? If he acts on your dictum it will be because you have spoken and not because of his understanding. The New Testament appeal for holiness and sanctification is always an appeal to the reason of the believing man: an appeal to work out the doctrine in terms of practical life. We must ask: Is it right for us to take the position of conscience to another? That procedure produces smug, self-satisfied Christians. It makes them think they have 'arrived' and therefore they stop thinking. It is a negative view of holiness. The thing that matters is not the figure we cut before people: but our 'pressing unto Him'. The more people live the dictated life (as also in Roman and Anglo-Catholicism) the poorer the spiritual life. When a man has to fight and think these things out for himself it makes him a strong man in Christ.[1]

On the last Friday in May, 1948 the subject was, 'What can I do to help and produce a revival?'. ML-J's conclusion was that while 'we are always to strive for purity of doctrine and life, and pray for revival, there is no technique that we can apply which will produce revival'.

Much of all this was new to most of those attending the Friday meetings. A departure from conventional evangelicalism was even more marked in the discussions which went on through the last three months of 1948 on 'What should be the Christian's attitude towards Politics and the ordering of society?'. On this subject the teaching of the Christian Brethren had become prevalent among evangelicals, namely, that the Christian is to avoid political affairs for he is a 'pilgrim and stranger' in this world. When alleged 'proof-texts' were offered for this view it was found that they only commanded an ethical and moral separation from the world and said nothing at all about Christians taking part in government. But, it was further argued, 'politics will not save a soul'. This brought on a discussion on the whole purpose of government as ordained by God, the obligation of Christians as citizens, the purpose of prayer for rulers, the relation between church and state and the headship of Christ over all things.

[1]Notes of Kenneth W. H. Howard on the meeting of March 12, 1948.

On the last point ML-J argued: 'Christ is not only head of those who recognise Him as such and submit to Him. He is Lord of all.' In the final summing up he emphasised:

The world is still God's world. He is not only interested in the saved but also in the unsaved. He has put bounds to sin and government is one of the ways in which He does it. There is common grace as well as special grace . . . We must be concerned about the world and not only about salvation . . . The difference between the Christian and the non-Christian in these things is that the Christian will never pin his faith in them as a means to bring ultimate and complete salvation to the race . . .

These Friday meetings certainly brought many in the Chapel to know one another, although the numbers who crowded the Institute Hall by the end of 1948 included Christians from other churches. Writing to Elizabeth on October 11, 1948 ML-J said, 'The Friday evening meeting was literally packed to the doors with people sitting all round the platform and many standing'. H. F. Stevenson, the Editor of *The Life of Faith*, gives the following impression of one of the meetings:

In a very full life, we have not found it possible, until recently, to attend the weekly discussion meeting which Dr D. Martyn Lloyd-Jones holds at Westminster Chapel. It was a stimulating experience to be present at this gathering, which has succeeded the famous Friday evening Bible School of Dr Campbell Morgan's days – a meeting which is surely unique, in this country, at least. It is held in the Institute Hall, which was filled to capacity – but we understand that Dr Lloyd-Jones thinks that the meeting would lose its essential, informal character if it were held in the church. It was a very representative gathering, of all ages – with a high percentage of young people; and almost as many men as women. There were several ministers present, and we recognized well-known members of various Churches, and of the Brethren. After an opening hymn, reading and prayer, Dr Lloyd-Jones, seated, briefly indicated the nature of the previous week's discussion, on the place of the feelings in the Christian life, and invited observations on the further aspect of the subject to be considered. A lively discussion was soon proceeding, guided firmly along constructive and helpful lines by the Chairman, who required scriptural support for statements made. The knowledge of the Scriptures which he revealed was truly amazing; he seemed to know not only the chapter and verse of every quotation made, but the exact context, and the precise meaning of every phrase.

We could not but compare this meeting with Dr Campbell Morgan's Bible lectures, when the church would be filled with eager Bible students, hanging upon the words of the peerless expositor; and we came away with the conviction that, as those lectures met the need of their day, so is the discussion of the more practical aspect of our Faith meeting the peculiar needs of this present day.[1]

There was one side effect to the Discussion meetings which no one anticipated. The rules for accurate thinking which were picked up by those in attendance (such as 'always interpret the uncertain in the light of the certain' and 'always argue from the general to the particular'[2]) could be beneficially applied by many in their daily employment. An example of this has been recorded by Ivor Williams who was a Special Branch officer at Scotland Yard when he first began attending the Chapel. As a result of listening to the Friday meetings and the Sunday sermons he began to find that he was beginning to apply the same kind of close, logical thinking to his police work:

On one occasion eight or so fellow colleagues of mine were involved in a serious case affecting the safety of the realm, each following a separate and distinct line of investigation which they carried through successfully. I was then given their reports and told to prepare one comprehensive report within 48 hours for submission to the Director of Public Prosecutions. Following the Doctor's line of reasoning, I dealt first with the main line of investigation and then with the complementary and supplementary lines of investigation in descending order of importance. So it was relatively easy to unravel the twists and turns in the overall investigations. Arrests followed and long prison sentences were imposed.

*　　　　*　　　　*

Dr Lloyd-Jones' letters to Elizabeth, generally written weekly during term time, do not give much news on home affairs – this was evidently left to Mrs Lloyd-Jones. Occasionally he spoke of their going out to dinner with friends in the evening or of the visits of relatives. With no car of their own, 'outings' were infrequent and, as

[1] *The Life of Faith*, March 23, 1949.
[2] See *Ephesians*, vol. 5, pp. 12–13.

a letter of June 7, 1948 reveals, he was still seeing some well-known places near London for the first time:

We have spent the day today with Dr and Mrs Wilson. They called upon us in a hired car at 10.0 a.m. We then 'did' Hampton Court until 12.40 p.m., then lunch at Staines and on to Windsor which we 'did' until 5.0 p.m. Then, after tea, we went to Stoke Poges and finally got home at 7.0 p.m. It was thoroughly enjoyable. I had no idea that Hampton Court was so interesting . . . For myself I was as impressed by Stoke Poges as by anything – I mean of course my thought of Gray and the Elegy . . .[1]

In one or two letters advice is given, firmly in one instance. His daughter had clearly written something about the view which was tending to be adopted by herself and others in the Oxford Inter-Collegiate Christian Union on attendance at their colleges' chapels. There was criticism of the chapel services, especially of the hymns sung. Her father replied:

Your attitude is not one that I can commend . . . Your duty is to show that your views and beliefs lead to a higher and finer type of Christian life and living. Then that will lead others to speak to you and to enquire as to your secret. To start a division on odd points and to raise difficulties especially in a matter like that of hymns seems to me to be the worst possible approach. It gives the impression that you are intolerant and that you regard yourselves as heresy hunters. Your duty it seems to me is to attend the services. If you find you cannot sing a hymn, just refrain from doing so . . . You must beware of falling into what appears to be the common evangelical trap and snare namely an over-punctiliousness about matters that are relatively unimportant and a tendency to neglect more vital matters such as love and charity . . .

In May 1948 Elizabeth wrote to her parents of the thought that she was being prepared for missionary work overseas and she questioned how she could be sure of the will of God. In the course of a letter of May 17, written when he was about to leave home to speak at a CIM Conference, her father replied:

I need not say that Mama and I were both much moved by your letter of last week and what you had to say in it about your thought and feelings concerning foreign mission work.

[1]It was this churchyard which had inspired Thomas Gray's famous 'Elegy Written in a Country Church-Yard'.

As far as we are concerned we are content with God's will for you whatever it may be. That is not easy, of course, but I thank God that we have had sufficient grace to commit you to His will. I have always tried to preach to myself what I have so often said to others that we are but pilgrims and strangers in this world. All we have is but given to us as guardians and custodians by God, not to keep to ourselves but to enjoy as from Him. This applies to our children and our business as parents is to prepare them for life and for God's purpose for them in life, regarding it as one of the greatest and highest privileges that they have been placed in our hands . . .

I say all this first in order that you may realise that all I am now going to say is quite disinterested and represents what I always say to people who put your question to me.

The one vital, all-important thing is to know the will of God. It is not as easy as it sometimes sounds. I was for over two years in a state of uncertainty and indecision before leaving medicine for the pulpit. But in the end it was made absolutely and perfectly clear and mainly by means of things which God *did*.

These are the rules which I would advise you to observe:

1. Never speak to anyone about it. Don't tell people what you are feeling and discuss it and ask for advice. That always leads to still more uncertainty and confusion. Make an absolute rule of this at all costs. Say nothing until you are absolutely certain, because we are all subject to self suggestion.

2. Do not even think about it and discuss the pros and cons with yourself. Once more this leads to auto suggestion and confusion.

3. In meetings, etc. do not start with the thought in your mind, 'I wonder whether this is going to throw light on my question or help in any way?'

4. In other words, you must not try to anticipate God's leading. Believing as I do that God does 'call' very definitely, and in a distinct and definite doctrine of a call, and a vocation is distinct from 'the need is the call' idea, I believe that God will always make His will and His way plain and clear. With reverence, therefore, I say leave it to God entirely as regards purpose, time and all else.

All you have to do is to tell God that you are content to do His will whatever it may be and, more, that you will rejoice to do His will. Surrender yourself, your life, your future entirely to Him and leave it at that . . . You must not go on asking God to show you His way. Leave it to Him and refuse to consider it until He makes it impossible for you not to do so.

Also remember, and especially in an atmosphere like OICCU and IVF which tends to be activist and to place such emphasis on works, that 'to be' comes before 'to do'. That is where we all fail. Our business is to make ourselves such instruments as shall be fit and meet for the Master's use. He always tells such people how and where and when He wants to use them. You prepare yourself and He will then show you what He wants you to do.

I urge you not only for your own sake but even for the work's sake to implement these principles.

The main impression given by these letters is of an unusually close spiritual relationship between father and daughter and of great singleness of mind on his part. In one sense, while there is much parental affection in evidence, he writes to her more as a Christian than as a teenage daughter and he shares with her some of his concerns about the work at the Chapel. 'The problem of Westminster as a church,' he says in one letter, 'is that people simply do not know one another and it is difficult to see how they can. It is the old question of a church or a preaching station or an evangelical centre. I feel that the only ultimate solution is to have a prayer meeting on a week night. That will test and sift people. But again one hesitates to call upon good and faithful people to travel such distances on another night and also in view of fares and the present cost of living. However, I am thinking much about it.' After briefer news of the Friday meeting, virtually every letter contained full outlines of both his Sunday sermons, repeated from memory. Here is one typical example:

On Sunday night I preached on Matthew 10:35, 36 ['For I am come to set a man at variance against his father . . . a man's foes shall be they of his own household'].

Most surprising, unexpected and at first most upsetting words our Lord ever spoke.

Spoke them in order to warn apostles who were over-sanguine and optimistic.

What He said was verified in disciples and has been in a sense ever since.

What accounts for this?

1   *Sin in those who do not believe*
Sin is not just a negation or refusal to do good. It is a positive evil and vicious spirit. Would have thought that all would rejoice when one is converted. But such is not the case. Converts are persecuted and ridiculed not only by outsiders but often by their own families. Nothing explains this but the nature of sin.

2   *The change that takes place in those who become Christian*
   (a) Must be a very powerful change to lead to such result.
   (b) A radical change involving the whole nature.
   (c) A change that differentiates us entirely from those who have not experienced it in same family.
   (d) A change that makes the gospel become the first and the controlling factor in our lives.
   (e) Makes us such that rather than deny Christ or gospel we are ready to forsake and lose all – friend, family, even life itself.

3   *The truth that leads to such a change*
   Makes us see the true character of the sinful life.
   Makes us see the terrible danger to our souls of that life in the light of God and judgment.
   Shows us the only way of deliverance in Christ.
   Shows us the new kind of life worthy of us and indeed makes it possible for us.
   Reveals 'the blessed hope' beyond this life and this world.

That ML-J took time each week to repeat to his daughter what he had preached to hundreds was a proof both of affection and of the supreme importance which the truth possessed in his daily life. It was not because they were *his* sermons that he repeated them to her. The fire in his heart for the Word of God was not kindled only on Sundays.

The closeness of his relationship to Elizabeth led him to say more personal things about himself than he would have said to others. On January 20, 1948 for instance, he wrote to her:

My report from Westminster this time is I fear not a good one. The damp muggy weather last week made me feel utterly dull and I fear that that must have revealed itself in my various activities.
   The Friday night meeting I felt was dull, largely due to me . . .

After the usual full outlines of both his Sunday sermons he added, 'I certainly had awakened a little by the evening service and it seemed to be a solemn meeting'.

In the letters of 1948 he mentions the increase in numbers and the re-opening of the gallery in May encouraged him. One of the visitors who happened to be in church on the Sunday the gallery was brought back into use was H. W. K. Mowll, the Archbishop of Sydney, who preached to the Queen in an evening service that same day in

Westminster Abbey. But, as the letters to Elizabeth show, it was not the size of the congregation which was the preacher's main concern. Speaking of the service on the evening of May 30, 1948, he wrote:

I was tired in the service and felt somewhat disappointed at the end. It should have been a better service I feel. There were well over a 100 people in the gallery . . .

What he looked for in the Sunday evening services especially is clear enough from other letters where he writes: 'It was a night of much conviction.' 'It was solemn and I think all felt a powerful service.' 'All seemed to be conscious of a spirit of deep conviction.' On yet another occasion, after giving Elizabeth an outline of an evangelistic sermon from Luke 12:13–15, he says:

Several came to see me at the end. It was certainly a night of much convicting power and I felt I was being used. But oh! how far short do we fall of Paul's description of the Christian. If only we knew more about and meditated more upon the glory that awaits us . . .

It was this consciousness of the presence of God in public worship which affected Westminster's congregation so deeply in the late 1940's, with many coming to the knowledge of Christ for the first time. Frequently in his letters to Elizabeth ML-J refers to individuals he had seen who were 'under conviction' or, he believed, 'definitely converted'. Such cases were not reported to the congregation, they were simply covered by a brief and general sentence in his annual letter. Looking back on 1948, he says in his letter to the members of January 1, 1949:

We thank God for the fact that during the year many have been brought to a saving knowledge of the Lord Jesus Christ. We do not press for decisions as we know that the Holy Spirit alone can do the work.

It has been a very great and real joy to receive many such friends into the membership of the Church, and we rejoice also at the coming into our midst of many others who by their lives and experiences have enriched our fellowship.

My own experience is that I am increasingly conscious of being surrounded and supported by a truly spiritual fellowship. I cannot thank God sufficiently for all who by their prayers and their labour of love in so many ways encourage and strengthen me in the work.

As to the future, I feel more and more that we have been called and set by God to witness together here in the heart of London, and to 'earnestly contend for the faith which was once for all delivered unto the saints'.

From words such as these it is clear that the uncertainty over remaining at Westminster was being taken from him. In a real sense he had been prevented from returning to Wales and from removing to other places which he might have chosen if left to himself. Speaking of 'a greater assurance that I am in God's hands' he referred to this point, in general terms, in a letter to Elizabeth of November 9, 1948:

Looking back, I thank Him quite as much for the things He has prevented me doing as for the positive leadings. See Acts 16:6–7 in this connection. More and more do I see that our supreme duty is to submit ourselves unreservedly unto Him. He will make His way plain and clear, and to attempt to anticipate or to be over-concerned about it all or even to think too much about it is lack of faith. How glad we should be that we are in God's hands and that He determines our ways. What foolish mistakes and blunders we would often make. How kind and good He is to restrain us and to order our circumstances as He knows best. Nothing is better or gives greater joy and happiness than to be able to say

> He knows the way He taketh
> And I will walk with Him.

If only we understood God's love to us and His concern about us!

Dr. Martin Lloyd Jones at Merthyr

"ONE OF OUTSTANDING PREACHERS OF OUR TIME"

Large congregations gathered on Wednesday last to listen to the Rev. Dr. Martin Lloyd Jones preaching at Pontmorlais C.M. Church.

It is inspiring to see in these days of dwindling interest in religion that there are ministries that attract and hold the attention of great numbers of people. Undoubtedly people came from the surrounding districts to listen to this famous preacher, but this only gives force to the contention that the Christian Gospel can command a following.

Dr. Jones has been in Merthyr many times, but his following does not diminish. It is sometimes suggested that his romantic entry into the ministry accounts for his popularity. Most people have forgotten that he left Harley-street at the height of his career to become the minister of a mission church at Aberavon, but they still come to hear his message.

Dr. Jones is something of a marvel and a mystery. His preaching cannot be termed popular in the sense that he appeals to emotion or depends on eloquence. He does not use the dramatic technique of the old preachers of Wales, yet he is surely one of the outstanding preachers of our time. There are those who would claim that he is the greatest preacher in London at present. It is not for Welsh people to claim this for one of their race, but there is no question about it that Dr. Jones is certainly amongst the front rankers.

His qualities as a preacher are conviction, forcefulness, and clear reasoning. He dissects his subject like a surgeon at work. He demands attention and creates respect for his views. No one would question that he is utterly sincere in his beliefs. Perhaps one of Dr. Martyn Lloyd Jones' secrets is that he tackles the urgent questions of our times. Materialism, self-expressionism, pseudo-science, theological liberalism all come in for ruthless treatment and uncompromising exposure. He brings everything to the bar of Christ's judgment and the Bible is always the supreme arbiter on all questions.

ALMOST LAST

Dr. Jones must almost be last of the Calvinistic preachers. Seldom do we hear in preaching the authoritative note so characteristic of the Divines of the School of Calvin. Perhaps this is the note that needs restoring. There should be a note of authority and conviction about preaching. People still listen to men with a message backed by genuine experience. Dr. Jones is a man of wide knowledge, great gifts and deep Christian experience.

It was a serious loss to Wales when England claimed him. We could ill afford to lose such an outstanding preacher, for I doubt if the English people are capable of appreciating his preaching as we do in Wales.

His visit to Merthyr brought inspiration and encouragement, and Pontmorlais are to be complimented on making his ministry available to a wide public.

—D. J. D.

Merthyr Express, *April 19, 1947.*

I0

'Last of the Calvinistic Preachers'

It was not coincidental that a new congregation was being built up at Westminster Chapel at the same time as Dr Lloyd-Jones' influence among students and graduates was at its height. In the late 1940's he seemed to be almost constantly engaged in the work of the Inter-Varsity Fellowship, chairing committees or public meetings, preaching for the various Evangelical Unions in the Universities, speaking annually at conferences of the Theological Students Fellowship or addressing meetings of graduates.

He spoke twice on 'the Authority of the Bible' at the Theological Students' Conference held at St Hugh's College, Oxford, in December 1946. The following spring he was at the annual Inter-Varsity Conference at Swanwick, Derbyshire (where several hundred assembled from all the Evangelical Unions of the various British universities). At least one conversion was known to have occurred following a long-to-be-remembered address which he gave on the atonement. Later in 1947 he shared in an evangelistic mission arranged by the London Inter-Faculty Christian Unions, usually known as LIFCU, at which it was not only students who were profoundly influenced. One of his hearers when he spoke at an evening meeting in the Great Hall of King's College on November 19, 1947 was R. V. G. Tasker, Professor of New Testament Exegesis in the University of London. Three years later, when ML-J was again at King's College for a similar meeting, Professor Tasker was no longer a mere hearer but a colleague in the IVF. He chaired the meeting and introduced the speaker with the words: 'I don't know who else heard Dr Lloyd-Jones speaking in this hall three years ago but I know one man whose whole life was revolutionised by that address. That man is your chairman tonight!'[1]

[1] An address given by Tasker for the IVF in Cambridge in August 1949 was published by them in 1950, *The Gospel in the Epistle to the Hebrews.* His most influential literary work was to be in editing and contributing to the Tyndale New Testament Commentaries.

In December 1947 ML-J was again at the TSF Conference speaking on 'The Application of Medical Principles to the Study of Theology'; in January 1948 he took an OICCU preterminal conference and in February addressed a LIFCU meeting held at the London Bible College on 'The Christian and the World'. There were also meetings at individual colleges as, for instance, his address on 'Theology and Preaching', already mentioned, at Spurgeon's College in January 1948.

For particularly sensitive issues ML-J was usually sought out by the Graduates Fellowship of the IVF. At their London Reunion on October 4, 1947 he was given the subject, 'The Position of Evangelicals in their Churches', and asked to make reference to the whole question of secession. At the conclusion of this address and the discussion which followed, he listed these questions:

Those who are contemplating withdrawal or secession should ask themselves continually:

1 Am I absolutely certain that Christ's honour is really involved, or that my basic Christian liberties are threatened?
2 Am I going out because it is easier, and am I following the line of least resistance?
3 Am I going out because I am impatient?
4 Am I going out because I am an egotist and cannot endure being a 'Brother of the common lot' with its disadvantages as well as its spiritual advantages?

Those who are staying in their Church should ask themselves:

1 Am I staying in and not joining others who may be fighting the Lord's battle because I am a coward?
2 Am I staying in because I am trying to persuade myself that I am a man of peace and because peace seems to be worth any price?
3 Am I staying in because I am just a vacillator or at a very low spiritual ebb?
4 Am I swayed by some self-interest or any monetary considerations?

We must all pray without ceasing both for those who trouble us and for our *own spiritual betterment*. We must seek in prayer and with patience that we may by all means save some. We must flee 'the leaven of the Pharisees and Sadducees'. We must shun all merely party spirit. 'The servant of the Lord must not strive; but be gentle unto all men, apt to teach, patient, in meekness instructing those that oppose themselves; if God peradventure will give them repentance to the acknowledging of the truth' (2 Tim. 2:24, 25).

The next year, at a Conference of the Science Section of the Graduates Fellowship held at the London Bible College in September, ML-J was asked to speak on 'The Christian View of God and of the World'.

The medical section of the Graduates Fellowship was also developing rapidly at this time under the inspiration of Dr Douglas Johnson, with ML-J's support. The latter chaired a discussion of the medicals in November 1948 when the subject was 'Christ and the Unconscious Mind'.[1] The next year the Christian Medical Fellowship was formed as a separate organization, several hundred strong, within the IVF. One of the first of many addresses by Dr Lloyd-Jones under the auspices of the CMF was on 'Healing: Miraculous and Psychotherapeutic'.[2] In order that difficult clinical, scientific and ethical problems might be considered in depth a 'Sub-Committee for the Exploration of Medical Problems', soon nicknamed SCEMP, was formed. It included some of the ablest consultants and general physicians in London in its membership. This committee, writes Johnson, later to be called the 'Medical Study Group', needed 'an able chairman with the necessary insight to give direction to the "team" and to get the best out of its members', and it was with 'great delight' that Dr Lloyd-Jones was secured for this role. The way in which he was to lead this group of full-time medicals was certainly a proof of the manner in which he had kept up with contemporary medicine. Dr Johnson writes:

When it is realized how many notes, memoranda and suggestions were passed on from the Study Group to the committees, speakers and individual authors, the importance to the Fellowship of the work of 'Scemp' becomes obvious. From 1953 Dr Lloyd-Jones nobly devoted a Monday evening bimonthly to lead the group. He continued to do so for 15 years.

The difference Dr Lloyd-Jones' presence made to the Group can scarcely be exaggerated. It was not only the constant challenge of his enquiring mind throughout every meeting which inspired the members, but his corrections and brief crystal-clear summings up at the end of each evening's business stimulated the members to bring increasingly accurate work to the next meeting! Nothing ill-thought, inadequately

[1] the *Christian Graduate*, Sept. 1949, pp. 81–84.
[2] *Ibid*, March 1951, pp. 22–24. This is sub-headed, 'Notes taken at a discussion conducted by Dr Martyn Lloyd-Jones', but the material is clearly the chairman's concluding address or summary.

documented or otherwise 'loose' was allowed to pass. Even constantly repeated statements copied from medical text-book to text-book would be challenged by the Chairman's comment – 'I wonder what the real evidence is for that!'

There could not have been a better mentor and a more practical example of all that CMF stands for. He greatly strengthened the pursuit of the Fellowship's aims, especially that each member should seek to attain to the highest standards in the Christian faith as recorded in Holy Scripture and also in scientific Medicine as practised by the leading members of the profession.[1]

As a result of the research done by this study group a number of papers were circulated within the CMF and a small but valuable publishing programme was initiated.

All the Colleges making up the University of London had Christian Unions in which Dr Lloyd-Jones' name became well known to successive generations of students. This was especially the case in the great teaching hospitals where medical students and nurses were often prompted by their seniors to visit Westminster Chapel. One Welsh student from Lampeter had already started attending Westminster Chapel when a chief, Sir James Paterson Ross, Professor of Surgery at Barts (and later President of the Royal College of Surgeons) asked him, 'What do you do on Sundays?'. On hearing that he was sitting under the ministry of Dr Lloyd-Jones, Ross expressed his approval and added: 'You know, I knew him very well indeed. I have always said that he was one of the finest clinicians I have ever encountered.'[2]

But if LIFCU students led the attendance at Westminster Chapel in terms of numbers, there was also at this period a very significant link with Oxford. A small group of Oxford students was among the first of a younger generation of men in England who were to understand the theological reasons why ML-J's preaching was not in the mainstream of contemporary evangelicalism. One of the leaders among this group was Raymond Johnston of Queen's College who returned to Oxford from the Swanwick Conference of 1947

[1] *The Christian Medical Fellowship – Its Background and History*, Douglas Johnson, 1987, p. 36.
[2] Another eminent surgeon, Sir Clement Price Thomas, who was active in the CMF, was once heard to say, 'I believe, or I'd like to believe, all that Martyn Lloyd-Jones says, only I cannot say it like him'. CMF *Quarterly Newsletter*, April 1973, p. 4.

enthusing about the addresses he had heard by ML-J. The next year Johnston and another student, Bernard Gee, were to cycle across France to be present at the IFES Conference at Lausanne, reported earlier.

James I. Packer was a friend of Johnston's who had become a Christian soon after he had won a place at Corpus Christi in 1944. He first heard ML-J speak at the TSF Conference at St Hugh's College, Oxford, in December 1946. Of that first meeting Dr Packer has written:

He struck me as grim and austere, but vastly impressive, with his magisterial mind and intense seriousness. I intercepted him, I remember, and asked him a question – I can't recall it for sure, though I know I thought it rather intelligent, but he was very short with me. His answer – worth noting, it was so typical, even if the question is gone beyond recall was this: 'Yes, that's to keep us humble.'

When Packer next heard ML-J, at a subsequent Conference at Lady Margaret Hall, Oxford, the subject was quite different and the different approach took him by surprise:

He gave a lecture, 'Psychology and Pastoral Work', which went on for 80 minutes and was full of funny stories – I never heard him raise more laughs. He wasn't being frivolous: the stories were the most effective way of making his points about the absurdity of pastors treating post-Freudian psychology as a kind of sacred cow.

In what order these Oxford students began to read the Puritans cannot now be precisely determined. In Jim Packer's case his interest was awakened through the pages of an old set of John Owen which had been donated to the OICCU Library. Elizabeth Lloyd-Jones, as already mentioned, was at Oxford at this period and ML-J recalls the day when she introduced Bernard Gee to him when he called and stayed for tea at their home in Ealing. As they sat down to tea, ML-J says:

I put him to sit at the table facing my bookcase – bottom row, John Owen, next row, Richard Baxter, and so on. I could see him looking at all this. In the end I said, 'Are you interested in these books?' He replied, 'What are they?'. I said, 'They are Puritan authors'. 'What are they? I have never heard of them.' So I talked to him for quite a long time and opened the books and told him quite a lot about them.

Before the end of 1947, Packer has written, Elizabeth, he and others 'belonged to a group who used to eat cheap food together in British Restaurants[1] and talked about revival; also about Calvin, Owen, the Welsh evangelical heritage and the Puritans'. Raymond Johnston seems to have been the first to put pen to paper and to give notice that a new note was soon to be heard in evangelical literature. The IVF magazine for the summer term, 1948 carried an article by him entitled 'John Owen: A Puritan Vice-Chancellor'.

Both Johnston and Packer exchanged Oxford for London in 1948 and became regular attenders at Westminster Chapel. Some of Johnston's notes of the Friday Discussion meetings still survive. Packer, tutoring at Oak Hill College, could only be present on Sunday evenings, about which he writes:

I was able to hear Dr Lloyd-Jones preach his way through Matthew 11. I had never heard such preaching and was electrified. I can remember at least the thrust of most of the messages still . . . All that I know about preaching I can honestly say – indeed, have often said – I learned from the Doctor by example that winter.[2]

Johnston and Packer were able to remain in London for only a year. The turnover of the student attendance at Westminster, as their courses were completed and they moved elsewhere, was inevitable. While it led to a scattering of influence, it also affected the problem of building up a church where people knew one another, for the numbers of students, nurses and other young people only temporarily in London could well have constituted a third of the entire congregation.

* * *

At the same time as ML-J was being given added influence in some circles he was losing it in others. There were those who had now heard him enough to dislike what he was saying. The growing

[1]Institutions inaugurated during the war to supply plain food. Food rationing continued in the immediate post-war years.
[2]Letter to the author, May 21, 1981.

distance between him and the Free Church leadership is observable in the columns of the *British Weekly*. After the end of John Hutton's editorship in 1946, news of the minister and ministry of Westminster Chapel gradually disappeared as the paper pursued a policy manifesting very different sympathies. In 1949 a series of articles on 'Giants of the Pulpit' included such liberals as Weatherhead and R. J. Campbell. It passed over ML-J in silence. The Correspondence columns also abounded in praise of Weatherhead and other liberals: 'In London, the most outstanding preacher is Leslie Weatherhead. He relates religion to life.' 'In London,' writes another, 'there is that brilliant triumvirate, Dr Sangster, Dr Soper and Dr Weatherhead.' A Scot reported: 'I had the good fortune last Whit Sunday to hear for the first time Dr Leslie Weatherhead preach at Marylebone . . . He took for his subject, "The witness of the Spirits [*sic*] with our Spirit", and in place of his second reading he substituted a short poem, "Some call it Evolution and others call it God", thereby illuminating the address that was to follow.'

Within the evangelical organizations and societies ML-J's influence seems to have been at its height at this period. The Children's Special Service Mission (Scripture Union), the most successful work among teenagers, republished his *Presentation of the Gospel* in 1948.[1] One effect of his influence was the maintenance of a resolve within the IVF and those agencies closest to it to see that a full commitment to the infallibility of Scripture was preserved by those who belonged. The IVF took the lead here and in so doing lost some of its ablest men who had slowly become sympathetic to a broader doctrinal position. Donald Coggan, Principal of the London College of Divinity, ceased to work with the IVF after 1946, not by his own decision but because he was not permitted to do so without signing a basis of faith which was narrower than his broadening views. 'He pointed out,' writes his biographer, 'that he had already, as part of his ordination vows, given his assent to Article 6 of the Thirty-nine Articles, would that not suffice? The IVF decided not; he and they parted company.'[2] Another significant loss was to occur in Scotland. In November 1948 ML-J was to lead a Mission to the University of Edinburgh with Alec Vidler. This was not simply an IVF mission, but when ML-J was unable to fulfil this commitment,

[1]'Some Dangers of Evangelism', *The Senior Teacher's Magazine*, April-July, 1948.
[2]*Donald Coggan, Servant of Christ*, Margaret Pawley, 1987, p. 87.

on account of a bad cold, another IVF speaker and author, Thomas F. Torrance, took his place. The organizing secretary for this mission was also an IVF man by the name of James Barr. Torrance, however, as was soon to be clear, was no longer in sympathy with the IVF position on Scripture. *The Scottish Journal of Theology*, which he launched that same year with J. K. S. Reid, was announced as a journal in which 'no theological position is represented exclusively'. Under Torrance's influence others in Scotland were to secede from the IVF, most notably in the Edinburgh Evangelical Christian Union.

The issue of 'narrow' versus 'broader' views of Christian doctrine was also present at this date in the work of the Evangelical Alliance and, once more, ML-J was closely involved. While preserving its original evangelical title, the Alliance (which was in its 101st year in 1948) had ceased to apply any doctrinal tests to those who spoke on its platform. The result seemed to be successful for it continued to have the general support of almost all Protestant churches. A dramatic example of the mixed character of the Alliance occurred when its 'universal week of prayer' was held, as usual, in January 1948. This was to begin, in London, with a public meeting at Westminster Chapel, chaired by Dr W. R. Matthews, the Dean of St Paul's, when 'the chief speaker' would be Sir Stafford Cripps, the Chancellor of the Exchequer. Another speaker announced to take part was Dr Lloyd-Jones.

The country at this date was still in the midst of post-war uncertainties and hardships and an address related to prayer from a leading politician was no doubt an attraction to many who gathered for the Westminster Chapel meeting on Monday, January 8. Dean Matthews spoke first, voicing the opinion that amidst much anxiety about the present condition of world affairs the church's need was to know the will of God for the hour which was, he believed, 'that Christians should be more united than they have been in the past; that they should work together and pray together'. Cripps then followed, speaking on Christian morality and on its preservation in society through prayer. On account of shortage of time, a Church of Scotland representative 'read prayers' but left out his address. It was then Dr Lloyd-Jones' duty to bring the proceedings to a suitable conclusion. From the record of his address which survives it is not possible to believe that he did what was intended. He introduced an entirely new note by asking what was the church's true calling. It was not, he said, to render assistance to the world in its problems but to

be 'the mouthpiece of God'. In the present conditions the church had
first of all to repent: 'She must acknowledge her departure from the
truth. She must acknowledge that, to a large extent, she has become
apostate; she must confess and admit it. Then the church must return
to the true doctrines that have always been preached by the church
when she has counted as a power in this land, to the doctrine which
emphasizes the fact that man is fallen. It is a sheer waste of energy to try
to induce an unregenerate man to apply the Christian ethics to his
life'.

The diary entry of one hearer, Mr Hector R. Brooke, written later
that night, gives a vivid idea of the impression made upon some who
were present:

I met 'Snippets' in the Strand at 6.20 to go to the Evangelical Alliance
meeting at Westminster Chapel. Chairman, Dean of St Pauls. Speakers,
Sir Stafford Cripps, Chancellor of the Exchequer and the Minister of the
Chapel, Dr Martyn Lloyd Jones. A call for spiritual action to combat
growing materialism. I expected a large crowd but not the teeming mass
we were confronted with at the chapel. We had tickets, but we had to
elbow our way to the first balcony and before the meeting started the place
was crammed, people standing everywhere. My fear was that Cripps
would not appear, but precisely at 7 the speakers entered. The Dean gave a
few introductory remarks, dealing with unity and referring to the packed
crowd as evidence of it. He introduced Cripps, a shorter man than I had
envisaged. Much to my disappointment he kept resolutely to his written
statement. He maintained that wars brutalised a people and lowered their
standard of conduct. Christianity was failing because Christians were not
applying faith to their human relationships. A rededication to prayer and
action would save us as a nation and save democracy. This was in fact the
theme of the address, prayer and action, one no use without the other. It
was a hard way, but Christ did not promise an easy one . . . It was very
sound in its way and coming from the man who is virtually our economic
dictator it was a thrilling experience, but I wish he had discarded his
written statement. Dr Martyn was the success. He welcomed all and then
entered the fray. Prayer was not a device to gain things for self or country,
prayer was worship, and we have largely forgotten God. Sin stood
between us and Him. Regeneration was the vital necessity. We wanted a
revival of true religion, the power of the Holy Spirit in evidence. He held
up Cromwell, the Puritans as men of God, Wesley etc. I trembled even to
look at Cripps or Matthews. He denounced those who weakened the
authority of the Bible and urged us to pray that the Spirit might be
manifested in a mighty revival.

In the published proceedings of that week of prayer nothing else was said by various churchmen which remotely resembled Monday's closing address. At a large luncheon gathering, sponsored by the Alliance on January 20, Dr Leslie Weatherhead spoke of the uselessness of 'scrapping' over 'theological points'. 'What we ought to do above everything else is to unite in action'. Mr H. Martyn Gooch, who had been the General Secretary of the Alliance for over 40 years, concluded the luncheon speeches by referring to Cripps' 'very moving address' of the previous Monday, and he believed that 'the secret of all that has been said today is to be found in that word "Evangelical"'.

We shall return later to the question of the Evangelical Alliance's role and membership. As Weatherhead's words above underline, the point which was to become the great issue in the years ahead was not so much *which* particular doctrines are necessary but whether *any* definite statements about the truth can be regarded as essential. Christianity, it was said, depends upon experience, not 'propositions', and therefore any contention for theological principles is not only uncharitable, it constitutes a failure to understand the true nature of Christianity. Using the word 'Fundamentalism' as a term to describe the viewpoint for which Dr Lloyd-Jones was the most conspicuous advocate, 'Ilico', a regular columnist in the *British Weekly*, wrote on 'Why Fundamentalism Will Not Do' (Dec 29, 1949). With obvious reference to the work of IVF he said: 'Fundamentalism, which seemed to most to be a lost cause yesterday, gathers in many today, not least amongst an educated section of the community. Not "Liberalism" but obscurantism would seem the greater danger in these days.' Fundamentalists, he believed, were basically wrong in their view of doctrine or theology. 'Theology' is but the human attempt to state the 'unchanging gospel'. God has not revealed 'theological propositions'. The reason why anyone clung to the doctrine of verbal inerrancy of Scripture was simply indefensible fear. There is no one set of statements which anyone may claim to possess as the truth: 'There have, in fact, been a good many doctrines of the Atonement as of the Person of Christ or of the Trinity, and none of them seems to us today to be fully adequate to the gospel.'

*   *   *

Given Dr Lloyd-Jones' family, his congregation, and such constant invitations from all parts of the country as are only received by very few preachers, it may seem absurd to describe him as lonely. Had he been able to multiply himself tenfold he could scarcely have fulfilled the hopes of the multitude of correspondents who sought his help on behalf of their churches or organizations. Yet loneliness was to be the accompaniment of his ministry. Not in any physical sense, nor in any lack of company. It lay deeper, in his conscious isolation from the prevailing thought of the church at large.

When people sought to explain what set ML-J apart in terms of his convictions they usually did so in terms of 'Calvinism'. 'Dr Jones must almost be last of the Calvinistic preachers,' reported the *Merthyr Express*, after he had visited Merthyr in 1947. Kenneth Slack, one of the rising leaders in the Free Churches, was thinking of the same thing when he said of the minister of Westminster Chapel, 'His systems of thought were too rigid to enter into the thought-world of others'.[1]

The present writer was at Hildenborough Hall in the summer of 1949 as a temporary helper on the staff. One afternoon, when several of us who were members of staff were relaxing in an office, the conversation turned to the spiritual blessings of the conference centre and I remarked with enthusiasm, 'All the best preachers in the country come here'. There was silence when a young woman calmly corrected me and assured me that I was mistaken. On my query of surprise, 'Who does not come here?', I heard the name of Dr Martyn Lloyd-Jones for the first time and, to my further question, 'Why does he not come?', I was given the simple reply, 'He is a Calvinist'. The explanation was then a mystery to me and possibly to all of us in that room.

The evangelical view to which we were accustomed was certainly not 'Calvinistic'. It was commonly supposed that the biblical teaching on human accountability means that man's decision is *the* crucial factor in his salvation, that human choice makes the difference between those who become Christians and those who do not, and that election means that God foresaw those who would choose to believe. Grace cannot be effective unless man will allow it to be so. If Calvinism differed from this then it had to be some form of 'fatalism'. The prevailing ignorance over the real meaning of Calvinistic belief in England was not surprising. It was the result of long years in which pulpits had been silent on the subject and when

[1]Part of a review by Slack entitled 'Puritan "Pope"' in *Church Times*, May 30, 1986.

publishers had virtually set aside all literature in that tradition. The label 'Calvinist' (or its variant 'Reformed') had no clear meaning attached to it and yet it was used both by liberals and by evangelicals to designate ML-J and to interpret his comparative isolation.

Certain things need to be said at this point. First, ML-J seldom used the label himself, nor was he interested to see any revival of its use. Further, he was utterly opposed to making the theology which he believed to be true Calvinism a requirement for fellowship among Christians. For an 'orthodoxy' which prided itself on its exclusiveness he had not the slightest sympathy. He knew that a Christian, dependent upon the death of Christ alone for salvation and trusting the Word of God, may have a very limited understanding of how God's grace came to him: 'What an impudence it is,' he says in one place, 'for any of us to expel or withdraw from a fellow sinner saved by the same grace because we believe that his deductions about how grace works are defective as compared with our own deductions.' Accordingly, as we have seen, he was ready to give assistance to a number of agencies which did not endorse some of his most deeply held convictions. And he likewise sought to maintain friendships with Christian leaders such as Fred Mitchell whose sympathies were much closer to the Arminian side of evangelicalism.

Yet, at the same time, Dr Lloyd-Jones believed that a restoration of the standpoint which is called Calvinistic was a fundamental need. It was needed because it was biblical; because it shows how the gospel begins not with man and his happiness but with God and His glory. 'In our churches we have lost this sense of the importance of the glory of God, even in those claiming to be evangelical. But the Bible is concerned for the glory of God and then, after that, for the good of man.'[1] True Christianity may exist where this is not understood but the resulting tendency will always be to weakness both in theology and in life. Wrong belief will ultimately produce error in practice. For this reason it meant much to ML-J when in 1949 the publishers James Clarke and Co. listened to his plea for a re-issue of Calvin's *Institutes of the Christian Religion*, and used his copy of the Beveridge edition for their photoprinting. A few years earlier Dr Lloyd-Jones had summarized Calvin's belief, and his own, in these words:

[1] See also *Romans*, vol. 5, p. 178: 'Any teaching . . . which starts with us and our needs, rather than with the glory of God, is unscriptural, and seriously unscriptural. That subjective approach, it seems to me, is what has led many astray for so many years'.

Calvin's main feature is that he bases everything on the Bible . . . he does not wish for any philosophy apart from that which emanates from the Scripture. It is in the *Institutes* that one gets biblical theology for the first time, rather than dogmatic theology . . . For him the great central and all-important truth was the sovereignty of God and God's glory. We must start here and everything else issues from here. It was God, of His own free will and according to His infinite wisdom, who created the world. But sin entered and if it were not for God's grace, there would be no hope for the world.

Man is a fallen creature, with his mind in a state of enmity towards God. He is totally unable to save himself and to reunite himself with God. Everyone would be lost if God had not elected some for salvation and that unconditionally. It is only through Christ's death that it is possible for these people to be saved, and they would not see or accept that salvation if God through His irresistible grace in the Holy Spirit had not opened their eyes and persuaded them (not forced them) to accept the offer. And even after that, it is God who sustains them and keeps them from falling. Their salvation, therefore, is sure because it depends, not on them and their ability, but on God's grace. The church is a collection of the elect.[1]

This faith which put God first was, he believed, 'the iron rations of the soul' for the men and women in the sixteenth century as well as for later periods. In matters of truth and error it taught them to regard the more comfortable pathway of expediency as impossible. To be faithful, to honour God and His Word – these things for such people became more important than life itself. It was a vision which set Christians free from all enervating concerns to please men.

Despite ML-J's concern for unity with fellow evangelicals it was inevitable that he should face problems on account of this conscientious adherence to Calvinistic principles. We have already mentioned his decision against accepting the Principalship of the London Bible College and against any further participation in Tom Rees' meetings. Similarly he twice declined the invitations of the Rev. W. H. Aldis, Chairman of the Keswick Convention, to speak at Keswick. Perhaps it was a hard decision for Aldis to understand. After all, Lloyd-Jones warmly co-operated with him in the China Inland Mission and sometimes had Keswick speakers to his own pulpit at Westminster Chapel. When Fred Mitchell became Chair-

---

[1] *Knowing the Times*, p. 35. See also p. 37 where the cover blurb by ML-J for the re-issued *Institutes* is reprinted.

man of Keswick Dr Lloyd-Jones even advised him with regard to addresses which he was to deliver at the Convention but persisted in not becoming personally involved. Keswick's traditional theology assumed the possibility of a person being a Christian with an 'unsurrendered life'. By a crisis of 'surrender' and of faith the 'victorious' life for such 'defeated Christians' might begin. For Lloyd-Jones that teaching rested upon a seriously defective doctrine of regeneration. He would not be the conscience of other men, but for himself to have been identified with Keswick would have been to compromise a major biblical truth.

ML-J found no enjoyment in standing apart nor in standing up for issues when others were silent. He felt keenly the lack of like-minded men. Certainly the number of men who in any true sense could be called Calvinists at this date was exceedingly small. When Philip Hughes, after being in touch with Continental Calvinists, wrote to ML-J about the hope of starting an English committee to co-operate with the Continentals, the latter was not enthusiastic. In part this was because he was suspicious of the cold intellectualism of some of the European brethren, but it was also because, as he explained in a reply to Hughes, dependable Englishmen able to make up such a committee simply did not exist: 'As far as names of other Reformed persons, there are really none that I know of of any standing at all, except Kevan.'[1]

A testimony to ML-J's frequent sense of isolation comes from Professor Tasker who could now sympathise with that experience. Tasker confessed to a friend that since taking a stand on Scripture as the Word of God in the theological faculty of King's College 'he felt as though he had been sent to Coventry' by his colleagues.[2] As well as his role in the University of London, he was Rector of Chenies in Buckinghamshire and as this was a country parish with no evening services he began to make a habit of travelling in to Westminster Chapel. How far his understanding of the truth had changed since his life was 'revolutionised' in 1947 was demonstrated by a memorable address which he gave for the IVF in May 1951 on 'The Biblical Doctrine of the Wrath of God'. After that address ML-J, who was present, commented to the Rev. Edwin King, 'I think he is a very lonely man in need of fellowship'. A few months later King happened to meet the Professor of New Testament Exegesis on the steps of Westminster Chapel at the conclusion of an evening service

[1]Letter of Dec. 27, 1952.
[2]'Sent to Coventry' = to refuse to associate with or speak with a person.

and they entered into conversation. 'This is preaching in the grand style,' exclaimed Tasker, 'by the time we Anglicans have concluded our little homilies the Doctor is just emerging from his introduction.' As they talked further, King had opportunity to refer to Lloyd-Jones' concern over the loneliness which, he believed, Tasker was experiencing. 'I am not lonely,' the Anglican protested, and then, after a pause, he went on: 'You know I think he is speaking out of his own heart's experience. He is the lonely man!'

In spite of all this, ML-J knew great encouragements in the late 1940's and none more so than the young men in whom he saw a real hunger for serious godliness and for truth.

There were other encouragements too which were often surprising. One of these was the way in which an older generation of Methodist ministers welcomed his ministry. J. Ernest Rattenbury, the retired minister of Kingsway Hall, and author of *The Conversion of the Wesleys* (1938) would frequently come to Westminster Chapel and let it be known that 'Dr Lloyd-Jones is the only man who preaches to my conscience'. Another senior Methodist was Dr Henry Bett. When ML-J was preaching at a large, mainly Methodist, rally in Leeds at this period, Bett was sitting on the platform with him, two seats away. At the end of the service, to ML-J's surprise, the Methodist leader leant across the man sitting between them and said, 'I would like you to know that a large number of us in Methodism are thanking God that you are in London to counteract the film stars of Methodism!'[1]

Another great encouragement to Dr Lloyd-Jones at this date, partly because it was so unexpected, came from the pen of an Indian by the name of Mark Sunder-Rao, who was the Assistant Editor of *The Guardian* of Madras. In the same year that the *British Weekly* ran its series on 'Giants of the Pulpit', from which ML-J's name was conspicuously absent, this writer was temporarily employed by that same journal while on a visit to Britain. For the issue of September 15, 1949, Sunder-Rao produced an article entitled 'An Indian Hears a Great Preacher in London'. He began by saying how he had been visiting various churches in a kind of pilgrimage in order to find the kind of church which had been responsible for the gospel ever reaching his own land. At Westminster Chapel, and in the ministry of

[1]Bett was referring, of course, to the 'brilliant triumvirate' mentioned earlier in this chapter.

Dr Lloyd-Jones, he declared, he had found that real source of foreign missions.

The physical appearance of ML-J in the pulpit, this Indian journalist wrote, reminded him of what was once said of William Wilberforce, who was a man of small stature yet 'as he spoke the shrivelled shrimp swelled to the proportions of a colossus'. 'But,' he continued:

what impressed me, in the end, was not the personal aspect of the famous preacher, though that made no uncertain impact. It was that as the preacher unfolded the theme he seemed to have been possessed, or to be discreet, perhaps, motivated, by One greater than himself, in Whom he lived, moved and had his being. All great preaching becomes a sacrament, nay, a miracle, when in and through it, it holds forth the indications and intimations of the presence of God . . .

It was small wonder, then, that the chapel was filled to capacity, unlike a church I went into a few weeks before. Here one did not see a few old women and tottering men only, but a goodly fellowship of persons of all ages with a generous sprinkling (I had almost said *sparkling*!) of the youth.

And why? Here one touches the significant point. Because in this typically Nonconformist chapel one realised at once the meaning of the 16th century reformation and the 18th century revival: that where the Gospel is preached within the congregation and taken out to the uttermost parts of the world, there the Church is. Important as they are, liturgy and church order are yet secondary; the primary thing, and one which renders a community dynamic and mobile, is the Gospel: the fact of the reality of God, His concern for our lives, His Love from which nothing in this world or the next can alienate us, His sufficiency. These were the points in the sermon of Dr Martyn Lloyd-Jones.[1]

When the preacher read these words I am sure he felt afresh that any little thing which he suffered was only part of the unspeakable privilege of being a servant of Christ.

[1]In another article on November 10, 1949 Sunder-Rao deplored the effect of short-lived modern theologies upon missionary work in India: 'The missionaries sallying forth from the Continental denominational churches took with them their confessional affirmations. But in the course of time they seemed to pass through the "theological epidemics" of the succeeding decades. Once Karl Heim was the fashion, then Rudolph Otto, later either Barth or Brunner. The Indian Christian must have wondered whether the friends coming from the West had more zeal in propagating the theological vogues than in preaching the unchanging Gospel.'

Annual Business Meeting

of

The Evangelical Library

78, Chiltern Street, W.I.

will (D.V.) be held at the Library on

Tuesday November 30th

at 5.30 p.m.

(Pre view of the Library during the afternoon)

PUBLIC MEETING

at The Welsh Chapel, 82, Chiltern St. Baker Street Station

at 6.30 p.m. when

The Inauguration of the Fellowship of

THE FRIENDS of THE EVANGELICAL LIBRARY

will be followed by a LECTURE

by

The Rev. Dr. D. MARTYN LLOYD-JONES

on

ISAAC WATTS and HYMNODY IN WORSHIP

Chairman :

Rev. E. J. POOLE-CONNOR

A short survey of the progress of the Library will be given by the Joint Honorary Treasurer, S. E. DENNING, Esq., F.C.I.S., and the Founder and Librarian, MR. GEOFFREY WILLIAMS.

A leaflet advertising the Evangelical Library Lecture of 1948 and the inauguration of 'the Friends of the Library'.

Nonconformity is in a bad way. The Chapel was once the rallying point or centre of gravity of the communal life in Wales. It has ceased to be so.

There is a serious dearth of preachers in Wales. This is most in evidence in the Presbyterian section of the church. Lack of funds again hampers many Welsh churches. They cannot support ministers.

What view or theory of the Hebrew Bible do we propose to teach? If it is the literalist theory then very few in these days will accept it. Biblical criticism has come to stay and we cannot ignore it.

There is hostility to religion and to the churches. It is no use ignoring it. One of your writers expressed a view that he could see signs of a spiritual revival. I hope he is right; but here in South Wales there is hardly a sign of it.

I and many others are bewildered, are completely in the fog when we search and read so many conflicting versions, opinions, and theories upon matters pertaining to religion and theology.

GLAN CONWY

writing on 'The Churches' Outlook in South Wales', the *British Weekly*, October 6, 1949.

11

Wales and the Summer of 1949

It is not easy in these pages to convey the extent to which Dr Lloyd-Jones was a Welshman. Certainly he condemned the 'carnal nationalism' which claims one's own country to be the only nation that matters and to be superior to all others, and he regarded any idea that nationality continues in heaven as 'dangerous speculation'.[1] At the same time he was opposed to the error which suggests that because a person is a Christian he should lose his national identity, or change his temperament, or leave the culture into which he was born. 'Greek and barbarian, male and female,' do not cease to be what they are by nature when they are made one in Christ. In other words, oneness in salvation does not mean oneness in every respect, and just as it is to the glory of God that all the variations between individuals are not removed by regeneration so the differences between national groupings and national characteristics remain among believers.

The great controlling principles by which ML-J lived were not Welsh but in a thousand secondary things he was Welsh through and through and proud to be so. Welsh was the language in which he almost always spoke and wrote to Bethan. He read Welsh newspapers and listened to Welsh radio. He deplored the Welshman who deliberately tried to lose his accent, regarding it as the attitude of a serf, *cymhleth y taeog*,[2] wanting to please his English masters.

Perhaps it is in his letters to his mother, written to her in London when he is on holiday in Wales, that the depth of his interest in his native background comes out. His letters to her when he was on holiday in Newcastle Emlyn are often so full of things Welsh —

[1] 'Nationalism, Tradition and Language', a Discussion between Dr Gaius Davies and ML-J, in *The Evangelical Magazine of Wales*, Aug-Sept, 1969.
[2] Literally 'the serf complex'.

relatives, farms, agricultural shows and so on – that it scarcely seems possible that he ever lived anywhere but in a rural locality.

In accepting preaching engagements I doubt if he gave any priority to the Principality, but it is remarkable how often he was there for that purpose. In 1948, for example, apart from holidays, commitments took him to various parts of Wales in no less than seven months of the year. A number of these engagements would frequently be far away from the large centres of population to be found in the South. The spiritual state of the countryside profoundly disturbed him. While taking one weekend off from Westminster in April 1948 he could not resist offering to preach on the Sunday afternoon in the hills above Newcastle Emlyn where they were staying. 'The congregation consisted of 15 people,' he wrote to his mother, 'most of whom did not know me.' Later in 1948 he had a commitment in Newcastle Emlyn, at Bethel Calvinistic Methodist Chapel which had formerly been a strong and lively congregation. After this visit to Bethel he wrote to Elizabeth (at Oxford) on November 3:

Never have I felt so much that the people down there are in a state of almost heathen darkness. They listened well but gave the impression that what they were hearing was altogether new. I preached in Welsh on the Tuesday night and the Wednesday afternoon and then in English on Wednesday night . . . I see no hope whatsoever for Bethel and for the whole district apart from a revival. A new minister would scarcely make any appreciable difference. It is really a most sad state of affairs. I feel increasingly, and said so in one of my sermons, that the real trouble is inside the church. The vast majority of the people are not Christian at all and do not know what it means. The work must start with them.

Roger Weil, who was a member of Westminster Chapel, recalls seeing a side of his minister's character in a new light when he happened to visit the Lloyd-Joneses during one of their summer holidays in Aberystwyth. They spoke together in the course of an evening on the state of the Welsh churches, past and present, and this was followed by family prayer which, as usual, closed the day. The English visitor writes:

I will always remember the deep note of sadness in that part of his prayer when he interceded for Wales, that God who had so signally blessed her in days gone by would revive His work there once more. It was that tone of sadness that stuck in my mind at the time – I did not realise how it grieved his heart. I suppose it was memorable, too, because while on our knees there together we were privileged to glimpse him on a more personal level than ever we could in the services at the Chapel. It was not so much the words but something more like a *groan* in how he said what he did.

Evangelical witness in Wales had been so largely amongst the churches of Calvinistic Methodism (the Welsh Presbyterian Church) that when these churches were overtaken by liberalism and worldliness the cause of the gospel went down in many areas. The last revival of 1904 had put a break on that descent and people involved in the '04 revival were, in subsequent years, those who kept prayer and fellowship meetings going in their chapels even where liberalism might be found in the pulpits. While ML-J was ready to admit some serious deficiencies had accompanied the work of 1904 he would also say, 'I tremble to think what the churches would have been like without the *plant y diwygiad*'.[1] By the middle of this century, however, such people were becoming fewer in number and the general condition of the country was well described by ML-J's brother-in-law in the words, 'the old religious background of our people is disappearing and a pagan generation is springing up'.[2]

While ML-J was widely respected in his old denomination it is scarcely surprising that the leaders of the denomination did not want him in a position of authority in their midst. We have seen how his possible appointment to Bala was blocked in 1938 and a similar thing happened with regard to the superintendency of the Forward Movement – the evangelistic arm of the Welsh Presbyterian Church – in 1947. When it was known that the Rev. R. J. Rees was retiring, after 54 years in the ministry, most of the men in the Movement wanted ML-J to succeed him. But, as already recorded, the hierarchy saw to it that he was never offered the post. 'You see,' as ML-J commented many years later, 'they were very clever, they appointed my brother-in-law.'[3]

[1] 'Children of the revival'.
[2] 'Forward Movement Notes', *The Treasury*, Oct 1947, p. 93. In 1964 ML-J is on record as saying, 'the conditions, religiously speaking, are worse today in Wales than in England.'
[3] The Directors and Officers of the Forward Movement, in a meeting on April 18, 1947, 'unanimously agreed to submit the name of the Rev. Ieuan J. Phillips B.A., Swansea, for the approval of the General Assembly, as Superintendent of the Movement', *Y Blwyddiadur*, 1948, p. 71. It was 'approved' when the General Assembly met in June 1947 at Liverpool.

It is hard to visualize how ML-J could possibly have fitted into the Forward Movement. While it was the most evangelical part of the denomination, its outreach methods and belief in campaigns were of the same type as those which he criticized in England. Instead of looking to their own Welsh background, and seeing the need for the theological preaching of the gospel which had witnessed the rise of Calvinistic Methodism, Welsh evangelicals (and Baptists even more so than Presbyterians) were conforming to the practices which were popular in England.

*   *   *

Scarcely had a door closed on ML-J in Wales in 1947 when a more important one opened. No one had appointed him a student leader in England, neither was he appointed in Wales yet he now came quietly into a position of exceptional influence among young people and the repercussions were to be far reaching.

As in England, this came about in large part through the Inter-Varsity Fellowship. Prior to the late 1940's ML-J had comparatively little contact with the Evangelical Unions in the University Colleges of Wales. This was partly due to his unwillingness to see the IVF become a stronger organization in Wales:

I felt it was not needed. I felt that our life was based on the Church, that we were not in sympathy with movements . . . We have been too ready to allow the English tradition to influence us . . . We have been too much influenced by English teaching, which has also been Arminian . . . I opposed the setting up of an IVF Conference in Wales, I opposed it for years.[1]

The nature of the IVF work in Wales bears out this comment. Through the 1940's the major emphasis was on student-led campaigns which followed the type of evangelism then usual in British evangelicalism. Such campaigns were held in the Rhondda Valley, in Carmarthen, Llanelli and – an unknown thing – even in ML-J's former church at Sandfields, Aberavon, in 1946. In the summer of that same year no fewer than six IVF campaigns were held in South Wales.

As some of the young student leaders came into touch with ML-J they noted a certain difference in his outlook. In the words of Gwyn Walters, who was to become the first IVF Travelling Secretary in

[1] See the discussion 'Nationalism, Tradition and Language' quoted above.

Wales, 'We understood that he had some antipathy to evangelistic campaigns – without quite understanding on what grounds'. ML-J was not a man to discourage young people with criticism. He approved their zeal, noted their prayerfulness with thankfulness and waited his opportunity.

The link between Welsh students and ML-J seems to have been strengthened chiefly by their attendance at English IVF Conferences where he was speaking. Referring to such Conferences, prior to 1946, Gwyn Walters again writes: 'Dr Martyn was warm toward us and expressed interest in what was happening in the Welsh Christian Unions – but we didn't discuss the campaigns. His encouragement of us as students, however, was significant, especially the exhortation to ground ourselves in the Scriptures and in the foundational doctrines of the faith, and to depend not on ourselves but on the Spirit of God.'

After the Sandfields campaign of 1946 ML-J invited Gwyn Walters to tea with him while on a preaching visit to Carmarthen and plied him, Walters remembers, 'with penetrating questions'. When they parted after a train journey together the following day, he pressed a ten shilling note into the younger man's hand. 'This,' recalls Walters, 'was symbolic of the many helps "practical" and spiritual he was to give to many of the young Welsh leaders in subsequent years.'

The number of Welsh students who came to IVF and TSF Conferences in England now steadily increased. 35 came together by bus from Cardiff to the annual Conference at Swanwick in 1947 – a conference which many remembered as a spiritual milestone, with ML-J speaking on the atonement as already mentioned. The next year, 1948, 12 Welsh students were at the IFES Swiss Conference, 'where,' says Walters, 'he again encouraged us to strengthen student witness in Wales'.

It was also in 1948 that developments of far reaching significance occurred in North Wales. At Bangor University College the Evangelical Union was the weakest in the country, with only three members. They were on the point of giving up when other students from outside the EU and of SCM background became interested. Elwyn Davies, a leader of this larger group, had been to some IVF meetings and even to the TSF Trinity College Conference of 1945 (where it is said he was 'very ill at ease'). Then, in 1947 Davies, who was preparing for the Independent ministry, entered into an experience of the gospel and, after evidence of the power of the Holy Spirit in meetings for prayer in which he and others were involved early in 1948, these men of SCM background proposed a union of forces with the small Bangor EU. But the union was to be on the condition that the group would be neither IVF nor SCM. After all, both organizations were English and they were Welsh-speaking students with the nationalism of North Wales in their blood. It was further proposed that Dr Lloyd-Jones and Gwyn Walters be invited to lead a mission among them in Bangor University College. In their burden for evangelistic outreach they were ready to side-step the principal issue which divided SCM and IVF, namely the extent of biblical inerrancy and authority. Nonetheless, there was some protracted debate on Scripture, not least when it was heard that the missioners declined to come unless the organizing committee's position was settled on that point. The result was a rejuvenated Evangelical Union, adhering to the IVF.

Nothing was to do more to strengthen their commitment to Scripture as the Word of God than the mission itself which was held January 23–26, 1949, with ML-J and Walters sharing the speaking. The customary appeals for immediate public profession of Christ were missing, but an unusual sense of conviction of sin was present in all the crowded meetings and the impact on the Bangor College (where the Biblical Studies Professor had scoffingly declined a presentation copy of an IVF book for the Library) was enormous.

There was much discussion in private at Bangor as students queued to speak personally to Dr Lloyd-Jones. Remembering the occasion many years later, he said: 'All sorts of men came to see me. They did not know where they stood or what they believed, and this included theological students.' Others have recalled how when speaking to those who already thought themselves Christians, or to those still under conviction of sin, he would ask the question, 'Have you been on your knees before God, thanking Him that Christ died for sinners?'.[1] Unannounced to the religious world in general, a stirring was taking place in Wales, and those involved began to wonder where it would all lead. Elwyn Davies, president of the Bangor EU in 1949, had already shared with others in the start of a new magazine, *Y Cylchgrawn Efengylaidd* (The Evangelical Magazine) and, concerned to reach fellow countrymen on a larger scale, it was proposed by another Bangor student that a tent be hired at the National Eisteddfod to be held in August 1949 at Dolgellau. The

---

[1] *'Excuse me, Mr Davies – Hallelujah!'* Evangelical Student Witness in Wales 1923–1983, Geraint D. Fielder, 1983, p. 140.

idea was to use the venue (where evangelical witness had hitherto been decidedly unfamiliar) to spread the magazine and its message.

*   *   *

The summer of 1949 in Wales was to prove one of the most remarkable in Dr Lloyd-Jones' life. Originally it was not his intention to be in Wales at all over the summer period for he was committed to spending July and August in the United States. From various churches (including Harold J. Ockenga's at Boston and Clarence Macartney's at Pittsburgh) he had received more invitations than he could accept. Among his engagements scheduled for this period were meetings at Stony Brook, Long Island, and Montreat Summer Conference in North Carolina. But before concluding at Westminster prior to this North American visit he was suffering from persistent catarrh and other symptoms of over-work. When he consulted his old chief, Lord Horder, he was firmly told to cancel the trans-Atlantic trip. It was high time that he took a proper holiday. Dr Lloyd-Jones was himself sufficiently concerned about his condition to accept the advice.

Thus, when another year's ministry – his eleventh – at Westminster Chapel ended in June 1949 Martyn and Bethan went down to Sunnyside, Newcastle Emlyn. Here in his beloved Cardiganshire he was free of engagements other than some which came unexpectedly in that quiet country town. Writing to his mother on July 8, he notes: 'I had to preach here morning and evening on Sunday as Nantlais Williams failed to turn up. I was none the worse for it.' He also wrote a letter of encouragement to O. R. Johnston at the same time as the younger man was about to leave London. Besides the readiness to encourage, there was another ML-J characteristic in this letter, namely, his care for other people's books: 'As I hope to continue with my sermons on the First Epistle of John after my return in the autumn I am taking the liberty of retaining your copy of Calvin's Commentaries which you kindly loaned to me. When I have finished, D V, I shall return it to you.'

At this time in Newcastle Emlyn, Dr Lloyd-Jones was going through a personal struggle of which he very rarely spoke and never in public. He was suffering from depression which he attributed to his low physical condition. With the depression, however, there came a temptation in the form of a 'fiery dart' of doubt. The doubt did not concern his faith or his ministry but it had to do with a person whose regard for him had long been of great support to his whole life. The temptation was to question the reality of this friend's regard. This suspicion was entirely without foundation and he did not give way to it, yet the power of the temptation put him into an agony of spirit: 'There are times,' he would later say, 'when the enemy concentrates on individual Christians, on Christian churches . . . when the devil makes a broadside attack upon you and would sweep you off your feet.' This awareness that the onslaught was from the devil did not, however, bring him comfort for the temptation had brought with it a discovery about himself. The attack had come at a point where it could have success: it was an appeal to his pride, 'Not my pride in the ministry but my carnal pride'.[1] More than thirty years later he could only speak of it with pain: 'It was a terrible thing, it was the thing that revealed to me ultimately the pride of the human heart. I knew I was a sinner without any hope at all, but I never realised the depth of the pride of the human heart. Eventually I saw it was nothing but pride. Carnal, devilish pride. And I was humbled to the ground.'

We do not know precisely what stage in the above temptation he had reached when they left Newcastle Emlyn on July 13. Bethan returned to London while he proceeded to a Nursing Home near Bristol where he had booked a place some weeks earlier for the treatment of his catarrh. This institution was run by Dr A. B. Todd, a highly individualistic physician of whose judgment he had a high opinion. Here he spent nearly two weeks largely on his own in a private room. For the first few days the inner tempest continued. Besides his usual reading of Scripture he had with him some of the writings of A. W. Pink which he had often found helpful, but now nothing seemed to give him any spiritual comfort. Then one morning he awoke soon after six a.m. in 'a complete agony of soul' and even feeling a sense of evil in the room. He once spoke of the well-known episode in the life of Luther in terms which he could have applied to his own experience at Bristol, 'He was deeply conscious of the devil's presence in his room and he could not get away from him'. Then, as he started dressing, and at the very moment when his eye caught just a word in a sermon of Pink's which lay open beside his bed – the

---

[1]'That sin of all sins, which runs through all ages, and through all the race of mankind, is pride . . . Now Satan, that knows this full well, labours with might and main to provoke all men to this sin; it was his own sin, the very sin that made him of a blessed angel a cursed devil.' Isaac Ambrose, 'War with Devils', p. 62, in *Complete Works*, 1674.

word 'glory' – instantly, 'like a blaze of light', he felt the very glory of God surround him. Every doubt and fear was silenced. The love of God was 'shed abroad' in his heart. The nearness of heaven and his own title to it became overwhelming certainties and, at once, he was brought into a state of ecstasy and joy which remained with him for several days.

Dr Lloyd-Jones never wrote of this experience, and he was very reticent to speak of it. He believed that the experience was the work of the Holy Spirit testifying to his sonship (Rom 8:16). In the similar experiences of others (to which he referred on a number of subsequent occasions) it is observable that two features, in particular, paralleled his own. First, there was the sense of light and glory. In the words of William Guthrie: 'It is a glorious divine manifestation of God unto the soul . . . It is a thing better felt than spoke of. It is no audible voice, but it is a ray of glory filling the soul with God, as He is life, light, love and liberty, corresponding to that audible voice, "O man, greatly beloved" (Dan 9:23).'[1] Another Puritan, Thomas Goodwin, writes: 'There is light that cometh and over-powereth a man's soul and assureth him that God is his, and he is God's.'[2] Secondly, there was the suddenness and the unexpectedness with which the assurance came. Speaking of such an occasion, Robert Bruce could say, 'I leapt no sooner on my horse but the gates of heaven were cast open to me',[3] while John Flavel and Christmas Evans were alone in the course of journeys when they similarly met suddenly with God.[4]

When he resumed his holiday with Bethan, together with Elizabeth and Ann, in the last week of July they were making their first of many visits to the farmhouse of Mr and Mrs Ellis Davies at Pant-y- Neuadd, Parc, near Bala. From there ML-J wrote a post-card to A. G. Secrett on July 29:

We had an excellent journey. You will be glad to know that I am feeling really better and I am sure that from now on I shall continue to gain strength.

We are staying right in the mountains. I had not realised that this farm was so situated. It is delightful to wake up to the sound of the running brook . . .

A note from Bethan to the Secretts some days later, gives a rather different view of her husband's health:

[1]*Romans*, vol. 7, pp. 341–2.   [2]*Ibid*, p. 344.
[3]*Ibid*, p. 339.   [4]*Ibid*, p. 315; *Ephesians*, vol. 1, p. 277.

I thought I should have written you many letters before this, but somehow or other it is the most difficult thing to *get at* and I cannot think why! I think that up here it has been because Martyn was so *low* that he has not been doing any reading at all and I have spent all my time pottering about with him. He has been pathetically content to do nothing but *laze* up till now, but now we are beginning to walk the hills and are enjoying it more and more . . .

It was on this visit to Pant-y-Neuadd that Dr Lloyd-Jones had a second experience akin to that described above. The Davies' farmhouse was busy with visitors and he had retired early one Saturday evening. Alone in their bedroom, he was reading the Welsh hymns of William Williams in the Calvinistic Methodist hymn book when he was again given such a consciousness of the presence and love of God as seemed to exceed all that he had ever known before. It was a foretaste of glory.

With the change of arrangements in their plans for the summer of 1949 it meant that ML-J, instead of being on Long Island during the first week of August, was less than twenty miles away from Dolgellau where the Welsh students, as mentioned above, were attempting a first evangelical witness at the National Eisteddfod. At short notice the Doctor agreed to help them. Mari Davies, the daughter of Mr and Mrs Ellis Davies, remembers vividly the afternoon of Thursday, August 4, when she drove the Lloyd-Joneses across to Dolgellau. ML-J chose the route, not the main road south-west, but one of his favourite drives in Wales, the mountain road – little more than a track – between Llanuwchllyn and Dinas Mawddwy, with breathtaking views and spiralling descents. This took them past Brynuchaf, a delightful hill farm at Llanymawddwy, which was to be Mari's future home after her marriage to John Jones in 1954. The subject of marriage was not on Mari's mind that August afternoon but it was in the minds of some of the other Christian young people at Dolgellau, and before the evening meal ML-J spoke to them as a group on an error (then circulating in student circles) that the single state was the state most consistent with true commitment to Christ. One or two courtships made definite progress from then on!

After the official events of the Eisteddfod were over on this Thursday evening, the evangelical students held an open-air meeting in the town square, and on its conclusion a *Noson Lawen* ('joyful evening') in a local chapel. The Eisteddfod was essentially for the preservation and furtherance of the Welsh culture, and a very old part of that culture was the tradition of the *Noson Lawen* when families and neighbours entertained one another with recitation, song and music. The meeting, which began at 10.30 p.m., was thus intended to put Christian content into this format and Dr Lloyd-Jones' part would be to speak at the conclusion. In the event, half-an-hour before midnight, he preached from Philippians 4:4, 'Rejoice in the Lord alway: and again I say, Rejoice', distinguishing between the kind of joy present at the Eisteddfod – happy but temporary – and the lasting joy of the true Christian.

It was novelty enough for evangelicals to be present in numbers at an Eisteddfod, but the events of August 4, 1949, were unusual enough to gain public attention which no one had anticipated. Mr J. O. Williams (a Welsh literary figure), speaking on the radio for the BBC the next day, referred to Dr Lloyd-Jones at the Eisteddfod and went on: 'We cannot but notice that something is moving silently in the lives of the youth of Wales in these days. That came to the Eisteddfod field . . . They love Wales passionately and long to see her emerging from her scepticism and materialism.'

Mrs Lloyd-Jones Sr, knowing that her son was convalescing near Bala, was surprised to hear this news of his activity at Dolgellau over the radio. In response to a letter from her, and in the course of other general news, ML-J gave his mother the explanation:

I was interested to hear that you had heard my name on the wireless. No! I was not in the Eisteddfod itself at all, but we went over to a meeting that was being held after the Eisteddfod on Thursday night. It was held in a chapel and was called '*Noson Lawen Grefyddol*'.[1] It had never been held before. I was described as '*Y Gŵr gwadd*'.[2] There were all sorts of people in the meeting and among them Elwyn Evans of the BBC, Wil Ifan's son. It seems that he was so impressed by the meeting that he decided an account of it must be given in the broadcast on the Eisteddfod. And it was he who got the man who did it to do it. The meeting had been organized by students from Bangor and Bala for whom I preached earlier on this year.

After Bala there was to be further rest and holiday, Bethan and Martyn going to the West of Ireland and the girls to Eastbourne. Ireland was an entirely new location for them and had come about

[1] 'A religious joyful evening'.
[2] 'The man there by invitation'.

because of a family who had begun to attend Westminster in 1947. The Catherwoods owned the Rosapenna Hotel in County Donegal, and Mr H. M. Stuart Catherwood's son Fred had been startled when his father announced that he meant to invite the Doctor to Rosapenna. Hitherto he had known ML-J from afar and could not imagine what the preacher/theologian would do at a place where guests generally came only to fish, golf or play tennis. The Lloyd-Joneses sailed for Ulster on August 24 and, after being six hours fog-bound and motionless off Belfast, they landed at 12.45 p.m. the next day. Stuart Catherwood was there to meet them and to drive the 120 miles, through Antrim and Londonderry, to County Donegal.

In the course of a letter to the Secretts, describing their enjoyment of this holiday (the first of a number at Rosapenna), ML-J wrote on August 28:

The scenery all round is beautiful. It is of a peculiar type – mountains and sea with innumerable little lakes dotted about here and there in the mountains. The hotel itself is on a little bay which opens out on to the Atlantic. Looking out to sea we are facing America and there is literally no other land between us and that country.

There is one thing however that I find depressing here and that is the extreme poverty of the people. They live in little hovels and eke out a bare existence on this rocky soil. I have never seen such a primitive type of life before. The contrast between it and the peasant life in Wales which I knew as a boy is striking. There is no sign of intelligence here or of any type of culture. It seems very sad to me. I have no doubt at all that it is entirely due to the domination of Roman Catholicism. It is a more powerful argument against that vicious system than anything I have ever read or even heard from you!

I am glad to say that I am feeling much better and I am quite sure that I am putting on weight.

This was not, however, the whole story. Notwithstanding the peacefulness of his surroundings and his physical improvement, the inner struggle which had begun at Newcastle Emlyn had returned. While the remembrance of the experiences of God which he had at Dr Todd's Nursing Home, and, again, at Pant-y-Neuadd, were to remain with him all his life, those days of joy had been followed by further severe conflict. On this account he spoke of the period of his first visit to Rosapenna as 'terrible' and said, 'I was in an agony throughout the time'. From Donegal he wrote to his mother on

September 5, indicating his expectation of being back in London on September 8 in time for another year at Westminster Chapel commencing on September 11: 'It will seem strange to be back again after so long an absence and especially to have to start working once more.' He did not tell her that he felt deeply apprehensive.

On returning to London after this long break, far from being ready to resume his ministry he felt utterly unable to preach. Various attempts to prepare a sermon for Sunday morning, September 11 all ended in failure, and so it continued until the preceding day when there was scarcely time left for preparation. In his own words: 'That Saturday afternoon in my study I felt I couldn't preach but the word came into my mind from Titus 1:2, "God who cannot lie", and I'll never forget it. I was absolutely overwhelmed, in tears, and I was given the sermon there and then.'

The sermon notes which he took into the pulpit the next morning bear their own witness to the abnormality of that week-end. Instead of the more usual four sides of notes, written in ink with heads and sub-heads, he had one scrap of paper (torn from an agenda of a London Bible College Committee meeting), with pencil notes hurriedly set down on the unused side. Only a few introductory words were written in full. They read:

Good to start with something great and fundamental. Always danger of becoming immersed and lost in details . . . Paul generally makes things plain at the beginning of every letter. Our whole basis and position rests on the fact of God and His great purposes. It is the only ground of confidence. The great thing is the 'hope of eternal life, which God, that cannot lie, promised before the world began'. Whatever may be happening to us and whatever our feeling, this is certain. But how can we be sure of it? Answer here . . .

These words thus led into his four heads:

The fact – God cannot lie. Incapable of it. *The explanation of fact* – His character, immutable, just, holy, antithesis of all that is false and deceptive. *Proof of the fact* – Bible and history, especially the sending of His Son and His work. *Comfort of the fact* – 'promised before the world began . . . in due times manifested'. Certain things delayed. The promises – 'I will never leave thee nor forsake'; 'When thou passest through the waters.' 'Let not your heart be troubled.'

The only addition, in a bottom corner, was the words of a favourite hymn:

> When darkness seems to hide His face
> I trust to His unchanging grace
> In every rough and stormy gale
> My anchor holds within the veil[1]

It may appear strange that the darkness in which Dr Lloyd-Jones struggled could persist even after the very conscious nearness of God which he had known on those two remarkable occasions. And the conflict was to go on until late in the year, though never with the same force after Sunday, September 11, when he was enabled to speak with much power and liberty. But to Dr Lloyd-Jones it was the marked contrast in the nature of his experience at this time which pointed to the real meaning of what was happening to him: 'In my opinion God wanted to do something new to me so He gave the devil liberty to attack like he did with Job. That was a real Satanic attack and the devil would get me right down but then God would lift me up. So the two went together. That is most important.'

*　　*　　*

It is not without significance that the demonic onslaught coincided with a period in Dr Lloyd-Jones' ministry when he was on the threshold of exercising a profound influence upon a younger generation. The beginning of that influence upon post-war students in England and Wales we have already noted. Almost immediately after the resumption of his ministry in September 1949 he was to take the leading part in another development in Wales. His first full week of work after Sunday, September 11 followed a typical pattern – a Westminster Fellowship on Tuesday afternoon, a service at Corsham (Wiltshire) on Wednesday, a CIM Council meeting on Thursday afternoon and a meeting for church members at Westminster the same evening. Then, after Sunday the 18th, he returned to Wales for the inaugural Welsh Inter-Varsity Fellowship Conference which was held from September 19 to 21, 1949.

---

[1]Written from memory, the words of the second verse of Edward Mote's hymn, 'My hope is built on nothing less', are not given with complete accuracy.

Hitherto the only option for students in the Evangelical Unions of the four Welsh University Colleges – Cardiff, Swansea, Aberystwyth and Bangor – had been to go to the conferences held in England. Evangelical youth work in Wales had remained more church-based than in England and there had been a certain resistance to any developments which would organize Welsh students into a more cohesive national entity. As early as 1941 ML-J had advised against the commencement of a Welsh IVF Conference, being convinced that the multiplication of movements was weakening the true role of the churches. It was partly for this reason that ML-J had not been a frequent speaker in the Welsh EU's; the Bangor mission of January 1949 was possibly the first in which he had taken part in Wales.

In the end, a group of Welsh student leaders, with the approval of Douglas Johnson, had decided to launch a Welsh Conference. This time Dr Lloyd-Jones was not consulted until after the decision was taken and then it was to ask him to come and speak on 'The Biblical Doctrine of Man'. His acceptance of the invitation to be the main speaker at this first Welsh IVF Conference was probably connected with a conviction that there was an unusual work of God evident among the Welsh students and with a reluctantly-reached persuasion that the churches were too weak and mixed to give the direction needed.

Some sixty Welsh students assembled for this three-day Conference at Pantyfedwen hostel in the seaside village of Borth, outside Aberystwyth. Wynford Davies, the student-chairman of the Conference, has retained several memories of these days at Borth. On the Doctor's arrival at Pantyfedwen it was Wynford who introduced him to the manager of the hostel. 'Oh, I know you,' said ML-J, 'you used to work in a travel agency in Aberystwyth before the War.' The man, who made no Christian profession, was so impressed at being remembered by someone who had only seen him a few times over ten years earlier that he came to the first meeting and remained for them all!

In his three addresses on the biblical doctrine of man ML-J first 'demolished' wrong views of man and of the biblical teaching, and then gave 'a very strong and powerful biblical exposition of the whole doctrine'. Although there had been marked growth in the Evangelical Unions, with many conversions since 1945, such teaching was very new to many who were present. Wynford Davies writes:

By and large there was no doctrinal understanding of the whole way of salvation and of God's grace as we understand it, especially from a reformed perspective. I remember at the end of the first day, when he had been dealing very much with the opposite views, several of the new converts, especially the girls, were not too sure of this. But then the second day, when he moved on and began positively to expound the Scripture, many people came to me and said what a tremendous feast it had been and how they had really begun to see in a completely new way. And what amazed me about the Doctor was that, though the conference was so small, he spoke with such conviction and passion as he would have done, I guess, at Westminster Chapel on an ordinary Sunday. His mind never seemed to tire. It was a remarkable conference. At the end I took the Doctor to the station to see him off. He said how much he had enjoyed it and added, 'I hope that you will keep these conferences moving in this direction especially for the benefit of the theological students'. He went on to say how in the English scene there had always been an aversion to doctrinal study.

* * *

We must pause at this point to ask what effect the experiences of 1949 had upon Dr Lloyd-Jones' life and ministry.

In the first place, it is clear that God permitted the sustained demonic assault in order to deepen ML-J's insight into the wiles of the devil and his knowledge of the only power which can counter such an adversary. In this way his ministry was to be made a greater means of deliverance and help to many other Christians in times of similar darkness. There were already indications of that purpose following his sermon on 'God who cannot lie' on that first Sunday back in the pulpit at Westminster. At the close of the service one future leader of the China Inland Mission came to the preacher to say that it had been 'the outstanding service of his life'. Then at the end of the same week, Dr Lloyd-Jones received a letter from a minister's wife who had been suddenly bereaved of her husband. She was writing to say that they had both been at Westminster Chapel the previous Sunday morning (September 11) and that her husband had gone there rather downcast and depressed. The sermon on Titus 1:2, she reported, had filled him with a joy such as he had never known the like before. He had gone home 'on the mountain top' and continued in that state until his death that Thursday. In the midst of her sorrow she was also still rejoicing in the help which they had received from the God 'who cannot lie'.

No small part of Dr Lloyd-Jones' ministry in the years ahead was to help Christians to know their enemy and how to resist him. His emphasis in this regard became akin to Martin Luther's. The knowledge which he had gained from experience was to illuminate many passages of Scripture first for himself and then for others. Thus his series of eleven sermons on Psalm 73, entitled 'A Soul's Conflict', to which we shall refer again, were not merely an explanation of how the Psalmist overcame a state of depression, rather the psalm was about the power of temptation and the subtlety of Satan whose might against us is 'second only to that of God'. 'This is the kind of thing to which God's people are subjected. Because they are God's people the devil makes a special target of them and seizes every opportunity to get them down.'[1]

His fullest treatment of this whole subject was to come in the course of his exposition of Ephesians 6:10–21. 'There is nothing which is quite so disastrous,' he was then to say, 'as not to accept in its fulness the biblical teaching concerning the devil. I am certain that one of the main causes of the ill state of the Church today is the fact that the devil is being forgotten. All is attributed to us; we have all become so psychological in our attitude and thinking. We are ignorant of this great objective fact, the being, the existence of the devil, the adversary, the accuser, and his "fiery darts".'[2]

With regard to his own spiritual life, the experiences of 1949 deepened his conviction both about his own superficiality as well as the superficiality of much evangelical religion. All that he allowed himself to say about himself was: 'I was brought to the end of myself in a way that had never happened before. I really saw the depths of sin and that man's ultimate problem is his pride.' He concurred entirely with the words of Sibbes, 'After conversion we need bruising by reason of the remainder of pride in our nature, and to let us see that we live by mercy'.[3] And the comfort which follows bruising, far from lifting men up with new confidence in themselves, makes them

---

[1]*Faith on Trial*, 1965, pp. 17–18. It is regrettable that the sermons originally printed in WR (March 1956-Jan. 1957) had their title changed when issued in book form. ML-J had little interest in the selection of titles, though the original one was no doubt his own and was identical with Richard Sibbes' title for his famous work based on Psalm 42:11.
[2]*Ephesians*, vol. 7, p. 292.
[3]Sibbes, *Works*, vol. 1, p. 44. In a brief reference to his experience in 1949 ML-J says that Sibbes' book 'quietened, soothed, comforted, encouraged and healed me'. *Preaching*, p. 175.

humble before God. The hallmark of a true experience of God, he would constantly preach, 'is a sense of awe, and accompanying it, a sense of unworthiness'.[1] 'The final explanation of the state of the Church today is a defective sense of sin and a defective doctrine of sin'.[2] As he was often to say, 'Modern Christians are much too healthy'.[3] Such statements he would qualify. He knew that in some Protestant traditions there was still a danger of people equating spirituality with morbid introspection, self condemnation and a profession of constant failure:

But that is by no means the danger today, especially not, if I may say so, here in London and in the circles in which most of us move . . . It is the opposite extreme. It is the absence of a true godly sorrow for sin, together with the tendency to spare ourselves and to regard ourselves and our sins, our shortcomings and our failures, very lightly . . . We heal ourselves so easily; indeed, I do not hesitate to say that the trouble with most of us is that in a sense we are far too 'healthy' spiritually.[4]

There was, it must further be said, a degree of change in the content of Dr Lloyd-Jones' ministry after 1949 in another respect. It was not a change in doctrine but of emphasis. From this date he was conscious of the addition of a larger measure of the experimental in his preaching and he came to see that this was the redressing of a balance which he had sometimes been in danger of losing after 1932. We have already noted the great influence which B. B. Warfield's volumes had on him in that year of his first visit to North America.[5] Warfield convinced him of the need to preach 'more theologically and intellectually . . . that I must have solid sermons and not rely on the inspiration of the moment'. Thereafter, he continued, 'Men could detect an intellectual, theological element that had not been there before'. One result was that, while still in Wales, ministerial students looked to him for a correction of the theology which they were receiving at College and increasingly, in many quarters, he was put into the role of an apologist for evangelical Christianity. In the

---

[1] See *Romans*, vol. 7, pp. 365–369 for a fine summary of ML-J's whole thought on what he regarded as so fundamental.
[2] *Sermon on the Mount*, vol. 1, p. 55.
[3] *Spiritual Depression*, p. 169. 'People who are not aware of indwelling sin are either the merest tyros or else are unregenerate.'
[4] *Faith on Trial*, pp. 67–68.
[5] See volume 1, p. 285 ff.

1940's, for instance, he was often the person asked by the IVF to review the major theological titles of neo-orthodoxy. Although his preaching between 1932 and 1949 never became mainly intellectual, he felt, with hindsight, that he had been in danger:

But then '49 I think was a real turning point. That is when I got my true balance. I had been becoming too intellectual, too doctrinal and theological, because when I came to London I suddenly found I was the teacher, the theologian, and it tended to make me lose my balance, although that had started in Sandfields by reading Warfield.

We would be wrong to make too much of the words 'turning point'. As noted earlier, some spoke of him as 'nothing but a Pentecostalist' *before* the events of July and August, 1949. And no one observed any major change in his preaching after that date. The address of truth to the mind remained primary and, instead of putting 'experience' in the place of faith in the Word of God, some of the strongest warnings against that error were delivered in the autumn of 1949 when he resumed preaching from 1 John at the words of chapter 4:7–8, 'Beloved, let us love one another . . . for God is love'. To know God, he said, is to know love and to know Him more is to love more; therefore 'let me beseech you, never put the love of God and doctrine as opposites'. For we need to know in order to love. On any supposed short cut to the assurance of God's love by the way of the mystics he said on October 23, 1949 (and therefore following his own remarkable experiences):

We must turn our back very resolutely upon every teaching of the Christian life which would lead us to try to obtain a direct vision of God. We must not desire ever to hear audible voices or to have such visions as will give us a kind of mechanical, material certainty. Now you know there were mystics who went in for that kind of thing . . . They did not like the idea of faith, they did not like the life which, as Paul describes it, says, 'we walk by faith, not by sight'. They wanted to see and hear, they wanted something tangible, and the result was they became victims of aberrations, of hallucinations and of all the manifestations which invariably accompany this craving for the immediate . . . We must not think of God in material terms.

At the same time he increasingly saw that truth is to be preached in a manner which affects heart and conscience: it has to be 'experimental' in the sense that it affects the experience of those who hear it, as well as their beliefs. And with greater clarity, tenderness and feeling, he urged that fellowship with God is *more* than orthodoxy. Love to God – a love that wholly possesses us – is *the* supreme need. After preaching on October 9, 1949, on the love of God in the giving of His Son, he said:

My beloved friends, I do not know what your feeling is at this moment, I will tell you what mine is. I cannot understand the hardness of my own heart. How could any of us look at all this, and believe it, and not be lost in love to God? How can we contemplate these things and not be utterly broken down? How can we do anything but love one another as we contemplate such amazing love? How can we look at these things and not feel that we owe everything to Him and that our whole lives must be given to express our gratitude, our praise and our thanksgiving?

From the latter part of this same year, 1949, there also comes one of the few scraps of what may be called autobiography from ML-J's pen. It appeared, written in Welsh, in Y *Cylchgrawn Efengylaidd* (Jan–April 1950):

I remember when I was a child that I had great difficulty in deciding what to wish for or what to choose when someone asked me to do so. But I do not have any difficulty with this request to state my desire for 1950.

Before everything else my chief desire is 'so that I should know Him'. Nothing surprises me so much as I look back as seeing the tendency to be satisfied with other objects. I do not refer to sins so much as to the 'poor idols of the earth' or to backsliding. It is so easy to satisfy oneself with truths about the Person. What gives more pleasure than theologising and being doctrinal about the faith, and even defending the faith? We are all ready to try to obtain and to thirst after special experiences – assurance of forgiveness and salvation, being freed from special sins, experiencing joy and peace, being able to live the full life and so on. All these things are part of the heritage of the Christian, but he must not live on them and be satisfied by them. To know Him properly is a life full of peace.

* * *

Dr Lloyd-Jones came to look back on 1949 as a year when he had been guided by God with unusual clarity. In 1947 a door had shut for him with respect to the Forward Movement, yet that event was soon followed by the beginnings of an extended usefulness among Welsh students. And such was God's sovereign overruling that he had found himself at the Dolgellau Eisteddfod and then at the Conference which shaped Inter-Varsity thought in Wales for the next decade. But, more than all this, was the humbling and the strengthening which he received for the long years ahead. He had learned more of what it means to enjoy the love of God. Dr Lloyd-Jones had not been praying for assurance, or for the Holy Spirit, when he was so unforgettably helped at Bristol and at Bala, but such dealings of God with those called to serve Him are not uncommon. In the words of Isaac Ambrose, three hundred years earlier: 'Sometimes when Satan is most busy, the Lord steps in with his own testimony, and stops the lion's mouth that he can say no more.'

PART TWO

WHEN THE TIDE TURNED, the 1950's

The 1950's brought both a widening and an intensification of Dr Lloyd-Jones' labours. At Westminster the congregation reached the number at which it would remain for the rest of his ministry and it was given the preaching from which the world would later benefit. His itinerant evangelism across Britain continued and his leadership in student work at home and overseas was at its height. Referring to the over 85,000 students then in the British Universities, the Editor of the Christian Graduate *wrote: 'God is working in a way we have not known before. This is the day for a general advance' (October 1951). In that advance no one was more closely involved than ML-J. Dr Oliver Barclay of the Inter-Varsity Fellowship writes: 'He had enormous influence. He taught a whole generation of Christian Union students to love doctrine and to be bold in declaring it.'*

As students for the ministry, conferences, books and magazines now multiplied, there were signs that the tide was indeed turning back to the older evangelicalism. But ML-J regarded any general optimism as premature. There was still no revival and a resurgent evangelicalism had greater problems ahead than it presently recognised. He was to be virtually alone in challenging ecumenism's insistence that a common Christian 'experience' must be put before the necessity of any common 'beliefs'. And his decision to stand apart from the Crusade evangelism introduced in 1954 was incomprehensible to the many who saw the development as a great opportunity for outreach and for increased evangelical influence.

12

A New Generation and New Thought

The 1950's saw a major change of direction in the thinking of a considerable number of people. There was a recovery of Calvinistic convictions in a manner and on a scale which has had few parallels in history. With hindsight it can be said that what occurred in the late 1940's was preparatory to this change, but when the decade began there was little observable indication of what was to happen. Christian literature provides one of the best means to measure the extent of the difference between 1950 and 1960. In 1950 publishers committed to the older theology had long since ceased to exist and the very few contemporary British authors of that outlook were virtually unknown. The writings of Arthur W. Pink were of no interest to any publishing house and when he died unnoticed in Scotland in 1952 there was no expectation that they would ever have a global readership. Yet by 1959 Dr Lloyd-Jones could speak of the 'tremendously encouraging fact' that 'there is obviously a new interest in Reformed literature and this seems to me to be true right through the world'.[1]

To profess to be able to trace the precise means by which this change took place would be to deny its real nature. As every true work of God, its origins were quiet and mysterious. A hunger for a more biblical and doctrinal Christianity occurred in a number of places simultaneously and in more than one country. In so far as any one instrumentality was involved, it was the prayers of Christian people, many of whom died before they ever saw the tide turn. Some of these people belonged to the few small British denominations which remained orthodox, yet it is clear that the resurgence of Calvinism owed little to these denominations as such. Those who looked for the cause of the change on the merely human level, and

[1]*The Annual Meeting of the Evangelical Library, 1960, p. 13.*

who were unenthusiastic at its progress, were often of one mind about the source from which it came. If the minister of Westminster Chapel was 'the last of the Calvinists' who else but he could be responsible for what was happening?

That was certainly not Dr Lloyd-Jones' viewpoint yet he did see it as his privilege to be closely involved in all the various agencies which were used in this re-awakening. By 1960, although still largely alone among his own age group, he was at the centre of a whole new generation of younger men who looked to him in a way in which they looked to no one else.

We have already spoken of how this change was first evident among young people, and particularly among a few English and Welsh students who belonged to the IVF in the mid- and late 1940's. In 1950 there was a development from that quarter which proved to be of major importance. In the IVF magazine the *Christian Graduate* published in September of that year, J. I. Packer wrote on 'The Doctrinal Puritans and their Work'. He contrasted the Puritans' thorough treatment of Christian experience with 'an endemic subjectivity in much modern teaching on the Christian life'. The article concluded with a low-keyed postscript drawing brief attention to a conference to be held at Westminster Chapel, December 19–20, 1950, under the general title, 'The distinctive theological contribution of the English Puritans'.[1]

'The Puritan Conference', as this new conference was inevitably nicknamed, was a novel idea and a direct result of the link between several Oxford graduates and Dr Lloyd-Jones. Raymond Johnston seems to have been the spokesman who put the idea to the Doctor. The proposal was for six sessions, spread over two successive days. Each session would be opened by a speaker dealing with a Puritan author or with some aspect of Puritan teaching, and would be followed by an approximately equal period of discussion. As well as making a large contribution (in terms of prepared addresses) at the first conference, Jim Packer became responsible for its arrangements in conjunction with ML-J who was to lead and chair all the sessions. Recalling the small beginning of 1950, Packer has written:

[1] The notice first appeared in the June issue of *The Christian Graduate* with the note, 'Speakers include the Rev. Dr. D. Martyn Lloyd-Jones'. For several years it was hard to find suitable speakers who shared this new enthusiasm for the Puritans. Until 1961 the Conference met under the auspices of the IVF's Tyndale Fellowship.

I simply wanted to share what my own reading had taught me, and was quite happy with the 20 or so folk who came on that first occasion. The Doctor, however, with whom as conference organiser I was now conversing for the first time, made no secret of his belief that what we were doing was of great potential importance for the Church: which struck me, for really I had never thought of it that way.

At this first Conference ML-J spoke on 'Puritan Preaching'.[1] The younger men taking part did so with all the enthusiasm of those who were possessed with a great discovery. They had no more idea of the encouragement they were bringing to the chairman than they had of the fact that the second day of the Conference marked his fiftieth birthday. On personal matters of that kind his reserve dictated silence; at the same time people were sometimes taken by surprise at the subjects upon which he did express his mind. Jim Packer recalls an instance of this kind which occurred in private at the conclusion of the first day of the 1952 Puritan Conference. ML-J was not interested in seeing numbers, as such, at the meetings. His concern was to reach men who would be future pastors and teachers of others. Accordingly when two young ladies attended the sessions of this third conference he was not wholly approving. 'They don't come to study the Puritans,' he said to Packer, 'they're only here for the men! I know one of them; she's a member of my church.' 'Well, Doctor,' the Conference organiser replied, 'as a matter of fact, I'm going to marry her' (Kit Mullett had accepted his proposal the night before). 'Without batting an eyelid,' Packer recalls, 'he said, "Well then, you see I was right about one of them; now what about the other?"' The humour in this repartee was probably only visible in his eyes.

*   *   *

In the early 1950's ML-J was giving much time to the strengthening of doctrinal commitment within the IVF. As well as continuing to speak at student and Theological Students Fellowship conferences, for four years he chaired a Summer School of the Graduates

[1]The other subjects announced on the programme were 'Historical and Theological Introduction' (Packer); 'The Puritan Use of the Old Testament' (Johnston); 'The Christian Life' (J. B. L. Gee); 'Pastoral Theology' (C. L. L. Binder). A closing session with subject unstated was also assigned to Packer.

Fellowship, which met at Tyndale House, Cambridge. These Summer Schools brought together some of the ablest men and speakers, including Cornelius Van Til from Westminster Seminary in 1950, and John Murray from the same Seminary in 1953. In 1950 the subject for the five-day conference was, 'Recent Theological Trends in the Light of Holy Scripture'. Marcus L. Loane (a future Archbishop of Sydney) who was present, says of ML-J, 'His mind was as sharp as a gimlet and he managed every session with very clear and acute thinking'. In the following years the subjects at the Summer Schools were, 'Justification by Faith' (1951) and 'The Principles and Practice of Biblical Interpretation' (1952).

At this period Dr Lloyd-Jones' influence in the IVF was at its height. He was president of the Fellowship again in 1952 and the hundreds of young people present at the annual conference at Swanwick that year are unlikely ever to forget him speaking on 'Maintaining the Evangelical Faith Today'. This address, or rather Dr Johnson's notes of it, was rushed into print to influence students throughout Britain. It was this publication which occasioned the first open attack on the preacher in the Christian press in a lengthy, unsigned editorial column in the *British Weekly* (March 19, 1953). The writer, who was Dr Nathaniel Micklem, Principal of Mansfield College, Oxford, began:

A little pamphlet entitled *Maintaining The Evangelical Faith Today* by Dr Martyn Lloyd-Jones (Inter-varsity Fellowship, 6d.) was, we gather, written with sorrow. It will certainly be read with sorrow by numbers of people who hold the author in high regard as a preacher of the Gospel. The pamphlet is an apologia for the refusal of the Inter-Varsity Fellowship to co-operate with any Christians who do not agree with them in their opinions, and is an attack on the World Council of Churches and the British Council of Churches. It is written with regret, without personal bitterness and as an expression of conviction . . .

In Dr Micklem's view this address advanced the thesis that Christians are committed to the whole gospel and that

the whole, full Gospel is to be identified with Dr Martyn Lloyd-Jones' definition of it; therefore he and his followers are precluded from co-operation with all Christians who do not agree with him, and both the World Council and the British Council of Churches are disloyal to the Gospel . . .

A New Generation and New Thought

Dr Lloyd-Jones writes in sincerity and charity, but it is time there was some plain speaking in this matter; for the Inter-Varsity Fellowship which, as utterly committed to the Gospel, might well be the spear-head of the Christian challenge to the world, is, in some places and where in this matter it follows the lead of Dr Lloyd-Jones, divisive, schismatic, obscurantist and quite un-Biblical.

The kindest thing to say about Dr Lloyd-Jones' position is that it rests upon downright theological ignorance. There may be no compromise in respect of the Gospel; we all agree about that. But we should hesitate to claim that Dr Lloyd-Jones or any other man has done more than glimpse the mystery of the grace of God, since it is only 'with all saints' that we may hope to grasp the length and breadth and depth and height of grace. There is a marvellous unity in the whole New Testament, but no scholar could maintain that there is theological and doctrinal agreement between St. Paul, St. John and the writer 'to the Hebrews'. Nothing could be more clear than that Dr Lloyd-Jones is a kind of Calvinist; and that the Apostle Paul was not. The Gospel is not in the least indefinite, but being God's Word to man, it can never be fully and adequately and finally caged and set forth in any human formula . . .

The sober truth is that Dr Lloyd-Jones offers a more or less arbitrary selection from the tenets of scholastic Calvinism, and tells us that if we presume to criticize these doctrines we deny the Gospel. 'We must be like Martin Luther,' he tells us, 'when he stood alone against the authority of the Roman Church, which had arrogated to itself such dictatorial powers for so many long centuries.' Quite, and unhappily we must follow Martin Luther and resist the authority of the IVF which, in the person of Dr Lloyd-Jones, arrogates to itself the same dictatorial powers. He may give us Protestant doctrine, but this is the same old Roman spirit. It is Romanism with its typical anathema on all who do not conform.

The tragedy of the situation is that Dr Lloyd-Jones cares nothing for himself, but only for the Gospel. We have great sympathy with him in his conviction that in many places the full Gospel is not being preached . . . But what ignorance, if it be not arrogance, it is, however unconscious and however unintentional, to suppose that the Gospel can only be expressed and can be adequately expressed in a particular brand of traditional Calvinist theology!

Dr Lloyd-Jones takes it upon himself to ascribe motives to those who support or co-operate with the ecumenical movement. We might better say that the World Council and the British Council of Churches exist for no other end than that together they may learn of Christ from one another and witness for Him before the world. They need the co-operation of the IVF.

[229]

As a review of the Swanwick address these words were patently unfair for, as ML-J replied in the Correspondence columns of the *British Weekly*, *Maintaining the Evangelical Faith Today* said not one word about Calvinism:

I have always asserted and argued as strongly as I could that evangelicals should not separate on the question of Calvinism and Arminianism. In the IVF, both here in Great Britain and on the international level, Arminians and Calvinists work most happily and harmoniously together, and it is my privilege to co-operate with all such . . . I pleaded for the maintaining of that Biblical Evangelical Faith to which Arminians, Lutherans and Calvinists subscribe. That is my position and for that I make no apology.

Neither do I make any apology for the 'ignorance' which hitherto has led me to believe, unlike you, Sir, that there is no 'theological and doctrinal disagreement between St. Paul, St. John and the writer to the Hebrews.'

He believed in co-operation with all who held to Scripture as the Word of God: the great cleavage was with those whose beliefs were not based solely on the authority of the Bible. Dr Micklem no doubt understood this but he also observed that Calvinism affected ML-J's whole outlook. In his case, at least, it was still the 'iron rations of the soul' and it seemed to put a resolution into his advocacy of the evangelicalism which was in resurgence among so many young people. Certainly the *British Weekly*, and other similar organs, regarded Lloyd-Jones as the man principally responsible for the opposition to the non-doctrinal Christianity in which they believed – a Christianity which 'charitably' credited everyone with a portion of the truth and which looked for unity simply on the basis of religious experience.

It was noticeable that no well-known evangelicals wrote to the Correspondence columns of the *British Weekly* in the weeks following Micklem's attack. There were undoubtedly some, even within the IVF, who held reservations on Dr Lloyd-Jones' influence and this was to surface a few months later at the fourth Tyndale Summer School in July 1953. ML-J was already conscious of a certain degree of coolness from some present who, like him, had been connected with the IVF over a number of years. In the 1952 School on Interpretation of Scripture one of these (a senior lecturer at an Anglican Evangelical College) gave an example of what he regarded as the correct use of allegory: 'When Gideon asked for the dew to be on the wool, he was saying, in effect, "Lord fill me with thy Spirit amidst a barren and lifeless people". But when he asked for the opposite it was, in effect, "Lord empty me of thyself, but pour thy Spirit upon all flesh"' (Romans 9:3 being quoted in support). In response to this ML-J queried whether he was being serious. The lecturer could not contain his annoyance and exclaimed, 'Indeed I am, I preached it last Sunday!'.

Clearer indication of the difference between ML-J's theology and that of others emerged when the subject in 1953 was 'The Plan of Salvation'. It was one which ML-J had not chosen but he was required to chair the sessions as usual and there was bound to be controversy. John Murray gave an address on definite (as opposed to universal) redemption. The subject was a bombshell to many and there was no senior man present who was prepared to support John Murray except ML-J. This the latter did with such effect that the same Anglican who had taken umbrage the previous year, finding himself unable to answer Lloyd-Jones' points, protested with some heat, 'I am not going to be ruled by your logic'.

ML-J, who did not lead another Summer School of the Tyndale Fellowship, believed that the younger men now coming forward should be encouraged. Jim Packer, particularly, he viewed in this light. He did all he could to encourage the tall, hard-thinking Englishman and to support a widening of his influence. Thus Packer gave an address at the Summer School in 1951 on 'Justification by Faith', and at the Annual Lecture at the Evangelical Library, the next year, on 'The Practical Writings of the English Puritans'. Only on one major aspect of the doctrine of salvation did a difference remain between them, namely, on the extent of the atonement. Still sympathetic with Richard Baxter's universal view (and working for a D. Phil. on Baxter at this time) Packer was silent on the issue at the Cambridge discussion of 1953. But he continued to think and ML-J was delighted at the outcome:

I will never forget one morning when the Puritan Conference was due to start. Packer came rushing up to me and said, 'I am now a complete Calvinist, Doctor!'. He had finished with Baxter and turned to Owen.[1] At first I alone was contending for limited atonement.

[1] i.e. on this point of doctrine. See the *Works of John Owen*, ed. W. H. Goold, vol. 10, p. 140 ff.

Something of a Paul and Timothy relationship developed between the two men, with Dr Lloyd-Jones becoming increasingly happy for Packer to enter into the role which he had hitherto played in IVF circles. At the same time the stiffening of resistance towards some of his convictions on the part of some of the IVF's leaders may have entered into his decision to lay down his chairmanship of the Summer School after 1953. Despite what some thought, he was not in his element in controversy, at least not when feelings were aroused (though debating, as such, he did enjoy). 'In public discussion,' writes Packer, 'he could be severe to the point of crushing, but always with transparent patience and good humour. I think he had a temper, but I never saw him lose it, though I saw stupid people "take him on" in discussion and provoke him in a manner almost beyond belief. His self-control was marvellous: only the grace of God suffices to explain it.'[1]

Dr Lloyd-Jones certainly did not believe that discussion of the doctrines of grace should be carried on in an atmosphere of controversy. To present those doctrines in an argumentative way to evangelical Christians of a different understanding, or to make a direct attack on their beliefs and practices, is unlikely to be beneficial. He thought that A. W. Pink had made a mistake at this point and that in so doing he had lost an opportunity to influence numbers who were incapable of suddenly receiving meat in the place of milk. Reflecting on this in later years, he was to say:

If I had behaved like Pink did, I would have achieved nothing. Nothing at all. I could see that the only hope was to let the weight of the truth convince the people. So I had to be very patient and take a very long term look at things. Otherwise I would have been dismissed and the whole thing would have finished.

A major example of how he believed Calvinistic doctrine should be presented was occurring at Westminster Chapel at this period. With some reluctance he terminated the Friday evening Fellowship and Discussion meeting in October 1952 and replaced it with meetings in the main auditorium of the Chapel at which he would give a series of lectures on 'Biblical Doctrines'. These Friday night

[1]*Chosen Vessels: Portraits of Ten Outstanding Christian Men*, ed. Charles Turner, Ann Arbor, 1985, p. 117.

lectures were to continue until 1955 when he began his monumental exposition of Romans.[1]

One major principle which governed his series on 'Biblical Doctrines' was that truth must be seen as a body, as a whole, and that to develop some special interest, whether it be with regard to holiness, or prophecy or Calvinism is always wrong. (For that same reason he did not favour societies which stood for one particular truth.) Usually error at one point is due to a failure to see the truth at another. After five evenings on the Doctrine of God he moved on to Angels, then to Creation, Providence, Man and to three evenings on the Fall and Sin. Then, after an introduction to the Doctrine of Redemption ('Redemption was planned before the foundation of the world, Eph 1:4. We were chosen before creation . . . The plan of redemption is perfect. There is nothing contingent about it.'), he went on to the Covenant and the unity of the Old and New Testaments before coming to twelve lectures on the Person and Work of Christ. On the first Friday in December 1953 he started on the Doctrine of the Holy Spirit, and it was under this general heading, in connection with the work of the Spirit in the application of redemption, that he took up the sovereignty of grace, at length, in January and February 1954. His lecture of January 29, 1954, which introduced the subject, was remarkable for a number of reasons. Using such terms as 'Pelagian', 'Arminian' and 'Reformed' (which he did not normally do) he showed that the view that salvation depends on man's co-operation is the result of an inadequate view of man's condition as a result of the Fall, and that the error of thinking that personal salvation begins with our faith or decision (instead of regeneration) is due to the same failure to realize man's real condition in sin. But equally notable in this address were the unusual number of personal references. He never normally said such things as, 'I have spent a great deal of my time this week in considering this great question' (the order of salvation). Still less did he normally mention Mrs Lloyd-Jones in the pulpit, but on this occasion he confessed that he had gone over the subject with her at 'a late hour of the night'. To the question, 'If there will be Arminians in heaven why should we bother about this difference in theology?' he also replied personally:

[1]These Friday meetings always ran from the beginning of October to the end of May, with a short break at Christmas and Easter.

I think that is a foolish question. We 'bother' about it, to use the term, because the Scripture has a great deal to say about it. Not only that. Any child of God should be anxious to understand as far as he can. I will go even further. If I were to give my experience in this pulpit tonight, I should have to put it like this: I know of nothing that is so strengthening to faith, nothing which so builds up my assurance, nothing which gives me such certainty about the blessed hope for which I am destined, as the understanding of Christian doctrine, the understanding of the way, yea the mechanism of salvation. And that is why I personally 'bother' with it.

   This lecture was to be followed by five on regeneration ('effectual calling') and union with Christ before he came to Conversion, Repentance, Faith, Assurance, Justification, Adoption, Sanctification and other subjects.
   Another feature of this whole series was the balance of the presentation. He warned, for instance, against hyper-Calvinism, as well as Arminianism, and here there was another unusual personal reference:

If you were asked to give the difference, or to define the difference, between a Calvinist and a hyper-Calvinist how would you do it? It is a question that is worth asking for this reason: I know large numbers of people who when they use the term 'hyper'-Calvinist generally mean Calvinist. In other words, they do not know what a hyper-Calvinist is; let me tell you what a hyper-Calvinist is. A hyper-Calvinist is one who says that the offer of salvation is only made to the redeemed, and that no preacher of the Gospel should preach Christ and offer salvation to all and sundry. That is a hyper-Calvinist. A hyper-Calvinist regards a man who offers salvation or who proclaims salvation to all as a dangerous person. For what it is worth, there is a society in London at the moment that has described me as a dangerous Arminian, because I preach Christ to all and offer salvation to all.[1] Well that is the difference between a hyper-Calvinist and a Calvinist.

   ML-J had always stressed the need for the Holy Spirit but it seems to have been in this series of lectures that he first introduced more specific teaching on baptism with the Spirit and the Christian's need for further fillings of the Spirit in personal experience. This subject took up three Friday evenings in October 1954. We shall return to it later and simply note here his balancing warning against 'experience seeking':

[1]He was referring to the Sovereign Grace Union which was at this time under hyper-Calvinistic leadership and, as a result, exercising very little influence.

Everybody wants blessing, of course; yes, but the peculiar mark of the child is that he is interested in the Person, he wants his Father, he wants to know his Father. He is more interested in the Giver than in the gift, in the Blesser than the blessing. He begins to know something of a hunger and thirst for God himself; as the Psalmist puts it, his soul thirsteth for the living God . . .

Seek not an experience but seek Him, seek to know Him, seek to realize His presence, seek to love Him and give yourself entirely to Him. If *He* is at the centre you will be safe, but if you are simply seeking for experience, if you are simply seeking for thrills, if you are simply seeking for excitement, well then, you are opening the door to the counterfeit and probably you will receive it.

The series of lectures on Biblical Doctrines closed with a lengthy treatment of unfulfilled prophecy which caused considerable excitement and stir. For many years the dispensational form of premillennial prophetic belief had been almost universal among evangelicals and was treated as virtually a cardinal point of orthodoxy. ML-J's demolition of dispensationalism was so thorough that many were simply stunned. The prophetic theory of the Scofield Bible lost its advocates literally by the hundreds.[1]

It was inevitable that younger men, coming to the doctrines of grace at this period, needed a good deal of guidance from ML-J and he was to give much time to this. One of these men, Raymond Johnston, who was working eagerly for the spread of a more biblical theology in the IVF, was frequently in touch. In a letter of January 6, 1953 Johnston reported to ML-J both the interest and the difficulties which he was encountering in the Graduates Fellowship of the IVF. In particular, he was finding the Keswick view of sanctification to be a very sensitive issue. (J. C. Ryle's *Holiness*,[2] recognized as taking an opposing view, had not been well reviewed in the *Christian Graduate*, the GF magazine). Johnston told ML-J that following an

[1]On a smaller scale this had also happened earlier when prophecy was discussed at the Westminster Fraternal. Edwin King recalls, 'A good proportion of the men realised that they had held to a doctrine without knowing why, and they changed their position'. One well-known Baptist was, however, heard protesting, 'I am not going to lose my millennium for the sake of a 2/6 book' (the reference being to *The Momentous Event* by W. J. Grier which was widely sold at Westminster Chapel).
[2]At the prompting of ML-J, who wrote a Foreword, James Clarke had reprinted this long-out-of-print classic in 1952. It has subsequently gone through many further reprintings on both sides of the Atlantic.

irenical discussion with the chairman of the Graduates Fellowship,[1] he was sending a further comment on Ryle to the GF magazine.[2] But, though convinced doctrinally of the older view of sanctification, Johnston went on:

One thing, however, I do find rather puzzling. It seems undeniable that through the Keswick and Ruanda types of holiness teaching, whatever else we may say about them,

    1. The cross of Christ, interpreted biblically, is most certainly uplifted.

    2. Large numbers of Christians *do* enter into a richer Christian life, with a renewed awareness of the sinfulness of sin and of the promises of God.

    In spite of the numerous failures, I feel that this points to the fact that these movements are not simply destructive, nor merely the originators of certain purely psychological transformations. I should be interested to hear what is your view of such cases on some future occasion.

In the course of a reply on January 17, 1953, ML-J wrote:

The republication of Ryle's *Holiness* seems to have accomplished even more than I had anticipated.

    I feel that Mr Packer and yourself are doing most important work which may well have a great influence in the future. But you must both learn to 'walk circumspectly'. I mean by this that there is a danger of their dismissing your teaching because of the manner in which it is presented. We must be patient and teach these people in a constructive manner. I write as one who has found it very difficult himself to learn this lesson, but as the years pass I have come to see more and more that the difficulty on the other side is really due to ignorance. We must keep on, and I think we shall find that the really striking change which has already taken place with regard to the views on prophecy will take place also with regard to this other matter.

    With regard to the difficulty about explaining the benefits that Keswick and Ruanda seem to give, there are two answers at least.

[1]The Chairman, Norman Anderson, was at this time of the opinion that there was only a difference of emphasis between supporters of the Keswick view of 'the victorious life' and 'the Lloyd-Jonesites'. This opinion he was candidly later to revise as he came to understand 'the teaching of Dr Martyn Lloyd-Jones, that it is God's fixed purpose that *every* Christian should be "conformed to the image of his Son . . ."'. See *An Adopted Son*, The Story of My Life, Norman Anderson, IVP, 1985, pp. 129–30.
[2]It was published in the *Christian Graduate*, March, 1953, p. 21.

1. Heresy is often right on many main essentials but goes wrong on just one point. In modern terms this is illustrated often in Pentecostal circles with regard to their doctrine of the Holy Spirit, tongues, healing, etc. While they are absolutely right and orthodox on all essentials and people have real blessing through them.

2. The argument from results and benefits is most dangerous. All the cults really thrive on this. I would also query very much whether Keswick really does give a true awareness of sin. I think it is at this point it really fails most of all.

You really must come back to London so that we can talk about these things instead of writing about them.

While the *Christian Graduate* was at this time printing a number of items favourable to the older beliefs, there were limits. A forceful review by Packer of the commentary of William Kelly, a Brethren writer, on Acts was considered too controversial to be published. But the stir which this review caused privately was as nothing compared with what was to follow. In a letter to ML-J of June 18, 1955, F. F. Bruce, the editor of *The Evangelical Quarterly*, referred to a forthcoming issue:

The July E. Q. has three articles on sanctification – all highly 'Reformed'. I expect some criticism from Keswick supporters, especially because of one of the articles, by Jim Packer, on 'Keswick and the Reformed Doctrine of Sanctification'.

Packer, with a curacy at Birmingham behind him and his doctoral study of Richard Baxter completed, was now a lecturer at Tyndale Hall, Bristol. Bruce underestimated the likely reaction to his fourteen-page article on Keswick. Readers of the *Quarterly* in England, long accustomed to regard Keswick as the citadel of evangelical orthodoxy, now learned that 'contrasted with the historic Reformed teaching . . . Keswick offers a salvation which, far from being "so great", is in reality attenuated and impoverished; that its teaching rests on a theological axiom which is false to Scripture and dishonouring to God', The Keswick message was Pelagian and delusive. 'After all,' Packer concluded, 'Pelagianism is the natural heresy of zealous Christians who are not interested in theology.'[1]

[1] For a later appraisal of Keswick teaching see the same writer's *Keep in Step with the Spirit*, 1984, pp. 145–163.

This was a bombshell and ML-J was inevitably implicated. He was, after all, chairman of the committee supervising the *Quarterly* and his name occurred in the first footnote in Packer's article.[1] As we shall see, more forceful words and strong reactions lay ahead.

In this same period the awakening among students to a clearer understanding of the grace of God was proceeding in Wales as well as in England. For two more consecutive years after the first Welsh IVF Conference in 1949 'Dr Martyn' remained the main speaker. In 1950 the second Conference was held in the Easter vacation at Cilgwn Conference Centre, Newcastle Emlyn and the subject given to him was 'The Doctrine of the Holy Spirit'. In these addresses he carried forward what he had given the students the previous year on man's state in sin. For a number present the knowledge that conversion begins, not with man's decision to repent and believe, but with the power of God in the imparting of a new nature, was a shock. Some questioned whether they were converted at all. Others were upset and disturbed. One future minister's wife, Eluned Rees, came close to breaking off her engagement to John B. E. Thomas, who was a student at the Theological College in Aberystwyth, when she discovered that he believed this teaching. She was one of the many to whom ML-J gave help in private. Wynford Davies recalls the conference as 'a time of real assurance' when many who had believed in Christ came to see how their conversion was due to the effectual work of the Spirit of God.

The third IVF Welsh Conference met in July 1951 at Pantyfedwen, Borth, and Dr Lloyd-Jones fulfilled a request that he should give three addresses on 'The Sovereignty of God'. That he agreed to do so is an indication of his belief that there was an unusual openness to the truth among these young people. As this subject was so crucial to the whole change of viewpoint now beginning among a younger generation, we must give a brief summary of what he said.

The first address, on Tuesday, July 24, was almost wholly taken up with the definition of divine sovereignty and with reasons why an understanding of the doctrine is so important. The sovereignty

[1]Principal Maclean had brought him on to the committee running the *Evangelical Quarterly* and his name had first appeared as an Associate Editor in 1942. He had succeeded Duncan Blair as chairman. Shortly after this, however, the *Quarterly* passed into new ownership and by 1956 ML-J's name had disappeared from its covers.

of God means that all that exists and happens does so because He wills it. Sovereignty is not to be considered as an attribute of God – in the sense of being a quality which exists in God (such as omnipotence and omniscience) – rather it is the result of His attributes. He acts sovereignly because of who and what He is, *God is God*. To assert divine sovereignty is to assert the supremacy of God.

By way of introduction, he then proceeded to the question, 'Why do we hear so little of this doctrine today? Why are sermons or articles on the subject so rare?' He believed that there were two main reasons:

First: *All* doctrine is at a discount today, both outside and inside the church. This doctrine particularly is disliked because of its implications to man. In his pride he has no wish to hear that God 'sitteth upon the circle of the earth, and the inhabitants thereof are as grasshoppers' (Isa 40:22). Therefore, men represent this truth as unfair and unjust.

Second: Human philosophy militates against this doctrine. Men start with their own ideas and thoughts and do not like the sovereignty of God. But the truth is that only as God graciously reveals himself can He be known: 'Canst thou by searching find out God?' (Job 11:7); 'The world by wisdom knew not God' (1 Cor 1:21). Philosophy is the greatest enemy of Christian truth.

He then proceeded to ask further, 'Why is divine sovereignty heard so little even among *evangelicals*?'. The answer, he believed, was that in their anxiety to present salvation in terms of the person and work of Christ, evangelicals had become unbalanced and tended to forget God the Father. There was a danger of 'Jesusology'. The worship of God as three Persons must always be remembered. In particular, the emphasis, 'I believe in God the Father almighty, Maker of heaven and earth', needed to be restored – not simply God the Saviour, but before that, God the Creator. He pointed out that modern hymns and choruses had encouraged the tendency which he criticized, a tendency which had reached a point at which evangelicals would rather have talks on 'Personal Work' than on the character of God.

Proceeding to the assertion that 'Nothing is more needed than this doctrine', the remainder of the first address was taken up with four reasons why this was his conviction:

1. There is no answer to the problem of history, and no explanation of the state of world affairs, apart from the sovereignty of God. With

[239]

illustrations from contemporary philosophers he demonstrated that the only alternatives are to believe that all is accident and chance or that all is in the hands of God.

2. The doctrine of God's sovereignty is necessary for the church. It will rid Christian people of the disease of pessimism as they face the future. For lack of this truth many Christians are depressed as they talk of Communism, materialism and of all the troubles and dangers of the age. Further, ignorance of the doctrine leads Christians to the adoption of certain methods of evangelism which are dangerous and unscriptural. If you feel the church is in your hands then you must do certain things to ensure its success. The main and chief offspring of a false doctrine of God is Arminianism and, worse, Pelagianism. The first need of the Church is true theology and this must govern preaching.

3. An understanding of divine sovereignty is necessary for the true living of the Christian life. The type of Christian living popular among evangelicals was, he believed, a major problem. The 'life' that was being presented was not one of 'godliness' (characteristic of the older type of evangelical Christian) but it was a life that was superficial and glib, defective in feeling and thought, lacking in virility and stability. A flabby generation of Christians had arisen because a sense of divine sovereignty had been lost. It was not so in the biblical accounts of Christians, nor had it been so at the Reformation and in subsequent times of revival. Instead of aiming to be godly and God-fearing, evangelicals were now so keen to have peace and joy. They had forgotten that the purpose of salvation is not, in the first place, to give men certain things or certain experiences, but to put them in a right relationship to God himself. In order to a recovery of godliness and strength in Christians there must first be a putting aside of subjectivism and a return to the knowledge of the sovereign God.[1]

4. All other doctrines derive from this. You can have no doctrine if this is not right. The sovereignty of God is the foundation doctrine of all Protestant and Reformed theology. If this is not understood then neither will the doctrines of justification, sanctification and glorification be understood aright.

He concluded this first address with personal counsel on how they needed to approach this truth. It should not be from prejudice or from the basis of being a 'Calvinist' or a 'non-Calvinist'. Nor should they *start* with questions on man's free will:

It will come up, inevitably, but you cannot start with *man* when you are

[1]Further on this, see *Romans, vol. 1, pp. 363–4.*

thinking about God. How common that is among Christians, even evangelicals. The approach must be to start with the Bible. Read the Bible concerning who and what God is, and only then take up the difficulties. You may not be able to answer ultimate questions of free will, but take what God shows you and leave the rest to Him. God has the answer, 'Secret things belong unto the Lord our God' (Deut 29:29). Habakkuk says 'the just shall live by faith' and faith sometimes means our being content not to know. The desire to know may be sheer intellectual pride. There are antinomies in the Christian faith so that the Christian must say two things at the same time – God is sovereign, man is responsible.

Above all we must remember we are standing on holy ground. Let us be little children and humble before Him (Matt 11:25).

In his second address ML-J proceeded to a lengthy exposition of the testimony of Scripture concerning divine sovereignty. All these addresses, it should be said, can hardly have been less than an hour's duration in their delivery. He started with the sovereignty of God in creation. In His self-sufficiency and self-existence God created all things because He chose to do so; nothing existed to persuade Him to do so. He was unaided and unadvised . . . Nothing in nature happens outside the control of God. ML-J then went on to divine sovereignty in the Fall and sin of man, with all the world's resultant disorder, disharmony, strife and bloodshed. 'Why God allowed the Fall and entry of sin to the world, why He permitted angels of light to rebel, I do not know. I do not understand. The mind of God is so great and eternal that I cannot understand (even if there were no sin in me, which there is). But by permitting it, and then doing what He has done, the manifestation of His sovereignty is the greater.'

There followed an extended treatment of many passages in Old and New Testament history – all showing that 'the Lord reigneth' (Psa 93), and that He acts against all mighty powers which oppose Him, manifesting His sovereignty both in the appointment of all times and seasons as well as in the details of individual lives. The beginning and the end are all determined by God. After showing from the books of Esther, Isaiah, Judges and Psalms that what is called 'secular' history is controlled by God – even sin and the devil himself – he began, in a general way, to deal with the sovereignty of God in the new creation, beginning with Abel, Abraham and Jacob, and proceeding to the manner of the gospel's first coming to Europe (Acts 16).

With his time more than exhausted, be broke off from this
marshalling of scriptural evidence, and pointed to the same lesson in
the history of the post-New Testament church, and in her revivals at
times when God had permitted her life to become almost dead. 'God
lets the church become moribund. The sceptics and scoffers say,
"Where is your God?". Then revival comes. I defy you to say that it
is anything but the sovereignty of God. In the last century men
worshipped preachers, so God withdrew them and you get the
position we have today.'

In the light of such truth, he concluded, it is not only sad but sinful
for the Christian to feel despondent. 'This is the victory that
overcometh the world, even our faith' (1 Jn 5:5).

On the afternoon of the next day – Thursday, July 26, and before
his final address which was at 8 p.m. – the whole Conference went in
two crowded coaches to Llangeitho, the scene of the ministry of
Daniel Rowland. Here ML-J led all the young people in a tour of
places connected with Rowland: first to the old parish church, scene
of Rowland's ministry before his ejection from the Church of
England and where his Bible was still to be found; then to the natural
amphitheatre where the great open-air communion services were
held; and finally to the Calvinistic Methodist Chapel, where
Rowland had continued his ministry (and where the Doctor himself
had attended as a boy). Here everyone sat down and heard ML-J give
an impromptu address on the beginning of the eighteenth century
revival in Wales and on Rowland's subsequent 50 years of ministry
in Llangeitho. The setting and the message of Llangeitho's history,
following as they did upon the expositions already given at Borth,
made the afternoon one of the most valued events of a lifetime for
many who were there. Geraint Fielder says, 'A lot of young minds
and hearts were opened that day to the value and meaning of church
history', and Wynford Davies writes:

It was a most moving experience and again one had the sense that the
people were seeing with new and clearer vision; that was one thing that
he gave to us, I think. There was always that marvellous balance
between his strong doctrinal understanding and yet his passionate
biblical evangelism.

In Dr Lloyd-Jones' third address that evening, as he came to
the question, How do people become citizens of the kingdom of

God? he gave a serious warning against approaching it in a spirit which genders heat and dispute. The question can only be approached aright in a higher spirit. He then proceeded to the truth that every part of salvation is all of grace and that the sovereign work of God in salvation is in order to the manifestation of His own glory. In the first instance, he affirmed, the whole plan of salvation demonstrates the sovereignty of God. Why is the sin of Adam imputed to all his descendants? Why was Adam made the representative of the whole human race? 'I answer, God so decided. It was all in the will of God. Why had Christ to die? It was because it was the Father's will. Why is the righteousness of God imputed to all believers? The only reason is that God decreed that it should be so. There is nothing in the world, nor in man, which dictated this. God alone is the reason.'

Divine sovereignty as it concerns individuals shows that salvation is altogether of grace. The sovereign will of God has chosen certain people to salvation. This is not a truth, he stressed, for unbelievers but for those who are already believers. He then put to them a series of verses 'to study later', namely, Acts 13:48 ('as many as were ordained to eternal life believed'); Romans 11:5–6; 1 Corinthians 1:26–29; Ephesians 1:3–5; 2 Thessalonians 2:13; 2 Timothy 1:9; 1 Peter 1:2; Romans 8:28–29 and 9:1–24; and Matthew 11:25,26.

The meaning of these verses, he argued, is confirmed by other negative statements: no man can save himself, he must be re-born (John 3:3); no man can come to Christ 'except the Father draw him' (John 6:44 and Matt 16:17); no carnal mind can be 'subject to the law of God' (Rom 8:7); no natural man can 'receive the things of the Spirit of God' (1 Cor 2:14), etc. Such negatives complement the affirmatives.

The doctrine of unconditional election is based on:

1. The biblical doctrine of sin. Man is at enmity with God and totally incapable. A defective doctrine of sin today regards sin as an act, but it is more radical than that, it is an attitude and condition. The natural man dislikes the God of Scripture, the cross and the blood of Christ. The modern doctrine of sin is defective. Man is diseased and dead (Eph 2:1) and the most ethical man in the world is in the same position before God as the drunkard or wife-beater.

2. The doctrine of the work of the Holy Spirit. Faith is the gift of God. Men without the Holy Spirit do not recognize the Lord of glory (1 Cor 2:8).

3. The doctrine of regeneration. Some people will persist in discuss-

ing election apart from regeneration, but the truth about regeneration is vital and essential to the whole doctrine of sovereignty. When a man becomes a Christian he is a new creature, he is born again. The natural man is not regenerate. He is an enemy and an alien in relation to God. He cannot see these truths. If he had the capacity to see them he would not need to be regenerate. We must think of man's condition in terms of life and death. We are passive until we are brought from death to life, as many examples of individuals in Scripture show (e.g. Lydia in Acts 16:14).

From this point, to the end of what was another long address, he proceeded to deal with possible objections. 'Does the Scripture not say, "*Whosoever* believeth in Him shall be saved"? and "Him that cometh unto me . . ."' The whole question, he replied, is this: What is it that makes a man believe? What makes a man come to Christ? What determines the 'whosoever'?

The argument is foolish and fatuous that says, 'A believes and is, *therefore*, chosen of God,' and 'B does not believe and is, therefore, not chosen'. Why does A choose to believe? What makes him believe? What makes B not believe? Here are two brothers, they hear the same sermon, the same preacher, in the same chapel, and yet they hear with such different effect. If it is not God who makes the difference, you must say that it is man's constitution, which means that they were born that way. You have thus handed yourself over to the psychologists. They say that some people are made religious and some are not. What can be more unfair than that? No, the difference is the result of His sovereign will.

To the further objection, 'If God is sovereign, and chooses who will be saved, no evangelism is necessary. We can sit back and do no preaching', he replied with another lesson from history. 'Do you not know of Augustine, of Luther, of Calvin, of George Whitefield, of Jonathan Edwards and of Spurgeon? All these men held the sovereignty of God. R. W. Dale, an Arminian, said that those who argue that the doctrine of sovereignty leads to inactivity are talking rubbish. Think of the missionary activity in modern times – of Carey in India, of Thomas Charles and the founding of the Bible Society. Nothing so promotes evangelism as the consciousness that salvation is all of God.'

In his final words he returned again to the manner in which this doctrine affects the believer's life and assurance. Repeating Romans 9:20, he insisted on the necessity of humility:

There are certain questions which we should not ask. To ask them is unbelief and an insult to God. No doctrine so glorifies God and so humbles man as this. Boasting is excluded. The lack of sobriety in Christians today, the readiness to joke and laugh so often, shows that something is wrong somewhere in us. Conventions and other meetings for 'holiness' are held and yet there is less true godliness. Why? I say it is because this doctrine is neglected.

We were lost and would be still but for this. Only divine sovereignty makes salvation certain. 'Therefore, it is of faith, that it might be by grace; to the end the promise might be sure to all the seed' (Rom 4:16). If salvation were not the work of God it would not be sure but uncertain. *Our* wills are uncertain. His will is the sure and the only guarantee. I would not be in His kingdom if left to myself. Weak and unworthy though I am, God has me in His hand and when He begins He never gives up. 'The foundation of God standeth sure, having this seal, the Lord knoweth them that are his' (2 Tim 2:19). Why does He know them? He knows them because He has elected them.

Remember this: you can be a Christian despite defective knowledge and understanding. What is utterly fatal is to fight against it, to reject it. Confess that you do not understand all the statements which you read in Scripture and say, 'Lord, I believe; help thou my unbelief' (Mark 9:24). And with Paul, 'O the depth of the riches both of the wisdom and knowledge of God! how unsearchable are his judgments, and his ways past finding out! . . . For of him, and through him, and to him, are all things: to whom be glory for ever. Amen'.

This address had a profound effect and some had few hours' sleep in the night which followed. Geraint Morgan says:

On the last evening of the conference I came under a tremendous conviction of sin, and joining the queue to see Dr Martyn, I reached him at just after midnight. In that conference I yielded gladly my Arminian views and came to rejoice in the doctrines of sovereign grace. That conference gave me an anchor.

Derek Swann, also a student for the ministry, writes:

When Dr Lloyd-Jones spoke on the sovereignty of God, many of us came to the doctrines of grace for the first time, myself included. He left the doctrine of the sovereignty in salvation to his last talk, having in the previous two talks laid down all the principles that he would apply in the final talk. I accepted everything in the first two talks and had eventually to accept them in the third. I remember it was early in the morning in conversation with Gwyn Walters that the truth of election dawned on me. I was so overcome with the wonder of it all that I had to fight back the tears. For many of us since, election has been an affair of the heart as well as the head.[1]

Gwilym Roberts, yet another future minister of the gospel who was present, and shortly to be the IVF's Welsh travelling secretary, says of the addresses on divine sovereignty:

I cannot express in writing what a tremendous impact these addresses made on the vast majority of those present at the Welsh IVF Conference in 1951. It changed our thinking about God (and, therefore, about man, salvation, evangelism and so on!). We were *prepared* for such things as the Graham Harringay meetings, etc. We saw where they fell short of the scriptural pattern because the Doctor had grounded us so firmly in the truth of God's sovereignty and all its implications.

It may sound surprising that, after such evident influence for good, Dr Lloyd-Jones was emphatic to the student leaders as the Conference ended that he would not be coming the following year. Wynford Davies recalls him saying: 'I think you are fairly launched. The time has come now that you can move ahead on your own'. The main explanation for this decision was undoubtedly a spiritual one. Within a few years ML-J had become an immense, almost determining, influence in the Welsh IVF. A new theological perspective had dawned and, for the first time, the meaning of genuine Calvinistic Methodism had come powerfully into the Welsh University Colleges. Where this would all lead ML-J did not know. What he did recognize was that, as the father figure and friend of many of the young people, an attachment to his person could all too easily become unhealthily central. His remark on the injurious consequences of the cult following of some of the great 19th century preachers was no mere aside. He believed passionately that the elevation of men – whoever they be – in the work of God is a snare and ultimately injurious to spiritual prosperity. Although the students did not see it at the time, it was, in part, the practical application of his Calvinism which made ML-J so decided on withdrawal from future Welsh student conferences. Borth, 1951 – where, in Douglas Johnson's opinion, he gave the best series he had

[1] *Excuse Me, Mr Davies - Hallelujah!* p. 157.

ever heard him give at any student conference – was to be his last IVF conference in Wales. The decision was characteristic of the man. Others might regard him, in Geraint Fielder's phrase, as 'undoubtedly God's man for the situation' but that is certainly not how he thought of himself.

There was, however, another reason for this withdrawal from further direct participation in Welsh IVF work. He still possessed his initial reservations over the development of conferences in Wales which were restricted to students. For, as we have said, separate youth work had never been traditional in the life of the Welsh churches. By the early 1950's a new alignment was emerging in Wales to which he preferred to give his time. South Wales and North Wales (where the Welsh language was strongest) had long been marked by separate interests, even in matters of religion. But the new magazine, Y Cylchgrawn Efengylaidd, begun by Elwyn Davies and others in 1949, had served to draw evangelical Christians together across Wales, and the Welsh IVF conferences had also brought the more distinctly Welsh students of the North (from the revived Evangelical Union at Bangor) into closer touch with those like-minded in the geographically separate Unions of the South. Interests and friendships were thus broadened and the Calvinistic evangelicalism represented by Dr Lloyd-Jones was now the basis for the shared hopes of these young people for the whole Principality. Initially the supporters of the magazine, known as pobl y cylchgrawn ('people of the magazine'), worked side by side with those whose background lay in the IVF, yet, as participation in the IVF was restricted to undergraduates, it was inevitable that another structure was needed to hold them together. Humanly speaking, this came about more by accident than design. The organizers of Y Cylchgrawn Efengylaidd organised a Welsh-speaking holiday conference at Bala in August 1952. It was open to all who wished to come. The response was enough to justify a further conference at Caernarfon in August 1953 which was designated as the conference of Y Mudiad Efengylaidd Cymru (the Evangelical Movement of Wales). At this Caernarfon conference there was a raised attendance as Dr Lloyd-Jones was present to preach three times from John 17. With this new conference now established, he returned to it in August 1955, when it was held in Lôn Swan Chapel, Denbigh, and spoke from Ephesians 1:13 on 'The Ministry of the Holy Spirit in the Life of the Believer'.

Writing to the Secretts of their time at Denbigh, Bethan Lloyd-Jones says: 'There were about eighty at the Conference – the great majority being young evangelicals – quite a number being ministers and getting real results in their churches. We couldn't help feeling it was well worth-while.'

This same year saw major steps in organization. The name first employed in Welsh in 1953, 'the Evangelical Movement of Wales', was formally adopted; the Rev. Elwyn Davies (until 1954 serving as a Welsh Congregational minister) was to divide his time between this work and that of travelling among the Welsh Colleges on behalf of the IVF; and a new magazine, *The Evangelical Magazine of Wales*, now appeared alongside its Welsh counterpart.

Of the young ministers mentioned by Mrs Lloyd-Jones above, the strongest nucleus was centered in South Wales and close to the Rev. I. B. Davies of Neath. Their natural leader was John B. E. Thomas, by this time minister of Dr Lloyd-Jones' former church at Sandfields, Aberavon. ML-J rejoiced at John Thomas' appointment to Sandfields in 1953 and had gone back to his old pulpit to preach at his induction. This group of Presbyterians had approached Dr Lloyd-Jones to ask if he would speak at a Ministers' Conference if they were to organize it. He affirmed that he would, but on one condition: it must not be restricted to Presbyterians. With the general decline of all the denominations in Wales, he was convinced that any new grouping should aim to draw in all evangelicals. With this in view, a Ministers' Conference was held in Barry in 1955, and again at Cilgwyn, Newcastle Emlyn, in 1956. The enthusiasm, vision and earnest doctrinal discussions which marked these early conferences was remarkable. The younger men felt and prayed as though a great revival might be close at hand, while some older men present could scarcely contain their surprise at the new direction which events were taking.

Opposite: The first of the two sides of ML-J's notes of his second sermon on Matthew 5:6, November 19, 1950, in his series on the Sermon on the Mount which began on October 1, 1950. Instead of small sheets (see p. 19 above) he came in 1949 to standardise his notes at this larger size, most of which were still only written in pencil. Although the above (as the notes on p. 19 above) were written in ink, this was not his general practice until 1953.

For the content of this page in printed form see Sermon on the Mount, *vol. 1, pp. 84–7.*

Return again to this beatitude, the drama(?) of the Chr.
Considered it in general last time in terms of the actual
words "righteousness", "hunger & thirst" & being "filled".

But this not enough.
The beatitude with its spiritual training of God most vital &
important. It is the only way of blessing.
But, alas one of the most convicting beatitudes which
we confront ourselves & our position.

① Test of doctrine
This one beatitude shows the double objection of the
tattoo(?) & gospel, yet both included in the one statement.
(a) that gospel is too easy with its free offer of reward
of grace.

(b) that gospel is too difficult & makes things impossible
— its demand for righteousness.
But clearly both go together & people who object to first
can reveal his understanding to actions of righteousness
He cannot one release the power that of God for (b). To
say that it is too easy and to object is to find that we
can do nothing & that we must receive it as a
gift just means that we are not Christian, that all.

② Practical test of our position.
Are we filled? In the case of having no misapprehend-
ing & prejudices. In the case of soreness of work of God
with try to effect
Is the fruit of the Spirit being manifest. Are any
reveal in to etc?
Are we enjoying peace & rest & joy in the Lord?
And all else that is said of the N.T. Christian.
We shall be according to this promise.

If not we are not hungering & thirsting after righteousness
But how can we tell that?
Shown in evidence in biographies of saints.
Read:—

Our coming together in public worship should be a foretaste of heaven . . . Public worship should be a gathering of the first fruits, a sampling of what is to be our lot in heaven.

ML-J
Ephesians, vol. 1, p. 308

We do not cater for any particular age or sex or social group, but at a time like this it is gratifying to be able to report that what impresses most visitors to our services is the high percentage of young people and the quite unusually high percentage of men. It is a high privilege and a great responsibility to be allowed thus to minister week by week to those who will be the leaders in many realms in life in the years that lie ahead.

ML-J
Annual letter to the members of Westminster Chapel,
January 1949

13

Sunday Mornings in the 1950's

From the late 1940's, and for the next two decades, there was such a degree of similarity about the work at Westminster Chapel that any strictly chronological description of successive years is unnecessary. I intend rather, in this chapter, to give some account of what it meant to be there on Sunday mornings in the 1950's.

The keenness with which 11 a.m., the hour of public worship, was awaited each Sunday will ever remain in the memories of those who were there. In a day in which church going was no longer fashionable, a certain sense of expectation could be found in the very streets approaching the Chapel as hundreds converged from all directions. A minority came by car, some on foot and others by bus to Victoria Street. Most travelled from various parts of London by the underground which they left either at Victoria Station or, more usually, at St James' Park where a general exodus from the tube brought a temporary congestion to the two-hundred yards of pavement in Petty France, the road which leads to the Chapel. On a smaller scale the scene was reminiscent of the nineteenth-century Sundays when, on the south bank of the Thames, crowds headed for the Metropolitan Tabernacle and tram conductors could call out that their passengers were going 'Over the water to Charlie.'

A comparatively small number of people met for prayer at the Chapel at 10.15 a.m. Dr Lloyd-Jones himself usually arrived around 10.30 and spent the time remaining before the service in his vestry. He would seldom have more than five minutes on his own. Deacons, and others closer to him, generally took advantage of speaking with him at this time before many others later in the day would seek to do the same. In an emergency he might see a member of the congregation about some pressing problem at this hour but not normally. One invariable caller at the vestry door was the organist. He had received the hymns from ML-J by phone the previous day, but there was now a final check on the tunes. Bethan Lloyd-Jones would also call briefly shortly before the service. At no more than five minutes to the hour of service the deacon on duty at the vestry door would see if the minister was ready and then all the deacons would crowd into the comparatively small room. The purpose of this meeting was for prayer (always led by a deacon) but if anything urgent required attention there could also be some short conversation. On one occasion, I recall, a deacon was in somewhat desperate need of advice on how to handle an unbalanced character who was disturbing, even alarming, some members of the congregation. In an instant the Doctor saw that the deacon was crediting the unfortunate man with a responsibility for his actions which he did not possess and his direction was as complete as it was startling, 'You must treat him like a dog' (i.e. with firmness and authority). There was always one particular feature present in the atmosphere in the vestry immediately before services, namely, the remarkable absence of any sense of tension. When a newcomer joined that circle it was the sense of calmness emanating from the minister which he was most likely to observe first.

Behind the vestry wall, in the church itself, it was different as stewards hurried or pointed people to vacant seats, the front seats on the ground floor always being the last to start filling up. In the pew rack before him a worshipper would find a Bible, a hymn book (*Congregational Praise*[1]) and a brief card. The card gave the times of service and other regular meetings and indicated Dr Lloyd-Jones' willingness to speak with anyone at the conclusion of services. These arrangements varied so little that the same cards lasted many months. There were no printed service sheets – in part for the very good reason that hymns and sermons were never finalized before the preceding day.

For visitors two things, particularly, were usually striking about the gathering congregation. The first was its diversity and cosmopolitan character. There were parents and children, young people and students (whose appearance denoted many different countries of origin), professional people and others whose appearance gave no hint of their occupation. While the percentage of older people was probably lower than in a normal city congregation, the ratio of men to women was definitely higher. In a sense there were two congregations present, the actual church members, and probably a

[1]First published in 1951, it was a considerable improvement on the *Congregational Hymnary* of 1916 and restored a number of older hymns.

larger number – including the sizeable student body – who for one reason or another never joined the church. A considerable proportion consequently did not know one another, and there would have been many surprises if they had. These were days when strangers did not commonly greet one another in church, and often one could only wonder at the identity of neighbours. Perhaps that middle-aged single lady, for instance, was a hairdresser, a member of hotel staff, a keeper of the Queen's linen at Buckingham Palace, a missionary on furlough, a hospital sister, a buyer at one of the large department stores or even a land-owner in town for the day. Of all the professions the medical was probably the most largely represented. Its personnel ranged from student nurses to a few of London's top surgeons and physicians, with a large group of medical students from Barts, Guy's, the London and other famous teaching hospitals.

But to conclude from this diversity that the congregation lacked all homogeneity and was only a mass of individuals would be entirely wrong. Along with the diversity there was a second feature equally observable. It was the unity of spirit and purpose, already mentioned, which was becoming apparent even as people approached the building. While the numbers were impressive, much more so was the evident spirit of eager anticipation which gave unity to the whole gathered assembly. Yet this animation bore no resemblance to the bustle and excitement of people awaiting a concert performance. The spirit was subdued as the organist began a quiet voluntary some ten minutes before 11 a.m. There was, therefore, no sudden hush as the deacons first emerged from behind the rostrum to take their places in the congregation and Dr Lloyd-Jones, having climbed the stairs at the back of the rostrum, crossed the six or seven paces to the pulpit desk where he would immediately slide the large and heavy pulpit Bible from its central position to the left in order to give himself room to lean his forearms on the desk as he bowed his head momentarily in prayer. In black gown (without hood) he looked small and slight in the large auditorium. A note from the organ then brought the whole congregation to its feet for the unannounced singing of the doxology, 'Praise God from whom all blessings flow'. This was immediately followed by the minister's opening words, 'Let us pray', as the people resumed their seats. It was a short prayer, addressed to God the Father, usually begun with thanksgiving and always concluded with the repetition of the Lord's Prayer. It led naturally into the first hymn – a burst of song which late-comers could readily hear as they neared the building. Undoubtedly ML-J had his own favourite opening hymns, none more so than Isaac Watts',

> How pleased and blest was I
> To hear the people cry
> Come, let us seek our God to-day!

The opening hymns were strong in their objective statements about God. To avoid a too-frequent use of any great hymn he kept a careful record of each Sunday's hymn numbers, minutely written on a sheet of paper which he could see at a glance. To the choice of hymns he always gave much care and they were chosen with reference to the unity of the service as a whole. The theme of the first hymn was one of praise, or very occasionally, of invocation (James Montgomery's, 'Command Thy blessing from above, O God, on all assembled here,' being another favourite). There was nothing in the way of a conductor. In so far as anyone led the singing he did. Not by voice (for his singing of the bass part could be heard only over the loudspeaker relaying the service to the vestibules and the rear halls) but by example. During all worship his whole being was a study of concentration; he never used times of singing as an opportunity to look round the congregation or to glance at notes. Unlike one or two of his predecessors, if there were celebrities in the congregation he neither knew nor cared. He was there to worship God and never raised his eyes from his hymn book. The idea that the minister should smile benignly at the people, or make them 'feel welcome' with some words of social greeting, was foreign to his whole conception of the grandeur of Christian worship. If the church were the minister's home and the people *his* guests, then, he argued, it would be permissible to say, 'Good morning folks; nice to see you, how good of you to come', but he regarded that whole approach as wrong: 'It is not our service; the people do not come there to see us or please us . . . They, and we, are there to worship God, and to meet with God. A minister in a church is not like a man inviting people into his home; he is not in charge here. He is just a servant himself.'[1]

The first hymn was followed by the reading of Scripture, usually from only one passage which was announced clearly and repeated. He read (always himself) at moderate speed, in ordinary tones and with

[1]*Preaching*, p. 263.

nothing resembling an affected elocution. But inflection of voice always drew sufficient attention to the sense of the words. One person who belonged to the Chapel for nearly twenty years during his ministry was later to say: 'I have never heard anyone else whose reading has been so blessed of God. At times, passages of Scripture which I had never really understood sprang to life and became full of meaning just as he was reading.'

The second singing was invariably part of a metrical psalm and as there are only sixteen contained in *Congregational Praise* most of them were used more frequently than many hymns. From such words as,

> The Lord doth reign, and clothed is He
> With majesty most bright   (Psa 93:1)

or,

> How lovely is Thy dwelling-place   (Psa 84:1)

the congregation moved on into what many regarded as the high point of the early part of the service, the main prayer. While only one voice was heard, it was unmistakably clear that Dr Lloyd-Jones was praying on the understanding that true public prayer is corporate prayer. He used no singular pronouns, but always the plural, 'We come into Thy holy presence and *we* come, O Lord, to worship Thee . . .'. Yet there was not a phrase nor a sentence which each Christian could not regard as his own. The worshipper often forgot the large congregation around him as prayer thus became individual as well as a corporate dealing with God. In Dr Lloyd-Jones' actual petitions there was often the blending of two seemingly diverse elements. There was both consciousness of sin *and* a thankfulness for what God is. Not one, or the other, but both. If the minister appeared to speak boldly with God it was clear that the most discouraged Christian in the congregation, or even one who was no Christian at all, might do the same, provided he came in the same way:

We come in the Name of Thy dear Son. We recognize we have nothing else to plead, we have nothing which we can present before Thee . . . O God, we see how poor and sinful and vile we all have become as the result of man's original disobedience and sin and fall, and our own misdeeds and transgressions. We have sinned against Thee. We have followed our own wills, been proud of ourselves, of what we are, not even recognizing that what we are was the result of Thy gracious gifts to us . . . So we come and we plead only the Name and the Blood of Thy dear Son, and we do thank Thee that in Him we know that we have this access . . .

It was not unknown for self-satisfied listeners to meet with conviction when hearing such prayer, while those who came with heavy and burdened spirits were often wonderfully uplifted. Not infrequently Christians spoke of being so conscious of God's help to them personally during the prayer that they could have been content to go home at its conclusion.

One reason that Dr Lloyd-Jones was against liturgies in prayer was that he believed that true prayer is *given* by God and, therefore, one must always be free to be led by Him at the actual moment of praying. In the words of A. M. Toplady (often sung at the Chapel) God is the 'Inspirer and hearer of prayer'[1]. ML-J did not prepare prayers (though he sought to prepare himself) and no two prayers were ever identical in thought and expression, notwithstanding general similarities.[2] In length the main prayer varied between ten and fifteen minutes. We never heard it commended for 'eloquence' or criticized either for verging on preaching or for being too long. It was prayer which left the impression that there is such a thing as first- hand communion with God.

Dr Lloyd-Jones' language in prayer was natural and unadorned. Although he had such large command of both Scripture and hymnology, he did not regard quotation as appropriate in prayer. If occasionally a quotation was introduced, it was used as a plea to God or as a profession of trust in Him. He might, for instance, when confessing the magnitude of our needs, repeat with much feeling the words of Oswald Allen,

> When all things seem against us.
> To drive us to despair,
> We know one gate is open,
> One ear will hear our prayer.[3]

[1] Verse two of 'A Sovereign protector I have'.
[2] 'You cannot pray to order . . . I have found nothing more important than to learn how to get oneself into that frame and condition in which one can pray.' *Preaching*, p. 170.
[3] From the hymn 'To-day Thy mercy calls us', 684 in the revised edition of *The Church Hymnary* (the hymn book to which ML-J was accustomed in Wales).

As much as half of the long prayer was generally taken up with intercession, in which there was usually a similar pattern in the order of the petitions and a greater identity of phraseology than at other times. 'The aged and infirm', those on 'beds of pain' and other groups were represented by the same terms week by week. Yet in the matter of intercession Dr Lloyd-Jones also believed in the possibility of the direct guidance of the Holy Spirit. One remarkable example of this concerned a Welshman who, having professed Christ, had later ruined his life and family. He ended up destitute in London, deserted by the woman who had taken the place of his wife, until finally a Sunday came when he solemnly decided to end his life by throwing himself into the Thames from Westminster Bridge. Such was his feeling of utter hopelessness. But when he arrived at the bridge the striking of 'Big Ben' suddenly reminded him that it was the hour of public worship and there and then he decided to go and hear Dr Lloyd-Jones again before he ended his life. Six minutes' walk took him to the Chapel which he reached as ML-J was leading the congregation in prayer. The very first words which he heard as he walked up the stairs and was about to enter the gallery were, 'God have mercy upon the backslider'. It was not a customary petition in that prayer. The man was restored in that very service and lived a consistent Christian life for a number of years before a glorious and triumphant death.[1] One testimony to Dr Lloyd-Jones' pulpit prayer comes from Emmi Muller, a German, who as a young Christian came to study at the London Bible College in the early 1950's. With the Second World War still a vivid memory, Muller was to encounter much prejudice and coldness even from fellow Christians. Still feeling very much a foreigner and an outsider, she came to Westminster Chapel and has described how it became a spiritual home:

In the beginning there was of course the language problem. For someone not yet fluent in English the sermons as well as the prayers were rather long. But this very difficulty made me all the more aware of the spiritual atmosphere in the services. The spirit of worship and prayer, the eagerness on the part of the congregation to listen, to receive God's message through His servant were a great blessing. I was very much aware of the Lord's presence in the services. What in the beginning was trying, in the long run proved to be a special blessing to me personally,

[1] This incident actually occurred in an evening service, *Preaching*, p. 302–3.

namely the pastoral prayer, which lasted longer than in most churches. As a foreigner the Doctor's pastoral prayer in particular made me feel included and truly part of the congregation because it usually embraced more than just Westminster Chapel and Britain.

The main prayer was followed by the only pause in the service. First the Church Secretary, Arthur E. Marsh, still in the frock coat and Edwardian dress of his pre-1914 years at Westminster, mounted the rostrum and, after clearing his throat, as he had done for fifty years, gave the barest minimum of announcements.[1] These all related to the next services of public worship at Westminster. No other notices were ever read, except for the intimation of the annual appeal for aid to various evangelical and missionary agencies. Notices of any special kind, or invitation to the communion (which followed the main service twice a month – once in the morning and once in the evening) would be given by the minister himself. The collection was then taken up by deacons and brought forward to the communion table, Dr Lloyd-Jones employing these few minutes to glance over his sermon notes. After a brief offertory prayer, when the deacons who had brought the plates forward stood at the communion table on the lower rostrum, the third hymn followed, its theme looking forward to the sermon either by invocation of the aid of God or by the relation of its subject matter to the subject about to be introduced. At close on thirty-five minutes after the commencement of the service Dr Lloyd-Jones would begin to preach. No title was announced beforehand and the opening sentence had liturgical uniformity, 'The words to which I should like to draw your attention this morning are to be found in . . .' and there followed a clear and emphatic announcement of the text upon which he intended to preach.

Through the Sunday mornings of the 1950's Dr Lloyd-Jones preached in consecutive series. The only exceptions to this procedure were the holiday periods when a number of regular hearers were likely to be away. On Sunday morning, June 4, 1950 he preached the 67th and last sermon on 1 John. A short series of six sermons on Habakkuk then followed and was concluded by the time of his summer break. On October 1, 1950 he began the Sermon on the Mount (Matthew 5–7) and this was to continue, apart from the

---

[1] Marsh was 'Secretary of Westminster Chapel' from 1907 to 1961, dying at an unstated age the following year (*WR*, Dec., 1962, p. 183).

breaks mentioned above, until April 6, 1952. The next passage for exposition was John 17 (May 4, 1952–July 19, 1953). Eleven sermons on Psalm 73 occupied the autumn Sunday mornings of 1953, concluding before the Christmas break.

He had intended following his series on Psalm 73 with a major series on Ephesians but before that series was finished something else had happened. As he recalled many years later:

I got up one morning, washed and was still half-dressed when quite suddenly that verse came to me, 'Why art thou cast down, O my soul? and why art thou disquieted in me? Hope thou in God . . .' There and then some seven or eight skeletons of sermons came to my mind on the subject of Spiritual Depression. I rushed down to my study to put them on paper and so powerful was the impression that I knew I had to do this series before Ephesians. I am not surprised it was so used. It was a pure gift.

There are a number of significant things to be noted in these words. This was not his usual method of obtaining sermons, which consisted of hard and sustained work. He was constantly putting down thoughts and outlines on scraps of paper or on backs of envelopes, some of which, in due course, he prepared more fully in larger outlines from which he preached.[1] He did not expect what happened in 1953 to happen every year. But experiences of this kind deepened his conviction that God does deal directly with men and that no preacher should tie himself to a fixed schedule. Freedom to be directed by the Spirit is vital to preaching. He held this principle in relation to the preparation of sermons and, still more, to their delivery. As he saw it, the pulpit message which contains precisely what the speaker has prepared and no more, with nothing extemporaneous, is a message which falls seriously short of biblical *preaching*.[2] This is the conviction which lies behind words which are

[1] On the importance of building up a stock of skeletons see *Preaching*, pp. 173–74.
[2] Further on this point see below p. 662. If any should deem his principle to be verging on the 'fanatical' let it be remembered that it was a Presbyterian Professor of Theology, writing on 'Extemporaneous Preaching', who said: 'Whenever any great movement has been produced, either in Church or State, it has commonly taken its rise, so far as human agency is concerned, from the unwritten words of some man of sound knowledge and thorough discipline, impelled to speak by strong feeling in his heart.' W. G. T. Shedd, *Homiletics and Pastoral Theology*, 1874, p. 212.

too easily missed in the Preface to his second volume of Studies in the *Sermon on the Mount*:

The fact that there are thirty sermons in this volume, as in the previous one, is quite accidental and not planned nor contrived. It has never been my custom to divide up a portion of Scripture into a number of parts and then to issue a syllabus announcing what will be done each week. That seems to me to limit the freedom of the act of preaching, quite apart from the fact that in actual practice I sometimes find that I succeed in doing only about half of what I had planned and purposed. In other words expository preaching must always be *preaching* and not merely mechanical exposition.

It was never my intention to preach sixty sermons on the Sermon on the Mount; I just went on from Sunday to Sunday and this turned out to be the result.

ML-J's series on 'Spiritual Depression' or 'A Miserable Christian' (these general titles, in this instance, were his own) began on January 10, 1954 and ran to July 18, 1954. The following day he wrote to Elizabeth and Fred (Catherwood) who had been married earlier that year:

Yesterday morning I finished off the series on Spiritual Depression by preaching the 27th sermon on that theme,[1] the text being Revelation 3:20, one of the most beautiful texts in Scripture but also one of the most frequently misapplied . . . At night I preached my 12th and last sermon on Isaiah 40, dealing with verses 29–31 . . . I must say that I have greatly enjoyed preaching both these series and many have said to me that they have received unusual blessing through them. What fools we are and

[1]A difference exists between the 27 preached sermons and the 21 ultimately published under the same title. The book contains only 16 of the original sermons, plus five others (preached at different times). One reason for this difference is that of the 11 original sermons which were unpublished, six were from Ephesians and three from Romans chapter 6 covering material which he had dealt with more fully in his expositions of those Epistles by the time that *Spiritual Depression* was published in 1965. The three sermons of the original series on Romans 6 (preached April 11, 18 and May 2, 1954) contained his new understanding of verses 1–14 of that chapter. Because he had previously been conscious that he was confused over the meaning of those verses, he had put off any thought of a series on Romans. The help he received towards the right interpretation of Romans 6 thus contributed to his decision to take up that Epistle on Friday evenings. With the conclusion of his Friday series on 'Biblical Doctrines' he began his expositions of Romans in October 1955. See below p. 639.

how slow to believe and to realise actively such glorious truths. Fancy forgetting our Lord!

With the Spiritual Depression series concluded he reverted to his former plan and, with the students reassembled in London for a new academic year, preached on the first verse of Ephesians chapter one on October 10, 1954. No fewer than 260 further sermons on Ephesians were to follow until the major Sunday morning expository series of his ministry finally concluded on July 1, 1962.

In the 1950's ML-J was virtually alone in England in engaging in what he meant by 'expository preaching'. For preaching to qualify for that designation it was not enough, in his view, that its content be biblical; addresses which concentrated upon word-studies, or which gave running commentary and analyses of whole chapters, might be termed 'biblical', but that is not the same as exposition. To expound is not simply to give the correct grammatical sense of a verse or passage, it is rather to set out the principles or doctrines which the words are intended to convey. True expository preaching is, therefore, *doctrinal* preaching, it is preaching which addresses specific truths from God to man.[1] The expository preacher is not one who 'shares his studies' with others, he is an ambassador and a messenger, authoritatively delivering the Word of God to men. Such preaching presents a text, then, with that text in sight throughout, there is deduction, argument and appeal, the whole making up a message which bears the authority of Scripture itself. Given such a conception, a faithful discharge of the teaching office necessitates the preacher being able to say, with Paul, 'We are not as many, which corrupt the word of God: but as of sincerity, but as of God, in the sight of God speak we in Christ' (2 Cor 2:17). If this involves a staggeringly high view of preaching, it was nothing more, Dr Lloyd-Jones believed, than is required of the ministerial office.

An example of his method will clarify the meaning. In his series on Ephesians, after treating the words of Ephesians 2:3 as they relate to human sinfulness, he went on, in a separate sermon, to take up the final words of that verse, 'and were by nature the children of wrath, even as others'. By way of introduction to the main theme of the wrath of God, he had three points to engage the minds of his hearers

[1]'Biblical study is of very little value if it ends in and of itself and is mainly a matter of the meaning of words. The purpose of studying the Scripture is to arrive at doctrine.' *Faith on Trial*, p. 88.

and to bring them into his train of thought. Proposing the question, Why should this subject be examined? he answered: (1) it is a part of Scripture; (2) it is a question of fact; (3) we never understand the love of God until we understand this doctrine. The attention arrested, he then proceeded to the actual teaching under two main divisions: first, all who are born into this world are under the wrath of God; second, we are all in this condition by nature. Filled out with reference to other Scripture, and brought home with application, this would have occupied some forty minutes, or more, in delivery. As a sermon it was a unity in itself, yet it dovetailed into the message of the following week on the next words, 'But God . . .'.

Such preaching demanded thought on the part of the hearer, but never thought which was abstruse or technical. And despite the intellectual content, it was not preaching from which the more intelligent present could gain the most. He pitched the level of his argument and paced its development in a way which even the many children present could generally follow. While some critics thought him guilty of repetition, he regarded repetition as essential to good preaching. He knew it was not enough merely to state a truth, one needed to 'walk around in it'. As with all great preaching the message was both profound and simple.

To say this, however, is to leave unsaid the most important part of what he was in the pulpit. In his view, one could possess the natural ability and the understanding of the truth necessary to follow the expository method, and yet still never be a preacher at all. The Holy Spirit must be active in true preaching, active not only in owning the truth as it is heard but active in anointing the preacher himself. Only then is his heart as well as his mind rightly engaged and the result is speech attended by liveliness, by unction and by the extemporaneous element already mentioned.

As with prayer, this element cannot be produced to order. It has nothing to do with the emotion affected by an actor to produce an effect (a preacher of that type is 'an abominable imposter'[1]). But it is the Holy Spirit so taking hold of the man with the truth of the message, and with love for God and man, that the messenger himself is lost in sympathy with his message and with his hearers: 'Preaching is theology coming through a man who is on fire. A true understanding and experience of the truth must lead to this.'[2] The only right

[1]*Preaching*, p. 93.   [2]*Ibid*, p. 97.

condition for preaching, he believed, was to 'be so absorbed in what you are doing and in the realisation of the presence of God, and in the glory and the greatness of the truth that you are preaching, that you forget yourself completely'.[1]

There have been periods in history when the anointing of the Spirit upon the preacher has tended to be identified with such things as tones of voice, mannerisms, gestures or even mere volume of sound. Dr Lloyd-Jones was careful to warn against such a confusion between pulpit style and powerful preaching. He knew that liveliness in preaching will not always take the same form; all he stipulated was that the expression of passion in the pulpit should be natural to the individual. In his own case he always began a sermon quietly and calmly, in the tones of an ordinary conversation. The voice usually rose gradually and quickened as the subject was opened until – as the message gripped speaker and hearer alike – his whole body became animated and began to add its own expression and emphasis to the message. It was movement and gesture in such harmony with what was being said that the hearer was scarcely conscious that the two things were not the same. The preacher and the truth became one and to repeat the words first used of William Wilberforce, the slight figure – the 'shrimp' – became 'a colossus'.

To attempt to state this in cold print is to risk a description sounding unnatural – just as the bare statue of Whitefield, depicting him in the full vehemence of preaching, looks scarcely real. Without the crowd of hearers and the truths being expressed, gesture and posture are nothing. But with Dr Lloyd-Jones, as with Whitefield, the manner of delivery and his 'action' became almost a part of the message. Thus in comparing and contrasting two positions – perhaps heaven and hell – he would cross and re-cross from one side of the pulpit desk to the other, his whole body visible and his hands outstretched in alternate directions as though both realities were almost within sight and touch. In extolling the attributes and unapproachable holiness of God his right arm was often extended high and quivering yet the gesture drew no attention to itself. His expression also harmonised with his theme and movements. His face, pale in middle age, would seem to turn ashen white as he spoke of the horror of sin, perhaps crouching slightly behind the desk and drawing his outstretched fingers down both sides of his face as he

[1] *Ibid*, p. 264.

spoke. At other times he nearly danced and the energy of his motion was such that it could be said, as it was once said of Samuel Rutherford, 'Many times I thought he would have flown out of the pulpit'. His voice, never harsh or unnatural, likewise toned with his subject.

When on one occasion an actor was brought by a friend to Westminster Chapel he was amazed at the speaker's action and gesture, exclaiming afterwards that he must have spent many hours before a mirror practising and rehearsing his movements. But when the same man returned the next Sunday he came to a conclusion which surprised him still more, namely that the preacher's gestures were all natural and entirely unstudied. It was perfectly true. So little importance did ML-J attribute to 'action' as such that he gives it only brief reference in his *Preaching and Preachers*.[1]

What has been said above raises the whole question of the relationship of oratory to preaching. Dr Lloyd-Jones repudiated oratory as an end in itself or as a kind of entertainment. He was equally against the deliberate use of oratory to condition or persuade people, condemning nineteenth-century pulpiteers who were 'experts at handling congregations and playing on their emotions'. He also knew that he had a gift of speech of very considerable power. He could describe a scene in such a manner that it virtually came to life. When people heard him sketch the scene of Paul before Felix and Agrippa, or the death of John the Baptist, whose head was brought to Herod 'on a charger', they felt as though they had seen these very things and actually been there. One hearer listening to him depicting the storm on Galilee, and the peril of the disciples in the boat, found himself stretching forwards involuntarily in the pew to lay hold of an oar. On another occasion, when ML-J was demonstrating how the eye is the most sensitive part of the body, and how when anything approaches it the lid shuts, the depiction was so vivid that when he suddenly thrust his finger, in gesture, towards his own eye, people visibly jumped in their seats.

But far from developing this gift, Dr Lloyd-Jones used it with much restraint. In the words of Philip Hughes: 'He was very

[1]'Do not cultivate or practise gestures. Everything that is histrionic should be avoided', p. 264. He would have agreed entirely with Spurgeon: 'The sermon itself is the main thing . . . the sacred anointing upon the preacher, and the divine power applying the truth to the hearer:- these are infinitely more important than any details of manner.' *Lectures to my Students*, Second Series. 1877, p. 96.

1. [Left to right]: *Dr. Campbell Morgan, Bethan Lloyd-Jones, Mrs. Campbell Morgan, M. L.-J. and Ann, Major Blackie.*

2. *In London, late 1930's.*

3. *Speaking for the World Evangelical Alliance at Westminster Chapel, January 5, 1948.*

4. *Platform party, [left to right]: M. L.-J., Dr. J. A. Jagoe, Sir Stafford Cripps, The Dean of St. Paul's, Mr. H. Martyn Gooch.*

5. *The interior of Westminster Chapel during repair of war damage.*

6. *The Evangelical Library and Geoffrey Williams.*

7. *Elizabeth and Ann, on the steps of St. Hilda's College, Oxford, where both girls studied, 1946-49 and 1956-59. Photograph taken around 1948.*

8. *Ann facing her father's bowling in their front garden at Mount Park Crescent.*

9. *The IVF Welsh Conference at Borth, July 23-28, 1951.*

10. *With Paul White* [left] *and Stacey Woods.*

11. *A Conference group at Tyndale House, Cambridge, 1956. The following can be identified in this group: Roger Beckwith, Dorothy Barter-Snow, Clement Connell, Morgan Derham, Philip Hughes, Ernest Kevan, M. L.-J., J. I. Packer, Alan Stibbs, Derek Swann and John Wenham.*

12. *With his eldest grandson, Christopher Catherwood, in front of the statue of Daniel Rowland at Llangeitho in 1957.*

13. *With Bethan, crossing the Atlantic in the closing years of the great Cunarders.*

14. *The family with Bethan's mother, Mrs. Phillips.*

15. *At the supposed site of Paul's imprisonment at Philippi, 1961*
[see page 467].

16. *Mars Hill, Athens, a light-hearted pose!*

17. *Preaching at St. Andrew's Hall, Glasgow, November 14, 1961.*

18. *Part of the congregation of 4,000 at the Kelvin Hall, Glasgow when M. L.-J.
preached, April 22, 1963.*

19. *'Friends of the Evangelical Library' in whom their President often confided
at their annual meetings. Taken in 1956.*

conscious of his gift of eloquence, and even afraid of it, as St Paul shunned excellency of speech, and desired his preaching to be not in persuasive words of human wisdom but in demonstration of the Spirit and of power (1 Cor 2:1–5)'. An example of this is the fact that although he was a master of story telling, he was very spare in his use of illustrations, believing that their frequent use, instead of effecting spiritual good, 'panders to the carnality of the people who are listening'.

At the same time, he knew that no subject was more worthy of true oratory than the Word of God and he believed that the truth needed to be presented in a form which could attract the interest of the non-Christian. Preachers *are* responsible for making people listen. When some heard him they undoubtedly went away impressed only with the outward, and reporters for the religious press were often of this kind. 'For real drama,' wrote one religious columnist, 'nobody can beat the Rev. Martyn Lloyd-Jones at Westminster Chapel, Buckingham Gate. Old fashioned Calvinistic preaching at its best.' Others, however, went away overcome by the message and not with the way in which it had been delivered. God had used the preacher and they felt like Emmi Muller, already quoted above, who says, 'Time and again coming home from church I went straight to my room, locked my door and went on my knees and prayed'.

*   *   *

The length of the morning sermon was around forty minutes, sometimes less and occasionally more. It was followed immediately by a short prayer and then the final hymn. This hymn he chose with special care, for it had to provide the congregation's response to the message, whether a response of penitence, of trust or of triumphant praise. It came as an 'Amen' to the whole service. The benediction was nearly always introduced with the words of Jude 24, 25, 'Now unto him that is able to keep you from falling . . .' and concluded, 'be with you throughout the remainder of this our short, uncertain, earthly life and pilgrimage and forevermore'.

A few things more need to be said about these services. The first is the silence which prevailed in the large congregation. The stillness generally deepened as the service proceeded, being undisturbed during the taking up of the collection and even, to a large extent, when the service was over. There were certain arrangements designed to encourage quietness. For the first part of the service ushers always stood at the doors and no one was allowed to enter while prayer or the reading of Scripture was in progress. A creche was provided for babies and infants. From about the age of three, children were usually in the church for the whole service (usually without colouring books or other things to 'occupy' them), but if they could not be quiet the parent and child were expected to remove speedily to a rear hall where the service could be heard by relay. Any failure to depart could earn an intimidating look from the pulpit! Remarkably, many young children were in the congregation throughout and they grew up believing that public worship was for them as well as for adults. By the age of ten it was not uncommon for some of them to be taking down notes on the sermon.

Regular worshippers at Westminster Chapel had no problem in explaining this stillness. In the words of Faith Linton, a student from Jamaica, 'It was as if I lost all count of time and space. The eternal truth that I hungered for so deeply was being revealed, and I was caught up body, mind and spirit in the sublime experience of receiving, finding, understanding, knowing . . . ML-J was only an instrument. What I experienced was the power of the Word and a deep, intensive, quickening work of the Holy Spirit.'[1]

Further, it should be noted that Dr Lloyd-Jones led public worship with an almost total lack of asides and informal comments. Hymns were announced, and calls to prayer were given, in precisely the same language week by week. As we have seen, even the flying bomb that nearly ended the service abruptly in 1944 received virtually no notice from the preacher. Similarly, if some civic dignitary was paying a visit to the Chapel it made no difference to the service. Practically the only occasions when he was provoked to comment during a service were when things occurred which he regarded as intrusions into the true spirit of worship. Thus he might, at times, if he thought a hymn was being wrongly sung, actually stop the people between the verses and warn them against singing the tune instead of the words. He would not tolerate, for instance, an exuberant and hearty singing of such words as 'False and full of sin I am' in Charles Wesley's, 'Jesus, Lover of my soul'. Neither would he tolerate gloomy and dragging singing.

---

[1] Sometimes members of the congregation, unable to wait to see ML-J after the service, would scribble a brief message to be passed to him. A Norwegian visitor once conveyed greetings from a mutual friend in Oslo in this way and added, 'Personally I will say I have been in heaven under this service'.

He did not like audible responses, or words of approval, during a sermon, and if enthusiastic visitors were present, unaware of this fact, they were liable to be informed. On one occasion the sermon had scarcely begun when vociferous 'Amens' were to be heard from a group close to the front of the congregation. When this happened more than once a number of regular attenders were beginning to surmise what the possible outcome would be when the preacher chose his own method. He had gained a temporary silence as he was speaking on man's fallen and ruined condition and, seizing the opportunity, he looked hard at the interrupters and exclaimed, 'I notice that there are no "Amens" now'. There were no more!

There were other times (these generally in an evening service) when he would add a word before the final hymn, or even while the congregation was standing awaiting the benediction after the final hymn. In such moments he might assure any in spiritual trouble that he was available to speak with them, or he might add a final plea to the unconverted to go to Christ without delay.

Some, reading the above account of a service at Westminster Chapel, might suppose that while it fitted with church life of the 1950's its whole concept is remote from the present day. Such thinking is a mistake for the truth is that this form of service was far from being representative in that era. The older views of divine worship were already being widely displaced. Edwin King, who first went to Westminster Chapel in 1946, writes: 'I had become accustomed to the propaganda for change. The emphasis was very much upon let us be bright and breezy, and above all don't let the service last too long, especially the sermon.'

The contrast between Westminster Chapel and the then prevailing church life is clear enough in various newspaper accounts of that decade.

Under the title, 'A stern preacher – but they flock to hear him', Norman Phelps wrote three columns on Dr Martyn Lloyd-Jones in the *Liverpool Daily Post* for June 8, 1954. They included the following:

This is, primarily, a preaching church where people from far and wide (as well as the big regular congregation) come to hear the sermon, a fact not unworthy of recognition in days when the rush of religious-social activities often tends to make a clergyman a sort of sanctified Master of Ceremonies, and to leave him such little time for sermon preparation that preaching becomes almost a postscript, a hasty fifteen minutes necessity, rather than the significant and crowning centrepiece.

Dr Lloyd-Jones gave us a good thirty-five minutes of full-packed, well considered, and well worked out exposition based on the last chapter of the Epistle to the Ephesians in which St Paul urged the readers of his letter to take unto themselves the whole armour of God.

And there was no restlessness among the congregation.

These big London churches have a continuous tidal wave of floating listeners – visitors from the provinces and the suburbs, strangers dropping in for one service and then perhaps, never seen again, sermon tasters with no steady religious roots – but here I was impressed with the number of families present. They came in – father, mother, daughter, son, and I think, engaged couples on the family perimeter – to their own special seats in that obviously accustomed manner which many of us believed had died with the Victorians.

There was, so far as I could see, no choir, but the congregation did not appear to need one. Philip Doddridge's opening hymn, 'Awake, my soul, stretch every nerve and press with vigour on,' set the key to the preacher's soldierly sermon on the loins girt about with truth, the breastplate of righteousness, the helmet of salvation, and the shield of faith. Words flowed in a fluent stream from the preacher's clipped, almost harsh voice as he compared the cults which offered a spurious perfection with Christianity, which was an eternal fight against principalities and powers, and the rulers of darkness.

'As soon as a man becomes a Christian' he cried, 'the powers of evil are immediately deployed against him with suggestions, innuendos, subtle temptations. They are always battling for his soul.'

Only a small minority, I suppose, now believe in the existence of that Satan, but Lloyd-Jones, pointing with upraised hand an invisible sword, putting on with gestures the helmet, the breastplate, the girdle, and the shield made us conscious of the immense, menacing presence of the dark, unresting forces of evil. We felt they were right there just outside the sanctuary walls in Victoria Street, in all the streets of London and of the world.

Similar observations occur in a *British Weekly* article for March 21, 1957, written by Derek Walker and entitled, 'Westminster Chapel Has a Great Tradition'.

Westminster Chapel is a church which thrives without making any visible effort to achieve success – or so it would seem at first sight. It is well filled every Sunday, morning and evening, although its activities are not widely advertised, and although the form of service makes no concessions to modern tastes . . . The service in the morning lasts for nearly an hour and a half, while in the evening it also runs to an hour and a half. Sermons are correspondingly long, often 40 minutes in the morning, and 50 minutes at night – this in addition to extempore prayers lasting for a quarter of an hour.

Hymns and metrical psalms form part of the service, of course, but there are no musical items, and no choir. Holy Communion is celebrated twice in the month, once after morning service and once in the evening.

It may be that in this very absence of any trace of 'modernity' we have the clue to the well-filled pews in Westminster Chapel. This kind of service, centred on the long, expository sermon, makes an appeal to a certain group within Nonconformity – the conservative evangelicals. These are the people who are drawn to Westminster every Sunday, and their numbers are added to by young people who have been influenced through the London Inter-Faculty Christian Union.

Looking at a typical Sunday morning congregation in Westminster Chapel, it is tempting to reflect that this is what a service in Cromwellian England might have looked like . . . There are only slightly more women than men, and the middle age-groups are well represented. About 16 per cent of the congregation are young people in their late teens and early twenties.

In the mornings, people in their fifties and over make up about 18 per cent of the attendance, but the proportion falls to nearer 10 per cent in the evenings. So, between two-thirds and three-quarters of the congregation are in the 25 to 50 age group.

It can thus be said that the form of worship at Westminster Chapel was not the result of conformity to a prevailing tradition; it was rather the result of convictions which had existed in an earlier age but which were already largely disappearing in the mid-twentieth century. Even with regard to the Bible version which he used, Dr Lloyd-Jones was not following a tradition, for the pew Bibles in the Chapel had long been those of the Revised Version whereas he had returned to the Authorised Version, regarding it as the best version for preaching. In the course of time, the pew Bibles were also changed to conform with the pulpit.

All powerful preaching has been accused of producing only a temporary emotional effect upon hearers. That temporary effects do follow such preaching in the case of some is not to be denied. Christ himself teaches us to expect it. But in others the effect is far from being a temporary emotion. Two instances of this from the 1950's will illustrate how the lives of Christians were affected by this preaching.

On Saturday, November 28, 1953, Ralph M. Hettrick arrived in London on a first visit from the United States. Recalling the event, nearly thirty years later, he wrote:

I had been given a three-month sabbatical as pastor of a church in central Washington State, and through a series of providential happenings was led overseas by ship to Southampton and then to London.

I had had part-ownership interest in a Bible Book Store in Washington and was familiar with publishing, so, as a point of contact I sought out Pickering & Inglis at 29 Ludgate Hill. I inquired about Spurgeon's Tabernacle and was told it was but a bombed-out shell. The managers, Mr and Mrs Gray, invited me to join them in their hall meeting (Brethren). I asked if there was not some evangelical center in London where I could hear the Word preached with power. They told me of Westminster Chapel and the effective work of the doctor. I straightaway made up my mind to hear this Dr Lloyd-Jones the following day. I had no idea I would be in for such a treat.

Problem after problem seemed to make it next to impossible to get to the Chapel. The final blow was when the cab driver delivered me to Westminster Abbey instead of Westminster Chapel. Running and walking down the Mall in a driving rainstorm, I finally arrived at the sanctuary and was seated in the center section, but a few rows from the very front. I had to look almost straight up to see the pulpit. After the singing had stopped the doctor began leading in the morning prayer. Never in my life had I heard a public prayer like that prayer. Then the message. What can I say? It was part of his series on the 73rd Psalm. Later I discovered his text that Sunday had been planned for the Sunday previous but that he was not able to finish it. He began dealing with verses 22 and 23, 'So foolish was I, and ignorant. I was as a beast before thee. Nevertheless I am continually with thee: Thou hast holden me by my right hand.'

Every part of the message was directed to me. I had traveled across the United States from the west coast, boarding a ship to take me to England. I had been traveling for more than five weeks. I was in a backslidden state and my heart was full of fear. My spiritual condition made me fearful that God would finally disown me and I would find myself lost and without hope. It was as though the Lord had been in detailed conversation with the doctor concerning my condition. Everything seemed to fit. I was weakened, greatly humbled and yet thrilled to think that God knew where I was (even if I didn't), and that He was again at work in my soul.

I met the doctor that afternoon at the Jr Carlton Club for tea. I told him briefly about the morning experience, and there began a beautiful friendship which has lasted over the years. I sat under his ministry on at

least five or six different visits to London. As I reflect today on that
November 29, 1953 experience at Westminster Chapel I have deep
appreciation and gratitude to God for His leading me to hear that
particular message. It was a life-changing happening.

God's timing was perfect, as is everything He does. There is no way of
my conveying what the ministry of Dr Lloyd-Jones has meant to me. It
turned my life around. I'm sure this same acknowledgement could come
from hundreds of others.

One of these 'hundreds' was Argos Zodhiates who, with his wife,
was in Westminster Chapel on Sunday morning, October 21, 1957.
Sad of heart, they were en route to Canada where they hoped to find
a new home. Behind them lay a much loved and fruitful work in the
Greek Evangelical Church of Katerini which Argos had served since
July 1946. The church at Katerini, on the Aegean Sea and not far
from the ancient town of Thessaloniki was one of the brightest lights
for the gospel in Greece, and for that very reason it had incurred the
anger of Bishop Barnabas, the local Greek Orthodox bishop.
Persecution of various kinds had been increasingly directed against
Argos and his preaching. When a dead bird was thrown down at his
door with a threat of murder attached to it, the possibility that
violence could proceed even to that length could not be dismissed. At
length, in the midst of this sustained opposition, the Zodhiateses had
come to the reluctant conclusion that it was time for them to leave,
and passing through London on their journey they took the
opportunity to visit Westminster Chapel. Their coming was, of
course, unknown to ML-J who that morning 'happened' to be
preaching on Ephesians 4:11, 'And he gave some apostles; and some
prophets; and some evangelists; and some pastors and teachers'. In
the course of his words on the pastoral office he was to say: 'The
shepherd shepherds his flock . . . looks after their safety and guards
them against enemies liable to attack them. It is a great office. A
pastor is a man who is given charge of souls . . . he is the guardian,
the custodian, the protector, the organizer, the director, the ruler of
the flock . . .'.[1]

Argos Zodhiates and his wife felt that the word was direct from
God to themselves, and turning to each other at the end of the service

[1]*Ephesians*, vol. 4, p. 193. He probably said more by way of application than is
included in the printed version of the sermon. The next sermon (pp. 196–208)
gives one of ML-J's finest summaries on the work of the ministry.

they said, 'That's our answer'. They went back to Greece, ready to battle it out, and Dr Lloyd-Jones heard nothing of the incident until he visited Kateríni four years later.

Such experiences confirmed all that he believed about preaching. To use the words of Gardiner Spring, 'The results of a preached Gospel are associated with the most interesting realities in the universe'.

Finally it should be said that there were at least two occasions when ML-J did take special notice of contemporary events during Sunday morning services in the 1950's. Both had reference to the death of eminent men. King George VI died, universally esteemed, on February 6, 1952. On the following Sunday ML-J told his people, 'Most people in this country today will have their minds centered upon the death of our late King,' and he went on to preach on what that event should say to Christians. The following year on Sunday, May 3, 1953 the news of the sudden death of a leader in another sphere reached ML-J shortly before he left home for Westminster. Fred Mitchell, Home Director of the China Inland Mission, had died in an air disaster on the previous day when the Comet in which he was travelling crashed near Calcutta. There were no survivors. ML-J was grieved at the loss of this true friend who combined a spiritual mind with an unusual insight into men and affairs. At the Chapel he spoke feelingly to the people of the news and reminded them of the need for thankfulness as well as sorrow. It says much of the position accorded to Dr Lloyd-Jones by the leadership of the CIM that he was asked to preside and preach at a Memorial Service held on May 26. At fifty-five years of age and as chairman of the Keswick Convention, Fred Mitchell had been one of the best-known evangelicals in Britain, and many were stunned that an accident could have cut short such a life. ML-J's sermon on May 26 was exactly suited to the occasion, with his text taken from the words of Job 1:20,21 which conclude, 'the Lord gave and the Lord hath taken away; blessed be the name of the Lord.' 'God cannot make a mistake,' he reminded the crowded assembly. 'There are no accidents in the case of God's children. Nothing can happen to us without our Father. "The Lord hath taken away," and therefore we must all say, "Blessed be the name of the Lord". Why? Because He is the Lord . . . His ways are always perfect . . .' In the words of the Acting Home Director reporting this Memorial Service to missionaries overseas, 'Dr Lloyd-Jones' closing message dispelled all doubts from questioning minds and exalted the Lord in our midst'.[1]

[1]The funeral sermons for King George VI and Fred Mitchell were both published, the former, *Honour to Whom Honour*, by The Bookroom of Westminster Chapel, 1952, and the latter, in abbreviated form, under the title 'Faith's Reaction' in *The Millions*, Journal of the China Inland Mission Overseas Missionary Fellowship, July–August 1953. The two sermons show how carefully he chose the message for different circumstances.

BUSINESS MEN PACKED CHURCH TO HEAR HIM.

One of the most remarkable congregations I have seen for some time gathered to hear Dr Martyn Lloyd-Jones at the lunch-hour service in Renfield Street Church on Wednesday.

Dr Lloyd-Jones rose magnificently to the occasion. I had heard him before, in London, as well as in Glasgow, but I never heard him preach with greater clarity, with more manifest and compelling power. He is neither rhetorical nor oratorical, but something better and greater. There is a real prophetic note in his utterance.

After the service, the Scottish Evangelistic Council gave a luncheon in honour of Dr Lloyd-Jones which was attended by a large and representative company of ministers and laymen of all denominations. Mr John Corbett presided and paid tribute to the guest of honour. The response of Dr Lloyd-Jones was marked by characteristic modesty – no man is more unconscious of his own greatness. He spoke of the visits which, through the kindness of his Scottish hosts, he had been able to pay to some of the beauty spots in Western and Central Scotland, and referred in particular to the inspiration he had received from being at Kilsyth and Cambuslang, the scenes of great spiritual awakenings in bygone days.

Tomorrow morning Dr Lloyd-Jones is to address a meeting of men and lads at Tollcross Y.M.C.A., and in the evening he will preach at the service in the Church of the Orphan Homes of Scotland, Bridge of Weir.

Evening Citizen,
Glasgow, September 11, 1948

14

Summer Travels

Dr Lloyd-Jones' vacation period was invariably from mid-July to mid-September, and throughout the 1950's it generally followed a similar pattern. Except for the years 1956 and 1958, he took his holidays in the British Isles or in Europe. Within Britain, Wales was usually the first destination and from there they frequently went on to Rosapenna Hotel, Co. Donegal where the hospitality of Mr and Mrs Stuart Catherwood (first extended in 1949) had led to a warm and life-long friendship. The two families were now still closer with the marriage of the Lloyd-Joneses' elder daughter to the Catherwoods' son Frederick.

Another friendship which also developed through an invitation to make a holiday visit (and preach!) was with the two brothers John and Alex Murdoch and their families in Gourock and Kilmacolm. The two men were well-known Glasgow business men and leaders of the Scottish Evangelistic Council. A first holiday with the Murdochs in 1948 had introduced the Lloyd-Jones family to the beauty of the Clyde and other parts of western Scotland.

Visits to the Continent were almost invariably combined with attendance at an IFES Conference or an executive committee meeting.

The vacation of 1950, while characteristic of these years, must have been one of the fullest he ever had. It began with the train to Liverpool, a boat to Belfast and then across to Rosapenna. After six days in the peace and quietness of that haven on the shore of the Atlantic he could write to his mother on July 24, 'I feel I have been away for several weeks'. From Donegal they crossed to Scotland, this time to explore part of the Highlands and the east coast. At Grantown-on-Spey in Morayshire he wrote to his mother on August 6:

We are now just half way through our Scottish trip and so far it has been excellent. We set out on Monday morning and we seem to have done just under 100 miles each day. Fortunately the weather has been excellent until yesterday when it rained a good deal. But it did not matter much, as we were staying here in any case. What impresses us all so much is the fact that this country is so much bigger than Wales in every respect. The scenery is certainly glorious. On the whole I was disappointed with Balmoral although the mountains round about it are very fine. The rivers are particularly good everywhere.

I much enjoyed seeing the old monasteries at St Andrews and Arbroath. The town of Aberdeen impressed us very much – it is certainly one of the finest in the country. Tomorrow and the following day until we arrive at Oban we shall really be in the wilds and we are looking forward to it very much.

From Scotland the next stop was the Continent where, along with engagements, they were also able to explore new ground. On August 22, 1950, ML-J wrote to the Secretts on a postcard from Venice:

This is certainly the most extraordinary place I have ever visited. It really baffles description. I have felt exactly as Paul must have felt in Athens seeing the art and beauty, the false religion and the utter worldliness. The noise is incredible, yet musical. They sing day and night. I am much impressed by the Italian cities and prefer them to the French.[1]

Five days later, at Adelboden, Switzerland, he wrote to his mother:

We have seen great sights during this past week, indeed never to be forgotten. Monday we spent sight-seeing in Venice. Fortunately the heat was not too great so we were able to enjoy it. We were taken to see a glass factory where some of the finest vases are made. The great cathedral is, of course, also wonderful.

We set off on Tuesday morning in sweltering heat but we soon reached the mountain passes and it got cooler. We spent the night at a road-side hotel which was just under 6,000 feet above sea level. It was right on its own in the mountains with a stream tumbling down outside. There was a great mountain with its peak covered with snow just outside. Wednesday we set off again and crossed two great mountain ranges with most wonderful scenery until we arrived at the Swiss border and then ran on to St Moritz. We saw a most wonderful glacier just before we reached St Moritz. I was not very impressed with St Moritz – I

[1]On the Sunday evening in Venice he preached on Paul in Athens in a Catholic church borrowed for the occasion.

prefer the smaller places in the country. After leaving St Moritz and climbing another mountain pass, as we were descending the other side our car broke down. We were able to glide into a little village called Bivio fortunately and found a very nice little hotel there. The garage man found that something had gone wrong with our water cooling system and that he would have to send for a spare part to Zurich. So we spent the whole of Thursday there. It was very delightful. We went for a walk into the mountains in the afternoon and Ann has taken a large number of photographs. The spare part arrived on Thursday night by express delivery, so we were able to continue our journey on Friday morning.

Their route took them to Chur, westwards to Andermatt (passing within a few miles of the source of the Rhine), then through the Sustenpass and Meiringen to Interlaken. After a detour to see the falls at Lauterbrunnen (in ML-J's view 'one of the greatest sights in the world') they finally arrived at Adelboden at 8.30 p.m. It had been a glorious drive. On Saturday they walked about Interlaken and took a chair lift up the mountain. They returned to Interlaken the next day to worship at the English church, morning and evening. On Monday they began the journey home via Paris and by Thursday, August 31, ML-J was in Cambridge for IFES meetings. Bethan, having taken a breath in London, joined him the next day. The meetings began with the executive committee and then, for the week September 2–9, the second General Committee Meeting. With twenty-one nations represented and full members, affiliated members and observers present, these General Committee Meetings were actually conferences and the accommodation both at Ridley Hall and Tyndale House was fully utilized. When the conference was almost over, ML-J wrote to Mrs Lloyd-Jones Sr on September 10:

I do not know that I have ever had a fuller week. We have been hard at it from morning to night. The programme has been roughly this. We were called at 6.45 a.m. Prayers in the Chapel [of Ridley Hall] at 7.30. Breakfast at 8.0. Then I had a committee meeting each morning straight after breakfast. The first regular meeting was at 9.30, the next at 11.30. Then each afternoon after lunch there was generally a committee meeting except Wednesday when we all went on a bus trip to see Ely Cathedral and Huntingdon. Then tea at 4.0. Another meeting at 5.0 Dinner at 7.0, and another meeting at 8.0. Then a final cup of coffee and bed.

You will see that it really has been a very full week and we are all feeling somewhat tired. As chairman I had to be present at all and I am to give the final address tonight at 8.0 p.m. We are leaving for home on the 9.27 a.m. train tomorrow (Monday) . . . It seems a very long time since we left for Ireland in July. We shall have to settle down again now to the winter's work.

Dr Lloyd-Jones' long and faithful correspondence with his mother (carried on whenever he or she was away from London) was approaching its close. Magdalene Lloyd-Jones died on June 22, 1951, at the age of 79. Referring to the event, a reporter in the *Western Mail* wrote:

Those who knew the late Mrs Lloyd-Jones, the mother of the Rev Dr Martyn Lloyd-Jones and Mr Vincent Lloyd-Jones, though she had spent so many years in Cardiff and London, were not surprised to learn that the burial took place at Llandyfriog. She was the daughter of nearby Llwyncadfor, a farm known not only to South Cardigan but to all parts of Wales where horse-lovers dwell. It was her father, a native of the Tregaron district, who first familiarised agricultural shows with the name Llwyncadfor . . . In their boyhood days Martyn and Vincent often spent their school holidays in the district, roaming the countryside from Henllan to Bryngwenith . . .[1]

At Westminster Chapel Mr Marsh paid a tribute to Mrs Lloyd-Jones which was printed in the *Westminster Record*. Speaking particularly of her overflowing sympathy and kindness, he said, 'Mrs Lloyd-Jones's outstanding characteristic may well be described as that of having been "interested in everyone and in everything", and she was never happier than when seeking to know why any member of the church was absent and to enquire after his or her welfare . . .'. They had been a close-knit family. Year by year, on the anniversaries of the deaths of his father and his brother Harold, ML-J never failed to refer to them in letters if his mother was away from home.

Other changes were also marking the passage of time. Bethan's parents had continued to live at Sunnyside, Newcastle Emlyn following the Second World War. After Dr Phillips had died in 1947 (at the age of 87), her mother continued the home until she came to live permanently with the Lloyd-Jones family in Ealing in the early

[1]Under the heading 'Horses and Sheep', *Western Mail*, July 10, 1951.

1950's. Thereafter Mrs Phillips became a familiar figure at Westminster Chapel and one much loved by every age group until her death in 1961 at the age of 91. Mrs Phillips' departure from Newcastle Emlyn brought to an end the many holidays which had been spent there. What was originally her husband's parents' home was no longer the same, its only survivors being an elderly uncle and a maid – now turned 80 – who had been there since the age of twelve. How to maintain the property soon became a problem, not least because the uncle was seriously of the opinion that dust should never be disturbed. Martyn and Bethan stayed in Mrs Phillips' section of the building for the last time in August 1954[1] and a letter from Bethan to the Secretts explains that their holiday activities had been rather different from the usual:

We had quite a job with the house, as it had been empty for 11 months and is really too old to be left empty. Anyway, believe me, it got a good do this time. Martyn was an invaluable assistant – quite adept at making fires, airing beds, shopping, making meals and more often than not washing up.

By the following summer both uncle and Hilda (the family maid) had died and clearly the old place, associated with so many memories, had to be sold. Before that could happen another week of cleaning up was to be necessary and when this was done Bethan wrote to the Secretts (August 29, 1955):

I must say I feel a sense of real relief when I remember that Sunnyside (Nos 1 & 2) are really cleared at last. We turned out more stuff than you would think it could hold, and as the Aunts, Uncle and maid had long before they died become quite decrepit, and had certainly turned nothing out for the past 50 years or so, the moth and rust had made the most of their opportunity! . . . The home help and her husband took away cartloads of rubbish with instructions to distribute anything possible to the oldest inhabitants, and to take the rest to a nearby field, pour a bottle of petrol and oil over it, and put a match to the lot – which they did! By the time we finished we only had one idea of luxury – a hot bath. Fortunately we have one relative remaining in that little town who put his comfortable house at our disposal for the week we were there.

[1]Sunnyside was, in fact, two semi-detached houses dating, probably, from the 1690's.

This meant that we could just stop work at meal times and creep by a back and unseen way to his house and sit down to an all ready meal at lunch, tea and supper times. It also meant that Martyn had great opportunities for reading in comfort, and only very infrequently did he have to be roped in to our assistance . . .

It was strange to think of Sunnyside, with no one sleeping there for the first time for 95 years.

With Newcastle Emlyn no longer a holiday base, and the shore at Aberystwyth no longer an attraction for the younger member of the family, the favourite holiday base was now the mountains around Bala – both Martyn and Bethan preferring mountains to seaside. Here their closest friends were the Davies family with whom they had first stayed at Parc in 1949. The summer day when they arrived at Parc in 1953 happened to be the day following the burial of the head of the family, Mr Ellis Davies, and ML-J was able to pay tribute to him in a society meeting. That same year Mari Davies was married to John Jones, who farmed on the other side of the pass of Bwlch-y-Groes in the beautiful valley which leads down past Llanymawddwy to Dinas Mawddwy. For the next near-quarter century the Bryn-uchaf farmhouse of John and Mari Jones at Llanymawddwy was to be a second home to the Lloyd-Joneses. At Brynuchaf he would enjoy every aspect of mountain farming, readily joining with John, shepherds and sheep dogs for truck rides over rough ground or entering into the bustle of sheep shearing. His interest in horses, his favourite animals, persisted and, on occasions, he would still mount and ride.

Although Dr Lloyd-Jones could drive a car from his youth he never owned one until 1952. He simply did not have the financial means until he benefited from his mother's estate. After that date they prized the greater freedom to travel at will in Wales (and elsewhere) as is clear from Bethan's letters to the Secretts. Speaking of the Welsh part of their holidays in 1954, she wrote:

The actual motoring gave us quite a lot of pleasure in itself, the countryside was beautiful . . . Most of our routes in Wales had many long ago associations for us, too, and we saw people this time that we had not seen for years. It was very pleasant and I enjoyed it all, but it certainly underlined the fact that we are *growing old*. In one family the children's children are now older than their fathers and mothers when we first knew them. The car behaved perfectly, except once when it faltered and groaned its way along for a mile or so, eventually stopping dead outside the garage where it was bought.

The next year there was more motoring in North Wales with glorious summer days, before leaving the car at Liverpool when they went on to Belfast by boat for a further visit to Donegal.

In 1952 they had been back on the Continent for IFES meetings at Darmstadt in Germany,[1] and in 1953 there were summer visits to France for the International Congress for Reformed Faith and Action at Montpellier (July 23–31), followed by more IFES engagements at Monti-Locarno in Switzerland.

In 1956 the Conference of the General Committee of the IFES was again convened in North America and so, after nine years absence, the Lloyd-Joneses began another Atlantic crossing on the 'Mauretania' on July 20. As the Cunarder approached New York on July 26, it passed through the area where a few hours earlier an Italian luxury liner, the 'Andrea Doria', had collided with the 'Stockholm' in fog. They were there to see the 'Andrea Doria' sink, with other boats standing around her. Three sailors had lost their lives. They disembarked early the following morning under a copper coloured sky and in the midst of a thunder-storm. The customs hall was crowded and busy. A lengthy delay seemed likely when a customs officer said to ML-J, 'Open everything up', and began to search their big hold-all while asking what they were doing while in the States. When he received the reply, 'Preaching and chiefly at a Conference', he stopped and Mrs Lloyd-Jones added, 'So you see you won't find any smokes or spirits'. The officer promptly gave up any further search with the exclamation, 'My! that'll be a mighty dry conference!'.

A two hour train journey then took them to Paoli, near Philadelphia. After services on the Sunday they left at 1.55 a.m. by train for Indiana, with Stacey Woods at North Philadelphia station to see them off despite the time. A twelve hour journey took them to a station close to Winona Lake Conference Center where Dr Muntz – ML-J's host in 1947 – was awaiting them. Other speakers that week included Dr Billy Graham. The following weekend they were in Chicago, for services at Moody Church (August 5), and the next day saw them on another train journey from 11 a.m. to 5.30 p.m. when they reached their stopping point at Rochester, Minnesota.

[1]'The German students were especially grateful to him', writes Agnes Collins (née Riley), a Welsh IVF representative. 'I remember them gathering early in the morning of his departure to sing their goodbyes to him'.

The chief point of interest en route had been the crossing of the Mississippi, 1,000 miles from its mouth, although Mrs Lloyd-Jones was less than enthusiastic when the train had stopped half way across the bridge which was seemingly 'a most flimsy affair of iron girders – looking down through the window you were gazing into the muddy flood and it looked very big and deep and strong!' At Rochester there was just time for dinner in the home of their medical host, Dr Waugh, before a service in the Presbyterian Church and then a meeting with about 30 doctors and their wives. The next morning (Tuesday) Dr Waugh, who was a surgeon at the Mayo Clinic, took ML-J to see that famous institution. Mrs Lloyd-Jones, reporting their father's reaction to the family at home, wrote, 'He had no words to describe it – it is quite superlative in every way. He watched a younger Mayo doing a gall bladder operation.'

In the afternoon the Lloyd-Joneses continued their journey, through Minneapolis, north into Canada, reaching Banff by rail at 9.30 a.m. on the Thursday. It was their first sight of the Rocky Mountains as they headed on a first visit to the West Coast. But before continuing westwards there was a detour east, through Calgary for a weekend at the Prairie Bible Institute. On Monday, August 12, they then resumed their train journey west for Vancouver from Calgary. There was only one near hitch. Knowing that the rail journey would take them back through Banff, ML-J had left two of their cases in the ticket office there, judging that he would have plenty of time to collect them as the train passed through. So on reaching Banff he left Bethan – a solitary passenger in the observation car at the rear of the train – to get the cases. He had scarcely left the carriage when to Mrs Lloyd-Jones' shock she found that it was being uncoupled and then shunted backwards until it came to a stop in a siding, leaving her entirely alone in a lone coach. 'After being turned to stone for some time,' she was to write home, 'sanity returned and I began to hope that I might yet be hitched on to a now lengthened train and so it turned out to be. There was an elaborate act of shunting various coaches off and taking others on. Finally the wretched monster hitched me on again, and in the far distance I could see a grinning Dada waving a carton of coffee in each hand!'

There followed a breathtaking run through the Rockies to Vancouver, where they had only a two-hour break before taking a ferry to Seattle, and then a long train journey south to San Francisco. The scenery between Portland and San Francisco was especially enjoyed: 'For about 200 miles we were on a plateau 6,000 feet up. It was a great Indian Reserve and all so marvellous that even Dada could not read. At least, not until it got dark.' They had one full day of sight-seeing in San Francisco, and a meeting with doctors, before the last stage of their journey down the coast to Los Angeles. ML-J was due there for services at the First Presbyterian Church of Hollywood on two Sundays (August 19 and 26), with the week in between being spent at Forest Home Christian Conference Center in the San Bernardino mountains.

Although this area was entirely new to them, there were some people whom they already knew. One was Dr Wilbur Smith, then teaching at Fuller Theological Seminary in the outer suburbs of Los Angeles. The two men had first met in 1952 when Smith had given the Campbell Morgan Lecture at Westminster Chapel, and they had become good friends. Mrs Lloyd-Jones, describing Wilbur Smith's greeting of her husband, says, 'He gave Dada a bear-like hug that almost lifted him off the ground'. In his autobiography, published in 1971, Wilbur Smith writes: 'During the last twenty years, there have been two men whose fellowship has always been especially refreshing to me. One is Dr Martyn Lloyd-Jones. His stimulating conversation, vibrant with his great love for the Word of God, so stirs up one's mind that one is meditating on what he has said for days to come.'[1] Smith claimed the privilege to drive the visitors to Forest Home Center, some 90 miles out of Los Angeles, after the first Sunday evening in Hollywood and so largely did he enter into the conversation en route – in four lanes of heavy traffic moving at high speed – that in Mrs Lloyd-Jones' words, 'We felt like chewed string when we arrived'. Writing about the week at Forest Home, the family correspondent continued:

There are about 700 people here all distributed around in little wooden cabins, hidden among the trees, with central dining rooms and auditorium etc . . . We are situated 6,000 ft up, surrounded by the mountains all round, 10,000 ft high. The road finishes here. The temp is 98° in L.A. all the week, and well in the 90's here . . . We get up about 7.30 and it is nice and cool, and then, in about 10 mins, the sun peeps at us over the edge of the basin and *immediately* it is blistering, sweltering hot, with no relief anywhere until it drops behind the mountains on the other side about 6.30 . . .

[1] *Before I Forget*, Wilbur M. Smith, 1971, p. 20.

I slept every afternoon in sheer self defence. One afternoon when I was really blotto, I woke up to see Dada sitting reading on the chair at the foot of the bed. Now I thought it was morning, getting up time, and I was so surprised I said, 'What are you doing?' 'Reading, of course.' 'But, *what for?*' 'What for?' said Dada, 'What do you mean, what for?' We got no further because in turning to take in the mysterious situation I fell out of bed – just straight out. He was so surprised and then gave a kind of gasp, 'I could have saved you,' said he remorsefully, 'if I'd known you were going to do that!' We laughed till we were nearly sick.

The people everywhere are very nice and friendly. They are drinking up Dada's teaching. They have certainly never heard anything like it before . . .

Two columns in a Los Angeles newspaper headed, 'British Cleric Pleads for Stress on Preaching', give some indication of the difference which people observed. The newspaper reported him as saying, 'Too little preaching and too much music, ritual and entertainment are leading to too much Christian superficiality'.[1] Evangelism, he told them, has to be church-centered and the churches need 'no special technique or advertising'. They are built up by sound preaching, 'preaching the word of God in a Christ-centered way, with conviction, and looking to the Holy Spirit to apply it . . . When the local church has a spirit of evangelism, members tell others about Christ, and through personal contact among friends, acquaintances and business associates bring many into the church.'

Writing to him after the Conference of how they had been 'refreshed and challenged', the Director of Forest Home urged that he return 'very soon'.

After the second Sunday at Hollywood First Presbyterian, supper with the Smiths and breakfast the next day (August 27) with Ralph Hettrick, they took the mid-day train east and, apart from one lengthy stop to see the Grand Canyon on the Tuesday ('not every place is as wonderful as it seems from reports, but this really is') and a short break in Chicago (where Stacey Woods and Douglas Johnson joined them), trains were their home until 5 p.m. Thursday when they reached Toronto. There were a further 100 miles to travel out to

[1] There were so many musical items in his first evening service at First Presbyterian Church, Hollywood, that it was impossible for him to conclude his sermon (which was being broadcast live) by the time that he was given a red warning light. He simply ignored the light. Following many complaints to the radio network there was far less music the following Sunday!

the IVCF Conference Centre at Glen Home among the lakes of Ontario for a General Committee meeting and Conference of the International Fellowship of Evangelical Students.

It was at this Conference that ML-J first gave the three addresses on 'Authority' which were later to be published. Giving news of the meetings, Mrs Lloyd-Jones wrote from Glen Home:

We are having an excellent Conference. One of the very best. Over the week-end there has been quite an influx of visitors and friends of IFES. We had our first hearing of Dr Tozer last night, and I must say that was quite an experience in itself – interesting and refreshing – like nobody else and with a complete lack of the showmanship which spoils so many of the good men this side. He is about 58 and his general build not unlike Dada . . .

Yesterday we all packed into all available cars and went 4 miles to the village church. It held 200 and was crammed to capacity. Dear Dr Pache opened the service and Dada preached and he had liberty and the truth penetrated. I think that some of the local inhabitants heard the gospel for the first time. Our people kept hearing various remarks – one old man said at the end, 'You know, that man is talking about something that he knows about'. Another heard an old lady say, turning to her daughter, 'I have never before in all my life heard a preacher like that.'

This was to be the only time that Dr Lloyd-Jones met A. W. Tozer whose books he had recommended in England since 1952. Speaking of the Conference at its close, he said:

I shall ever look back to it as being unique in my experience because I have had the privilege of sharing in the ministry with Dr Tozer. Ever since I read a book by him I have felt that he is one of the very few great prophetic voices in the Church today, and in the modern world, and I have looked forward for years to meeting him and to have the privilege and pleasure of listening to him. His books have whetted my appetite, but having heard him now actually in the flesh I see that even his books do not do him full justice.

They left Glen Home on September 11, 1956, taking a train to New York and then the 'Queen Elizabeth' back to England.

*   *   *

Most of his vacation period for the next year, 1957, was spent in Wales and it included attendance at the first English-speaking

Conference of the Evangelical Movement (held at Sandfields, Aberavon) when he preached from Ephesians 3:14–19. But there was also a short visit to the Continent and to Rome where he preached in the Methodist Chapel. This was his only visit to the city so closely connected with early Christian history, and the sight of Colosseum together with other antiquities moved him deeply. A part of this continental holiday was also spent at Huémoz, Switzerland where, with Bethan and Ann, he was a guest of Francis and Edith Schaeffer whose L'Abri Fellowship had begun there just two years earlier. The Schaeffers were delighted that the Lloyd-Joneses could be there for the marriage of their eldest daughter Priscilla to John Sandri. At the wedding in the old parish church of Ollon where William Farel had once preached, ML-J 'gave a splendid talk on Christian marriage', and then in the evening, Edith Schaeffer further recalls, as they sat round the fireside, their visitor spoke of what it had meant to him to be called into the ministry.[1]

*   *   **

In the summer of 1958 Dr and Mrs Lloyd-Jones made their only visit to the southern hemisphere, sailing on the 'Arundel Castle' to Cape Town which they reached on July 31. They especially enjoyed this Union Castle liner – 'steady and well built, with no vibration' – in which they spent two weeks on the outward voyage of 6,000 miles. There was even a small library close to their accommodation. Bethan wrote home: 'I have read more than I have done in 20 years I'm sure. I've finished the closely written and detailed *Life of Lady Glenorchy* and am half way through *The Rise of Puritanism*.'[2] They discovered that sitting on deck while crossing the equator (which they did on July 25) was a different proposition to the North Atlantic route and the sun burnt them 'good and proper'. Noticing their lobster-like appearance, the Scots Captain, Dan McKenzie, can hardly have soothed their feelings by professing that 'there is some truth in "Mad dogs and *Englishmen* go out in the mid-day sun"'. Their first contact with the captain seems to have been after they had declined to attend a cocktail party. He then recognized who Dr Lloyd-Jones was and frequently spoke with them during the remainder of the voyage.

[1] *The Tapestry*, Edith Schaeffer, 1981, p. 475.
[2] *The Life of Willielma, Viscountess Glenorchy*, Edinburgh, 1822, and William Haller's *The Rise of Puritanism*, 1938, and paperback, New York, 1957.

Disembarking at Cape Town the Lloyd-Joneses were met by the Rev. A. S. ('Sandy') Gilfillan who had been chiefly responsible for arranging their visit. Mr Gilfillan was one of the first of a number of London Bible College students to go to South Africa and was then Principal of the Bible Institute of South Africa at Kalk Bay. From Kalk Bay (Cape Town) Mr Gilfillan drove them the 665 miles to King William's Town on August 1. 'It was,' wrote Mrs Lloyd-Jones, 'beautiful all the way, with very blue skies and incredibly blue Indian Ocean which we had in sight off and on all day. You should see some of the passes we crossed – steep up and steep down, like a corkscrew . . .' There was little time to see King William's Town, which they thought resembled 'the feel and smell of Newcastle Emlyn though much bigger', as they had another 500 miles before them the next day to reach their destination at Durban. Describing the second day's travel in a letter home, Mrs Lloyd-Jones said:

Our first 3 or 4 hundred miles was through the native reserve – thousands of square miles given to the Africans, where they live according to their ancient custom. Dada has found one thing in common with them – they all wear ancient overcoats or brick-red blankets on the most sweltering days![1] These reserves are great, rolling, brown-baked hills, rolling away from each side of the road to the distant horizon – nothing but scrub, with an occasional tree and the little 'rondavel' native huts dotted about in thousands. Someone told us that the ones which have white paint round the doors and windows belong to the Christians (which may mean nothing more than that they no longer observe heathen practices) . . . About 200 miles from Durban our good tar road petered out and we were on a dirt road for 100 miles. Words fail me to describe the roughness and the dust. To pass anyone else, or to be behind them, was quite blinding and choking and the dust got everywhere, even *inside* our cases in the boot.

Having left King William's Town at 8.30 a.m. they reached Durban at 8 o'clock at night, having averaged 50 mph in their host's Opel Kapitan.

The week in Durban was to be very full. There were meetings on five nights, gatherings with ministers, old friends from Britain calling on them (including two doctors whom ML-J had taught at Barts), a

[1] ML-J's addiction to wearing a heavy overcoat, even indoors, especially after preaching, was proverbial in Britain. It was perhaps not so noticeable in South Africa. Despite the fact that it was winter there was no heat in many houses and, together with their hosts, the Lloyd-Joneses would sometimes sit in their coats buttoned up to the chin!

Welsh Society welcome, a visit to the Indian market and much else. It seems that Bethan was disappointed in her hope of getting a photograph of her husband in one of Durban's innumerable rickshaws, pulled by men dressed like Zulu warriors with horns and feathers.

At one of the evening meetings in Durban ML-J was surprised to see Dan McKenzie in the congregation and he asked Mr Gilfillan to invite the captain to lunch with them on the next day. McKenzie was glad to accept. 'After lunch,' Sandy Gilfillan recalls, 'I drove him to the docks and pulled up beside the gang-way leading to his ship which was to sail in an hour or two. Captain McKenzie seemed reluctant to go and sat chatting to me. He said something very like this – "I have been at sea all my life, and am due to retire very soon. I have served on many of the great liners as a senior officer, and have had at my table almost all the 'great men' of our day. Mr Gilfillan, I give you my considered opinion that the greatest man I have ever met is Martyn Lloyd-Jones."'

They left Durban on Sunday afternoon, August 10 by road to be in Pietermaritzburg by the time of the evening service at Chapel Street Baptist Church where he preached from 1 Samuel 5:1–12, 'And Dagon fell down'. The next day they continued on to Pretoria, via Ladysmith, and stopping *en route* to see the spot where Winston Churchill was captured as a journalist during the Boer War. In Pretoria, capital of the Transvaal and of Afrikaner power, ML-J preached for four evenings, beginning on the Tuesday, when there was an estimated attendance of 1,400. Numbers increased and there was a final 'grand wind-up' in one of the large Dutch Reformed churches on Sunday afternoon, August 17.[1] The next week was to be a complete holiday, and one of the most unusual and fascinating which they ever experienced. On the Monday Dr and Mrs Paul Bremer of Pretoria drove them the some 250 miles into the Kruger National Park, where they were to be sight-seeing until Friday. From Satara Camp in the midst of the Kruger Mrs Lloyd-Jones wrote to Ann, Fred, Elizabeth and Christopher[2] on the Wednesday evening:

You wouldn't believe it if you could see us now. Dada and I are sitting in a small, round, thatched 'native style' hut, with small oil lamp, and we are sitting one each side of a little trestle table – Dada reading and me writing to you. Outside we can hear jackals barking – it is now 8.20 p.m. and I have *never* felt so near the wilds. There are camp fires for cooking and

[1] One known conversion through these services was that of one of the richest farmers in Natal.
[2] Christopher Catherwood, their eldest grandchild, born in 1955.

boiling water just outside our door and the black 'boys' are talking loudly to each other as they stoke-up, in some African language . . .

We got into the Reserve just before closing time on Monday. That camp was almost civilized, and so was last night's with electric light, etc. and a little bathroom in our Rondavel or hut, but tonight is much more like the real thing! We leave camp at 6.30 a.m.! when the gates open and are fined if we are not in at 5.30 p.m. when they shut. We then coast along these gravel roads – not allowed to leave the road, or to get out of the car. As you go you look out for animals. We saw a great variety yesterday, including Giraffe and hippos . . .

Things had become more exciting when, continuing the same letter two days later, Bethan described what had happened on the Thursday:

We coasted about all the morning, seeing lots of interesting things, then Dr Bremer said about 12.15, 'Would you like to have lunch or shall we go and look for lions?'. Of course, Dada immediately said, 'Oh, look for lions'! So we went – and did we see them?! We drew up where a loop road joined the main road and we had seen some cars parked, and then we saw them – padding along between the cars, like great aloof cats – not even looking at us! My heart was knocking like a hammer. As soon as the last one had passed, and gone into the bush, Dada said, 'Quick, go on the road to the next loop and see if they come along again – off we went and waited and sure enough before long they hove into sight – all nine of them – padding home from the kill, with blood on their jaws. Dada was thrilled with them and kept making us rush ahead to intercept them . . . at last they padded right into the bush and I was just breathing a sigh of relief when some idiot in a car poked his head out and said there were elephants about 6 miles further on and off we went! The road ran parallel with a river and apparently the elephants were going down to drink, crossing the road as they went, a herd of 30 or so. When we got to the place the man had said, I was so thankful, there was nothing to be seen but we could hear bashing and crashing down by the river and see the lumbering backs of one or two of them. We turned the car round and Mrs Bremer, looking back, said, 'Oh, stop, look!' and there was a great tower of a beast coming straight towards us on his way to the river! He was 50 yards away, 40, 30 and the Bremers fumbling with cameras and all talking together. Meanwhile he was just about 20 yards away and his great ears flapping. He stopped for a minute and then raised his trunk, half-blew, half-bellowed at us, and stamped his foot, and without any doubt preparing to charge. All this time we were still talking together and nobody listening to anybody – I gave Dr Bremer such a push and said Go, *Go on*, and I think he thought he had better so he went . . . Let me tell you now, as far as elephants are concerned, I am *not* in favour of them, they are *out* – they are too big and very nasty. Nothing would ever induce me to put myself in that position again. I kept seeing it all night. Dada loved it all and his only regret is that he didn't have a tape recorder in the car!

From the visit to the Kruger, which ended on this high note, they returned to Pretoria for the night of Friday, August 22, before leaving at 8.30 the next morning for Bloemfontein, capital of the Afrikaner heartland, the Orange Free State. Here there was another series of services, with many asking for interviews, before the long train journey (the first of their visit) back to Cape Town on the following Thursday. At Cape Town there were more services, sight-seeing, and long conversations late in the evenings with the Afrikaans family with whom they enjoyed staying. For the last service on Thursday, September 4, the great Groote Kerk was entirely packed out. As their ship left Cape Town the next day, ML-J was very moved as all the ships in the harbour sounded their sirens in tribute to them.

The weeks spent in South Africa were among the most significant which Dr Lloyd-Jones ever spent overseas. He was in a land divided not simply along lines of colour but divided also within the white community, the Afrikaans-speakers of the Boer and Dutch Reformed Church tradition being on one side (preponderating in religious and political influence) and the English-speaking churches, generally hostile to the reformed tradition, on the other. Dr Lloyd-Jones was probably the first preacher in this century to appeal to both groups and to win the support of both. Hitherto *joint* services and joint ministers' fraternals had been practically unknown.

The reason for his appeal to the Afrikaners was, of course, partly theological. Here was a visitor from Britain who, as they soon found out, was no supporter of the Arminianism which prevailed in the evangelical circles of the English-speaking churches. Brian Darroll recalls hearing him near the beginning of his visit where the audience – himself included – at least initially, was largely of English background and very unfamiliar with the emphasis of his message:

I first heard Dr Lloyd-Jones preach in the Durban City Hall. This is a large auditorium, seating several thousand people, and on this occasion it was well filled. While the Doctor is not a large man and the stage of the city hall is, he was not lost in its vast expanse. He stood at a lectern at the very front of the platform and behind him stretched out the stage, the orchestra and choir stalls, and finally the great organ loft. He had a quiet dignity and presence that immediately imposed its authority on the scene.

His quiet, but forceful, voice is with me to this day. But it was the physical effect which his preaching had on the audience that remains more vividly in my memory. Twenty-one years later I can still feel the physical 'shock waves' his preaching produced. 'Shock' is the right word, for he indeed *shocked* his hearers with his repeated, apparently heretical, certainly objectionable, statements.

His text was from Ephesians 2:4, 'But God'! As each doctrinal truth in the context was stated, the entire crowd seemed to surge forward as one angry wave in a protest of disagreement. The effect was heightened by the simultaneous intake of breath by the few thousand people as if to roar out a protest. Then as the Doctor, with calm deliberation, proceeded to explain and demonstrate the truth of the statement, the wave slowly subsided in nodding agreement until the calm was re-established. Only to surge forward again with the next statement and again to be stilled by the quiet but relentless argument. So the sermon proceeded with these successive waves of indignation alternating with quiet submission to the relentless reasoning of the exposition.

Dutch Reformed people present saw that the truth of divine sovereignty, preached in this manner, could be used to win the assent of other Christians. One hearer of English background, writing of Dr Lloyd-Jones' Durban services to a friend in the United Kingdom on August 15, reported:

Without hesitation I would say the visit was all too short – he could easily have had two weeks in Durban when a build up would have packed our biggest hall – such searching ministry is seldom if ever heard in this country.[1]

Mrs Lloyd-Jones, in writing home from Durban, had particularly noted the rising tide of interest from the Afrikaner side. She wrote on August 5: 'Everything is I believe spiritually very dead – nonconformity weak and Dutch Reformed powerful . . . They have taken to Dada in a big way and at this moment he is with them – the pastors

---

[1] W. H. Maxwell writing to George Gray, the owner of Pickering and Inglis Ltd., Ludgate Hill, London. Mr Maxwell says that the meetings started 'with 450 or so – then 550 in City Hall, then double the last number in the City Hall, and finally the Baptist Church was absolutely crammed everywhere'.

came and asked him to come and meet them to discuss some of their acute problems and to advise. The other ministers are holding their breath in a state of stunned, though delighted, incredulity.'

This entrée with the Dutch Reformed pastors increased throughout the visit. It was not, it should be said, entirely based upon a common theological foundation. His interest in Afrikaner views, in the Voortreker Monument at Pretoria and in museums of the Boer Wars at Bloemfontein, was accompanied by a measure of understanding unusual in Britishers. Speaking of this nearly thirty years later, Dr Paul Bremer (himself the son of a former South African cabinet minister) writes: 'I frequently think of him in our present situation here in South Africa. He had so much insight into the situation when he was here and he had such an appeal to the Afrikaner because he understood them. His Welsh background and his understanding of the Welsh national feeling gave him immediate insight into some of the more emotional aspects of the Afrikaner. They are an emotional people and unless their emotions are understood, they are not understood.'

This is not to say that the Lloyd-Joneses agreed with everything they heard from the Afrikaner side, even though they had been brought up as Liberal pro-Boer sympathisers. After one afternoon's sight-seeing in Bloemfontein, when they were told of little save the atrocities committed against the Boers, Mrs Lloyd-Jones says she became 'positively pro-English' and firmly of the opinion that Douglas Johnson 'must never be allowed to come to South Africa, he would burst!'. They appreciated seeing something of work being done among the black peoples and especially at the Training School of the interdenominational Dorothea Mission, near Pretoria. ML-J was to leave South Africa convinced of the wrongness of the glib generalisations which people offer on the nation's problems, and convinced that the gospel was the only possible solution to its racial and political problems.

It was Dr Lloyd-Jones' opinion that the most profitable work which he was able to do in South Africa was in many ways in the gatherings of ministers which he addressed at each centre. He spoke with much force to pastors who, although often orthodox in their doctrine, were beginning to take up modern evangelistic methods in order to promote church growth. The real need, he argued, was not for 'campaigns' but for the renewal of the inner life of the church and for a restoration of faith in the power of preaching, anointed of the

Spirit of God, leading to revival. In this connection an incident in the Pretoria meeting of ministers and students was long to be remembered. At the end of the meeting, one of the professors of the Dutch Reformed Church, in moving a vote of thanks, took the opportunity to express his disagreement with the visitor's emphasis and he pointed to the 'Tell Scotland' campaign as a recent example of effective mass evangelism. Had the criticism been personal, ML-J would have ignored it but, believing that an issue vital to the work of the ministry was involved, he asked leave of the chairman to respond. He then spoke further with much authority and displayed, in doing so, a close knowledge of the 'Tell Scotland' campaign which he described as 'an artificial, paper campaign'. Speaking of the professor who had moved the vote of thanks, A. S. Gilfillan comments, 'The Doctor must have demolished him and later expressed to the chairman his fears that he had gone too far. The reply was, "Not at all. The students were delighted to see their professor laid flat!"'

Subsequent letters to ML-J from ministers spoke particularly of these fraternals. One pastor in Durban wrote to say, 'It is with praise to the Lord that I thank you for what has been to me a great encouragement, an uplift of spirit, a correction of fault and a deliverance from drift'. He explained how he had come to waver in his attachment to the views held by ML-J 'and Dr Tozer of Chicago':

It was just in these matters that I was beginning to lose out, for I was succumbing to the 'popular' idea that perhaps a different sort of 'programme' was after all the sort of approach one should make in these days, while in my heart of hearts the very idea was unsatisfying. I wish that I had not needed the rebuke and that I had been more established in the points of view which you have now underlined for me. But I see where the fault lies now. Pressure upon the prayerless must inevitably bring collapse and having known its power (i.e. that of prayer) in service in days gone by, I determine to seek more time for communion with the Father, and to spend less time in nervous effort and wasteful thinking.

Another minister wrote similarly from Bloemfontein:

I shall not forget the correction of your powerful utterance at the joint ministerial meeting on Monday morning. To know that it is the power of God which alone can save, and not the ingenious techniques which we can devise. That has welled up in me again and again, until I want to turn from the tedious details of circuit administration and give myself just over to this business of preparation and preaching. You have taken me back to the vivid days of my own call to preach and I give all the glory to God who has so mightily used you in these all too few days in our midst.

Nothing has so inflamed my spirit anew as the fellowship that has been ours this week. Interestingly enough, I picked up a copy of Smeaton on *The Holy Spirit*, purely because your recommendation was on the cover, and it is first-class.

It is noteworthy, also, that young people who were to be future leaders were permanently influenced by Dr Lloyd-Jones' visit. One of these – later to attend Westminster Chapel as a student in London – was Robin Wells, a future General Secretary of the Universities and Colleges Christian Fellowship (as the IVF was to be renamed). Another was John Temple. He was fourteen when he heard ML-J preach on 'But God' in Pretoria and writes:

I was a Christian but the reality of Christ came to me in a new way and from then on I lived differently . . . I recall so vividly my first meeting with him. It was after a service in the Central Baptist Church, Pretoria. He had preached a mere 40 minutes and I was moved out of this world. As he stood below the pulpit to speak to any who desired to see him whilst the congregation left, I quickly made my way forward. I thanked him and told him of how God had spoken to me. I was struck immediately by his presence – his humility. I had been used to seeing visiting evangelists in South Africa – many from the USA – and they were hard-driving, powerful personalities. After a short hesitation he said just, 'Thank you'. He may have said more but I do not recall it. He apparently didn't feel that I needed more.

Despite a commonly felt hope that 'God will send you back to us', Dr Lloyd-Jones never returned to South Africa, nor to the West Coast of the United States. Many shared the view that the visits were too brief and would have agreed with the opinion of Archbishop Mowll of Sydney (expressed at the IFES Harvard Conference of 1947) that ML-J needed to be freed from his pastoral commitment in order to play a full international role. But ML-J was never drawn to such a view. He believed that Christian leaders needed to be pastors, and that preaching and teaching to *one* congregation is the first work of the ministry. He did not, however, foresee that it was precisely that conviction which was to lead, ultimately, to the widest international influence. It was the week by week preaching that the Westminster Chapel situation demanded which, when issued in printed form, was to do more than any personal travelling could ever have accomplished.

The so-called Ecumenical Movement will, of necessity, cause all Evangelicals to re-examine and reconsider their position more and more. It has already done so in many countries, and there is much uneasiness in many minds in this country.

ML-J

in his Foreword to *Evangelicalism in England*
by E. J. Poole-Connor, 1951.

Dr Martyn Lloyd-Jones said recently that Dr Schweitzer was a very good man, and that he had accomplished excellent work, but in spite of that, he was not a Christian . . . If being a Christian is to be orthodox within the confines of the historical creeds, then I am afraid that Dr Lloyd-Jones is correct. I do not think that Dr Schweitzer could accept all the Christian dogmas and ignore his own great achievements in the field of theology. But I could name dozens of other great men who have enriched our lives both philosophically and spiritually who are in exactly the same boat.

It is fair to ask whether Dr M. Lloyd-Jones would accept them at all? Perhaps the Pope of Rome would not call Dr Lloyd-Jones a Christian . . . I say this to show that the custom, with Christians, to curse each other leads us to very sticky mires until we don't really know where we are.

May I say that I am willing to believe that the present Pope is a sincere Christian. And of course I believe that Dr M. Lloyd-Jones is as good a Christian as he.

It is a pity that people of strong convictions in religious matters are led to express such an uncompromising opinion of others who believe differently from them.

Translation from Welsh, '*Hawl ac Ateb*'
Y *Goleuad* (the weekly newspaper of the Calvinistic Methodists),
May 22, 1957

15

The Changing Religious Scene

In Dr Lloyd-Jones' view the 1950's and the early 1960's witnessed the greatest degree of change in the Christian world during the 20th century, a change which was to affect both the churches in general and evangelicalism in particular. A glance at the evangelical papers and magazines of the early 1950's compared with those of a decade later indicates the extent of the transformation in evangelical attitudes and interests. At the beginning of the second half of the century the *English Churchman* was probably the principal weekly organ of Anglican evangelicals, and *The Christian* and *The Life of Faith* supplied the evangelical constituency as a whole with news and comment much as they had done thirty years before. Ten years later a new evangelical mood – self-consciously contemporary in outlook and critical of what it was now coming to regard as the obscurantist isolationism of the older evangelicalism – favoured different publications, *The Church of England Newspaper* for Anglicans, and the monthly *Crusade* magazine for evangelicals in general. The advantages of the change seemed obvious to many: in the 1960's evangelicalism was more influential, more respectable and more competent to meet differing views with tolerance and understanding. As we shall see, evangelical Anglican clergy, whose numbers and position gave special prominence to their voice, were leaders in this change, motivated by a concern to give a new image to evangelicalism in the national Church.

Behind this change lay the inspiration of a new ethos, introduced largely by the ecumenical movement which by the 1950's had already made Christian unity the major theme of the religious press. 'The Holy Spirit is leading us to a Wider Union' was the most often repeated sentence of the decade. It affected Anglicans and Nonconformists equally. When the Free Church Federal Council co-operated with the World Council of Churches at Amsterdam (1948) and again at the WCC Evanston Assembly (1954), the justification for its separate existence was soon called in question as the British Council of Churches took up the leading role in ecumenical endeavour.[1]

The strength of ecumenical opinion was to challenge the whole structure of English evangelicalism. As already noted, since the decline of historic Christianity in the previous century, while generally continuing in their respective denominations, evangelicals had found their chief support and encouragement in activities which lay outside the control of the denominational bodies. Accordingly, their main influence was exercised not in the denominations as such – where they might be cold-shouldered and criticized – but rather in such evangelical institutions as Keswick, the non-denominational missionary societies and the Inter-Varsity Fellowship. Here, if not elsewhere, evangelicals could insist upon an acceptance of the Bible as the inerrant Word of God.

At a later date James Barr was to describe the evangelicalism or 'fundamentalism' to which he once belonged as follows:

While fundamentalism in Britain is not represented by major denominations in the traditional ecclesiastical sense, it has nevertheless produced its own special forms of organization, and these are of the greatest importance in any attempt to understand fundamentalism as a phenomenon . . . though undenominational in this sense, they are commonly very exclusive and non-co-operative towards non-conservative evangelical organizations which work in parallel with them. The classic case is . . . The Inter-Varsity Fellowship . . .

Thus, though conservative evangelicals do not form a church or a denomination, they do have an organizational base which in some ways comes close to being a conservative evangelical denomination, though one of a peculiar kind.[2]

As we have seen, Dr Lloyd-Jones was himself critical of the 'movement' character of evangelicalism in England but he understood very well why it had occurred. Given existing church conditions, evangelicals had to put the Bible and fellow evangelicals first even

[1]In the *British Weekly*, March 8, 1956, Ernest A. Payne (General Secretary of the Baptist Union) wrote on 'What is to Become of the Free Church Federal Council?'. The British Council of Churches was formed in 1942 under the presidency of the ecumenical Archbishop William Temple.
[2]*Fundamentalism*, 1977, pp.21–22.

[298]

though it brought the accusation that they were not men conspicuous in denominational loyalty. Painful though that charge was, evangelicals at least had the consolation of believing that they were putting *Christian* unity before denominational unity. But it was precisely that belief which the ecumenical movement now challenged, for it also claimed to represent a greater Christian unity which transcended all denominational differences. Evangelicalism had now either to justify its existing position or concede the claim that it represented a kind of sectarianism. Inevitably this was to be a key issue in the second half of the 20th century. Evangelicalism was at a cross-roads.

It is interesting to note that Dr Lloyd-Jones was closely involved in some of the earliest attempts to address this question of where evangelicalism stood in regard to ecumenism. Perhaps it is not surprising that the Evangelical Alliance, with its stand for evangelical (i.e. Christian) unity, was one of the first agencies to be put under pressure. We have already noted the mixed nature of its speakers in 1948. That same year Dr Lloyd-Jones had a private meeting with Martyn Gooch, the General Secretary of the Alliance. Gooch was perhaps awaking to the danger of ecumenism and he wrote to ML-J, 'How greatly I enjoyed that talk with you, and how important I feel the present to be in relation to the future!'.[1] A further meeting was arranged with a number of key men, the Rev. Hugh R. Gough of Islington (soon to be Bishop of Barking) representing the officers of the Alliance, and Lloyd-Jones being asked to invite others whose names he had evidently mentioned. They were W. H. Aldis, Colin Kerr, E. J. Poole-Connor and G. W. Kirby. It should not be overlooked that the first two men named in this list were Anglicans, though they represented an older viewpoint than that of Gough.

Nothing seems to have been settled at this April, 1948 meeting. After the World Council of Churches was founded later that same year, the Evangelical Alliance was asked to state publicly its policy on ecumenism. It replied that its attitude to the World Council of Churches was one of 'benevolent neutrality'. When Poole-Connor wrote a letter to the *Christian* expressing his regret over this statement, the publication of his letter was declined. 'I then,' writes Poole-Connor, 'inquired of the Editor of the *English Churchman* whether he would print it, and he cordially agreed to do so. But once more my efforts were frustrated, for the Bishop of Barking (Hon.

[1]March 25, 1948.

David Martyn Lloyd-Jones: Volume Two

Clerical Secretary of the Alliance) intervened, with neither apology nor explanation, to prevent its publication.'[1] Later Poole-Connor came to believe that the Alliance 'had made up its mind to follow a policy of "benevolence" toward the World Council which carries it far beyond "neutrality"'. When an article appeared in the Alliance's magazine *Evangelical Christendom* (May 1952) which, in Poole-Connor's words, 'conveyed the impression that the World Council was strongly swinging over to Evangelicalism', he resigned his Alliance membership.

The Inter-Varsity Fellowship made no similar claim to 'neutrality' and, accordingly, faced frequent opposition on account of its articulate defence of evangelicalism and its 'isolationism'. As we have seen, it was Dr Lloyd-Jones who was especially blamed for the movement's 'divisiveness' and 'intolerance'. Certainly no one else spoke as forcefully in defence of the IVF's position. One of the best examples of this was at the annual meeting of the IVF in London on October 1, 1954. There was no common ground with ecumenism, he argued, with its claim that it is 'experience' of Christ which unites and not any common body of truth. For the issue behind that claim was really this: 'In spiritual affairs, does theology really matter at all? Does it, in the last analysis, matter what a man ultimately believes?' An avoidance of that question, he believed, lay at the heart of the ecumenical movement. Dr Lloyd-Jones' charge in this 1954 address was that ecumenism was not facing the real problem. Certainly church attendance was about a third of what it had been in 1901, but why was this the case?

We have been repeatedly told that the cause of the state of the Church today was the result of two world wars and their consequent aftermath of political, economic and social changes. Obviously, they say, increasing social pressures of various kinds, greater movements of the population and a hundred and one other factors have all combined to take people away from places of worship. Such an explanation is constantly given and this superficial diagnosis all too easily accepted. But is it *true*?

There is only one adequate explanation for the state of the Christian Church today, it is the *apostasy of the Church herself*. The crucial damage was done by that fatal destructive Higher Criticism movement which came into being during the 19th century. The one essential

[1] *E. J. Poole-Connor*, D. G. Fountain, 1966, p. 182.

question in the mind of anyone who investigates such a matter must be, 'What robbed the Church of its authority?'. The certainty of its message was undermined. This is why the Church lost its hold upon the masses. That is the real explanation of the present position . . .

It is being said that the chief need of the Church is to repent because of its 'lack of unity'. That is being asserted widely today. It was, in effect, the message of Evanston – 'The Church needs to repent for her disunity'. We would suggest that before she repents of her disunity, she must repent of her apostasy. She must repent of her perversion of, and substitutes for, 'the faith once delivered to the saints'. She must repent of setting up her own thinking and methods over against the divine revelation given in Holy Scripture. Here lies the reason for her lack of spiritual power and inability to deliver a living message in the power of the Holy Ghost to a world ready to perish!

He then went on to show from various Scriptures that there are certain, definite cardinal doctrines, 'by which ye are saved' (1 Cor. 15:2). Unlike the current emphasis, he asserted, the New Testament is polemical. It appeals to doctrine and argument:

In Jude 3, we read, 'Beloved, when I gave all diligence to write unto you of the common salvation, it was needful for me to write unto you, and exhort you that ye should earnestly contend for the faith which was once delivered unto the saints'. Here we are given a stirring call to the defence of the Faith. Such a call is not popular today. It is not popular today even in some evangelical circles. People will tell you that it is all 'too negative'. They continually urge that we must keep on giving positive truth. They will tell us that we must not argue and we must never condemn. But we must ask, 'How can you fight if you are ever afraid of wounding an enemy?' 'How can you rouse sleeping fellow-warriors with smooth words?' God forbid that we find ourselves at the bar of judgment and face the charge that we contracted out from love of ease, or for fear of man, or that we failed to do our duty in the great fight of the Faith. We *must* – we *must* fight for the Faith in these momentous times.[1]

In 1954, the same year that ML-J gave this address, an event had already occurred in London which he came to regard as a watershed in evangelical history, though he was virtually alone among evangelical leaders in holding that opinion.

Two years earlier, the Evangelical Alliance, while still uncertain of

[1] I am quoting from Douglas Johnson's notes of this address which are given in *Knowing the Times*, pp. 51–60.

its role with regard to unity, underwent a change. Martyn Gooch was no longer in office, and a new Secretary, Roy Cattell (formerly a worker with Tom Rees), aided by the support of Bishop Gough, was intent upon giving the Alliance an evangelistic role. When, about the same time, a little-known American evangelist by the name of Billy Graham visited England and was unable to obtain the support of denominational leaders for a projected campaign, the Evangelical Alliance stepped in. Under Gough, the Alliance provided an Executive Committee to back 'the Billy Graham Greater London Crusade' and plans were made for the spring of 1954.[1]

After widespread publicity the Crusade began at Harringay arena in North London on March 1, 1954. It continued for eleven weeks during which time 37,600 people had responded to the evangelist's invitation to go forward to 'receive Christ'. Unlike later crusades, Graham came without the sponsorship of any official church bodies, for as Shaun Herron, Editor of the *British Weekly*, reminded him, their doors were 'politely but firmly closed on many of your British sponsors'. In other words, the visiting evangelist would have to choose whether he wanted the support of evangelicalism or of the denominations. He could not have both. Herron's own paper had opposed Graham's coming.

But the success at Harringay brought a remarkable change in the attitude of non-evangelicals. During the Crusade church leaders, hitherto never known to stand for biblical convictions, suddenly offered their support and approval. In 'An Open Letter to Billy Graham', Shaun Herron himself changed his position. Men not previously identified with evangelicalism were now to be found as distinguished visitors on the platform of the Harringay arena. Herron went further and promised the goodwill of ministers all over the country, and expressed the hope that the Crusade might 'become something of great value to *all* the Churches', provided Graham would distance himself from the 'self-righteous censoriousness' of

---

[1] In the opinion of Gordon Landreth, a later Secretary of the EA, Dr Lloyd-Jones had more influence upon the Alliance in these years than my narrative might suggest. Writing in *Idea*, the Quarterly Bulletin of the EA, Summer 1981, Landreth says of ML-J: 'It is not generally known that in the immediate post-war years it was his initiative which led to the strengthening of biblical convictions within the Evangelical Alliance leadership at the time, indirectly preparing the way for the subsequent invitation to Dr Billy Graham to conduct the Harringay Crusade of 1954, though Dr Lloyd-Jones himself did not publicly support that event.'

his 'followers' who were 'denouncers of their fellow Christians'. The question Graham had to face, said Herron, was whether the Crusade would end with a greater gulf between 'a large body of uncharitable and self-righteous evangelicals and the rest of the Church', or whether the evangelist would resist these 'followers' and contribute something creative to the British churches as a whole. 'You still have time,' the Editor wrote, 'to make it clear to the zealots that the consignment of all other Christians to hell is not a part of what you preach or what you wish . . . You should say it loud and clear, at Harringay, every night, and wherever else you may.'[1]

Put in this form to a visitor with little knowledge of the British scene, the appeal proved well-nigh irresistible. The suggestion was that English evangelicalism, with its bad dogmatic spirit, had hitherto achieved little. Its results were seemingly insignificant compared with the published figures of Harringay converts. 'You have been a common talking-point in the Churches of Britain,' Herron said to Graham, 'in a way that no one and nothing else have been for many years.' In order to achieve yet greater success all that was needed was a 'better' relationship with non-evangelicals. As the Crusade came to its conclusion, with the doors now wide open that had been 'closed' only a few months earlier, Jerry Beavan, its Executive Secretary, affirmed his hope that no 'divisiveness' would 'be stimulated by the campaign'. As though to confirm the same point, when the great final meeting was held at Wembley Stadium on May 22, Geoffrey Fisher, the Archbishop of Canterbury, was there to give the benediction.[2] Henceforth, in Britain (and elsewhere), the Graham crusades would be open to the co-operative support of all churches and their leaders irrespective of theology.

In this way a new alignment was introduced into the British evangelical scene, an alignment supported by 'success' on a scale unparalleled in the present century. The question now before evangelicals, which time was to make clearer, was whether their former insistence on certain doctrinal standards as a basis for co-operative effort was still tenable. Those of ecumenical persuasion already believed that agreement on such questions as the Person of Christ, the nature of the Atonement and the authority of Scripture was unnecessary in order to Christian unity. The British Council of

[1]The *British Weekly*, March 25, 1954.
[2]*Billy Graham*, John Pollock, 1966, pp. 170–72.

Churches, for example, included the Unitarian denomination in its membership. If evangelicals – among whom Graham was naturally seen as a leader – could drop their former standards with respect to co-operation in work *outside* their denominations, why could they not also drop them *within* and thus share with denominational leaders in the ecumenical quest? If it were possible for evangelicals to be ecumenical in evangelism, then why not in the regular life of the churches? While any discussion of these questions had not yet surfaced in England it is of importance to note that they had in the United States. Billy Graham, with strong financial backing, was now poised to back a new policy in North America. A network of organizations, in which Fuller Theological Seminary, the National Association of Evangelicals and a new journal, *Christianity Today*, were centre-pieces, would deliberately seek to move evangelicalism away from the 'militancy' of fundamentalism and to gain better recognition in the main-line denominations. There would be a new scholarship, a new openness and a new spirit of inclusiveness. Speaking of the vision of the founders of *Christianity Today*, George M. Marsden writes, 'Apparently their proposed strategy was that for the first two years they would emphasize points of commonality with ecumenical Christians, thus establishing the widest possible hearing for the magazine'.[1] When Carl Henry was being sounded out for the role of the journal's first editor the question was whether he saw the need for 'an entirely new approach'. In reply to a letter from Graham, Henry pointed out that 'Liberalism and Evangelicalism do not have equal rights and dignity in the true church'.[2] Henry was appointed although he declined to be as concessive as the formulators of the new approach desired. Nonetheless the policy, both at Fuller and elsewhere, was to go forward, with Graham now committed to accepting the sponsorship of non-evangelicals. What had happened in England in 1954 had clearly affected the evangelist's judgment. Marsden writes:

During campaigns in England in 1954 Graham received broader church support than his fundamentalist supporters would have allowed him in the United States. Such successes in culturally influential religious circles were leading Graham toward the conviction that he could make

[1] *Reforming Fundamentalism*, Fuller Seminary and the New Evangelicalism, Eerdmans, 1987, p. 161.
[2] *Ibid, p. 160 (Letter of June 20, 1955).*

marvellous inroads into America's major denominations if he could only jettison the disastrous fundamentalist images of separatism, anti-intellectualism, and contentiousness.[1]

Graham probably did not understand the extent of differences on the two sides of the Atlantic in 1954 (evangelicalism in the UK was not identical with fundamentalism in the United States) but from now on a similar policy was to be at work in both countries. 'Co-operation without Compromise', a phrase in use among new evangelicals in the States by 1956, was to become a slogan of English evangelicals in the sixties.[2] Similarly the Graham statement, 'The one badge of Christian discipleship is not orthodoxy but love', which by 1957 was repeated so often in the States, says Marsden, that it 'was becoming a refrain',[3] was before long to be echoed by evangelicals in Britain.

*   *   *

In the meantime perhaps no one in England in 1954–55 anticipated precisely what the new coalition which emerged from the Harringay Crusade would do to evangelicalism. The position of the Evangelical Alliance, as we shall see, was to become crucial at this point. After the Crusade the Graham organization developed its own work in Britain and thus made the position of the Alliance in inaugurating mass evangelism unnecessary. This led to a further change both in personnel and in policy within the Evangelical Alliance. When the Rev. Gilbert W. Kirby, a Nonconformist minister and a member of the Westminster Fellowship, became its Secretary in 1956 he sought to renew the old role of the Alliance in the promotion of evangelical unity. On this subject and others he was in frequent consultation with Dr Lloyd-Jones and, for a time, Lloyd-Jones was to return to being a principal speaker for the Evangelical Alliance. Already, however, there were signs of tensions which lay ahead. After Dr Lloyd-Jones had been the main speaker at a day conference of the

[1] *Ibid*, p. 159.
[2] It was used as the title of a book by James DeForest Murch in 1956 and also as the title of the first chapter in A. T. Houghton's *Evangelicals and the World Council of Churches*, a booklet published in London in 1962 by the World Dominion Press.
[3] *Reforming Fundamentalism*, pp. 164–65. The statement belongs with that of E. J. Carnell, the most popular professor at Fuller Seminary, 'Jesus names *love*, not defense of doctrine, as the sign of a true disciple' (p. 138).

Alliance held at Westminster Chapel on June 18, 1957 E. J. Poole-Connor wrote to him:

> 39, Palace Road
> London S.W.2
> 20/6/57
>
> Oh, my dear Doctor – I do so heartily thank God, and thank you, for your address at the Alliance meeting on Tuesday last! You always manage to say the thing that needs to be said, but which nobody else will say.
>
> I attended the morning meeting; and while Kirby was excellent, and Sir Arthur good, Bishop Gough presented the vaguest platitudes; except that he hinted at kinder feelings toward Rome, and left the door wide open for co-operation with the World Council – all in the most dulcet of tones.
>
> How my heart went out to your words about revival! There lies our only hope. Oh, for the Lord Jesus to pray over again in heaven the prayer recorded in John 17, 1 & 2!
>
> Yours gratefully
> E. J. Poole-Connor

Here was the main problem: how could bonds be strengthened among evangelicals while they remained disagreed among themselves whether or not ecumenism was a danger to the gospel? For the time being at least the old attitude towards non-evangelical Christianity was prominently represented in the Alliance and the Alliance was agreed about the danger of the new openness towards the Church of Rome in the Church of England. Changes in the Canon Law of the Church of England, in order to allow the use of vestments identified with the idea of a sacrificial priesthood, were currently being put forward and Kirby, on behalf of the Alliance, drafted a letter to the Archbishop of Canterbury expressing 'the apprehension that is felt by evangelicals generally'. 'We deplore,' he wrote, 'any revision of the Canons which would make co-operation between the established Church and the Free Churches more difficult, or which would in any sense compromise the reformed character of the Church of England . . . We are concerned that the position of the Bible as the supreme and final authority in all matters of faith and conduct should be zealously safeguarded.' If this proposed Alliance letter was sent it was probably the last time that evangelicals unitedly attempted to affirm what had been the traditional evangelical

Anglican view of the Protestantism of the national Church. Archbishop Fisher, to whom the protest was addressed, as well as giving his blessing to the Graham Crusades, was soon to be the first man holding his office to visit the Pope since the Reformation.

A further danger, at least in the view of some evangelicals, had to do with the whole work of overseas missions. For many years strategists in the missionary world had seen the need for far greater unity. Too often traditional denominational differences between Protestants had been maintained on the mission field to the injury of young churches. Evangelicals did not doubt that a greater measure of biblical unity would clearly be to the advancement of the gospel. But by the 1950's there were missionary statesmen already convinced that the movement represented by the WCC provided the best hope for greater unity. They accepted that the ecumenical movement was, in the words of the WCC statement at Evanston (1954), a response 'to the call and action of their Divine Lord'. When a London Mission Convention of sixty British missionary societies was held in March 1957, this viewpoint was strongly presented by Bishop Stephen Neill. Surveying the forces arrayed against the Christian message, he argued that it would be folly not to commit the whole missionary effort to the ecumenical principle.

The Alliance again took a lead in responding to this situation as Gilbert Kirby reported to Dr Lloyd-Jones in a letter of February 12, 1959:

I thought I would like to keep you posted with developments, particularly regarding the emergence of the Evangelical Missionary Alliance. The interest in this direction has been most encouraging and there are just on forty Societies in membership, plus a futher eight Training Colleges. I thought you might be interested to see the draft constitution. You will notice that we have adopted the IVF basis . . .

I felt I would like to share these matters with you as I have always so greatly appreciated your counsel.

But despite this move by the Evangelical Alliance to create an alternative to ecumenism in missionary endeavour it is significant that not all its participants assessed the situation in the same way. It was becoming apparent that a number of evangelicals saw no conflict between adherence to the IVF Basis of Faith *and* participation in the World Council. The International Missionary Council already had evangelical participation and, when this Council was integrated with the WCC at the Third Assembly which met in New Delhi in November 1961, not only the integration but the Assembly itself received evangelical support. In *What of New Delhi?* the Rev. A. T. Houghton, a leader in the most orthodox of the Anglican Missionary Societies (the Bible Churchmen's Missionary Society), argued that the only alternatives were participation in the WCC or 'splendid isolation'. In favour of evangelical participation, he believed that the day had passed when evangelicals 'who spoke the truth as they saw it were neither welcomed nor tolerated'.[1] Further, Houghton urged the illogicality of staying outside new developments, remarking that evangelicals in the Church of England were already committed by their denomination 'to indirect membership and involvement in the World Council of Churches'. To avoid that membership they would need to leave the Church of England altogether. They should also face the inconsistency of not objecting to participation in Anglican diocesan affairs, yet drawing the line at the WCC: 'the former participation may be more frustrating and even "compromising" than the latter, for it is possible for the Church of England to take official action of which we thoroughly disapprove, but which we have to accept whether we like it or not '.[2]

These words, as we shall see, are a key to understanding what was to be the new evangelical policy of the 1960's. A. T. Houghton was presenting views which would soon be commonplace. The implications of this position were, however, wider than Anglican evangelicalism and even before the end of the 1950's it was putting a strain on relationships between Dr Lloyd-Jones and some Free Church members of the Westminster Fraternal. Though the strain did not surface in public at this date, ML-J was conscious of its existence and among its consequences was a gradual weakening of the once close connexion between ML-J and the leadership of the London Bible College. Since its small beginnings the College had prospered. By 1953 its old building on Marylebone Road was 'bursting at the seams' with 100 full-time students and another 400 attending evening classes. In a sense it was the increased numbers which gave rise to a difference in view between ML-J and the Principal. Since the College was non-denominational its men had no ready access into

[1] *What of New Delhi?*, A. T. Houghton, Bible Churchmen's Missionary Society, 1962, p. 22.
[2] *Ibid*, p. 57.

the ministry of any denomination, yet its success in placing growing numbers of students in churches was clearly crucial to its reputation. Ernest Kevan, though of Strict Baptist background, saw a better future for his students in such larger bodies as the Baptist Union churches. Initially the Baptist Union would not accept London Bible College men for its ministry and it had become a primary object of Mr Kevan's policy to change that decision. This he did by putting as many as possible of his students through the Bachelor of Divinity course of London University in order to win for the College recognition as an educational establishment. The Baptist Union opened its doors[1] and by the 1960's the leadership of the London Bible College was on good terms with members of the Baptist Union Council. Concerned at the common view once expressed by H. L. Ellison (a former London Bible College lecturer) that 'the typical conservative Evangelical is seldom a good denominational man', Kevan expected his men who entered the Baptist Union to live down that reproach: 'When our men settle in Baptist pastorates they never cause trouble'.

Dr Lloyd-Jones did not share Mr Kevan's confidence in this policy development. In the first place it meant the encouragement of denominational loyalties just at a time when the ecumenical movement was already endangering the distinctiveness of evangelical convictions. In the Free Churches, as well as in the Church of England, it was becoming virtually impossible to be pro-denominational without also being pro-ecumenical. In the second place, he did not believe that the London Bachelor of Divinity course was the best means of preparing men for the work of the ministry. Certainly he saw that to bypass the credentials conferred by theological degrees could exclude students from places of influence, but he feared that a greater influence was being jeopardized by subjecting future preachers to the unbelieving and liberal studies approved by the Universities.

This background is necessary if we are to understand the implications of an address which Dr Lloyd-Jones gave on the occasion of the opening of the new premises of the London Bible College at 19 Marylebone Road on Saturday, May 10, 1958. A fine day in early summer, it was a grand occasion in the evangelical calendar of that year. Earlier in the week Professor E. J. Young of Westminster Theological Seminary had given four 'Inaugural Lec-

[1]It did, however, retain one or two special stipulations for candidates for its ministry from the LBC.

tures'.[1] On the day itself the crowds of visitors were welcomed with the gift of a splendid brochure on the College, but for many there was no hope of getting a seat in the Chapel which was early crowded with official guests for the service at which Dr Lloyd-Jones was to preach. Every corner of the whole building seemed to be crammed with people and, happily, the proceedings from the Chapel were relayed by loudspeakers. It was one of the most powerful sermons which ML-J ever gave. His text was 2 Timothy 2:15, 16, 'Study to shew thyself approved unto God, a workman that needeth not to be ashamed, rightly dividing the word of truth. But shun profane and vain babblings . . .'.

In the course of this address he spoke of the contemporary lack of concern over error in the religious world, yet Paul says it 'will eat as doth a canker' (2 Tim 2:17): 'It kills, robs of life and leaves a festering mass at the end. The church today is a travesty of the word "church" all because of this cancer.' The call to evangelicals, he went on, is to concentrate on 'the word of truth'. 'Our message is not uncertain. Men are not all going the same way, worshipping the same God. We are to teach *revealed* truth and not shift our position according to the state of the world . . . It is because it believes that, that this institution is called the London *Bible* College. If our Lord's return does not take place for a hundred years I hope it will still be teaching the same thing.'

He then took up the meaning of the phrase 'rightly dividing'. The dividing of the truth which the Apostle required was not the division which liberalism introduced into the Bible, nor was it the dividings of those who were 'always on prophecy or sanctification or always evangelistic', but it meant the right use of the whole of Scripture: 'We must know the whole counsel of God and deliver it all. We must avoid nothing out of compromise, we must keep the balance and proportion of faith, and always *apply* Scripture to the conscience . . .'

ML-J's application of his message that day consisted in pressing the question, How may the College know if it is attaining this object and 'rightly dividing the word of truth'? 'The tests,' he said, are these:

Are the men more certain of the truth at the end of their studies than at the beginning? Are they more steadfast? Do they know God better and desire to serve God better than when they came in? Ah, how many lose this!

[1]Subsequently published under the title *The Study of Old Testament Theology Today*, James Clarke, 1958.

Have they a greater zeal for God? a greater love for the lost and
perishing? What is the purpose of doctrine and knowledge if it is not to
know God? . . . You may have more BD's than any College in the
country but only if the result is that your people know God better!

. . . We are a remnant today, but others have been through the same
situation – 'If we suffer, we shall also reign with Him'. Paul encouraged
Timothy with this, 'The foundation of God standeth sure, having this seal,
The Lord knoweth them that are his'. Remember that He is taking special
interest in you. He will be with you in some lonely village, and when the
end seems to have come, remember that you are preaching a Saviour who
rose again; 'Remember that Jesus Christ was raised from the dead' . . .

It was a thrilling peroration. E. J. Young told a group of students
afterwards that he had heard nothing equal to it since the death of
Gresham Machen and back in the United States he wrote of that May
afternoon at the London Bible College: 'The dedication service was
impressive, and the highlight came in the address by Dr Martyn
Lloyd-Jones. To hear Dr Lloyd-Jones preach is a memorable experience. Like few others he has the ability to expound the Scriptures in
such a manner that what he says stays with one. His words were very
appropriate for the occasion.'[1] But Professor Young, and no doubt
others present, had not seen the implications for the College which
lay behind the preacher's theme. The Faculty certainly saw them and
received the sermon coolly. When the possibility of its publication
was discussed at the next Faculty meeting, it was firmly turned down.
Later that same year (1958) the same controversial issue appeared
again at the Puritan Conference, though not at ML-J's instigation. In
the course of discussion on the existing state of theological education, Jim Packer expressed his conviction that even the evangelical
colleges 'turned out anything but preachers of the Word'. It was a
general statement, but Kevan rose to deprecate it and to speak of the
usefulness of the framework of the BD course. Dr Lloyd-Jones, well
aware of the sensitiveness of the issue, did not prolong the debate,
but asked whether it was not true that when the theological degree
courses were taken in evangelical colleges it led to an over-concern
with the apologetic at the expense of the positive. After 1958, in
contrast with earlier years, ML-J was asked to take little part in the
affairs of the London Bible College.[2]

[1]'A Visit to Britain' in *The Presbyterian Guardian*, September 15, 1958, p. 114.
[2]Surprisingly his name is not even mentioned in the short biography, *Ernest
Kevan, Pastor and Principal*, Gilbert W. Kirby, 1968.

Behind these differences of view now emerging within evangelicalism there was a deeper general difference with respect to the
whole condition of evangelical Christianity. Dr Lloyd-Jones believed that there was a serious condition of decline in the churches
and that evangelicalism was itself weakening rather than gaining in
spiritual power. He was thus not optimistic with regard to the
direction of events and, as in the London Bible College address
above, he could speak of evangelicals 'being a remnant'. This
assessment was out of keeping with the prevailing evangelical
mood. Even in 1951 when Poole-Connor's *Evangelicalism in England* was published, a reviewer in *The Christian* took exception to
the statement, 'In most Protestant denominations some evangelicals
are found but they are in a minority'. On the contrary, the reviewer
believed, 'At no time have evangelicals been so numerous in the
world as they are today'.

The Graham crusades notably strengthened this mood of hopefulness. It was not only men of liberal persuasion who were impressed by the numbers which attended the crusades; evangelicals
themselves began to believe that the future was with them. After
Harringay the Bishop of Barking spoke of 'the glorious possibilities these coming years hold for us',[1] and Billy Graham of his
'belief that Britain is on the verge of the greatest spiritual awakening in her history'. This kind of optimism was strengthened by
the greater sense of welcome which evangelicals began to receive
both in the denominations and in the World Council of Churches.
A. T. Houghton, while admitting 'some disquietude' over how far
the WCC was ready to admit evangelicals 'in its inner councils',
seemed to believe that liberal influence was in retreat and he noted
how 'Dr Billy Graham and Dr Paul Rees, whose names are household words among evangelicals all over the world', were both
present and welcomed at the Third Assembly of the WCC at New
Delhi.[2]

As we already know, Dr Lloyd-Jones read this whole situation
differently. He did not see the highly organized and much publicized crusades as proof of 'harvest time in England', and he believed
that churchmen, in their new 'openness' and readiness to welcome
evangelicals, were not being motivated by a shared love of the

[1] *Billy Graham*, p. 173.
[2] *What of New Delhi?*. See pp. 27 and 51.

truth.¹ For years he had been saying, 'There is nothing more tragic or short-sighted or lacking in insight than the assumption, made by so many, that the Church herself is all right and all she has to do is to evangelize the world outside'.² At the end of the 1950's this comment was less welcome than it had been at the beginning. It was not that evangelicals in the main denominations denied the need for change in the churches, but it was not change at a fundamental level. There was certainly a recognition of the need for evangelicals to attain a higher standard of scholarship. There was also the development of a feeling – soon to sweep all before it – that a main hindrance to the church effectively reaching the world lay in her out-of-date Bible version and in her forms of worship which had changed so little in centuries. The climate of thought – not uninfluenced by the secular world – was swinging against all things 'traditional' and 'old fashioned'.³

*   *   *

For an accurate understanding of Dr Lloyd-Jones' position there is further information which needs to be inserted here. How his increasingly controversial role within evangelicalism in these years is assessed will depend to a large degree on how far he may be said to have understood the true nature of the ecumenical movement. Some supposed that he had few, if any, personal contacts outside a narrow circle of conservative evangelicals. That was far from being the case. In fact he had the responsibility of taking the foremost part, representing the evangelical side, in discussions with leaders of the British Council of Churches over an extended period.

These discussions arose directly out of the Graham crusades of 1954–55 in Britain. Ministers and church leaders of liberal beliefs quickly saw the significance of the welcome which they received as they began to participate in the tide of evangelistic success. If such an international leader of evangelicalism as Dr Graham accepted their co-operation, there was surely reason to hope that British

¹If this sounds cynical, let it be remembered that A. M. Ramsey, who became Archbishop of Canterbury in 1961, urged his clergy, 'whatever we think of the theology', to receive those referred to them by the Graham crusades (*Canterbury Diocesan Notes*, April, 1966, p. 2).
²*Sermon on the Mount*, vol. 1, p. 54.
³'If one looks at Britain today,' wrote an acute observer, 'one must come to the conclusion that discontinuity rather than continuity is the order of the day.' *On Britain*, Ralf Dahrendorf, (London: BBC), 1982, pp. 37–38.

evangelicals would soon follow the lead which they had now been given. Evangelicals had either to justify their former intransigence with the alleged 'partisanship' of their separate identity, which was so contrary to the whole ecumenical spirit, or they had to abandon it.

The organizers of the British Council of Churches were particularly interested in this development and they were not slow to take the opportunity created by the dilemma among evangelicals. On October 6, 1954 the Rev. Kenneth Slack as its General Secretary sent a letter to Dr Lloyd-Jones and a few other key evangelical leaders asking for discussions. Slack reported that the Council had received a report from their Committee on Evangelism proposing a consultation 'between those with differing Biblical pre-suppositions to discover what co-operation in evangelism may be achieved despite such differences'. A first meeting was eventually proposed for November 5, 1956, from 11 a.m. to 5 p.m.

Dr Lloyd-Jones accepted the invitation and from the outset took the meetings very seriously; in fact, except for his friend, Leith Samuel, he was the only evangelical who remained in regular attendance throughout the whole period of their continuance. About sixteen ministers were present for the first session when the chairman, the Rev. John Huxtable (Principal of New College, London), as ML-J recalled, said:

They had invited us because he felt now, as a result of the Graham campaigns and of Barthianism, that the only point of difference between us was our view of the Scriptures. There was then some talk about this statement. I had not intended speaking but he called on me to speak. 'Well,' I said, 'seeing you ask me to speak I must, and I entirely disagree with you. I don't think we agree about *any* of the cardinal doctrines, so I would end with the Scriptures.'

When ML-J was then queried over where he thought their discussions should begin if not on Scripture, he proposed the atonement and was accordingly asked to make a statement in order to open the discussion at their next meeting on February 4, 1957. This he did, affirming that bound up with a substitutionary atonement (Christ 'being made a curse for us') was the whole question of the character of God. Such is the wrath of God against sin that He cannot forgive, except in a just manner. Propitiation was essential in order to forgiveness. ML-J's words were met with polite but almost universal opposition (there being only two other definite evangelicals present). The majority held that the cross did not effect a change in God's attitude to the sinner as 'it is always God's nature to forgive', rather it was intended to 'make God's forgiveness credible to us'. Others thought that no 'theory' of the atonement was necessary for co-operation in evangelism and that so long as there was a 'unity in the desire to present Christ' there was no need to insist on anything more. By introducing 'theology', Derrick Greeves, the Methodist minister of Central Hall, Westminster,[1] complained, Dr Lloyd-Jones was making 'effective evangelism dependent on man's understanding of the message'.

At the next meeting in April 1957, the subject for discussion was 'The New Life in Christ' and was introduced by an Anglo-Catholic, Father Kenneth Ross.[2] ML-J remained silent through a lengthy statement on the sacraments – 'the means whereby Christ is in us' – and through subsequent discussion. When he then reminded the gathering that the purpose of their meeting was to consider the possibility of co-operation in *evangelism*, the discussion soon turned to the relevance of evangelism for those who are already baptized. Methodist and Anglo-Catholic alike agreed that the evangelistic message to baptised people should be an exhortation 'to possess your possessions'. ML-J responded that such a message could only be appropriate to those who were *already* believers. 'He said that it is not possible to call people to Christ who, according to the Anglo-Catholic theory of incorporation at baptism, are already in Christ and questioned whether it was really possible to preach justification by faith if this theory were held.'[3]

Only a month later, a third meeting followed. The subject was 'The Church' and once more ML-J was silent for the first half until the discussion came round to the question as to what it meant to be a Christian. Hugh Gough, Bishop of Barking, thought that it was essentially a matter of 'the spirit' and that people could be one 'in Christ' though differing profoundly in theological beliefs. The Evangelical Alliance, he said, 'was concerned with the unity of the spirit, compared to which such questions as whether or not the Anglican Church and the Church of Scotland came together is of secondary importance'.

[1] Dr W. E. Sangster had concluded his ministry at Central Hall in 1955.
[2] Vicar of All Saints, Margaret Street, London.
[3] I am here and elsewhere quoting from summaries of the discussions which were provided for the group members by the organizers, supplemented by personal notes from Leith Samuel.

Another minister asked how far it was necessary for a person to be aware of God and His presence in the soul in order to be recognized as a Christian:

> Dr Lloyd-Jones said that he thought this was a very important point. He pointed out the danger in the Bishop of Barking's assertion that it was possible to 'feel' or 'sense' when a person was a committed Christian. He felt that this was applying a purely subjective test, and the result of that test might have its roots in something physical or psychological. Dr Lloyd-Jones would rely far more on the specific words or actions of a man. He explained that if the purely subjective test were held to be sufficient, devout Hindus and Buddhists might well come into the same category . . . The group continued to discuss the question of how it is possible to recognise a man who is 'in Christ' and Mr Jamieson asked whether it is the things to which a man gives assent, which provides the clue, or whether it is what he is himself. To this Dr Lloyd-Jones replied that it is both. The Chairman then asked Dr Lloyd-Jones to indicate more specifically how he would decide whether to admit someone to membership of his congregation. The answer given was that it would first be necessary to talk with such a person and ask certain fundamental questions; this, however, would not be entirely sufficient and Dr Lloyd-Jones said he would need to know something of the life of the person concerned. He also admitted that it was possible for mistakes to be made in admitting people who were not ready for church membership . . .
>
> Dr Goodall asked Dr Lloyd-Jones to elaborate on his division of Christians into the two classes of evangelical and non-evangelical and Dr Lloyd-Jones said he felt it was illustrated within the group itself. He pointed out that the Bishop of Barking was really nearer to himself than he was to a non-evangelical member of his own Church.

At following sessions in 1957 and 1958 discussion moved on to justification by faith and then to man as a sinner. On each occasion the same division in the meeting was apparent, with ML-J invariably being the one who had to demonstrate how wide the difference was. Notes of the group's conversation on the Fall are a good illustration. Father Mark Gibbard, having given his thoughts on sin and Adam, opened further discussion as follows:

GIBBARD   'We are clear aren't we, that we did not all sin in Adam?'
ML-J   'We are not. To me this is essential to the parallel that Paul is draw-ing. I am arguing that when Adam sinned, we sinned. Sin brought

in death. Sin renders us guilty. The punishment of that sin is death. Genesis is clear. Death is the punishment of Adam's sin. Death would not have entered in without sin. "And so death passed on all men, because all sinned" (Rom 5:12) – in that one act. Paul realises that there is a difficulty in understanding this thought, so there is the anacoluthon concerning those who died before the Mosaic Law. It is obvious that sin had been imputed prior to the Mosaic Law or people would not have died. Why do infants die? Paul's explanation is that they sinned in Adam. This is the only way to explain the death of infants. (If conscious sin is the cause of death they should never die). To constitute a sinner is a forensic term. Romans 5:19 refers to our standing before God.'

CYRIL BOWLES[1] 'Romans 3:22,23. Sin is the same word in Greek as 5:12. Would it not refer to actual sin or conscious guilt?'

ML-J 'Romans 5 amplifies and elaborates Romans 3 as is so often the case with the apostle Paul. How can we explain this reign of death among other people who have not sinned themselves apart from that involvement in the one sin of Adam.'

KENNETH ROSS 'Death is the consequence of Adam's sin.'

GIBBARD 'I find it hard to believe that "all sinned" means in Adam.'

ML-J 'Why all this Pauline stress on this one act of Adam if it is not so?'

ROY MCKAY[2] 'I could not accept the Augustinian relationship between us and Adam is physical. Surely the link is sin, as the link between us and Christ is faith.'

ML-J 'As God in His grace imputed to us the righteousness of Christ, so He imputed to us the guilt of Adam. Isn't Romans 5 a principle of seminal identity? Your argument is not with me but with the Epistle to the Romans.'

BOWLES 'Paul is not just thinking about sins but sin, as Leith Samuel said earlier.'

ML-J 'Why does a child disobey?'

BOWLES 'Romans 7.'

ML-J 'You cannot explain the world by Romans 7. You need Romans 5. This is not just a matter of relationship to the Law. It goes back to Adam.'

MCKAY 'How do you explain our connection with Adam?'

ML-J 'I cannot but look on Adam as a man, personal.'

GIBBARD 'I am going to accept this universality of death and sin.'

---

[1]Principal of Ridley Hall, Cambridge.
[2]Canon McKay was head of the Religious Broadcasting Department, BBC, 1955–63.

ML-J 'You are not being generous!' [Roars of laughter].

ERIC TINKER 'Sin does not imply guilt. Only sins imply guilt. We have no moral responsibility until we sin.'

BOWLES (TO ML-J) 'If you are right, we are sinful before we have sinned.'

TINKER 'Where do you find guilt imputed without conscious sin?'

ML-J 'Romans 5:10–13 is not subjective. War has been declared. Romans 5:12, "*all sinned*". 5:19, all "were constituted sinners". This avoids the subjective element. Adam has constituted us sinners.'

E. W. ODELL 'How would your theology work if Adam were only a generic concept (and not a person)?'

ML-J (TO GIBBARD) 'There was a good deal of Nygren this afternoon, wasn't there?'[1] ['Yes'] to Odell – 'I would not know where I was at all. I do not understand C. H. Dodd – he says a thing and then withdraws it or qualifies it.[2] The glorious parallel in Romans 5 is lost if there is no Adam.'

ODELL 'Adam is shaky ground. People say, "What right had God . . . ?".'

ML-J 'We must be careful not to join the scoffers. You are speaking in the interest of science, not the Bible[3] . . .

BOWLES 'We must put the teaching of Jesus in Mark 7 alongside this.'

ML-J 'Why this universal sinfulness?'

ODELL 'I do not know. The explanation in Genesis is such-and-such if you are interested.'

ML-J 'Was man ever perfect?'

ODELL 'I feel he must have been, but I do not know. We are all created capable of falling.'

ML-J 'No! We are all *born* fallen.'

BOWLES 'We have here a clear point of cleavage.'

GIBBARD 'I cannot accept as literal history Genesis 1–3. I have got to demythologise it and remythologise it. To preach all the New Testament says is a real problem.'

ML-J 'Where is my authority if the Apostle is not divinely inspired?'

[1] Anders Nygren, *Commentary on Romans*, 1949.
[2] *The Epistle of Paul to the Romans*, London, 1934, a much acclaimed work of which ML-J had a low opinion.
[3] At another meeting when ML-J affirmed that his whole theology rested upon the historicity of Adam as a person, Principal Huxtable 'wondered how Dr Lloyd-Jones reconciled his position with what the scientists say'. ML-J, probably the only scientifically trained person in the room, replied that 'scientists are very fallible gentlemen'. He regarded the theory of evolution as 'the biggest hoax in the world in the past 150 years'. Further on Genesis chapters 1 to 3 as history, see *Knowing the Times*, pp. 291, 343 ff.

It was not often within the group that differences in discussion came at once, and head on, but that was the case when Kenneth Slack gave an opening address on the character of God, instancing the Old Testament's claim that Uzzah was struck dead for touching the Ark (2 Sam 6:7) as 'not only shocking, but immoral'. Such a God would not be the same God as the Father of Christ. He believed that the story represented the 'imperfect morality' of the Old Testament. ML-J replied that Slack had missed the whole point of the story.

Man's attitude to God, Dr Lloyd-Jones said, is of primary importance. In this instance God had given exact instructions about how His Ark was to be handled. Uzzah disobeyed God's command and put God's revelation on one side. Therefore, his whole action was wrong. Dr Lloyd-Jones believed that this kind of disobedience is exactly what is happening in the Church today. In this instance God took action in order to teach people that He is to be worshipped and that His work is to be carried out in His way. Dr Lloyd-Jones said he could find many examples of this intervention running through the Scriptures. Periodically God seemed to take striking action, to act as a finger-post to men . . . Whenever people substitute their own ideas for God's declared way, Dr Lloyd-Jones believed, He is liable to deal with them in a drastic way.

Mr Barrett said he found difficulty in believing that it could really matter to God how the Ark was carried. He asked for further clarification from Dr Lloyd-Jones. Dr Lloyd-Jones gave the explanation that man's motive in this instance was to pit his mind against the will of God to the point of rebellion against that declared will. Although he was not able to interpret all the complex instructions about the handling of the Ark, it was quite clear to him that their purpose was to safeguard the sacred things of the holy and to emphasise that holiness. As he saw it, God is teaching us that He is the Lord. We are to obey His laws implicitly and surrender our own ideas and will.

Dr Lloyd-Jones said he thought a fundamental difference between the Group with regard to the nature of God had emerged from this particular discussion. Mr Slack said he was wholeheartedly in agreement with Dr Lloyd-Jones that this was the focus of division.

After twenty such meetings, the twenty-first meeting (on April 17, 1961) decided to recommend to the Committee on Evangelism that it wished to disband.[1] Interest had markedly declined since the initial

[1] Instead it was reformed on a smaller scale and continued for a further three years, but no longer discussing any resolution of differences. ML-J remained in attendance.

proposal for co-operative evangelism in 1956. The group was a mere half of its original number and of the 16 present at the second meeting (February 4, 1957) only ML-J and Leith Samuel remained. At the twenty-first meeting ML-J, tongue in cheek, 'wondered if it were possible to discover why in fact the group had "died"'. Neither Huxtable nor Slack was present to comment but Principal Bowles thought that part of the answer was that members lacked the time to attend. 'Dr Lloyd-Jones said that all the members of the group were busy people, but that some had regarded this conversation as so important that they had put everything else on one side.'

The truth was, as ML-J was to say later, 'We had demonstrated that no co-operation was possible'. But as these meetings were entirely unreported, the lessons they confirmed remained unknown to evangelicals at large. In a sense ML-J was to suffer from the ignorance of evangelicals concerning the manner in which he had patiently and courteously for five years debated the biblical position with those of differing views. Many who, in the mid-sixties, came to regard him as an unrelenting opponent of ecumenism had no idea of the time and energy he had expended to see that misunderstandings were avoided and to confirm that the differences were real and fundamental. As we shall see, by that date the climate of opinion was changing and the ecumenical leaders were to find more success with other evangelicals who were less intransigent than the minister of Westminster Chapel.

Opposite: The first of the three sides of ML-J's pulpit notes for his first sermon in the series on Romans, October 7, 1955. See Romans, *vol. 1, pp. 1–7.*

Introductory aresewal. Will learn a lot from this before
we come to detailed consideration.

1st epistle = N.T — Why? Has been there from beginning
W.B chronologically. 1st = Thessalonians.

Because of its importance & its clear statement of
basic & foundation truths.

This confirmed by its place in history of Church

Conversion of Augustine.
Basis of Augustine's refutation of Pelagius.
Led to Luther's conversion. His lectures on Romans
in 1515. "Inspired by faith" "Live in God"
— Bunyan.
Wesley & the reading of the Preface to Luther's Commentary
Robert Haldane & the revival on the Continent,
including D'Aubigné, Malan, Gaussen & others

Confirmed also by specific statements

Chrysostom — Had it read to him twice every week.
Luther :— "This epistle is the chief part of the N.T
and the very purest gospel, which indeed
deserves that a Christian not only know
it word for word by heart, but deal
with it daily as with daily bread of
the soul. For it can never be read or
considered too much or too well, and the
more it is handled, the more delightful it
becomes, and the 'better it tastes."
Coleridge :— the profoundest piece of writing in
existence

Author — Paul. General consideration, note what he says in v.1.
— Remarkable fact the he should write to a church =
Rome, mainly Gentile.
His story :—

A man cannot with real composure face death and eternity apart from consciousness of reconciliation with his Maker. We all need peace with God. We are getting older. Some of the colleagues whom I see here today are those whom in earlier years I taught in our Medical School. Speaking for myself, I can only face God in Jesus Christ, by spiritually dying and rising again in Him, by being reconciled through Him, and by living day by day in Him. It is from Him that I hear the liberating words: 'Thy faith hath made thee whole.' It is this spiritual element which ultimately matters to us. This goes on into eternity and, in Christ, I am ready for eternity.

ML-J
in an address on 'Medicine and the Whole Man' at the Annual
Breakfast of the CMF at Brighton, July 12, 1956

When a series of compliments to her husband's powers were one day being paid, Mrs Lloyd-Jones (herself medically qualified from University College Hospital) quietly remarked 'No one will ever understand my husband until they realise that he is first of all a man of prayer and then, an evangelist!' Those who knew him best will recognise the accuracy of this insight.

DOUGLAS JOHNSON
In the Service of Medicine, The Journal of the CMF, July, 1981,
p. 2

True evangelism, I would maintain, is highly doctrinal.

ML-J
1954, *Knowing the Times*, p. 58

16

Evangelism

The fact that at least half of Dr Lloyd-Jones' preaching was directly evangelistic can easily be overlooked. For one thing, the preponderance of sermons which have been published do not convey that impression. In the large majority of cases the published sermons consist of material prepared for the instruction and help of those who are already Christians, that is to say, they were first preached on Sunday mornings or Friday evenings at Westminster Chapel. These expository volumes give the reader only slight indications that in the same period in which they were first preached ML-J was also constantly engaged in the work of an evangelist. As a matter of principle he believed that in every congregation preaching that is primarily evangelistic 'should take place at least once each week'.[1] In his case, as already noted, the Sunday evening service was always set aside for this purpose.

Even after 1952, when the Friday night lectures commenced, the amount of time given to evangelism in his total ministry took up considerably more than a third for there was his other ministry constantly going on away from Westminster. Those who heard him in his own pulpit on Friday evenings had no idea that, since the previous Sunday, he might have been preaching two or three times in almost any part of the United Kingdom. These sermons, away from his own pulpit, were commonly of an evangelistic character. Initially prepared for Sunday evenings at Westminster Chapel, they were re-used elsewhere, the best ones on scores of occasions. The actual percentage of time given to evangelistic preaching was thus almost the opposite of the impression gained by anyone restricted to reading his published works currently available.

In form the Sunday evening service at Westminster Chapel was

[1]*Preaching*, p. 63.

virtually the same as the morning service already described. It was the nature of the sermon which constituted the main difference. In the morning the content of sermons ranged over many subjects arising out of the passage of Scripture currently being expounded as part of a consecutive series. In the evening the intention was narrower. Attention was focussed on such texts, or features of a text, as have pointed relevance to non-Christians. Not that such relevance was expected to be immediately apparent to his hearers; on the contrary he usually began (on Sunday nights) with the assumption that he was addressing those for whom Scripture might have no point or interest. It could well be some way into the sermon before the casual hearer began to come to the conviction that the text – perhaps from a book of Scripture that he could not even find – was speaking to him. Prior to that point, however, there was something in the preacher's introduction that had led the hearer into a train of thought and argument which was patently important enough to demand his attention. Perhaps the introductory words had to do with some familiar problem of the times and then, after the examination of popular but superficial proposals for the solution of that problem, it was related to the text and to the fundamental question of man's relationship to God.

But while ML-J's method of speaking to non-Christians was always logical and intended to engage their minds, it was in no sense based upon the idea that people can be reasoned into the kingdom of God. He believed absolutely that all saving hearing of Scripture came from God alone. That did not lead him, however, to suppose the exposition of any part of Scripture is as likely to be as effective as the preaching of any other part. Such a supposition he regarded as destructive of true evangelistic preaching. All Scripture is not equally profitable to the unconverted, rather there are certain primary truths which are essential to gospel preaching and which are most likely to be used in leading to conviction of sin and then to repentance and faith. The immediate purpose of evangelistic preaching is to drive men from all hope in themselves, and the scriptural means to that end is the proclamation of the truth about God and His holy law. Reflecting on Lloyd-Jones' Sunday night preaching, and comparing it with the message of other well-known London pulpits, an observer once said, 'Soper preaches love, Weatherhead preaches Jesus, and Lloyd-Jones preaches God'. For ML-J his emphasis was not a matter of personal preference, it was *biblical*. He believed with

B. B. Warfield that 'the staple of Paul's preaching was God and judgment'. That must be the starting point, for it is man's wrong attitude and his enmity to God which is the essence of his sin. Repentance is, primarily, a change of attitude to God. 'The worst sin of all is the false thinking about God of which the natural man is so terribly guilty.'[1] 'The trouble with people who are not seeking for a Saviour, and for salvation, is that they do not understand the nature of sin. It is the peculiar function of the law to bring such an understanding to a man's mind and conscience. That is why great evangelical preachers three hundred years ago in the time of the Puritans, and two hundred years ago in the time of Whitefield and others, always engaged in what they called a preliminary "law work".'[2]

This proclamation of God he saw as much more than the teaching of orthodox statements. It required the sense and experience of God both in the preacher and, if hearers were to be saved, in the pew. The presence and power of God Himself must be there. In this connection a number have spoken of the awesome element in the services at Westminster Chapel. The ultimate impression was not of the preacher, and yet the ambassador was so one with Him for whom he spoke that, in the consciousness of hearers, messenger and message merged into one. After listening to nearly a year of his evangelistic preaching, Jim Packer could speak many years later of what he remembered most:

I have never heard another preacher with so much of God about him . . . His approach is habitually Isaianic: having surveyed man's pretensions, his fancied greatness and adequacy, moral, religious, cultural, intellectual, he punctures them, humbling man and exposing his weakness, futility and sin, in order then to exalt God as the only Saviour. The thrust of Lloyd-Jones' sermons is always to show man small and God great . . . Application has been going on throughout the sermon; in one sense, it has all been application. He will have searched us, analysed us to ourselves, diagnosed us into self-despair, shown up sin and weakness and failure in vivid forms. Now, in conclusion, he points us to the God of all grace. With intense compassion he urges us to cast ourselves on the mercy of God in Christ, and his last words are likely to be an assurance about the life and glory we shall find when we do. Thus the preacher slips

[1] *Romans*, vol. 7, p. 44.
[2] *Romans*, vol. 6, p. 114.

out of the picture and leaves us with the God whom he would have us know.[1]

For Dr Lloyd-Jones to preach the real peril of man's guiltiness before God meant to preach the certainty of divine wrath, wrath which is already upon the unconverted and which is yet to come in the punishment of sin in hell. Far from believing that because modern man does not like this truth it should not be preached, he regarded warning as an essential part of biblical preaching. Hell is not a theory, and he saw the idea that for the ungodly there is no immortality (which was quietly gaining acceptance in some otherwise evangelical circles) as a dangerous error. 'Perish means perish; it does not mean go out of existence. It is the opposite to eternal life. It is the same as that place where their "worm dieth not and their fire is not quenched".'[2]

Another truth which he regarded as necessary to evangelistic preaching was that of human helplessness and inability in sin. To teach men that they possess the ability to turn from sin when they choose to do so is to hide the true extent of their need. Certainly the offer of salvation is to be urged upon all, and men must be told the necessity of their believing and repenting if they are to be saved, but faith and repentance are given to those who come to an end of themselves.[3] If men could choose to turn themselves from enmity to love, and from death to life, their conversion would not be the immense and supernatural thing which Scripture represents it to be. Commanded to believe though he is, man's preference for self and sin is such that any saving change in his condition must come from the direct action of God. The true condition of every non-Christian is such that

he cannot desire to love God, he cannot desire to obey Him. He cannot choose to do so, he is totally incapable of any spiritual effort. I am not saying this; it is the Apostle Paul who says it. The popular teaching which says that we have to preach the gospel to the natural man as he is, and that he, as he is, decides to believe on the Lord Jesus Christ; and that then, because he has believed, he is given new life, is regenerated – this, I say, is a complete denial of what the Apostle teaches here.[4]

[1] Quoted in *Twenty Centuries of Great Preaching*, vol. 11, Clyde E. Fant Jr and W. M. Pinson Jr, 1971, pp. 269-71.
[2] *Romans*, vol. 2, p. 107.
[3] 'The ultimate defect and error in the Arminian argument and all that has emanated from it is that it excludes the Holy Spirit from the real decision, and asserts that man is able to convert himself'. *Puritans*, p. 19.
[4] *Romans*, vol. 7, p. 14.

The time of regeneration is, therefore, not in man's control. What Scripture does make clear is that God first humbles through the truth those to whom he is pleased to impart life and a new nature. The only proof that believing is genuine is that the *life* is changed. These simple facts he saw as having immense bearings on evangelism. For one thing, it means that an evangelist must exercise care lest by a mere appeal to self-interest he induces a 'decision' which, far from being saving, is perfectly consistent with a person remaining in an unregenerate condition. A presentation of the gospel chiefly in terms of its ability to fulfil man's need of happiness and other blessings, and which fails to show that man's wrong relationship to God 'is much worse than everything else' in his condition, may well receive a considerable though temporary success. A salvation conceived 'not as something primarily that brings us to God but as something that gives *us* something'[1] requires no real conviction of sin in order to its acceptance. ML-J was not surprised that such evangelism could be carried on with glibness and lightness and that its result was to add the unspiritual and the careless to the churches. The true convert always wants deliverance from the power as well as the guilt of sin.[2] He viewed with sadness the type of evangelism which supposes that the ethical and moral change associated with sanctification is something which Christians can receive at some point later than their conversion and justification. Rather, the most decisive influence for holiness comes from the rebirth itself.[3] By obscuring the meaning of

[1]*Romans*, vol. 1, p. 363.
[2]'In true conversion there is always some degree of realization of the horror of sin within and the desire to be delivered from it' (*Romans*, vol. 7, p. 215). Preaching which gives people the impression 'that all they have to do is to say that they believe in Christ' is 'a non-ethical message. True evangelism is always ethical' (*Romans*, vol. 5, p. 195). See also his important sermon on 'Sanctification and Evangelism' in *Sanctified Through the Truth*, 1989.
[3]'Nothing is so unscriptural, so utterly wrong, as to place or create a division between justification and sanctification' (*Romans*, vol. 5, p. 217). For ML-J, it must be understood, regeneration is an instantaneous act of God that radically changes a man's nature: conversion (i.e., the exercise of faith and repentance) is the process following that act. That the conversion is genuine is not to be judged by the time element (whether quick or slow) nor by the degree of assurance professed, but rather by whether or not the whole life has been made new. ML-J agreed with J. C. Ryle's assessment of the evangelism which became popular in the later 19th century. It was marked, says Ryle, by 'an extravagant and disproportionate magnifying of three points in religion – *viz.*, instantaneous conversion, the invitation of sinners to come to Christ, and the possession of inward joy and peace as the test of conversion' (*Holiness*, 1952 reprint, p. 74).

regeneration, modern evangelism had separated two things which Scripture always puts together, namely forgiveness *and* a new life of fellowship with God. To suppose we have received one and to know nothing of the other is to be in a state of delusion. On the effects of this kind of teaching he sometimes spoke very strongly. For example, in a sermon on 'False Prophets' he includes the following as an example of false teaching:

It does not emphasize repentance in any real sense. It has a very wide gate leading to salvation and a very broad way leading to heaven. You need not feel much of your own sinfulness; you need not be aware of the blackness of your own heart. You just 'decide for Christ' and you rush in with the crowd, and your name is put down, and is one of the large number of 'decisions' reported by the press. It is entirely unlike the evangelism of the Puritans and of John Wesley, George Whitefield and others, which led men to be terrified of the judgment of God, and to have an agony of soul sometimes for days and weeks and months. John Bunyan tells us in his *Grace Abounding* that he endured an agony of repentance for eighteen months. There does not seem to be much room for that today. Repentance means that you realize that you are a guilty, vile sinner in the presence of God, that you deserve the wrath and punishment of God, that you are hell-bound. It means that you begin to realize that this thing called sin is in you, that you long to get rid of it, and that you turn your back on it in every shape and form. You renounce the world whatever the cost, the world in its mind and outlook as well as its practice, and you deny yourself, and take up the cross and go after Christ. Your nearest and dearest, and the whole world, may call you a fool, or say you have religious mania. You may have to suffer financially, but it makes no difference. That is repentance. The false prophet does not put it like that. He heals 'the hurt of the daughter of my people slightly', simply saying that it is all right, and that you have but to 'come to Christ', 'follow Jesus', or 'become a Christian' . . . They offer an easy salvation, and an easy type of life always.[1]

* * *

We turn now to give two descriptions of Dr Lloyd-Jones' preaching at Westminster. The first was written by Dr Wilbur M. Smith in

[1]Preached on Feb 3, 1952. *The Sermon on the Mount*, vol. 2, pp. 247–8. The warning was to continue throughout his ministry. Preaching on Nov 11, 1960, he said, 'There is no greater danger to our highest interests than this kind of "easy believism" which is not the work of the Spirit at all' (*Romans*, vol. 7, p. 212). See also his 1967 address on 'Sandemanianism' in *Puritans*, pp. 170–190.

Moody Monthly, while spending six Sundays in London in the summer of 1955, three of which he spent in hearing various preachers. In his subsequent article entitled 'Preliminary Thoughts on Contemporary Preaching in London' he wrote on W. E. Sangster, John Stott, and finally, at length, on Martyn Lloyd-Jones:

Any minister of this church who expects week by week to hold the audience of Westminster Chapel and to draw to this side street men and women from all over London, must first of all be a preacher with unusual gifts. The present minister, Dr D. Martyn Lloyd-Jones, has had just such gifts abundantly conferred upon him by the Lord Himself.

It is commonly said among evangelicals in London that he is the outstanding preacher in Great Britain today. I have heard it stated since coming to London, not by anyone connected with Westminster Chapel, that no less a person than Brunner himself, the Continental theologian, has stated that Dr Martyn Lloyd-Jones is the greatest preacher in Christendom today. This would be a great deal for Brunner to say about anyone, and especially about this person, because Dr Lloyd-Jones is a staunch defender of the plenary inspiration of the Holy Scriptures. After hearing him again, twice within three weeks, I am easily persuaded that both of these statements are probably true.

One Sunday morning I heard him preach his thirty-eighth consecutive sermon from the first chapter of Ephesians. I wonder if any minister with expository gifts in America has preached thirty-eight consecutive sermons from this chapter in our generation. He preached on one clause: 'That ye may know . . . the exceeding greatness of his power to usward who believe, according to the working of his mighty power.' He spent the first ten minutes of his sermon developing the idea that the Greek word here translated 'according to' means 'because of,' 'on account of'; and that this great power Paul is speaking of is not something given after conversion, *but power exercised by God that we might believe.*

He then went on to establish his thesis that it was absolutely necessary for such divine power to be displayed, because of the powerful forces which prevent the natural man from believing – his darkened mind, the pressure of the opinions of the world, man's innate enmity against God . . .

Man can only believe by God's grace. How fitting was the last hymn:

> Lord, I was blind: I could not see
> In Thy marred visage any grace;
> But now the beauty of Thy face
> In radiant vision dawns on me.

Two weeks later, on a Sunday night, before a great audience, I heard him preach from a text that I had never noticed before: 'Heal me, O Lord, and I shall be healed; save me, and I shall be saved: for thou art my praise. Behold, they say unto me, Where is the word of the Lord? Let it come now' (Jer. 17:14, 15). Here, said this great defender of the faith, we have two contrasting attitudes toward the Word of God: in verse 14 the believer speaks; in verse 15 the scoffer and unbeliever speak.

He then went on to say how that these are the only two groups there are in the world in the sight of God. Men create various groups, according to our ancestors, the race to which we belong, intellectual training, wealth or poverty, etc., etc., but in the sight of God there are only two groups, those who believe His Word and those who disbelieve. No one can pronounce the word *Scriptures* with such force as this great expositor. You cannot hear him preach for three minutes without realizing that he believes God is speaking in His Word, that the Word is infallible, and that what we do with the Word of God will determine our eternal destiny.

Over and over again he illustrated the meaning of the scoffers' sarcastic challenge, 'Where is the word of the Lord? let it come'. 'Ah,' said Martyn Lloyd-Jones, 'it came.' What the prophet uttered came to pass, and it was not long before these people were in chains marching to Babylon. The Jews said the same thing when they heard Christ's prophetic words, 'Let it come'. Indeed, they went further and flippantly, with a shuddering boldness, cried out, 'Let his blood be upon us,' and it came upon them! In forty years their city was in the dust, and those who were left from the terrible slaughter of Titus were being marched to Rome as slaves.

So, too, will come an end of this age. Man may speak scoffingly of the second advent of Christ and of the day of judgment, saying, 'Let it come,' but, oh, it will come. Then he pleaded with the souls before him to believe *that very night* in the grace of God revealed in the cross of Christ.

I have not heard such preaching for years. One thing I determined in my own soul. I would never be satisfied again, as long as I live, with preaching anything but the very best that I have in deadly earnestness and, pray God, in the power of the Holy Spirit. This is preaching.

My fellowship with him at dinner one night while in London was one of the red-letter days of my life, though I had spent hours with him on a former visit. Some things we talked about are too sacred to record in print.

I wish every minister of the Word in America could have heard the sermons I have heard from this anointed servant of the Lord this summer. My own language is utterly inadequate to communicate the experience of sitting under such Spirit-anointed proclaiming of the eternal truths of our holy faith.'[1]

[1]*Moody Monthly*, October 1955, pp. 31–32.

A second description is from the pen of Mati Wyn, writing for the weekly Welsh newspaper *Y Cymro* (The Welshman) in its issue of August 21, 1958. Its interest is perhaps increased by the fact that the writer, the wife of a sub-editor of *The Daily Telegraph*, did not apparently share the preacher's understanding of his work:

It was extremely hot here the other Sunday and a great percentage of my fellow citizens were sunbathing on chairs and on the grass as I walked through St James's Park. I left them a little before six o'clock and turned through Buckingham Gate to the Sabbatical peace of some of London's most beautiful and historical houses.

Some of the streets of Westminster on Sundays have that same tranquil peacefulness as is found in any village in Wales. And as in Wales, it is only in the chapels that one finds any signs of life. So here was Westminster Chapel before me, and I was making my way to the service.

'Where would you like to sit?' asked one of the deacons, with a welcoming smile. 'Well, where may I sit?' I asked, being used to a chapel where all the seats were designated to various families. 'Wherever you wish,' the deacon said.

And I chose the gallery, where I would be able to get a wider view of this enormous chapel and its congregation. There is room in it for a congregation of around three thousand people. By 6.20 p.m. the 'floor' was packed and the rest of the congregation flowed into the gallery.

I was amazed by the variety of people who came to fill the seats around me. Nurses in their uniforms, a great number of sick and handicapped people, young families, and students of all colours and races. On both sides of me sat Burmese people, and I could not but wonder quietly that these people, who had been brought up on the religious traditions of the East, should come and listen to the message of the man from the West.

At 6.30 p.m. precisely, the Doctor appeared. And it is high time that I should have introduced him to you. No other than the famous Dr Martyn Lloyd-Jones. This great Christian and evangelist, who turned his back on the medical world after attaining great heights in that field, to answer his Master's call is well-known enough to readers of *Y Cymro*. And here was I, having heard so much about the blessed meetings in Westminster Chapel, at last having the privilege of being present myself.

As I listened to the beautiful Welsh accent of the Doctor, I could not help but guess that this was in part the reason for his appeal and charm for many of his listeners, especially the foreigners amongst us. I felt that we were hearing a Welsh sermon being preached in English as the Doctor spoke.

I also felt that there was some Welsh *hwyl* in the hymn-singing here, by a congregation of over one and a half thousand. The service was 'live' from start to finish, and there is no finer experience than such a service.

When the Doctor stated his text, I saw the students around me pulling out their notebooks and writing for their lives, taking notes of the sermon. I used to see this happening in Welsh chapels years ago, but there is very little such enthusiasm there today.

The Doctor chose his text from the fifth chapter of John's Gospel and the 44th verse. There was very little mention of theology in the preaching. It was a flood of eloquence with the stream flowing fully and naturally as a river after heavy rains. This was preaching about sin and salvation without a doubt. This was the sincere milk of the Word without being watered down or being thinned down in any way by any other addition.

The Doctor hurled his truths at the congregation, and the congregation was highly pleased by this. He called us fools, stupid fools if we rejected God and refused Christ. And he emphasized the word 'fools' again.

He chastised us for running after some of the world's empty and vain glories and for ignoring the only glory and honour which is worth having, and that entirely free.

I have not been 'shaken to the foundations' by preaching for many a year as I was shaken by this sermon. And I could not help feeling great pity that that sort of unction is missing from our Welsh services generally today.

After the service, I went in search of the way to the back of the chapel, in order to try and get a word with this great evangelical. Or maybe I should have said to the back of this village, because this chapel is similar to a village because of all the various activities which go on in the different rooms.

There were rooms there for the young and old and for the younger children, and there was also tea and a welcome. And I could not help feeling the extremely happy atmosphere which the place had. There was a seraph-like smile on the faces of everyone around me, as if the Doctor had cured everybody both physically and spiritually.

I got nearer to the Doctor's parlour and joined the queue which was waiting to talk to him. And before long my turn came to go in. The Doctor stood there in his flowing robe and he addressed me in fluent Welsh, thanking me for coming to listen to him.

For some reason I could not speak freely as I am accustomed to doing on such occasions. I felt as if I had been struck dumb with reverent fear, and I could do nothing more than thank the Doctor for his sermon.

I felt that there was some sort of aura about the man, some special feeling which draws you to him and also keeps you at bay. It is difficult for me to express my feelings, apart from saying that I was thoroughly convinced of the Doctor's greatness and sincerity.

When I went out a queue of people were slowly moving into a cinema nearby. Well, we had had a congregation of 1,500 and that on a hot summer's evening. It was unlikely that a cinema could draw such an audience.

It is to be noted how the above writer, like others, was struck by the mixed nature of the congregation. And this was true not merely racially and socially but spiritually. Many non-Christians were present. A report of the Open Air Mission in 1952 gives an illustration of this fact. An evangelist by the name of Mr G. Harris had been preaching in Hyde Park one Sunday afternoon in June, in which work he was harassed by a group of men who placed themselves at the front of the crowd and constantly interrupted with shouting and singing. Despite this Mr Harris was able to make contact with one hearer who came with him to the evening service at Westminster Chapel. 'To the evangelist's astonishment, there, on the opposite side of the gallery, was the leader of the gang that had caused the disturbance.' It is believed that he became a Christian.

Dr Lloyd-Jones was so averse to the announcement of conversions that he was inclined to the opposite extreme. He never asked those who had come to faith in Christ to identify themselves to him and there are indications that not a few who came to rejoice in their salvation never thought that they needed to 'trouble' him and to accept his invitation to those needing help to go to his vestry. It was not unusual for members of the congregation to meet with cases of conversion which were unknown to him. Sometimes people wrote to him, and among such letters the following happens to have survived:

> C/o 12, Herne Hill
> London, S. E. 24
>
> Dear Dr Lloyd-Jones,
>   I hope that this letter will reach you. This evening I came to hear you, and God has spoken to me through you. I entered Westminster Chapel a Pharisee and came out as the Publican in our Lord's parable of the Pharisee and the Publican. I have now been truly 'born again'. For three years now I have professed to be a converted Christian, but now I realize I was only a Pharisee.
>   May the Lord abundantly bless you in your ministry for Him.
>   Yours very sincerely,
>   Charles E. Wilkinson.

As already noted, the one time when ML-J referred to conversions taking place was in some of his annual letters to members and then it was only in very general terms. Looking back on 1948, he wrote in 1949, 'During the year many have been brought to a saving knowledge of the Lord Jesus Christ. We do not press for decisions as we know that the Holy Spirit alone can do the work.'

The annual letters of other years contain similar brief statements. In 1954 he said slightly more:

The work of direct evangelism goes on regularly, and the histories and background of those brought to a saving faith in our Lord is quite astonishing. At one extreme are those who literally had no religious background whatsoever. At the other end are those who were brought up as Roman Catholics. The commonest type, however, consists of those who had always regarded themselves as good Christians, but who found after attending the services that they had never known the truth at all. But, coming thus in various ways, they have all arrived at the same knowledge of our Lord and Saviour Jesus Christ.

*   *   *

As already indicated, it was Dr Lloyd-Jones' usual practice, on his itinerant ministry around Britain, to preach evangelistic sermons which he had first preached at Westminster Chapel. Many of these services will ever be remembered by those who were present. One occasion of this kind which had not been intended to be a 'service' at all, occurred in 1953 and nothing could illustrate more clearly ML-J's concern for the salvation of all to whom he had opportunity to speak. The Annual Meetings of the British Medical Association were held in July that year in Cardiff and the Christian Medical Fellowship took the opportunity to advertise a breakfast to be held in The New Continental Cafe, Cardiff on July 15 to which all doctors were invited. The speaker would be Dr Lloyd-Jones and his subject, 'The Doctor Himself'. There was, even at the hour of 8.30 a.m., a large gathering of distinguished guests, including such men as Dr William Evans, the cardiac physician of The London Hospital, who had been a friend of the speaker's since school days. Evans, who sat next to ML-J, recalls the occasion in his autobiography and how he noted a certain nervousness in Lloyd-Jones before he rose to speak: 'He was restless and ill at ease because he was expected to speak from the floor and not from a platform or pulpit. Here was the eloquent preacher and talented teacher craving for this additional advantage so that he might give of his best to those who had come to listen to him.'[1] Though an intelligent guess at the reason for his friend's less-than-usual composure, it was wrong. The truth was that ML-J was struggling over the subject he should take up under the title given to him. He had, of course, prepared an address relevant to the gathering but during breakfast he decided to lay it aside and, instead, to preach the gospel as simply as he could. There and then he settled on a sermon he had often preached on the parable of the rich farmer (Luke 12:13–21) which he introduced with an explanation which gave no indication of his change of purpose. His choice of subject, he told the gathering on rising to his feet, had been governed by the principle that 'the rule for our action must always be that which is best for the patient'. He believed that men belonging to the medical profession had particular temptations, one of the chief being the peril of objectivity. They could treat dying patients and forget that they too would one day be in the same condition:

Somewhere in Pembrokeshire a tombstone is said to bear the inscription 'John Jones, born a man, died a grocer'. There are many whom I have had the privilege of meeting, whose tombstone might well bear the grim epitaph: '. . . born a man, died a doctor'! The greatest danger which confronts the medical man is that he may become lost in his profession . . .

These words led him to his text concerning the man who seemed to have provided for everything but to whom God said, 'Thou fool this night thy soul shall be required of thee'. The burden of his words was to show why God calls such a 'successful' man a 'fool'. He had stopped thinking at a vital point, he made no provision for death. And he had an unworthy view of himself. Making money, having a bigger car, building a reputation is a life fit only for a mere reasoning animal. But man is a far higher being, created for fellowship and communion with God, and one for whom this is possible through Christ. If there were any cynics there they did not reveal it. Tears ran upon some faces and gravity marked all. 'I don't know any preacher,' says Paul Tucker (who was present at the invitation of a local

[1]*Journey to Harley Street*, William Evans, an autobiography, London, 1968, p. 181. Evans introduced the anecdote in the course of advising future teachers on the advantage of a platform.

doctor), 'who would have been as faithful as the Doctor that day and as powerful.' But it was the power of compassion rather than of denunciation and none could doubt the sincerity of the speaker's closing words: 'I have tried to counsel you as a one-time medical man and one who still loves the profession and the men and women who belong to it. I beseech you not to allow the profession to make you forget yourself, that you are a man and not merely a doctor.'[1]

It happened to be in Cardiff a few years later that another of Dr Lloyd-Jones' most memorable evangelistic sermons was preached. This was at a Civic Service broadcast from Wood Street Congregational Church on January 1, 1957. The sermon, from Isaiah 22:8–14, with special emphasis on verses 12 and 13 ('And in that day did the Lord God of hosts call to weeping and to mourning . . .'), he had first preached at Westminster Chapel on Sunday, November 25, 1956 – an evening marked by an unusual solemnity in the congregation. It was the time of 'the Suez Crisis' and ML-J seized such opportunities to demonstrate that the gospel is always a contemporary message. The sermon showed both the relevance of God's former dealings with nations to the present day and the supreme need for the salvation of the individuals blind to the true cause of national troubles. This was the message which he preached again in Cardiff. Instead of thanking the civic dignitaries for their attendance he told them that repentance 'does not mean just attending a Civic or some other formal service annually'. True repentance, he went on, involves a great deal more and he drew his final appeal to a conclusion with the words:

Turn back to God. Recognise your need of His forgiveness. Recognise your need of a new life, a new start, a new nature, a new heart, a new beginning. Ask Him for the gracious influence of the Holy Spirit. Submit yourself entirely to Him and surrender your life to Him. And then get up and walk in obedience to His laws . . .[2]

This sermon did more than cause temporary headlines in the

[1]Douglas Johnson's notes on this address are reprinted in *The Doctor Himself and the Human Condition*, 1982, pp. 9–14. One statement he did not get down is remembered by Paul Tucker, 'One day you will face God and it will not be a post-mortem, it will be a living examination'.
[2]Under the title, *Sound an Alarm*, the sermon was published by the Westminster Chapel Bookroom in 1957.

[336]

Evangelism

Welsh newspapers.[1] The Rev. J. T. Evans wrote to him a month later from Swansea concerning the effects of the broadcast sermon on January 1: 'You have left a very lasting and uplifting effect. It has been much discussed and has caused a universal stir. From what I gather it must have been one of your most successful meetings in South Wales.'

*   *   *

There is another aspect of the effect of Dr Lloyd-Jones' preaching which must be mentioned here. Both at Westminster Chapel and at services elsewhere, hundreds of men who were preparing for the Christian ministry, and being required by their training to struggle with liberal theology, were rescued from that blighting influence. Testimonies as to how this occurred generally have a common feature, as the two following examples will illustrate.

Fred Arnot, grandson of the missionary pioneer in South Africa, arrived in London confused and uncertain after a year in the liberal Baptist Theological College at Rüschlikon in Switzerland. Though he had heard ML-J once in his home-country of South Africa the service had possessed no particular significance for him but his first visit to Westminster Chapel was of a very different order in his experience: 'There was such an awareness of God in the church, and hearing someone speak from the Word of God as though he believed it, was so overwhelming after studying in a liberal theological college that the tears ran down my cheeks. It reminded me of the fruitfulness of an evangelical ministry which liberal theology can never have.'

Basil Howlett also trained for the ministry under liberal influences. He writes:

I had gone to college from a typical Baptist Union Church where we had no teaching and in my first year there I was completely bowled over by the modernistic lectures, to the extent that I hardly believed anything and my spiritual life hit rock bottom. I did not pray or read the Scriptures devotionally for months. But then one memorable Monday evening in

[1] The *Western Mail* reported the service under the headlines, 'Famous Divine Hits at Frivolous Britain'. In a major article on another page Harry Green gave a character study of ML-J with the title, 'A physician in search of our hearts'. Ordained a missioner at Aberavon thirty years earlier, wrote Green, 'he remains a missioner'.

October 1961, a fellow student urged me to go with him to the Free Trade Hall, Manchester to hear Dr Martyn Lloyd-Jones. In my ignorance, I replied, 'Who is he?' As long as I live I shall never forget that night. There was spiritual power in the meeting and I sat gripping the seat as the Doctor preached on 1 Corinthians 2 with such unction and authority. In the first half of the sermon all the doubts and delusions of modernism were smashed to the ground and so was I! In the second half of the sermon I was lifted up and set on my feet by the glory of the gospel. Almost 27 years later the memory of it is still vivid.

*   *   *

Before we leave the subject of evangelism we must touch on the question of Dr Lloyd-Jones' position in regard to the Graham Crusades. It is said that he 'would have nothing to do with Billy Graham and all his works'[1] and that misleading statement by the former Secretary of the British Council of Churches indicates the need for an accurate record to be put down. When the Evangelical Alliance was organising the first Graham Crusade at Harringay ML-J was asked to take part in meetings for ministers which were to be held in conjunction with the Crusade. He quietly declined, but he was certainly not opposed to what was planned for 1954. He heartily wished the Crusade well and when it began on March 1 his intercessory prayer at the Chapel included the 'brethren' from overseas, 'ministering in another part of the city'. Writing from Belfast to Fred and Elizabeth on March 9, 1954, he said, 'The reports coming of the Billy Graham campaign are most confusing. Some are critical, some feel it must be of God. We must refrain from criticising and wait and see.'

Such was his initial view. A few weeks later he went, incognito, to the Harringay meetings for the first time. That visit dismayed him. He did not doubt that individuals were being converted but the idea that the Crusade represented a great spiritual harvest – in the words of one enthusiastic counsellor, 'Pentecost multiplied by seven'[2] – he regarded as entirely unwarranted. In particular one feature that is always the characteristic of powerful evangelism seemed to be missing although, strangely, it was this very lack which a number

---

[1] Kenneth Slack writing on ML-J under the title 'Puritan "Pope"' in the *Church Times*, May 30, 1986.
[2] Erroll Hulse, *Billy Graham – The Pastor's Dilemma*, 1966, p. 7.

thought to be most praiseworthy. Speaking on this point he was later to say:

I remember how a few years back when there was a great evangelistic campaign in London, a man who was a leader in religious circles came to me one day and asked, 'Have you been to the campaign?'. I said, 'No, not yet'. 'This is marvellous,' he said, 'marvellous'. He continued, 'People are going forward by the hundred. No emotion you know – marvellous'. He kept on repeating this 'No emotion'. What to him was so marvellous was that all these people who went forward in response to the appeal showed no emotion.

ML-J's own visit confirmed this impression, but led him to the opposite conclusion. Neither in Scripture nor in the whole of church history did he know of any period when the power of the Holy Spirit had been specially evident without emotion in those affected by his power. 'Can a man,' he asked, 'see himself as a damned sinner without emotion? Can a man look into hell without emotion? Can a man listen to the thunderings of the Law and feel nothing? Or conversely, can a man really contemplate the love of God in Christ Jesus and feel no emotion?'[1]

ML-J believed there and then what many came to consider only months or years later, namely, that to base the claim for the Crusade's extraordinary success on the numbers going forward to 'receive Christ' (3,000 every evening) was an entirely unscriptural assessment. People will be converted when the gospel is preached, but conversion does not take place through a physical response to an 'appeal'. It was not the walk to the front which made anyone a true convert. But the 'appeal', or 'altar-call', to use the American term, was responsible for confusing conversion with a decision to come forward. Because unregenerate people, for all manner of reasons, are capable of responding to the call to the front, an impression of spiritual results far beyond the reality was being created. At the same time the virtual identification of saving faith with the decision to walk forward was bound, in many cases, to confuse individuals as to their real spiritual condition. It was a wrong theology – 'God has given to every man the ability to believe'[2] – leading to a wrong practice. Certainly the evangelist is to appeal for faith and repent-

[1]*Preaching*, p. 95.
[2]Billy Graham, *Peace with God*, 1954, p. 134.

ance, but the time when the truth is made effective unto salvation belongs to God alone.

Dr Lloyd-Jones believed that he could have worked with evangelists of the old Wesleyan Arminian type who, while calling men to repentance and faith, knew that assurance is something that only God can give. The Graham Crusades, on the other hand, by relating assurance to 'making a decision', were promoting a type of evangelism in which he could not share.[1]

He did not come to this conclusion lightly. He knew he was the only prominent Protestant minister in South-East England who would be seen not to be giving his support. He knew, further, that he had far more in common with Graham than men such as Leslie Weatherhead who, after visiting the Crusade, commended it with the words, 'I could not find anything in the whole service that was psychologically unsound'. His motives would be misunderstood and by some he would probably even be accused of being 'against evangelism'. Painful or not, he had no choice. He made no public statement about the Crusade which continued until May 22, 1954 but reference to it dropped out of his public prayer and there was one comment which he made in the Friday night meeting at the Chapel on May 7, 1954 which, as we shall see, was to be very significant in the light of later developments:

There are certain people at the moment who, in expressing their views on the campaign at Harringay are saying something like this: 'Of course, we don't agree with this man's theology, but what does that matter? What does it matter what his theology is as long as there is a crowd and he is able to bring people to Christ?'. Now what such people are really saying is this, you see – that truth does not matter, they are only interested in results.

He was not denying the existence of encouraging results. By the end of 1954, for instance, the circulation of Scripture Union notes was to see an increase of 60,000 new readers.[2] Churches and

[1] For full treatment of his reasons against 'Calling for Decisions' see *Preaching*, pp. 265–82.
[2] *No Mere Chance*, John Laird, 1981, p. 165. On the other hand, of about seventy people referred to Westminster Chapel from the Harringay meetings, and all contacted by the Chapel, very few are said to have maintained any interest in spiritual things.

evangelical agencies similarly received new strength. But ML-J was warning against the attitude which supposed that in the presence of results so apparently impressive all cautionary considerations could be set aside.

To ministerial friends who raised the subject of the Crusade he was ready to express his mind. Wynford Davies, at this time Presbyterian minister at Tonypandy, South Wales, recalls how ML-J was preaching at Pentre, Rhondda, during the Harringay period and how he and Hugh Morgan (then minister in Ton Pentre) raised the subject of the Billy Graham Crusade with him:

All we had were reports of people who had been up and had come back with glowing stories to tell, and we thought this was really a tremendous thing. We were talking to the Doctor about it, quite enthusiastically, and were taken aback when he said that he did not share our feelings and went on to tell us why. I think what gripped us at the time was the fact that there were such great numbers attending and we had had land-lines down in South Wales which had led to very real conversions. The Doctor's answer to that was, 'Well, these people were obviously on the way beforehand and they were on the way because they had been listening to you fellows preaching regularly over the years', which, on reflection, was surely right. But there was that aspect of his character that his concern for truth brushed aside everything and he would get right to the heart of the problem. I suppose the conversation could only have been five minutes that Hugh and I had with him and in that five minutes he made us put on the brakes and think very seriously from a completely new direction. And then we saw how right he was and how wrong we had been.

One thing further is vital to an accurate record. ML-J refrained from any public disagreement over the Crusade because it would have done more harm than good. Large numbers who lacked the discernment to judge *issues* would have seen any disagreement as a difference between personalities.[1] But, more than that, he had a genuine wish to help Dr Graham whom he regarded as 'an utterly honest, sincere and genuine man'. The difference between the two evangelists was not personal and at this time, as always, ML-J was

[1]Some prominent supporters of the Crusade attended Westminster Chapel. It was only as they came to understand more clearly what ML-J was teaching that they began to agree with his different position on evangelism. One of this number was Leonard Reeve, associate producer of the Graham film, 'Souls in Conflict'.

following his practice of seeking to befriend fellow Christians with whom, on some important issues, he might strongly disagree. He was equally ready to give such help as he could to members of the Graham team. The meetings for ministers which were arranged in connection with the Crusade were led by Dr Paul Rees of Minneapolis and held at Westminster Chapel. ML-J made it his business to attend at least one of these sessions. Unable to be present at Rees' final meeting at the Chapel, he left a letter for him in his vestry which he knew the American would be using. From Minneapolis Paul Rees responded:

June 8, 1954

My dear Dr Lloyd-Jones:
    Here I am back in my own study after these extraordinary days and weeks in London and Britain.
    I am doing now what I should have done much more promptly, namely, reply gratefully to the gracious note that you left for me in your vestry the last day that we had our Bible class at the Chapel. It was thoughtful and gracious of you to leave me this farewell note.
    My dear friend and brother, I shall always be grateful to God for the privilege of meeting you and having fellowship with you. It is the touch and tone of your spirit that moved me and brought its benediction to me.
    I realize that there are differences of terminology and of approach that may stand between us, but the deeper and more significant realization is precisely that which you have expressed in your note when you say that we are both concerned about 'a deeper experience of God's love and a desire to live to His glory'. Please give my cordial greetings to Mrs Lloyd-Jones.
    Thank you again for the exceedingly brotherly hospitality that you accorded me in your church.

Yours in the love that never faileth,
Paul S. Rees

*   *   *

In concluding this chapter there are a few general observations which need to be made.
First, as these pages have abundantly shown, ML-J was an evangelist, indeed saw himself primarily as an evangelist. To a critic who once asked him, 'When did you last have a campaign at Westminster Chapel?' he could reply, 'I have one every Sunday'. It

was his decided conviction 'that there should always be one evangelistic service in connection with each church every week'.[1]

Second, his belief that special campaigns are not the best means of evangelism was settled well before the Harringay Crusade of 1954. 'I have watched so many campaigns,' he said in February 1953, 'and the situation of the church has gone steadily down in spite of them all.'[2]

Third, the difference between him and popular evangelicalism was not so much over methods and types of evangelism as over theology. 'It is our whole idea of evangelism that is wrong.'[3] He believed that the common view of gospel preaching could not be harmonized with the apostolic approach laid down in the Epistle to the Romans. Effective evangelism requires that profound biblical principles be held in their true relationships. When he came to be regarded, as he did, as a 'teacher', not an 'evangelist', he saw the assessment not as a reflection on himself but on the current view of evangelism – 'a measure of the terrible spiritual aberration of these days', as he wrote to a friend.[4]

Fourth, he regarded the preaching of Christ to the unsaved as the most demanding of all work. For not only does it require a discriminating understanding of the truth, it looks for an 'impossible' response as far as man is concerned. In the hope of attracting people, and to lessen the possibility of failure, the modern practice was not to start as Paul did with man in sin and under the wrath of God. 'Perhaps,' it was said, 'you could do that sort of thing one hundred years ago, but you just cannot now.'[5] In ML-J's view the supreme need was for men full of faith and the Holy Spirit who, sent by God, would be owned in the recovery of apostolic gospel preaching. With the word of the gospel there can be, there has to be, almighty power to awaken the dead. If he had not believed that, as he would often say, he would have given up in despair.[6]

---

[1]*Preaching*, p. 151.
[2]*Sanctified Through the Truth*, p. 27.
[3]*Ibid*, p. 30
[4]Letter to Peter Golding, January 11, 1961.
[5]*Romans*, vol. 1, p. 329. ML-J discusses evangelism in many places but in my view the most important summary of his teaching will be found in his sermons on Romans 1:16–18 contained in this volume.
[6]*WR*, Feb. 1968, p. 30.

My concluding words take me back to the start of this work. When I began collecting books for this undertaking, the Puritan authors were one of my two chief quests, the other was for books on true revivals of religion and in particular the great awakening in the eighteenth century under George Whitefield, Daniel Rowland, Howell Harris, and other like-minded men. I had a burden for revival and I shall never forget the cries that went up to God as I walked along the railway bank pathway near the spot where the idea of this now world-wide Library first came to me. I cannot express what I felt and even now there are times when the fervency of desire for revival overwhelms me, when the subject is touched upon with the kindling power of the Spirit of God. Few will understand the depth of feeling that shake one at such moments. But here is the point I want to come to. I have a hope that God has a purpose for these precious writings beyond what we yet realize. Will the dawn of a fresh day of God's power, such as George Whitefield knew, bring with it a far greater interest in the rich heritage of spiritual works which are here preserved and shall we have yet more abundant reason to bless God that He brought this work into existence? Pray that it may be so and that the Holy Spirit will descend upon us and bring about such a blessing!

GEOFFREY WILLIAMS,
The Annual Meeting of The Evangelical Library, 1961,
pp. 14–15.

17

'Great Purposes of Grace'

In the recovery of a more scriptural and doctrinal Christianity in the 1950's it may be that Dr Lloyd-Jones' own writings played a comparatively small part for very little of his work was then in print. The explanation for the absence of his books at this date needs some consideration. Basically it lay in his conviction that ministers are called to be preachers, not writers. He did not view the readiness of contemporary Christianity to allow the pulpit to be overshadowed by other means of communication as a wise adjustment to modern conditions but as a loss of faith in *the* means to which God has attached the special promise of His power. It was because the church was being conditioned by the world that the testimony of John Knox was no longer commonly believed: 'What efficacy hath the living voice above the bare letter read, the hungry and thirsty do feel to their comfort'.[1]

It may, however, be asked why ML-J's sermons, once preached and recorded on tape, could not then be printed – as, in fact, was being done in the *Westminster Record* month by month? The answer lies in the whole practical problem which arises when the spoken word is transferred into literary form. Some of the features of the most effective speech become blemishes when put into print and therefore even in literature where the sermonic form is retained – as, for instance, in the case of Spurgeon's published sermons – a great deal of revision is necessary.[2] Despite Mrs Lloyd-Jones' aid and later that of Elizabeth, Dr Lloyd-Jones was often hard pressed to find the

[1]*The Works of John Knox*, 1895, vol. 5, p. 519.
[2]Spurgeon had spent several hours each week on the revision of a sermon for publication. As J. C. Ryle says: 'English composition for speaking to hearers and English composition for private reading, are almost like two different languages, so that sermons which "preach" well "read" badly' (*Christian Leaders*, 1978 reprint, p. 51).

time to do the minimum work required on the monthly published sermon. On his voyages to the States in 1956 and to South Africa in 1958 it was this kind of work which he had to take with him.

Although several publishers were constantly asking Dr Lloyd-Jones for books they all entertained the view that titles which were patently sermonic in form were unsaleable and that considerable changes would have to be made before anything issued in the *Westminster Record* could reach a wider readership.

This was a problem which ML-J often discussed with Douglas Johnson and it formed part of a conversation which the two men had on December 4, 1946. Pickering and Inglis were eager at that time to print nine sermons which he had preached from Ephesians on 'God's Plan for World Unity' which had recently appeared in the *Westminster Record*.[1] Arthur Marsh, on ML-J's behalf, had entered into negotiations with these London publishers and in November 1946 they had returned the sermons (as printed in the *Westminster Record*) so that the author could 'look them over' before their publication in more permanent form. But, as ML-J reminded Johnson, more than a 'look over' was needed and he had no time to attend to it. Johnson followed their conversation up with a letter the next day in which he said:

During the Christmas period I will gladly look at the MSS or printed addresses which you propose to publish on Ephesians. It will be a good thing to employ Christmas helping on the cause, rather than just playing with the twinkling lights on a Christmas tree!

With regard to the Editor for the sermons to be printed in the monthly *Record*: the ideal would be to have someone with real literary 'feeling' resident in West London so that you can easily be consulted on the various points where an editing is suggested. If you are unable to find anyone I will abstain from reading the newspaper or one of the theological journals in favour of doing it for you. Please use this offer as a last resort because it will be much better if you can have a real 'literary fan', in fact one wishes one could provide you with a private secretary trained in literary form – a junior Miss Cable[2] – who could make it her great concern to give the truest expression of your message to the world.

No such 'Editor' was forthcoming and the results of Dr Johnson's

[1] Preached at the Chapel in the autumn of 1944.
[2] Mildred Cable, a well-known missionary author, was a member at Westminster Chapel.

self-imposed labours over Christmas, 1946, seem to have found a final resting place in a bottom drawer in ML-J's study. Pickering and Inglis, who had already announced the publication of this new title, wrote despairingly to the preacher in October 1947 to say that they had no idea how to answer the many enquiries they were receiving on the date when the book would appear. In the outcome the nine sermons were never published in book form at all! Lutterworth Press in the next decade fared even worse. Through Arthur Marsh they negotiated a contract with Dr Lloyd-Jones for his sermons on 'The Soul's Conflict' from the *Record* and to avoid, as they hoped, the problems of which they had probably heard rumours, they proceeded to have the type set without giving ML-J the opportunity to 'look over' what they had taken upon themselves to do by way of editorial revision. 'I think,' wrote their editorial secretary, 'that when you see the book in proof and look at the way in which our very skilled editor has brought the material into the right compass you will be very pleased indeed. Mr Marsh is anxious to have copies for this summer season and we are doing our best to push ahead with the book . . .'

Far from being 'pleased' when he saw the proofs, Dr Lloyd-Jones terminated the whole proposal!

The main problem in this oft-repeated difficulty was not any wish on the preacher's part to retain his exact words. He understood the need for some revision very well. Disagreement centered on the extent to which the authoritative preaching style, at times discursive and repetitious, ought to be retained. Dr Lloyd-Jones was himself unsure how effectively he could be put into print: he had certainly made up his mind that he would forego publication altogether rather than accept the extent of the curtailment which publishers commonly considered necessary if the books were to find a market. His five addresses at Wheaton on 'Truth Unchanged, Unchanging' in 1947 were less sermonic in form and that may be part of the reason why they were his first post-war book to be printed. Yet even those addresses did not appear until four years after they were given.

In 1951 Fred Mitchell also attempted to encourage the publication of a major volume of sermons by ML-J. By December of that year the first nine sermons in a long series on 'The Sermon on the Mount' had been printed in the *Westminster Record*. Mitchell, having ascertained that Leslie Lyall – a CIM missionary well accustomed to editorial work – was willing to help, wrote to ML-J proposing that

Lyall start work on these sermons. The preacher was willing to give it a trial but once again the revision foundered on the fundamental issue of how far the chapters would keep their original character.

As a result of this persistent difficulty, coupled with ML-J's own lack of time, it was not until 1959 that volume one of *Studies in the Sermon on the Mount* was published. Its text stayed very close to the text first printed in the *Record* and these words of apologia from the author are to be found in the Preface:

A sermon is not an essay and is not meant, primarily, for publication, but to be heard and to have an immediate impact upon the listeners. This implies, of necessity, that it will have certain characteristics which are not found and are not desirable in written studies. To prune it of these, if it should be subsequently published, seems to me to be quite wrong, for it then ceases to be a sermon and becomes something quite nondescript. I have a suspicion that what accounts for the dearth of preaching at the present time is the fact that the majority of printed books of sermons have clearly been prepared for a reading rather than a listening public. Their flavour and form are literary rather than sermonic.

In so far as any publisher had Dr Lloyd-Jones' confidence it was the Inter-Varsity Fellowship, and that was certainly appropriate for Douglas Johnson was about the one person – outside the family circle – who never ceased to press the need for the preacher's work to be in print. From among a number of Johnson's letters on the subject I quote the following, written to ML-J on December 11, 1956:

I have a letter from the Rev. Marcellus Kik in which he asks whether a sermon or sermons of yours were available that they could publish in *Christianity Today*. He enquires whether I could persuade Dr Lloyd-Jones to let him have any sermon or sermons for publication in this paper. He says, 'As yet we have not succeeded in getting one from him', and then goes on to ask me to use my earnest persuasions.

I cannot quite make up my mind about this paper. If it is your opinion that *Christianity Today* will be a worthy contribution and may shift ministers in the right direction then I would sit up at nights or rise early in the morning to try to put two or three of your sermons into the form that Kik would want for publication. In my reply I have explained your right attitude in these matters, viz. that the preacher must go on preaching with the sole idea of the audience and not worry about how it will read . . .

To this request, along with similar ones, ML-J was probably unable to give any attention. Even the IVF in 1956 had only one small paperback and one booklet bearing his name in their catalogue, and these publications, like the *Westminster Record*, had no extensive circulation. But if Dr Lloyd-Jones' writings played no major part in the doctrinal change which was now beginning, they were certainly not without effect. The Rev. Peter De Jong of the Christian Reformed Church writes of how 'the little book of Lloyd-Jones *The Plight of Man and the Power of God* had an incalculable amount of influence on my thinking, life and labour as a minister of the gospel'. John Reid Miller, of First Presbyterian Church, Jackson, Mississippi similarly told ML-J in a letter of May 3, 1956:

I have profited greatly by reading your books and various messages you have published from time to time. Your ministry has been an inspiration to hundreds of evangelical pastors throughout the English speaking world . . .

Dr F. Crossley Morgan, another well-known American preacher and one of the sons of Dr Lloyd-Jones' predecessor, wrote from Texas in 1956 urging Dr Lloyd-Jones to issue a weekly sermon because 'a month seems a long time to wait for the next *Westminster Record*'. There were others helped by the *Record* whose lives were spent far from public view. A lady of ninety-nine years wrote:

I thank God who first led a friend to pass your *Westminster Record* on to me . . . I have through your teaching been helped to realize fully the deeper meaning of revelation and it has been a joy through all the days of being house-bound. God has graciously given me His abiding presence, day and night.

Another receiver of the *Record* was a blind man from Smethwick, Staffordshire, from whom ML-J heard as follows:

For many years now a friend has been spending an evening with my wife and myself, to read to us your sermon which is printed each month in the *Westminster Record* and I feel so strongly that it would meet a very real need if the sermon could be made available in Braille, and I now write and ask if you would use your good offices to explore how best this may be done . . . I remember a word in one of your sermons which reminded us never to flatter the Lord's servants, but it would ill befit me if I now

missed this opportunity of thanking you for all the blessings your
messages have brought to us . . .

*　　　*　　　*

At this same period when Dr Lloyd-Jones could give little time to his
own publications he was constantly urging and advising a number of
Christian publishers on what ought to be made available. In 1951
Marshall Morgan and Scott, at his prompting, published a British
reprint of B. B. Warfield's *The Inspiration and Authority of the
Bible*, using a recommendation from ML-J to 'try to create a new
interest'. But Warfield's *Biblical and Theological Studies*, which he
also encouraged them to re-issue, was not accepted. As early as 1952
Lloyd-Jones was urging Marshall to take up A. W. Tozer's writings
but about these, as well as other titles, it was frequently said that
'economic difficulties' stood in the way. There was, evangelical
publishers believed, little sale for the older authors or for unknown
Americans. While they admired Dr Lloyd-Jones' ministry, and
observed its evident influence, they did not understand his vision for
the *theological* change which was needed in the church at large. Even
the IVF shared in this limitation, for while they did more than other
publishers towards a recovery of serious reading, 'they were,' in
Dr Lloyd-Jones' words, 'very careful to say that this was not a
theological matter primarily, but of biblical studies, so they concentrated on commentaries and books of a general apologetic nature'.[1]

Remarkably, in Dr Lloyd-Jones' view, a greater influence for
change, as far as literature was concerned, was not new books at all
but the older reformed and Puritan classics which, though now
becoming very scarce, could still be found in the second-hand
bookshops. It was as hunger for these books grew, stimulated by the
Puritan Conference, that the Evangelical Library now came into its
own. In 1948 the Library had moved to its present site at 78 Chiltern
Street, which is close to Baker Street and in the heart of the West End
of London. The location also had the major advantage of being only
a few hundred yards from the London Bible College in Marylebone
Road. The Library premises were in many ways an extraordinary
place, situated on the second floor of an old building and to be
approached only by three flights of stone steps akin to the entrance of
some Victorian workhouse. A notice on a landing two-thirds of the

[1]*The Annual Meeting of the Evangelical Library*, 1966, p. 27.

way to the top advised the climber to 'Pause and Pray'. The top landing once reached, a heavy door opened into a large upper room, some seventy feet long by twenty broad, with a pitched roof rising immediately from the high walls to an apex twenty-two feet above the floor, with windows letting in some light on the southern slope of the roof. It would have been comparatively airy had it not been for some 25,000 volumes, crammed into the shelved partitions which divided the floor space, and climbing like creepers up every conceivable inch of wall with the exception of the spaces occupied by portraits of the old divines. Looking at the sheer weight and substance of these old quartos and folios it was not hard to imagine how Richard Baxter once narrowly escaped a shortening of his life when similar books fell from a crazy height above his head. Immediately inside the entrance door, on the right, was an office where at almost any time Geoffrey Williams and Marjorie Denby, his secretary, could be found with barely enough room to sit amidst books and papers and, if it happened to be lunch time, the delicious smell of toasted brown bread. This was the inner sanctum. On a mantelpiece above a disused fireplace stood one concession to modern times, a photograph of Dr Lloyd-Jones[1] and in the corner, to the left of the fireplace, was a glass bookcase containing the Librarian's favourite books on revival. In a sense the whole purpose of the Library was contained in that small bookcase.

Another surprise to newcomers to the Evangelical Library was the age of those who were overseeing its work. Geoffrey Williams was 70 in 1955 and Miss Denby some six years younger. A graduate of the London School of Economics, and engaged in business, her life was already well advanced when she had come to the knowledge of Christ under Dr Lloyd-Jones' ministry. Thereafter he could say of her: 'Miss Denby just lives for the Library, she seems to spend most of her life here and is forever willing to put herself to trouble in the interests of the Work. She is always ready to find books and to carry them down to me at Westminster Chapel – in fact, I sometimes wonder if I overtax her strength as she carries heavy books back and forth . . .'[2]

---

[1] It attracted attention because virtually nobody outside his family circle possessed a photograph of ML-J at this date.

[2] *Report of the Annual Meeting of the Evangelical Library 1959*, p. 7. Miss Denby, a pile of books in her hands, was a familiar sight outside ML-J's vestry door on Friday evenings. For an example of ML-J pleading the importance of books and of the Evangelical Library see *Romans*, vol. 1, p. 240.

However improbable it might sound, it was to this archaic place that young people were now coming in increasing numbers. It was not the finest Puritan library in England but it was probably the only one where the works of many seventeenth-century authors could be seen and even, given a careful use of ladders, handled and borrowed. Ten years later Dr Lloyd-Jones was to look back on the mid-1950's as a time when the Evangelical Library made 'a massive contribution' to the beginning of something new and he regarded its work as 'a living illustration of the fact that out of the smallest – almost despicably small – beginnings, God can bring a great power into being'.[1]

It would appear to be from the year 1955 that we have ML-J's first recorded conviction that a major spiritual change had begun. By that date it had become a tradition that as President of the Evangelical Library he should speak to the circle of friends who gathered every November for the Annual Meeting. In numbers they were few, but ML-J regarded them as an inner circle of friends (both of the library and of his ministry) and he would often express his personal thoughts to them in a manner which he would seldom do anywhere else in England. In the course of what he had to say at the 1955 Annual Meeting, after commending Geoffrey Williams' remarkable gift in tracking down some of the rarest volumes, he proceeded:

But there is another remarkable thing to which I must refer; I feel that we are witnessing a true revival of interest in the Puritans, and a number of young men are studying their literature constantly. There is held annually a Puritan Conference which is attended by some sixty people, and this library has played a very central part in it. All the men involved come here, or to the branches, in the course of their quest. As I see things, it is of supreme importance for the future of the Christian faith in this country that we should experience a revival of interest in the literature of the great Puritans of the seventeenth century, and to this end the library is absolutely central and invaluable.

Twelve months later, after his visit to the United States in 1956, he could report to the same gathering that what they were beginning to see in Britain was also to be found across the Atlantic:

I spent some time in the United States and Canada recently and I can tell

---

[1]*The Annual Meeting of the Evangelical Library*, 1966, pp. 27–30.

you something about the religious situation there. I found one thing there which is the most encouraging trend I have encountered for many a day. Among the leaders in evangelical work, and especially among the students, I found something which really did amaze me. After a meeting a number of young men came forward to speak with me, and every single one talked to me about Puritan literature and asked whether there was a possibility of getting Puritan books from this country. It is true of increasing numbers of them; they, like us, are turning to the Puritans, and for the same reason. We are all tired of the typical periodicals and books and are not being helped by the literature of today. They felt that they wanted something solid for their souls . . .

I was also at the International Students' Conference, and there were delegates from many other countries – Europe, Korea, Japan, the Philippines, and three or four countries in South America – and there I found the same thing – 'Where can we get hold of some deeper literature?' they asked. They can see that excitable evangelism is not enough; it tends to be transient, and if you are to have solid and lasting work it must be based on a deeper knowledge and understanding of the Gospel.

As a result of this experience, I have a feeling that we are going to witness a change. We are all getting tired of going round and round in circles and are conscious of a need of deepening our understanding mentally and spiritually.

I am sure this library is playing a part in bringing this conviction into being, and I rejoice in it. For, it seems to me, we shall never see a spiritual revival except along these lines – as people come back to these works and are searched by them.

I am not advocating that people should spend all their time in reading, but there is a great need of more familiarity with the Scriptures and their teaching in order that we may be crushed to our knees with a sense of humility and be made to cry to God that He would visit us again.

*   *   *

It was at this point that another agency suddenly came into prominence which was destined to carry forward on a larger scale what had already begun. Mr D. J. W. Cullum was a well-known acoustic consultant in London and the head of two London companies which he largely owned. Financial success and international business had followed his invention during the Second World War of mufflers to reduce the noise of jet aircraft when they were being tested on the ground. Yet this prosperity had brought no inner peace to the nominal Methodist who had long since ceased attending church, and when two evangelical Christians, Mr and Mrs Stanley Clarke, spoke of Christ to him during a trans-Atlantic crossing on the 'Queen Elizabeth' in 1955 their words reached his heart. On returning home from New York Jack Cullum resumed church attendance in his former denomination, but, after trying one or two Methodist churches in North London he remained confused and under conviction of sin. The Rev. Joe Blinco (Methodist minister at Highgate) was perhaps conscious that here was someone who was being prepared of God for future usefulness and he advised him to attend Dr Lloyd-Jones' ministry. The only thing about Westminster Chapel known to Cullum was its roof for he had scrambled over it twenty years earlier in the course of some acoustic work. Soon after the commencement of his attendance at Westminster Chapel, in December 1955, he accepted an invitation from the Clarkes to visit them in their home at Jerusalem, and it was there, at a morning service in St George's Cathedral, that he received what he later came to understand as the assurance of salvation. His first introduction to ML-J was as follows:

> 59 Highgate West Hill,
> London, N.6
> Christmas Eve, 1956

Dear Dr Lloyd-Jones,
   I have at last plucked up the courage to write to you. The devil has driven me beyond doubt and I now feel that the battle is more spiritual than physical.
   Little more than a year ago when I first came to your church I had not accepted Jesus as my Lord and Saviour. Last Christmas by a merciful provision of God I spent in Jerusalem. I have enjoyed many visits to Westminster and many messages through you. Now I should like to see you if you will be so kind . . .
> Yours sincerely
> Jack Cullum

My first extended conversation with Jack Cullum was just a few weeks later. But here, perhaps, some explanation is needed of how I came to be at Westminster Chapel at this time as Assistant to the Minister. I had first come to know Dr Lloyd-Jones personally in 1954 while spending a few months in London. Prior to that time I had lived in the north of England and knew very little of what is reported in these preceding pages. Quite independently of southern influence, a re-awakening to the Puritans and to Jonathan Edwards had occurred among some of us who were students at Durham University in the early 1950's. Through old books we discovered the meaning of the word which had mystified our little staff meeting at Hildenborough Hall in 1949. To Tom Rees' work at Hildenborough I owed both my first hearing of the gospel and my meeting with my future wife.[1] In 1955 we married and settled in Oxford, 60 miles from London, where I had opportunity to assist the Rev. Sidney Norton in a small church as well as pursuing private study in a city which is so rich in spiritual history. Close at hand, buildings, libraries and monuments were reminders of those eras when from Oxford's ancient Colleges the doctrines of grace flowed to the whole nation. Those former days of power, along with the truths which then moved multitudes, all seemed forgotten amidst arid academic theology and a modern evangelicalism which seemed to know nothing of William Tyndale, John Owen or George Whitefield.

Mr Norton, my senior colleague, emphasised that our primary need was to seek the face of God and it was in connection with prayer and frequent discussion of Psalm 60 that the decision was reached to issue *The Banner of Truth*, a little, twenty-page magazine which appeared in September 1955 bearing the text, 'Thou hast given a banner to them that fear thee, that it may be displayed because of the truth' (Psa 60:4). At this time there was already a longing in our hearts to see the start of a new work of book-publishing. When we visited London in September 1955 to enquire into the cost of printing presses our findings came as a shock, but subsequent conversation with Dr Lloyd-Jones on Sunday, October 16 (which happened to be the 400th anniversary of the burning of Latimer and Ridley in Oxford) strengthened belief that such a thing was possible. There were no financial resources available known to us, and although it meant a great deal when ML-J personally offered £100, a vastly larger sum was required even for a beginning.[2] It was an idea of ML-J's which possibly contributed most at this stage. Given the facilities at Oxford, he urged me to concentrate on writing a book to demonstrate the Calvinistic convictions of the English reformers. My

[1] Affection for the memory of Joe Blinco prompts me to add that he was the speaker at the first Hildenborough Conference which I attended.
[2] At this time he also encouraged the Westminster Chapel deacons to provide half the sum necessary for the printing of the second issue of the *Banner of Truth* magazine.

manuscript was finished by May 1956, by which time it was also clear that the very slender finances of our little congregation could no longer support an assistant. The outcome was that ML-J, who read the manuscript that same month, proposed that I came to Westminster, not as Assistant Minister, but as *his* Assistant, a position which did not require any formal call on the part of the church. The deacons agreed to the appointment and the decision was conveyed to a church meeting on July 12, 1956. Two reasons lay behind this proposal, as ML-J told the meeting. First, he was concerned that there were too few meetings for members during the week on account of his journeys to various parts of the country. His Assistant could, therefore, help in this area by leading a prayer meeting and a Bible Study Class on Monday and Wednesday evenings respectively. Second, I could spend further time in study and writings on the Puritans 'with a view to creating interest in these men and their teaching'.

Before we came to Westminster, in September 1956, ML-J had a further idea. My Wednesday night meeting should take the form of an address on church history. As far as I was concerned, this was where Jack Cullum came into the picture. Six foot four in height with jet-black hair, it was impossible not to notice his attendance and his rapt attention when these Wednesday night meetings began in October, 1956. It was a few months later, however, that we first talked personally when my wife and I accepted an invitation to visit his home in Highgate on January 26, 1957. As we walked that day on Hampstead Heath he put a question to me the repercussions of which were, in due time, to touch the ends of the earth. Thankful for his growing understanding that salvation is all of God, he was also finding the witness of church history to be full of excitement and his question was, 'Why is it that all the history and teaching of the English Reformers and Puritans is so little known today?'. When I replied in terms of the long period during which their works had been unavailable through booksellers, I had no idea that I was speaking to someone whom God was calling to support their republication. Since his conversion Jack Cullum's prayer had been that he might be enabled to do something useful for the remainder of his life. At first he had thought of giving of his considerable means to advance evangelical agencies in general, and had founded a charitable trust with that in view, but the testimony of leaders from the 16th and 17th centuries had stirred him deeply and, on hearing of the vision of a new publishing venture for the advancement of historic and Calvinistic Christianity, he seemed to be instantly committed to it. By mid-March 1957 plans were developed between us, and ML-J gave his approval to a publishing work which, as its existence was unrelated to any question of financial profit, should also be a charitable trust. As the intention was to continue on a larger scale the message of the little magazine of 1955, the name became 'The Banner of Truth Trust'.

Only at one point did Dr Lloyd-Jones express some misgivings. He doubted the wisdom of the projected re-issue of so many books in a short space of time. Not without reason, he was concerned lest organisation and promotion would run ahead of the spiritual change which was slowly increasing in influence. I think that he also understood more than we did of the difficulties in the market. Certainly he had been advised by some in the publishing world, who heard rumours of what was planned, that such an enterprise with unknown authors could not possibly succeed. He was also inclined to think that Jack Cullum's resources would be better employed if they were not concentrated into one channel and (at Cullum's request) he had spoken to him of the needs of the Evangelical Movement of Wales and of The Evangelical Library. Some help was given to these bodies, but a letter from Jack Cullum to ML-J on July 19, 1957, indicated that the new Trust was unlikely to move more slowly with regard to its main intention:

I find no one else with your experience and wisdom to whom we can turn. The assistance you gave Iain Murray in drawing up the Articles of Faith for the Trust, and your promise of further support is a great encouragement to us.

I am more and more persuaded that the funds should be used to support the bold presentation of the Puritan position as defined in the Trust Deed, and if it should be God's glorious purpose to revive his Word in a mighty re-awakening, as we pray for, some needs may arise which cannot now be estimated. To this end you will be glad to know that all dividend so far distributed has been transferred to the new Trust.[1]

Thanks be to Him who has given us an illustration of His providence. May He mightily bless this movement by the raising up of powerful preachers and writers again.

[1]The deeds of the Banner of Truth Trust were formally signed three days after this letter was written.

By November 1957 two books were printed and at the binders, with a further nine in the course of production. When the first two books became available early in 1958 their sale was remarkably rapid, and especially at Westminster Chapel, where ML-J spoke as follows on the first Friday evening after they became available:

I want to call your attention to two books available in the Book Room. *A Commentary on The Song of Solomon* was published at my personal suggestion. It is one of the choicest books I have ever read in my life . . . I cannot speak too highly of this book and exhort you all to read it. It is republished by a new Trust and the price of ten shillings and six pence is quite amazing. Old classics are to be reprinted at a cheap rate. The second book is Thomas Watson's *Body of Divinity*, sermons on the Westminster Catechism. As you read this book you will be brought face to face with the essentials of the Christian Faith. I am not a member of this Trust; I am speaking warmly of these books because of my esteem for them. I am extremely happy that this is being done so that modern Christians can read some of the great Christian classics.

These two books were quickly followed by *The Select Sermons of George Whitefield* and *The Select Works of Jonathan Edwards*, vol. 1. The latter work Dr Lloyd-Jones recommended to the congregation on Friday evening, March 7, 1958, and pointed out that the month marked the bicentenary of Edwards' death. It was this same month that he wrote a Foreword to Robert Haldane's *Exposition of the Epistle to the Romans* which the Banner of Truth Trust had in hand for publication. In this Foreword he quoted the words of Dr Reuben Saillens concerning the revival which had followed Haldane's work on the continent of Europe. The quotation also expressed very clearly the objectives both of ML-J's own ministry and that of the Trust: 'The three main characteristics of Haldane's Revival, as it has sometimes been called, were these: (1) it gave a prominent emphasis to the necessity of a personal knowledge and experience of grace; (2) it maintained the absolute authority and divine inspiration of the Bible; (3) it was a return to Calvinistic doctrine against Pelagianism and Arminianism. Haldane was an orthodox [preacher] of the first water, but his orthodoxy was blended with love and life.'

The first Banner of Truth titles had become ready for publication before any premises for the Trust had been found. At Dr Lloyd-Jones' suggestion to the deacons, the problem was solved by the loan of a room at the Chapel situated at the back of one of the rear halls. This was used both for storage and despatch until the arrangement could shortly be changed for a better one. Keith Lloyd, a member of Westminster Chapel who was helping at the Evangelical Library, drew our attention to the fact that the large ground floor of 78 Chiltern Street was currently empty. An enquiry to the owners (St. Paul's Church, Portman Square) revealed that they were willing for the Trust to use it on a rented basis. This was in February 1958. The new location thus brought the two agencies which shared a common purpose together under one roof. The utmost cordiality prevailed between us as each helped the other, and the numbers of visitors to Chiltern Street swelled as books, both old and new, were now available at the same address.

By October 1958 the sale of the first eleven titles was a matter of general astonishment. Even the least successful, in numerical terms, of the titles had sold 1,200 copies, and others were far outstripping all expectations. The 2,000 copies of Watson's *Body of Divinity* printed were soon exhausted, and over the next twelve years sales of this title were close to 17,000 copies. By 1960 there were more than 35 Banner of Truth Trust titles available.

In the 1970's *Crusade* magazine, reviewing developments in evangelical life in the previous 21 years, referred to 'the revival of Reformed theology sparked off largely by the setting up of the Banner of Truth Trust which flooded the market with inexpensive reprints of Puritan classics'. As the preceding pages have shown, this is not an accurate statement of what occurred. The Trust's work was met with success in 1958 because a hunger already existed. No one can flood a market with unwanted books. The change was already there, stimulated by the few reprints already available and, more so, by copies of the older books to be found at the Evangelical Library and elsewhere. At the Annual Meeting of the Library on November 29, 1960 Dr Lloyd-Jones could say:

We rejoice in the fact that now we can get so many really good books, brand new and beautifully produced, with glossy, shiny covers. You see, the daughters are much more up-to-date and attractive in appearance than the older ones. But do not forget the mother! The best books were available here, and almost exclusively here until two or three years ago.

But not only had the work of the Evangelical Library preceded the

Trust, still more important was the effect of the preaching and teaching of Dr Lloyd-Jones in preparing the way for a new climate of opinion. The seemingly sudden demand for a different type of book was directly connected with the accumulated influences of Westminster Chapel. 'It is very interesting to note,' said ML-J on one occasion, 'how the type of theology you hold will decide whether you are a reader or whether you are not.' *His* theology, as it was preached, made people readers. The preaching had to come first and had it not done so the response to the older literature might well have remained as feeble as it had been ten years earlier. The spoken word thus had a profound effect in opening the way not only for ML-J's own books but for a whole school of literature to which a superficial evangelicalism had long been oblivious.

By the late 1950's there were hundreds of people, and notably young people, whose thinking and theology had been permanently changed through the pulpit of Westminster Chapel. For a few years their numbers seemed to be constantly multiplying. It was, to a degree, reminiscent of the days when John Knox could write of God 'raining men from heaven', or when Thomas Goodwin could speak of the gospel being at 'full-tide' among the students at Cambridge. Swelling numbers were a characteristic of these years. From sixty at the Puritan Conference in 1955 the attendance was soon to reach a couple of hundred. Similarly, the Westminster Fraternal held in the Parlour at the Chapel until 1955 had to move to the much larger Institute Hall. One older member of the fraternal, Angus McMillan, absent from the Fraternal for more than a year on account of illness, wrote to Dr Lloyd-Jones of his impression when he was able to return in October 1958: 'It was a great joy to me to be able to attend the Westminster Fellowship again . . . What a thrill to see that large group of influential young ministers (and older ones too) at Westminster Chapel. The influence for good must be simply incalculable . . . .'.

The same growth was evident in the Sunday services. In November 1959 Jack Cullum could write to ML-J of his 'thankfulness that the numbers at Westminster Chapel seem to increase continually'. While not confined to students and other young people, the change, as already noted, was most marked in that age group. By 1959 there were 220 students at the London Bible College, and 25,000 in the various Colleges and Medical Schools of the University of London. Few of these institutions can have been unrepresented at the Chapel on Sundays.

Many of the students at the London Bible College in the 1950's have spoken of what Westminster Chapel meant to them. Emmi Muller from Germany, already quoted, regarded Dr Lloyd-Jones' sermons and Bible studies 'of great complementary help and value to studies at London Bible College'.

John Brencher recalls:

Nothing surpassed the regular doctrinal teaching of the Friday nights. For those of us who were living and studying within reach of Central London it was like attending a Seminary without paying the fees! That great auditorium holds a special place in my affections, for it was there that I so often met with God. Sitting regularly under such a ministry my theological thinking was to be changed, a taste for church history was to develop and under God my call into the ministry began to take shape.

The same writer provides a personal comment on the link between Dr Lloyd-Jones' ministry and the influence of literature which we have already noted:

In my late teens the Doctor introduced me to the Evangelical Library and to the value of good reading. Previously I had little time for books, but when I saw his enthusiasm I felt compelled to see what I was missing. I began to read Puritan and other writings and these were to become an incalculable asset to me. In 1957 the Banner of Truth Trust came into being and when their early reprints were heartily commended, with other books, on Friday nights I was usually found in the rush to the Bookroom at the close of the service.

David Potter, who came to London to study theology in the late 1950's, has written of his surprise at the new influences with which he found himself suddenly surrounded:

I felt thoroughly provincial, even though my home was only fifty miles away. It was not, perhaps, surprising that I had not heard of some of the names which were common talk among my fellows — names like John Calvin, George Whitefield, and Richard Sibbes. They were from another age from my own. But who was 'the Doctor' who seemed so popular? Even when I learned that he was Dr Martyn Lloyd-Jones I was no wiser. I had never heard of him before.

At first I resisted the pressure to join the crowds to Westminster Chapel each Sunday. Eventually I succumbed, but made my way alone to 'the Chapel'. Many things surprised me. The size of the congregation was something quite new to me, and the hymn-singing was moving in a way I

David Martyn Lloyd-Jones: Volume Two

had rarely experienced. And there seemed to be hundreds of other students. The Doctor came quietly into the pulpit. His seeming insignificance belied his command of the situation. When he came to preach, it was ministry such as I had never heard before . . . His method, approach and theology were all new to me, in spite of my evangelical background.

Without question, there was an observable movement now present in England and Wales. One way in which it was now reflected was in the marked increase in sales for ML-J's own books. His *From Fear to Faith* was reprinted in 1958. In the same year his three IFES addresses were published in March with the title *Authority*. By the end of May 4,200 copies had been sold and twelve months later the figure was close to 12,000.[1] A month after the publication of volume one of *Studies in the Sermon on the Mount* in 1959 the IVF reported, 'We are very encouraged by the response'. The American publishers, it would seem, were not yet awake to what was happening, for Eerdmans took only 3,000 copies of this volume for the North American market. Within months, however, the Book Club Guild in the United States was to take on a special printing of around 10,000.

*   *   *

Inevitably what was happening in England led to an increase in the kind of controversy which followed Dr Packer's criticism of Keswick teaching in 1955. The current evangelicalism suddenly found itself under seeming attack, not from liberalism, but from its own side. In 1957 James Packer and Raymond Johnston brought out a new edition of Luther on *The Bondage of the Will*, with an 'Historical and Theological Introduction' of nearly fifty pages. In this Introduction they concluded: 'Much modern Protestantism would be neither owned nor even recognized by the pioneer Reformers . . . We are forced to ask whether Protestant Christendom has not tragically sold its birthright between Luther's day and our own. Has not Protestantism today become more Erasmian than Lutheran? . . . Do we still believe that doctrine matters?'[2] Packer went still further in his

---

[1] It was characteristic of his attitude to the ministry of literature that ML-J gave the royalties due to him to the IVF for the first 6,000 copies.
[2] *The Bondage of the Will*, Martin Luther, translated by J. I. Packer and O. R. Johnston, James Clarke, 1957, pp. 59–60.

'Introductory Essay' to John Owen's *The Death of Death in the Death of Christ*, published by the Banner of Truth Trust in 1959. He believed that modern evangelicalism 'conspicuously fails to produce deep reverence, deep repentance, deep humility, a spirit of worship, a concern for the Church' and he traced all this to the evil of man-centeredness. A gospel which depends for its success upon man's will and man's response is not, he argued, the gospel of the New Testament.

Many other young men were now saying the same thing but not always as maturely as the above writer. Tom Rees was one who deplored the disturbance which was being caused and the 'serious division amongst evangelical Christians'. 'Extreme Calvinism,' he warned in a booklet, 'has spread to many parts of the country, particularly amongst the younger evangelical ministers and under-graduates'.[1] That older men of the stature of Tom Rees had some room for complaint cannot be doubted. Controversy was wide-spread and it was largely due to young men. But those who were shocked by the change were too often unaware of its doctrinal origins or its real meaning, and their attempts to restore 'balance' were consequently bound to fail.

In the minds of some, Dr Lloyd-Jones had to bear the principal part of the blame for the controversy. The attachment to him and virtually to no one else was clear for all to see. Tom Rees wrote in the same booklet of 'the impressionable young undergraduate' who 'speaks of Dr Martyn Lloyd-Jones with a reverence and awe that ought properly to be reserved for Deity'. It strained the grace of some of the lecturers at the London Bible College to hear students refer to Westminster Chapel as 'the upper sanctuary' and make no secret of their preference for the pulpit over the classroom. When a change in College regulations required students to be indoors on Friday evenings and, therefore, not to be at Westminster Chapel for the addresses on Romans, the obedience rendered was not always exemplary.

The strength of this attachment to ML-J needs some comment. In part it was, of course, the hero worship of youth which time would cure. In fact, some who admired him excessively as students would become very cool towards him in later years. But in the case of many others there was an overriding explanation for what Dr Lloyd-Jones

[1] *Election and Biblical Evangelism*, n. d., p. 20.

meant in their lives. When they read of the Puritans, of Whitefield or Spurgeon, they found themselves in a different universe of thought from that of modern evangelicalism and of the churches with which they were familiar. In the vast majority of cases the old creeds and confessions of a doctrinal Christianity had long been in limbo and such words as 'unconditional election' and 'effectual calling' had not been heard for generations. If young people throughout England had been able to find pastors who, in their own measure, were standing for the old principles there would not have been the looking to Dr Lloyd-Jones that there was. Westminster Chapel and its pulpit, as we have seen, stood comparatively alone as the one prominent church where the old truths could be heard in their power in the modern world. It is no wonder then that those whose eyes were opened to a great heritage felt a unique thankfulness for Westminster Chapel. Nor is it surprising that those who were first led to the doctrines of grace through books felt, when they came to Westminster Chapel, like the Psalmist and could say, 'As we have heard, so have we seen . . .' (Psa 48:8).

When due allowance has been made for the excesses of youth and legitimate criticism is allowed for a measure of idolatry, it remains true that the fundamental reason for the strength of attachment to Dr Lloyd-Jones' ministry was the truth he preached and the position which he represented. We have already noticed that he had paid a cost in terms of loneliness over a number of years because he had believed that the truth required him to do so. His faithfulness in that regard was one of the chief reasons why younger men came so to love and admire him. Many of them in later years, scattered about the world, would also know something of hardship and loneliness, for their love of the truth was not to end with the days when, in John Bunyan's phrase, it walked in 'silver slippers' in Westminster's large congregation.

Dr Lloyd-Jones had now to give more time than ever to the guiding, advising and, often, restraining of these younger men. But he exercised no dictatorial control, not even over his Assistant nor over the Banner of Truth Trust which was, in these years, so closely connected with the Chapel. Had people understood this he would have been blamed far less. The new circumstances certainly placed him in a difficult situation. He wanted evangelical unity. He eschewed any kind of Calvinistic sectarianism which would break fellowship with fellow Christians of Arminian persuasion and, in this regard, he often pointed to the example of Whitefield's brotherly relationship with John Wesley. Yet at the same time he had worked and prayed for evangelicalism to be moved to a stronger doctrinal position and he believed passionately that the greatest need of the church, namely a true revival, was closely related to a recovery of those biblical truths associated with the Calvinistic tradition. It was thus his belief that, despite some excesses among the younger men, the contemporary return to the older tradition was of God. The spontaneous manner in which the change had occurred had the marks of a work of the Spirit of God. So, while he was sometimes embarrassed and pained by instances of unwise zeal, he would not disown the younger men even though such action would sometimes have been beneficial to his reputation. When a senior IVF committee, anxious to reduce the existing controversy, entertained a proposal that anyone belonging to 'a party' should be excluded from speaking to the Christian Unions, ML-J immediately indicated that such a ruling would put them all out for they all belonged to parties in matters of belief.

It was in part to aid a better balance that yet another literature work began in connection with Westminster Chapel in 1958. The prime mover was Elizabeth Braund who in 1956 and '57 had given addresses at the Puritan Conference.[1] Miss Braund had been converted earlier in the 1950's in connection with the ministry at Westminster Chapel, at a time when she was preparing the script for a British Broadcasting Corporation programme on the history of the transmission of the Bible. In 1958, encouraged by ML-J and in conjunction with Jim Packer and Paul Tucker, she launched *The Evangelical Magazine*. With a strong devotional and pastoral emphasis, this bi-monthly soon established itself as an influential journal. *Knowing God*, one of the more widely read Christian books of the present century, originated as articles in *The Evangelical Magazine*.[2] The new magazine also gave expression to the emerging unity between the work in Wales and in England. For several years a group of the younger Welsh ministers had made the Puritan Conference an occasion for an annual visit to London and Dr Lloyd-Jones had introduced some of us to the Conference in Wales. It was

[1] She was only the second woman to do so. Miss E. R Hilton had spoken on 'The Gospel Hypocrite' in 1953.
[2] This Packer title first published in book form in 1973, soon climbed to a circulation of more than a quarter of a million copies.

now agreed that the quarterly *Evangelical Magazine of Wales* (started, as mentioned earlier, in 1955) should partially merge with the new *Evangelical Magazine* so that henceforth the two magazines would carry the same material in two-thirds of their content. Both countries benefited and the greater unity which the arrangement signified was another of the hopes which stirred expectation for the future as the 1950's drew to their close.

Signs of a turning of the tide were thus multiplying. At the Evangelical Library annual meeting in 1960 Geoffrey Williams could report that during the year 6,700 books had been borrowed from Chiltern Street and that a total of 84,077 books had now been sent to overseas branches. The words with which ML-J concluded his prayer at the end of that meeting are also a fitting conclusion to this chapter:

And now, O Lord our God, we ascribe unto Thee all praise, all honour and all glory, and it is Thine alone, and we do not desire to give any portion of it to anybody else. Lord, it is Thine; we but humbly thank Thee that Thou hast ever given any of us a part and a place in Thy great purposes of grace.

It must not be thought that Dr Lloyd-Jones is merely concerned with setting out evangelical principles in a detached, intellectual way. He is not concerned to establish a cold, classical orthodoxy. One of the powerful contributions made during the last decade has been his emphasis on the need to consider the work of the Holy Spirit in a more vital and experimental way. The need for revival and renewal in the church today is a theme of which the Doctor never tires and the sermons preached during 1959 (the centenary of the 1859 Revival which swept the English and Welsh speaking world) are heart warming to peruse. He feels very strongly that a demonstration of the power of the Holy Spirit is the only answer to the moribund state of the church today. That there is an increasing awareness of this need in many quarters of the world can in a measure be traced to ministry at Westminster Chapel.

WYNFORD A. DAVIES
on 'A Modern Prophet: Dr D. Martyn Lloyd-Jones' in the Evangelical Presbyterian, *New Zealand, July, 1963.*

18

1959 and the Burden for Revival

In most respects the pattern of Dr Lloyd-Jones' work in 1959 was the same as in any other year. One factor, however, made that date of particular significance to him: it was the centenary of the widespread awakening which occurred in the British Isles in 1859. While the mere commemoration of an anniversary, as such, did not concern him, he saw the contemporary disinterest in history among evangelicals as an important part of the explanation of their weakness. Ignorance of what the church had been in the past entered directly into the failure to assess present conditions and what should be her present priorities. The belief which led him to say, 'We have passed through one of the most barren periods in the long history of the church',[1] was one which few took seriously. That was why he was virtually alone among evangelical leaders in believing that the church needed to be called to repentance. He thus saw the anniversary of 1859 as an opportunity to draw special attention to the whole subject of revival.

With this concern in view, Dr Lloyd-Jones interrupted his Sunday morning series on Ephesians to commence, on January 11, 1959, twenty-six sermons on revival. What he taught on this theme will be summarised later but here it is important to note what he was also preaching at the same time. For a while, the subject of revival was to become an all-absorbing theme in the minds of some but ML-J never allowed his thinking to run in one channel. January 16 saw the resumption of the Friday night meeting with his 100th exposition on the Epistle to the Romans. He had reached verse 16 in chapter 6, the chapter in which the Pauline emphasis falls so heavily on what Christians *are*. All believers are baptised by the Holy Spirit into Christ,[2] all are sanctified and have 'died to sin', all are indwelt by the

[1]Sermon on March 14, 1959 (*Revival*, p. 129).
[2]*Romans*, vol. 5, p. 35.

Holy Spirit.[1] Thus at the same time as he was speaking of the subjective need of the churches on Sunday mornings he was equally emphasising the truth that for a Christian to think of himself and his experiences only in subjective terms is entirely wrong. Glorious things are true of the Christian whether he feels them or not! Faith in objective truths is the starting point for both Christian holiness and for service.[2] 'The real explanation of the trouble in most Christian lives is the fact that believers start thinking about salvation in terms of themselves, and not in terms of God, the Holy Trinity.'

As usual, most of his preaching in 1959 was to be evangelistic and it would appear to have been a particularly fruitful year in this regard, both at Westminster and in his itinerant journeys. On the first Sunday night of the year the emphasis in his gospel preaching was on sin; on the second, the value of the soul; and on the third, the atonement. The freshness of his approach in preaching basically the same message, and the variety of the passages which he used, were remarkable.

In January and February, ML-J normally did less travelling than in other months, the wintry weather usually being at its worst. But his engagements included meetings at Walthamstow, Cambridge, Kenton, Bournemouth, Bath and Camberwell. In March he was in Bedford, Colwyn Bay, Hemel Hempstead and then, at the end of the month, he went to Ireland where his itinerary had been arranged by a united committee of Irish Churches for the 'Revival Centenary Commemoration'. The first of these meetings was in the Metropolitan Hall, Dublin, on March 31. The next day 1,500 people crowded the Wellington Hall, Belfast for a second meeting which was reported in the Belfast press under the heading, 'People turned away from churches rally'. The final meeting, on the third successive day of services was in the First Presbyterian Church in Londonderry. *The Derry Standard* (April 7, 1959) wrote of the sermon, from Acts 12 on prayer in the growth of the church, as 'an inspiring message'. They were not there merely to commemorate 1859, Dr Lloyd-Jones told these Irish congregations: 'While I am a great advocate of looking to the past, I would warn everybody against living in the past. The only justification for looking to the past is that we may learn great lessons from it and apply them.' Arguing that 'the gospel is literally the only hope for the world today', he showed how the gospel always makes a

[1]*Ibid*, pp. 139–40, 156, etc.
[2]*Ibid*, pp. 43–44, 174–77, etc.

powerful effect upon the world *after* there has first been a distinct quickening in the life of the church. The modern church was bypassing her primary need. She was adopting 'methods of big business and advertising' instead of praying for a visitation of God. As the Belfast press reported his words: 'The Church has never tried so hard to deal with the situation as she has tried in this century. We have never had so many organisations, we have never worked so hard, but we are not touching the situation.'

Following these services ML-J had his first free Sunday of the year prior to returning to Westminster and more meetings in England and Wales before the end of the month. In May he was preaching in Glasgow on the 12th and for the Liverpool City Mission in Liverpool the next day. In the words of the Superintendent of that Mission, the Liverpool Rally 'was one of the greatest meetings that we have had'.

May and June were always his busiest months, with many churches asking him for afternoon as well as evening services mid-week. Over these same weeks of early summer he was continuing to preach on Revival on Sunday mornings and was also enjoying exceptional liberty in preaching from John chapter 7 in the evening services. A marked feature of the evening services at Westminster Chapel was how *Christians* benefited from them. One who commenced attending in March 1959 wrote to the preacher to say: 'Your presentation of the gospel has done much to establish me in the way and to intensify and deepen my faith. It is all too wonderful really! Last evening I almost jumped to my feet to shout, "Hallelujah, I have been born again!".' Many could have said the same.[1]

By this date it had become traditional that the members of the Westminster Fraternal looked forward to an annual day's outing every June. In the early 1950's the numbers going could all be taken on one small coach, and there were occasions when ML-J would stop the coach to buy everyone ice cream! Later in the decade the scene for the outing became the old manor house of 'Guessens' at Welwyn with its beautiful gardens and the evangelical church nearby which contained the pulpit once used by John Gill. There must have been well over 100 men who arrived in a fleet of cars at 'Guessens' on June 17, 1959. A pattern for these meetings had now become established with ML-J usually giving a major address at a morning

[1] It was ML-J's conviction that if Christians were not helped by the evangelistic preaching of the gospel there was something seriously wrong, in the pulpit or the pew, or in both (see *Romans*, vol. 5, p. 218).

session in the church. This was followed by a splendid lunch at the house, half an hour of relaxation in the garden and then an afternoon session of discussion. For the address this year the Chairman gave an exposition of Romans 6 which was profoundly helpful. The teaching in that chapter was now fundamental to his whole view of the Christian life.

The following week the Welsh Ministers' Conference was held at Cilgwyn, Newcastle Emlyn from Monday to Thursday. It was a time of year when Wales was to be seen in all its beauty and nowhere more so than on the border of Cardigan and Carmarthenshire where this conference centre was situated. Various subjects were on the Conference agenda, including an address by ML-J on 'Nervous Strain', in which he spoke on the need to distinguish in counselling between the insane, the mentally defective, the neurotic and those whose primary problem is spiritual. There were also addresses and discussion relating to 1859 and the subject of revival. ML-J urged the need to begin with ourselves, our own relationship to God and what is wrong there. We fail to spend time in prayer, he believed, because we do not sufficiently *desire* Him and we do not desire because we do not know Him. There were memorable evening prayer meetings, particularly on the last night of the Conference when at one point he stopped the meeting and exhorted us for several minutes on the manner in which we should be praying. He had detected a note of despair in some petitions: urgency there ought to be, he said, but never despair. Our lack of confidence in prayer was due to failure to see the *victorious* Christ and he pointed to Isaiah 63:1–7. Our praying needed to be closer to scriptural models and, in particular, we needed to pray, with Moses, 'I beseech thee, shew me thy glory' (Exodus 33:18).

This last prayer meeting had started half-an-hour early because Dr Lloyd-Jones had to return to Port Talbot that same evening as he was to preach the following day at a new church on the Sandfields estate. It was an evening of rain and mist and his friend the Rev. Luther Rees of Llansamlet, who was to drive him, believed that they needed to leave about 9 p.m. Accordingly the two men sat together so that they could leave promptly. But Rees recalls how, after ML-J had interrupted the meeting about 8.30 p.m., they lost track of time:

I felt, and so did the Doctor, that God was near to us then. How we longed for revival! It was after 11.30 p.m. when we got on our journey. As we left he took my hand and said, 'Mr Rees' – as friendly as we could be he would always call us 'Mr' – 'we couldn't leave sooner could we? We were dealing with eternal things.'

When we arrived at Morriston we were unable to get through and had to take some back roads. We reached Port Talbot about 1.30 a.m. What humour the Doctor had! The next day, seeing my wife, he said to her, 'Did you let him in this morning?'. I got to my bed at 2 a.m.

This was one of the last Ministers' Conferences to be held at Cilgwyn because the following year the Evangelical Movement of Wales decided to purchase Bryn-y-Groes, a conference centre of their own in Bala, and thus Bala became the new venue for the annual conference.

In mid-July 1959 Dr Lloyd-Jones returned with Mrs Lloyd-Jones to Wales for their annual holiday. As usual, there were opportunities to preach, once in English and eleven times in Welsh. One of these services took place at Caernarfon on August 6 during the Eisteddfod and was held to commemorate the revival of 1859. Exactly one hundred years earlier on August 6, 1859, one of the most remarkable days of blessing in that revival had occurred in ML-J's own village of Llangeitho when the Holy Spirit had come in power upon a gathering of some 18,000 people. This summer, as in so many other summers, they stayed with John and Mari Jones at Brynuchaf and ML-J preached in the Welsh chapel nearby at Llanymawddwy. Mari Jones, recalling such occasions, writes:

He would give as much effort in presenting the gospel in our little church to a handful of people as he would to the hundreds, and sweating just as much. I remember one Sunday night he had been preaching here and some friends came with us for supper after the service. In the course of conversation he asked whether we were conscious of the heavenly presence at the service. He felt it was not his effort but rather he watched someone preaching by his side. It was for this anointing he yearned.

One Sunday morning we were having a prayer meeting at our small chapel at Llanymawddwy. When we were on the doorstep of the chapel the Doctor suggested, 'Would you like me to give a word this morning?'. As we hesitated to give an answer, being afraid of taxing his energy on his holiday, 'Let him,' was the comment of his wife, 'preaching is his life'. Oh how very true, and what a gracious wife the Lord gave him in Bethan Lloyd-Jones!

An unusual occasion when the service at the chapel in Llanymawddwy was held in English rather than in Welsh deserves mention here as recorded by Elizabeth Braund. With the development of *The Evangelical Magazine*, Miss Braund had been offered a disused chapel, near Clapham Junction, for the work of the magazine. But its location, among gangs of youths in the unchurched sub-culture of Battersea, gave rise to an unplanned outreach among these needy young people. The chapel also became a youth club and in the late 1950's Elizabeth saw the value of introducing a party of these youngsters to a holiday away from the only world which they knew. John and Mari Jones, knowing of this, offered the use of the old farmhouse at Brynuchaf which they had recently left for a newly-built house close by. The first visit was enjoyed so much that it was repeated in eight successive years, and it was on one of these holidays that their leader found her minister and his wife staying at the new house. Usually, on these holidays, the party from Battersea had their own meeting on Sunday but ML-J was to preach at Llanymawddwy that Sunday and he readily agreed to preach in English so that the youngsters from London could attend. Miss Braund was not without some apprehensions:

The tiny chapel, which scarcely held fifty people when full, would have half of its congregation made up of cockney lads who were ignorant of any form of church worship or religious conformity, the other half would be Welsh-speaking locals from a totally different background and culture . . .

The boys' first astonishment as the service began was the volume and fervour of the singing that burst forth. After an uncertain giggle, they saw that many of the men of the valley were there and, like John, singing loudly. This was not a meeting for a few 'old dears', as they thought of church-goers at home, and it was not long before they were gruffly joining in, though without Welsh tunefulness. Wisely, the Doctor explained to the boys that he was going to speak in Welsh to the people for a minute, and after that the service would be in English. The boys sat still, fascinated by the strange sounds, as the Doctor thanked the Welsh people for sharing their service, and reminded them of where the boys came from. With good-will established all round, the meeting continued.

There was spiritual power in the service that night. The Doctor took as his text the story of Paul preaching on Mars Hill, and explained in everyday terms the sort of people who listened to Paul, who their counterparts were today, what he had to say to them, and what it meant for us. There was not a long or complicated word or sentence in the whole sermon, and although the boys sprawled along the pews as they would anywhere else, they listened.

'That was good,' several remarked as they bunched out of the doorway afterwards. Two went further as they walked back to the farm beside me. "E's all right, that bloke. I could understand wot 'e said,' declared one.

'Yeah – it's the first time I ever 'eard anything ter do with religion that made sense,' replied the other.

Another lad joined us and remarked: 'I could 'ear that bloke again. It were interestin' – 'E didn't talk down to us.'[1]

*   *   *

'How did ML-J relax on holiday?' we once asked Mari Jones. To which she replied that as far as reading was concerned he never did relax, 'He had the same satisfaction penning in his memory the mind of an author that a shepherd gets in penning a difficult flock of ewes and their lambs that had not been within an enclosure before'. And his enthusiasm in reading affected the whole household at Bryn-uchaf: ' "Listen, listen to what Jonathan Edwards has to say on this," he would call to us in the kitchen, with a special emphasis on the 'E' in Edwards. And with joy glowing on his face, he would read of how that great man underlined some truth or other.'

For weeks before the arrival of their friends, John and Mari Jones would collect contemporary Welsh religious magazines and periodicals which ML-J would always read carefully. Wales was very near his heart and as family worship closed the day, 'he would be pleading with as much earnestness as he would in front of any congregation for God's visitation in our land'.

There were also many lighter moments in these holidays at Brynuchaf. Although still ready to mount a horse, physical exercise was not his idea of a vacation, 'When we would urge him to come for a walk,' says Mari Jones, 'he would say with a smile, "I do my physical exercise in the pulpit"'. But he could be active enough when he thought it necessary, as on the occasion when John, Mari and others were working in a hay field some distance from the farmhouse when a thunder-storm and heavy rain began. To their surprise the workers saw ML-J hurrying towards them with his arms full of dry coats. Of course, he did take some walks in the hills and one of these, when Bethan and he had set out for the source of the river Dyfi, became a subject of amusement. In Mari's words:

[1] *The Young Woman who Lived in a Shoe*, Pickering & Inglis, 1982, pp. 95–96.

One length of the path traversed quite a steep ravine, and about halfway down this path he became paralysed with fear. He could neither go on nor retrace his steps. As far as I could gather, he came back by flattening himself against the slope, holding on to the turf and every clump of coarse grass. His respectable black suit was in a sorry state on his return, and he laughed heartily as he related the incident. He was to preach that night at Llanrhaeadr-ym-Mochnant, and whilst holding on there above the ravine he was wondering who would go to preach in his place. But he got there safely, of course.

Most evenings on these holidays were spent in the family circle around the log fire, with the day's work done. In the picture idiom of Mari's Welsh tongue: 'The Doctor would start pulling the strings of his memory. Oh, what a memory he had, it was as if he was unravelling an endless ball of wool. There were stories of childhood days and the horses at Llwyncadfor whose very names he remembered, or of recent travels and of people he had met in various places. He could rock with laughter as he spoke of unfortunate experiences such as the time when preaching in a barn, shared by swallows, in the north of England. As he was reading the Scriptures he suddenly received a warm splash on his hand – a few inches nearer, on his face or nose, and it could have been a real calamity!'

As indicated above, ML-J's dress for this Welsh hill farm was virtually the same as it was in London. 'I never once saw him in a sports jacket,' Mari Jones writes. 'He was always tidy, neatly dressed in collar and tie and clean shaven'. But the reference to shaving needs a qualification. He used an electric razor and sometimes in earlier years at Brynuchaf, when electricity depended upon an uncertain supply of water to work the turbine, it was put out of action. 'Whiskers again', he would remark with a mischievous smile as he arrived at breakfast.

From the mountains of North Wales Dr and Mrs Lloyd-Jones went to the different world of Paris at the end of August 1959. Here meetings of the Executive Committee of the International Fellowship of Evangelical Students were followed by sessions of the General Committee and a Conference. Stacey Woods recalls an unusually difficult situation arising at the General Committee – also chaired by ML-J – when a number of representatives from different countries protested at a decision taken by the Executive Committee: 'In a masterly way Dr Lloyd-Jones controlled the situation and persuaded the militants to ask no further questions but to respect the integrity of the Executive Committee.' Certain things could not be disclosed to the General Committee without breaking confidences. On one Sunday during this time in France ML-J preached in the Scots Church in Paris and the message he chose was no doubt influenced by the memory of the time when he had sat in the same congregation as a visitor. Stacey Woods describes what happened:

The Church was crowded. The Doctor's text was, 'Strait is the gate and narrow is the way that leadeth unto Life and few there be that find it'. In an extraordinary way, the presence of God was in that Church. I personally felt as if a hand were pushing me through the pew. At the end of the sermon for some reason or the other the organ did not play, the Doctor went off into the vestry and everyone sat completely still without moving. It must have been almost ten minutes before people seemed to find the strength to get up and, without speaking to one another, quietly leave the Church. Never have I witnessed or experienced such preaching with such fantastic reaction on the part of the congregation.

✳   ✳   ✳

The week after Dr Lloyd-Jones returned from Paris he was back in Wales for another service before a new year of work commenced at Westminster with a Members' Meeting on September 17. As usual ML-J gave a short account of his vacation at this meeting. His main impression arising out of the strenuous period in Paris was of 'the crying need for Christian literature in all parts of the world'. This meeting marked the 21st anniversary of Dr Lloyd-Jones' coming to Westminster Chapel and a fine speech was given by the senior deacon, Mr Donald Hattersley, who spoke of what they owed to God for the ministry which had begun in their midst at the time of the Munich crisis of 1938. By reference to questions and answers in the *Shorter Catechism* of the Westminster divines Mr Hattersley reminded the people of the nature of the work of the ministry and urged the duty of thankfulness to God and of continued prayer: 'If we wish men to preach the holy Word with power, then we should continue to wait upon our heavenly Father'. Tribute was also paid to Mrs Lloyd-Jones for the wonderful help she gave her husband, her Bible class and for her ever-willing counsel given to large numbers of people. He then asked them both to accept with the love and appreciation of the church the gift of a Georgian mahogany dining table and chairs.

In reply ML-J spoke of how they had been preserved through World

War II and of what it meant to him to have a united church. 'God has given me a people who are in accord. Let us go forward together.' And he testified that he enjoyed preaching the gospel more than he had ever done in the whole of his life.

Although recommencing his Sunday ministry on September 20, 1959, he waited, as usual, until the students had returned to London for the University term before taking up his expository series. On the morning of October 4 he then resumed Ephesians at chapter 5 verse 14 and on the following Sunday he took the first of ten evangelistic sermons on 1 Peter 1:13 to 21. During the next weeks the mid-week periods were to be spent away from London according to his usual autumn routine. In mid-November his mid-week engagements were in London when he took part in a London Inter-Faculty Christian Union mission to the University Colleges of London. This IVF Mission had been preceded by an unusual degree of controversy, for in a number of the Colleges Christian students were being so influenced by the recovery of the doctrines of grace that there was a general disillusionment over modern evangelism. The knowledge that the giving of faith is God's work had led to a rejection of the popular evangelistic techniques which had ignored that truth, and there were even doubts whether there was any place for 'special efforts' in evangelism (as distinct from the regular witness of churches and Christians). It was to help in this new turmoil of discussion that Jim Packer was asked to speak to a Pre-Mission Conference on 'Evangelism and the Sovereignty of God' at Westminster Chapel on October 24, 1959. He gave a masterly address which was virtually a summary of ML-J's own thoughts.[1]

Without question Dr Lloyd-Jones' energies were being taxed to their limits at this time. In addition to so many public engagements there was the usual weight of correspondence (with appeals for visits from as far away as Australia). There were also the committee meetings of the Evangelical Library, the British Council of Churches,[2] the IVF and his own diaconate, not to speak of the weekly private interviews with all and sundry at Westminster Chapel.

[1] In enlarged form it was published as a book by IVF in 1961. Packer did not agree that evangelism was being weakened by 'the current revival in many places of faith in the sovereignty of divine grace' and 'fresh emphasis on the doctrines of unconditional election and effectual calling'. On the contrary, 'regarded as a human enterprise, evangelism is a hopeless task' (*Evangelism and the Sovereignty of God*, p. 109).
[2] These were the committee meetings referred to above, pp. 314–320.

Communion services were held at the Chapel, following the service on the first Sunday of the month in the morning and every third Sunday in the evening. These were often times of profound devotion. Before the distribution of bread and wine ML-J always spoke for a few minutes by way of comfort and exhortation to the believers assembled. But in the communion service following the evening service on November 15, 1959 he shared his feelings with his people at this point in a manner which was very uncommon for him. He explained that the weather that day, which was dull and rainy, was about the worst for his poor blood circulation and he had left home in the morning with such tiredness of body that he feared he would not be able to preach in a manner worthy of the Lord. God had given him strength, but after the exertion he felt even weaker and during the afternoon he did not know how he could possibly proclaim the Word of God at the evening service. What troubled him most, he said, was that he was to preach on the very heart of the gospel, the death of Christ the Son of God (1 Peter 1:18–19). He then, as he told the people, prayed and pleaded that the Holy Spirit who had been sent to glorify Christ would help him who was supposed to be preaching Christ, and that if he was left to himself the Lord Jesus Christ would not be glorified. In the mercy of God, he thought he could say that these pleas for the Spirit's aid had been heard. 'The congregation,' said one who was there, 'very noticeably and audibly assented to this statement. It was as though the Lord disclosed Himself in a fuller measure to those present.'

This brief reference to himself with respect to the demands of preaching provides an opportunity to observe that ML-J was not immune from what Spurgeon calls the minister's 'fainting fits'. He knew what it was to have trying and difficult experiences in the pulpit when he felt alone. While in his own view he never attained to the true biblical standard for preaching,[1] there were times when he could be very cast down over the degree to which he believed he fell short. After one Good Friday service it is said that he went home and told Mrs Lloyd-Jones that he was not preaching any more. There was no further conversation between them on the subject but he went to the Chapel as usual on the Sunday and preached what some considered to be 'two of his greatest sermons'. On another occasion,

[1]For his view of his own preaching see *Knowing the Times*, p. 263, and his Preface to *Preaching*, 'I can say quite honestly that I would not cross the road to listen to myself preaching'.

after an evening service, he spoke to one of the deacons of his consciousness of being oppressed by the devil and (half-seriously) of handing in his resignation. As in the episode of November 15, 1959, related above, we can well believe that these other experiences also drove him to earnest prayer.

For the remainder of 1959 his diary continued to be full. A visit to Scotland for services in commemoration of 1859 in Glasgow and Edinburgh and further LIFCU meetings were his main public engagements before the Puritan Conference which met, as usual, the week before Christmas. From this year until near the end of his life, it became a tradition that he gave the closing address. Attendance was probably never higher than for this final session when he addressed the crowded gathering in the Institute Hall on 'Revival: An Historical and Theological Survey'.

The following Sunday he passed his sixtieth birthday. The Christmas Day service was held as usual on the following Friday. Then, after Sunday, December 27, his help at a Theological Students Fellowship Conference closed the work of a very full year.

*   *   *

As we turn now to a summary of Dr Lloyd-Jones' teaching on revival and the work of the Holy Spirit in Christians, perhaps the first thing to observe is that his convictions on this subject were thoroughly settled by the 1950's. A failure to notice this was later to contribute to his views being interpreted in an entirely wrong context. Indeed there is only one point in his teaching in the 1950's which was not prominent before that date and it relates to the meaning of the foretastes of glory which he was given in 1949. The experiences of that year contributed to a deepening of his appreciation of what happens to the church in a time of revival, namely, that there is an overwhelming sense of God's love and a full assurance of salvation, accompanied by awe and joy and praise:

The essence of a revival is that the Holy Spirit comes down upon a number of people together, upon a whole church, upon a number of churches, districts, or perhaps a whole country. It is, if you like, a visitation of the Holy Spirit, or another term that has often been used is this – an outpouring of the Holy Spirit . . . When God acts in revival everybody present feels and knows that God is there. Of course, we believe this. We believe this by faith. Yes, but we should *know* it. We should be conscious of His nearness. And that is what revival does for us.[1]

But, further, those experiences also clarified his conviction that what happens to many in a time of revival may happen to individual Christians at other periods.

Dr Lloyd-Jones' understanding of the work of the Spirit in believers was as follows. As already noted, he taught that the Spirit is united to every Christian in regeneration and yet Christians need more of the Holy Spirit. Why else would they be promised more in answer to prayer (Luke 11:13)? The Acts of the Apostles shows that there were further enduements of the Spirit after Pentecost. The Jerusalem church, baptized with the Spirit as we read in Acts 2, was filled again as recorded in Acts 4:31. This relates to another great truth. It is through Christ that the Spirit continues to be given and there is an important distinction made in Scripture between 'the measure vouchsafed to men and the inexhaustible fulness in the resources of the fountain'.[2] Christ remains the 'immense, eternal, living spring or fountain of all grace' and gives further communications of the Spirit in terms of love, light, strength and assurance (Rom 5:5; Eph 1:17; 3:16; Rom 8:16; 15:13).[3] Believers are thus dependent upon Christ for 'the supply of the Spirit' (Phil 1:19) for, in Owen's phrase, the Spirit is not 'bestowed immediately on us, but, as it were, given into the hand of Christ for us'. As Bishop Moule says on Ephesians 1:17: 'We are not to think of the "giving" of the Spirit as an isolated deposit of what, once given, is now locally in possession. The first "gift" is, as it were, the first point in a series of actions . . .'

This, ML-J believed, was the key to understanding such large variations both in the life of a single Christian and in the history of the church. There have been times when full assurance, fervent prayer and joyful testimony have been almost commonplace – times

[1] *Revival*, pp. 100, 123.
[2] George Smeaton, *The Doctrine of the Holy Spirit* (1882), 1974 reprint, p. 32. At most, the Christian in this life enjoys only 'the first fruits of the Spirit' (Rom 8:23), 'the plenitude of the Spirit' awaits the consummation'. See John Murray, *The Epistle to the Romans*, vol. 1, p. 307.
[3] See John Owen, *Works*, vol. 2, pp. 334, 199–206; vol. 11, pp. 336–51; vol. 4, p. 388. The believer, says Owen, needs to pray daily for the Spirit and to be in earnest 'for new breathings and operations of the Spirit of grace, to renew and revive . . .'.

[381]

when, as John Knox said in explanation of the Reformation in Scotland, 'God gave his Holy Spirit to simple men in great abundance'.[1] Jonathan Edwards repeats the same idea in speaking of 'remarkable effusions [of the Spirit] at special seasons of mercy'.[2] A biblical metaphor for such large communications of the Spirit is that of the 'floods' of heavenly influence with which men are baptized and accordingly, in the older evangelical tradition, 'the outpouring of the Spirit' was a phrase synonymous in meaning with 'the baptism with the Spirit'.[3] These terms were so generally employed in this sense that such preachers as Whitefield and Spurgeon could take for granted that their meaning was understood as could such hymn writers as James Montgomery, author of 'O Spirit of the living God' with its verse,

> Baptize the nations; far and nigh
> The triumphs of the cross record . . .

This is not to deny that they believed, as ML-J believed, all Christians are baptized *by* the Spirit into the body of Christ at regeneration. But they saw that a similarity in language should not be allowed to confuse that once-for-all event (1 Cor 12:12), of which the Christian is unconscious,[4] with subsequent experiences of the Holy Spirit.

ML-J held the old definition of revival as being, firstly an 'extraordinary enlivening of members of the church' explained in terms of a larger giving of the Spirit. Where only one person was

---

[1] Knox's *Works*, 1846, vol 1, p. 101.

[2] Edwards' *Works*, vol. 1, p. 539. It has been said that Edwards and ML-J differed from the Puritans in that there is nothing of the 'cyclical' view of revival in their writings. But that such an idea was not introduced by Edwards is surely clear enough in the Works of John Owen, vol. 9, p. 514; vol. 16, p. 492, etc.

[3] The last-century Presbyterian historian, Thomas Murphy, describes the Great Awakening of the 18th Century as 'a wonderful baptism of the Holy Ghost' (*The Presbytery of the Log College*, 1889, p. 445). George Smeaton writes: 'The history of the apostles shows that not once, but on many occasions, they were made partakers of the baptism of the Spirit and fire.' Because Pentecostalism misused the same phrase, ML-J saw no reason to abandon a term which had long had a correct usage. Too many, he believed, 'are so afraid of Pentecostalism' that they mishandle the Scriptures (*Romans*, vol. 7, p. 310).

[4] A person discovers by the evidence that he has been regenerated but 'no man can tell you the moment when he was regenerated'. *Joy Unspeakable*, 1984, pp. 22, 52, etc.

involved the word 'revival' was not traditionally used, but he came to see that those experiences of the Spirit which mark many lives in times of revival are essentially the same in their nature as those which may be known by individuals at other times. It is a question, primarily, of the enjoyment of a full assurance of salvation.[1] That enjoyment does not belong uniformly to all Christians any more than revival belongs to the church in all eras. As biblical support for this position he pointed to the fact that a person may be a Christian without assurance and that the Spirit's work in this regard is additional to His work in regeneration. The texts upon which he laid stress were 'the sealing' of the Spirit spoken of in Ephesians 1:13 and 'the witness of the Spirit' described in Romans 8:16. These words, he believed, referred to a larger giving of the Spirit and so were synonymous in meaning with the 'baptism with the Spirit'.

As already mentioned, this teaching on the work of the Spirit appeared in his Friday night series on Biblical Doctrines in October 1954. It was expanded more fully on Sunday mornings in March and April 1955 when he was preaching on Ephesians 1:13. There was thus no sudden change after 1949 and only in terms of ignorance of the older evangelical and reformed tradition can it be said that he was preaching a novelty. It is true there were some differences in that same tradition over the meaning of 'sealing' and whether Romans 8:16 speaks of a higher form of 'immediate' assurance, but the *thing* which ML-J was preaching about did not depend on one or two verses. It involved the whole subject of knowing God, personally and experimentally, and how the Christian may experience 'sudden and sovereign manifestations of His love'.

This experimental approach to the doctrine of assurance was, however, so unfamiliar that it caused much surprise. Some wondered whether the 'new teaching' was a peculiarity of Pentecostalism. Others supposed that he had changed his view on sanctification. Raymond Johnston heard a rumour that he had so revised his teaching that he wished his IVF booklet *Christ our Sanctification* to be withdrawn. Wisely, Johnston wrote to ML-J for clarification and received this reply:

The simple answer to your question is that *Christ our Sanctification* still expresses fully what I feel on this question. The confusion arose as a

[1]'The "baptism" with the Spirit, the "sealing" of the Spirit ... is mainly concerned with the question of assurance.' *Ephesians*, vol. 6, p. 41.

[383]

result of a series of sermons I preached on the Sealing of the Spirit in Ephesians 1:13. In doing so I said that the interpretation of Acts 19:2, which I gave in the booklet, I would no longer hold, but that it made no difference to what I believed on sanctification, and that in any case that particular interpretation made no difference to the argument of the booklet. The booklet is still on sale in the Bookroom at Westminster Chapel . . . I have a feeling that I shall have to publish my five sermons on the Sealing of the Spirit because in one of them I deal at considerable length with the fact that this does not refer directly to sanctification at all.[1]

This leads us to a very important further point. The New Testament is never to be interpreted in terms of any *one* truth. To suppose, as some evidently did, that what he was saying on assurance cancelled out all he taught on sanctification was absurd. Truths must be held *together*. For this same reason he was careful to warn of the danger of giving exclusive attention to the subject of revival. He knew that the church can be blessed by God, conscious of His help and enabled to do His work, when there is no revival. To ignore everything apart from revival is the same as thinking that the extraordinary work of the Spirit is His *only* work. A few in 1959 were so absorbed with revival that they organised all-night prayer meetings and looked for ML-J's support. They did not get it but, as we have seen in this chapter, most of his year was spent carrying on his normal work and there was no reduction in his evangelistic preaching. Speaking in December 1959, he criticised people who

always talk about revival and only about revival. They are only interested in the exceptional and unusual, and they tend to 'despise the days of small things', the regular work of the church and the regular work of the Spirit in the church.[2]

In the same address he quoted, with approval, James Buchanan's lack of sympathy with those who 'make no account of the multitudes who are added, one by one, to the church of the living God, merely because their conversion has not been attended with the outward

---

[1] Letter dated Feb 4, 1956. This remained his position although the rumour was to persist. Regrettably, the sermons were not published until 1978 (*Ephesians*, vol. 1, pp. 243–300).
[2] *Puritans*, p. 15.

manifestations of a great religious revival'. God has more than one way of working.

An over-concentration upon the subject of revival was, however, very far from being the common problem in the 1950's. The truth was that very little at all was being heard either on the Holy Spirit or on the subject of revival. Dr Lloyd-Jones believed that a whole dimension of New Testament teaching had been largely lost. There was, in general, no recognition either of the need for revival or of what revival meant. The silence of contemporary evangelical literature was one proof of his point:

Look at many books which have been written in this present century on the doctrine of the Holy Spirit and try and find for me a paragraph, or a section, or a chapter, on revival . . . Now if you go back and read books which were written on the person and the work of the Holy Spirit, say, round about 1860, by Smeaton, for example, and others, there you will find sections on religious awakenings, religious revivals. They deal with it specifically. In the past they always did, but during the last seventy to eighty years, this whole notion of a visitation, a baptism of God's Spirit upon the Church, has gone.[1]

This point was so apparent to his hearers at the Puritan Conference that it did not need further proof, and a main part of ML-J's address at the 1959 Conference was to analyse why Christians had given up thinking in terms of revival. His general answers were dealt with under these headings: (1) The decline in Reformed Theology; (2) The influence of the writings of C. G. Finney which had confused revivals with evangelistic campaigns; (3) A wrong emphasis in the setting aside of men for the ministry, in which learning had been put before spirituality.

He then proceeded to give these reasons why 'men belonging to the Reformed tradition, of all traditions, have apparently lost interest in revival': (1) Resting in orthodoxy and 'growing negligent about your own spiritual life and the life of the church'; (2) An over-concern with apologetics in answering Modernism; (3) The dislike of 'emotion' and 'an excessive reaction against Pentecostalism'; (4) A wrong deduction drawn from the Puritans whose 'primary interest was pastoral and experiential in a personal sense'.

[1]*Revival*, pp. 53–54.

In view of his audience at this Conference (who were mostly already familiar with his teaching) he said little about the main *theological* reason for the prevailing indifference to revival, namely, the argument that because the Holy Spirit was given once for all on the Day of Pentecost, He cannot be poured out again and prayer for revival is therefore wrong and needless. He had referred to this argument often in his twenty-six sermons on revival preached earlier in the year. Those holding that view, when they read the experience described in Acts 2, say: 'Yes, that was the baptism of the Holy Spirit. But we all get that now, and it is unconscious, we are not aware of it, it happens to us the moment we believe and we are regenerated. It is just that act of God which incorporates us into the Body of Christ. That is the baptism of the Spirit. So it is no use your praying for some other baptism of the Spirit, or asking God to pour out His Spirit upon the church . . .'

'It is not surprising,' he concluded, 'that, as that kind of preaching has gained currency, people have stopped praying for revival.'[1] He also pointed out how, just as the wider work of the Spirit in revival had been forgotten, so all that was needed in the individual had now been reduced to two points. A person has only to go to an evangelistic campaign to get saved and then to a convention to learn that 'the fulness of the Spirit' is to be 'taken by faith' in an act of 'full surrender'. He feared that this outlook set aside much that was characteristic of New Testament believers. It virtually made assurance a non-experimental thing. While paying

lip-service to the work of the Holy Spirit [it] really pins its faith on what man does himself, on what man organizes. You first of all get your men to go to the evangelistic campaign to get them saved . . . take them to the right places and the results can be expected to follow. 'What more do you need?' say such people. 'Why are you talking about revival? Things are going well. Look at the crowds, look at the masses of people who are coming; isn't this enough?'[2]

It was on this kind of view, principally, that he blamed the absence of any expectation that God may work in an extraordinary and remarkable way. The effect of this outlook upon preachers particularly troubled him. Few things concerned him more than the fact that

[1] February 2, 1959, see *Revival*, pp. 51–2.
[2] *Puritans*, p. 7.

people confused unction in preaching with mere natural warmth or even with 'Welsh rhetoric'. He saw this as the same mistake as the view which attributed the number of revivals in Celtic cultures to the supposed proneness of the Celts to emotionalism or mysticism. In a discussion at one Puritan Conference a participant offered his opinion that Celts were 'revival prone'. ML-J replied drily that it was only the letter 'C' which he had got right. It was in countries where Calvinistic views of God were strong that people knew more of depending on God. The great danger   church in the present day was to attempt to do God's work   energizing power of the Spirit. On this point he   brief it is well summarized in the report of a   ve to Baptist ministers on 'Evangelical Prin   1956:

In consideration of the   he affirmed that much   g interpretations con   ave this baptism, or   sarily as witnesses. F   od than the Old Tes   ve.

Citing inst   pouring forth of the Spirit upo   g else could ever produce – a burnin   or the lost souls of men. Have we a sense   e Lord and for souls? Present-day conditions   urch if she is baptized with the Spirit.[1]

I close this chapter by indicatin   wo other ways in which ML-J's theology entered into his convictions about the work of the Spirit.

First, because God is sovereign, there are no formulas which will *ensure* that He will work in a particular way. The believer is indeed responsible not to grieve or quench the Holy Spirit. He is responsible for his beliefs and his conduct and in this connection Dr Lloyd-Jones indicated how reformation in the church has often been a prelude to reawakening. But we are never to speak of revival as though it is something to be brought about by the fulfilment of conditions. The time and measure and manner in which God works are wholly in His hands. ML-J urged prayer, and urged ministers to encourage prayer

[1] *The Life of Faith*, Feb. 7, 1957. The occasion was the Baptist Revival Fellowship Conference of November 1956.

among their people by the circulation of books which drew attention to the records of revivals. He did not do this, however, in terms of any exercise on our part being sure to lead to any certain results. He pointed out in one address how 30 years had elapsed between the doctrinal recovery in the Presbyterian Church in Ireland and the revival of 1859.

Secondly, his theology led him to keep one point in the forefront of attention. Prayer for the Holy Spirit is not to be made so that the problem of church attendance might be solved, or so that Christians can be happy and enjoy experiences. The primary motive has to be that God and His glory be made known.[1]

The concern has to be God-centered. To start with ourselves and to view God as an agency to supply our needs is always wrong. 'We must start with God and His glory.'[2] Because God was not being glorified, there ought to be grief and sorrow akin to that brokenness of heart to be found in the Psalmists because His name was being ignored and dishonoured. 'It is because men are not glorifying Him that they need to be saved, not to have some little personal problem solved.' It is thirst for God and for His honour which is the true basis for prayer. 'When we look at the prayers in Scripture, we find that God's glory, the church's growth and welfare, her holiness and progress, were ever higher in the thoughts and breathings of the saints than personal considerations.'

[1]*Revival*, pp. 88–89, 119–20, etc.
[2]*Ibid*, p. 192

Opposite: ML-J's 'skeleton' of an address on 'How evangelicals unconsciously deny that the Bible is the Word of God'. The notes include only one sentence more than the obliterated bottom line; it read, 'implying that it really does not matter what we believe about the Bible and the Atonement'.

How evangelicals occasionally deny the the Bible is
the word of God.

Say this & not all others.
but not what ourselves.
Yet very common & surprisingly so.

Failure to read & study it.

Dislike of doctrine & refusal to study it and
to learn it.

No time. Like retirement "interval"
meetings & testimonies etc
(Maria fake & Oswald Smith)   Time
habit is not tested because it is God's word   element

Dislike if definitions & discipline

Dislike of polemics & prattle about being +

Too much separation bet O.T. & N.T
Feeling the O.T. has nothing to do with us now &
failure to see the there is but one covenant
∴ ignoring of O.T. except as devotional reading

More practical

Trusting in sanctification the well ignores
the argument & appeal of the epistles

Worse . . Modern ideas put before clear
        & plain teaching
    "Temporary & not to count" etc

II Methods of Evangelism -- A je flush devoid of
            1 for 1 & 2 & Pastoral
V Using & working with men the deny the unique authority
   & living message to guide them. "fellowship" on the text & the he

Never have I been more deeply conscious of the high privilege of being the Minister of such a Church. The many-sidedness of the work is quite astonishing.

ML-J
Annual letter, 1954

The plain and clear teaching of Scripture is that every single Christian person is an evangelist.

ML-J
Sanctified Through the Truth, p 21

The church is not meant to be a place in which one man does everything and nobody else does anything. The church is not a place in which one man alone speaks and the others just sit and listen.

ML-J,
Feb. 24, 1956
Romans, vol 1, pp 238–39

19

The Ministry of Others

If any record had been kept of the number of activities in the way of Christian outreach and service which went on amongst those in attendance at Westminster Chapel it would have been a remarkable document. But such witness was often undertaken spontaneously, without any publicity, and even without Dr Lloyd-Jones himself being aware of it. When, for example, an Anglo-Catholic church in the Westminster area complained that young people belonging to the Chapel had been leaving tracts on its premises ML-J could reply that he knew nothing of it.

We have already mentioned forms of Christian work which had their beginnings under Dr Lloyd-Jones' ministry. In this chapter we will seek to give a few representative accounts of other activities which had far-reaching consequences.

Albert Waghorn, or 'Wag' as he was affectionately known, was a wholesale dealer in children's toys who lived at Dulwich Common in South London and joined Westminster Chapel in the 1940's. A bachelor who possessed a special gift in talking to teenagers and in winning their confidence, he kept open house on Saturday evenings for many years for boys from Dulwich College and Emanuel School, Wandsworth. On Sundays he could be seen amidst a crowd of these boys at the Chapel, generally occupying one or two pews about five rows from the front of the church on the preacher's left. One of the teenagers who became a Christian by this means was David Fountain who, in the 1950's, became Secretary of the Puritan Conference and entered upon what has been a life-long pastorate at Sholing, Southampton. Another was Christopher Porteous who, recalling Mr Waghorn's hospitality, has written:

He would gossip the gospel over a meal or while cutting bread in the kitchen. He explained to me for the first time how God would forgive even the worst of us and that none of us could reach heaven by our good works. This was underlined by the Doctor's preaching too. I became a Christian when hearing the Doctor preach on Sunday mornings to Christians rather than through the evening service when he made an assumption that those present might not be Christian.

Yet another of 'Wag's boys' was Brian Gerrish who, as Professor of Historical Theology in the University of Chicago in later years, was one of the hundreds of students from Westminster Chapel who became a teacher of others.[1]

Mr Waghorn's interest was not restricted to boys from public schools. For 25 years he was Superintendent of Thomas Cranfield Children's Mission, Southwark, where he gathered children week by week from a slum area near the Old Kent Road. His young men converted at Westminster he would encourage to aid him in this work. 'In its day,' writes Christopher Porteous, 'the Mission was a power for good in the area and Wag would teach children the Bible in old fashioned but effective ways. The Doctor became president of the Mission and he used to go there each year for an annual meeting when the building would be very crowded.'

Roger Weil, of Jewish background, was taken to Westminster by a fellow student on November 2, 1952, and came to know Christ in the evening service of that same day. He became linked with the young men who met at Dulwich Common on Saturday evenings and was soon a worker in the Thomas Cranfield Children's Mission which he served from 1953 to 1964. More far-reaching, however, in terms of Christian service, was the link Roger Weil formed with another behind-the-scenes leader who attended the Chapel, Robert Currie Thomson.

Colonel Robert Thomson, a Scot, had joined the Foreign Office in London shortly before the First World War and when his distinguished civil service career ended after the Second World War he gave himself fully to the spread of the gospel in Eastern Europe. It was an area well known to him and he could speak many of its languages. When a close German friend, Ernest Priefert, was looking for spiritual food in London 'Uncle Robert' (as he was also known) took him to Westminster Chapel and became a regular attender himself at about the same time. Colonel Thomson was a great

[1] Of the group which met at Mr Waghorn's home another three became ministers of the gospel and three have become distinguished in medicine.

encourager and stirrer of young men. Roger Weil was drawn into his low-profile Christian agency working in Eastern Europe (The Slav Lands Christian Fellowship), and through it, as well as through other means, the Westminster Chapel ministry became linked with brethren behind the Iron Curtain. Thomson travelled extensively in Poland, Romania, Yugoslavia and Hungary, introducing many pastors in these countries to the best Christian books. One of these pastors was Simo Ralevic whose work of evangelization at Pec in Yugoslavia, as we shall later note, was to bring so much encouragement to ML-J. Thomson, at more than eighty years of age, was carrying his usual heavy suitcase when he suffered a heart attack at the railway station at Budapest. On his death in the 1960's Roger Weil and others were able to carry on the same quiet and effective work.

There were many at Westminster Chapel like Waghorn and Thomson whose faithful work was unknown to Christians at large. Mrs André (mentioned earlier for her hospitality to servicemen and women) served a mission in the East End of London over a long period. Other voluntary helpers gave leadership in such Christian Unions as the Lawyers' Christian Fellowship, helped with the supply of accommodation for Christians passing through London, served on the committees of missionary Societies and orphanages, maintained prayer meetings in their homes, gave evenings to the short-staffed Evangelical Library and so on.

The one exception to the rule that no publicity was given to activities being undertaken by members of the Chapel was the work of the church's overseas missionaries. Valedictory meetings, always mid-week, were often memorable occasions when the Institute Hall was packed, and information from the missionaries was regularly given in a duplicated Supplement to the *Westminster Record* intended for members of the church. When home on furlough the missionaries were always asked to speak at a church meeting. Fourteen missionaries or missionary couples went overseas from the membership at Westminster in the years 1947–1967, being attached to various missions. The earliest of the couples, Dr and Mrs W. C. Lees, who went with the Borneo Evangelical Mission, subsequently named their Tri-Pacer missionary aircraft 'Westminster Chapel'! Another of the longest serving missionaries during ML-J's ministry (and still in Brazil today) was Jack Walkey, who joined the West Amazon Mission in 1953. Mr Walkey had been invited to

Westminster by a friend a few years earlier. Writing of what Westminster Chapel meant to him, he says:

From the first moment I started listening to 'the Doctor' I could not stop going there. I soon learnt that the modern Church had shifted from objective to subjective preaching, with all its emphasis on man. The doctrines of grace were new to me, and of these I became convinced, as one always does of the truth when it is applied by the Holy Spirit. God used Dr Lloyd-Jones to revolutionize my life and open my mind, not to an '-ism', but to the truth of the Bible. I deem it one of the greatest privileges of my life, not only to have profited from his exposition of the Word, but also to have observed for myself that when preaching honouring to Christ is central in the church, nothing more is required . . . What I learned there was to transform my method of presenting the gospel in Amazonas. The doctrines of grace for the first time I had come to understand, love and teach. They provided a solid basis for evangelization in a land where gimmicks and radical Arminianism were too frequently the order of the day, and where in many churches great pressure would be brought to bear upon sinners to accept the gospel, in an avid concern to see and register results.

Because of the Doctor's influence upon my missionary work, the books in my library, that I use for study and sermon preparation, are all those holding to the God-glorifying doctrines of the Reformation. Such teaching I have ever strived to pass on to the Brazilian Church through the Westminster Confession of Faith and the Shorter Catechism. What satisfaction to be able to share with the simple humble saints of the Amazon some of these precious truths! It has been possible to pass on to the Tapaua Church a digest of his teaching on Romans.

It will already be apparent that Westminster Chapel's connections with the world scene were far larger than the number of its own missionaries. Scores of men and women attended the Chapel while in training for the mission field in London or on refresher courses. (During ML-J's ministry the financial support given to missionary agencies and to individuals steadily increased until, in 1967, the number of Societies and individuals being helped stood at fifty-nine).

Still larger was the number of students and others who went or returned to all parts of the world following their days at Westminster Chapel. There can be few countries in either hemisphere which would not have to be included in any full list. Leigh Powell went to teach at Toronto Baptist Seminary; William Nadvi to heal the sick in Poona, India and Donald Kidd to Adelaide, Australia to follow the same ministry; Margaret Hayes went to the Republic of Niger and F. Kefa Sempangi to Uganda; Cecil Siriwardene became a pastor and an evangelist in his native Sri Lanka; Albert Nessim (first taken to the Chapel by Robert Thomson) went to Italy and Israel and his brother, Elie, to Vancouver; A. S. Gilfillan, Murdo R. Gordon and Clive Tyler were each to serve the Bible Institute of South Africa, successively, at Kalk Bay, Capetown.

These names provide but a few examples and instead of extending this list it will be of more interest to the reader to select a few portraits of men from different parts of the world.

Brian Wood was a young New Zealander, a first-class rugby player and sprinter, who worked for a period as a young school master in the East End of London. In looking for a church he took the advice of some friends and made his way to Westminster Chapel. Although Wood's home church in Auckland had been evangelical he had received little doctrinal teaching and by the end of his first morning service at Westminster he knew he had never heard anything like this before. At the young people's Bible Class at the Chapel in the afternoon the impression deepened. Faith in the sovereignty of divine grace was new to him and it was only after much searching of the Scriptures – prompted in part by the conversation of the young people he met at Westminster – that he came to see what he had previously missed. For the next two years Westminster Chapel was his home and when he then returned to New Zealand he could say (as reported by his friend, Wynford Davies): 'I was a completely different fellow. I was much stronger and my biblical understanding was so much deeper.' At the same time, as Wynford observed: 'His evangelistic cutting-edge was not blunted in any way. He had a marvellous capacity for personal evangelism and could get alongside the most radical of people. Through his participation in sports, music and many cultural activities there were points of contact which he used in a really wonderful way.'

Brian Wood then went to serve with the BMMF in Nepal where he became the headmaster of the school at Pokhara. He had already climbed extensively in the Alps and now loved mountaineering in the Himalayas as he had opportunity. After five years in Nepal he returned to New Zealand and then back to his adopted home where he was tragically killed in a climbing accident at the age of forty-two. On Wynford Davies' last meeting with Brian Wood in New Zealand the two friends talked again of the ministry in Britain to which they both owed so much and Wood remarked on how he never failed to receive a reply when he wrote to ML-J. Wynford Davies writes: 'He said that he owed more to that two years that he spent at Westminster Chapel as a young school teacher than to any other area of his Christian training and background.'

Felix I. D. Konotey-Ahulu arrived in London from Ghana as a young Christian in 1953 to study medicine. His father, David Andrews Konotey-Ahulu was a teacher and pastor among the Krobo people who had received German-Swiss Basel missionaries as early as 1836. Felix found accommodation in the Alliance Club (run by the IVF for overseas students) and never forgot the day at the Club when he expressed a wish to 'hear a man called Lloyd-Jones'. A Britisher, Richard Alderson, 'sprang to his feet', and, with an exuberance more African than English, 'shouted, "Beloved, come along!"'. At Westminster Chapel the Ghanaian medical student found others no less ready to welcome him and his diary entries from this period reveal something of what the services came to mean to him:

Martyn Lloyd-Jones in the morning. 1 Peter 3:11–12. The best New Year message I've heard in English.
. . . Heard the Doctor on Ephesians 2:1–3. Oh, I have never heard a sermon like that before. What a blessing this man is to his congregation . . .
. . . There is nothing like fellowship with God and with the Saints! Tremendous day of worship. The message of the gospel came down with mighty power . . .
. . . The morning service in the Chapel was shattering. I was humbled to the very dust and indeed blessed . . .

Other diary entries bring out features which were common among many young people in London University at this period. There was an evident hunger for Scripture and the eagerness to hear the Word preached was by no means restricted to Westminster Chapel. At All Souls, Langham Place, the ministry of John R. W. Stott[1] was also attended by many young people, with a frequent coming and going between the two congregations. 'We tended to go to All Souls in the morning,' Dr Konotey-Ahulu writes, 'and Westminster Chapel in the evening, or vice versa. Should one of us spend the whole day in one place we rang up friends and compared notes.' His practice

[1] John Stott, curate at All Souls since 1945, had been appointed Rector in 1950 at the age of twenty-nine.

changed after he became a member at Westminster (in October 1956) but the fellowship between the two churches continued and one of its consequences was to be a number of marriages. Felix found his future wife, Rosemary, at All Souls. The young lady who was to become the wife of Michael Harper (one of John Stott's curates) was converted under Dr Lloyd-Jones' ministry and many other couples could report a similar story.

There was also much evangelistic zeal among these young people. 'I made it a point,' says Dr Konotey-Ahulu, 'to take as many people to Westminster Chapel as possible – atheists, professing Christians, Moslems, anyone who would yield to persuasion.' Among those 'gloriously saved' were George Prawl (now a doctor in Australia) and Brian Williams. One Jew who came confessed, 'I never heard a more moving preacher, not even in the synagogue', but he would never come again. This evangelistic concern was not confined to taking people to church. One of Felix's closest friends was Dr Barry Jones of Guy's Hospital, President of the London Inter-Faculty Christian Union in 1956 and a member of Westminster. The two men would often pray together and visit hospital patients on Sunday afternoons to speak to them about Christ and to distribute literature. 'Eternity was constantly before Barry's eyes,' wrote Felix of his friend when the latter died in 1962 at thirty years of age.[1]

Felix Konotey-Ahulu returned to Ghana in the early 1960's at about the same time as his father came to London for three years study at the London Bible College. As his son before him, the Rev. David Konotey-Ahulu was to be greatly helped by the ministry of Westminster Chapel. 'This is Holy Ghost inspired preaching,' he would write home and for the remainder of his life he would always speak of Ernest Kevan and ML-J with 'great regard and deep emotion'. Dr Lloyd-Jones' close link with this one Ghanaian family is an example of how spiritual blessing is spread. Through David Konotey-Ahulu's powerful preaching in four different languages in Teshie, Accra and other places until his death in 1980, multitudes were to be influenced in the churches. Attaining distinction as a consultant physician and medical author, Felix Konotey-Ahulu (who took some 200 tapes of Dr Lloyd-Jones' back to Ghana with him) has been given many opportunities to witness in his own

[1] A tribute to Dr Barry Jones, by Felix, entitled *The Lord is King* with a Foreword by Dr Lloyd-Jones, was published in London in 1963 and in Ghana in 1969.

country and in other parts of Africa. In 1981 when he was asked by a group of Christian Ugandan and Kenyan medical students (at a conference in Kenya), 'What single factor has contributed most to your progress in the Christian life?' he replied, 'The greatest single factor God used was the ministry of a man who has just gone to glory. He was Dr Martyn Lloyd-Jones'.

Jeevan Joshi came from Malaysia to London where he was brought to know Christ through the witness of other students from Malaysia in the summer of 1961. They were all members of the London Chinese Church and with these brothers and sisters Jeevan enjoyed a fellowship which he felt was 'just like those early Christians in the New Testament'. The pastor of the Chinese Church, Stephen Wang, was a Barnabas-type leader who, conscious of the short time many of his young people would have in London and of what their missionary influence could be in the Far East, wanted the very best for them. He accordingly fixed the hour of worship for the Chinese Church (which met in one of the halls of the Central YMCA) for 3 p.m. on Sunday afternoons so that the congregation could also be at Westminster Chapel both morning and evening if they chose to do so. Pastor Wang's biographer says that because he loved that preaching himself, 'he liked his young people to go to Westminster Chapel to hear Dr Martyn Lloyd-Jones on Sunday mornings, but when they returned bubbling with enthusiasm he warned: "Do not build up your heads if you have little legs to walk on"'![1] Jeevan writes:

Like many others from the Chinese Church, I shall never forget those years of such warm fellowship. We were from many parts of the world. A good number consisted of students mainly from Hong Kong, Malaya and Singapore.

While we regularly attended the morning sessions at Westminster Chapel, when the Doctor was preaching on 'the Christian Warfare' we also took every opportunity to hear him on Friday nights on 'Romans'. I can still remember how we used to rejoice and literally jump for joy as we made our way home after those meetings. We would discuss what we had been learning over supper and then a time of prayer together.

A whole year at least had gone by before I first went along with some of the others to hear the Doctor preach on Sunday evenings. I shall never

---

[1]*Stephen the Chinese Pastor*, Mary Wang with Gwen and Edward England, London, 1973, pp. 164–5. 'On several occasions,' the authors note, 'Dr Lloyd-Jones showed especial kindness to him'.

forget that first time. It brought home to me a number of things. I was to learn that evangelistic preaching could and should be thoroughly expository, faithfully Calvinistic and that the message of the Bible is always up to date! It was such preaching that clinched the matter for me that Calvinism was doing justice to the whole Bible – that it was Christianity rightly understood. Thus it was through his *evangelistic* sermons that I was settled in the matter of Calvinism.

As in the case of the medical students already mentioned, these young people of the Chinese Church were themselves eagerly involved in evangelistic work and led the work of the Malayan Christian Fellowship and the Hong Kong Christian Fellowship which met once a week and sought to reach fellow nationals. It was typical of ML-J that he would seek to encourage these small groups and he agreed to speak at one of their meetings before Easter 1963 on the subject, 'Why Good Friday?' The organizers of this meeting, full of enthusiasm, promised one another a sight of the 'pyrotechnics' of Westminster Chapel on Sunday evenings in the basement of Malaya Hall but they were to be mistaken. For an audience which included many who had no Christian background – some Hindus, Buddhists and a few Muslims – ML-J did not speak as though in the pulpit at Westminster. 'Thankfully,' as Jeevan observed later, 'the Lord was clearly in charge of the proceedings.'

The men present in that basement meeting were to be scattered across the earth: Dennis Yeo, the chairman, to a Reformed seminary in the United States after being married at Westminster Chapel; Basil Jayatilaka, the pianist, to Perth, Western Australia; and Jeevan Joshi back to Malaysia where for several years he was able to give himself to scattering the God-honouring books, including the four titles by Dr Lloyd-Jones then in print. Writing of this book ministry in 1983, Jeevan says:

They were well received. This is due *partly* to the fact that there were those who were already Christians in Malaya who had gone to London as students, had sat under the Doctor's ministry, and who on returning to Malaya passed the word to others. Hence in this way the name of Martyn Lloyd-Jones became dear to many Christians in Malaya and Singapore.

Among the Malaysian Christians who heard Dr Lloyd-Jones in person I recall one elder who told me that the very memory of those years under his ministry had proved to be a source of encouragement and inspiration throughout the years.

[399]

This chapter has provided only an indication of the usefulness that resulted from the blessing which so many received at Westminster. Because of the quietness in which the work of many was done it was easy for some critics to allege that the Chapel had a congregation of sermon hearers who undertook little in the way of Christian witness. In a sermon on 'Being and Doing' ML-J observed: 'You know what is often said, "Ah, yes, but those Christians do nothing, they just sit and listen, they do not do anything"'.[1] He was not deterred by the criticism for he was convinced that lives moulded by Scripture will ultimately be the most useful. The best incentive to faithful and fruitful labour is the truth rightly understood and felt.

There is, however, one aspect of the testimony of this chapter which could be misunderstood. Dr Lloyd-Jones was against making the practice of evangelism or the number of 'full-time' Christian workers *the* test of a church's witness. *Every* Christian is involved in a calling. Ordinary daily work and 'spiritual' living are not two different things and he believed that the way in which Christians act and speak in their daily employment is the real test of a church's true strength. A cleaner, a mechanic, a secretary, or a housewife are all called to work for God as Christians. Poor work, he would say, is 'a thoroughly bad testimony'. And, similarly, students who spent time evangelizing when they should have been preparing to be qualified had no encouragement from him. Perhaps a sentence which Felix Konotey-Ahulu noted in his diary from a sermon he heard on May 5, 1957, sums it all up: 'As you walk the streets of London remember you have got the reputation of God in your hands.'

[1] *WR*, Dec., 1961, p. 140.

Affectionate in look
And tender in address, as well becomes
A messenger of grace to guilty men

WILLIAM COWPER
The Task, Book II

. . . *All this did he do according to the singular gift of wisdom that was bestowed on him. And so eminent was the apostle Paul in this gift, and so successful in the management of it, that his adversaries had nothing to say but that he was subtle, and took men by craft and guile, 2 Cor. 12:16. The sweetness, condescension, self-denial, holy compliance with all, which he made use of, mixed with truth, gravity, and authority, they would have had to be all craft and guile. And this gift, when it is in any measure continued unto any minister of the gospel, is of singular use unto the church of God; yea, I doubt not but that the apostle fixed it here in the first place, as that which was eminent above all the rest.*

JOHN OWEN
on 'the word of wisdom' in 1 Corinthians 12:8,
'A Discourse of Spiritual Gifts', *Works*, vol. 4, p. 456.

20

Pastoral Counselling

Next to the pulpit, Dr Lloyd-Jones throughout his ministry was constantly engaged in seeking to help individuals and it is to his work in that role that we turn in this chapter. I will use the word 'counselling' for convenience, but it must be remembered that the term was virtually unknown in Christian circles in Britain until the mid-1950's and the spiritual direction which ML-J gave to individuals in private throughout his ministry scarcely conformed to much that often goes by that name.

Writing in 1977, ML-J contrasted Paul's method of helping Christians 'and that which is becoming increasingly popular – indeed the vogue – at the present time under the name of "counselling"'. The difference between the two was the large admixture of the psychological and medical which was entering into modern 'counselling'. On occasions, of course, these elements do enter into individual cases but he was convinced that 'much that passes among Christians now as psychological problems is essentially spiritual'.[1] 'My experience is that most of the people who come to ask for the name of a Christian psychiatrist need spiritual help rather than psychiatric treatment.'[2] He viewed this confusion of spiritual with psychological as serious because the psychological and the biblical approach towards helping an individual are fundamentally different. Psychology teaches a person how to look within and how to analyse one's mind and motives. It assumes that the primary need is to possess a knowledge of oneself. According to Scripture this is entirely ineffective in dealing with spiritual problems because the starting point has to be knowledge about God.[3] The only truly practical way to provide help for the individual is, therefore, by means of teaching

---

[1]*Ephesians*, vol. 8, pp.5–6. [2]*Preaching*, p. 112.
[3]*Ephesians*, vol. 1, p. 357.

or doctrine, and because that teaching is the same for all he regarded the whole idea that every person needs a spiritual adviser as entirely fallacious. The one universal need is for spiritual understanding: 'Looking back over my experience as a pastor for some thirty-four years,' he said in 1961, 'I can testify without the slightest hesitation that the people I have found most frequently in trouble in their spiritual experience have been those who have lacked understanding.'[1]

Dr Lloyd-Jones' view of counselling thus followed his view of the true role of the work of the ministry. The work of the pulpit is to bring people to know the truth in its power. Through such preaching the truth is applied by the Spirit to individual cases and problems 'without the preacher knowing it at all'. 'It is quite astonishing to find that in expounding the Scriptures you are able to deal with a variety of differing conditions all together in one service.' Dozens, perhaps hundreds, of people are thus helped 'at one and the same time'. This was not theory. It was not uncommon for individuals at Westminster Chapel, experiencing some spiritual problem, to consider going to Dr Lloyd-Jones only to find that their difficulty was met in a sermon and there was no longer any need for them to do so.[2]

The idea that ministers should 'preach less and spend more time in doing personal work and counselling and interviewing' ML-J thus regarded as a failure to understand both the true nature of preaching and of biblical counselling. The contemporary trend to more counselling was, at root, a failure to understand the real problem. 'We are so subjective, and we live in this unhealthy "psychological" generation that starts with man and ends with man. Most of our troubles are due to that.'[3]

At the same time it may be doubted whether any minister of a large church was ever more ready to speak with individuals than ML-J. As already mentioned, he let it be known that he was available without prior appointment after every service, which meant twice every Sunday and after the Friday evening meeting. People wishing to see him made their way to the church parlour to be shown, in turn, into his vestry by the deacon who was on duty for that purpose. ML-J would never leave until everyone waiting for him – perhaps ten people at a very rough average – had been seen. In this way he must

[1]*Ephesians*, vol. 7, p. 114.   [2]*Preaching*, pp. 37–39.
[3]*Ephesians*, vol. 8, p. 29.

have talked with considerably more than a thousand people at Westminster Chapel every year.

It was observed by one of the medical members at Westminster Chapel, Dr Helen Gunn, that ML-J ran his vestry interviews as a specialist runs his consulting rooms. To an extent that was true and had it not been so the numbers whom he was able to see would have been far less than they were. Few people succeeded in taking much of his time unnecessarily. Those who came simply to meet him and to exchange pleasantries were always welcome, but after a few minutes they were liable to be propelled gently backwards to the door with a warm handshake. As this procedure was obviously unworkable if a visitor was seated, ML-J had to make an instant decision as each person was shown into his room. He was always standing as someone entered and would move at once towards them to greet them. If he judged that a short conversation was all that was needed (perhaps with someone whom he saw regularly) he would remain standing with them. On the other hand, if the individual was a stranger who had come with a spiritual concern, he or she would be asked to sit down on the leather couch while ML-J would sit opposite, either in a favourite leather armchair beside the electric fire or on a swivel chair beside his desk. He never spoke to anyone from *behind* a desk.

If ML-J's austere pulpit appearance probably served to keep some who had no real need to see him from his door, it also gave a measure of difficulty to the nervous who had reason to seek his help. Donald Elcoat, for example, from the North of England, spent a year in London in 1957 and felt he had been 'converted all over again' as he attended the Chapel. But he never spoke face to face with the preacher who helped him so much. 'I had opportunities to meet him personally,' he writes, 'but I was too shy to avail myself of them, though I longed to do so . . .'. Ten years later, however, he was able to revisit the Chapel and determined to '*take* his courage in both hands after the service'. Accordingly he made his way to the Church parlour and was, in due course, ushered into the minister's vestry. The deacon on door duty, however, somehow failed to announce him and he was left standing silently within the door while 'the venerable figure' of ML-J stood, back towards him, drinking a cup of tea beside the fire. 'At length,' Elcoat writes, 'I cleared my throat. He turned and, on seeing me, was full of apologies.' In a moment the preacher's cordiality made all his previous hesitations seem absurd.

Another hesitant first-time visitor to the vestry was Joan Hougham who writes:

Through the kindness of friends I was able to see Dr Lloyd-Jones in 1949. At that time I was nervously strained, depressed and confused spiritually; my condition had been diagnosed by a G.P. as physical exhaustion, by a psychiatrist as needing psycho-analysis and by others as Satanic indwelling. I was fearful as I sat in the Parlour of Westminster Chapel awaiting the Doctor, not wanting to expose myself to another diagnosis and very sceptical of his being able to understand or help. But how wrong I was! His gentle, caring love soon relaxed and assured me.

From a meeting with ML-J multitudes went away with a sense that they now had an enduring part in his friendship and few can have had any apprehensions about meeting him a second time. His sympathetic interest, humility and total lack of professional mannerisms, together with his calm and relaxed manner – these were invariably among the features in his make-up which people noted on a first acquaintance. There was nothing contrived in this on his part. He was committed to people and, aided by his prodigious memory, could follow up accurately a conversation with anyone he had met months or even years later.[1]

In interviewing a person who had come for help ML-J followed some basic procedures, beginning with diagnosis. There were certain broad questions which he always asked himself such as: Was the person a Christian or non-Christian? Was the problem spiritual or were there indications that the individual had physical or mental problems requiring medical advice or treatment?[2]

Preliminary diagnosis of this kind ML-J regarded as far from easy and he often emphasised to fellow ministers the harm that could be done by wrong evaluations: 'We are dealing with souls, with persons.' His method was to listen, at length if necessary, and with occasional questions which might, at times, cut at right angles across the speaker's own line of thought.

[1] Joan Hougham, for example, in her account of their meeting (written in 1981) says: 'Thirty years later he preached in Cheltenham and a friend asked him if he remembered me. Without a moment's hesitation he said, "Oh, very well; she came to see me in 1949!"'.

[2] Although, as already stated, those in the latter group were a minority, he regarded the recognition of their existence as vital. On distinguishing the spiritual from the physical or mental see vol.1, p. 267; *Ephesians* vol. 7, p. 206 ff; and *Healing and Medicine*, p. 137 ff.

One minister supplies the following example of a lady from the congregation to which he belonged when he was still training for the ministry in London. This Christian woman suffered much mental distress over wrongs done to her much earlier in her life by her employer. It affected her whole life and thinking to such an extent that she had no spiritual peace or assurance and all who sought to help her met with no success. Of Dr Lloyd-Jones' meeting with the student minister and the person in need the former writes:

I will never forget how he dealt with her. She was a somewhat delicate personality but the Doctor spoke almost fiercely to her telling her that she needed to put these things behind her; however, despite the force with which he spoke she kept returning to the same incidents in her past until the Doctor almost brought her to tears. Suddenly when he saw that he was making no impression, he softened and became extremely kindly and comforting in his words to her. As we went out he called me back and said, 'I want you to understand the problem here, it will save you a lot of time and effort in your future ministry'. He then explained to me that the woman's problem was not spiritual but psychological. The incident in her past had become a fixation and it was of so longstanding that nothing would remove it. 'Did you notice', he said, 'how she kept returning to this one thing no matter what I said to her. That should have given you the clue. The problem is psychological and I doubt at this stage whether anything can be done about it.' He was right, nothing could be done: but that day I learnt one of the most important lessons in pastoral work, the necessity of correctly identifying the nature of a problem and of sometimes appearing to be cruel to be kind.

Where the problem of those who sought help was not psychological and they professed to be Christians, perhaps considering that they need sanctification or assurance, he set no great store by such self-assessments. The first thing was to make certain of their foundation. He therefore looked for the features of a regenerate mind, such as a concern to be God-centered instead of self-centered and where this was missing the starting point had to be conviction of sin. A defective understanding of sin he regarded as the main hindrance in stopping people depending on Christ *alone* for justification. 'If you talk to a man about sanctification only, when his great need is to be shown the way of justification, you will aggravate his troubles.' If he believed he was speaking to a non-Christian he would simply repeat the same truths he preached, looking to the

Holy Spirit to give the necessary light for a saving response and, because the timing of the Spirit's work is not in our hands, his vestry was not commonly the place where anyone professed to have been 'led to Christ' in the usual sense of that statement. Some were converted almost instantly at Westminster Chapel, others very slowly. There was no stereotype.

Whether or not an individual was a Christian made a fundamental difference to Dr Lloyd-Jones' whole approach to their particular problem. The Christian and the non-Christian may, of course, experience the same kind of problem, but while the latter is spiritually helpless, the Christian is in possession of a strength which is not his own. He has 'died to sin'. He has the ability to resist sin and must do so. 'Every Christian who falls into sin is a fool.' If a *Christian* feels he is in a state of defeat it is because he is being controlled by his subjective feelings instead of by an understanding of the truth. Deliverance from this condition, therefore, depends upon a total change in approach: Christians are to look not at themselves and their problems but at what God had done for them; their need is not the 'hospital' but the 'barracks' where they will forget their own 'troubles and ills' and learn to fight in the army. 'We must get rid of that notion of the clinic and the hospital; and we must look at these things more in terms of God and His glory, and the great campaign which He inaugurated through the Son of His love and which He is going to bring to a triumphant conclusion.'[1]

Many Christians have testified to the practical effects of ML-J's counsel along these lines when they were looking for a quite different solution. Joan Hougham, quoted above, who had received such conflicting advice from others gives this statement of the counsel she received from ML-J:

His five-word prescription was unbelievably simple, though he well knew it was the hardest thing for me to do. 'Refuse to think about yourself'. I felt like Naaman shattered by his instructions from Elisha, but like him, as I obeyed, I found release and gradual healing. I saw the Doctor several times; his humility was such that on one occasion he told me that my experience and struggles had helped him in his preaching. He encouraged me to write to him, each letter was answered personally,

---

[1] *Romans*, vol. 5, p. 175. The whole subject is dealt with at large in this his exposition of Romans chapter six and again in the sermons on the second half of Ephesians chapter four (i.e. *Ephesians*, vol. 5, 141).

written in his own hand, and enclosed a repeat prescription. Never shall I forget his kindness and encouragement.

Another Christian writes as follows:

I was converted young. All seemed to go well until my twenties, when I was assailed with blasphemous thoughts, which plagued me day and night for some years. Several ministers advised me to 'trust the Lord' or 'pray about it' – but the more I did so, the worse it became! I seriously contemplated suicide. It was at this juncture that I asked the Doctor for help. He did not help me until he was satisfied that I was a Christian. He then diagnosed my problem immediately! He advised me (rather surprisingly) not only never to think about the problem again but never to pray about it either. I was not really 'praying', simply reminding myself of my problem.

The next week things became infinitely worse! I returned in distress to the Doctor, who said he had expected it! It was proof that Satan was behind it all, seeking to take control of my thought life. He added a warning not to let Satan do so with any other problem whatsoever.

I thank God that the Doctor gave me that advice – the best pastoral advice I ever had. Satan was crushed under my feet – and remains so after all these years. I still wonder at the Doctor's extraordinary insight – unquestionably God-given. The advice others had given had led me into the grossest bondage.[1]

A final illustration of this same kind of approach comes from the experience of a Christian lady and the stress she suffered on being appointed head of a large secondary school. She lost the poise and confidence which marked her earlier career as a teacher and began to suffer from a sense of fear. The morning school assemblies were a trial which she particularly dreaded. She would try to prepare herself for these by identifying herself with the promises of the twenty-third psalm, which she repeated to herself with emphasis on the personal pronouns: 'The Lord is *my* shepherd; *I* shall not want; He maketh *me* . . . he leadeth *me* . . .'

This was of no avail and in desperation she went to ML-J to seek his help. As usual, he listened carefully then began to call her attention to the need to change her emphasis. It should not be on 'My, I, me' but 'The Lord' – the great God of all creation, the Lord of

---

[1]ML-J refers to a similar case to this in *Ephesians*, vol. 5, p. 142.

heaven and earth – the shepherd and His love and care. She soon began to see the point, and the next morning it was of the Lord, the living God, that she deliberately thought before the hour of assembly. Her burden was lifted and she was able to undertake the duty in a different spirit.[1]

The help in the three cases above, though so apparently simple, was the result of biblical, theological thinking. Each individual received, not some kind of slogan or formula, but an explanation of the truth they needed and this took more time than the above summaries might suggest. ML-J was thoroughly opposed to any kind of advice which consisted of exhortations and attempts to inspire confidence without any sound reasons and explanations. Simply to cheer a depressed Christian up with such words as '*Of course* you are a Christian' can only give short term relief. The fundamental need, in the case of Christians, is to see the relevance of Christian doctrine to the practical problems of daily life. In other words, what ML-J did with such individuals was to help them understand the particular truths which they had to learn to preach to themselves. 'The whole art of Christian living is to know how to talk to yourself.'[2]

An instance of the depths of depression and confusion into which Christians can fall as the result of muddled theology is worthy of inclusion here. Ron Edmonds began attending Westminster Chapel in 1953. He was a young Christian and his gifts and zeal to share in evangelism found him a position in the organization set up to prepare for the Graham crusade of the following year. He was not long engaged in this work when word reached him that 'Dr Lloyd-Jones was not sympathetic to the mass evangelism that was to take place in London.' Edmonds thereupon decided to leave the Chapel – a decision which, years later, he came to view as 'a grave mistake. Had I continued to sit under that ministry I might have been spared the considerable trauma that was to come.'

For the immediate future Edmonds had no hesitations over 'decisionist' evangelism and, with the crusades over, he was one of the Britons who went to the United States to serve in the Billy Graham organization. This saw him sharing in evangelistic work in North America through the years 1957–62. His testimony continues:

[1]Further on this point see *Spiritual Depression*, p. 266 ff.
[2]*Ephesians*, vol. 5, p. 145. 'We should spend time every day preaching to ourselves' (*Ephesians*, vol. 3, pp. 102, 269).

It was during that time I experienced very deep and painful reservations about the success of the evangelism in which I was involved. I found that I was not a 'soul-winner', as much as I tried, which eventually contributed to doubts about my own salvation. But even more perplexing was the reason for the falling away of those who had made professions of faith in Christ (some with very credible testimonies). What had gone wrong? Was it possible for regeneration to take place and then be undone? I soon began to wonder if I had been saved, and whether it would be my lot to lose that salvation. Not being associated with a church, or under pastoral care, I was soon overwhelmed with my fears and unable to cope with them despite a considerable knowledge of the Scriptures. As I could not see my way forward, I decided to return to the UK.

My spiritual perplexity intensified until I became convinced that I was 'Gospel hardened' and could never have been saved. I was so disturbed that I began seeking out former friends and ministers in London. None was able to help me with my problem. One minister refused to pray with me, saying I was calling God a liar because, if I had asked Christ into my heart then He must surely be there. I walked in Regents Park for hours trying to console myself with the Scripture that I had memorised in former years but to no avail. I had procured a job in a London Department Store, and one day, during a lull in the work, I remembered an account told me by a medical student some years earlier. This friend had described to me how he had once been waiting in the parlour at Westminster Chapel to see Dr Lloyd-Jones about IVF work when another man was assisted into the room in a state of great agitation and looking for all the world as though he were 'demon possessed'. The poor man's condition gave him priority in the queue of those who were also waiting and he was soon hustled into the Doctor's vestry. Some time later, to the astonishment of all present, the same individual emerged, perfectly composed and tranquil. Upon recalling this incident I began to reason that if Dr Lloyd-Jones had the time and inclination to attend to someone in such a dire state he might, perhaps, be able to help me.

Resolving to attempt to see the Doctor, I went to Westminster Chapel the following Sunday morning. After the service and sermon – which was above my head – I nervously made my way to the parlour, apprehensive over the possibility of obtaining a hearing from this prominent preacher. A very gracious deacon immediately informed me that the Doctor would see me when my turn came.

Ron Edmonds received the same kind of welcome as has already been described by others, but the advice he was given in that first interview surprised him a little. He was encouraged to attend every service that he could on the grounds that preaching was the main means through which pastoral help is to be received. At the same time he was told to feel at liberty to return to the vestry for further personal conversations. Though Ron began to find that the pulpit teaching was helping him, his inner turmoil and anxieties were not speedily resolved and calls at ML-J's door, both on Sundays and on Friday evenings, became a regular part of life in the next few months:

He dealt with my every question and apprehension and never, at any time, showed any impatience. In a pang of conscience I finally said to him one evening, 'Doctor, aren't you getting weary of my constant appearance at your vestry?' To which he replied, 'Not at all, my dear friend, you keep coming for as long as it takes to resolve the problems'. He never treated my questions (usually arising from what he had preached or what I was feeling) as trivial, although there is no question that they sometimes were. His whole approach was to teach me to reason in and from the Scriptures.

In the early months of 1963 I providentially began working at the Banner of Truth Trust in London, and between the theological discussions (in the course of packing books for shipment) and the visits to the Doctor I became more settled in heart and mind as the reformed faith gave me the needed assurance. The Doctor's pastoral care had accomplished its end and I am eternally indebted to the loving and patient care that I experienced under his ministry.

As so often happened, the help which Mr Edmonds received did not terminate with himself and for the past seventeen years he has been enabled to serve in the Christian ministry in the United States.[1]

＊　　　＊　　　＊

A number who were in very evident moral trouble when they first saw ML-J to confess their need, observed how he never reacted with shock or disapproval. Speaking on this point to Christian doctors, he once said: 'We must always be careful to avoid condemnation – especially in the case of a sick or agitated person. If the plain truth of the situation comes home to the patient that is one thing; but it is not our place to condemn.' 'For people in difficulties of their own

[1]Pastor Edmonds' testimony, from which I have quoted above, was supplied to me on request in 1987.

making,' writes Geoffrey Thomas, 'his tolerance was inexhaustible . . . He was the very antithesis of the unworldly "churchy" person destitute of knowledge of worldly problems.'

It would give a misleading impression, however, to imply that ML-J in private was nothing but charm and affability. He could be otherwise. His patience had limits in the case of those who caused difficulties for themselves or for others when, he considered, they ought to have known better. At such times he could speak very plainly and, as some of us close to him found, with an occasional touch of anger. I should add that, when on the receiving end of a 'dressing down', we usually felt that the 'anger' was more feigned than real. Perhaps it would be better to say that it was not of a type which ever made us doubt his underlying affection. Referring to this side of Dr Lloyd-Jones, Geoffrey Williams has written:

The Doctor could be ruthless and the effect of his treatment of those he loved could be crushing and at times cruel. Only afterwards could one perceive God's wisdom in bringing about a measure of needful sanctification through the seemingly unkind and strangely rough handling of one for whom he had a depth of sincere affection beyond anything I have known.

Sometimes his abruptness could be the result of personal reserve as well as of theological conviction. A young person going to the vestry to tell the preacher of his conversion since coming to Westminster could well be met with the response, 'Don't thank me, thank God'. As an example of the kind of 'rough handling' to which Mr Williams refers above mention may be made of a lady who once came to the vestry for help. She had recently become a member of the church and in the preceding service had heard ML-J preach on the need for Christians to be humbled and to remain humbled. The record is best given in her own words:

I well remember being greatly moved emotionally, and could hardly wait to rush round to the vestry and say, 'I want to be brought low Doctor'. While I waited expecting him to put his hand on my shoulder and say, 'Well done, I will pray for you', or something like that, nothing happened! The Doctor stood looking thoughtfully at me, but not a word passed his lips! After an embarrassing silence there was nothing left to do but back out of the room and walk away, decidedly like a deflated balloon!

From lower standards than his one might have expected that he would say something, even a little encouraging, so as not to lose a member. Not so Doctor, and now I do indeed thank God that he didn't encourage anything so superficial and worthless as the thing I was looking for.[1]

This Christian lady, and her husband, were to remain much respected members of Westminster Chapel over many years.

There were times when people were puzzled at the apparent contrast in the way in which ML-J dealt with different individuals. He might be hard on some who expected his support and encouragement and yet unceasingly cordial towards individuals whose behaviour seemed to warrant a different treatment. Referring to this point, Geoffrey Williams writes:

In the early stages of our Library Committee [chaired by ML-J] a certain member became so wilful and difficult that I feared disruption and wondered why the Doctor appeared to be treating him with unbounded courtesy. Far from calming the spirit of this man he became more and more difficult and finally handed in his resignation because the Committee's decision did not coincide with his own. Thus the good Doctor proved a master at diplomacy.

Quite as much as diplomacy, I believe ML-J's behaviour in the above instance was designed to win the individual to a better state of mind, though it failed on this occasion.

Another illustration of a similar nature comes from the diaconate at Westminster Chapel. Mr M. J. Micklewright recalls that when he and others were elected to the diaconate after the Second World War they were surprised to find that one frequent attender at their brief gatherings in the Doctor's vestry immediately before the services was a man who had never been appointed to their number and who, indeed, was not even a member of the church.[2] If signs of the disapproval of the church officers were sometimes visible so also was the great allowance being made for him by ML-J. Occasionally, when the would-be deacon was absent for several weeks he would

---

[1] A somewhat similar example is given by ML-J: 'I remember a man saying to me, "You know, my greatest ambition is to be a holy man." I said to him, "Yes, that is the trouble with you!"' (*Sanctified Through the Truth*, p 79)

[2] He was one of many who in the days of Dr Campbell Morgan's ministry had attended the church regularly without ever joining the membership.

return with reports of visits he had been making to churches in the United States until eventually, to everyone's surprise, he announced that he had been called to be the minister of a group of Methodist churches in the Midwest. Micklewright records:

One Sunday evening prior to his departure to take up this appointment something happened to produce an effect quite unexpected. The Doctor, while quietly adjusting his gown, turned towards him and assured him of his own (and even including *our*) good wishes for the blessing of God on his venture and work. I noticed the strong emotion this kindly act produced. The man, almost overwhelmed and at the point of tears, hurried from the vestry unable to speak.

This type of action by the Doctor so often administered a lesson to us all on Christian consideration for others and behaviour becoming the gospel. While people were near him he was ever watchful to turn such acquaintances to true opportunities for opening the closed heart towards the ministry he exercised. This man afterwards returned some years later and attended the services but never again joined us in the vestry.

*　　　　*　　　　*

The range covered by ML-J's pastoral counselling was extraordinary. For example, at a time when persecution was threatening Christians in Ghana, Joseph Hamidu, who was training at Sandhurst to be an officer in the Ghanaian army, received the following advice: 'Be careful what you say, when you say it, to whom you say it and how you say it'. This was then circulated to others in Ghana who, in Felix Konotey-Ahulu's words, owed their godliness and zeal for the Lord chiefly to the preaching which they had heard at Westminster Chapel during their own time in England. Their number included at least one senior member of the police and a Lt Colonel in the Ghanaian armed forces.

A very different case of counselling concerned a whole group at Westminster who were engaged in various forms of outreach among young people. Some helped in the Sunday School at the Chapel itself, others at the Thomas Cranfield Children's Mission or at the boys' club established by Elizabeth Braund at Clapham. In February 1963 some twenty to thirty people who had links with youth work decided to seek a meeting with their minister to obtain his guidance on problems of mutual interest. Questions were prepared beforehand in writing. 'I thought this meeting was likely to be a complete waste of time,' writes Mr Weil, 'for what could the Doctor of all people know about Sunday School work? I was amazed at how wisely he dealt with our questions and we had a most profitable hour together.' The following are some notes of what ML-J said at that meeting:

1. Try to avoid controversy even with RC children. The main thing with children is to give them the general impression (not in a false and superficial manner) that the Christian faith is the greatest, most wonderful thing in life.
2. Q. Should you have a specific 'call' to Sunday-School work?
    A. On the whole you ought to have a call; it is a gift, some have it and some do not.
3. Q. Do you agree the Christian parent *only* ought to teach their own children?
    A. It is part of their duty to do so – but not only them! Parents *and* Sunday School teachers. Some teachers are better at this than some parents. It is very strange but nonetheless a fact that it often happens that spiritual matters are most difficult to share with those nearest and dearest to you. Some parents find their children antagonistic to learning from them.
4. Use 'Thee' and 'Thou' when referring to God to establish a clear difference between this and all other subjects. Make children ask the question, 'Why the difference?'.
5. Q. Are we Sunday School teachers to be preachers?
    A. The Holy Spirit takes a message from Scripture and gives it to the preacher *for* the people – a burden; God addressing a company of people. This is the difference between the teacher (who imparts information) and the preacher. Teach but be ready to respond to the Spirit's message.
6. Q. Should we use Catechisms?
    A. The danger is that people (e.g. the Dutch) tend to think they are Christians because they know their Catechism. Try to use Scripture memory passages very much.
7. Q. How should we advertise our Sunday School?
    A. Your children are your best advert. They're ready to do it if they enjoy what they see and hear in your School.
8. Q. Have you any guidelines about what methods we should use to attract the children?
    A. If your heart is right you will not go far wrong. It is not the 'mechanics' which matter but your ultimate aim and object that counts.

It will already be apparent from the above that ML-J was an adviser to a circle far wider than his own members at Westminster. Ministers sought his counsel on the needs of hundreds of people, some of whom he would see himself. During the week and on Friday evenings there were also many engaged in all kinds of Christian work who came to discuss their needs and problems. On this point Douglas Johnson, who knew the various evangelical organizations better than anyone, has written: 'I believe that ML-J was used of God to give advice and to restore evangelical confidence in a number of Secretaries of Societies and various other office-bearers of churches and organizations. I have met several who talked of him as if he were their chief friend and adviser. I came to the conclusion that these lonely souls, struggling with evil and the devil's attempts to spoil their committees and organizations regarded ML-J as their elder brother always ready to come to their aid.'

A large number of overseas missionaries could be included in this category, receiving his time when home on furlough or his response to their letters when on the field. Natalie Castle, serving in Northern Nigeria, was representative of so many in speaking of ML-J 'as though he was my father'. The words of the Rev. D. K. Williams, who with his wife came to know ML-J at Westminster during the Second World War, well illustrate why missionaries felt this way:

Over the years nothing has more amazed me than the fact that he, in his very busy life, deliberately kept in touch with my work. I could always count on his prayers and encouragement, and his wise counsel. His ministry made a profound impression on my own, and to see him again after being years away was a spiritual tonic. But one incident stands out in my memory.

In May 1960 I went back to Nigeria to translate the New Testament into the Bassa language. On account of ill-health, my wife was not able to accompany me, and for over four years we did not see each other. Those four years were tough and trying ones indeed. One difficulty followed another. There was endless opposition to the work I was doing. Part of it appeared to be from jealousy. But the greatest blow came when the Bassa New Testament was complete and I was making preparations to come home with it. A group of white missionaries who knew nothing of the Bassa language tried to prevent the British and Foreign Bible Society publishing the long-awaited Bassa New Testament. When I received this news from the Bible Society I was deeply shaken, to say the least. All the bitter opposition and the unkind criticism of the previous four years seemed like school-boys' banter compared with this. Shortly afterwards I came home.

Within two weeks of my home-coming my wife and I were in London one Sunday evening. We put our luggage in the hotel at Victoria where we were staying, and hurried off to Westminster Chapel. After the service we went round to the minister's vestry. Quite a crowd of folk were waiting to see the Doctor who was feeling – and looking – very tired after a busy day. After a time the Deacon came and mentioned the Doctor's tiredness to those of us who still remained, asking those of us who could put off our seeing him to another time if we would do so. He came to my wife and me, and I told him it would be all right. We would be up in London again. But when he learned that we were missionaries he said, 'I must go in and tell the Doctor you are here'. He returned with the message: 'Under no circumstances were Mr & Mrs Williams to go until he had seen them'. A few moments later we were ushered into his vestry.

The Doctor came forward, shook my wife warmly by the hand with the greeting, 'Well, it's lovely for you to have him back safely, isn't it'. Then he turned to me, put his left hand on my shoulder, and in that delightful Welsh accent said, 'So the work is completed. Now my boy, tell me all about it.' It was an emotional moment for me, especially after the emotional strain of the events of the previous few months. For a moment I didn't know whether to burst into tears or to put my arms around his neck and hug him. His dignified manner fortunately prevented either. Although obviously tired, his face lit up eagerly as he waited, and I realised again that this busy servant of God really wanted to hear about the bit of work I had been doing. So I collected my thoughts, and gave him a brief account of the trials and triumphs of those years of working on the translation. I made no mention of the attempt to prevent the publication of our Bassa New Testament. Somehow or other during those moments in the Doctor's vestry I suddenly realised their action had become – and would remain – absolutely of no consequence whatsoever to me. The tension and the emotional strain had gone – completely. When I had finished, he took my hand again and said, 'God bless you, my boy'. Eileen and I went back to our hotel room that evening very deeply moved. Those moments in his vestry had been precious ones indeed. I came out feeling very different from when I went in. I felt I had grown several inches spiritually.

While so many missionaries could give a similar testimony, there can be no doubt that those with whom ML-J spent the most time in the way of giving counsel and guidance were colleagues in the pastoral ministry and students for the ministry. I have never heard of a case where he took the initiative in encouraging a man to consider the ministry. In his preaching he did not urge Christians to enter 'full-time Christian work' and believed that those who preached in that way were confused over the whole meaning of the call to the ministry.[1] But he spoke with large numbers of men who were uncertain whether this was their calling. A number he definitely discouraged.[2] Others who were hesitant he urged to go forward. John Waite had some doubt over the validity of his call because he had aspired to the ministry while still unconverted. ML-J, who had observed this young man sharing in the life of the congregation, swept that doubt aside and said to him, in effect, 'Not at all, now go and preach the truth'.

James Murdoch at the age of 53 believed that God was calling him into the ministry in Scotland. When ML-J was visiting his uncle, Alexander B. Murdoch in Glasgow, James took the opportunity to discuss this major decision with him. His account of their meeting reads:

The Doctor's first words were: 'Well, Jim, I am so pleased to hear how the Lord has been leading you in this matter, just tell me more about it.' After I had done so, he asked me some questions, which were so practical and looking back on it, so sensible, but not quite what I had expected! The first one was: 'How does your wife feel about this?' I could assure him that she was right behind me, for she felt the Lord had been preparing her, in that she had been asked to work amongst women in one of the new housing areas, for the past eight years. 'That's fine', he said, 'now tell me; will your children suffer in any way?' We had had to look at this carefully because our two boys were still at private schools where the fees were rising each year, and we knew it would be difficult to keep them there on a Baptist minister's stipend of £750 per annum! However we did have some money laid aside for this purpose, and so I was able to say that while they might lose out on some of the luxuries, all their needs would be met. He then commented: 'You see! It is all very well for you and Betty to be sure that this is God's will for you, but it is necessary to remember that He has given you these children and you now have a prime responsibility to see that they are properly cared for and made fit to go out into life for themselves. It is quite a different

[1] See *Ephesians*, vol. 6, p. 350.
[2] For an example see *Preaching*, pp. 112–13.

matter for a single man, or even for a couple without children.' The Doctor then went on to encourage me and counsel me as to studies, etc . . .

This practical emphasis was typical of many aspects of ML-J's counselling. Perhaps more than anything else the factors which made him such a support to men in the ministry were his unbounded sympathy and sincere interest. Men felt they could speak to him about problems as diverse from each other as being single when one wanted to be married to dealing with hostile church officers or members. The lengths he would go to help a brother minister are illustrated by the case of an evangelical pastor who served an inner London church in the years 1956–62. It had once been a notable congregation but this man received such opposition from some of his people that the continuation of his ministry among them was often in doubt. The emotional strain was such that twice this pastor had to leave his pulpit during a service, and he began to think that he needed psychiatric help. Turning to ML-J for help, he was assured that the problem was spiritual and that he could receive the necessary strength to continue. But the man was so nervously shaken that for a period of several months, as he records, 'Dr Lloyd-Jones telephoned me at home, each Sunday, quoting appropriate Scripture texts to enable me to enter the pulpit and minister'. Sometimes fifteen minutes before his own service ML-J would be on the phone to this colleague. Finally, for reasons concerning his health and that of his wife who had also suffered in the situation, this ministerial friend decided that he must resign: 'When my wife and I visited Dr Lloyd-Jones in his vestry at Westminister Chapel to tell him our decision, he not only prayed with us but wept.'

On another occasion when a Christian couple revealed the heart-ache they were suffering from their children who were unbelievers he simply listened and wept. 'Nothing', they were to say to friends, 'had ever brought them so much comfort as his sympathy.'

The subject of books often came up in ML-J's advice to ministers, sometimes in response to letters on that question. When a man who was to become Principal of the Elim Bible College wrote for advice on books, ML-J replied as follows on September 19, 1950:

Dear Mr Russell–Corsie,
    The delay in replying to your letter of August 17th is due to the fact that I have been away on holiday.

With regard to the books which I would recommend to you I would suggest the following:- *Systematic Theology* by Charles Hodge, 3 vols. This can only be obtained second hand and it is very difficult even then. On the Word, I recommend *Revelation and Inspiration* by B. B. Warfield, or else *The Infallible Word*. It would also be good for you to obtain the recently re-published *Institutes of the Christian Religion* by John Calvin, 2 vols. price 30/-. If you master these you really need no more, but of course there are many lesser books which are of great value. I think it would be a good thing for you to write to Dr Douglas Johnson, the InterVarsity Fellowship, 39, Bedford Square, W.C.1 and he may be able to help you to get the Hodge volumes and I believe that they have the other volumes also in stock. Please write to me again if you find trouble in obtaining these books and also let me know if you desire further suggestions at any time. I hope that if you should visit London again you will be good enough to come in to see me. I pray that God may bless you more and more in your ministry and in your personal life.

At a much later date (November 17, 1973) he responded to a similar question on his own reading:

Dear Mr Spears,
    Many thanks for your most kind and encouraging letter. I was delighted to receive it. I am so glad that my books are proving to be of some help to you. Nothing gives me greater joy than to know that a young preacher like yourself is helped in this way.
    With regard to books that have meant a great deal to me, I think I would have to put at the very top of my list the works of Jonathan Edwards. I have also been much helped by the works of John Calvin, especially his *Institutes*, also by some of the Puritans such as Sibbes, Thomas Goodwin and John Owen. You will also find that C. H. Spurgeon will act as a great tonic and stimulus to you.
    May God greatly bless you in all your ways and use you mightily to His glory.

There was much more that ML-J would say to ministers about reading. He always urged the importance of balance and warned against an over-concentration upon any one type of Christian literature or any one school of authors. Books, he would also say, had to be assimilated with meditation so that their thought became our own, to be expressed in our own language – not reproduced like a gramophone record. Similarly, he constantly encouraged the reading of the great Christian biographies but, at the same time, cautioned against living 'a kind of second hand spiritual life on books . . . We may do this for years without realizing that we are living on books instead of living on Christ.'[1] For ministers, as well as other Christians, he regarded a lack of balance as one of the main dangers. Preachers need to know themselves and to counter every tendency to lop-sidedness in character or interests.

*   *   *

In conclusion, comment needs to be made on two aspects of ML-J's work in advising others which he regarded as important. One was the definiteness with which he gave advice when it was asked for. Geoffrey Thomas writes:

Dr LJ never regarded merely assisting one in weighing up the pros and cons of a situation, so as to clarify one's mind leaving you to take the ultimate decision, as giving proper advice in a situation. He would have the courage, having discussed the various aspects of the situation, to say, 'and this is the course which I advise you to take'. He then gave his advice with an authority that made one immediately feel it to be right. More than this, this force of authority gave one the courage to act upon it and carried one through the problem. The writer's debt to Dr LJ in this sphere particularly as a young man is incalculable.

By following this course ML-J undoubtedly exposed himself to criticism for, need it be said, his counsel was not invariably correct. Yet his readiness to commit himself on matters where practical action had to be taken one way or another was of enormous help to so many in perplexing situations.

A second feature of his counselling, at first sight, might not appear to be in harmony with what we have just said. It was his concern not to make *his* conscience the ground upon which the person being counselled based his actions. In his own words: 'We must be very careful not to foist our opinions on others. The counsellor is not a dictator, he is simply there to give help. While he may give his views and, with care, put them quite strongly if asked, yet . . . as counsellors we must never be in the position of dictating to another person's conscience . . .'[2]

[1] *Ephesians*, vol. 3, p. 261.
[2] *Healing and Medicine*, pp. 53–54.

Pastoral Counselling

The above quotation is from an address to Christian doctors, relating primarily to ethical issues in medicine, but the point is true for all counselling. The person counselled has to live with their own conscience and, therefore, they should never be prompted to take a course of action of which they themselves are not persuaded. Thus, before giving definite guidance, ML-J would always seek to see that relevant scriptural principles were understood. He would have agreed with the words of the CIM missionary, D. E. Hoste:

What is the essential difference between spurious and true Christian leadership? When a man, in virtue of an official position in the church, demands obedience of another, irrespective of the latter's reason and conscience, this is the spirit of tyranny.

When, on the other hand, by the exercise of tact and sympathy, by prayer, spiritual power and sound wisdom, one Christian worker is able to influence and enlighten another, so that the latter, through the medium of his own reason and conscience, is led to alter one course and adopt another, this is true spiritual leadership.[1]

[1]Quoted in Dr John Laird's autobiography, *No Mere Chance*, 1981, p. 97.

PART THREE

SIFTING TIMES

For Dr Lloyd-Jones the 1960's were undoubtedly to be the hardest decade in his life. In general he was convinced there was a worsening of spiritual conditions in Britain and, instead of sharing in the self-confidence of an evangelicalism which spoke as though revival was at hand, he feared 'we still have a long way to go' (Revival, p. 182). There were now problems to be addressed on several fronts at once. Some had to do with excess among those with whom he had much in common. Among the younger men who had shared in the doctrinal recovery of the 1950's there was now a dangerous tendency to trust in orthodoxy. This led him to modify his former emphasis on the need to study doctrine and to insist that 'doctrine is not enough'. There were others who had heard his call for renewed faith in the power of the Holy Spirit and who came to allege a sweeping restoration of the charismata. In so doing, as we shall see, he believed that they were imperilling the essential meaning of revival.

But the main difficulty lay elsewhere. The ecumenical movement was not only questioning the priority of truth, it was challenging the argument of evangelicals that they could remain scattered in various denominations because their spiritual unity did not require any external oneness. By aiming to bring denominations together, ecumenism claimed to be working for a unity which was both spiritual and church based. It was to be left largely to ML-J to answer that claim and his answer was to reveal a fundamental split in evangelicalism. His words spoken at the annual general meeting of the Evangelical Library in 1964 were to be verified:

'There is going to be a time of real sifting amongst us, and there are indications even in these present days that the sifting is going on. A number of men are becoming dissatisfied. They are obeying their consciences and they are taking action. If there is to be a period of yet greater sifting (and I venture to suggest there will be) well then, it will be of inestimable value to be able to read what men in past centuries did under the guidance and inspiration of the Spirit in their similar new situations.'

21

Unity: Ecumenical or Evangelical?

For evangelicals in England the 1960's were not to be a decade of revival but of controversy and, paradoxically, it was the question of unity which was a principal cause. Churchmen of other persuasions had already settled their position on this subject. A flood of ecumenical articles, books, 'conversations', commissions and conferences could all take the view that the hope of transforming the existing denominations into one church was a good and proper thing. In 1964 a Conference of the British Council of Churches at Nottingham would commit itself to 'one Church . . . not later than Easter Day, 1980'. All that remained, it seemed, was discussion over the means by which this was to be brought about. For evangelicals, however, the fundamental questions were only beginning to be faced.

How the need for true unity was to be met was much more important to Dr Lloyd-Jones than mere opposition to the ecumenical movement, yet, holding the position which he did, it was inevitable that he would have to take a leading role in opposition to the latter. He differed with ecumenism on its fundamental principle, namely, that all dialogue should proceed on the understanding that it was between fellow *Christians*. He objected to this because it meant giving a breadth to the meaning of 'Christian' which was unknown in the New Testament. The fact was that the movement for the reunion of the denominations had grown up in conditions where the liberal view of Scripture was so pervasive that the idea that anyone needed to *believe* certain definite truths in order to be a child of God was no longer taken seriously. In theory some kind of recognition of Christ as 'the Son of God' might be required as a statement of belief, but the willingness of leaders to dispense with any doctrinal test of Christian profession indicated an underlying attitude. Thus when Aneurin Bevan MP died in 1960, despite his atheism and public indifference to Christianity, a Memorial service was held in Westminster Abbey. The following year Michael Ramsey, Fisher's successor as Archbishop of Canterbury, was reported to have pronounced 'Heaven is not a place for Christians only . . . I expect to meet some present-day atheists there'.[1]

Such a view was not the temporary aberration of one leading Anglican. The same basic attitude was in all the churches, as may be seen by the way in which Albert Schweitzer, Nobel Prize winner and medical doctor at Lambaréné in Gabon, was commonly regarded as a very eminent Christian. Yet Schweitzer was a self-confessed agnostic without a shred of Christian belief. A prominent article in the *British Weekly* (July 28, 1960) by Professor John G. McKenzie discussed, 'Is Schweitzer a Christian?' and concluded that there ought to be no hesitation in saying that he was. 'Life is bigger than intellect,' McKenzie wrote. Schweitzer had 'the spirit of Christ' and anyone who has that is a Christian regardless of what is believed or disbelieved. Professor John Baillie of Edinburgh had argued the same point in his book, *Our Knowledge of God*. According to Baillie an alleged atheist who denies God with the top of his mind may nevertheless believe in Him in the bottom of his heart even though he does not know it.[2]

Instead of regarding this interpretation of unbelief as a happy advance in the spirit of charity, ML-J saw it as an error denying the exclusiveness of the Christian message and threatening the very life of the churches.

Dr Lloyd-Jones took up this subject at length in two addresses which he gave to the Westminster Fellowship at the annual outing to Welwyn in the summer of 1962. In expositions of John 17 and Ephesians 4 he argued that the biblical definition of what it means to be a Christian must precede an understanding of the unity in which Christians share:

There is no real fellowship and unity in a group of people where some believe in 'the wrath of God against sin' and that it has already been 'revealed from heaven' (Romans 1:18), and others not only do not believe in the wrath of God at all, but say that it is almost blasphemous to teach such a thing, and that they cannot believe in a God who is

[1] *The Daily Mail*, Oct 2, 1961.
[2] In a review of Baillie, John Murray speaks of his 'plausible yet fatal charity' (*Collected Writings*, vol. 3, 1982, pp. 295–300).

capable of wrath. Fellowship exists only among those who believe, as the result of the operation of the Holy Spirit, these essential truths concerning man's lost estate – that we are all 'by nature the children of wrath' (Ephesians 2:3) – and the action of God in Christ Jesus for our salvation and restoration. There is no fellowship between people who believe that and those who believe something else, which they may call a gospel but which, as Paul tells the Galatians, 'is not a gospel' (Galatians 1:6, 7).[1]

Both in these addresses, and elsewhere, what is noticeable in his definition of 'Christian' is that he stipulates the necessity of both belief and experience. Christians are people who have experienced conviction of sin, who know repentance and who possess new life as the result of a rebirth. But the experience and the doctrine they believe belong together. If a person does not love fundamental truths, and desire to know them more, he has no claim to be regarded as a Christian. 'There is an irreducible minimum, without which the term "Christian" is meaningless, and without subscribing to which a man is not a Christian ... There is to be no discussion about "the foundation". If men do not accept that, they are not brethren and we can have no dialogue with them.'

Christian unity is the result of a common faith in the gospel of Christ and while he did not regard *all* beliefs associated with evangelicals in the 1960's as tests of a person's Christianity, he considered the word 'evangelical' rightly understood to be synonymous with 'Christian'. Evangelicals, in the historic sense of the word, are 'gospellers'. Certainly he believed that a man might be a Christian who did not employ the name 'evangelical' and he knew that it does not belong to us to be the final judges of a person's Christian profession. But the fundamentals of evangelicalism are the fundamentals of the gospel, and to concede the title 'Christian' to those who deny those fundamentals is to undermine Christianity itself: 'Those who question and query, let alone deny the great cardinal truths that have been accepted through the centuries, do not belong to the church, and to regard them as brethren is to betray the truth.'

It was pre-eminently because of this point that ML-J drew such criticism from ecumenists. He was denying the validity of their main

[1] *The Basis of Christian Unity*, IVF, 1962, p. 46. The two addresses, taken down from a tape recording, were published in the autumn of the same year. They are reprinted in *Knowing the Times*.

presupposition. We noted the antagonism of the *British Weekly* to his *Maintaining the Evangelical Faith Today* in 1952. In the 1960's the opposition was to increase. When some evangelicals shared in the ecumenical discussions of the First British Faith and Order Conference at Nottingham in September 1964, to which we have referred above, they spoke of being 'keenly conscious of the prejudice and even hostility' towards the IVF's position (of which ML-J remained the chief spokesman).[1] At that Nottingham Conference it was ML-J's convictions which John Huxtable attacked. 'Not the least of my difficulty with the Conservative Evangelicals,' Huxtable said, 'is their characteristic insistence that, unless the Faith is expressed in their particular way, it is not truly expressed at all . . . that, unless we believe in a substitutionary theory of atonement, it is doubtful if we believe in salvation at all . . . if we do not agree with their reckoning of what Scripture amounts to, we are only questionably Christians . . .'.[2]

Huxtable was more guarded than another ecumenist, Douglas Jones, Lightfoot Professor of Divinity at Durham University. In his book, *Instrument of Peace*, Professor Jones deplored that ML-J's 'influential book, *The Basis of Christian Unity*' taught that 'the true believers are those who believe in the historic fall, the wrath of God against sin, the substitutionary atonement, the physical resurrection of Jesus Christ, and . . . a fundamentalist approach to the Scriptures'. He applauded the words of the Archbishop of Canterbury that, 'Christians do not "believe in the Creeds" but, with the Creeds to help them, they believe in God'. 'Dr Martyn Lloyd-Jones,' he complained, 'is trying to persuade us that there are precise doctrinal distingushing marks of Christians, that we can distinguish him who believes from him who does not believe . . . In this respect he has learnt nothing from the greatest evangelical theologian of modern times . . . [i.e. Karl Barth]. There is no greater scandal in this complex situation than the refusal of Christians to accept their fellow Christians.' It is plain that the Durham Professor of Divinity differed in his whole conception of salvation. Denying ML-J's conviction on the Church as separate from the world, he argued, 'The Church is the emergence within the body of mankind of the unity to which not only Christians but all men are called – more than

[1] *Evangelicals and Unity*, ed., J. D. Douglas, 1964, p. 5.
[2] *Ibid.*, p. 14.

that, in which they already exist in Jesus Christ. Christ is the head of every man . . . the Church is . . . never possible to define.'[1]

Still stronger words were to follow. Dr Lloyd-Jones' position, it was to be said, was akin to that of the self-righteous Pharisees. Such antipathy was to persist. A decade late James Barr was to direct his readers to ML-J's *Basis of Christian Unity*, 'For an example of a harsh and rigid opposition to any participation by conservative evangelicals with non–conservatives'.[2]

Criticism of this kind did not worry ML-J but what did concern him deeply was the cleavage appearing within evangelicalism on how the ecumenical movement should be treated. In the thirteen years from 1954 to 1966 there was a major shift in evangelical opinion on this point. The background to this shift we have touched upon earlier. Clearly a change of some kind in English evangelicalism was inevitable, because ecumenism had raised new issues and was endeavouring to alter the denominational boundaries in a manner hitherto unknown. Congregationalists were in active discussion with English Presbyterians with respect to union, the Church of Scotland (Presbyterian) was in consultation with the Church of England and the Methodists were likewise engaged in plans for re-union with the Anglicans. If the church structures were thus changed there was obviously no way in which evangelicals could remain exactly as they were. Uneasy though they had often been in staying in their respective denominations, at least they had known what those denominations were. For long years the boundary lines had been static. Now, amidst the general call for new alignments and for visible 'Christian unity', the old evangelical *status quo* was scarcely tenable. One way or another there was bound to be movement.

Dr Lloyd-Jones believed that this situation presented evangelicals with a great opportunity. Instead of simply adopting delaying tactics in their denominations, evangelicals should themselves take up the New Testament emphases on unity and on the evil of schism. Opposition to error and warnings over the growing doctrinal

---

[1]The above quotations from Jones are taken from *Instrument of Peace*, 1965, pp. 69–74. Gilbert Kirby, under the heading 'Ecumania' reviewed this title in *The Life of Faith*, Sept 2, 1965, pointing out how the author 'singles out for particular attack Dr Martyn Lloyd-Jones', and concluding, 'Those critics of the ecumenical movement who have expressed disquiet at the thought of the coming "super-church" may well feel, from reading this thesis, that there is some justification for their fears'.
[2]*Fundamentalism*, 1977, p. 362.

indifferentism were not enough in this new situation. If men were orthodox and yet content to remain separated and divided from one another then they were not, he argued, taking the New Testament with sufficient seriousness. In 1961 he spoke of this as one of the main problems facing congregations which were concerned to be faithful to Scripture: 'How are we to draw the line between allowing heresy and apostasy on the one hand, and being guilty of schism on the other?'[1]

For Dr Lloyd-Jones the correct answer to this question depended upon a true understanding of the nature of schism. Schism, he argued is the division of *Christians*, that is to say, of those who are agreed on fundamental truths. The Reformation was not schism because it was a division from an institution in which the meaning of 'Christian' had been lost. There can be no unity without the gospel. It is, therefore, to those who are one in the gospel that the New Testament's commands on unity and its warnings on schism belong. ML-J believed that evangelicals had long taken these commands too lightly and that the ecumenical movement was showing them to be in a position of inconsistency. Evangelicals said that they were 'one in Christ' at such gatherings as the Keswick Convention, and 'one' in the many evangelical organisations (whose work was too important to allow the membership of non-evangelicals), yet in the corporate responsibility for unity required of *churches* in the New Testament they were not one at all. Now, with the denominations themselves in a ferment of change, ML-J believed that the scriptural duty for evangelicals was to translate their oft-affirmed oneness into practice: 'If we have not a burning desire and longing for this unity of true believers I say we are false to the New Testament.'[2]

This was the burden behind Dr Lloyd-Jones' address at the Puritan Conference in December 1962 – the year which marked the tercentenary of the ejection of some 2,000 Puritans from the Church of England. He argued that the Puritans, united in the fundamentals of the Faith, lost their cause in 1662 because they were disunited in secondary matters, and he seized on this point as a lesson for the present:

The movements around us today, the ecumenical movement in particu-

---

[1]Sermon on 'Schism' from Ephesians 6:10–13, Feb 5, 1961, *WR*, June, 1963, p. 85.
[2]*Puritans*, p. 230.

lar, are forcing us to ask this question: what is our view of the church? Is it right that we belong to the same company, calling itself a church, as men who deny almost everything we stand for . . . What is the gospel? Our whole position is based upon this, that we say the gospel can be defined, can be stated in propositions. We *do* believe in Confessions of Faith, we *do* believe in Creeds. It is just there that we are differentiated from the majority of people in the Christian church at the present time . . . Is it right that we should be more associated in general, and in our total life as Christians in the church, with people with whom we do not agree, than with people with whom we do agree about these central vital matters?[1]

The need for a more biblical unity among evangelicals was the subject he took up and elaborated in speaking to the Westminster Fraternal outing to Welwyn on June 19, 1963. Reading Haggai chapter 1, he commenced by pointing out a parallel between Haggai's time and the present situation. Both were periods of reconstruction and new beginnings, yet both then and now God's cause was at a low ebb. The text he repeatedly emphasised was, 'Is it time for you, O ye, to dwell in your cieled houses, and this house lie waste?' (Haggai 1:4). His main theme he introduced with a seven-point survey of 'certain unique features' of the day:

(1) We live at a time when everything relating to the church is in the melting pot. It is more similar to the Reformation than anything that has happened since. Everything is once more being queried. (2) Unions between different sections of the Christian church are taking place (e.g. South India) and many are involved in movements for union. (3) On the mission field there is a new nationalism. People are no longer ready for us to impose our pattern upon them but are going to think out the whole problem of the Church for themselves. (4) I am impressed with what has happened amongst the Exclusive Brethren. Here are numbers of people who have come out of the bondage in which they have been held for so long, and they are scattered all over the country not quite knowing what to do nor where to turn. What is going to be our relation to them? (5) The blatant unbelief in the official churches is coming into the open. And there is evidence of a subtle change of emphasis in evangelical thinking — an acceptance of looser views of the early chapters of Genesis and of miracles, a new atmosphere in book-reviewing, a disinterest in doctrine and a tendency to gloat in scholarship.

[1] *Puritans*, pp. 68–70.

(6) There is the whole moral condition of the country. There is need of prophetic statement but we seem to be living in our 'cieled houses'. (7) There is an appalling need of evangelical preaching. Evangelicalism is concentrated in the Greater London area. We forget the appalling conditions that prevail in the great bulk of the country.

This is a great challenge and unique opportunity. It is we alone who can give the message. But we seem to be ineffective and silent . . . Our statements are tepid and harmless. Evangelicals in all the major denominations are in the same position. Why?

The main answer is that we are so divided up that our witness is diluted. We have avoided the Church problem by contenting ourselves with movements.

This principal statement he proceeded to analyse and some of his observations were as follows:

Our testimony has been inevitably inconsistent because it is scripturally defective. We have criticised those in error yet continued to belong to the same church and have acknowledged them as members and dignitaries. This more or less nullifies our criticism. With intellectual dishonesty rampant in the church, how can we speak to the nation?

Non-evangelicals are generally consistent. They say the same things at all levels. We do not. For example, evangelicals advocate separation at the student level (recommending attachment to IVF, not SCM) and then at the church level evangelicals do the exact opposite and advocate participation in the WCC. If separation is right on one level should it not be right on the other? This makes the evangelical position almost untenable.

Movements have led to the sheer indiscipline of evangelicals. That is inevitable because movements are voluntary associations, they cannot and do not discipline. If you have gifts and power, no one can stop you from doing what you like. The tendency is to chaos. Further, because evangelicals have tried to solve problems by getting into movements they have by-passed the whole question of the church. Our grandfathers went wrong. They met in 'little conclaves' and more or less retired from the church situation. They avoided church questions because they were afraid of disharmony in the movement where they said, 'We are all one in Christ'. Disharmony would wreck the movement so out of fear of division they evaded the church question.

Has the time not arrived when we must re-examine the whole thing? Many of the movements are running to seed. Here is a unique opportunity to re-examine the position and see whether we have not to start anew and afresh.

This led him to his second main heading, the statement that the nature of the church had become the major problem.

All evangelicals agree that they can only decide issues according to Scripture but, in practice, their decision here is so often influenced by tradition and history. They start with the *status quo* and their main argument becomes one of expediency.

We must go back to New Testament teaching.

(1) What is a church? It is an assembly of true believers, those who have been born again, the association of people who are the body of Christ and who meet conscious of His presence. They are a spiritual society (Acts 2:41; Eph 2:19–22). (2) What are the marks of a true church? An assembly where true doctrine is preached; where the sacraments are faithfully administered and where discipline is exercised. The 'power of the keys' is to be exercised in admission and excommunication, without which there can be no guarantee whatever of purity of life or doctrine (Matt 18.15 ff; John 20:22–23; 1 Cor 5; Gal 5:12; 2 Thess 3:6; Titus 3:10–11). Is this teaching compatible with saying, 'My church is a good place to fish in?' Is the church a place where members need to be evangelized? The popular exposition of the parable of the tares is to justify the absence of church discipline but this makes the parable contradict other teaching in the New Testament. John Owen gives five reasons why Christ instituted discipline in the church.[1]

We need to concentrate on this question of the nature of the church. It would be tragic if we let this go by default because of fears of upsetting people.

It is astounding that we should be in this world at such a time as this, when we see the breaking down of things once regarded as unmovable in the realm of the church. One possible reaction is to be depressed at it all and to wring our hands over such degenerate times. Another reaction is to say, 'Well, as far as my particular church is concerned, at any rate, everything is all right'. Haggai ought to put us right on that once and for ever. We cannot contract out of this situation, for the essence of the gospel is at stake. We must be clear about the one big, grand objective or we will lose everything. We need an over-all strategy and must refuse to allow ourselves to be side-tracked by matters of lesser importance . . . We must be ready to say that men are not Christians and are enemies of the Faith. But how can you if you belong to them and to the same church?

We have an opportunity which has not confronted evangelical people for a long time.

I have no cut-and-dried scheme but it behoves us to face this question of the nature of the church together. We need positive, constructive

[1] These he quoted. See *The Works of John Owen*, vol.15, p. 519.

thinking. We must approach the situation theologically. The position is moving very rapidly and if we do nothing we shall have to crawl out of a terrible wreckage. The first thing is to *clarify* our minds. We must stop avoiding this central doctrine. That time has gone.[1]

The reaction within the Westminster Fellowship to Dr Lloyd-Jones' Welwyn address revealed what he already knew: instead of leading the way in terms of biblical unity, evangelicals were themselves going to be divided.

To the causes of this impending division we must now turn. In the first instance, what has already emerged in the preceding pages needs to be underlined. Within English evangelicalism there was now a major difference in mood with respect to the whole scene. By this date Dr Lloyd-Jones had travelled the country ceaselessly for over thirty years and he knew the general conditions as did few others. In addition, instead of spending long summer breaks abroad (as many wished him to do), he was generally in many different parts of Britain and seeing churches from the pew rather than from the pulpit. As an ordinary member of the congregation attending for worship on a Sunday, the impression he received was often very different from that of a mid-week service where many attended from other places when he was preaching. His summer holidays in 1960 and 1962 sharpened his conviction that the whole country was involved in a spiritual decline of vast proportions. Whether in East Anglia or Oxfordshire, Cornwall or Somerset, the north of Scotland or Wales, everywhere conditions were much the same. 'The tragedy,' as he told members at Westminster, 'lies not merely in the smallness of the congregations, but in their utter deadness and their apparent dislike of the truth when presented to them'. Meeting with forty or more ministers in the Highlands of Scotland, he noted their view that 'even in the last five years there had been a deterioration in the situation'.[2]

Almost everything he saw outside London confirmed his impression that the situation was profoundly serious. To his friends at the Annual Meeting of the Evangelical Library in 1961 he said: 'I think it

[1] My quotations from this address are from my own abbreviated notes. The full text (taken down from tape) is in *Knowing the Times*, pp. 164–97.
[2] This meeting occurred in connection with special services at the Free Church of Scotland in Dingwall in September 1960, the church which C. H. Spurgeon had opened for his friend Dr John Kennedy in 1870. ML-J enjoyed being in the same old manse in which Spurgeon had stayed, but this visit led him to think that belief in the possibility of revival was weak even in the Scottish Highlands.

is more than likely that the times will get worse and that there will be a great searching even amongst us who are called evangelical. We will be driven back to certain foundations; we may become a very small company.'

The basis for these opinions, and the fact that these were held by a man who ministered to what was probably the largest regular congregation in London, were things passed over by most evangelicals who still believed that the success of recent evangelistic campaigns was a warrant for optimism. They were confident that evangelical influence was growing. Far from accepting ML-J's diagnosis, they believed that an evangelicalism with a modern image and an up-to-date presentation of the Christian Faith could even yet win the centre ground in the denominations. It was consequently, in their view, a very inopportune time to be thinking of any kind of 'withdrawal'. Conservative evangelicals in the Church of England were the most prominent in this mood of hopefulness and, because of their numbers, their colleges and their traditional place of leadership in English evangelicalism, their decision with respect to ecumenism was bound to be widely influential. From 'the benevolent neutrality' advocated by Bishop Gough and others in the early 1950's, numbers of Anglican evangelicals now began to move to the position of active involvement in ecumenism advocated by A. T. Houghton. 'Cooperation without compromise', the phrase we noted in the United States in 1956, was now applied to the new policy in England. If the evangelical voice was to be heard in the corridors of power where it could count, there was, they argued, no other alternative. The 'Choice before evangelicals', to use the headlines of a report of an address by A. T. Houghton, was 'Isolation or involvement'.[1] Ecumenism was the discussion of the age and if evangelicals did not speak from within that discussion their opinion would count for nothing. 'The fault of evangelicals who eschew dialogue,' wrote John Stott, is to assert their evangelicalism in an 'inflexible way which is quite irrelevant to the modern confusions and perplexities of the Church'.[2]

Those who took this view were confirmed in their belief in its rightness by the welcome now being accorded to them in various congresses and commissions for ecumenical discussion. J. D. Douglas

[1] *Church of England Newspaper*, May 18, 1962, p. 3.
[2] "Evangelicals in a changing world', *Church of England Newspaper*, Nov 1, 1968, p. 12.

(Church of Scotland) applauded the 'notable gesture' of the organizers of the 1964 Nottingham conference who 'encouraged the attendance of a number known to be conservative evangelicals'. He believed that the Nottingham invitation 'reflects a graciousness of spirit that augurs well for the future' and noted that 'one of the evangelicals, the Rev. A. T. Houghton, was asked to give one of the major addresses'.[1] Anglican evangelicals similarly received invitations to join the various forums for ecumenical discussion within their Church. Soon it was to seem a far cry from the comparatively recent days when evangelical Anglicans, in Stott's words, were 'a rejected minority, a despised minority movement'. In 1964 the Rev. John Weller, Secretary of the Faith and Order Department of the British Council of Churches, could report that: 'The dialogue between "conservative evangelicals and others" is going on at the moment here in Britain more widely, more vigorously and more fruitfully than perhaps at any time in these last few years.'[2]

Here, then, was a very major difference of view among evangelicals. Instead of believing that those who took an opposing view were gaining a real influence for biblical Christianity, ML-J considered that they were actually contributing to the existing decline and confusion. The main problem in the nation was the unbelief in the church. As he told an Evangelical Alliance Rally, held to commemorate the 350th anniversary of the Authorised Version of the Bible, in the Royal Albert Hall, London, it was the *church* which had engaged 'in undermining the faith and belief of the masses of the people in this Book as being the Word of God'. He instanced 'a recent statement to the effect that we can "expect to meet atheists in heaven"'. Everyone knew that he was referring to the words of the Archbishop of Canterbury. "If a man can go to heaven who does not even believe in God,' he went on to ask, 'why should we ask him to believe in the Bible? Why should we have a Christian church at all?'[3]

To ML-J it was a plain matter of fact that most of the church leaders, Anglican and Free Church, did not believe the Confessions of Faith of the denominations to which they belonged. By the mid-sixties the Labour leader in the House of Lords could not be

[1] *Evangelicals and Unity*, p. 13.
[2] A letter to the Council's Group on Differing Biblical Presuppositions, indicating its final closure, October 6, 1964.
[3] This address, 'How Can We See a Return to the Bible?' given on October 24, 1961, is reprinted in *Knowing the Times*.

contradicted when he said that there was not one bishop holding to a Protestant position; mass vestments, prayers for the dead and stone altars had the approval of all. Meanwhile, on the liberal side of the Church of England, John Robinson, Bishop of Woolwich, was propounding an impersonal God according to the ideas of Tillich and Bultmann.[1] In the Methodist Church, involved in reunion negotiations with the Church of England, things were no better. *The Methodist Recorder* could report that one of its best-known leaders Dr Donald Soper proposed a ban on Bible reading for the year 1965 and for this reason: 'The present situation with regard to the Scriptures is intolerable. They represent an incubus that cannot be removed until an almost completely new start is made . . .' Far from regretting that 'the traditional Nonconformist Sunday is dying', Soper professed to be glad: 'Let it die. Better still, kill it off'. In an article entitled, 'The Methodism Gone Forever . . .' also published in *The Methodist Recorder*, John J. Vincent argued that all the doctrines of justification, of saving faith, assurance and holiness, 'belong to an intellectual and theological world which is no longer ours. They describe experiences which are no longer normative for Methodist people.'[2]

When an evangelical at the Methodist Conference in Plymouth in 1965 moved an amendment to recall the Church to its own articles of faith it was defeated by a vote of 601 to 14!

Yet the price for ecumenical dialogue was that the very men who tolerated, or even approved, this state of affairs had to be regarded by evangelicals as fellow Christians. As one of the evangelicals, after the Nottingham Conference of 1964, was to declare: 'The real question at issue in the whole discussion of the ecumenical movement is one of trust. Are we or are we not willing to trust the Christian sincerity of those who name the name of Christ, who call Jesus Lord, but differ from us in doctrine?'[3] This was indeed the question and to ML-J's amazement many evangelicals – led by the Anglicans – decided there had been a serious mistake in the way in which they had previously been answering it. The issue was thus becoming clear: either the

[1] In a booklet, *Keep Yourselves From Idols*, a discussion of 'Honest to God' by John A. T. Robinson, 1963, J. I. Packer wrote: 'All that is distinctive of the *Christian* faith in God, as opposed to that of a Moslem or Hindu, seems to have gone from the bishop's theology.'
[2] *The Methodist Recorder*, Sept. 7, 1961.
[3] *Evangelicals and Unity*, pp. 29–30.

former evangelical attitude was wrong, narrow and bigoted, or the new policy was a move away from Scripture. If it was the latter, what could account for such a change of direction? Dr Lloyd-Jones saw two main reasons.

First, doctrinal commitment had become so weakened in evangelical circles that the judgment of leaders was being shaped by considerations of success and wider influence in a manner hitherto unknown.

The position of Dr Billy Graham and his Crusades made a critical difference at precisely this point. In contrast to Graham's early unwillingness to co-operate with liberals (which explained the shut doors he encountered in England in 1952) he was now ready to receive the support of virtually any well-known religious leader. Men whose teaching had been disastrous in its spiritual effect were thus being given an identification with a message which their ministries opposed.

On this point ML-J talked with Graham face to face. They met in the vestry of Westminster Chapel early in July 1963, and at the request of the American evangelist who came to seek support. The Graham organization was planning a first 'World Congress on Evangelism' to meet in Rome and wanted ML-J to be the chairman of that Congress. The latter's reply to this appeal has been recorded as follows:

I said I'd make a bargain: if he would stop the general sponsorship of his campaigns – stop having liberals and Roman Catholics on the platform – and drop the invitation system, I would wholeheartedly support him and chair the Congress. We talked for about three hours, but he didn't accept these conditions.[1]

In attempting to show Dr Graham the inconsistency of his policy, ML-J instanced how the evangelist had introduced Dr John Sutherland Bonnell of New York as a helper in the All Scotland Crusade of 1957 even though Bonnell was a known liberal in his theology. When Graham replied that he could have more 'fellowship' with Bonnell than with a number of evangelicals, ML-J advised him that true fellowship was based upon something other than a likeable, warm personality. Graham had capitulated to the ecumenical idea of

[1]'Martyn Lloyd-Jones'. An interview by Carl F. H. Henry, *Christianity Today*, Feb. 8, 1980, p. 29. Reprinted in *Martyn Lloyd-Jones: Chosen by God*, pp. 96–108.

Christian 'fellowship' without agreement in the truth of the gospel and his example inevitably became an influence, to use ML-J's words, in 'shaking people's convictions as to what exactly it means to be an evangelical'.

Shortly after this meeting and when ML-J was on the eve of his fifth visit to the United States, Graham wrote:

July 18, 1963

Dear Dr Lloyd-Jones:
 Just a note to thank you for the wonderful time of fellowship with you in London, and even more for your kindness and thoughtfulness in taking me to the doctor. You will be interested to know that the lump in my throat has improved considerably due to the medicine that I am taking faithfully. I know that the advice you and the doctor gave me was sound.
 We are praying constantly for your ministry here in America. My wife is eager to have you in our home for a meal when you come to Montreat. My only regret is that I must be away in our crusade in Los Angeles at that time. It would be the greatest joy for us if we could welcome you to the Los Angeles crusade after you have finished your meetings.[1]
 I have been giving much thought and prayer to our discussion, and I am sure that it was ordered of the Lord.
 With my deepest personal affection for you in Christ, I am
Most cordially yours,
Billy

When ML-J reached the States later that same month it was to find that his unwillingness to act as chairman at the projected 'World Congress on Evangelism' had not been taken as final. He and Bethan were met as they disembarked from the 'Queen Mary' by John Bolten with whom a friendship had been formed in the work of the IFES since the first meetings at Harvard in 1947. Bolten, along with J Howard Pew and a few others, was one of the chief financial backers of the Graham organization and of the 'new evangelicalism'. The latter term was, in fact, originally coined by Bolten's own minister, Harold J. Ockenga of Park Street, Boston, and Fuller Seminary.

The network led by Ockenga and Graham was now facing something of a crisis as it risked losing the support both of the older

---

[1]Graham had been suffering from throat trouble when he saw Lloyd-Jones who personally took the evangelist to see a medical friend. ML-J did not appear at the Los Angeles crusade.

fundamentalism and of the main-line denominations. The whole policy, related as it was to obtaining wider acceptance and approval, was in danger.[1] ML-J would know a little of this through Wilbur Smith (who was later to resign from Fuller Seminary) and others but he was taken by surprise when Bolten used the occasion of their three days of holiday together at his seaside home at Gloucester, north of Boston, to press the importance of his agreeing to Graham's proposal. Bolten was one of many who admired Lloyd-Jones yet failed to understand that he was held by a theology which left him deaf to the pragmatic argument of 'wider influence' when it came to questions affecting fundamentals. The preacher's mind was closed and when the Congress was finally held in Berlin, not Rome, in 1966 he would not be there.[2]

The next twelve months after the summer of 1963 also confirmed that Dr Graham would not change his direction. In a televised interview with Cardinal Cushing of Boston, he spoke of the 'new day of understanding and dialogue'. 'You've made a great contribution to this ecumenical spirit,' Cushing replied. When Graham returned to London in 1964, for preliminary talks on a further Crusade, his biographer tells us that his first engagement was with Archbishop Ramsey and that soon after he was to see the Bishops of London and Southwark. The latter (Mervyn Stockwood), a supporter both of John Robinson and of re-union with Rome, was asked to serve on the Council of Reference which was to support Graham's 1966 Earls Court Crusade.[3]

The acceptance of this ecumenical patronage on the part of Graham could only have one effect upon those who had confidence in his judgment. If the evangelist was so impressed by the 'brother-liness' of non-evangelicals, then there was surely reason to say, 'Well, I wonder whether these doctrines we've been emphasizing are so important after all'.

To say this is not to make Dr Graham out to be the main cause of

[1] On this whole subject Marsden's *Reforming Fundamentalism* is the most important work to date.
[2] Carl Henry is mistaken in saying that ML-J was there as an 'unpublicised observer' (*Confessions of a Theologian*, 1986, p. 258).
[3] The 1966 Crusade was perhaps the first in England to have the public support of Roman Catholics. In the words of Mr N. St John Stevas, MP, 'Mr Graham's mission is not to make converts to his own faith but to send them back to the churches of their own tradition .. his efforts should have the support of Catholics' (the *English Churchman*, June 17, 1966).

the doctrinal weakening in Britain. If weakness had not already been present, evangelicals would never have been carried away, as they were, by the new policy of co-operation. What would once have been called compromise was now being openly justified. An example from the realm of Christian literature will illustrate this. Dr William Barclay of Glasgow was one of the best-known religious figures of the 1960's. As an author and broadcaster he had mastered the art of communicating ideas in a popular manner to the average person. But although Barclay spoke much about the Bible he had no belief in its authority as the Word of God and his views on the person and the birth of Christ were not those of historic Christianity. Barclay's biographer quotes ML-J as affirming that Barclay was 'the most dangerous man in Christendom'.[1] It is probably an accurate quotation. ML-J believed that people were confused by the attractiveness of Barclay's presentation and because of some of the good things which he did say. But what concerned him more, in terms of encouraging confusion, was that Professor F. F. Bruce was now working in harness with Barclay in the production of a series of 'Bible Guides' of which Lutterworth Press were the publishers. Bruce, Rylands Professor of Biblical Criticism and Exegesis at the University of Manchester, remained a signatory to the IVF Basis of Faith and yet saw no inconsistency in being publicly identified with one whose beliefs were far removed from that basis. This disturbed ML-J so much that in November 1962 he referred to the point in a sermon at Westminster Chapel. 'Was he forgetting,' asked one indignant correspondent, that 'both editors are Christian men' and that Bruce 'exercises a wide influence for great good in the world of biblical scholarship?' 'If I may say so,' continued the same writer, 'I am surprised that you have taken the liberty of mentioning the name of *any* writer in a critical way from a public platform.' In ML-J's view, the writer was missing the main point. What is the value of evangelicals affirming a statement of faith if they see no harm in making common cause with those who teach the opposite? By action, if not by word, such a policy treated evangelicalism as a party rather than a biblical position.[2]

[1] *William Barclay*, The Authorised Biography, Clive L. Rawlins, 1984, p. 651.
[2] Bruce's autobiography does not address itself to this question either. He speaks of the IVF needing to be 'specially sensitive to the climate of opinion in the evangelical world' because of 'its constitution and clientèle' but expresses thankfulness for the 'academic freedom' of Universities 'where it is quite irrelevant whether a man is conservative or liberal in theology'. *In Retrospect, Remembrance of Things Past*, 1980, pp. 187, 143.

The second factor which ML-J saw as contributing largely to this change in direction among evangelicals is closely related to the first. Alongside an unwillingness to insist upon Scripture, there came an excessive fear of being thought negative, controversial and belliger-ent. Criticism of almost any kind had become very unpopular among professing Christians. A loving attitude was thought to be one which accepted everyone for what they appeared to be. If discernment between truth and error and the need to 'beware of men' were still counted as Christian virtues they were now low down the list of priorities. The duty of 'contending earnestly for the faith' was put still lower. To emphasise these things was to risk losing the increased acceptance for which evangelicals hoped. Those who defended this change generally did so in terms of the hard, unattractive contentious-ness which had formerly, so it was said, too commonly prevailed. In one form or another the words Professor McKenzie had used in defending Schweitzer were repeated endlessly: 'A man may believe the whole creed, every letter of it and be an eternity away from the spirit of Christ'. It is true that there have always been cases of orthodoxy divorced from compassion, but it was now implied that anyone who took 'the fight of faith' seriously was bound to be such a person. If there was one thing left which was still considered worthy of condemnation it was 'lack of love'. Such was the atmosphere into which evangelicals were being drawn in the 1960's and it goes far to explaining why Dr Lloyd-Jones was so often alone in what he said.

It is significant in this connection that Dr Lloyd-Jones' Sunday morning sermons in the early 1960's gave much time to an exposition of 'the wiles of the devil'. The Bible, as he reminded his people, warns us that things are often not what they *seem* to be and that vigilance and a suspicion of human nature, because of the Fall, are constant duties for the Christian. Included in these sermons were several on the devil's use of error and deception and when one of these, on Roman Catholicism, was printed in the *Westminster Record*, it caused no small comment.[1] Some professed to be critical over not so much what he said as the way in which he said it. The minister of Highbury Quadrant Congregational Church wrote

[1]Preached on Jan. 29, 1961, it was published in *WR*, May 1963. For reasons of space, this sermon (along with several others in the series) was omitted by the preacher from his published volumes on Ephesians. It was reprinted separately as a booklet (Evangelical Press, London, 1967 and, translated into Welsh, Evangelical Movement of Wales, 1971).

to him: 'Whilst much of your criticism of the Roman Catholic Church may be true, the terms in which you present it seem to me to be appalling. I am sorry you should ever think it right to speak in such a way.'[1] The same writer went on to express his fears over what such a sermon could do to hinder reconciliation among the churches.

More strange was the attitude of those who regarded his sermon as irrelevant to evangelicalism. At the Islington Clerical Conference of 1960 the Rev. M. A. P. Wood saw no danger from Roman Catholicism and, as late as 1962, the Rev. A. T. Houghton was denying that the direction of ecumenism was towards re-union with Rome. Yet within a few years evangelicals were to use the same argument which they were now adopting to support co-operation with liberals, namely, a shared spiritual experience, to justify a friendly response to the overtures which came from Vatican II.

Instead of backing off from the convictions expressed in his sermon on Roman Catholicism, Dr Lloyd-Jones returned to the subject in 1964 and related it to the general change which he saw taking place in evangelicalism. On June 10 in that year he gave the concluding address in the series of Campbell Morgan Memorial Lectures which had been delivered annually over 16 years. His subject, 'The Weapons of our Warfare', based upon 2 Corinthians 10:4, provides one of the most important statements of his thinking at this date. He saw three main dangers confronting evangelicals. The first was 'to think that there is no warfare any longer' because there was no more battle to be waged. Many Christians now thought that 'all is changed, even Roman Catholicism is changing'. He went on:

Here was something, people thought, that would never change. The conflict and the fight between Protestantism and Roman Catholicism was assumed to be something that was permanent; whatever changes might take place within Protestantism there would always remain this fundamental difference between the Roman Catholic and the Protestant outlook. But we are told that even that is changing now, that Rome is changing. Was not this quite obvious in the appearances of the late Pope John on the television screens? What a fine, kind, and benevolent-looking man; and all he said was full of such a loving Christian spirit!

[1]On the other hand, a converted ex-Roman Catholic wrote to thank him for 'a balanced and very true exposition . . . Your booklet is so far removed from the many publications which seek to denounce the errors of Rome but rather create a laughing stock on account of the elementary errors about fundamental beliefs'.

Moreover the Roman Church, we are told, is now advising and urging her people to read the Bible. We must give up those old ideas of conflict; we are all becoming one, and those old differences are no longer there. So we must not talk any longer about a 'warfare'.[1]

It should be said that ML-J read a good deal by Roman Catholic authors both in books and journals. He was familiar with such authors as Hans Küng and even read the monthly *New Blackfriars* edited by English Dominicans, of which most evangelicals had never heard. A frequent contributor to Roman Catholic journals, Mr H. W. J. Edwards, records how he went to hear ML-J preach on one occasion and afterwards 'dared' to enter the vestry: 'to my very great surprise Dr Lloyd-Jones beamed upon me and said (in Welsh), "H. W. J. Edwards? Why, I am so glad to meet you".'[2] ML-J was never an advocate of any personal hostility to Catholics and the possibility of being a Christian and a Roman Catholic he would never deny, 'such people are Christians in spite of the system to which they belong and not because of it'. But he regarded the Roman Catholic system as the ultimate form of anti-biblical comprehensiveness.

Of course, as ML-J went on to say in his 1964 Campbell Morgan Memorial Lecture, there was change in Rome but that had happened many times before. It is part of her distinctive nature to accommodate to different circumstances. The one form of evidence that would justify a new hopefulness, namely change in her fundamental doctrine and repentance for her former apostasy, did not exist. Evangelicals were being influenced by the mood of the times, not by scriptural convictions. They were acting as though a better image and a more 'brotherly' approach would win influence for the truth, as though all the historic differences were chiefly due to misunderstandings and a lack of mutual confidence. Speaking on this point in an address on the fourth centenary of the Scottish Reformation in Edinburgh, ML-J represented the modern approach to differences in these terms: 'We will have a friendly chat and discussion, we will

---

[1]*Knowing the Times*, p. 201 The other main points of this address were 'the danger of avoiding the warfare' and 'the danger of fighting with the wrong weapons'.

[2]From a letter to the author, November 1, 1981, which began, 'I am not the only (Roman) Catholic to grieve upon hearing of the departing of Dr Martyn Lloyd-Jones, now I believe, in glory'. Far from being an ecumenist, Mr Edwards considered that Vatican II moved his Church closer to the Pelagianism opposed by Augustine.

show them that after all we are nice, decent fellows, there is nothing nasty about us, and we will gain their confidence.' And he went on: 'Was Knox a matey, friendly, nice chap with whom you could have a discussion? Thank God he was not! Thank God prophets are made of stronger stuff!'[1]

It remains to be said that isolated though Dr Lloyd-Jones was as a leader, he was not altogether alone and although Anglican evangelicals came to feel that they were under his criticism, there were some among them who gave their support to what he was saying. The Rev. Gordon Murray, Editor of the *English Churchman*,[2] was one of this group. When Anglican evangelicals involved in ecumenical discussion accused ML-J of wanting a 'pure' church of a perfectionist type, Murray replied:

There may be those who would like their Church to be one field of unblemished wheat but we have never met any Christian who has expected that this side of eternity. What we have met are Christians who are concerned to keep their doctrine of the Church as scripturally pure as they know how and if that is not a biblical, evangelical and reformation idea we do not know what is . . . There is all the difference in the world between the mixed Church of Scripture and the kind of mixed Church we are getting now, and which is found within the ecumenical movement, a mixing of biblical doctrine and teaching which is clean contrary to Scripture.

If it is true that the strength of evangelicalism in England is overwhelmingly in the Church of England, then evangelicals generally have a right to expect a strong scriptural lead to be given them by us on these matters. We believe, however, that such a lead is not being given . . .

This failure to act positively against doctrinal error is our greatest weakness at the present time. We refuse, apparently, to decide whether or not we believe others to be preaching another gospel in case the answer proves to be too embarrassing. Yet this is the question which must be asked and answered if we are to know what to do.

A Church only exists where the true gospel is proclaimed . . . *and only those who preach the gospel should be allowed to minister in it.* Is this true of the Church of England today? Of course it is not. All sorts of different messages are being proclaimed, and if we are as scriptural as we claim to be we would rebuke those who preach another gospel and after the second or third admonition reject them, refuse to have fellowship with them . . .

[1] Address in the Usher Hall, Edinburgh, April 5, 1960, published in *Knowing the Times*, pp. 90–105.
[2] From October 1965 to Jan. 1971.

It is our candid opinion that the policy which is being followed at the moment far from high-lighting the uniqueness of the gospel is simply confirming others in their view that we have a few valuable insights to contribute to the understanding of Christ's truth as a whole.

Another who stood close to Dr Lloyd-Jones was Dr J. I. Packer, although he knew that the preacher's 'peers in official Christianity treated him as scarcely more than an extremely able freak'.[1] When *A Report to the Archbishops of Canterbury and York and the Conference of the Methodist Church*,[2] prepared by representatives of both denominations, was issued in 1963, with recommendations for the reunion of the two denominations, Packer and five colleagues went into print with serious objections. Packer believed that the proposals for reunion rested on theological foundations which were 'opportunist, equivocal and dissonant at several points both from Scripture and from the theological standards and traditions of the two churches'. He saw the negotiators who wrote the Report as double-minded and considered that they showed no serious desire that the two churches should be reformed by the Word of God. To expect a renewal in health in the Church of England and the Methodist Church — 'neither noted for soundness and depth of doctrine, or sanctity of life' — simply by reunion was, he believed, as unrealistic as 'to expect two consumptives to get better simply through getting married'. In particular, Packer criticized the way in which the report represented 'the Church of England as containing "evangelicals" and "catholics" side by side on an equal footing, without a mention of the fact that its authorized formularies exclude some things for which Anglican "catholics" stand'.[3]

To this book the Methodist leader, Professor Gordon Rupp, replied with a stinging missile in which he asserted that Dr Packer and his friends were 'putting the interests of an ecclesiastical party [i.e. evangelicalism] before the welfare of the whole Church of Christ'.[4] At this same time Packer's convictions also involved him

[1] *Martyn Lloyd-Jones: Chosen by God*, p. 42.
[2] This was the sub-title of *Conversations between The Church of England and the Methodist Church*, February 1963.
[3] See *The Church of England and The Methodist Church, A Consideration of the Anglican – Methodist Report*, edited by J. I. Packer, Marcham Manor Press, November 1963.
[4] *Consideration Reconsidered*, An examination of *The Church of England and the Methodist Church*, The Epworth Press, 1964, p. 58.

in an open difference with some fellow Anglican evangelicals. Six conservative evangelical leaders who were Anglicans, including A. T. Houghton and Maurice Wood, had published their own response to the proposals for reunion with the Methodist Church entitling it, *The Anglican–Methodist Conversations: An Evangelical Approach.*[1] This book Packer reviewed and argued that a question mark needed to be added to the authors' use of the word 'evangelical'. He complained that they had adopted 'an unusual role for evangelicals, and not a very becoming one':

They view their evangelicalism as simply a party view in the Church of England, and do not object in principle to the Church's official ecumenical actions being determined by Anglo-Catholic convictions about the ministry . . . To be sure, most of them wish to maintain that saying 'yes' to the report involves no real sacrifice of Evangelical principle at all; but their special pleading fails to convince, for it neither faces all the facts nor reaches the heart of the issues handled.

Clearly, they care very much for evangelism, and that is good; but they seem so obsessed with 'practical politics', and the desire to show themselves good and shrewd diplomats, as to be quite lacking in concern that the Church of England, in its public actions, should be obedient to the truth of the gospel.

This lack, along with their occasionally imperfect grasp of the meaning of biblical authority and their readiness to justify a seemingly unprincipled comprehension, leaves one wondering whether 'Broad Church pietists' would not be a better description of some of them than 'Evangelicals'.[2]

Such words were a help to Dr Lloyd-Jones on another front. In Wales a well known figure in the broadcasting world, Aneirin Talfan Davies, one-time member of the Calvinistic Methodist Church, was becoming a leading spokesman for ecumenism. He had joined the Anglican Church believing that, in its possession of a common tradition and a common principle of authority, it offered a security not to be found elsewhere. Dr Lloyd-Jones' belief that evangelicals should come together and leave the denominations to unite he criticised as 'a load of cynicism'. In a lengthy reply ML-J pointed his fellow-countryman to facts which could hardly be harmonized with Davies' belief that episcopacy could solve disunity:

[1] Edited by Peter Morgan, S.P.C.K., 1964.
[2] 'An Evangelical Approach?' *Church of England Newspaper*, July 17, 1964.

What union can there be between the Catholic element and the evangelical element in the Church of England? From week to week, in their papers, their conferences and congregations, they continually contradict each other completely. I regularly read articles by my friend, Dr J. I. Packer, and others, articles which attack the majority in the Anglican Church as being wholly unscriptural and out of touch with the Articles and the Book of Common Prayer in their ideas concerning bishops, the sacraments and the way of salvation. There is no authority within Anglicanism. Indeed, there is more confusion, disorder and a breaking of rules within that church than any other of the religious bodies.[1]

By 1964, for the reasons we have considered, Dr Lloyd-Jones knew that there could be no expectation of any general evangelical unity. The truth was that evangelicalism itself was beginning to break up. But he still entertained hopes that a new grouping of some strength could emerge which might rise to the challenge of the hour.

[1] *Barn* [Opinion], June, 1963, p. 237. This was the second of two long letters, in Welsh, debating ecumenism with Mr Davies, both entitled, *Yr Hyn a Gredaf* [That which I believe]. The first was published in the same journal, April 1963, pp. 171–73.

A MARATHON LECTURE

The one totally unequivocal London celebration of the Great Ejectment, of 1662, may well prove, when the tercentenary year ends, to have been neither that of the Unitarians in the spring nor the meetings planned by the Free Church majority for August and October but a remarkable gathering in the Welsh Church, Chiltern Street, on Tuesday night, for the annual lecture of the Evangelical Library. The lecturer was Dr Martyn Lloyd-Jones, of Westminster Chapel, and he gave a marathon performance of 2¼ hours.

The church, its porch, and a small room behind were packed with men and women of all age groups. After he had read for two hours, Dr Lloyd-Jones's voice seemed not to have flagged a bit, and he did not shrink from a peroration that embodied the whole of Wordsworth's sonnet 'Milton, thou shouldst be living at this hour, England hath need of thee,' and a long list of ways in which Christians should respond to the 'fen of stagnant waters' that Wordsworth saw when he wrote and Dr Lloyd-Jones sees in the England of today. And his audience was still there. A few left after two hours, but the great majority stayed to sing 'Our fathers were high-minded men, who boldly kept the faith' and receive the lecturer's benediction.

The Guardian, July 6, 1962

22

Conversations and Journeys

In the 1960's, although no longer at Westminster Chapel, I was sometimes with Dr Lloyd-Jones for longer periods than in earlier years. When he had preaching engagements away from London from which it was possible to return by car the same night we would occasionally drive together in my car. No matter what the hour, conversation would flow (and more rather than less if we were not home before midnight!).

With regard to routes to and from our destinations, there was never any need to be concerned about maps, even in the depths of the countryside. There seemed to be scarcely a road which he had not travelled and remembered, and there were few places about which he could not offer information, either from books or from his own experience. On this point the Rev. E. W. Hayden has written:

On one occasion I had to meet 'the Doctor' off the London train at Hereford, give him hospitality at our Manse in Leominster, then drive him to Llandrindod Wells for an afternoon ministers' meeting and an evening rally. What a passenger for such a journey! As we passed through Radnorshire (now Powys) he knew every chapel (New Radnor, Abbey Cwm-hir, Llanfihangel, Builth Wells, Newbridge-on-Wye, Rhayader, Pant-y-Dwr, etc.) and how the Welsh revivals had affected them, or if not, why not! I have never known the hour's journey from Leominster to Llandrindod Wells pass so quickly, so entertainingly or with such inspiration.

From the variety of places to which I drove with ML-J it was not always evident why he had accepted any particular engagement. The numbers likely to be present certainly did not determine his decision. Sometimes our destination might be a crowded united service, with a large congregation, but he was not at all averse to preaching in an

[453]

out-of-the-way village or country chapel. In the latter case the need to encourage a young, or perhaps struggling, pastor was often in his mind. In one or two such places, as I have sat among a chattering, largely female, afternoon congregation awaiting the service, it seemed that the atmosphere would be far from helpful to the preacher. But preaching is not dependent upon 'atmosphere' and within minutes of the start of the sermon there could be a great transformation in those who had seemed so thoughtless.

Harold J. Rodwell's record of how ML-J first came to preach for him at Yelling, a quiet backwater in Huntingdonshire, illustrates the variety of influences which led to ML-J's engagements. Rodwell had been indignant to read in a printed sermon by the minister of Westminster Chapel that agricultural workers were among the most difficult when it came to preaching the gospel. 'Perhaps because they spend so much of their time in the open air,' ML-J was reported as saying, 'they tend to slumber in not-too-well ventilated churches.' When the opportunity to meet the preacher occurred, Rodwell expressed his disagreement over the statement and promised ML-J that he would have an alert congregation of farmers and their employees if he would come to Yelling! 'The Doctor was so amused,' says this country pastor, 'that he agreed to take up my challenge.' Thereafter ML-J was to be a very welcome visitor to Yelling on a number of occasions.

Another thing which was observable at times, on the occasions when I drove him to services, was the very different manner in which he could treat chairmen. Once or twice in my hearing a layman who was chairing the meeting would make comments on his person or ministry of a fulsome type which he would never tolerate from a minister. He would not embarrass a well-intentioned Christian who was doing his best,[1] but if a fellow-preacher transgressed he would not be spared. On a June evening in 1962 I was with him at an old chapel almost buried in the Hertfordshire countryside. Its age was one of the principal reasons why he was there, because the congregation had its origins in the period of persecution which followed the Great Ejection of exactly three hundred years earlier. When the service began, and before ML-J could get down to preaching on 'So great salvation', he had to endure hearing the young pastor (whom he did not know) congratulate himself on his success

[1]One nervous chairman in Cornwall, in introducing the preacher, promised the people that 'after the next hymn Dr Lloyd-Jones will *sing* to us'!

in bringing such a distinguished preacher down from London. We were told of the surprise of the pastor's friends, who had asked him, 'How did you do it?'. There was no way that ML-J would let this pass, and we had not long to wait. Rising to his feet, after this introduction, he said:

Before I call your attention to the words in the Scriptures I would like to say just a word and to vary my normal procedure. There seems to be a bit of a mystery about why I am here. The explanation is quite clear. The minister was wise enough to indicate that we might bring to mind 1662. I am an unbounded admirer of those great men of God and any little thing I can do to perpetuate their memory is something which is done very gladly. What led them to sacrifice all? I want to consider this in the light of the first four verses of Hebrews 2:1–4 . . .

It was about the least painful way which he could have adopted to set the record straight, and if our host felt any hurt I am sure the Doctor's kindness in the manse later that evening removed it. The same man was to become a valued member of the Westminster Fraternal.

There were one or two occasions when ML-J was known to clash far more seriously than this with a minister chairing the service. He did not normally preach for liberals unless he had reason to think that they were themselves looking for spiritual help. Of course, there were times when he knew little about a minister who had invited him. I do not know the background to a service where he preached at Ton Pentre in South Wales in the 1950's and was not present, but what happened at its conclusion was long to be remembered. After listening to a powerful sermon from ML-J on the uniqueness of the gospel as the only way of salvation, the local minister rose to give out the last hymn. Before doing so, however, he took the liberty of telling the people, in effect, that the gospel was only one 'solvent' among a series of other possibilities. With the final hymn sung, instead of allowing the benediction to follow, Dr Lloyd-Jones, pale and tense, stepped forward in the pulpit and told the congregation to be seated. He had determined not to allow the meeting to close on such an uncertain note, and for almost ten minutes he proceeded to declare that the gospel is the *only* solvent. Then he pronounced the benediction himself.

ML-J was never so occupied with his message that he could not speak naturally about other things. I recall for instance a visit with him to Harston, near Cambridge, in the early sixties, when he took some time between the services to enquire about the availability of houses in the neighbourhood. He was seeking to help Fred and Elizabeth who were now looking for a family base for themselves away from the rush of London. Their search was finally ended in 1964 with the purchase of the old rectory in Balsham, a quiet rural corner of East Anglia, where there were to be countless happy family holidays and gatherings in the years ahead.

ML-J was astonishingly stimulating in conversation and, like a good Celt, never more so than in the late evening. No matter what the distance from London, when returning with him from services, the time was always short. The only night I can recall my mind straying momentarily from the subject in hand was when I had some fear of running out of petrol when it was past midnight and we were still in the country with no garages open! The range of his interests never ceased to surprise me. He might speak, for instance, of recent discussions or of music which he had heard on radio or television. One of his favourite programmes was 'Desert Island Discs' in which some well-known public figure would be interviewed and his or her favourite recordings played. Mozart was unquestionably his own first choice as a composer. He could not get on with Bach. He greatly enjoyed beautiful voices, Gigli and Callas were favourites, although they never replaced Caruso who had the first place in his admiration. He confessed how a recent broadcast on Caruso had reduced him to tears. Discussing on one occasion Sir Thomas Beecham's choice in 'Desert Island Discs', with which he was in full agreement, he went on to say how he knew what a musician felt when he had created some piece of music because sermon preparation also involved creativity. The most important part of the sermon is its outline and this is also the most creative part. (Because ML-J rarely announced 'heads' in his sermons people often underestimated the importance which he gave to the need for every address to have a good 'skeleton').

Most classical music he could enjoy while reading at the same time, unlike Mrs Lloyd-Jones. He usually watched the main television news and liked programmes on current affairs, especially if they possessed an element of debate. He seldom watched or listened to 'religious' discussions unless he had reason to respect the participants. For other relaxation on television nature films and sheep dog trials were among his top choices. His childhood love for cricket and soccer never left him and he sometimes watched these on television. He had rather less interest in tennis and there was only one family visit ever made to Wimbledon.

While conversation on our trips might range over many such things, the majority of time was usually spent on contemporary church issues and problems. One issue, particularly, which has not yet emerged in these pages, tended to recur in our private discussions at this time.

It had to do with the recovery of Calvinistic convictions which, as we have seen, became such a movement among young people in the late 1950's and for which ML-J was credited with the main responsibility. He heartily disliked the word 'movement'; it smacked too much of a programme organized around personalities. In so far as he was thankful for the change in the 1950's, it was to the extent that he believed it to be a work of God. 'Thank God our efforts are producing results,' he said to those who shared his vision at the Puritan Conference of 1959, 'and far be it from any of us to despise them or under-estimate them'.[1]

But he knew human nature well enough to know that nothing is an unmixed good and there was one thing, above all else, which began to disturb him. He was concerned lest the recovery of serious reading and of sound theology was going to produce nothing more than men who were theoretically correct but whose orthodoxy was not balanced by spiritual depth and power. Instead of a generation of 'activists' the danger he saw now was that of young people who stopped at being students: 'Reading is vital; but if a man simply lives to read, he can end by being completely useless.' His concern was based, in part, on reports he received, at least one complaint per week, as I recall him telling me in 1961. Older ministers sought his help over young men in their congregations whose reading seemed to begin and end with John Owen. Christians, who now had some of these young men as their pastors, reported the length of the 'expository' sermons to which they had to listen. Others wrote to him of suffering under preaching which resembled a recording from the seventeenth century. ML-J knew that such reports were often coloured and, in part, some troubles – as they concerned younger ministers – were simply the result of youth not knowing that they cannot begin at the point reached by others only after years of

[1] *Puritans*, p. 20.

experience. As William M. Taylor points out, a young minister is prone to try to attain by one jump the height which others have reached 'by a long series of single steps in the labour of a quarter of a century'.[1] Nonetheless, there was enough truth in what he heard, and sometimes saw, to justify the disquiet he felt. His own men were putting too much emphasis on the intellectual and giving too much weight to 'authorities', to Confessions of Faith and to arguments on how the church was to be reformed. Sometimes they seemed to speak as though, given study, every problem could be solved and there was too little awareness of how those united in the doctrines of grace can all too easily become divided if they begin to insist upon the same certainty for such secondary truths as baptism and church government. Having himself done so much to impress upon these men the necessity to *think*, this was a classic case of over-reaction.

Other ministers tried to deal with these problems either by dismissing these young men or by blaming them for too much zeal for 'Calvinism' and, not surprisingly, they made little impression. ML-J saw that the danger had to be faced, but not by playing down doctrine. He knew that, to use his own words, 'When a man's whole ministry has been transformed by discovering the true theology, he is of course prepared to sacrifice anything for it'. But the emphasis needed now was that even truth, of itself, is not enough. More spirituality was required, more attention to the New Testament's call to dependence on God and, particularly, more of the joy and praise which should belong to those who are the heirs of glory. It would be absurd to consider this as a new note in ML-J's ministry: it is simply that it was, for good reason, to be more prominent in the 1960's, and it is well illustrated in his Puritan Conference addresses for 1960 and 1961 which are now in print.

*   *   *

There was a further reason why ML-J became apprehensive over a number of the younger men who looked to him for leadership and we shall find this recurring in later pages. It concerned the whole question of evangelical unity. He was convinced that the gospel itself had to be kept as the main issue if ecumenism was to be effectively countered. Important though it was that Calvinistic belief should be

[1] *The Ministry of the Word*, 1876, p. 4.

recovered, it was the broader unity of all who stood for the heart of the gospel that had to be seen as the true alternative to ecumenical unity. For evangelicals to allow themselves to be divided over secondary truths at this serious juncture in history would be like men arguing over which was the best room in a house when the whole was in danger of being burned down. It was with regard to this emphasis upon evangelical unity that some of the younger ministers close to him began to drag their feet. They did not believe, any more than he did, that an understanding of all the truths commonly called Calvinistic was a prerequisite to Christian fellowship, but they questioned any attempt at achieving an organisational unity among *ministers* which left those truths as an open question. This was their main objection to the Fellowship of Independent Evangelical Churches providing a model for a new alignment among those considering withdrawal from the major denominations.[1] ML-J's response was to say that both the congregations he had served were Arminian when he went to them and that patient, biblical teaching was able to win those whose hearts were right. To make a detailed statement of faith the starting point for the new alignment which was needed would be to cut off many who could be helped, given time, to clearer understanding.

It was understandably aggravating to Dr Lloyd-Jones that his concern for the broader unity of evangelicals was hindered by the very organisation which he had helped to establish and strengthen. While the Banner of Truth Trust republished many books of spiritual quality which were not directly related to the controversy between Calvinism and Arminianism, there was no denying that the overall influence of their reprints – and of some contemporary articles in the *Banner of Truth* magazine – was unconducive to any organisational unity between churches taking different sides in that controversy. ML-J was also apprehensive about the percentage of Presbyterian and Scottish thought which seemed to be present in the Trust and he was not pleased when the Trust organized a three day Conference for ministers at Leicester in July 1962, with two Highland Scots, Professor John Murray (not yet retired from Westminster Seminary) and Kenneth MacRae, among the main speakers. Nor did it help that this new conference coincided with the Annual Lecture of The Evangelical Library. A number of us were absent who would

[1]The Basis of Faith of the FIEC (see above p.95) was little different from the minimum statements adhered to by the evangelical societies.

normally have been at the Library Lecture and so missed hearing one of ML-J's masterly historical addresses entitled, *1662–1962: From Puritanism to Non-Conformity.*[1]

The Banner of Truth Trust gave ML-J both encouragement and problems. He remained immensely enthusiastic about the spread of the doctrines of grace but, for reasons already given above, he feared that the youthful leadership of the Trust was contributing to the danger of intellectualism and that it insufficiently recognized the need for a broader evangelical unity. He did not think that it was the business of publishers to organize conferences and he was concerned lest a doctrinaire Presbyterianism was being encouraged. On the latter point he had misgivings over the extent to which John Murray's leadership might become a force in England – a country with which the American-domiciled Scot had little acquaintance. At the same time he thought highly of Murray's gifts. When the professor gave the Evangelical Library lecture in 1964 ML-J was in the chair as usual and his welcome to the speaker included the words:

Whenever Professor Murray writes an article in *The Westminster Theological Journal*, or publishes a book, he puts us greatly in his debt. His half-commentary on the Epistle to the Romans has been a great help to many. I speak for many when I say that I hope we may expect the second half before very long, for it will cover some difficult points in the Epistle on which some of us would like some help [Laughter].

On many occasions in these years the question of the right approach to evangelical Christians of Arminian persuasion was discussed between us and with others. He was not averse to being argued with. We urged that if priority was given to the need for a broader evangelical unity then there was a danger that the doctrinal witness revived in the 1950's was going to be weakened. He replied that this was not the *present* danger and it was mistaking his whole policy to think that he favoured any weakening. 'Who understands me if even my own children misunderstand!' he exclaimed to five of us in his vestry on January 9, 1963. He went on to point out that we had to learn what he had had to learn in the mid-1930's. At first his

[1]'Essential Puritanism', he argued, 'was not primarily a preference for one form of church government rather than another; but it was that outlook and teaching which put its emphasis upon a life of spiritual, personal religion, an intense realization of the presence of God, a devotion of the entire being to Him.'

interest had been confined to Welsh Calvinistic Methodism without any wish to be involved with English evangelicals. Then he had been brought to see that it was his duty to help and not dismiss them. To which we replied that we were not dismissing anyone but whereas he might hold together a broad spectrum of evangelicals, over against ecumenism, that kind of unity was not likely to survive his absence. We also urged him to consider whether he was not over-estimating the extent to which Calvinistic convictions had taken hold. There were a number of men who were more attached to his person than to his doctrine.

It was during this discussion that he surprised us with a remark that we can better understand now than we did then. When one of the men commented on the loneliness in the work of the ministry, ML-J responded, with feeling, 'You speak of loneliness! I am the loneliest man in this room.'[1]

He continued to be troubled over the danger of which, he believed, many of us were too little conscious yet the fact that he came to speak at the second Banner of Truth Conference for ministers at Leicester in July 1964 is indicative of the basic 'family' relationship. It was an outstanding conference, with Dr Lloyd-Jones preaching from the words of Moses in Exodus 33, 'I beseech thee, shew me thy glory', and John Murray lecturing on 'The Nature and Unity of the Church'.[2] It is not common for ministers to weep in public but it happened at College Hall, Leicester, that summer.

*   *   *

Before the mid-sixties, when meetings of the Westminster Fellowship came to be overshadowed by the issue of the evangelical response to ecumenism, many subjects continued to be covered in the monthly meetings. The standard of debate and discussion was often high, helped by the contribution of a few of the older members who were better able to hold their own with ML-J. Ernest Kevan was one of

---

[1] Dr William Nadvi of Poona, India, also recalls ML-J saying with reference to his work, 'I am alone in this world'. It was not, Nadvi could see, loneliness for any personal reasons but rather the kind of loneliness which Paul knew as he stood for the Word of the gospel.

[2] ML-J's sermon was adapted from his seven sermons on Exodus 33 which were part of his series on revival, see *Revival*, pp. 148–249, and Murray's address can be read in his *Collected Writings*, vol. 2, 1977, pp. 321–35.

that number and it is a matter of regret that his attendance was less frequent from the mid-1950's. Additional work, declining health and, perhaps, the measure of difference which came to exist between him and ML-J over the vision to be imparted to young ministers, all contributed to our seeing less of him at the Fellowship and at Puritan Conferences. Some of the good-humoured exchanges between him and ML-J were long to be remembered. On one occasion, for instance, when the discussion was on the best way for ministers to present the truth to their people, Kevan was insisting on the thorough preparation of sermons. He was in full command of his audience as he insisted that a good cook saw to it that food was not only well prepared, it had also to be well presented if it was to be enjoyed. But he then made the mistake of asking his listeners to consider what this proved and before he could advance beyond his rhetorical question ML-J interjected, 'It proves you are a gourmet!'. If the Principal's ample build gave a semblance of substance to the repartee everyone knew that no such reflection was intended.

Incidents such as these were part of the appeal of discussion sessions chaired by ML-J. More was lost, however, by Ernest Kevan's gradual withdrawal from these meetings than we realized at the time. The Principal's 'spare' hours in the late fifties and early sixties were going into an intense study of the Puritans, a field in which his breadth of knowledge considerably exceeded that of ML-J. The special area of his interest was the Puritan teaching on the relationship between grace and law, involving the correct definitions of 'legalism' on the one hand and of Antinomianism on the other. On this subject he produced two valuable books, the first, *The Moral Law*, was based on the volume by Anthony Burgess, with the same title (1647), and the second was his thesis, *The Grace of Law*, A Study in Puritan Theology. For the latter he received the University of London Doctor of Philosophy degree. The extreme difficulty which he experienced in finding publishers was indicative of a very general disinterest in such seemingly obscure subjects. The Banner of Truth Trust declined both titles and so did other publishers.[1] It was the non-evangelical Carey Kingsgate Press which finally brought out *The Grace of Law* in 1964.

The fact was that despite the resurgent interest in the Puritans Dr Kevan had few to believe him when he urged that the Puritan opposition to Antinomianism was still very relevant and important.

---

[1] *The Moral Law* was made available in the United States by Sovereign Grace Publishers, Jenkintown, 1963.

Seventeenth century Antinomians had argued that it was 'legalism' for Christians to look for any 'signs' of grace in themselves for assurance instead of looking to Christ alone; and it was legalism, also, they judged, for preachers to believe that the law has any part in the conversion of sinners or that it has a function in the life of the believer. These points seemed to be very theoretical in the early sixties for such opinions were virtually unknown among Christians of Reformed convictions.

If Dr Lloyd-Jones at this date had been more familiar with the history of Antinomianism I think he might have been more guarded on a point closely connected with this long-forgotten 17th-century debate. With regard to assurance of salvation, he held that there were three ways in which it may be gained: first, by the Christian's consciousness of his own faith in the promises of Scripture; second, by self-examination in the light of such 'tests' of spiritual life as are found in the First Epistle of John; and third, by the testimony of the Holy Spirit. The only respect in which this formulation differs from the *Westminster Confession of Faith* (chapter xviii) is that the *Confession* says nothing for or against the belief that the testimony of the Spirit provides a third way to full assurance, distinct and separable from the first and second. ML-J regarded the witness of the Spirit not only as distinct but as the true secret of revivals and he concurred heartily with the words of Dr John Duncan that 'experimentally it goes into the very essence of religion'.[1]

Speaking of the 'three main ways in which assurance comes to us,' ML-J said in 1957, 'Often in these days, unfortunately, only the first one is stressed'.[2] He certainly did not neglect the second – the evidence of a changed life – but he stated the third in a manner which could too easily be disparaging to the first and second. The first two grounds of assurance, he would say, come from the Christian's own deductions drawn from his faith in the promises of salvation or from the signs of the grace of God in his life, whereas the third is a

[1] *In the Pulpit and at the Communion Table*, Edinburgh, 1874, p. 57. Speaking of the three means of assurance Duncan says of the third: 'Not only does the Spirit of God bring out His own graces into vivid exercise (No. 1); and not only is He pleased, especially at times, to shine upon these – without which the believer's perception of them (No. 2) is dark and indistinct – this testimony is something more. It is the Father and the Son communicating with the souls of believers by the Holy Ghost by means of the truth; and in this lies very mainly the secret of experimental religion.'
[2] *Authority*, 1958 (1984, p. 76).

'direct' assurance, 'immediately' given by the Holy Spirit. So stated, this distinction could readily be employed – as it had been by 17th century Antinomians – to render the first two forms of assurance needless and worthless: 'having assurance by God's Spirit,' said the Antinomians, 'what need is there of evidences by inherent graces? This is to light a candle when the sun shines'. The answer of many of the Puritans to this was to emphasise the truth that Christians are dependent upon the Holy Spirit for *all* forms of assurance.[1] The conscious activity of true faith, and the presence of grace in the believer's life, are equally the work of the Spirit; and therefore a testimony of the Spirit to the Christian's sonship, which appears to come direct from heaven, without reference to his faith or life, is not to be sought or regarded as something vastly superior to the assurance which is connected to faith and sanctification. Conscious communion with God is heaven on earth but in the teaching of Scripture it is not separable from believing and obedience. 'The testimony of the Spirit,' writes Anthony Burgess, 'and the evidence of graces make up one complete witness and therefore are not to be disjoined, much less opposed'.[2]

If all this should appear to the reader as a distraction, the relevance will be better understood by later developments which none of us anticipated at this date. The teaching contained in the titles by Dr Kevan which fell almost stillborn on to the market in the years

[1] ML-J, of course, also believed this and could say, 'It is a great fallacy to think, that God must always work directly or he is not working at all' (*Sanctified Through the Truth*, 1989, p. 58). But I am speaking above of the emphasis in his teaching.

[2] *A Treatise of Grace and Assurance*, 1652, p. 48, see also p. 672. For ML-J on 'indirect' and 'direct' assurance see *Authority*, pp. 76–78; *Ephesians*, vol. 1, pp. 274–79; *Romans*, vol. 7, pp. 302–4; *Puritans*, pp. 198–200 etc. Thomas Horton (*Sermons on the Eighth Chapter of Romans*, published posthumously in 1674) uses the same formulation as ML-J on 'the witness of the Spirit' but later Puritans became more guarded (e.g. Thomas Brooks, *Works*, vol. 2, p. 518 f; vol. 3, pp. 251–52, 469 f; John Owen, *Works*, vol. 6, p. 594. See also *Jonathan Edwards*, A New Biography, Iain H. Murray, 1987, pp. 489–90, and the testimony of Welsh Calvinistic Methodists against treating the testimony of the Spirit as a separate witness: 'An occasion was found to notice the indispensable necessity of walking with God, and of living a spiritual life, in order to retain an assurance of hope as to our eternal state . . . the witness of the Spirit is given to those who are led by the Spirit, and who live according to the Spirit. The confidence that we are children – and the obedience of children – and the nurture of children, *go together inseparably*' (Minutes of an Association at Llanvair, 1796, in *Essays and Letters of Thomas Charles*, ed. E. Morgan, 1836, pp. 468–70).

[464]

1963–64 was going to be greatly needed before the end of the next decade.

*   *   *

Before leaving these memories from the early years of the 1960's there are two other meetings which must be mentioned. Ex-members of Westminster Chapel could become 'Friends of Westminster Chapel' and an annual occasion which these 'Friends' who lived in the greater London area never missed, if they could help it, was the 'At Home' held every September when everyone could meet Dr and Mrs Lloyd-Jones personally over tea and then hear him give an account of their summer holidays. These were bright occasions. His résumé of their doings was always full of interest, not without humour, and concluded with some brief lessons and words of exhortation. No matter what his subject he had an incredible ability to send people away uplifted and encouraged. Regrettably, on his orders, these accounts of holidays and travels were never taped or taken down in shorthand, but some of us did take our own notes and from these I can report his two summers abroad in 1961 and 1963.

In 1961, with Mrs Lloyd-Jones and Ann, he made his first and only visit to Greece and his account of the weeks there, from August 1 to 28, was one of the finest which he ever gave on these occasions. The principal invitation had come from Argos Zodhiates, the pastor at Kateríni, whose departure to Canada had been so instantly reversed by the sermon he heard in Westminster Chapel in October 1957. Since that date there had been some reduction of persecution and the church had prospered so that Mr Zodhiates was now assisted by a graduate of London Bible College who was a former member of the congregation at Westminster.

The first part of their journey across Europe was by train through Paris and Milan to Genoa where they boarded a boat which sailed at 6 p.m. To ML-J's disappointment as an admirer of Napoleon ('not as a man but from the standpoint of human greatness') they did not see Corsica or Elba. This was more than compensated by six hours ashore at Naples the following afternoon when they were able to visit Pompeii, so amazingly excavated after its destruction in AD 79. Drusilla, named in the passage in Acts 24:24–25 from which ML-J had so often preached, had perished there. He would have liked to spend days in Pompeii. Naples impressed him with its beauty and poverty, 'a typical Roman Catholic city'. They reached the Straits of Messina by 8 o'clock the next morning and spent the rest of that day, Friday, crossing the lower part of the Adriatic. Saturday morning brought a wonderful first sight of Greece, with its brown mountains rising behind the vivid blue of the Bay of Corinth, and at 2 p.m. 'in indescribable heat', second only to the heat he remembered in Los Angeles, they landed at the port of Athens. After 'siesta time' and tea, there was time before sunset to visit the monument to the 'Sea God', erected on a promontory south of the city to terrify invaders.

At this point in his address ML-J digressed to remind everyone why the history of Greece was so important. The Greeks were a remarkable people, very intelligent and the civilizers of the ancient world. Their marvellous literature included the historians, Herodotus and Thucydides, the latter with his marked care over facts. And yet the glory that was Greece all came to an end three centuries before Paul had landed there.

Sunday, August 6 he preached in the morning in the First Presbyterian Church and at the Second in the evening. The next two days were spent sightseeing in Athens, beginning with the Parthenon on top of the Acropolis. This temple to the goddess Athena built five or six centuries before Christ and yet with its roof preserved until bombarded by the Venetians in 1687, he viewed with 'sheer astonishment'. But the less-noticed rocky hill called the Areopagus, below the western foot of the Acropolis, interested him far more and fortified with a bottle of peach juice in the 'tremendous heat', they climbed up to the spot where Paul had stood and visualized the scene described in Acts 17:22. From there it was down into the old market place, the Agora, with the ruins of temples still showing how the men of Athens were 'too superstitious'. Then on to the Pnyx, the place for public discussion in ancient Athens, where the great statesmen and orators from Pericles to Demosthenes had all spoken.

Anticipating the enquiry, 'How does Athens compare with Rome?', ML-J thought it a difficult question: 'I still think I have to put Rome first. There is more of the ancient world in Rome, with buildings from a longer period and you can see the development of the church. Greece became a tragedy. They fought one another and ruined themselves. It is a picture of the glory of man which does not last and comes to nothing. "For all flesh is as grass, and all glory of man as the flower of grass." Man is an amazing creature and Greece is a monument to his greatness and to his failure.'

On Wednesday morning, August 9 they set off by car, crossed the Corinthian canal and lunched in the new Corinth before driving south into the Peloponnese. The remainder of the day was spent visiting the ruins of Mycenae, where King Agamemnon flourished about 1200 BC, and then the great amphitheatre seating 1,600 people at Epidaurus. The next morning they returned to Corinth and explored the remains of the old city, including 'the judgment seat', before which Paul stood. 'It gave me great pleasure,' said ML-J, to tread in places where he must have put his feet and to mount the steps' (cf. Acts 18:17). They could not have lingered long for the same day, after a two hour journey by ferry, they made the steep ascent to Delphi on Mount Parnassus. It would fill a page to attempt to give ML-J's vivid description of Delphi – 'an astounding place' – with its temple, amphitheatre and stadium (combining religion, drama and athletics) and the modern museum. Commenting on the hill-top positions of Greek temples, he said: 'When they made worship involve a climb and an effort they at least knew that it was to be regarded as a privilege. We have made our religion too cheap. They understood that much.'

After spending Thursday night at Delphi, most of Friday was spent in a car journey to Kateríni, their destination on the east coast below Thessaloniki. The route included the crossing of three mountains and the great plain of Thessaly before they reached the Zodhiateses at eleven o'clock at night. The Presbyterian church which Argos Zodhiates served was made up almost entirely of refugees forced to flee from Asia Minor in 1923, and ML-J was perhaps surprised to face a congregation 1,200 strong on the Sunday morning. Monday was spent quietly with a visit to a peach farm before further travel on Tuesday, August 15, which was to be one of the most memorable days in his life as far as sightseeing was concerned. First there was the 60 mile drive to Thessaloniki, then on through Amphipolis to the ruins of Philippi, the birthplace of the church in Europe. Here they saw the remains of the Agora and of the prison (which he believed to be authentic) where Paul and Silas were held, with a cell which they entered. 'But,' said the speaker, 'the thing at Philippi that moved me more than anything else that I saw was the river, flowing as it always has, and it did not need any imagination to picture the scene which Paul saw when he "went out of the city by a river side" (Acts 16:13). I would like to have spent a week walking up and down that river bank. It saw the first preaching in Europe, to a few women, and yet out of it came all the churches of the West!'

They were now 165 miles from Katerini, but as they were to return the same day, ML-J took the wheel back to Thessaloniki, and the fact that they were on the same road that Paul travelled probably made it none too long for him. After a rest on Wednesday he preached on Thursday in the struggling little evangelical church in Berea and then, on Friday at Leptokaria, a church camping centre on the coast at the foot of Mount Olympus, a ten day conference began with some 400 people present, including a number of ministers and elders. One of ML-J's main impressions of this conference was of the spiritual hunger shown by the people and their evident thirst for the Word of God. Meetings began daily about 7 o'clock and, apart from a siesta every afternoon from lunch until 4 p.m., they went on until about 9.45 at night. ML-J preached every morning at 11 a.m. On the final Sunday, August 27, he preached at Thessaloniki in the morning before returning for the final service of the conference the same afternoon. He spoke of those days beside the Aegean as ones never to be forgotten, and felt it had been 'a great privilege' to be among people who were not only warm and hospitable, but ready to endure hardships for Christ's sake. 'They asked me to ask you to pray for them and they wanted books.'[1]

All this is but a glimpse of an address that lasted two hours in its duration, with illuminating excursions into Greek history, national and spiritual, ancient and modern. He did not miss underlining the significance of the fact that the Greek Presbyterian churches still suffered persecution from the Greek Orthodox, even though both bodies were supposedly united in the World Council of Churches. He admired the special charm and beauty of the scenery, but was 'convinced that the beauty of *England* remained supreme'. Whether there was a slip of the tongue in the last sentence we never asked him! Perhaps one example of ML-J's humour should be included from his narrative. He reported how Professor R. A. Finlayson, of the Free Church College, Edinburgh, had also visited Katerini a few years earlier. One day when travelling with a Greek friend, whose English was somewhat imperfect, they stopped at a roadside cafe to eat.

[1] Argos Zodhiates was a Greek Cypriot who held a British passport. He was always refused a Greek passport and in 1962, on the instigation of Bishop Barnabas of Katerini, the authorities compelled him to leave the country. Attempting to re-enter in 1963, he was turned back at the border. Many of his parishioners migrated to North America and in 1969 there were sufficient of them in Boston to call Argos to be their pastor. This work he fulfilled for the last ten years of his life.

Being 'none too robust', Professor Finlayson's concern for his digestion led him to play for safety and ask for soup. But when the soup at length arrived the Professor was scarcely put at ease by its appearance, and particularly by one or two small bones which were visible. Whatever the smell was, it gave away nothing as to the soup's true identity and so, with some apprehension, the Scots visitor enquired of his friend, 'What is this soup?'. 'Oh, very good, our best,' was the reply. Then, seeing that Finlayson was obviously still hesitant, his fellow-traveller added, 'It is citten soup'. 'Did you say *kitten?*' responded the startled professor. 'Yes, very good!' 'You mean kitten, *miaow-miaow?*' 'Oh, no!' said his host, struggling to find words, 'chitten, *cock-a-doodle-doo . . .*' With some variations, this story was to go round the British Isles.

The Lloyd-Joneses left Greece on Monday, August 28 by train and the same train took them through Yugoslavia, Austria, Germany and Belgium to Ostend which they reached on Wednesday morning, to be home again at Victoria Station, London by 4.15 p.m.

*   *   *

Dr Lloyd-Jones' only other visit abroad in the first half of the sixties was to the United States in 1963. He had not been there since 1956. The fact of that visit has already been mentioned in these pages. He gave one of his usual accounts at the 'At Home' on September 19, 1963, and from that source, chiefly, I give the following summary.

Their voyage out in July was followed by the three days spent largely at the Boltens' seaside home, as already mentioned. Of this ML-J said nothing to the people at Westminster but he did tell them of their enjoyment of a visit to the reconstructed settlement of the Pilgrim Fathers at Plymouth while they were in New England. From there they took the long train journey to Winona Lake Conference Center in Indiana. It was their third visit but due to some confusion in communication, they were a day early and consequently arrived while another conference on 'Rescue Missions' was still in progress. With characteristic American cordiality, the strangers from Britain were welcomed and they were not entirely unknown, for someone was aware that ML-J's name appeared on the notepaper of the Thames Embankment Mission.[1] That evening the late-comers to the

[1]ML-J was a vice-president of the organisation, as he was of a number of other evangelical agencies.

Missions conference were invited to an evening banquet, at which
the chairman drew attention to their presence with the words, 'I am
very delighted and honoured to introduce Mr and Mrs Jones of the
Thames Embankment Mission'. (Later in their travels an unexpected
elevation was to follow. As ML-J stood among a number of people
who wished to speak to him beneath the pulpit after a service, a lady
was heard to remark, 'I do not want to be a busybody but I do think
that a chair should have been provided for the bishop!').

Once the conference for which they had come (Fuller Summer
Seminary) began, their anonymity disappeared and he had to speak
eight times within a week. In four morning sessions, which were the
Campbell Morgan Memorial Lectures, his subject was 'The Preacher'.
From this beautiful spot they moved on – via Washington ('one of
the greatest cities I have ever been in') – to another conference, this
time in Asheville, North Carolina, for six days. A further long rail
journey brought them back to Newark (New Jersey) just in time to
alight from a train at 9.30 on a Sunday morning with no time to do
anything but go straight into the pulpit of the church in Hawthorne
where he was expected. In reporting this he explained: 'I had never
heard of it, my arrangements were all made for me. Friends send me
where they think my ministry will be most useful.' There was to be a
week of meetings in the Hawthorne church followed by a Sunday
with Stephen Olford at Calvary Baptist Church in New York.

The following week the meetings of the Sixth General Committee
of the IFES, which were the main purpose of his visit, began at
Nyack and continued from August 21 to 31. The Lloyd-Joneses had
the novel experience of travelling the 20 or so miles to Nyack, up the
Hudson, in a speedboat. There were 86 delegates from the 26
national movements which then formed the IFES. Other speakers
came from as far as Latin America, India and the Philippines. Special
subjects discussed included 'Ecumenical Problems and Their Relationship to Evangelical Christianity', 'Roman Catholicism Today'
and 'Christian Unity'. In a printed report of the conference in *His*
magazine there are several quotations from ML-J, including the
following: 'There is a pernicious doctrine abroad that we can receive
Christ as Saviour without receiving Him as Lord. You cannot receive
Christ in bits and pieces.' 'Our great danger today is to start with
ourselves and end with ourselves. We are so subjective.'

In the midst of this very busy period there was also time for a visit
to a house where Whitefield once stayed and to the grounds of the

Rockefeller mansion. At its conclusion the next engagements were in Philadelphia before a three-day car journey via the Niagara Falls to Toronto. They arrived in Toronto on September 6 in time for the wedding of Leigh Powell, a former member of Westminster Chapel. On Sunday, and on the evenings of Monday and Tuesday, there were services at Knox Church where William Fitch had been the minister since 1955. Dr Fitch, who had served in Scotland until the age of forty-four, has written of how, in his decision to emigrate, God used Martyn Lloyd-Jones' insistence that he should take the call to Knox.[1] Leaving Toronto after the evening service on Tuesday, September 10, they were just in time to catch the 'Queen Elizabeth' sailing from New York the next day.

Despite the strenuous nature of this fifth visit to America, ML-J returned refreshed and invigorated. Two things had especially interested him. First, there was the movement (not yet called charismatic) which, having begun in California, was now widespread in the States. His comments on this, given at the Evangelical Library meeting of December 5, 1963, we will notice in the next chapter. Second, that amid much confusion, there were evident signs of a new interest in Reformed and Puritan teaching and of the part which Westminster Chapel was playing in it. He said at the 'At Home':

I never imagined the effect of the two volumes on the *Sermon on the Mount*. Many have said that these books have changed their ministries . . . Numbers of people read the *Westminster Record*. I say this so we may realize the responsibility which rests upon us. People are utterly bewildered. They want scriptural exposition. Ministers are looking to us, after finding an absence of what they want in their own country . . . This visit has done me great good. It has made me see our peculiar task, more than ever before. We need the Holy Spirit. The times are desperate and really urgent. There is the whole problem of the emerging nations. Our responsibility is almost crushing. But with the Word of God open before us, and the power of the Spirit, we shall be sufficient. It is frightening to think of others looking at us. If we make a false move the consequences upon others may be incalculable. I have just finished my twenty-fifth year. I need physical and spiritual strength, and spiritual wisdom to discern the signs of the times. The times are desperate and the time is short.

[1] *Knox Church, Toronto*, 1971, p. 108.

I am speaking particularly to those good, honest, spiritually-minded men and women who are longing for revival and reawakening, longing to see the church speaking with power in this evil age . . . For it is your very anxiety to know the fullness and the baptism of the Spirit that constitutes your danger and exposes you to this possibility of not using your critical faculties as you should . . . You may say, 'Well now surely anything that makes me feel greater love to God must be right'. Robert Baxter, to whom I have already referred in connection with the Irvingite movement, used to say that he had never felt so much love, the love of God in his heart, as he did at this period . . . but he came to see that it had all been misleading him.

Feb 14, 1965, *Prove All Things*, pp. 67–68

23

Cross-Winds

Dr Lloyd-Jones' choice for what was to be his last major series of Sunday morning sermons at Westminster Chapel points to his uppermost concern for Christians in the 1960's. On October 4, 1962 he began to preach from the first chapter of the Gospel of John, indicating to the congregation that what he had in view was not a verse-by-verse exposition but rather an application of the teaching 'which is found in this Gospel to the state and condition of the Christian in this world'. The theme of that teaching, he believed, is 'the fullness of the Lord Jesus Christ available for His people', and it demanded sustained attention because 'there is no doubt that the greatest trouble at the present time is that we are living so far short of what we should be, what is offered us here and what is possible to us'. The church was failing because 'we are ever reducing this Gospel, making something small of it, and so giving non-Christians the impression that Christianity is something small, narrow, cramped, confined, instead of being this glorious thing that is here indicated by our blessed Lord'. 'The main trouble in the Church today – and I am speaking of evangelical churches in particular at this point – is the appalling superficiality.'[1]

This state of things, as we have already seen, he connected directly with the prevalent lack of personal acquaintance with the power of the Holy Spirit and a consequent lack of joy and of full assurance. In his sermons on Revival in 1959 he had taught what he claimed was 'the old evangelical view' of the work of the Spirit, namely, that although the Spirit is present in all Christians there are times when His influences are outpoured in an extraordinary manner. But virtually no other evangelical leader was preaching this and almost the only books available on the subject were the older works of

[1]*Romans*, vol. 7, p. 278, a sermon preached on December 16, 1960.

George Smeaton and Octavius Winslow reprinted, with ML-J's encouragement, by the Banner of Truth Trust.[1]

While part of the answer to the existing conditions which ML-J saw had to be a clearer understanding of particular texts, there was the greater need for a broad view of the whole subject of Christian experience. This he now took up from the Gospel of John. How he *approached* the theme is of particular significance for it contrasts sharply with the approach subsequently taken by others when, after long years of neglect, the Holy Spirit again became a subject of general interest. He began by dealing mainly (Oct 1962 – June 1963) with the two truths in the Prologue of John's Gospel which he considered to be 'basic to our full enjoyment of the gospel'. These were, first, what God has done in His Son and, second, the fallen, sinful state of man which alone explains the need for what God has done.

In order to the possession of full assurance these great objective truths had first to be understood. Summarizing the ground already covered, he said on January 13, 1963, 'We have tried to see – and I think we have succeeded – that so many people are lacking in this joy and assurance because they have never fully realised what salvation has done to them, what they have been saved from, both in themselves and in their relationship to the law of God'. He then went on to preach on the privileges the believer already possesses, including sonship and the indwelling of the Holy Spirit. 'It is not primarily a matter of experience, it is primarily a matter of understanding. We have no right to come to the subjective until we have understood the objective . . . You start with your doctrine.' Although the deepening of true Christian experience was his main concern he knew very well that the scriptural method of teaching is not to concentrate on experience as such.

It was entirely undesigned that ML-J began this series from the Gospel of John at virtually the same time as news broke in England of what was claimed to be the beginning of a remarkable revival in California. The events which were reported bore similarities to what was familiar to Pentecostalists but the context was very different, for the two clergymen initially involved, Dennis Bennett and Frank Maguire, served parishes in the Episcopal Church. Both men believed that they had been 'baptised in the Spirit' and also that they

---

[1] *The Doctrine of the Holy Spirit*, George Smeaton, 1882, was reprinted 1958, and Winslow's *The Work of the Holy Spirit*, 1843, in 1961.

had received the gift of tongues. In April 1960 some 70 people in Bennett's Church of St Mark's at Van Nuys gave the same testimony and 'many sick were now healed by the power of God'.[1]

With the inauguration of *Trinity* magazine in 1961 news began to spread of these unexpected happenings in churches which had no history of Pentecostal tradition. More than anything else, however, it was the pen of ML-J's friend, Philip Hughes which first alerted attention in England. Hughes was then living in London and was the Editor of the evangelical Anglican journal the *Churchman*. While visiting the USA in 1962 he was invited by Jean Stone, founder of *Trinity*, to visit California and to judge what was happening for himself. Hughes accepted and as he reported to ML-J on his return, he was impressed and enthusiastic. In an editorial in the September 1962 issue of the *Churchman* he described his Californian visit and concluded:

There are already indications of a new movement of the Holy Spirit within the Church at the present time. Is this something for which we are ready? Are we willing, do we long for a divine tide of blessing to flow over us? That tide is even now on its way.[2]

The Westminster Fellowship was probably the first forum in England where this report from the United States was discussed. At the meeting of October 8, 1962, ML-J introduced the subject and read part of the testimony of Dennis Bennett. He expressed no kind of verdict on what was being reported but used the subject to lead into our need to know more *conscious* dealings with the Spirit of God. There was, he urged, an important distinction between the work of the Spirit which is normal, on-going and less consciously experienced (i.e. Ephesians 5:18) and that which may suddenly happen as in Acts 4:31, 'And when they had prayed, the place was shaken where they were assembled together; and they were all filled with the Holy Ghost, and they spake the word of God with boldness'. The latter verse describes precisely what happens in a revival yet we were failing, he believed, to keep this possibility in the forefront of our minds. Our danger was to

[1] *As at the Beginning*, The Twentieth Century Pentecostal Revival, Michael Harper, 1965, p. 63.
[2] These are the words quoted by Harper (*Ibid*, p. 86). The article was reprinted in a pirated edition with, says Harper, 'over 60,000 copies being sold in the autumn of 1962 and in 1963'.

be so afraid of wrong experiences or to be so absorbed in our own routine and activities that we look for nothing beyond the ordinary.

In the heart-searching discussion which followed ML-J referred to what had happened to him in the summer of 1949. It was, as far as I know, about the only reference he made to those experiences in the fraternal and it was very brief. He said nothing of the date or the circumstances and his hesitation in saying anything at all was so obvious that the question was put to him, 'Should we not make such experiences known?'. To this he promptly replied that it is the doctrinal message of the possibilities of such knowledge and communion with God which must go first. Further, while we may, as preachers, indicate in a general way our knowledge of these realities, it is the people's consciousness that we are speaking from experience which makes our words convicting. There is, therefore, no need for a preacher to introduce his own personal experience directly.[1]

We have noted, many years before this, ML-J's private words to Philip Hughes, 'I pray daily for revival', and it had long been his attitude to listen eagerly to any reports that pointed in that direction. He was, for instance, greatly encouraged by news passed on to him by missionaries of an evident work of the Spirit in the Congo in the 1950's. He was similarly hopeful of what he heard from the West Coast of the United States and unprepared to question the existence of a true awakening solely because of the presence of features which were unusual. He knew that in every revival excesses can be found alongside what is undoubtedly of God. And he was not prepared to exclude, in principle, the possibility of any restoration of extraordinary gifts.

The year 1963 brought further developments and these were much closer at hand. St Mark's, Gillingham, a dockland parish in Kent, has been described as the parish where 'the charismatic renewal first surfaced in the Church of England'.[2] David Watson believed it was in February 1963 that a number engaged in nights of prayer for revival at St Mark's 'were gently aware of being filled with the Spirit'.[3] Watson (formerly a curate at St Mark's) knew a similar experience in Cambridge at about the same time while another Anglican, Michael Harper, who was a curate with John Stott at All

---

[1]There are experiences, he says in *Romans*, vol. 7, pp. 367–68, of which the Christian is 'almost afraid to speak'. Glib speech about 'great experiences' is a sign of the counterfeit.
[2]*David Watson, a portrait by his friends*, ed. Edward England, 1985, p. 55.
[3]*You are my God*, D. Watson, 1983, p. 54.

Souls in London, believed that the same thing had happened to him some months earlier.

On April 9, 1963, Watson and Harper, along with their senior, John Collins, the rector of St Mark's, Gillingham, went to tell ML-J what was happening and to speak of their hopes. They went to him clearly because it was his preaching more than anything else which had heralded the need of revival. Harper was frequently at Westminster Chapel for the Friday night meetings in the 1950's and Watson regarded him as 'a man whose ministry we immensely respected and whose concern for revival was well known'. [1] I believe that ML-J was stirred by what he heard from these men. Their attitude and testimonies concerning the Holy Spirit were in marked contrast with much that was customary in evangelical Anglicanism. After listening to them, Watson records that he said, 'Gentlemen, I believe that you have been baptized with the Holy Spirit', and he encouraged them to press on. [2] Further contacts between him and these young Anglicans were to develop. Harper became a member of the Westminster Fellowship and ML-J made a personal visit to St Mark's, Gillingham.

As has now been documented in various books, these years mark the start in England of what has since become known world-wide as the charismatic movement. What has not been explained is why Dr Lloyd-Jones' name barely appears in these same records of a movement in which he had this initial interest. There is no reference to him at all in Michael Harper's *As at the Beginning*, The Twentieth Century Pentecostal Revival, 1965, nor in Andrew Walker's *Restoring the Kingdom* published exactly twenty years later. Peter Hocken, in the fullest account to date, *Streams of Renewal*: The Origins and Early Development of the Charismatic Movement in Great Britain, 1986, mentions ML-J only three times and then as a very marginal figure. When it is remembered that charismatic literature has never been slow to publicise the support of well-known figures – as exemplified by the Hughes article of September 1962 – this silence cannot be without significance.

[1] *You are my God*, p. 56.
[2] *Ibid*, p. 57. The accuracy of Watson's memory is not perfect for he dates ML-J's summer experiences in 1949 as being 'shortly after the Hebrides Revival' which did not begin until November 1949. On the so-called 'Lewis Awakening' see *Diary of Kenneth MacRae*, edited by Iain H. Murray, Banner of Truth, 1980, p. 443 ff.

I will touch on the explanation here and say more in later chapters. During 1963 ML-J had further opportunity to consider the claims increasingly being made on both sides of the Atlantic. In May 1963 he heard Frank Maguire of California when he spoke to a private meeting of ministers in London and, later that summer when he was himself in the States, he met a number who were connected with the neo-pentecostal or 'tongues movement' as it was being commonly called.[1] Philip Hughes, also, was further involved as he accepted an invitation from Jean Stone to fly to Los Angeles to speak at a major congress lasting several days. Of this second visit to California Hughes writes to me:

I learnt that they had me marked down to be the leader of the charismatic movement in Great Britain! But it was a time of disillusionment for me. The insistence that everyone could and should speak in tongues and that it was the evidence of the 'reception' of the Holy Spirit was unbiblical, also the opinion widely accepted that it was open for a person to have all the gifts; and I was appalled to see them inducing glossolalia by telling people to make noises as they laid hands on them, in fact placing the ear to the candidate's throat to listen and encourage it. I told them what they needed was a week of solid Bible study rather than a week of the sort of meetings we were having. The signs of true revival were missing and I saw no evidence of powerful preaching, no sense of the awesome majesty of Almighty God, and no concern for purity of doctrine in conformity with the canon of Holy Scripture.

ML-J was not in California during his 1963 visit to the States but what he had heard and read led him to the same conclusion as Hughes. Both men considered that there was a genuine element in the events in America. There was reason to hope that numbers had been converted but conversions were being wrongly interpreted as second experiences of the Spirit. Instead of regarding themselves as spiritual babes, these Christians (under the influence of Pentecostal theories) claimed to know a special 'baptism of the Spirit' which they considered proved by the evidence of their speaking in tongues.

Of particular concern both to Hughes and ML-J was the influence at this point of the South African pastor, David du Plessis, who had become closely associated with *Trinity* magazine and its message.

[1]These descriptive terms were to remain in general use for some time. On November 19, 1964, for instance, ML-J's friend, Pastor R. G. Tucker, in a letter to him, said, 'I think we shall be in the "Tongues Movement", for a while' (meaning that he feared it was going to be more than a passing phenomenon).

Lecturing at Princeton in 1959, du Plessis criticized the many missionaries he had seen who took such pains to make Africans 'Roman Catholics, Lutherans, Calvinists and Methodists'. 'My whole being,' he proceeded, 'rebelled against this kind of mission. Our Pentecostal Mission flourished because we did not have books or creeds or catechisms to teach Africans. We gave them the Bible . . .'[1] But, with all his disparagement of doctrine, du Plessis did thorough work in inculcating Pentecostalist views upon Christians in California and elsewhere and it was his interpretation of the 'movement' in America which was broadcast around the world.[2]

Disappointed by the second visit of Philip Hughes, the *Trinity* magazine organization found the spokesman they were looking for among the English Anglicans in Michael Harper and it was Harper who invited du Plessis to speak to another private meeting of ministers in London in October 1963. The Pentecostal pastor accepted and to those who gathered to hear him he made no secret of the fact that he had just come from the opening meetings of the Second Vatican Council.

Several factors were now combining to increase ML-J's apprehensions. Until the autumn of 1963 the men in England who had spoken to him of their new anointing by the Spirit had known nothing of any tongues speaking but following the visit of du Plessis, and others from the States, these same men now began to regard their experiences as part of a greater work of the Spirit of which the visitors spoke – a work in which tongues were the visible proof of the supernatural. While ML-J did not rule out in principle the possibility of any restoration of the gift of tongues, the means by which 'the gift' was promoted in the States (as he had heard from Hughes), together with the circumstances of its appearance in England, disturbed him. In a letter of November 29, 1968, looking back to 1963, he says on the subject of tongues:

I felt that a psychological element seemed to have come in in that connection in several people known to me in this country. I mean by that that several who had had the baptism with the Spirit and had rejoiced in

[1] *As at the Beginning*, p. 94.
[2] I do not mean, of course, that du Plessis introduced Pentecostal ideas to Maguire, Bennett, Stone and others for it is now clear that those ideas were present from the outset but, as Hocken says, du Plessis had 'a quite distinctive role. More than any other leader, du Plessis contributed to the self-understanding of the new movement and demonstrated its international character.' *Streams of Renewal*, p. 134.

it for several months only began to speak in tongues when the Pentecostal pastor, David du Plessis came to this country. Then suddenly they all began to speak in tongues. I cannot quite reconcile that with the Lordship of the Spirit in this matter.[1]

At this point in time it was not clear that du Plessis, more than anyone else, was going to be the spokesman for the new movement but ML-J feared that his teaching both on tongues and on the baptism of the Spirit amounted to inducing experiences which were nothing more than psychological. He was still more concerned at the encouragement which du Plessis gave to the ecumenical down-grading of the importance of true doctrine.

It was this latter point which ML-J took up in his address at the Annual Meeting of the Evangelical Library on December 5, 1963, when he spoke at some length on his visit to the States during the previous summer:

The thing everybody is talking about in America today is the recrudes-cence, if you like, of interest in the gifts of the Holy Spirit. In certain old sections of the Christian Church, such as the Anglicans, Lutherans, Methodists and so on, there has been this revival of interest in the gifts of the Holy Spirit, with a very special attention being given to the whole question of tongues. In other words, if you listen superficially in America you come to the conclusion that the old denominations in America are rapidly becoming Pentecostalist. I do not think that is true, but that is the general impression you get.

But there is another side to this picture – and this is what interested me – and that is that amongst the Pentecostalists there is more definitely an awakening interest in Reformed theology and a great desire and craving for these very books that our Library possesses, and which it loans to various people in different parts of the world. This is not only confined to America as it happens. It is equally true in this country. I have with increasing frequency had the pleasure of meeting either men who are in the Pentecostal ministry or training for it, and who come to me to tell me that they have started reading Reformed theology. This has led to a real crisis for some of them. I know certain men who have actually gone out of the ministry of the Pentecostal Church because of this and there are others who at the moment are reading, and reading very deeply, and anxious to be more and more instructed. It is very interesting to observe how these things work. They feel that the Pentecostal movement, and especially as it is represented in their churches, seems to be waning in this and in most other countries, and they are beginning to wonder, some of

[1]To J. A. Schep at Geelong, Australia.

them, why that is; and the conclusion they have arrived at is that it is due to lack of teaching. The only teaching they have found which can satisfy them is the teaching which is known as the Reformed Theology. So they are reading this with great avidity both in America and in this country. Last week I was in Scotland and a well-known minister was telling me that he had gone into a certain bookroom and found two young men browsing round and picking out some of the recent Banner of Truth publications. He began to talk to them and found that they were two Pentecostal ministers. They told him precisely the story that some of them have told me.

So, you see, there is this extraordinary change taking place. Some of the older denominations seem to be looking more or less in the direction of Pentecostal teaching, whereas the Pentecostalists themselves in their dissatisfaction are looking in the direction of Reformed Theology. Now the tragedy is this, that the older denominations which, because of their own utter bankruptcy are looking to this Pentecostal teaching, do not look also to the Reformed teaching. It would give them the satisfaction they need, but refusing to do that, they are now turning in the other direction.

There is a minister in America – he has published it in a book so I can refer to it – a well-known Pentecostal leader, David du Plessis originally a South African. He was a well-known Pentecostal minister in the U.S.A., but he now spends the whole of his time going round speaking under the auspices of the World Council of Churches. He has been greatly befriended by the late President of Princeton Theological Seminary, Dr John A. Mackay, who had him to address the students at Princeton. He has also been present at and addressed Assemblies like the Faith and Order Conferences which have been held in St Andrews, and this last year in Montreal in Canada. This man has now got open doors amongst these leaders of the old denominations who constitute the World Council of Churches. They are obviously very ready to listen to his message. Unfortunately, in that message he says that doctrine does not matter, that what matters is a living experience. That is what they are ready to believe in their bankruptcy because they are not Reformed in their doctrine. They are ready to listen to a man who can speak in an authoritative manner on the basis of personal experience. Doctrine is being discounted and experience is being exalted at its expense.

Now this is an extremely interesting phenomenon, because while all that is going on, this other movement to which I have referred is going on as well. That is where we come in, in particular. The people who have been for years in that movement which placed all the emphasis on experience and who are most thoughtful and intelligent, are very dissatisfied and are looking to us. So in the providence of God who knows how all this may work out?

Well, that is one thing which to me is really encouraging. Another thing I met there – and I want to report this also – is that there is obviously an increasing number of people in that country who are more and more dissatisfied with the superficiality of the life of their churches, and who are longing for something deeper. There is no doubt that this new interest in the Pentecostal phenomena is entirely due to that. It is an expression of bankruptcy, but thank God there are people there who, without going that way first and then coming back round this long circle, are turning immediately and directly to the Reformed theology and teaching for which we stand, and for which this Library stands in particular.

The meeting at which these words were spoken was always a small gathering, held in the Reference Room of the Evangelical Library, and those who customarily attended constituted something of an inner circle to whom Dr Lloyd-Jones could speak his mind more freely than he was inclined to do elsewhere. After this December 1963 meeting he may not have felt so free again for the *English Churchman* was to give to its readers a full report of what he had said. This led to a long letter in the correspondence columns of that paper (May 22, 1964) from Pastor George Canty who was responsible for Public Relations in the British Pentecostal Fellowship. Obviously unclear about what ML-J meant by 'Reformed theology', Canty professed to be puzzled by 'the good doctor's surprising slant'. Speaking for the older Pentecostalists, he admitted that 'pre-occupation with theological enquiry has not had time to develop' but biblical doctrine, he believed, was not downplayed in their churches: 'In fact Dr Lloyd-Jones would be most surprised, obviously, if he knew how large a following he has among the Pentecostals for the sake of his abilities as a Bible expositor'.[1] The writer went on to defend du Plessis though he had nothing to say on the recent events in the United States with which the international traveller was associated.

The unexpected appearance of ML-J's words at the Evangelical Library's Annual Meeting of 1963 in the Christian press probably made it more difficult for him to help some of the young leaders of the emerging charismatic movement in England whom he had been

[1] It is true that ML-J had little personal acquaintance with Pentecostal churches, and had, I believe, generally declined invitations to speak among them to this date. George Jefferies had been unsuccessful some years earlier in urging him to come and share a meeting at the Albert Hall which they 'would fill to capacity'.

hoping to influence. David G. Lillie of Devon, who was becoming one of the movement's senior advisers, wrote to Michael Harper on August 23, 1964:

A copy of an address by Dr M. Lloyd-Jones at the Annual Meeting of the Evangelical Library has come into my hands. I don't know how widely it was intended that this address should be publicised, but it is, to me, a very painful revelation of the Doctor's real position in relation to the things of the Holy Spirit, and it is quite different from what I had been led to think. He presents what he terms a 'recrudesence of interest in the gifts of the Holy Spirit' in a wholly unfavourable light, and sets over against this the revived interest in the Reformed theology as being the thing which really matters and which alone can meet the spiritual need of serious, intelligent and spiritual people.

I find it hard to reconcile what the Doctor said in this address with all that I had previously heard as to his views. I begin to wonder what his motive was in cultivating your fellowship. Did he want to lead you gently into the sure paths of the Puritans and away from these American enthusiasts?

*   *   *

We must return now to ML-J's series on the Gospel of John with which this chapter started. His regular Sunday morning expositions kept him on John chapter one for the three years following October 1962. These sermons included many on the person of Christ, His offices and His glorious fullness. Only at the start of the third year in October 1964 did he come to verses 26–33 of that first chapter, the words which include the promise concerning Christ, 'the same is he that baptizeth with the Holy Ghost'. From this text he took up the theme of how the fullness of Christ becomes known to us in experience. Twenty-four sermons which he preached on this theme (from November 15, 1964, to June 6, 1965) have now been published under the titles, *Joy Unspeakable* and *Prove All Things*. That these sermons, which appeared posthumously in the mid-1980's, became the most controversial of all his published material is due in considerable measure to ignorance of the context in which they were preached. Some have spoken as though their contents show at least a measure of support for the burgeoning charismatic movement. Had they been preached ten years later that supposition might have been understandable but the fact is that there

David Martyn Lloyd-Jones: Volume Two

was no 'charismatic movement' in England in 1964. The very term was still unknown. Certainly there was talk of 'baptism in the Spirit' and of a 'tongues movement' in its early stages. There were also a few scattered articles in the Christian press on the subject but no public meetings were held in London to promote the new teaching until Jean Stone spoke in April 1964 and anything like a popular movement was still a good way off. The formation of the Fountain Trust by Michael Harper at the end of September 1964 saw the beginnings of some organisation yet influence was still so comparatively insignificant that 'Edward England hails the courage of Leonard Cutts of Hodder and Stoughton' for publishing Harper's *As at the Beginning* in 1965.[1] It was not until November 1965 – months after the ML-J sermons referred to above were over – that the first large meetings were seen in London with the term 'charismatic renewal' now being introduced.[2]

To judge ML-J's assessment of what were later developments from his statements in the winter of 1964–65 is thus to misconceive the situation which then existed. Apprehensive though he was over aspects of the new teaching, his main theological concern lay in another direction, namely in answering those who believed that there was no larger giving of the Spirit – no 'baptizing with the Spirit' – to be expected in the church apart from the conversion of individuals. This was the prevalent view among evangelicals. What George Smeaton had called 'the modern notion propounded by the Plymouth Brethren that believers are not to pray for the Holy Spirit because He was once for all given on the day of Pentecost'[3] was now, eighty years later, the generally accepted belief. From Pentecost onwards, it was said, all Christians are 'baptized' and filled with the Spirit at their rebirth. ML-J, as already noted, believed with the older teaching in those larger givings of the Spirit both to churches in days of revival and to individual Christians at other times. It is only to Christ that the Spirit is not given 'in measure' (John 3:34). Certainly the Spirit is present in the weakest Christian but He is present more fully in His influences when 'the love of God is shed abroad in our hearts' and when His witness to the believer's salvation is made

[1]*Streams of Renewal*, p. 247.
[2]*Ibid*, pp. 184–85. Meetings sponsored by the Fountain Trust at Southwark Cathedral in November 1965 were entitled, 'The Twentieth Century charismatic renewal' (p. 247)..
[3]*The Doctrine of the Holy Spirit*, 1974 reprint, p. 52.

[484]

gloriously clear. To ML-J it was patently evident that one can be a Christian without being 'filled with the Spirit' just as churches can be churches without knowing the Spirit being outpoured upon them. 'Outpouring' and 'baptism' he saw as synonymous terms for the overwhelming flood of heavenly influence which Christ is pleased to give to His people from time to time.

That ML-J was not misjudging the prevalent view at this time is clear enough from the way in which evangelicals were now reacting to the claims of the new Pentecostalism. As Peter Hocken says, 'The opposition in Britain was strong among leading evangelicals'.[1] The most widely circulated response was that of John Stott whose own parish was inevitably involved in what he called 'a recrudescence of "Pentecostalism"' on account of the activities of Michael Harper, one of his curates.[2] Stott spoke on 'The Baptism and Fullness of the Holy Spirit' at the Islington Clerical Conference on January 7, 1964 and this was published in expanded form in a forty page booklet by the Inter-Varsity Press in July 1964. The Rector of All Souls argued that the sense of 1 Corinthians 12:13 ('by one Spirit are we all baptized into one body') must determine the sense of the promises which speak of Christ baptizing His people with the Holy Spirit. Therefore as the Corinthian text refers to regeneration so must the others, and as the baptism of the Spirit in Acts secured 'the fullness of the Spirit' in Christians that same baptism (i.e. regeneration) now ensures that every 'newborn babe in Christ is filled with the Spirit', is assured by the Spirit 'of his sonship and of God's love', and this fullness of the Spirit is to be regarded as 'a continuous blessing, to be continually and increasingly appropriated'.[3] Stott did not deny that there are such things as special anointings and unusual experiences but they should not be referred to as baptisms of the Spirit nor be regarded as 'the secret of either holiness or usefulness'.

Apart from one introductory sentence, the booklet on *The Baptism and Fullness of the Holy Spirit* said nothing of revival, nor how it is to be understood biblically. The main drift of the argument was to defend the existing position against any view that Christians may need to be baptized with the Holy Spirit.

---

[1] *Streams of Renewal*, p. 258.
[2] Harper's curacy at All Souls concluded in August 1964.
[3] See *The Baptism and Fullness of the Holy Spirit*, 1964, pp. 12, 21. A second edition, with considerable revision and enlargement, was published in 1975.

David Martyn Lloyd-Jones: Volume Two

ML-J had read and annotated Stott's booklet before he began the series on baptism with the Holy Spirit referred to above and it confirmed his fears. He believed that the biblical teaching on the work of the Spirit in the church was now threatened on two fronts. On the one side there was the new pentecostal or tongues-speaking movement, commonly associated with people who claimed to have been 'baptized with the Spirit', and on the other, those who offered no theological reasons why the church was suffering a serious absence of the Holy Spirit's presence and power. The danger of the first view was its tendency to excess and fanaticism, the danger of the second to defend the attitude which saw no need for any major change in the evangelical churches. Both sides were wrong but of the two dangers, the second, which had obscured the meaning of revival and permitted Christians to be 'satisfied with something very much less than what is offered in the Scripture was the greater at the present time'.[1] He judged that the false teaching that all Christians should speak with tongues was far less widespread than the opinion that Christians have received all that they need of the Holy Spirit at their conversion and that thereafter they can continue to be filled by faith. The early church, because of her life and vigour, had the problem of going to excess in the spiritual realm but, as he asked in a sermon on November 15, 1964, 'Would anyone like to claim that, speaking generally, that is the danger in the church today?' In other words, deadness was more common than excitement. It would be a disaster for evangelicals, and for men of Reformed convictions, if they became preoccupied with answering the new Pentecostal claims instead of recognizing that 'the greatest need of the church is to realize again the activity of the Holy Spirit'.[2] Only when his thought on the relative strength of these two dangers in the years 1964–65 is appreciated can the main burden in ML-J's twenty-four published sermons from those years be appreciated. While the sermons repeatedly counsel caution and give warnings about the new claims[3] their main burden lay elsewhere. In his words of December 6, 1964:

[1] *Joy Unspeakable*, p. 18. Unassigned quotations from Stott will be found on pp. 37, 53.
[2] Ibid., p. 120.
[3] Ibid., p. 18; *Prove All Things*, pp. 47–49, 57ff., 76ff., 85, 95ff. The sermons in *Prove All Things* were originally preached *between* the sermons now published as chapters 7 and 8 in *Joy Unspeakable*. As these are more cautionary in their nature it is arguable that the posthumous re-arrangement and separation into two books has affected the original balance of his presentation.

[486]

Our greatest danger, I feel today, is to quench the Spirit. This is no age to advocate restraint; the Church today does not need to be restrained, she needs to be aroused, she needs to be awakened, she needs to be filled with a spirit of glory, she is failing in the modern world. These are no days for restraint.[1]

Or again, in the same series, on March 21, 1965:

Let me say again that one of my main objects in this whole series of sermons is to safeguard the doctrine of the baptism with the Holy Spirit. There is a tendency on the part of some, because they dislike the gifts and the manifestations and the excesses, to throw out the doctrine of the baptism of the Spirit with it.[2]

To summarize what ML-J teaches on the 'baptism with the Spirit' in these sermons: it is an experience of the Spirit which gives the full assurance of faith and which is to be identified with the 'sealing' of Ephesians 1:13. This same experience results in the power and boldness which are the prerequisites for truly effective Christian witness. Far from moving his position in sympathy with what had recently been said by others (as it has been alleged that he did), he could affirm: 'I am more or less repeating from this pulpit what I was saying nine years ago. People seem to think that this is some strange new doctrine'.[3] With regard to special gifts he warned that claims for their existence should not be rejected out of hand. He was particularly concerned lest some of his own young people of Reformed convictions should be found quenching the Spirit in their zeal for orthodoxy. At the same time, as he kept repeating, gifts are *not* the main thing and any movement which becomes excited about gifts is repeating the error of the church at Corinth. Yet, as he cautioned those on the other side of the debate to remember, the Corinthian church was a true church which knew the power of the Holy Spirit.

In the sovereignty of the Spirit He can give any one of these gifts at any time; we must therefore be open. But we must also always be cautious and careful.[4]

[1]*Joy Unspeakable*, p. 75.
[2]*Prove All Things*, p. 146.
[3]December 6, 1964. By an editorial slip the first sentence does not appear in *Joy Unspeakable* p. 67.
[4]*Prove All Things*, p. 144.

The main difference between these twenty-four sermons and his earlier treatments of the same subject – apart from the increased warnings now given to the counterfeit – was his larger use of the Acts of the Apostles to justify the baptism with the Spirit as a post-conversion experience. In particular, he put more stress upon the argument that it was the baptism of the Spirit which was given by the laying on of hands in Acts 8:17, 9:17 and 19:6.[1]

I would offer the opinion that the connection which Dr Lloyd-Jones made between full assurance and these three Acts passages was a mistake and that it contributed to a confusion over the main intent of his teaching. The one great essential which he longed to see recovered was the recognition of need for the experimental work of the Holy Spirit and this, *not* for the sake of experiences as such but in order that God might be known and served more truly. This emphasis is always in the forefront in his sermons.[2] Cults, he would so often say, 'can give people experiences, can make people happy'; Christianity is far more than that. It involves a personal, on-going relation with God, with experiences which are necessarily subject to degrees, to variations and to growth. No *single* experience is to be standardized and made the rule for others. He can say: 'There are people who may feel that they have never received this baptism with the Spirit because they have not had certain particular experiences. That is quite wrong, quite false.'[3] There is, he taught, no baptism with the Spirit which is once-for-all and no crisis experience which leads to a permanently higher stage in the Christian life. 'This experience is not permanent,' he says,[4] referring to what he meant by the 'baptism' or full assurance. To claim that it is, he calls 'a great error'.[5] The only instance known to me where he refers to the baptism of the Spirit as 'the second experience' is where he is deliberately quoting and opposing *false* teaching on the subject.[6] In

[1]The same arguments are in his *Ephesians*, vol. 1, pp. 251–54 (preached January 1955).
[2]See, for example, *Ephesians*, vol. 1, p. 297; *Romans*, vol. 7, pp. 24, 334, 365; *Joy Unspeakable*, p. 227; *Prove All Things*, p. 138. An abundance of similar references could be given.
[3]*Joy Unspeakable*, p. 85.
[4]Ibid., p. 244.
[5]*Ephesians*, vol. 1, p. 291. See also p. 286 where he emphasises the variations of intensity in spiritual experiences and *Puritans*, p. 293 where he underlines the stress of Howell Harris on the 'importance of *new* experiences, *fresh* experiences'.
[6]*Romans*, vol. 7, p. 93. There are again warnings against any 'standardized' experience to be found on pp. 328–32.

stating his own view, there is, he says, a first time when a Christian is filled with the Spirit and given an abounding assurance (and this may be at conversion) but that first experience, while memorable, is not to be regarded as anything unique. To use his own illustration:

When something happens for the first time – well, you cannot go on repeating the first time, but you can repeat what happened on that first time. I first entered the pulpit of Westminster Chapel on the last Sunday morning of the year 1935. I cannot repeat that particular occasion, but I have repeated the action many hundreds of times since.[1]

Yet while such words as these warn against any concentration on *one* experience his constant use in these sermons of the phrase 'the baptism with the Spirit' is suggestive of *one* event which is as definite as regeneration or justification in the salvation of the Christian. It may be relevant to note that the New Testament language about the work of Christ in 'baptizing with the Holy Ghost' is put in terms of a verb: 'baptizing' refers to what Christ does. If it is legitimate to think of the consequence of that action as 'a baptism with the Spirit', and to use the noun form, there is no biblical warrant for putting weight upon any use of the definite article 'the'. The Scriptures no more speak of '*the* baptism with the Spirit' than they do of '*the* effusion of the Spirit'. But once the three Acts passages noted above are used as proof texts then the case for the idea of one distinct experience of the Spirit inevitably tends to become dominant for those verses do refer to a crucial receiving of the Holy Spirit through the laying on of hands. ML-J reasons that because regeneration was never imparted by the laying on of hands the reference must be to the baptism with the Spirit (i.e., full assurance). But was full assurance itself ever imparted by the laying on of hands? And was there not 'great joy' in Samaria *before* the apostles laid hands on any of the new believers (Acts 8:8)? The case that it was spiritual gifts which were imparted at least in Samaria and at Ephesus (Acts 8:17–19 and 19:6) is stronger than ML-J seemed willing to consider. He accepted, of course, that gifts were involved but maintained (over against Pentecostal claims) that they were not a necessary part of what occurred. This becomes hard to establish if the experiences at Samaria and Ephesus are treated as an example and description of full assurance or 'the

[1] *Joy Unspeakable*, p. 272.

baptism with the Spirit'.[1] Further, on the basis of his interpretation
of these passages, it is questionable whether he was warranted in
treating the Pentecostal practice of the laying on of hands to impart
the Spirit as unfavourably as he did.[2] ML-J's whole case does not, of
course, stand or fall on the correct interpretation of these three Acts

[1]On his refusal to identify the baptism of the Spirit with gifts see *Romans*, vol. 7,
pp. 305, 328. Yet he allows a close connection and that tongues may be one
proof of a person having received 'the baptism' (*Prove All Things*, pp. 24, 133).
But the Bible appears to indicate that special gifts (tongues, prophecies, healings
etc.) far from being an accompaniment of full assurance may be possessed by
those who have no saving experience at all. King Saul, Judas and others exercised
such gifts while still being unregenerate (see 1 Sam. 10:11–12; Matt. 7:22–23;
10: 5–8 etc). If it seems an imposition on the words of Acts 8:17 to read 'they
received the Holy Ghost' as, 'they were endowed with the miraculous influences
of the Holy Spirit', it should be remembered that elsewhere the meaning of brief
references to the Spirit has to be interpreted by the context and the general
teaching of Scripture (e.g. John 7:39, where the original reads 'Holy Spirit was
not yet because Jesus was not yet glorified'). In any case, to interpret 'they
received the Holy Ghost' as 'they received full assurance' is also a gloss on the
text. It was clearly not the sight of full assurance which led the unregenerate
Simon Magus to wish that he also might 'receive the Holy Ghost'. ML-J says that
'fallen' with reference to the Spirit (Acts 8:16) equals 'baptism' but the same term
is applied to the gift of prophecy in Ezekiel 11:5.

Michael A. Eaton defends ML-J's use of the Acts passages while noting that if
the passages in question do refer to the receiving of full assurance (i.e., 'the
baptism with the Spirit') they scarcely support the Doctor's view that a lengthy
time-gap between conversion and such full assurance can be normal (*Baptism
with the Spirit, The Teaching of Dr Martyn Lloyd-Jones*, IVP, 1989, pp. 236,
246–47).

The dependability of Eaton's scholarly work is affected by his failure to put
ML-J's teaching on *one* aspect of the Spirit's work into the context of his whole
theology. How far Eaton disagrees with that whole theology is illustrated by the
question of conviction of sin. ML-J believed that a shallow experience of
conviction was the main reason why contemporary evangelicalism has rested in
superficial views of assurance. But Eaton argues that to look for conviction of sin
is to *hinder* assurance because it makes people introspective. He fails to note the
difference between the error which makes conviction the *warrant* to permit a
sinner to believe on Christ and conviction as the *motive* which leads sinners to
rest on Christ alone as He is offered in the gospel. The latter represented ML-J's
position and that of the Puritans.

[2]Speaking of Christian leaders in revival periods of the past who knew what he
meant by 'baptism with the Spirit' ML-J said: 'I do not know of a single instance
among such men where they received the blessing as the result of the laying on of
hands of someone else . . . This whole idea of giving the gift by the laying on of
the hands has been restored by the Pentecostal movement in this present century'.
Joy Unspeakable, pp. 189–191. See also *Romans*, vol. 7, pp. 281–82.

passages but I think that the emphasis which he puts upon them in *Joy Unspeakable* is liable to confuse and it increases an element of tension in his teaching – the tension between seeking God and seeking one distinct experience which is to be called *the* baptism with the Holy Spirit.

*   *   *   *

In 1964–65 Dr Lloyd-Jones, not for the first time, was in the position of trying to address simultaneously two different schools of teaching and on subjects which had been little considered for a long time. Biblical teaching on knowing the full assurance of salvation was possibly the most neglected of all subjects among evangelicals. As he repeatedly said, experimental dealings with God had been too largely reduced to a formula, and faith (generally thought of as 'accepting Christ') and assurance were treated as one and the same thing. In the broad emphasis of his preaching on this theme and on the closely related subject of revival, he was speaking for the old evangelicalism. It is regrettable however, that there was no closely reasoned debate with the position represented by John Stott and that virtually nothing of ML-J's preaching on these things was to be in print until many years later.

With many new ideas about the Spirit's work and gifts suddenly in the air at once, and given a degree of looseness about ML-J's teaching at certain points, it is not altogether surprising that some people have supposed that he was giving measured support to the movement whose title – by ingenious promotion – was to be switched from 'tongues' to 'charismatic'. But whatever some have thought the movement's leaders knew differently. They have noted how he 'dealt rather negatively with "a recrudescence of interest in gifts of the Holy Spirit"'[1] and despite his warnings with respect to du Plessis it was du Plessis' thought that they followed. In private ML-J continued for a time to seek to encourage some of them and to attempt to dissuade them from accepting the framework of thought which was being imported from America. He esteemed them and they were undoubtedly included in his thought when he said on March 21, 1965: 'There is at the present time amongst many good,

[1]*Streams of Renewal*, p. 228.

excellent Christian people a great deal of interest in the whole matter of speaking in tongues.'[1] But his counsel was not heard or followed by several with whom he was in touch and they began to move away from the whole orbit of his labours and witness. As we shall see confirmed later, there is good reason why the charismatic commentators on this period of history should pass over Martyn Lloyd-Jones in comparative silence. As Peter Hocken shows at length, the principal figure in what was happening was the man against whose teaching ML-J initially warned in his address at the annual meeting of the Evangelical Library in December 1963.[2]

For those who believed that an awakening had arrived, the preacher who had previously done most to point to that need seemed to be in danger of choosing to remain in a backwater.

[1]*Prove All Things*, p. 142. In another reference to what was currently happening he said, 'to form movements with respect to the gifts of the Spirit is utterly unscriptural' (p. 124).
[2]While emphasising the major influence of du Plessis, Hocken in *Streams of Renewal* seeks to show that the charismatic movement in England was a spontaneous 'movement of the Spirit' and not something imported from America. It is true that there was a concern for revival present in England prior to the arrival of du Plessis and other trans-Atlantic visitors but Hocken misses the extent to which that was connected with the ministry of ML-J and draws no attention to the change of interest which occurred in 1963 when the introduction of tongues and the development of a movement brought about a new situation and the parting of the ways as outlined above. Michael Harper's *As at the Beginning* shows how far the American framework of thought had been accepted by 1965 and significantly he begins his account of what was new in England in the 1960's in a chapter entitled 'Atlantic Crossing'.

Opposite: ML-J chose hymns carefully and kept a record of their use at Westminster Chapel. This is part of his pencil-written record from September 17, 1961 to July 11 1964. The hymn book was Congregational Praise, *Independent Press, London, 1951.*

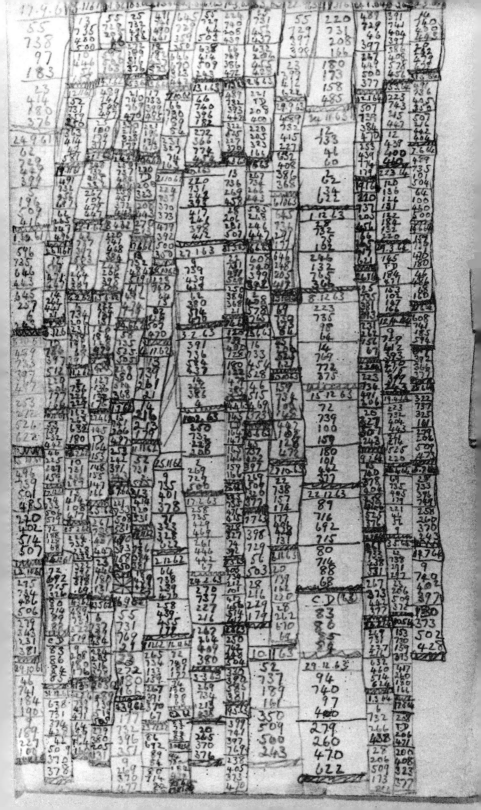

It is my considered opinion that we are at a turning point in the history of the Church such as has not been known since the Reformation of the 16th century

ML-J

Annual letter to the congregation of Westminster Chapel, 1964

I thank the Lord who has given to you to believe in Him, that you too may have eternal life with the saints. But because there are certain persons who, while they affirm that they do not hold with Arius, yet compromise themselves and worship with his party, I have been compelled to write at once . . . For when any see you, the faithful in Christ, associate and communicate with such people, certainly they will think it a matter of indifference and will fall into the mire of irreligion. Lest, then, this should happen, be pleased beloved to shun those who hold the impiety of Arius. We are specially bound to fly from the communion of men whose opinions we hold in execration. If then any come to you, and, as blessed John says, brings with him right doctrine, say to him, All hail, and receive such an one as a brother. But if any pretend that he confesses the right faith, but appear to communicate with those others, exhort him to abstain from such communion, and if he promise to do so, treat him as a brother, but if he persist in a contentious spirit, him avoid.

Letters of Athanasius,
Nicene and Post Nicene Fathers,
vol. 4, 1891, p. 564.

24

1965: The Approaching Crisis

On the first Sunday of 1965 Dr Lloyd-Jones was not at Westminster Chapel. Not to be in his own pulpit on that date was abnormal for, apart from one Sunday after Easter and his summer break, he was always to be found there, mornings and evenings, month after month. But on January 3, 1965, he rested before taking up the work again on the following Sunday. To many of us who had never known London without his being at Westminster, he seemed almost ageless, with neither his health nor spirits subject to change. We did not take seriously enough such occasional remarks as were quoted at the end of chapter 22 on his need of strength and of responsibilities which were 'almost crushing'. In January 1965 he knew very well that all was not changeless. He had just passed his sixty-fifth birthday and was conscious that he had reached the point when most men retire. Douglas Johnson had retired as General Secretary of the IVF in 1964. And old friends were becoming fewer in number. E. J. Poole-Connor had gone home in 1962, E. F. Kevan was to die later in 1965. Family circumstances, also, were at a point of change. Ann was to marry Keith Desmond in April and there seemed little point in Bethan and himself continuing to live in the large house at Mount Park Crescent, Ealing, as they had since 1945. They moved to 49 Creffield Rd, Ealing, the first and only home of their own, in the summer of 1965.

ML-J's calmness of manner hid the constant problem he faced with respect to the demands made upon his time. He allowed nothing to interfere with his pulpit preparation, but with respect to other duties it had long been impossible to deal with the multiplicity of items which sought his attention. Some of the consequences of this pressure had results which a number never understood. For example, it prevented him developing such close personal friendships as would have otherwise been natural. Though attached to many friends, he lacked the leisure to keep in close touch. Social calls even by telephone were an infrequent part of his routine. To Peter Golding, one of his own young men who was going into the ministry, he wrote: 'It is to me a matter of constant regret that, owing to the indescribably busy life that I have to live, I do not see more of you in private. Please do not hesitate to come to see me whenever you would like to do so.'[1] These words say a great deal. He depended on his friends to approach him. But often their very affection for him made them hesitant to take his time, and this would be true of a number of the more senior members at Westminster Chapel in the 1960's.

Another problem area for him with respect to time was the old question of getting his sermons and addresses into print. *Studies in the Sermon on the Mount* had proved that expository sermons could sell but no further books had appeared since the second volume of that title in 1960. Two other books were at the printers at the beginning of 1965, *Spiritual Depression* and *Faith on Trial* (the 11 sermons from the *Westminster Record* which Lutterworth had failed to obtain for publication in the 1950's). These books, however, were to be his only volumes for the rest of the 1960's. Douglas Johnson despaired over the Lloyd-Jones material which, although taped and transcribed, was lost in the endless queue of items awaiting the preacher's attention. In a letter to Dr Lloyd-Jones on this point, Johnson referred to an important address which ML-J gave for the Christian Medical Fellowship and which was needed in print. The transcript was 'a valuable weapon lying idle whilst the enemy is rampant'. He continued:

I still think that it is a tragedy that you have not a literary editor i.e. someone very accurate who (from hearing you constantly and sharing your views) would take off you the reading of MS proofs, etc. He would be made, on pain of death, responsible to make no changes other than typists' verbal slips etc. and to bring back to you all the proposed changes (i.e. where elision or change of phrasing has been done). This would save you reading reams and reams of MS and proofs – which you *ought* not to do!

It seems to us "mad" for your time to go on chores. Is there no one who can be trusted to do what every publisher has for any author of note?[2]

[1]Jan 11, 1961
[2]Letter of June 27, 1962.

The effect of the non-publication of some of ML-J's more controversial material was more serious than anyone realized at the time. Except for those who belonged to the Chapel, his views on such subjects as revival, the sealing of the Spirit, and unity among evangelicals, were chiefly circulated by hearsay and rumour. His crucial Welwyn address of June 1963, for example, was taped and transcribed but never printed. Consequently no one was able to study his words on an issue which was of vital and immediate relevance. This failure came from multiple causes. There was, no doubt, some lack of vision in the Westminster Chapel diaconate and there was also a slowness to delegate on ML-J's part. At the same time it has to be remembered that his early experience with publishers gave justification to his reluctance to trust any editors except those in his own family.

Dr Lloyd-Jones certainly saw the need for more books. In a personal discussion which he had with a few of us in his vestry on November 26, 1964, he said that he might be inclined to retire from Westminster, undertake world travel and prepare his Romans sermons for the press, 'if it were not for men like us'. By which he meant (for this was a main theme under discussion that day) the need for a structure which would hold men together in work and witness in later years. Any association which depended on a personal attachment to him was the last thing he wanted, yet the need for closer unity was such a priority in his thinking that he was willing to continue at Westminster if it would serve that purpose.

Unity was a subject which, we have already seen, was taking increasing amounts of his time. A change in the meetings of the Westminster Fellowship illustrates this fact. Until January 1960 the Fellowship usually met monthly on a Tuesday afternoon. With the larger numbers now attending it became difficult for Westminister Chapel ladies to serve tea on Tuesdays when a women's gathering was meeting elsewhere on the premises at the same time. The ministers' meeting was accordingly moved to a Monday afternoon. Then, at the critical meeting at Welwyn in 1963, it was proposed and agreed that, in view of the need for more time to discuss the pressing issues of ecumenical or evangelical unity, the Fellowship should add a morning session to its regular meetings. This meant for ML-J that once a month he went straight from his heavy weekend of ministry at the Chapel to virtually a full day of meetings as well as to interviews, for there were always ministers from a distance at the fraternal who sought his advice over particular problems while they were in town.

With the introduction of this morning meeting of the Fellowship, there was also a new arrangement in the meetings themselves. In order to follow up his Welwyn address it was arranged that a number of speakers from within the membership of the fraternal would give addresses at the morning session as a basis for discussion. These men represented the denominational differences to be found in the Fellowship, the intention being to re-examine these differences from Scripture in the hope of there being sufficient common ground to lead to a much wider and closer association. ML-J selected those who spoke but again, in part through pressure of time, there was insufficient planning. Addresses were never made available. The same points tended to re-emerge and to be left unresolved. No drafting work was ever done by committees. In part the slowness of the procedure was deliberate for ML-J wanted to give men time to think and confer. By the autumn of 1964 he had made up his mind to make the mid-summer meeting at Welwyn in 1965 the occasion when he would give a final challenge to men to put a new evangelical unity *before* traditional denominational affiliations. In some cases, at least, he knew that such a decision would necessitate men leaving their present denominations and what this would cost some men weighed heavily upon him. He thought much about the question of timing and was critical of the Elizabethan Robert Browne's attitude of 'Reformation without tarrying for any'.[1] To the Rev. Charles Hilton Day, a friend who had known long gruelling years seeking to exercise a biblical ministry in the Presbyterian Church of England, he wrote on April 12, 1965:

With regard to your main feeling about what should be done at the present time, I have just to say that I am in entire agreement with you. I have all along felt that it is wrong simply to call men out without having thought the matter right through. In any case these matters are never to be done in cold blood, there must always be some very definite leading and sense of constraint. I am sure that we need to exercise great patience

[1]'There is timing in these matters; history proves that very eloquently ... We must always consider the preparation and the readiness of the people. Do not rush them ... Educate them, train them, show them the dangers; do not rush ahead at once the moment you see a thing ... Through forgetting that, the story of many men who have separated has been a sad one. They have been able men and great men but they have divided at the wrong point, and they have just gone off into a little cul-de-sac where no one has ever heard of them and their excellent testimony has been of little value.' *WR*, July 1963, pp. 109–110.

in this extremely complex situation in which we find ourselves, and I am
sure that at the end we shall be shown the way.

I cannot tell you how much I feel for people situated as you are, and it
grieves me much to think that I cannot be of more active and positive
help . . .
Some of the younger men have never really had to face the true
position as it is and are therefore liable to jump to conclusions based on
purely theoretical considerations.

There was, however, another factor besides patience which now held
ML-J back from what might have become a more definite challenge
in the summer of 1965. Counter-proposals (which is basically what
they were) emerged from men within his circle and with whom he
had long had close relations.

The Evangelical Alliance, of which Gilbert Kirby remained the
General Secretary, now began to take its own steps to meet the
problem of the endangered unity of evangelicals. It announced a
'National Assembly of Evangelicals' to be held in London at the end
of September 1965 – a move which was linked with a significant
change in the organization of the Alliance. Hitherto it had stood for
'spiritual unity', with membership restricted to individual Christians. Now, to help meet the charge that such unity was a great deal
less than what is required by the New Testament, local churches or
assemblies could become associate members of the Alliance and the
National Assembly conference sessions (as distinct from public
evening meetings) would be 'reserved for those who come as
representatives or delegates of local churches or of Christian
societies'.[1] Instead of regarding this as a move in the right direction,
ML-J believed that it would bypass the whole issue of whether a true
unity of evangelicals could be maintained if it included those who
simultaneously believed in the possibility of ecumenical unity. His
belief was confirmed by his observation that the programme for the
Alliance's 'National Assembly' contained no mention of anyone
speaking on this issue. He saw the change as a compromise which
was bound to fail.

For different reasons, April 1965 was to be a dark month for
ML-J. From Monday, April 5 to Thursday, April 8 he attended the
third Conference for Ministers organized by the Banner of Truth

[1] *A Study of the Evangelical Alliance in Great Britain*, J. B. A. Kessler, (Goes,
Netherlands: Oosterbaan & Le Cointre),1968, p. 105.

Trust at Leicester. This was a considerably larger conference than the earlier ones, in part because it had been announced that attention would be given to seeking agreement upon a 'Confession of Faith and Order which would provide a basis for bringing to expression the unity of the body of Christ according to the Scriptures'. There had been some meetings of men in smaller groups prior to the Conference. John Murray and ML-J were expected to be the main speakers, though the majority of the time was to be given to discussion.

In terms of its announced intention, this Conference was a failure. In part the fault lay with those of us who organized its programme. Two addresses took up the possibility of a Confession which would be deliberately 'open' on the issue of Arminianism and they both opposed it. The present writer did so chiefly on the basis of lessons from 18th century church history, and John Murray from the standpoint of Scripture and theology. Speaking on 'The Creedal Basis of Union in the Church', Professor Murray concluded: 'Though Reformed evangelicals and non-Reformed evangelicals may embrace one another in love, in the bond of fellowship with Christ, and co-operate in many activities that promote the kingdom of God and the interests of Christ's church, yet it is not feasible, and not feasible in terms of commitment to Christ and to the whole counsel of God, to unite in creedal confession as the bond and symbol of ecclesiastical communion.'[1]

For reasons already given, ML-J did not agree that the best way forward at this point in time was the preparation of a creedal statement which would exclude evangelical ministers of Arminian views. At this Conference, however, he gave no address on the subject and declined to lead a discussion on it because, as he said in private, 'I am too tired'. He had come straight to the Conference from the work of the weekend and concern for the issues involved had interfered with his sleep. He was deeply disappointed over the Conference. I believe that there was some real misunderstanding which more adequate consultation beforehand might have reduced. No sharp words were exchanged between him and John Murray. They were men of very different gifts, yet – had they only known each other – of the same heart. One thing they had in common, in terms of temperament, was that they were both reserved and they had never had the time to become friends. ML-J left the Conference

[1]See *The Collected Writings of John Murray*, vol. 1, 1976, pp. 286–87.

before John Murray preached at its conclusion from Acts 1:1–2, on Christ's *continuing* ministry through the Holy Spirit on behalf of the church. He probably never heard him preach.[1]

The difference between these two men had a beneficial result for some of us of which we were unconscious at the time. Both men were leaders. In a sense, they were *the* world leaders of those who loved the doctrines of grace and, being over a quarter of a century older than the new generation of younger ministers, they tended to be viewed with a confidence akin to that which should be accorded only to infallibility. That two such men so likeminded in doctrine should *disagree*, was a salutary lesson to us. One of them had to be wrong! Perfectly obvious though that will be to most readers, those who knew the spiritual stature and authority of these two Christians will well understand what I am saying. We loved them both, and regarded them as Titans, but we needed to be more persuaded that they were also men.[2]

At virtually the same time as this third Leicester Conference a book entitled *All in Each Place* came on the market and gave ML-J a greater disappointment from another direction. As we have seen, in the debate over participation in ecumenical proposals much depended on the evangelical Anglicans and, notwithstanding the policy of what seemed to be a new majority, ML-J had been encouraged at the position taken by Jim Packer who represented the more Calvinistic of the younger Anglican evangelicals. But between 1963 and 1965 (when he became a member of the Anglican–Methodist Unity Commission) something happened to Packer's assessment of the situation, as was apparent in *All in Each Place, Towards Reunion in England*, Ten Anglican Essays, with Some Free Church Comments.

[1] I give some further comment on this Conference in my biography of John Murray, see *Collected Writings*, vol. 3, 1982, pp. 132–33. The difference between Lloyd-Jones and Murray has some likeness to the difference between Thomas Goodwin and John Owen as observed by Robert Halley: 'Goodwin and Owen are valuable expositors; but Goodwin well interpreted Scripture by the insight of a renewed heart – Owen, distrusting his own experience, by the patient and prayerful study of words and phrases' ('Memoir of Thomas Goodwin' in his *Works*, vol. 2. p. xlvii).
[2] Dr Oliver Barclay, who succeeded Douglas Johnson as the General Secretary of the IVF has made a similar point in another context: 'In my own view Lloyd-Jones' (to many people impossible) exegesis of "the sealing of the Spirit" was a real blessing. After that people did not follow him so slavishly but judged whether he was truly expounding the Bible. It broke a near idolatry of the man and did no harm' (letter to the author, Feb. 2, 1981).

Dr Packer edited this work and contributed the major opening chapter on 'Wanted: A Pattern for Union'. Along with much that was good, the book showed unmistakable signs of a major shift towards the very position which Packer had earlier criticised as inconsistent with evangelicalism. He now wrote of 'the debate on union between evangelicals and others', these others being described as our 'catholic' brethren (meaning Anglo-Catholics) and 'non-episcopal brethren'. The non-episcopal included such Free Church-men as John Huxtable (who contributed to the volume), although he had chided evangelicals at Nottingham for holding 'a substitution-ary theory of the atonement'. To Anglo-Catholics it was promised that the authors intended to create no 'conscientious difficulties'; all plans for reunion must 'safeguard' the consciences of Anglo-Catholics, even to the point of allowing 'the right of Anglo-Catholics to abstain from eucharistic fellowship of which as individuals they cannot approve'.[1] The 'deeply unorthodox' should be excluded from official positions in a united Church but who such people might be was left in obscurity. The overall impression given by *All in Each Place* was that the common quest for unity with non-evangelicals was right after all.

To understand how Dr Lloyd-Jones felt by the time of the Westminster Fellowship outing to Welwyn on June 16, 1965, one needs to turn to Psalm 74 – the Psalm which he read at the opening of the morning meeting. In view of what had happened in the preceding months he had laid aside his thought of challenging the men to reach a decision. Instead, after the reading of the Psalm, he reviewed the scene as he saw it:

This Psalm sums up what I feel about the present situation . . . Two years ago I tried to make a statement. I appealed for unity, a unity at the church level. I spoke of the inadequacy of movements and the error of allowing movements to become hardened and persistent. My case was that we were facing the situation in terms of movements and not in terms of the church. So we decided to look into the nature of the church and to consider: Can we reconcile our position with the New Testament? Is there a pattern set in Scripture? Do we stay as we are or come out? And if we do come out into what are we coming? I was convinced two years ago that many were not convinced of schism and so should be given the opportunity to be convicted . . .

[1] *All In Each Place*, pp. 30, 37, etc.

What is the position at which we have arrived? Is there any hope of evangelical unity at the church level and of grasping a unique opportunity? I can only give you my conclusions. My conclusion is that there is no hope at all at the church level. Why? Because there is no agreement among evangelicals. There is less today than two years ago.

I see at least six groups.

1. Easily the largest is those who are a bit unhappy about their denominational affiliation and the ecumenical movement but who feel the answer is still in movements.[1] Their view is the exact antithesis of what I was trying to say two years ago. The proposed Evangelical Alliance Conference expresses this attitude . . . 'There must be no suggestion of leaving denominations – it will wreck the movement'. The Conference is not even considering evangelicals coming out.[2]

2. Those who are controlled by denominational thinking. A distinct group of evangelicals has been emerging in the last three or four years who are advocating active participation in the WCC, etc. They are quite logical for their denominations are member churches in the WCC.

3. A more recent group who are increasingly vocal, evangelicals in favour of the Church of England but they suggest modifications . . . They, J. I. Packer, Gervase Duffield and others, want a modified episcopacy, and a state church comprehensive enough for Anglo-Catholics yet without room for liberals. Whether this is realistic or not is not our concern this morning.

4. Those who are already out, who belong to the Fellowship of Independent Churches or other independent churches.

5. Those who would like to come out, who feel that they should but believe that their churches are not yet ready to follow a lead. They are intellectually convinced. My greatest personal predicament is to assess the numbers belonging to this group.

6. Men belonging to groups already described but who are so doctrinally rigid as to make Evangelical unity impossible . . . Some are in this

[1]'Movements' here, of course, means the non-church evangelical organisations and societies. 180 such Societies had shared in an Evangelical Alliance exhibition in 1951. They were generally regarded as the most hopeful way of achieving biblical action. Thus, as late as the winter issue of 1962/63, the Alliance's *Evangelical Broadsheet* noted: 'Whilst evangelical Christians are happy to have fellowship with all who sincerely love our Lord Jesus Christ, they believe that active co-operation can only be effectively enjoyed with those who are agreed upon basic Christian truth.'

[2]i.e. the first 'National Assembly of Evangelicals', referred to above, which was scheduled to meet in September 1965.

position because of Calvinism, because of Arminianism, because of baptism or because of Presbyterianism.

So it is idle to talk about evangelical unity.

He then went on to say that the 'most tragic' aspect of the current general scene was the changed attitude to the importance of doctrine:

A new climate of opinion has come in very rapidly . . . Large numbers of evangelicals profess to be very satisfied. They say our Colleges are full, they appeal to the influence of the Graham Crusades and believe it is 'only a question of time', 'we are capturing the denominations'. So they are utterly impatient with those who demand true doctrine . . . they have a hearty dislike of prophets. They want innocuous, harmless men who won't upset anyone at all. The whole climate of thinking has ceased to be evangelical . . . For example, they say, 'The vestments issue is no longer relevant'. They have a fear of being regarded as negative. The Baptists have not had a word to say on Howard Williams – 'We mustn't get at him!' He can get at the Lord Jesus Christ but not a word about him . . . Look at the way in which insults are offered, as in Williams' Presidential address and Ramsey did the same in Australia.[1] They speak of us in a way they would not speak of Hindus!

Yet evangelicals say, 'Always be positive'. Even with regard to Rome a new language is coming in. The Church of England is being called 'a bridge church' and there is a readiness to believe that Rome is changing . . .

ML-J spoke of other examples of changes among evangelicals. Posing the question, 'Why has it all happened?' he answered: 'I am not quite sure but it has happened in the last eleven years'. As representatives of most if not all of the six groups listed above were present, he addressed a series of questions which were relevant to each:

To Anglicans: What is the value and object of occasional protests if you don't follow it up by action? Saying and doing nothing – saying the Bishop of Woolwich is not a Christian and is teaching idolatry and then continuing to be a member of the Church and even having to recognize such men as 'Fathers in God' . . . Is this any honest position to be in at all? Should you not move heaven and earth to get that man out or go out yourself?

[1] Ramsey had criticized the evangelicals of the conservative Sydney diocese.

To Anglicans and others: Is there any conceivable point at which some would even consider coming out? I have asked this for four years and had no answer. It is a policy of drifting and postponement. Surely the logic of the present position is back to Rome and to one world church.

To Independents and others: Some find yourselves in the happy position of having your churches agreeing with you. You say, 'Of course, if anyone tried to stop me preaching I would do something' – I ask you, are you asking *this* question, 'Am I my brother's keeper?'

To those who say their churches are not ready: Are you educating your people?

To the final group: Remember your priorities! When the whole house is on fire you don't argue about the best room in the house. We are fighting for the *whole* evangelical faith. To me, the big thing is the faith *in toto*. It is almost criminal to divide evangelicals on Calvinism – Arminianism, Presbyterian or non-Presbyterian, immersion or non-immersion. If we do this we are going to be atomized and destroyed one by one.

In concluding he apologized that his final remarks would be more or less purely personal. He was being forced to say some things. He denied rumours that he was about to launch a new Calvinistic, Presbyterian Church or a new Pentecostal Church, and went on:

I have no *personal* interest in all we are discussing. I have not proposed a new Church. I am not an organizer – it is probably one of my greatest defects. I am almost driven to think I ought to write an autobiography in the interests of truth! I could have been President of the Free Churches Council or the Congregational Union years ago. I could have had it all.[1] Every man will have to answer to God for himself . . .

I still feel that evangelicals are missing an opportunity which will probably never recur. A world Church is coming and evangelicals will be faced with a *fait accompli*. The situation is not hopeless but it is very grievous. I never expected anything else, but I am sad. What do we do?

1. All I have to do is to go on preaching the gospel.
2. 'Fight the good fight of faith' – it is the whole fight of forty or fifty years ago but we have to fight it this time in evangelical circles. (What amazes me is that any evangelical should think there is anything new in this situation!)

[1]See p. 61–2. Others besides J. D. Jones had wanted him in these roles.

3. We have to exhort the people to pray for revival . . . I am going to
   spend my time urging people to pray for the outpouring of the Spirit.
   Many of these difficulties would then be swept out of existence.
4. We need to encourage the formation of local independent evangelical
   churches . . . Greater London is not representative of the country.
   I know I shall be misquoted. That does not worry me. We shall all
   stand before the judgment seat of Christ, and knowing something of
   the terror of the Lord I have tried to persuade you concerning some of
   these things.

In the concluding remarks of this 1965 address he also raised a
question about the future of the Westminster Fellowship which, as
he reminded those present, he had not started. It had been carried on
through the years in an undefined manner. It had never passed
resolutions and it was not its purpose to try in a subtle way to
manipulate the situation. He also confessed that, on account of all
these things, the last three months had been the most unhappy in all
his ministry. Upon further discussion on the change of climate and its
origins, he traced the 'eleven years' to which he had already referred
back to Harringay and to the blurring of evangelical distinctives
which the policy of the Graham Crusades had introduced.

This Welwyn outing (the last of many happy summer days at that
beautiful location) concluded in a very sombre spirit. ML-J was of the
opinion that the Fellowship in its present form had fulfilled its usefulness. No further meeting was to be held until Monday, November 29.

Sometimes, about this period, Bethan Lloyd-Jones would find her
husband sitting silently, without a book, rapt in thought and
seemingly cast down. If he had any special struggle with a temptation to depression at this time, he was enabled to overcome it. There
was nothing gloomy about the address which he gave to mark the
centenary of the opening of Westminster Chapel on July 6, 1965. He
said on that occasion, 'I think that God expects us to feel an affection
for the very precincts of the place because He has been pleased to
meet with us here, and has honoured us by His presence.' But the
bricks and mortar as such, he went on, meant little. It was what the
building stood for that mattered, and he was certain that God would
preserve it as long as 'that evangelical faith, which is alone true
Christianity, is proclaimed'. If his spirits needed to be further rallied,
they were the following week, when his friend the Rev W. J. Grier of
Belfast gave the Annual Lecture of the Evangelical Library on 'Hus

and Farel, Heroic Pioneers of the Reformation'. As usual, ML-J was the enthusiastic chairman.

In August 1965 an incident occurred which provides an interesting glimpse both of a private conversation and into the kind of man ML-J was. During that month he was on holiday with Bethan, staying with their good friends Ray and Megan Ellis at Wappenham Manor in the English Midlands. After a Friday in the open air, sightseeing, when Martyn and Bethan arrived back in time for the evening meal they heard that the Rev Kenneth W. H. Howard was to preach at 7 p.m. in the local Methodist Chapel. Howard had been a friend for many years and ML-J wanted to be there, though it meant postponing dinner for a few hours (which was no problem to his hostess). The preacher, who was himself on holiday, was thus surprised to see Dr Lloyd-Jones among his twenty-five or so hearers. Far from being inhibited, Howard felt that the senior preacher's presence had a liberating effect on his own spirit as he preached on 'the preciousness of Christ'. Another old friend of ML-J's, Charles Lawrence, was also there and afterwards both men joined the party at the Manor. The Doctor was relaxed and the conversation flowed. There was description of some of the places they had recently visited, including the Civil War battlefield at Edgehill and the village of Weston Favell where James Hervey had ministered. Discussion also covered reminiscences of preachers, including Whitefield and his differences with the Erskine brothers (ML-J taking Whitefield's side in that division while admiring the work done by the Erskines). From Howard's notes of this time of fellowship we quote:

The serious part of the conversation centered on the ecumenical movement and the situation now confronting evangelicals and their churches. The Doctor did not think there would be any repudiation of the 39 Articles or the historic creeds but that they would be retained with 'liberty of interpretation'. The recent proposals for the union of the four denominations in Wales were following this line . . . I asked if the Doctor thought that congregations were ready to follow ministers if they seceded. He thought not and that perhaps the task of the next five years would be to prepare people quietly for such a step. He feared that some ministers would never be willing to sever their denominational connections.

He agreed with my view that the only cleavage we ought to recognize, in the present historical situation, is that between evangelical and non-evangelical. The Westminster Fellowship in the Presbyterian Church of

New Zealand was shortly to seek the Doctor's opinion on their leaving
the Presbyterian Church of New Zealand because of its impending
union negotiations with the Anglican Church. 'I shall have to tell
them,' he said, 'that I am not interested in a continuing Presbyterian
Church. We are now in a new historical situation, such as has not
existed before in the church, when continuing evangelical remnants of
denominations is not the answer. There must be not only a coming out
but a coming together of evangelical people.'

I said that either we must constitute an Evangelical Church on
Reformed lines or a general and inclusive Church. To do the former
seemed to me to be an act of schism, to do the latter seemed to present no
option but to co-operate with the Fellowship of Independent Evangelical
Churches. With this general line of thought the Doctor concurred,
pointing out that he was himself 'Reformed' but advocating patience
with others. But he thought that the longstanding prejudice against the
FIEC – due to various churches (chiefly Baptist) having joined on
inadequate grounds – argued for the assimilation of the present FIEC
with a new body on similar lines. He thought that the present leaders of
the FIEC would be very ready to come in on such a scheme.

One of the most encouraging things the Doctor had found for a long
time was the tendency among the Plymouth Brethren to set up churches
with pastors – in contradiction to their earlier views against the 'one
man ministry'.

This discussion concluded at 12.20 a.m. and ten minutes later,
after prayer, Howard and Lawrence were seen off by their hosts
and Dr Lloyd-Jones from the back door of the Manor!

Dr Lloyd-Jones did not go to the Evangelical Alliance's National
Assembly of Evangelicals in September 1965 but a report of that
Assembly, followed by discussion, occupied the Westminster Fellowship at its one further meeting in 1965 on November 29. ML-J
already knew the main facts. Although not convened to discuss
church issues, the National Assembly had accepted a resolution
from the Rev Don Davies (a member of the Westminster Fellowship) for the setting up of a Commission 'to study radically the
various attitudes of Evangelicals to the Ecumenical Movement,
denominationalism and a possible future United Church' (i.e. a
United Evangelical Church). Gilbert Kirby had informed ML-J of
this decision in a letter of October 14, 1965 and asked for his
participation in the discussions which the Commission intended to
set in motion.

Dr Lloyd-Jones and other members of the Westminster Fellowship accepted invitations to speak to the nine-member Commission and it was therefore agreed that the Fellowship would postpone any move of its own until the Commission's findings were published. The date already fixed for publication was October 1966 which would co-incide with a Second National Assembly of Evangelicals again organized by the Evangelical Alliance. In the meantime the fraternal would continue its own discussion of the issues and, accordingly, the usual monthly schedule of meetings was arranged for 1966.

The theme which had been receiving such attention during the previous twelve months was also the subject for the addresses at the Puritan Conference for 1965, 'Approaches to Reformation of the Church'. With one exception, the papers given on December 14 and 15 dealt with the history of the sixteenth century and were predictable in content. The exception was ML-J's concluding address, 'Ecclesiola in Ecclesia', which broke new ground. He traced a number of examples from the Reformation onwards of evangelicals who had sought to organize a nucleus of churches within a larger territorial church ('little churches within a church'). In his view these attempts at reformation from within had all failed to come to grips with the New Testament teaching on the nature of the church. They had put expediency before principle and he was convinced that current events were again illustrating the decline which occurs when a concern for influence is put first: 'We are forgetting the doctrine of the remnant. We are trusting to expediency and expedients and not saying that, if we are faithful, the Holy Spirit has promised to honour us and our testimony however small our numbers and however despised by "the wise and prudent".'[1]

For Dr Lloyd-Jones, at the end of 1965, the lines of a coming division were clearly drawn. As he wrote to Philip Hughes in the United States on December 21:

[1] *Puritans*, p. 147. He thought the words of Robert Hall to be relevant to the situation. Hall, after commending the 'godly simplicity and fidelity' of the men who restored evangelicalism in the Church of England in the 18th century, expressed these fears of later representatives of the evangelical party: 'We cannot dissemble our concern at perceiving a set of men rising up among them, ambitious of new modelling the party, who, if they have too much virtue openly to renounce their principles, yet have too little firmness to endure the consequences: timid, temporizing spirits, who would refine into insipidity, polish into weakness, and, under we know not what pretences of regularity, moderation, and a care not to offend, rob it utterly of that energy of character to which it owes its success.' (*Works*, vol. 4, 1834, pp. 122–23).

I have been having an exceptionally busy time travelling in various parts of the country as well as my work at Westminster. The position here is still very confused and I am sure that we are heading up during this next year to a real crisis on what is to me the fundamental issue, namely, do we believe in a territorial church or in a gathered church of saints? You will know about or have seen the symposium edited by Packer – *All In Each Place*. This I think indicates clearly the dividing points between evangelicals. Some of us cannot understand this attitude to make accommodations for 'the Anglo-Catholic conscience', for that is surely to make accommodation for 'another gospel which is not a gospel'. However, I must not pursue this in a letter.

I gather that the position is something similar out there with evangelicals increasingly prepared to compromise on the Scriptures and on other matters. It is to me nothing less than tragic that evangelicals do not see that they have a unique opportunity at the present time if they but stood together. They still fondly imagine that they can infiltrate the various bodies to which they belong and win them over.

In concluding this chapter there is one point which needs to be stressed if the reader is to grasp ML-J's thought in what is to follow. It must be understood that neither now nor at anytime was he advocating the formation of a new evangelical denomination as the right response to ecumenism. To the question, 'Are you proposing to set up a new denomination?' he could reply, 'That is the very thing I am not saying'.[1] If he had given his weight to supporting one denomination – either one already existent or one to be newly formed – and pressed his own view of church order, namely Congregationalism or Independency,[2] there can be no doubt that he would have received considerable support. But he was against such a procedure for a fundamental reason. The crisis in the church was not over different forms of church government, a subject about which, in his view, the Scriptures allow no final certainty. It was over the issue, 'What is a Christian?' The need of the hour, therefore, was not for the emergence of a new denomination which would either enforce one view on church government or convince all participants to accept some kind of compromise over traditional denominational distinctives – excluding all others. Such a course of action would never achieve greater evangelical and Christian unity. It would only perpetuate the mistakes of the past.

[1] *Revival*, p. 167.
[2] For further comment on his churchmanship see Appendix 3, pp. 789–91.

As we have seen in this chapter, men who were close to him sometimes used such terms as a 'future United Church' or 'a general and inclusive Church' but ML-J never used that language.[1] Such a 'Church' in the end would mean nothing more than another denomination. He was pleading rather for bigger and bolder thinking, and especially for thinking which would keep obedience to the gospel as the decisive issue. Let men retain their differences over the secondary issues of church government but at the same time they must see the need to act with fellow evangelicals in a manner which showed unity in the gospel to be their *first* commitment. His hope therefore was for a basis of association in which churches, whether independent or already linked in a denominational grouping (where the ministry was sound on essentials), could 'work and operate together' with a minimum of control. Dr Lloyd-Jones' thought here seemed to be so new that many failed to grasp it, yet, as he pointed out, it was not new. It was basically the same vision pursued and for a time implemented in the days of Cromwell. Advised by such men as John Owen, Cromwell worked for a unity among churches which was not based upon the elimination of differences over church order. The one demand was that all ministers be orthodox Protestants and be tried by a common standard as to their fitness for office. On that point there has to be an over-all control. After commenting on this 17th-century programme for unity ML-J said: 'That is exactly my position on these matters. I do not care whether a man is a Presbyterian or a Baptist or an Independent or Episcopalian or a Methodist, as long as he is agreed about the essentials of "the faith".'[2] The way to unity was not through the removal of all secondary differences. It was for churches to submit themselves to Scripture on all the fundamentals and, provided that submission existed, ML-J could say, 'I have no interest in denominations'.[3]

[1] Imprecision in language was to be a part of the cause of confusion in the ensuing controversy. Don Davies, who moved the Evangelical Alliance resolution for a Commission to study 'a possible future United Church' was a well-known member of the Westminster Fellowship and might therefore have been assumed to be speaking for ML-J. Not unreasonably the Alliance interpreted the words to mean 'a united evangelical Church on denominational lines' (see the *Report of the Commission on Church Unity to the National Assembly of Evangelicals*, Evangelical Alliance, 1966, p. 10.

[2] Sermon on 'Division – True and False' in *WR* July, 1963, p. 111. For fuller comment by ML-J on the Cromwellian experiment see 'Cromwell' in the Index of *Puritans*.

[3] *Revival*, p. 152. 'Belong to a denomination,' he says elsewhere, 'but do not stand fast in denominationalism.'

There is scarcely anything else ever heard in the church, speaking generally, but this whole question of unity; every day you see some reference to it in the newspapers. One section of the church holds a conference or a council to promote it; and another one does the same until all are talking about this. This has become the great theme of the Christian church at the present time.

ML-J

on Romans 12:4, 5, January 28, 1966.

25

1966: The Call to Decision

The year 1966 began for Dr Lloyd-Jones no differently from so many others. For the first Sunday at Westminster he departed, as usual, from the passages which he was expounding in sequence and preached from two individual texts, in the morning from 2 Chronicles 7:12–14 ('If my people . . . shall humble themselves, and pray, and seek my face . . .') and for the evening evangelistic sermon from Ezekiel 33:30–33. The following Friday evening, January 7, he resumed the Romans series at Romans 12:3, which was his 307th exposition of the Epistle. Sunday, January 9, saw him back in the two New Testament books from which his Sunday texts were to be drawn until the end of his ministry: in the morning he commenced the third chapter of John and in the evening the fifth chapter of the Acts of the Apostles.

Although the pattern of his ministry thus remained the same, he was personally convinced that the year ahead was to be one of the most crucial in his life. For one thing, a decision was imminent on whether or not Westminster Chapel would enter the proposed re-alignment of the Congregational Union Churches of England and Wales which was to be called 'The Congregational Church in England and Wales'. Of much more concern to him was the outcome of the discussions continuing in the Commission of the Evangelical Alliance. It was certain that Westminster Chapel would not enter what was to be an intentionally short-lived 'Congregational Church';[1] what was far less clear was the extent to which evangelicals would recognize the need for corporate action in the face of the changing church scene.

One result of ecumenical pressure in both Scotland and Ireland had been the formation of 'Evangelical Fellowships', intended to give the evangelicals in different denominations in those countries a closer inter-denominational contact with one another. Both of these

[1]Proposals for union with the English Presbyterian Church were already well advanced.

Fellowships looked to ML-J for leadership,[1] and his first engagement away from Westminster in 1966 was to speak at the Evangelical Fellowship of Ireland in Belfast on January 18. As at other times, he stayed with his friends the Rev and Mrs W. J. Grier at Knockdene Park South, Belfast. On the afternoon of this visit he addressed a ministers' meeting in Grosvenor Road Reformed Presbyterian Church, arguing that for evangelicals to answer the ecumenical call for church unity solely in terms of the organization of 'Fellowships' was to fall short of Scripture. Adam Loughridge recalls how 'under some pressure from questions he said that he thought that the time had come when evangelicals could no longer stay in denominations that belonged to the World Council of Churches, a viewpoint that was not unanimously received'.[2] The evening meeting held in the large Wellington Hall was the first public meeting of the Evangelical Fellowship of Ireland. Such was the support it received that, even with provision for an overflow meeting, hundreds had to be turned away – including Mr Grier's own wife and family.

Two days later, on Thursday, January 20, 1966, the first Westminster Chapel members' meeting was held in the new year. It included a baptism, a financial statement, report on news of members and, finally, an address by ML-J on the question of the Chapel's relationship to the proposed new 'Congregational Church' – the constitution of which he had already studied and considered with the deacons. According to this constitution, one of the Church's aims would be 'to further the unity of the Church and to foster ecumenical relationships with other Christian Churches and communities through such agencies as the Free Church Federal Council, the British Council of Churches and the World Council of Churches'.

Quoting these words, as reported in the Minutes of the meeting, ML-J went on to say:

Here was a clear-cut issue. To enter into covenant to form the new Church would be to pledge ourselves to further that object.

As a church we had always regarded the ecumenical movement as being anti-evangelical and therefore against the interests of the Gospel as

[1]The Scottish Evangelical Fellowship had been launched with a Rally in Edinburgh on November 26, 1963, at which ML-J had been the preacher.
[2]The organizers of both the Irish and the Scottish Fellowships do not seem to have known that ML-J's thinking had now gone beyond the old inter-denominational co-operation between evangelicals.

we understand it. This had become still clearer recently in the fraternization that was taking place between the World Council of Churches and the Church of Rome. Observers from the World Council of Churches had been officially present at the recent Vatican Council meetings and Roman Catholic representatives attended the meeting of the World Council of Churches. Something was to take place the following night (January 21st) which was almost incredible – namely, a Jesuit priest was to preach in Westminster Abbey in connection with what is called 'The week of prayer for Christian Unity'. And the Archbishop of Canterbury, attended by high officials of the Church of England, was soon to visit the Pope. Moreover, it was clear that the Congregationalists and the English Presbyterians were soon to amalgamate and negotiations between the Methodist Church and the Anglican Church were well advanced. It was clear that the ultimate object was to have a single comprehensive church in this country and that would obviously include eventually the Church of Rome, basically unreformed though perhaps modified in certain outward respects . . .

When the motion was proposed and seconded that Westminster Chapel should not enter into covenant with other churches to form the proposed Congregational Church in England and Wales, it was overwhelmingly carried, not a hand being raised against it. The Minutes of the meeting record Dr Lloyd-Jones' reaction: 'He was overwhelmed, humbled, and mightily encouraged and he had a feeling that something of profound significance not only to us as a church but to other churches also had taken place.'

In the same Institute Hall in which this meeting was, as usual, held, the Westminster Fellowship also met on March 21, 1966 for what was to be the last in the whole series of addresses on questions of church polity and evangelical unity. As though to mark the importance both of the occasion and of the decision to be faced by all Anglican evangelicals, Dr Packer was invited by ML-J to speak. He came with a well-prepared address. He knew that *All in Each Place* had not been well received by the majority of those listening to him and took evident care not to say anything which would add further tension to a relationship already strained.

The case which Dr Packer put for involvement in the Anglican ecumenical agenda and for not making common cause with ML-J's plea for a new visible unity between evangelical churches was twofold. First, he argued that evangelical Christians were already united in the great matters of the gospel and that a formal, organisational or denominational unity was not essential. Second, as evangelicals differed over secondary matters, such as church order, he believed that they were justified in remaining in denominations which accorded with their views on those secondary matters provided they retained their freedom to preach the gospel. 'Am I,' he asked, 'separated from my friends in a way which is needless and which could be remedied? I am not sure that I am. Though we agree on essentials, there are other points on which we are divided . . . I do not see how the facts of the case can be met except by evangelicals maintaining fellowship while at the same time [continuing in] different denominational alignments.'

As Packer had spoken at the afternoon session, there was, regrettably, no time to discuss his address that day and the value of the debate which took place at the next meeting was much reduced both by his absence and by the fact that copies of what he had said were not available. But it was clear that disagreement was not over details, rather the whole assessment of the current climate of opinion in the denominations seemed to be different. Anglican evangelicals spoke optimistically about what could be done to retrieve the situation within the denominations. As one of the contributors to *All in Each Place* had confessed, his case was 'based throughout on the assumption that there is real concern for biblical Christianity in the English churches of today; that there is real conviction of the divine authority of the word of God'.[1]

Packer's address on March 21, 1966, had no alternative to offer with respect to wider church unity. His hopes lay in what might be obtained from working within the ecumenical programme, and he asked those of a contrary view to set forth the more biblical form of visible unity which they envisaged. Writing of a private conversation which he had with ML-J about this time, Dr Packer says: 'I once asked Dr Lloyd-Jones whether he was not really saying that we should all join the Fellowship of Independent Evangelical Churches; he replied that that would not do, but did not say why

[1]R. T. Beckwith in *All in Each Place*, p. 142. Although Dr Packer no longer spoke of the condition of Anglicanism (and Methodism) in the terms he had used in 1963, he clearly had misgivings and was to say, in 1969, 'It is now clear that no union at present proposed will bring much in the short run in the way of protestant and evangelical reformation'. And, speaking of his 'Independent brethren', he conceded, 'It may in time appear that they read the signs of the times correctly.' Address at the Islington Clerical Conference, reported in the *English Churchman*, January 10, 1969.

not, nor what the alternative was, save that something new was called for.'[1]

*   *   *

On March 22, 1966, the day following the Westminster Fraternal, ML-J was engaged to preach at a combined meeting of churches in the market town of Melton Mowbray in the English Midlands. It was one of the occasions when I drove him, partly to give us time to talk and partly so that he could be back in his own home by the early hours of the following morning. Our conversation included the fraternal of the previous day and the form which the new grouping of evangelical churches might take. But the message he preached that night overshadowed all else. His text was Acts 24:24–26, especially verse 25, 'And as he reasoned of righteousness, temperance and judgment to come, Felix trembled . . .' The congregation which had come to the parish church in Melton Mowbray that evening were as affected as everyone else at that date by the excitement over the general election which was to be held the following week. But as Paul's message to Felix was preached all else suddenly seemed trivial. The silent and packed congregation, whose feet rested on ancient flagstones covering the dead of other centuries, were not being addressed as voters but as immortals whose chief interests belonged to another world. The truth that all is transitory save the Word of God swept aside every other thought and seemed to hold all captive to its power.

It was characteristic of Dr Lloyd-Jones' generosity that, although it was about 1 a.m. when we reached Ealing after that service, I had to come in while he proceeded to the kitchen and cut in half the huge Stilton cheese which had been presented to him that evening!

ML-J often gave thought at this date to the old problem of the number of his commitments. The most obvious thing to reduce was his mid-week preaching engagements, but this was not an option he entertained. As already said, he viewed these meetings as part of his calling as an evangelist. Gospel preaching remained his first love. He did, however, withdraw from the Advisory Committee of the Inter-Varsity Fellowship. As Dr Oliver Barclay, the General Secretary of the IVF, wrote to tell him, it was a resignation very reluctantly received for he had played a principal part in that work for so long:

[1] *Martyn Lloyd-Jones, Chosen by God*, p. 49.

I myself have a vivid memory of the first Advisory Committee meeting I attended under your Chairmanship. I suppose it was in 1941 in Cambridge and ever since then we have owed a lot to your wise guidance and policy in many ways. I am sure the IVF would easily have made a number of important mistakes if it had not been for your help. We are deeply grateful and thank God for the gifts He has given you and for the fact that you were able to help us with your time and advice, etc. over these crucial years.[1]

The only Sunday when ML-J was not in his own pulpit – except for his summer break – was the first Sunday after Easter. It did not necessarily mean that he was on holiday for he usually combined some additional services with these breaks. On Easter Monday, April 11, 1966, he went by train to Glasgow with Mrs Lloyd-Jones to the home of their old friends, Mr and Mrs Alex Murdoch in Giffnock. The Murdochs had arranged another preaching tour under the auspices of the Scottish Evangelistic Council. The next day took them all 177 miles by car through the Scottish Highlands, via Glencoe and Fort William to Inverness. Here ML-J was to preach on the following day in the Free North Church – once the pulpit of his friend Principal John MacLeod. On Thursday the journey with the Murdochs was resumed, with a Rally that evening in Aberdeen. Friday took them back to Glasgow, with a cruise on the Clyde up to Loch Fyne on the Saturday, followed by a quiet Sunday. Then on Monday night he preached at a 'Bible Witness Rally' in the Tent Hall, Glasgow before returning to London the next day, April 19. Tiring or not, it was the kind of holiday he thoroughly enjoyed, and the crowded congregations were a testimony to the esteem in which so many in Scotland had long held his ministry.

The period between Easter and his summer break was usually the busiest of the whole year and 1966 was no exception. In these weeks he visited at least fifteen different parts of England or Wales where he preached once or twice. There were also the usual church meetings, committee meetings, interviews in his vestry on week days, correspondence, and the annual Evangelical Library lecture in June when the lecturer was his friend Dr Wilbur Smith.

ML-J's last Friday night on Romans was on May 27 and his last

---

[1]March 18, 1966. I am inclined to think that this withdrawal was also due to a concern not to embarrass the IVF over the issues which lay ahead and which he knew would be divisive.

Sunday at Westminster before his summer break on July 10. The next day, the first of his summer break, he was in Oxford to attend the Second International Congress of Christian Physicians. Some 700 delegates were present and heard him speak on the three evenings, Tuesday to Thursday – the last night from the pulpit of St Mary's, the University church – on the importance of biblical theology as the only sufficient basis and guide for contemporary medical practice. Sir Herbert Seddon, who chaired the Congress, told its members that ML-J had tried to teach him some medicine when he was a student and had reprimanded him on one occasion for singing in a laboratory. On a more serious note, he also spoke of how a service at which ML-J had preached in the Rhondda Valley had been the turning point in his life.

Dr Lloyd-Jones returned from Oxford late on the Thursday night with just one day free before leaving with Bethan on a first visit to Finland, via Sweden. He had not been in Scandinavia since 1946. After a rough weekend at sea in which his sea sickness remedy failed (and Mrs Lloyd-Jones forgot the Marzine until it was too late!), they reached Gothenburg and then Stockholm on Monday morning, July 18. In the six hours before they sailed for Finland at 5.30 that afternoon they saw enough of the Swedish capital to be impressed with a sense of its majesty and greatness. The view of Sweden behind them in the sunset that evening across a satin sea, he was to speak of as 'one of the most glorious sights I ever saw'. Disembarking the next morning, they were met by friends and driven half-way to Helsinki, their stopping point being the country home of a Professor Sarisala, who taught Hebrew at the University of Helsinki. The subject of diet was, however, one of the professor's great interests and after an initial 'speech' from him on the subject the two men proceeded to debate the benefits of such things as sour milk, porridge made of rye and a low meat consumption. Sarisala's build possibly added some force to his arguments, for he was the thinnest man they had ever met. Bethan was not as interested in the discussion as she might normally have been. She explained in a letter to Keith (her son-in-law) and Ann: 'With the heat and the driving, I slept three times (*without* falling off the chair!) before I was rescued to have a sauna bath.'

The next day, Wednesday, they reached Helsinki, 'a very beautiful city', where ML-J preached that evening in the Lutheran church. From there they proceeded the day after to Lahti where a conference of students was convened for five days. Speaking through an interpreter, ML-J was impressed by their seriousness and was interested to meet a man who had been at Westminster Chapel. After a day's break in which it was possible to see more of this land of 60,000 lakes, and also the birthplace of Sibelius, there was a three-day conference for student leaders (July 28–31). Such was the eagerness of these students that on the Saturday night after he had spoken (with the interpretation) for two and a half hours they still wanted more time to question him.

Their last week in Finland was spent at a conference at Tampere. Announced as being 'for young people', ML-J was to find some 2,000 people of all ages crowded into a great marquee. From here they went to Copenhagen, Denmark, as guests of John Madsen (once a member at Westminster) who, with his brother Paul, had arranged a conference in a seaside hotel which could accommodate 600–700 people. At all these gatherings the one question repeatedly raised concerned the present state of the church in the world and what evangelicals, who often lacked spiritual food, should do.

On August 12, 1966, these labours ended with their return to Britain. There was nearly a month's complete relaxation at the new Catherwood home at Balsham before his ministry at Westminster resumed on Sunday, September 11. This was the start of his twenty-ninth year at the Chapel. The first church meeting on Thursday, September 15 was the usual 'At Home'. It was a meeting keenly anticipated each year, and no one who attended ever doubted whether ML-J had a sense of humour. On this occasion the humorous part of his address (not given in the short written account later published for church members) concerned the taking of sauna baths. The subject, he confessed, was one of which he had no personal experience, but he was able to give his 'travelling companion's' vivid description. Despite the fact that the benefits of the sauna had been 'proclaimed for 1,000 years', it was, he said,

contrary to one of my physiological principles. They say it does everyone good. The first rule in dietetics is to remember

> Jack Sprat could eat no fat,
> His wife could eat no lean . . .

The same is true with respect to the application of heat to the body . . . (I believe in health. Thirty-five years ago an old minister who saw me putting on two coats said, 'You are careful of your health though careless of your life'). When last in America in 1963 I met Dr Erdman in Philadelphia who teaches that people are divided into two groups, those to whom heat does good and those to whom cold does good. His whole theory is based on the fact that hot fomentation is good for some while cold is good for others. If you get red you should not sit in the sun. I follow Dr Erdman, that is why I did not have a sauna. Since getting back I have read of a Welsh miner who was advised to have a sauna: he went down to Swansea and died while having it! . . . The Finns take the sauna very seriously. I tried to make a joke about it to a man who has one every day. Seeing he was very hoarse from a bad cold, I said to him, 'Ah, the sauna does you no good . . .'.

The truth, as all his listeners knew, was that he did enjoy heat but, faced with the choice of red-hot stones in a little wooden hut full of steam or more debate with Professor Sarisala, he was bound to prefer the latter.

The main spiritual lesson which he drew from the Scandinavian visit, as he told the members of Westminster Chapel, concerned the same issue that was now before them in England. He explained that he had been invited to Finland by the Free Church, not the national Lutheran Church, and he outlined the part which Lord Radstock had played in the origins of that Church as well as in the conversion of Prince Bernadotte of Sweden. But the problem in Sweden was that they had no alternative to the national Church and that, he believed, was the reason why spiritual conditions were worse in that country. What he had seen in Finland and Denmark confirmed his conviction that present developments were going to lead to a major division – with a 'world church' on one side and on the other such churches as made up those who have 'a living relationship with the Lord Jesus Christ and who have His life within them'. His holiday reading, he also said, had been in the field of the Reformation and he had particularly enjoyed a first volume of a history of Protestantism. 'The same thing is happening again – people are examining themselves to find out where they stand. We must understand our own position and the truth concerning the church. I have come back very encouraged. We are part of a movement of the Spirit of God calling people together who are agreed about the gospel and the way of salvation.'

The next week Dr Lloyd-Jones recommenced his usual travelling with three separate visits to Wales within ten days. The first was to preach for his old friend Eliseus Howells in Bridgend; the second to

Pontardawe, and the third to Tonypandy and Carmarthen (the latter having now been an annual engagement for 38 years).

In order to speak at the Second National Assembly of Evangelicals organised by the Evangelical Alliance to begin at Westminster Central Hall on Tuesday, October 18, 1966, he had to cancel preaching in Lancashire.[1] To the general public it could have seemed that his speaking for the Alliance was simply another of many such meetings. The leaders of the Alliance and a number of ministers knew that this occasion was to be different, though how different in terms of precipitating a division within evangelicalism, they scarcely anticipated.

Dr Lloyd-Jones was scheduled as the speaker at the opening meeting of the Second National Assembly of Evangelicals on October 18. Two more days of addresses and discussions were to follow, with a concluding communion service on the Thursday evening. The main thing before the Assembly was known to be the question of Christian unity and, particularly, the finding of the Commission set up after the First Assembly. In a 12 page Report, published in time for the Second Assembly, the Commission announced its finding:

There is no *widespread* demand at the present time for the setting up of a united evangelical Church on denominational lines . . . This does not mean that there could not be an effective fellowship or federation of evangelical churches at both the local and national level.[2]

As the leaders of the Alliance were both familiar with this finding and with Dr Lloyd-Jones' differing views (which they had heard in private), it may seem surprising that he should have been asked to restate his position as the main speaker at the Rally which marked the Assembly's opening. They obviously thought that it would be good to bring 'into the open a difference of opinion within the evangelical world which had been known about for some years'.[3]

[1] It is an indication of the calls made upon his time that he had also been asked to preach in York Minster that same evening.
[2] *Report of the Commission on Church Unity to the National Assembly of Evangelicals*, The Evangelical Alliance, 1966, p. 10.
[3] *Unity In Diversity*, ten papers given at the National Assembly of Evangelicals in 1966, The Evangelical Alliance, 1967, p. 7. In view of doubts expressed to the contrary, it is important to observe that this Alliance publication records that he was 'asked to say in public what he had said in private' (p. 8).

This would hopefully show that the Alliance was big enough and tolerant enough to present all sides, and there was probably the expectation that a public airing of ML-J's views would show that they had comparatively little support and thus reduce pressure for action according to those views. The printed programme for the Assembly announced that it was expected that Dr Martyn Lloyd-Jones would speak on Christian Unity. The Chairman that evening was the Rev J. R. W. Stott who also knew the general nature of what ML-J would say, having had a personal conversation with him on the subject at the International Congress of Christian Physicians in Oxford that summer. Stott was scheduled to take ten minutes before the main speaker in order to state his own, i.e. the evangelical Anglican, point of view on unity so that the meeting would clearly understand that ML-J was not speaking for all evangelicals.

The evening of October 18, 1966, did not, however, go according to plan or, at least, not from the point when the Chairman introduced the main speaker as 'in every particular my elder and better; I hold him in great esteem and affection in Christ'. ML-J spoke with much point and force, summarizing his beliefs as already given in these pages: evangelicals could no longer follow their traditional view on unity because the ecumenical movement had introduced an entirely new situation – 'We are confronted by a situation today such as has not been the case since the Protestant Reformation'. But instead of facing the doctrine of the church, 'The impression is given that evangelicals are more concerned to maintain the integrity of their different denominations than anybody else in those denominations'. If evangelicals were presently prepared to be 'evangelical wings' in their denominations, the question they needed to face was whether they would be an 'evangelical wing' in a national, ecumenical and, eventually, Roman Catholic church.

The main issue, he said, was whether evangelicals should try to modify and improve the existing situation in the denominations or meet the ecumenical challenge by going back to Scripture and asking, What is the Christian church? 'Here is the great divide. The ecumenical people put fellowship before doctrine. We, as evangelicals, put doctrine before fellowship.' The church is the body of those who have believed and experienced the fundamental truths (Acts 2:42), people who give daily evidence by their lives that they are Christians – 'that is the evangelical view of the Christian church . . . the church consists of living people'.

He proceeded to speak of schism and to assert that people who do not believe the essentials of the faith cannot be guilty of schism. 'They are not in the church. If you don't believe a certain irreducible minimum, you cannot be a Christian, and you are not in the church. Have we reached a time when one must not say a thing like that? Have evangelicals so changed that we no longer make an assertion like that?'

Evangelicals were united with men in their denominations with whom they only agreed on secondary issues, while their true unity with fellow evangelicals was never expressed in terms of the New Testament doctrine of the church.

What reasons have we for not coming together? Why is it that we are so anxious to hold on to our inherited positions? . . . Don't we feel the call to come together, not occasionally, but *always*? It's a grief to me that I spend so little of my time with some of my brethren, I want to spend the whole of my time with them. I am a believer in ecumenicity, evangelical ecumenicity. You and I have been called to a positive task. We are guardians and custodians of the faith, the faith that's been given once and for ever to the saints, and tradition tells us that we evangelicals have been the guardians and custodians of our New Testament heritage. We believe the Bible. We take it authoritatively. We don't impose our philosophies and ideas upon it, and we're the only people who are doing this. God has given us this solemn task of guarding and protecting and defending this faith, in this present evil age in which we find ourselves. But, my friends, we're not only the guardians and custodians of the faith of the Bible itself. We are the representatives and the successors of the glorious men who fought this same fight, the good fight of faith in centuries past. We are standing in the position of the Protestant Reformers. Are we accepting this modern idea that the Reformation was the greatest tragedy that ever happened? If you want to say that it was a tragedy, here was the tragedy, that the Roman Church had become so rotten that it was necessary for the reformers to do what they did. It wasn't the departure of the reformers that was the tragedy. It was the state of the Roman Church that was the tragedy. And we are the modern representatives of these men, and the Puritans, and the Covenanters, and the early Methodists, and others. Can't you see the opportunity? I believe that God is calling upon us to maintain this ancient witness, not occasionally, not haphazardly, but always putting it to the people of this country.

I know that there are men, ministers and clergy, in this congregation before me who, if they did what I'm exhorting them to do, would have a tremendous problem before them, even a financial, an economic problem, and a family problem, and I don't want to minimise this. My heart goes out to such men. There are great problems confronting us if we act on these principles. But has the day come when we, as evangelicals, are afraid of problems? The true Christian has always had problems. The early Christians had grievous problems – cast aside from their families. My dear friends, we are living in tremendous times. We are living in one of the great turning points of history. I have said already, and I say it again; there has been nothing like this since the sixteenth century. It is a day of glorious opportunity, unique opportunity, unexampled opportunity, if only we could see it, and rise up and take it. We may be small in numbers, and that seems to deter some people. Since when has the doctrine of the remnant been forgotten amongst evangelicals? It is one of the most glorious doctrines in the whole of the Bible. As a well-known American put it last century, 'One with God is a majority'. Evangelicals are not interested in numbers. We are interested in truth, and in the living God. If God be for us, who can be against us? Go home and read the story of Gideon again . . . We shall need great grace. We shall need to be filled with the Spirit. We shall all need to be humble. Who knows but that the ecumenical movement may be something for which, in years to come, we shall thank God, because it made us face our problems on the Church level, instead of on the level of movements, and really brought us together as a fellowship or an association of evangelical churches. May God speed the day![1]

So Lloyd-Jones had done what he had been asked to do. He had kept to his brief and set before the Assembly the situation as he saw it. But what followed had neither been planned nor commissioned by the Assembly. The Chairman rose not to close the meeting but to offer further impromptu counsel:

There, brethren, is dialogue . . . We are here to debate. I would think appeal should have come at the end [of the Assembly]. I believe history is against what Dr Lloyd-Jones has said . . . Scripture is against him, the remnant was within the church not outside it. I hope no one will act precipitately . . . We are all concerned with the same ultimate issues and with the glory of God.

[1]A summary of this address was printed in *Unity In Diversity*. The whole is given in *Knowing the Times*. The events of the evening of October 18, 1966, have been variously misunderstood. One recent author says that Dr Lloyd-Jones urged 'Anglican Evangelicals to leave their compromised Church and join him in a pure Reformed Church. He got a dusty answer, delivered publicly, by John Stott' (Michael Saward, *Evangelicals on the Move*, 1987, p. 11).

Though calmly spoken, John Stott's intervention to repudiate the case which had just been presented could not be other than sensational. It polarised the densely packed meeting. Many who were only beginning to consider the issues under debate were suddenly faced with the easier choice of following one evangelical leader or another. It was not the worst possible conclusion to an historic meeting – that would have occurred if ML-J had followed his natural instinct to debate then and there – but it was a long way from the result for which the Assembly planners had hoped. Feelings were profoundly stirred. Perhaps, as John Stott evidently thought when it was too late, it was a mistake to pre-empt all debate by having Dr Lloyd-Jones speak with such authority at the Assembly's first meeting but the programme order had not been of his choice. As ML-J and Stott left the tense gathering, the latter murmured apologetically that he was afraid that some of the Anglican clergy might have left their churches the next morning had he said nothing more. Both John Stott and the Evangelical Alliance leaders had clearly underestimated the difference between hearing the Doctor's views in private and the same views *preached* at the Central Hall.

The second day of the Assembly was designed to give further time to the subject of unity, but there was no real continuance of the issues opened the night before. The major address relevant to the matter was by a young Anglican, the Rev Julian Charley, who was given time to balance the time given ML-J. His case that they should all be seeking 'a united, territorial church rather than advocating secession' was far removed from reality and debate fell flat. ML-J was there for some of the day but he took no part. The organizers were mightily relieved that the remainder of the Assembly passed without more controversy. The fact was that the line had already been drawn and many nonconformist evangelical churches proceeded to withdraw from the Evangelical Alliance.

Inevitably the religious press concentrated all their interest on the public division revealed on the night of October 18. Under a bold heading, 'Evangelicals – Leave your Denominations', *The Christian*, October 21 announced that Dr Lloyd-Jones had given 'an impassioned plea . . . to form a united Church'. The next week the same journal published an 'Evangelical Alliance Protest'. The protest might have been that the heading did not correctly summarize ML-J's address. Instead the EA's objection was that the words of the heading had appeared above a photograph of the front row of the platform party, which could cause the men concerned 'serious embarrassment in their own denominations . . . The men who appear in the photograph are, with one exception, opposed to such a policy.' One of the 'platform party' was David Winter who, reporting the Assembly in *The Life of Faith* (October 27), said that the public rally

in dramatic fashion, dragged into the open a subject normally avoided in evangelical debate – secession. Dr Martyn Lloyd-Jones made an eloquent plea to evangelicals to leave their denominations and join a United Evangelical Church and the Chairman, the Rev John Stott, publicly (firmly but politely) disagreed with him . . . Feelings ran high . . .

The Baptist Times reporter (October 27) spoke of 'A sharp clash of views . . . with Dr Martyn Lloyd-Jones seeming to be encouraging evangelicals to secede from their denominations and the Rev John Stott challenging his address by claiming that division was not the way forward . . . it was clear that evangelicals are divided theologically . . .' Across the border, the Editor of the *Monthly Record of the Free Church of Scotland* (December 1966) asserted that 'A plan for the formation of an evangelical church was passionately put forward at the opening public meeting by Dr Martyn Lloyd-Jones, and just as forcibly resisted by Rev John R. Stott from the chair!'

It was left to the Anglican paper *the English Churchman* to get the emphasis of what ML-J said right:

He was not putting forward some negative scheme into which we are to be reluctantly forced, but rather was pointing us to the glorious opportunity of taking positive action because we realise we ought to if we are to be true to our evangelical convictions. Non-evangelicals have realised that visible disunity among Christians is sinful and a breakdown of the unity which our Lord willed for His people. We as evangelicals make much of our spiritual unity but are content to let it be disguised effectively by our visible disarray.

Anglican Evangelicals would appear, on the evidence of the Assembly to be the most intransigent on this matter. Although it was allowed by some that the time might come when they would be forced out of the Church of England they were content to wait until that time comes, rather than take some positive steps towards evangelical union now. A few gave the impression that nothing would move them at all. But is it not a misunderstanding to look at this problem only as one of secession? Does entry into a scriptural union with other Christians deserve that

[527]

name? We feel sure it will not be applied to those who enter a united Anglican-Methodist Church.

Few seem to accept the fact that whether we like it or not our present denominations are doomed, and if present tendencies are anything to go by they are doomed to be swallowed up by Rome. Some will label this talk as defeatist and perhaps it is, but we are more inclined to regard it as realistic . . . Who is really giving a definite lead in the Church of England at this time? Who will define the line beyond which we will not go? We have already surrendered on a number of issues which in earlier days would never have been accepted. We have heard it said that when the Articles go then will be the time to depart, but we believe that the authorities are quite capable of devising a formula which will enable those evangelicals who so desire to remain in the Church of England without straining their consciences unduly.

In these circumstances it is not enough to attack the idea of evangelical union as an attempt at perfectionism. The Scriptures never give us any excuse for failing to seek the best in our own lives or in the life of the Church, and those who use the perfectionist argument as ammunition seem to us to be in danger of condoning sin. We recognise that there will be no perfect Church on earth but we are nevertheless meant to keep it as pure as we can, and this we are very far from doing at the moment.[1]

*   *   *

The first meeting of the Westminster Fellowship after the Evangelical Alliance Assembly met on November 28, 1966, and it was evident from the abnormally large attendance that an important occasion was anticipated. Dr Lloyd-Jones commenced the meeting, as usual, by asking one of the brethren to lead in prayer. His choice was the Rev William Wheatley, a retired missionary of the Qua Iboe mission in Nigeria and a man highly esteemed by all who knew him. Mr Wheatley's opening prayer included a petition for God's richer blessing upon ML-J 'in these closing years – they must be closing years – of his ministry'. Given the Doctor's apparent vigour, the remark, interjected into the petition, came as a surprise to those who heard it.

The morning session of the fraternal then proceeded with ML-J asking men to give their impression of the recent Assembly's deliberations on unity. Morgan Derham, the new General Secretary of the Evangelical Alliance, thought that an opportunity had been provided for views held in the Westminster Fellowship to be given a public hearing for the first time and that this had been helpful in

[1]*English Churchman*, Oct. 28, 1966.

forwarding a discussion which was still in its early stages. Another speaker believed that it would take two years to measure the reaction to the Doctor's address. But some were of the opinion that the Assembly had shown that it was not a forum where these issues could be resolved. It contained too many men – notably Anglicans – who seemed unprepared at any stage to face secession. Others cautioned against being too pessimistic and pointed to the fact that the Assembly had passed a resolution (proposed by Leith Samuel, a member of the Westminster Fellowship) that 'the movement towards the Roman Catholic Church is a movement away from biblical Christianity'.

Dr Lloyd-Jones listened to this free flowing comment for some while before rising to give his own conclusion. The time had come for action and the first practical step, he believed, was to bring the present Fellowship to an end:

At Welwyn eighteen months ago I said I saw no hope of evangelical unity and said that this Fellowship had come to an end. I postponed that decision . . . When we met in November 1965, in view of the proposal of a Commission arising out of the first Evangelical Alliance Assembly, I said I was prepared to wait for another year to see if the Commission could do what we failed to do. We have waited. The issue has been settled: there is a fundamental cleavage among us. There are two positions: first, those who believe in staying in and, second, those who see no purpose in doing that. There is the division. It is unmistakable. The same cleavage is here in this Fellowship.

He went on to describe how the fraternal had begun 25 years earlier when, being in touch with both Free Churchmen and Anglicans, he was asked to conduct a Seminar. He believed that its original purpose had been fulfilled. If they now went on, without change, there was the danger of the gathering degenerating into strife and wrangling: 'There has been strife already in these discussions; some of us have been given grace and restrained ourselves with difficulty.' The meeting, he further explained, had never possessed any constitution and it was an embarrassment that it should centre around him. 'I am not surprised at what has happened. I am saddened but not surprised.' Then, with a momentary touch of humour, he alluded to the remark which had caught everyone's attention in the opening prayer. 'Mr Wheatley in his prayer was announcing that I am coming to the end of my ministry. Naturally one is influenced by that. But "we must all appear before the judgment seat of Christ". You may go before me. Don't depend on calendars, diseases are no respecters of age! We have all got to appear before the judgment seat of Christ. This is uppermost in my mind.'

With regard to the future, he went on:

I am very ready to do anything to help men who are out of the denominations or who are thinking of moving out, but I cannot see the point of meeting with men who are adamant on staying in . . .

We must never lose charity. We must recognize the honesty of those with whom we differ and recognize that others do not see it as we do. People say, 'He is quite right but . . .'. I am prepared to accept that. I have been severely criticized for years from two sides. Some say, 'He is much too quick'. Others, 'He moves much too slowly'. I *have* been holding back and delaying. I have been thinking especially of the difficulties for men and their families. I said this at the Evangelical Alliance meeting. I don't know if that was said in the report of my address – I never read reports of what I have said.

Our personal relationships will remain what they were before. We can help one another, but we cannot go on in regular association.

I am not going to organize anything. I have no personal interest. If I had wanted to start a denomination I would not have left it till now. I have had few letters [since the Assembly] but I had one from a minister – you would be amazed if he was named – saying there were many all over the country ready for a Reformed Evangelical Church![1] Well, produce the evidence . . . I am not impressed with the numbers here this morning [as some present had said they were]. I remember a meeting with T. T. Shields of Toronto, with whose contendings on personalities I was not and am not in agreement. When invited to lunch I had the opportunity given me to tell him he was doing no good by his contendings and tirades. 'But,' he answered, 'the circulation of the *Gospel Witness* has rocketed, how do you explain that?' I replied that I was not a bit surprised. Where there is a dog fight a crowd always comes. People are ready to look on, but there is a great difference between looking on and taking part. Those of you who say I am too pessimistic, all right, produce your evidence!

All I can do is help. I am not going to organize, lead, or suggest anything. I trust I shall be a helper. I feel I have done what I have been called to do. The question is what are *you* going to do?

[1]The letter was from Tom Rees, who wrote (on October 20) to thank him for his message in the Central Hall and to add: 'With respect, may I point out that you do not seem to realise that many evangelical ministers look to you for a lead . . . Why not leave your Church and start the Evangelical Reformed Church? I feel sure there are many men who would readily join you. Thank you again for your ministry.'

1966: The Call to Decision

It must have cost him a great deal to give this address. He knew it meant a virtual farewell to a number long associated with the fraternal. With respect to any future fraternal, as he told the morning meeting, he had no plans. If men wished to discuss further they could have the use of the room or another room after lunch but he would not be present. If any further meeting was able to draw up a basis with which he felt free to be associated he would give support. But, he concluded, 'the present Westminster Fraternal must be considered as disbanded'.

As we have seen, criticism of ML-J's conviction that there must be a new evangelical unity of *churches* had drawn attention to the absence of practical proposals for its implementation. In 1964, and probably earlier, ML-J had spoken in private of his vision for a unity of evangelical churches and denominations which would include such bodies as the FIEC in England and the Free Church of Scotland. At what point a further idea occurred to him, or was put to him, I do not know. It is clear from the conversation at Wappenham Manor in August 1965 that he had spoken with some leaders of the FIEC and particularly, I believe, with one of the best-known of their pastors, the Rev T. H. Bendor-Samuel. Mr Bendor-Samuel was also a leader of the British Evangelical Council, an organization launched in 1953 in order to represent churches and bodies that were unwilling to be connected with the ecumenical movement.[1] E. J. Poole-Connor, another of the founders of the BEC, had resigned from the Evangelical Alliance in 1952, as recorded earlier. Hitherto Dr Lloyd-Jones had never participated in the BEC, chiefly on account of his fear that its primary purpose might be too negative. The BEC had small support in England but, including as it did the Free Church of Scotland and the Irish Evangelical Church (those denominations being represented on its Council by two of his friends, the Rev G. N. M. Collins and the Rev W. J. Grier), there was the potential for a wider appeal. The question which now occurred to him was whether the BEC, and its member churches, could provide the structure for a move towards the positive unity of evangelical churches. The BEC leaders with whom ML-J consulted believed that it could and by the autumn of 1966 the idea had surfaced among men connected with the Westminster Fellowship.

[1]Twelve months earlier the personnel of the Council had come together to represent the International Council of Christian Churches in Britain but their perception of the direction which that movement was taking had led to their early withdrawal and to a separate organization.

It is interesting that ML-J himself said nothing of the BEC in speaking on the morning of November 29, 1966, the occasion when the original Fellowship was disbanded. He clearly believed that it was time that others took up leadership and grappled with the issues. For that same reason he was not present when a considerable number of the old fraternal reconvened on the afternoon of the same day and in the same hall at Westminster Chapel. The meeting began at 2 p.m., fifteen minutes later than the usual hour for the afternoon session, and commenced with a season of prayer. A proposal that a smaller group of men be appointed to draw up a constitution for a new fraternal was not carried. Another proposal was that two Fellowships be formed, one to deal with discussions of church issues (perhaps under the auspices of the Fellowship of Independent Evangelical Churches or the British Evangelical Council), and a second for spiritual questions of pastoralia and other matters of concern to all conservative evangelicals. In this way narrower and broader purposes could both be pursued. But this proposal also did not gain any significant support. Following much discussion a resolution was finally framed expressing a readiness to respond to the Doctor's appeal of October 18 and affirming a commitment to the policy outlined in his address on that date. To this it was objected that we should avoid a statement which could look like a personal following of ML-J. Further, as the Doctor's address was unpublished, it might be premature to express commitment until the precise issues involved could be studied. There was already some difference of opinion over what he had actually said at the Central Hall meeting. But the opinion that the issue should be presented in terms of the Doctor's appeal was strong even though a measure of uncertainty persisted over what the resolution 'to endorse the appeal made by Dr Lloyd-Jones at Westminster Central' entailed. The temporary chairman (the Rev T. H. Bendor-Samuel of the FIEC) believed it was a statement of *intent* rather than a commitment to immediate action. Finally, along with a decision to call another meeting at which ML-J be invited to take the chair, the resolution was carried. The vote was 96 for, 13 against and 31 abstentions. There were certainly a few who voted against, and others who abstained, who were to stay closer to ML-J in the days ahead than some who voted in favour.

The first of two sides of notes for his Evangelical Alliance address, October 18, 1966. For transcription see 'Evangelical Unity: An Appeal' in Knowing the Times.

As for myself, my name, reputation, and esteem with the churches of God, I commit the whole concernment of them to Him whose presence, through grace, I have hitherto enjoyed, and whose promise I lean upon, that he will 'never leave me nor forsake me'.

JOHN OWEN
in 'A Review of the True Nature of Schism'.
Works, vol. 13, p. 275

26

Controversy

As a theme for his annual letter to the congregation, dated January 1, 1967, Dr Lloyd-Jones wrote of 'the relationship between the local church and the general situation'. No doubt he did so partly because of some who wondered whether there was any need for the Chapel and its minister to be so involved in the wider debate. Given the degree of encouragement at Westminster Chapel, was there not a case for at least a measure of withdrawal from the problems of others? There were probably times when the same thought came to ML-J himself during this twenty-ninth year of his ministry in London. Perhaps the annual letter of January 1967 was an answer to his own temptation as well as those of others. 'There is always,' he wrote, 'the danger of living only to ourselves, and for ourselves, in the local church . . . We are part of a larger whole, and we are responsible for what happens there also. Failure to realise this accounts for much of the confusion at the present time. The feeling too often is that as long as we are happy and all is going well with us locally that nothing else matters.'

He went on to point out the great changes which were taking place in the direction of a 'world church': 'We are living in momentous times, undoubtedly one of the great turning points of history'. To contract out of wider responsibilities at such an hour was impossible. 'As "no man liveth unto himself" no church can live unto herself.' As he had done many times before, he sought to show his people both their privilege and their responsibility. He concluded the letter with thankfulness and the prayer, 'May the Holy Spirit shine upon the Word and in our hearts more and more, building us up and making us strong to fight the battles of the Lord'.

At the next two meetings of the new Westminster fraternal of ministers on January 23 and March 13, 1967, the discussion centered largely on what the terms of membership would be. ML-J was once more in the chair. Despite all that had already occurred, some were still confused on elementary points of difference. One speaker on January 23 declared: 'I would be unhappy about belonging to a Fellowship which is opposed to the ecumenical movement. We might have a contribution to make'. Yet ML-J had opened the meeting by saying the issue was whether men were in favour of the ecumenical movement and were convinced denominationalists or whether they put the need for evangelical unity, expressed at a church level, first. By this he did not mean, he explained, that there needed to be a secession from all denominations. There was a clear difference between, for example, the Strict Baptists and the Pentecostalists and those 'mixed denominations' where commitment to ecumenism and doctrinal indifferentism prevented any possibility of the discipline of false teachers. Even so, he was careful to add, this did not mean pastors should necessarily leave mixed denominations at once. There were their people to consider. The people needed to be brought to see the issue and that would take time.

He was convinced that the outlook of men who believed that the main denominations could be 'won' for evangelicalism was so different that division was inevitable: 'We are not disagreeing on details, our whole language is different.'

In the end it was in terms of this general difference that the new terms of membership were fixed. After a preamble which said, 'We recognize that all conservative Evangelicals do not see eye to eye with us over the issues we refer to', the Statement of Principles governing membership read:

Because of the serious situation developing in the conversations between the major denominations, and because of our belief in the need for true evangelical unity at church level, the fellowship shall be composed of men exercising a recognized ministry in a local church, or among the churches, whose position is described in the following terms:

1. We are all conservative Evangelicals whose first loyalty is to the conservative evangelical faith, rather than to any inherited traditional position.
2. We are all already dissatisfied with the denominational position, and are grieved with what appears to us to be compromise on the part of many Evangelicals in the doctrinally mixed denominations.
3. We see no hope whatsoever of winning such doctrinally mixed denominations to an evangelical position.

4. We are calling on all Evangelicals to come together on an uncompromising Gospel basis, which involves us in opposition to the ecumenical movement because of its obvious overall trends.
5. Those who are at present in denominations linked with the World Council of Churches are agreed that separation from such denominations is inevitable, and seek to know the mind of God concerning the steps which they should take.
6. Recognizing the urgency of the times, we desire to express our evangelical unity by meeting in this fellowship, and to discuss prayerfully together the principles upon which our unity may be expressed at church level, moving in the direction of a fellowship of evangelical churches.

In the meantime debate in the Christian press on the implications of the division among evangelicals continued and, with reference to this, a significant new factor was added in February 1967 with the appearance of a newsprint monthly, *The Evangelical Times*, in popular illustrated format. With the exception of the *English Churchman* – now selling to a diminishing Anglican readership – the Christian papers which majored in news had never been close to the standpoint of the minister of Westminster Chapel. But the Editor of *The Evangelical Times*, Peter Masters, a former member of Westminster Chapel, was a young pastor who had been helped into the ministry by ML-J and possessed the gifts and energy to promote a cause. Masters became a publicist for the policy which was being articulated in the new Westminster Fellowship. The first issue of *The Evangelical Times* was dramatic enough. Its front page announced that in a large new housing development in the Thames Mead area of Woolwich, in London, Christian worship was likely to be confined by the Greater London Council to an ecumenical centre with 'No sites for Independents'. The chief proponents of the ecumenical centre were the Bishops of Southwark and Woolwich. This news (dubbed 'the Woolwich affair') instantly became a *cause célèbre* in the Christian papers. While a writer in *The Life of Faith* denied that any such danger existed, other writers majored on the 'Threat to Religious Liberty'. The Editor of *The Evangelical Times* was not exaggerating when he spoke, in the March issue, of 'a very considerable stir in many quarters'. It was through this stir that many evangelicals now heard of the British Evangelical Council for the first time, as a 'Protest Rally' was announced to be held under BEC auspices in South London on March 1 with Dr Lloyd-Jones as the speaker. At that meeting, attended by an estimated 900 to 1,000 people at Plumstead, Dr Lloyd-Jones made reference to the local press which had referred to him as 'an opponent of interdenominational activity' – a complete misunderstanding of his position. He went on to say that this was a type of meeting none of them had ever attended before. His theme was the character of ecumenism and the need which the situation demonstrated for evangelicals to stand together if their voice was to be heard. The address was widely reported. The *Church of England Newspaper* gave it the heading, 'Woolwich protest, Dr Martyn Lloyd-Jones repeats his call to (Evangelical) unity'. But *CEN* was against evangelicals attempting to form a united evangelical Church to serve the new Thames Mead development, and called the idea 'divisive, obscurantist and impractical'.

*   *   *

There was certainly no lack of controversial news in this Spring of 1967. For two-and-a-half days in early April the first National Evangelical Anglican Congress met on the campus of Keele University, the delegates being 519 clergy and 481 laymen and women. The Congress under the chairmanship of John Stott had, of course, been planned well before the public differences of the previous six months. The policy which was now to be popularized with reference to ecumenism was already operative.[1] There was to be no confrontation with non-evangelicals. But it was the Keele Congress which first publicized the new approach on church issues as its own publication, *Keele '67*, made clear. In an introductory chapter, John Stott was quoted on the change then occurring in the Church of England. He went on to say:

Evangelicals in the Church of England are changing too. Not in doctrinal conviction (for the truth of the gospel cannot change), but (like any healthy child) in stature and posture . . . We have acquired a reputation for narrow partisanship and obstructionism . . . We need to repent and change.[2]

[1]Colin Buchanan, Bishop of Aston, is ignoring what had been happening over the years when he says, 'In three days a whole constituency turned round'. Quoted in *The Church Scene*, Melbourne, May 27, 1988.
[2]*Keele '67*, The National Evangelical Anglican Congress Statement, edited by Philip Crowe, 1967, p. 8.

The extent of this change in 'posture' was immediately visible, for Dr Ramsey, the Archbishop of Canterbury, was the preacher invited by the evangelicals to open the Keele Congress. It was Ramsey who in the mid-fifties had criticised English evangelicalism as 'heretical' and 'sectarian', who expected to meet atheists in heaven, who took a liberal position on Scripture and a sympathetic view of reunion with Rome.[1] In his short address to evangelicals at the Westminster Central Hall the previous October, John Stott had argued that evangelicals were 'the constitutionalists' within the Church of England, but there was not a hint of this at Keele. There evangelicals listened submissively as the Archbishop reminded them of what their proposed fuller participation in the life of the church would mean. Emphasizing that 'experience' goes before 'theology', Ramsey pointed to what he thought they needed to learn:

Let us recognize that amongst us Anglicans some may have experienced the centrality of the Cross in ways different from others. For instance, those who value, as others do not, such things as sacramental confession or the eucharistic sacrifice . . . We are called as Christians and as Anglicans to be learning from one another . . .[2]

Nor was the 'learning' process to stop here. Followers of Rudolf Bultmann, and the 'de-mythologizing' of the Bible, were equally to be viewed as participants in the life of the church:

We may find fault with his [Bultmann's] treatment of history and with the arbitrariness of his philosophy, but he is not wrong in helping us to see that our knowledge of Jesus must always be an encounter . . . Many people are puzzled by these critical questions. We shall help them by learning with them, and our evangelical calling should make us the more ready to do this.[3]

The Keele statement on doctrine and practice which the Congress was to adopt was in many ways admirably evangelical but, at the same time, its compilers took considerable pains to avoid the kind of exclusiveness which was the anathema of ecumenism. They wrote:

[1]Ramsey's view of the authority of Scripture may be judged by his belief that 'the Fourth Gospel includes authentic historical records' (*The Churchman*, Summer 1967, p. 92). He had made an official visit to the Vatican in 1966.
[2]*The Churchman, op. cit.*, p. 93.
[3]*Ibid.*, p. 94.

We have been slow to learn from other parts of God's Church . . . The initial task for divided Christians is dialogue at all levels and across all barriers. We desire to enter this ecumenical dialogue fully . . .

The World Council of Churches' basis of faith was agreed to be a sufficient statement for all engaged in ecumenism to 'have a right to be treated as Christians'. 'We do not believe secession to be a live issue in our present situation . . . We recognize that the Roman Catholic Church holds many fundamental Christian doctrines in common with ourselves. We rejoice also at signs of biblical reformation.'

After the Congress the *Church Times* reported, 'Their [Evangelicals'] new image has been beaten into shape by a thousand people in three gruelling days'. The change of evangelical Anglican posture was so great that even some observers who were present seemed to doubt it was happening. Canon D. M. Paton, Secretary of the Missionary and Ecumenical Council of the Church Assembly, queried, 'Have evangelicals fully grasped that to play a real part in the corporate life of the Church of England involves taking very seriously (positively as well as negatively) the existence and views of those in the Church of England who are not conservative evangelicals?' John Lawrence, Editor of *Frontier*, believed that the evangelicals had indeed grasped their new role and he rejoiced that the old 'wall of partition' was now truly down:

Now this wall is down Evangelicals will be heard in a new way, but this would not have happened if they had not shown that they are now ready to listen to others. For ten years I have been hoping and praying for something like NEAC, and I thank God for the new stage that is now opening.[1]

It is difficult to convey the extent of the ferment in England over ecumenism at this date. When the Baptist Union Assembly met on April 15, 1967, the published 'Report of the Council' concentrated on the subject and referred to the closer ties developing between several denominations and the Church of Rome. This Report also warned against Dr Lloyd-Jones' idea of congregations withdrawing from their existing denominations 'with a view to the formation of a

---

[1] This quotation, and those in the previous paragraph, were given by the Anglican evangelicals themselves in *Keele '67*, pp. 12–16.

new one, whose theological basis and church structure remains at present undefined'.¹ About the same date the Union also published a 60-page paperback on *Baptists and Unity*. Already in print was *A Proposed Basis For Union* from a joint committee of the Congregational and the Presbyterian Churches which passed the May Assemblies of those denominations and brought nearer what was to be the United Reformed Church. *Towards Reconciliation, The Interim Statement of the Anglican–Methodist Unity Commission*, a document of 78 pages, was also published in 1967.²

These writings manifested the ecumenical openness to all doctrinal views, except any which stated the gospel in exclusive evangelical terms. While Congregationalists and Presbyterians were to be required to 'acknowledge' the formulations and declarations of faith belonging to their Churches in the past, that did not mean they were to *affirm* them. As Caryl Micklem wrote after quoting from the *Savoy Declaration*, 'To accept it as a valid declaration for today would be unthinkable'. Similarly, Methodists must submit to episcopacy, but there was no question of their having to assent to the 39 Articles. The Baptist position was equally against any requirement of creeds which would be 'tests for exclusion or shackles on interpretation'. The one thing which must not be done was to cast doubt on the Christian standing of others on the grounds of 'theological differences'. Thus the authors of *Baptists and Unity* objected to the Evangelical Movement of Wales defining evangelicals as 'those who resolutely endeavour to be faithful to the Gospel', declaring the statement to be 'offensive and wholly out of relationship with the realities of ecumenical discussions'.³ Baptists needed to be on their guard 'lest any come *unawares* into the position of denying that another – even a fellow Baptist – is a child of God in Christ'.⁴ Instead of heeding 'a plea by Dr Martyn Lloyd-Jones' it

¹*The Report of the Council* for the year ended 31st December, 1966, p. 9.
²After various views on the authority of Scripture, including the Anglo-Catholic and the liberal, the Commissioners affirmed 'there can be no question of the exclusion of any of the views outlined above from the life of our Churches . . .' (p. 10).
³*Baptists and Unity*, p. 36. One well-known Baptist minister, who was to be the next Moderator of the Free Church Federal Council, cancelled an arrangement for ML-J to preach for him in October 1967, advising him that 'a different attitude from yours towards the ecumenical movement does not necessarily mean for one moment a weakening of evangelical conviction'.
⁴*Ibid*, p.46.

would be better, the writers believed, to adopt the aim of Abbé Couturier, the Roman Catholic ecumenist, namely, 'the unity of Christians "such as Christ wills and by the means He wills"'.[1]

In terms of the extent of potential controversy, the English spring of 1967 had scarcely any parallel in modern times. On this point at least, Morgan Derham the hard-pressed General Secretary of the Evangelical Alliance was speaking for everyone when he wrote in June that this was 'a period of speedy development and far-reaching change; everything is, so to speak, "on the boil"'.[2]

It is indicative of the tensions that even within the Westminster Chapel membership a measure of controversy had now appeared and that from a quarter where it might least have been expected. In his annual letter to members of January 1, 1967 ML-J had given notice that the Chapel's formal relationship to other evangelical churches would be considered at the Church meeting of March 16. At that meeting he spoke of what was happening in the Congregational Church and of the rapid advance of ecumenism, instancing 'the Woolwich affair' as pointing to the possible future plight of evangelicals if they did not act together. Setting aside the possibility of the formation of a Reformed Evangelical Church, he went on to propose that they joined the Fellowship of Independent Evangelical Churches. These churches, he argued, followed the original independency of the founders of the Congregational Churches, that is to say, such men as John Owen and Thomas Goodwin; furthermore by joining the FIEC the Chapel would necessarily become officially involved in the British Evangelical Council of Churches (to which the FIEC belonged) and which had such leaders as G. N. M. Collins and W. J. Grier who had both preached at Westminster: 'If this body [i.e. the BEC] can be strengthened and enlarged it can deal with problems such as that at Woolwich.'

When comment and questions were invited, a number of the younger members who held firmly to their minister's Calvinistic convictions wished to speak. One wanted to know, if the FIEC was only a fellowship rather than a denomination, why the objective of 'fellowship' could not be achieved without joining the organization. Another asked why the Chapel could not simply join the British Evangelical Council. Some speakers spoke on behalf of

[1] *Ibid*, p. 37.
[2] 'We Need One Another', a Comment in Current Trends, *The Life of Faith*, June 15, 1967.

the FIEC but doubts were not allayed. One asked how a church which stood for the Reformed faith could belong to a body which was not committed to those doctrines. Another speaker pointed out how, following the last Graham Crusade supported by the Bishop of Woolwich, the Council of the FIEC had passed an unqualified resolution expressing their thanks to Almighty God for the blessings and the results. On a point of church order, it was asked where the FIEC found its biblical justification for their annual 'President' of the churches.

Dr Lloyd-Jones was scarcely prepared to find these young men, who loved his teaching and his person, stand in his way in this manner and it is said that in responding to some of them he lacked his customary patience. Probably an element of the displeasure which he felt was connected with his knowledge that these questions perhaps owed something to some of the more Calvinistic ministers in the Westminster Fellowship from whom he had heard similar objections.

A resolution to delay a vote to join the FIEC was seconded and finally put to the meeting at 9 p.m. 42 voted for it, with a clear majority – perhaps 60 per cent of the members present – against. In view of the numbers who were holding back, ML-J asked the meeting to agree that a decision ought to be delayed and this was approved.[1]

The next church meeting was brought forward to April 13, 1967. In his opening prayer the Doctor referred to 'those of us who have worshipped in this place with the sound of guns firing and bombs falling around us'. The atmosphere was noticeably tense at the outset, with a number clearly expecting more disagreement. But this time ML-J was not only prepared to deal with the questions previously raised, he was at his conciliatory best as a chairman. There was even some disarming humour. When one member likened the benefits of joining the FIEC to his own experience of the coffee trade, where the majority of merchants belonged to a central buying agency, ML-J confessed that he knew the Scripture spoke of milk and meat but was coffee quite relevant? He assured the meeting that everyone was welcome to speak and there would be as much time given to discussion as was wished, for he remembered how it took

[1]Allowing for the inexactness of the number recorded as present at this meeting, the numbers present at church meetings never amounted to as many as half the membership (828 in 1967) and they illustrate the old problem of 'a church within a church' at Westminster.

David Martyn Lloyd-Jones: Volume Two

him some time to persuade his wife to marry him! His reasons for wanting to join the FIEC were that it would give regular information of other churches; it would be better to help other churches financially by supporting a central fund; it would give guidance to ministers in the Westminster Fellowship who were asking, 'What do we do if we come out' of this or that denomination; and it would silence 'the almost weekly attacks made upon him by Anglican newspapers, charging him with a desire to start a new Evangelical Church'. He then went on to speak of the wider unity which would be found in the BEC, where there would be Presbyterians as well as Independents.

When the question of Calvinism and Arminianism was once more raised ML-J responded with some care, stressing that the FIEC did not define its position on this issue, nor on baptism. With support from references to Calvin and Spurgeon, he argued that commitment to the doctrine of election was not necessary to our personal salvation and, therefore, it should not be made a term for church fellowship. He then invited a member of the church, the Rev Omri Jenkins, who was to be the next annual President of the FIEC, to speak on this point. Mr Jenkins told the meeting of the growing number of Calvinists in the FIEC and gave his opinion that this was of vital significance in connection with the proposal under consideration. Two former members of Westminster who were now connected with the FIEC were mentioned, David Fountain, biographer of E. J. Poole-Connor, and Peter Masters whose new monthly paper ML-J commended to the meeting.

By 7.45 p.m. there were no more speakers and, with only five against, the meeting voted in favour of applying for membership in the FIEC.

At the May 1967 meeting of the Westminster Fellowship reports were given of both the Keele Congress and the recent Baptist Assembly by members of the Fellowship who had been present. Keele confirmed, ML-J believed, that the Anglican evangelicals had made concessions from which they could not withdraw – 'it is not just what a man says but what he *does* that counts' – and the Baptist Assembly showed how 'the integrity of the Baptist Union is the chief thing to be maintained'.

There was no June meeting of the fraternal but Dr Lloyd-Jones gave a major address on the current situation at the Evangelical Movement of Wales annual Ministers' Conference at Bala. As well as

[544]

reviewing the ecumenical literature of the previous months, and the surprising critique of ecumenism which had come from Scotland,[1] he gave a broad world survey illustrating how the same issues were present in many countries – in New Zealand (the case of Professor Geering), in the Netherlands (the changes at the Free University of Amsterdam) and in the United States where the testimony of the Christian Reformed Church was weakening and the United Presbyterian Church was introducing its new Confession of Faith. A similar pattern was emerging world-wide. 'One thanks God,' he said, 'that the position is becoming clearer, but only at the expense of dividing evangelicals'.

After speaking of their own need of closer unity in the Evangelical Movement of Wales he turned to Acts 6:4 and emphasized that the priorities must always be prayer and the preaching of the Word. And preaching should lead to *results*. Their preaching was in danger of being too formal, too perfect – 'We must be more direct. There ought to be more of the element of exhortation.'

At the next meeting of the Westminster Fellowship on July 3, 1967, he also gave an address which concentrated on the nature of the unity to be sought among those who were agreed in their opposition to ecumenism. At this point they faced, he believed, a danger which was the very opposite of the threat from ecumenism. Ecumenical leaders worked on the principle of minimum doctrinal statement, they sought to say something so loosely that no one is excluded. 'Among us, on the other hand,' he went on, 'in our desire to safeguard orthodoxy we tend to become too precise. We go to the opposite extreme of the ecumenical mentality. Even the detailed statements of the 16th and 17th centuries have not been able to safeguard the faith. You can never safeguard the truth by statements on paper or guarantee continuing orthodoxy by paper declarations.'

Two main things, he proceeded, should govern our attitude:

First, it is spiritual life, the experience of the grace of God, which creates the desire for fellowship (Acts 2:46). This was primary in the unity of the early church. If we do not say this we are in danger of scholasticism. An interest in theology which is not based on life is dangerous . . . Such was the position of the Pharisees and of many since. Sound theology can be taken up as a great system in the same way that some people take up crossword puzzles.

[1] *Power Without Glory*, Ian Henderson, Hutchinson, 1967.

David Martyn Lloyd-Jones: Volume Two

Second, the seriousness of schism, rightly defined and understood. Schism means separations among those agreed on fundamentals on account of secondary matters. It is constantly condemned in the New Testament. Unless we have a burning desire to preserve unity we are in a dangerous position.

He believed that the crux of the present position had to do with the recognition of the distinction between truths which are essential and those which are not essential. To be anti-ecumenical was essential because the ecumenical movement was deliberately guilty of doctrinal indifferentism. Its chief concern was a kind of organisational fellowship.

Ecumenical thinking is to take the churches as they are and to bring them all together. So they take up a minimal statement of faith and even that they do not apply . . . The first thing we want to know with regard to a man who comes to us for fellowship is, What is his attitude to this. To have fellowship with men who deny the truth is to deny the truth by implying that the truth does not matter.

Foremost among the doctrines he listed as 'absolutely essential' was the sole authority of Scripture in faith and practice. We do not receive tradition as being a subsidiary authority. There must be a full acceptance of revelation: 'We have no fellowship with a man who does not submit himself as a little child to Scripture. It is no use for a man to profess he believes in the "supreme authority of Scripture" in general and then question the foretelling aspect of prophecy or the historicity of creation and of Adam as the first man.' A new tendency to do this among evangelicals he described as 'one of the saddest things I have known in my ministry'. Then among the chief doctrines taught in Scripture he specified: the Trinity; the devil and evil powers; the plan of redemption; the person and work of Christ; man (born spiritually dead, having died in Adam); regeneration by the supernatural power of the Holy Spirit; justification and sanctification, with the necessity of good works.

He then turned to non-essentials, which he did not understand to mean truths which are unimportant, 'but they are not so important as to divide us'. 'You notice that I did not put in my list of essentials the doctrine of election. I believe the doctrine of election. I cannot interpret Scripture without it and I preached it last night as none of

[546]

you has ever done, but I cannot say that a man who does not believe it is not a Christian, or that I cannot have fellowship with him. I say he is seriously defective in his understanding. I do not say that Arminianism is "another gospel". It is rather another understanding of the mechanism of how salvation is given to us.' Among other subjects upon which Christians differed in their understanding he instanced views on baptism, assurance, church polity, unfulfilled prophecy and charismatic gifts. 'On such issues we may hold to our convictions, but with love and patience towards others. We must not break fellowship. We must condemn all wrangling. We all realize that we are saved in spite of ourselves. Not one of us is perfect in our understanding of these matters.' He concluded:

I have never proposed a united evangelical Church. What I have believed in is fellowship for mutual edification and encouragement and perhaps certain other activities. There may be groups of churches even in such fellowship who are disagreed on some of these non-essential matters: I cannot see the impossibility of a loose fellowship including those who are Presbyterian, those who are independent, and those with varying views on baptism.

In subsequent discussion at this same July 1967 fraternal ML-J indicated that the Chapel had made application for membership in the FIEC and had been received 'but', he added, 'to me that is not the big thing. The British Evangelical Council is the bigger thing because its scope is bigger.' Hitherto as evangelicals they had all been in movements which were too nervous to discuss the church – 'it would disintegrate the movement'. Now, he believed, the position was changed. The BEC was primarily an association of *churches*.

*   *   *

The July issue of *The Evangelical Times* – under ML-J's influence – reflected the same priority. While an inside page announced 'Westminster Chapel and Above Bar Church Received into the FIEC', the front-page headline was, 'BEC Goes into Action'. Virtually unknown to the general Christian public until a few months earlier, the BEC now suddenly sprang into prominence. *The Evangelical Times* announced that the BEC was to hold a major Conference in London in the autumn, that a paid General Secretary would soon be appointed, that it had opened a fund to help pastors and churches withdrawing from denominations on doctrinal grounds and that numbers adhering to the BEC were multiplying. The same issue reported that the Evangelical Movement of Wales, which it described as 'another church body',[1] had joined and that several Strict Baptist area Associations were looking towards formal affiliation.

There was now an element of excitement in the air, fanned by conflicting opinions in the Christian press, which made any assessment of what was actually happening among evangelicals very hazardous. Keele was generally regarded as a great success among the Anglicans. In the words of one of their spokesmen: 'Evangelical Anglicans are conscious that they are on the crest of the wave; they are quietly confident about the future of their church, and they are recognized by plenty of non-evangelicals as the coming force in the Church of England. In contrast, morale is much lower amongst evangelical Free Churchmen ... those following Dr Lloyd-Jones' line are in a smallish minority.'[2]

An uncommitted evangelical observer was not nearly so sure of the relative strength of the two groups. Morgan Derham believed that the Evangelical Alliance – considerably criticized since October 18, 1966 – had

provided Dr Lloyd-Jones with a most effective platform from which to expound his case; and the consequent publicity carried a summary of his message around the world. Developments since then have revealed just how effective this was.[3]

Derham's words were written before support for the British Evangelical Council reached what to some was a near-incredible high-point at the London Conference on October 31 – November 1,

---

[1] *The Evangelical Magazine of Wales*, June–July, 1967, announced that the General Committee of the Movement 'has allowed churches to become affiliated'.
[2] G. E. Duffield on the 'National Assembly of Evangelicals' in *The Christian*, November 3, 1967.
[3] *The Evangelical Alliance Broadsheet*, Autumn 1967, pp. 1–2. Derham observed that the Alliance was getting criticism from two opposite directions – some alleging that it had been supportive of ML-J's stand, others that it was unprepared to take any position on ecumenism. The Alliance had certainly lost a lot of support.

1967. This was, of course, not the first BEC Conference. But the last one which met at Swanwick in 1966 had gathered an attendance of some forty members while this, held at Westminster Chapel, drew an estimated two to three thousand to its final meeting when ML-J spoke on 'Luther and his Messsage'.[1] The occasion of this Conference was the 450th anniversary of Luther's nailing of the 95 theses to the door of the Castle Church at Wittenberg. In the view of one member of the BEC, the numbers 'were far in excess of the Council's wildest dreams'.[2] With eight sessions, there were speakers from all parts of Britain and the Rev the Hon Roland Lamb, the General Secretary (formerly a Methodist minister), gave an inspiring evening address on the first day on 'Revival and Reformation'. Inevitably press reports concentrated on Dr Lloyd-Jones. His Luther address took the front page of *The Christian* (November 10), with the heading, 'Attack on Ecumenism'. *The Evangelical Times* led with the heading '"Here I Stand!" 2,700 at Westminster Chapel'. The report in *The Life of Faith* (November 9), entitled, 'Authority and Power', was enthusiastic. After describing the proceedings, its writer, David R. Smith, concluded:

Although Dr Lloyd-Jones did not know it then, his address to the Alliance Assembly in 1966 was an historic act; he was laying the foundation of a spiritual movement whose size cannot be assessed, so does it grow apace. Even the organisers of this BEC conference did not appreciate the volume of the tide, and so were almost overwhelmed by it. We have, on our hands, a colossal anti-ecumenical movement which is (despite its failings) scripturally inspired. What will it perform, as it hastens to its destiny, none dare prophesy. But its existence is no longer a matter for conjecture.

Dr Lloyd-Jones did not share this confidence. Certainly the number present at the BEC Conference was encouraging, but he put little weight on it. It was issues not numbers which concerned him most. He meant what he had said about being 'a remnant' at the

[1] Published as a booklet by the Evangelical Press, 1968. The Evangelical Press was another publishing venture commenced from within the membership of Westminster Chapel. It was founded by Robin Bird in 1965 and concentrated initially on the publication of booklets, a number of which were produced in conjunction with the BEC.
[2] J. Elwyn Davies, 'British Evangelical Council Conference' in *The Evangelical Magazine of Wales*, Dec. 1967–Jan. 1968, p. 6.

Evangelical Alliance meeting of October 1966 and on a number of other occasions. The majority, he believed, were looking the wrong way and asking the wrong questions. As he told the BEC Conference on November 1, 1967:

We should not be asking, 'How can we have a territorial church, how can we have unity and fellowship, or how can we find a formula to satisfy opposing views?'. We should be asking, 'What is a Christian? How does one become a Christian? How can we get forgiveness of sins?' and 'What is a church?'.

The *English Churchman* saw the point and, after Archbishop Ramsey had preached on unity in the Roman Catholic Westminster Cathedral, shrewdly observed: 'In certain respects Dr Martyn Lloyd-Jones and the Archbishop are saying the same things. It is on the question of defining the word "Christian" that they would differ, but what a difference this makes.'[1]

[1]'Two Sermons', *English Churchman*, Feb. 2, 1968.

*Although Martyn Lloyd-Jones is not a leader in the BEC, or
one of its spokesmen, he is its charismatic voice; without his
outspoken challenge in the autumn of 1966, we may still never
have heard of the BEC. If we wish to know of the purpose and
aims of this nebulous body, it is better to listen to its most gifted
supporter than to its officers.*

DAVID R. SMITH
'Comment on the BEC Conference'
The Life of Faith, Nov. 8, 1969

*It is irrefutable that the veteran Welsh preacher's views on
separation have split evangelical ranks.*

J. D. DOUGLAS
Christianity Today, December 19, 1969

*Neither are we to be concerned for separation as such; indeed I
would go further and say that our object should be, not to
exclude people, but to include as many as possible, and yet to be
careful that we are maintaining our principles and our land-
marks.*

ML-J
1971, *Knowing the Times*, p. 317

27

Controversy: An Assessment

The public controversy which began in 1966 was unquestionably the most serious in Dr Lloyd-Jones' ministry and while we shall have to return to it again some evaluation is necessary here.

For the first time he was now, and subsequently, exposed to open criticism from fellow evangelicals on the grounds that he was responsible for 'dividing evangelicals'. The basis for the criticism was that he had changed the long-held ground rules which governed fellowship among them. As illustrated by the Evangelical Alliance since the 1840's, evangelical Christians had been able to share in corporate activities while agreeing to differ on secondary matters affecting their denominational affiliations. By urging secession upon members of the Alliance and by excluding 'convinced denominationalists' from the Fellowship at Westminster, ML-J was said to be introducing a new interpretation of 'evangelical'. Never before was a person's evangelicalism treated as dependent upon his denominational alignment – not, at least, since the secession movement inspired by the Brethren in the previous century.

Dr Lloyd-Jones' reply to this was twofold. First, the main denominations were in a condition such as had never been seen in England before. They were all in various stages of preparation to sink their distinctive identities in the interest of 'one church', and the influence bringing this about was not anything to do with secondary issues, it was the ecumenical betrayal of the gospel itself. The issue was not whether a man could stay in one of these mixed denominations and be an evangelical. ML-J knew very well that he could. He also believed that genuine pastoral considerations might well keep men in their existing congregations for the present. But if men intended to support the ecumenical policy of the denominations, and to accept the presuppositions of ecumenical dialogue, then, he argued, they were doing something hitherto unknown in historic evangelicalism. To put denomination first in this situation was to treat evangelicalism as only a 'party' viewpoint – a contribution among others which were all to be regarded as equally allowable. While some objected to his criticism that the new policy among Anglican evangelical leaders meant that Anglicanism was being put before evangelicalism, the evidence seems to be indisputable. For instance, when Dr H. R. Gough (closely involved as we have noted in evangelical policies since the 1950's) resigned from his position as Archbishop of Sydney in 1966 he made no secret of his dissatisfaction with those in that traditionally evangelical diocese 'who are evangelical before they are Anglican'. Should that attitude succeed, Gough believed, 'it would result in the Diocese of Sydney becoming a small and increasingly ineffective splinter group of the Anglican Church . . . I am an Anglican first but one who believes the Evangelical interpretation of Anglicanism.'[1]

Second, Dr Lloyd-Jones believed that Anglican evangelicals, or at least their best-known spokesmen, had themselves deliberately introduced a new policy on ecumenism which inevitably put them in conflict with other evangelicals. His position with regard to doctrinal indifferentism had not changed, but theirs apparently had. Some of the evidence for this belief has already been covered in these pages. The invitation of Michael Ramsey to the Keele Congress by the Anglican evangelicals was a blatant example of expediency taking priority over principle and of Anglicanism taking precedence over evangelicalism. When the Archbishop had lectured the evangelicals at that Congress on their need of greater openness towards Anglo-Catholics and liberals there had not been the slightest whisper of disagreement. No chairman's dissociation from a speaker's remarks was heard then! Instead the evangelicals' own published report of the Congress was at pains to underline how changed they were. 'Dr J. I. Packer,' it recorded (who ten years earlier had shown how different his position was from that of Ramsey), 'took up the often repeated phrase of Dr Ramsey: "Our concern must be as wide as God's".'[2]

The old Anglican evangelical attitude to errorists in the Church was now viewed as a form of 'pietism'. Keele was not a temporary aberration. Rather, in the words of John Stott, it 'marked a turning point' in the thinking of evangelical churchmen. It registered their

---

[1]*Nation*, Sydney, June 11, 1966, p. 13; *Sydney Morning Herald*, May 30, 1966.
[2]*Keele '67*, p. 10. In his book, *'Fundamentalism' and the Word of God*, 1958, Packer had quoted examples of Ramsey's antipathy to evangelicalism at length, pp. 10–14.

public acceptance of change. With no consideration given to the possibility that the accusation of intransigence levelled against earlier Anglican evangelicals might have been related to the offence of the cross, Stott wrote:

Keele expressed the formal public, penitent, renunciation by evangelical Anglicans of that pietism which for too long had marred our life and our testimony. And by pietism, I mean an exaggerated religious individualism, a withdrawal from both the church on the one hand and the world on the other, into a personal godliness and a tight-closed ecclesiastical 'in' group, a retirement into a self-made security with God and with one another, a contracting out of our responsibility both to the visible church and to the world . . .

Pietism is an immature protective attitude of those who have not yet attained their majority. I don't think therefore it is an exaggeration to say that the Keele Congress marked the coming of age of the current generation of evangelicals. Keele was the conscious emergence of evangelical Anglicans into maturity in the wider life of the church and the world. Keele marked for many of us our conversion from the negative and the defensive . . .

The opposite of pietism is involvement. We must say, therefore, that pietism is not the hallmark of true evangelicalism but rather a denial of it. Historically evangelicals have often been pietists but when they have been pietists they have not been true to their nature and calling.[1]

ML-J had himself occasionally used the word 'pietism' to describe a certain type of evangelicalism of the quietistic type, associated with Keswick, but he regarded the application of the word in a pejorative sense to all earlier Anglican evangelicals as a confusion of the issue now in controversy.[2] The argument of the older evangelical constitutionalists had been that the Church of England was limited by her own standards to a biblical and Protestant religion. Stott had himself formerly taken that position and had appealed to it as late as October 18, 1966 when he spoke at the Central Hall meeting.[3] But the old

[1]'Evangelicals in a changing world', *Church of England Newspaper*, Nov 1, 1968, p. 12.
[2]'I am getting very tired of evangelicals attacking pietism' (*Knowing the Times*, p. 333).
[3]An example of Stott's former position can be seen in his book *What Christ Thinks of the Church*, Lutterworth, 1958, where he says: 'We cannot have Christian fellowship with those who deny the divinity of Christ's person or the satisfactoriness of His work on the cross for our salvation . . . to preach any other gospel than the gospel of Christ's saving grace is to deserve Paul's anathema . . .' (p. 56).

position (that of such men as John Charles Ryle)[1], and indeed all thinking which would not allow commitment to ecumenical fellowship was now to be considered 'pietism'.

Another example of the new Anglican evangelical policy occurred in the week following ML-J's address on Luther in November 1967. In the Anglican House of Laity the evangelicals shared in the 'warm approval given to the motion asking that a Committee be set up to explore the possibility of finding a form of words for prayers for the dead which would be acceptable to the consciences of all major sections of the Church of England'. Commenting that 'this would presumably have to be such a form that it need not necessarily be taken as praying for the departed, but could, at the same time, be interpreted in that way if desired,' the *English Churchman* of November 17, 1967, observed: 'Here is another instance of Anglican evangelicals, as a whole, following a different line from that of their nonconformist brethren.'

Dr Lloyd-Jones had some justification for thinking it strange that he should be charged with dividing evangelicals.

There was, however, a second line of criticism which he encountered. It was claimed that by bringing together the questions of Christian unity, secession and a 'united evangelical Church' he was creating a new sectarianism, for this envisaged, not a toleration of different denominational distinctives, but a body which would claim to be the one, true manifestation of Christian unity. In other words, ML-J was thought to be heading towards the same kind of exclusive unity once espoused by J. N. Darby and the Brethren, a unity condemned by Spurgeon in the words, 'Call yourselves nothing at all, but insinuate that you are the only ones who are really *the church of God* and you have scattered seed which will produce a harvest of strife'. Reflecting this criticism, a member of the Westminster Fellowship, which had just been dissolved, wrote to ML-J on December 14, 1966:

On receiving from John Caiger the notice of the closure of the Westminster Fellowship, I feel I must write to send you my personal thanks for the benefits I have received at so many meetings in the past. They gave me a much needed stimulus to thought on a wide range of topics, and they were unfailingly illuminating. All this was through your own leadership – under God as I recognize – and I am very grateful.

---

[1]See *Charges and Addresses*, J. C. Ryle, 1903 (Banner of Truth Trust, 1978 reprint, pp. 30, etc.).

It is a matter of all the greater regret to me, therefore, that this Fellowship has been brought to an end, and that there is no longer any welcome except for those who are anti-denominationalists! The lessons I thought I had learned from most of a life-time in Brethren meetings were that only poverty comes from this sort of division; and that in an uncanny way one can, while trying to be thoroughly scriptural in certain particulars, become anti-scriptural in one's resulting attitude. J. N. Darby's slogan – "separation from evil is God's principle of unity" – illustrates this, and has produced results which seem to be the very negation of true godliness.

The writer of the above letter was not speaking in terms of what he had heard at the fraternal. He seems to have been an irregular attender. His information came from elsewhere and reflected the misunderstanding that had arisen in connection with the Evangelical Alliance's discussions over a 'united evangelical Church'. As we have seen, ML-J was not advocating a new denomination for which evangelicals were to abandon all the existing ones. He still held firmly to the position of his 1962 booklet, *The Basis of Christian Unity*, which treated Christian unity as essentially spiritual, not organizational and formal.

Yet the charge that ML-J was being 'denominationalist' if not sectarian has persisted and been repeated more recently by J. I. Packer. Dr Packer argues that evangelical unity means either spiritual, inter-denominational unity or it has to be a unity of a denominational nature. There is no third alternative. Speaking of the controversy of the 1960's, he writes:

I believed . . . that the action for which the Doctor called would be, in effect, the founding of a new, loose-knit, professedly undenominational denomination; and that he, rather than I, was the denominationalist for insisting that evangelicals must all belong to this new grouping and no other. His claim that this was what the times and the truth required did not convince me.[1]

Dr Packer, making the same point, says elsewhere that Dr Lloyd-Jones 'never gave substance to his vision by producing, or getting others to produce, a blueprint for the new para-denomination (the "non-denominational" denomination) that he had in view'.[2]

[1] *Chosen Vessels*, p. 112.
[2] *Martyn Lloyd-Jones, Chosen by God*, p. 49.

This argument did not escape the attention of Dr Lloyd-Jones, though it was not put into print at the time. His response was that there *had* to be a third alternative. Staying permanently in the major denominations and adopting dialogue with ecumenism was not a real option for, as events were already showing, the price would be the weakening of evangelical Christianity as a whole. But neither was it an option to advocate secession into a new grouping which would follow traditional denominational lines. Ecumenism, with its appeal to the oneness of the New Testament church, could not be answered by denominationalism.

Packer finds ML-J's position vague and obscure. He calls it a 'campaign of words without plans'. He even confesses to wondering 'whether he was not more interested in making the gesture of calling for separation . . . than he was in seeing the gesture succeed'.[1]

It was no 'gesture' ML-J was talking about between 1963–67. His conviction was that obedience to Scripture in the existing situation demanded new and bigger thinking from evangelicals. An unprecedented situation confronted the churches. Christianity, with a gospel of supernatural power for the salvation of sinners, was being challenged at its foundations. The old denominations were in the process of breaking up. The way forward could not be by a dialogue which required a compromise with the very unbelief which had brought on this situation; rather it was to answer the ecumenical call for unity with another unity – a unity closer to Scripture than that represented either by the existing multiplicity of denominations or by the evangelical organisations. But he did not underestimate the size of the problem and he had an inner conviction that he was not called to lead the churches into a new situation. 'I am Moses, not Joshua,' he said, with feeling in private. He spoke the sober truth when he re-iterated such words as, 'I am not an ecclesiastic', 'I have no plans'.

What he saw clearly, he said clearly. If, along with others, he was ignorant of things he would have wished to know, that did not mean that a great challenge and opportunity should not be faced. God leads His people and, as in every crisis and turning point in history, faith has to rest on God alone. The absence of light on the precise nature of a stronger evangelical unity was no reason to stand still. There had to be a way forward which was more honouring to God than an acceptance of the existing conditions.

[1]Ibid., p. 50.

There was nothing contrived about the absence of more detail in ML-J's call to fellow evangelicals. He frankly accepted the limitations of his own understanding. To this it may, however, be answered that Dr Lloyd-Jones' view provided the definite programme for evangelical unity which was actually taken up. It was his support which transformed the British Evangelical Council from its former largely anti-ecumenical role into a connection of churches with a vision for unity on the basis of essential truths. The FIEC could not provide such a connection because, on one point of church polity at least, it made a secondary issue a term of participation. It believed in independency. The BEC, on the other hand, was open to all congregations and denominations not affiliated with the World Council of Churches, and the Calvinistic commitment of some of its best known leaders would give it an appeal to a number in England who were doubtful of the FIEC. This was certainly his hope and he therefore gave every help he could to the BEC although he never held office on its Council. Yet his opinion on making the BEC the link in a wider unity was followed, largely because, when he urged others to take on a more active role, none came forward with any alternative.

*   *   *

Dr Lloyd-Jones was at his strongest and his most persuasive when he was enunciating principles which could be seen to possess biblical authority. In the whole debate on ecumenism and secession he held principles which were of that order. No one ever attempted to answer the booklet *The Basis of Christian Unity* from Scripture. But there were points in this controversy where I believe he was open to some criticism and I shall mention these briefly.

First, in the presentation of his case the argument at certain points seemed to rest too much on his interpretation of the existing situation, with the result that it looked more like a matter of judgment than of biblical principle. The question of when it is right to leave a denomination or break with ecclesiastical connexions is notoriously difficult. He had himself, as we have seen, long given support to such mixed bodies as the Free Church Federal Council. Only slowly had his conviction deepened that the older denominations were committed to the vision which had gathered such momentum since the World Council of Churches was formed at Amsterdam in 1948 and that union with Rome was the intention of the ecumenical movement. Other good men of less experience could be forgiven for still doubting that assessment and, accordingly, being hesitant to leave their 'mixed' denominations for a reason which was not as obvious as a biblical principle. They were not sure whether the position in those denominations was irretrievable, or whether, in Packer's phrase, 'renewal remains possible'. But the rules for membership of the new Westminster Fellowship, from which we have quoted, drew the line in terms of 'we see no hope whatsoever of winning doctrinally mixed denominations'. Right or wrong it would have been better had the line been drawn in less subjective terms. As ML-J himself often showed, the issues of the hour were the nature of the church and the *practice* of the principle of the purity of the church. These truths are easier to demonstrate than is the correct time for secession. In large measure because of circumstances over which he had no control, the debate too often became a question of the right interpretation of the existing situation instead of the necessity of facing biblical principles.

Second, it is my opinion that the element of vagueness attending the question how the evangelical churches, or denominations, not involved in ecumenism were to express their unity had regrettable consequences. The lack of any 'blueprint' for a new evangelical unity could be defended as I have defended it above. Dr Lloyd-Jones' case was that the *main* issue needed to be faced first, which was that unbelief within ecumenism made its programme impossible for evangelicals. Having accepted this, evangelicals could then, with the help of God, deal with their lesser differences within an overall commitment to fundamental truths.

But this call to go forward in faith did not cohere easily with another argument which ML-J used in urging the necessity of separation. If evangelicals endorsed the existing situation then, ML-J argued, they were approving a state of 'schism'. For they were often united at a church level with those who made no profession of biblical Christianity yet disunited at the church level from many fellow evangelicals. That this situation was anomalous could be seen by all evangelicals but that it was actually schismatic seemed to require that two other propositions be shown to be true. First, that the guilt of schism cannot be avoided simply by pleading the truth that all Christians are spiritually one regardless of their congregational or denominational affiliation. Second, that participation in *some kind of association* between churches is necessary to the avoidance of schism. On this second point evangelicals who did not interpret the general situation in the same light as ML-J had some justification for feeling they could not be fairly charged with 'schism' without being also told the kind of association they had to join in order to be relieved of that charge. A spiritual unity, enjoyed by all who hold the essential gospel truths and transcending denominational differences, was a familiar concept. Upon that there was no debate. It was basic to the inter-denominational evangelical unity represented by such organisations as the Evangelical Alliance. But ML-J appeared to be challenging the adequacy of this unity without saying clearly what was to be put in its place. His argument naturally had the effect of focusing attention upon the *alternative* which was envisaged.

It may be said that for someone holding Congregationalist or Independent views of the church, as ML-J did, there could not be any alternative apart from independent local congregations, in which case the charge of schism could hardly be sustained.[1] A congregation maintaining a relatively independent existence, free from coercion, within a 'mixed' denomination might be accused of compromise but scarcely – if pure independency be true – of schism. Dr Lloyd-Jones, in speaking of schism, clearly believed that there had to be more visible unity – primarily in the faith yet including powers to preclude the participation of errorists or to discipline them if they arose from within. The British Evangelical Council constituted a move in the *direction* of what ML-J wanted, but as things stood in 1967 it was not clear how, at the point of biblical principle, the BEC was more capable of providing unity 'at the church level' than the Evangelical Alliance. The BEC was an attempt to express greater doctrinal unity among many evangelicals but its claim to express Christian unity 'at the church level' could scarcely do other than give the impression that those who did not join were putting themselves outside some superior form of evangelical unity. If the charge of 'schism' was sound then it seemed that to stay outside the BEC was tantamount to being guilty of that charge and to being indifferent to true Christian unity. But as it was certain that large numbers of Christians would remain outside, or not be permitted to join,[2] this gave the BEC the

[1]ML-J was impressed with John Owen's writings on schism and put much weight on defining schism as a division over unnecessary things *among Christians*. But he does not seem to comment on Owen's argument that schism is a division within *one* congregation and that different considerations are involved when it comes to relationships between churches.

[2]Membership was not at this time open to evangelical congregations which remained in such bodies as the Church of England or the Baptist Union.

appearance of sectarianism. The wholesale withdrawal of BEC supporters from the Evangelical Alliance and the exclusion from the reconstituted Westminster Fellowship of those who, while opposed to ecumenism, could not express an intention to leave the 'mixed denominations' increased this same impression.

If ML-J had not introduced his argument based on the duty of resolving 'a state of schism' there might not have been the same urgency to bring forward a visible alternative unity. This could have come gradually and in conjunction with a developing understanding among evangelicals of the true spiritual position. Instead the BEC was suddenly brought into the forefront of attention in 1967 and the impression was given that to belong to its organization was the right and only means to end a state of schism. This brought a shift in the debate and in the attention of the participants. Prior to this shift, an Anglican, the Rev D. R. Hill could write (January 1967), 'Those who talk of secession appear to be in the vanguard of biblical unity because they have ceased to focus their eyes on earthly centres of ecclesiastical organization'. In other words, Dr Lloyd-Jones' main contention had to do with the spirituality of the church and with the gospel itself. But in the following months very considerable attention, as we have seen, came to be fixed on the BEC alternative for a visible unity, with the Evangelical Alliance and the BEC now in rival positions. The debate and controversy was now too much directed to questions of organisational unity which, as one writer says, were everywhere in the air, 'like German measles in the time of epidemic'.

Dr Lloyd-Jones was certain that there had to be a division among evangelicals for too many would not make a stand at any point. He was not, therefore, entirely averse to the polarisation which occurred and saw those who had control in the Evangelical Alliance and in Anglican evangelicalism as being responsible. But at least some damage might have been averted if the alternative unity presented from his side in 1967 had been understood to be more fluid and open than the BEC claims seemed to suggest.[1]

The impression of sectarianism might have been avoided if it had been said that, without any reflection upon the evangelicalism of others, steps were being taken to strengthen unity among *some*

---

[1] In this connection it should also be noted that Dr Lloyd-Jones was not answerable for all that was said by spokesmen for the BEC. The Rev Peter Masters one of the BEC's strongest advocates was later to become one of its leading critics.

evangelical churches. But so much emphasis was put upon the need to answer the dominant ecumenical unity with a strong evangelical unity that it seemed imperative for the BEC – or whatever the BEC became – to try to act for evangelicalism as a whole. This mistake arose because to have opted for less would have been too much like the formation of yet another denomination.[1]

As in all major controversies, the course of events at this period ceased to be manageable. Prior to the Central Hall meeting of October 1966 Dr Lloyd-Jones often emphasized the need for more time and patience. Many churches, both Anglican and Nonconformist, were seeing only the beginning of a stronger ministry and a more spiritually educated people. The effects of the doctrinal recovery of the 1950's were by no means widespread and were still largely to be found in pulpits rather than in congregations; but if there was to be a movement of secession ML-J looked for the action of churches, not simply of individuals (which was why the new terms of membership for the Westminster Fellowship required only a statement of 'intention' and no instant separation from the denominations committed to ecumenism). But the collision of opinion at the Central Hall meeting precipitated a polarisation and the pace of the consequences thereafter could not be checked. Dr Lloyd-Jones, sensitive to the charge that he was aiming to lead a new denomination, was perhaps himself more hurried than he would otherwise have been. At any rate in early 1967 the alternative structure provided by the BEC was in place. Time was to show that some of the basic ideas associated with its message had not been thought through adequately.

At the end of the very controversial year 1967 Gordon Murray, the Editor of the *English Churchman*, wrote a perceptive editorial on 'United We Stand . . .'. He grieved over the hardening of differences between Nonconformists and Anglicans and believed that the main blame for 'the present situation rests on the side of those who have not responded sympathetically to the Doctor's call'. Yet not all the responsibility, he considered, rested there:

Those who are doubtful about the depth of unity which would exist among Evangelicals after their coming together have seen nothing since

[1]To appreciate this the profound disillusion with all forms of denominationalism in England and Wales in the 1960's has to be remembered.

1966 to dispel their suspicions that it might very soon be shattered by disagreement on theological differences . . . The point is that the genuine differences of theological interpretation among us require careful and detailed consultation to take place if there is to be any real hope of a lasting form of unity brought about in this country.

It is too easy simply to say of those who remain in their denominations that they are compromising and that they are not as Evangelical as they ought to be. This represents a failure to understand why there are Evangelicals in the mainline denominations at all, a failure to realise they belong to those denominations through the conviction that they represent truths which may not readily be seen in other Christian groupings. In other words, if they leave their particular denominations they want to ensure that these truths go with them. The Independent easily recognises the folly of inviting him to accept membership of the Church of England as it is at the moment, with all that this would involve in sacrifice of his convictions. Similarly he must realise that it is equally foolish to invite a member of the Church of England to become an Independent where this, too, would mean forsaking much which the Anglican holds to be scriptural.[1]

This Anglican editor did not blame ML-J for what he considered the weakness of the alternative unity thus far proposed. On the contrary, as already seen above, he whole-heartedly supported the need for the bold vision that was prepared to recognize the need for a new beginning:

In the present state of affairs there exists a wonderful opportunity for Evangelicals to work towards the display of an outward expression of their spiritual unity and to show the sceptics that they really do believe the Bible. Many have already dismissed such a vision as impossible of realization, but we would encourage those who believe it to be of divine origin to go on working at it. Only we would beseech them not to narrow their vision so that it excludes large numbers of fellow Christians who are unable to join with them on the present basis.

* * *

A foremost characteristic of the 1960's was the multiplicity of problems that arose simultaneously. It was impossible for Dr Lloyd-Jones to maintain his own principle, 'Insist always upon controlling the place where the battle is fought'. Evangelicalism was threatened from several directions at once and not least by the counsel being

[1] *English Churchman*, Dec. 8, 1967.

given by some of its leaders. Confronted by the evident retreat from the convictions of the older evangelicalism, ML-J found himself forced into a new role. He had never made Calvinism the test for Christian fellowship: he had always preached that to be a Christian takes precedence over everything else. And, despite the distinctiveness of his position, such was his character, and such the esteem for his ministry, that he was held in well-nigh universal regard among evangelicals. No one else could command such a cross section of support. It is not surprising, therefore, that he became so closely involved in the defence of a broader evangelicalism – for supernaturalism over against deviant forms of Christianity.

ML-J was drawn into counter-proposals on Christian unity by the certainty that the new evangelical policy of tolerating a co-existence with the proponents of error was hastening, not reversing, decline:

We have evidence before our very eyes that our staying amongst such people does not seem to be converting them to our view but rather to a lowering of the spiritual temperature of those who are staying amongst them and an increasing tendency to doctrinal accommodation and compromise.[1]

True evangelical unity and ecumenical unity could not co-exist and he believed that if the evangelical organizations were going to persist in calling for neutrality on ecumenism (for the sake of preserving their own unity) they were guilty of shirking the main issue of the hour.

But, as we have seen, he tried to avoid any leadership role in the formation of new structures. In part this was because he had neither the gifts nor interests of an ecclesiastic. In part, also, it was because he knew that the *essential* need at this stage was no mere re-organization of churches or denominations: it was for on-going reformation and a true revival in *all* churches. Secession, as such, was no solution. Important though the need was for united action in facing the crisis of unbelief in the main denominations, his fundamental conviction was that the success of such action would not *depend* on membership in the same organization. It would depend rather upon the depth and reality of spiritual life of the participating churches, upon the closeness of their fellowship with Christ the head, for therein lies the source of true catholicity and of readiness to practise the truth in its fulness and power. In other words, an

[1]Spoken at the Puritan Conference, December 1965 (*Puritans*, p. 147).

external unity is not an entity to be sought in and of itself. This was the note upon which he finished the case he argued forcefully in *The Basis of Christian Unity*: 'The greatest need of the hour is a new baptism and outpouring of the Holy Spirit in renewal and revival . . . The ultimate question facing us these days is whether our faith is in men and their power to organize, or in the truth of God in Christ Jesus and the power of the Holy Spirit.'[1]

Nonetheless, he never used the need for revival as an argument for doing nothing. Another principle which he always urged was that 'we have to deal with the situation as it is and not as we would like it to be'. While he did not, therefore, intend to be diverted into becoming the organizer of a movement, he believed that something had to be done and that the BEC offered a better alternative than the beginning of a new denomination. He understood very well that this was no final solution and the need for further thought on unity and a greater longing for its attainment continued to be one of his uppermost concerns for the remainder of his life.

Amidst the strain of these years, which was undoubtedly now telling on his health, he never ceased to be an example in the tenor of his life and spirit. He believed in God. He was ready to confess his ignorance over the outcome of events but he did not hesitate to remind men that Christians are often called to action without a clear view of what the consequences will be. In many momentous periods of history believers have been required to act in obedience to God without knowing where it would lead them: 'By faith Abraham . . . went out, not knowing whither he went' (Heb. 11:8). ML-J believed

[1]See *Knowing the Times*, p. 163. His conviction that a recovery of greater unity is bound up with revival was no mere theory. A Presbyterian author writing on 'The American Awakening and the Revival of Religion' in *The British and Foreign Evangelical Review*, 1858, p. 924, said: 'The problem of "Christian Union," is one which has of late been receiving no small amount of consideration. One theory after another has been propounded for its solution; and many semi-mechanical efforts have been made to realise it in positive fact. But the very imperfect measure of success which has rewarded these endeavours, has shewn with tolerable clearness that it is not by dint of controversy or persuasion that we shall soon attain to uniformity of belief; it is not by diminishing the number of articles in our confessions that we shall manage to combine all the sects into one large and liberal-minded denomination, nor is it by getting members of different churches to meet together and talk in a friendly way over a breakfast table that the spirit of sectarianism is to be exorcised and banished forever into the deep. The evil may be mitigated by these expedients, but it will never be cured by them. The present experience of the American churches reveals to us the only effectual remedy. – WE MUST HAVE A BAPTISM OF THE HOLY GHOST.'

that, as in the time of the Reformation, the truth could not be recovered, and distinguished from error by the people at large without major controversy. In such controversy, however, as he repeatedly stressed, charity, humility and patience are essential for 'we must remember that men who are equally honest may differ'.[1]

Above all else he continued to pray and to look for such a recovery of the churches as only God could send. He hated the publicity and the controversy of these years and his reputation was to suffer for the stand which he took, but he went into it deliberately because he believed that evangelicals were being tempted to a path of compromise which could only lead to yet greater barrenness.

[1] See *Puritans*, pp.148, 169, etc.

What things we have experienced! To a preacher nothing is so wonderful as to feel the unction of the Holy Spirit while preaching, and to hear of souls being brought under conviction of sin, and then experiencing the new birth. Thank God, that has often been our experience. But not only that, one remembers marriages, births, deaths, even war and bombing, reconstruction of buildings and many other matters faced together; but above all I shall treasure the privilege of ministering to those with grievous problems of various types and enjoying the trust and confidence of those passing through dark and deep waters.

ML-J
Letter to the members of Westminster Chapel
May 30, 1968

28

The End of an Era

It might be supposed that the controversy of 1966–67 was so major
that it entered into Dr Lloyd-Jones' entire ministry. This is far from
being the case. His normal work proceeded as usual and in a number
of meetings where he might have taken up the issues he dealt entirely
with other subjects. To the 'inner circle' at the Annual Meeting of the
Evangelical Library on December 6, 1966, he spoke of the great
improvement which he had seen in England with reference to serious
reading over the previous thirty years. He attributed the change to
the work of the IVF, the Evangelical Library, the Puritan Conference
and to the Banner of Truth Trust. At the same meeting the following
year he was to speak of the United States. For his address at the
Puritan Conference in 1966 – the year being the 350th anniversary of
the founding of the first Congregational church in England – he
spoke on 'Henry Jacob and the First Congregational Church'.

As already said, there was no let up in his preaching engagements.
One, particularly, stands out in my own mind. On July 4, 1967, I
drove him from London to a service where he was to preach that
evening at Catbrook near Tintern, Monmouthshire. I expected him
to be somewhat tired for it was Tuesday and the previous day –
immediately after his Sunday work – he had given the major address
at the Westminster Fraternal meeting referred to in the previous
chapter. But far from being tired he was in fine spirits and reminded
me that while physical effort exhausted him he had great stores of
nervous energy. Mrs Lloyd-Jones was more tired on Sunday nights
than he was! There was no motorway to Wales at this date and we
took the same road that he had seen on his first car journey from
London in 1908, a fact which led to a whole series of reminiscences
recorded in the opening chapters of the first volume of this
biography. From his childhood and the death of his brother Harold
in 1918, conversation went on to his first visit to Canada in 1932.

Then the subject of books came up. Though he read all through the year he looked forward to his summer break to get through some larger works. The books he was looking forward to reading that summer were A. F. Scott Pearson's *Thomas Cartwright and Elizabethan Puritanism* and a major biography of Napoleon by a Dutch author. Observing my surprise at the latter choice, he confessed to his enjoyment of books on battles and that there was still enough of the boy in him to have heroes and to regret their falls. He illustrated this same point from his recent experience in watching a cricket match. A few weeks earlier, on his annual day outing to Lord's, he had looked forward to seeing the Indian celebrity, the Nawab of Pataudi, who had batted brilliantly at Leeds. But to his regret the famous batsman was out quickly before they could see him in action. His disappointment, however, was more intense, he recalled, over a similar incident in 1948. In that year he had the opportunity to see Don Bradman bat for Australia against Middlesex in one of his last matches in England. Bradman scored over 2,000 runs that summer but on this occasion Compton caught him at backward short leg for a mere 6 runs: in ML-J's view the crowd were 'fools' for erupting in applause instead of realizing what they had missed seeing from the world's greatest batsman!

We had left London soon after 2.30 p.m. for the evening service at Catbrook at 7. Having made good time, a notice advertising 'cream teas' as we passed through the centre of Marlborough brought us to a halt. An observation from me on his devotion to scones, cream and jam, and that before a preaching engagement, prompted him to recall the amusing anecdotes on the appetite of another preacher he had known, John McNeill.[1]

This particular engagement was to a place where he had never been before and when we reached Catbrook, with ten minutes to spare before 7 p.m., it was to find a large marquee erected in a hay field – not the easiest place in which to preach on a summer's evening. The chairman, however, was quick to tell us of a more serious problem. One attraction for the evening was to be 'The Songsters' from Bristol and, though coming from a place a good deal nearer than London, they had failed to arrive. The chairman's anxiety was profound. There was no help but to start the service without them, with care taken that the front seats be kept free should

[1] See vol. 1, pp. 256–57.

they arrive late. I suppose we had all forgotten 'The Songsters' by the time the sermon began from the closing verses of Hebrews 4. Within five minutes, however, no one could think of anything except these Bristol singers. A coach had just driven up the hillside to our hay field and an excited crowd of young people announced their arrival with no little talk and noise. Seemingly oblivious to the absence of any sound-proofing properties in canvas, they simply stood around the tent conversing loudly with one another as though they knew nothing of any service in progress so close at hand. There was general relief when the chairman rose and tiptoed (on the long grass!) down an aisle to the exit. But this turned to mystery when he returned without the Songsters whose noise continued as before. On only one other occasion did I see Dr Lloyd-Jones completely lose the attention of a congregation. Preaching in Glasgow, by way of illustrating the bankruptcy of modern thought, he gave several lengthy quotations from contemporary scientists and philosophers. Realizing the situation he then quickly regained the wandering minds of his hearers with the words, 'I see you are finding this more difficult than watching your televisions!'. At Catbrook, with the Epistle to the Hebrews almost completely forgotten, it was not so easy. At length, with the chairman reseated on the platform and the talk and giggles of the late arrivals unabated, the preacher stopped abruptly and told the chairman in the hearing of the whole congregation: 'I would rather they came in. They are neither in nor out. It reminds me of the condition of the church of Laodicea, neither hot nor cold, and I don't like it'. Then to the now silent Songsters, at last conscious of being a distraction, he said in stronger tones, 'Come in or go away!'. This was done with that humour and severity which only he could blend. As the party hurried in and down the aisle to their seats he eased their embarrassment with, 'We are very glad to see you friends', and then proceeded with his text where he had left off.

On the way home that night conversation was on the Epistles and he commented on how he felt that he really knew Paul and had 'got inside him'. 'Do you not think,' I asked, 'that anything approaching Arminianism was quite alien to Paul?' 'Yes,' he agreed. 'Archbishop Temple,' he recalled, 'had said that he could not understand Paul, but he thought – wrongly – that he could understand John!'

As usual, there were many visits to Wales in 1967. One of these engagements he was to describe as the most extraordinary service he had been in. This was in Aberfan, a place suddenly known across the world on account of the terrible disaster which occurred there on October 21, 1966. The register had just been marked that morning in the village school when, at 9.15 a.m., a great heap of coal slurry which over-shadowed the building suddenly slipped and, with a rumble like thunder, engulfed nearly a whole generation of the local children. One hundred and sixteen died, along with twenty-eight adults. The coal-mining areas of South Wales knew something of disasters but a tragedy of this nature, above ground, took the community into an abyss of sorrow from which it seemed it would never recover.

Dr Lloyd-Jones was asked to preach on the first anniversary of this disaster, November 15, 1967 in the Welsh Presbyterian church, Capel Aberfan. All denominations, however, gathered for these services on the afternoon and evening of that day. In the evening the Welsh Baptist chapel, Smyrna, across the road was also packed for worship and to hear a relay of the sermon. The evening message was one of glorious comfort for believers from the words of Romans 8:18–23, 'For I reckon that the sufferings of this present time are not worthy to be compared with the glory which shall be revealed in us . . .'. At the conclusion of a profoundly moving service, the Rev Wilfred Jones, the Vicar of Aberfan came forward to tell the preacher that this was the message for which Aberfan had been waiting. Two years later a woman wrote a postcard to say she would never forget those services at Aberfan and many others confessed the same. 'I have heard the eminent preachers of all the Churches,' said one Anglican hearer, 'but have never heard a sermon or address to compare with what I heard at Aberfan.' A letter written to ML-J by one of the ministers present, the Rev John Phillips of Merthyr Tydfil, on November 19, 1967, gives a vivid impression of the effect which this preaching had upon the community:

Your visit was eagerly awaited at Aberfan and had been the subject of all our prayers over the past weeks. Once again our prayers have been answered, praise His Name, for I know that, through your messages, inspired by Him, we have all received, not only a wonderful blessing, but renewed courage and determination. After the services I saw mothers, who had lost little ones, and fathers also, smile with renewed hope in their faces. I know they will face the future now with more confidence. God bless you, for all you have done for these dear people here and indeed for us all.

The whole series of services, culminating in your visit, has sparked a flame amongst the churches in Aberfan. Since the disaster everything has been so utterly dormant that it is wonderful to see a re-awakening. After our experiences of the past week there is more of a spirit of unity, and care for the church and the work of Christ, than has existed for many a long year. I am determined that I shall devote my life and my energies to see that the flame which has been kindled shall not die, but shall grow and spread for His everlasting glory.

*　　　　*　　　　*

At Westminster Chapel the expository and evangelistic ministries continued in the manner now familiar for so long. There were many young people present whose own parents had once been youngsters under the same ministry. Except at holiday periods, there were never visiting preachers at the Chapel. Dr Lloyd-Jones was as regular as Big Ben and almost – it seemed – as fixed in his pulpit as the great clock was above the Houses of Parliament. But those who supported him most in prayer did not take the ministry for granted. Another postcard writer sent him this anonymous message: 'Thank you a thousand times for that most wonderful message last Sunday evening! May the Lord graciously bless you, and preserve you to continue this most vital ministry in London.'

By the summer of 1966, ML-J had been through Acts 5 and 6 on Sunday evenings and he commenced chapter 7 on October 16. For the morning sermons he was in John 4. A year later, on October 8, 1967, he began Acts 8 in the evenings but was still in John 4 for the general sermons he was preaching on the Christian life. In the Romans series he concluded his expositions of chapter 12 on Friday, November 11, 1966. The next Friday he started on Romans 13 and remained with that chapter to May 26, 1967. He resumed the series at Romans 14:1 on October 10, 1967.

The press still took notice of Westminster Chapel from time to time. *The Observer* magazine for March 19, 1967 carried a survey of preachers and congregations. The reporter of the service at Westminster Chapel was still mystified, as others had been, at what he found:

On ordinary Sundays you have to hunt for vacant seats in the lower galleries and the central area.

Lloyd-Jones is the last, in London anyway, of the great oratorical preachers. People call it 'Hell and damnation tub-thumping' when they think they have to be funny about it.

You could call his message seventeenth-century Puritanism.

His sermons start quietly. The variations in delivery come later. Slow, slow, quick, quick, slow. He has a Bible in front of him and can locate texts like a computer. Nobody so much as coughs . . .

After hearing him preach many people go to him for help and get it. In private he is quiet and kind. Whether it's what he says, or how he says it, *something* is terribly convincing.

It was this issue of *The Observer* which provided photographs which were later to be put to good use by the Banner of Truth Trust.[1]

In the summer of 1967 Dr Lloyd-Jones made his sixth visit to North America, his fifth with Bethan. These were to be their last Atlantic crossings by boat and the voyage out, on the 'Queen Elizabeth', was one of the best they ever had, with a spacious cabin on the main deck and a 'dead calm' sea all the way. The age of the great Cunarders, with their grand main staircases and ample space, was almost at an end and, although they spent little time in enjoying the facilities of the ship, they both felt the same about its future. 'I do think it is sad to think they are going to scrap this lovely boat', Bethan wrote home. The same letter (to Ann and Keith) reported: 'I have done nothing but go through your father's 2 Peter sermons. They do take time and I could never do them except on an occasion such as this.'

This visit began with two-and-a-half weeks' holiday at Green Pastures, Salisbury in Connecticut, where they were the guests of Mr and Mrs Frank H. Cordes. After this rest in New England they had three days in Montreal, one of these being spent at 'Expo '67' which impressed them, as it did the world, by the new standard it set for such exhibitions. The whole of Canada in 1967 was celebrating the centennial of its confederation and Knox Presbyterian Church, Toronto, planned to mark the occasion with ten days of services in August when ML-J would be the preacher. Thus, after the 400 mile rail journey to Toronto and an address to the Christian Medical Society of the USA and Canada, these meetings in the church of his friend, William Fitch, followed. At a later date, in his history of Knox Church, Dr Fitch was to write: 'No one who shared in these services will ever forget them. There was standing room only . . . Who will ever banish from his memory the tremendous exposition of the 107th

[1]Its photograph of the congregation from the pulpit end of the church was the basis for the well-known drawing used on the dust-jackets of ML-J's *Romans* series.

Psalm which was given on the closing night of this very special series? Truly these were high and holy days.'¹

The Lloyd-Joneses left Toronto on August 21 by plane for Cincinnati. The flight, in a six-seater Beechcraft belonging to their Cincinnati host Mr A. M. Kinney, was Bethan's first. After a week of holiday with the Kinneys another flight took them to Grand Rapids where ML-J was engaged to preach on Sunday, August 27, and for three week nights under the auspices of the Christian Reformed Church. It was his first visit to the 'Jerusalem' of the American Dutch, and the CRC paid him the honour of suspending an extraordinary session of their Synod – meeting to discuss the Dekker case – in order to attend one of the week-night services at which he was preaching.

From Grand Rapids a car journey of 608 miles, with their friends Mr and Mrs Marvin Muller brought them to Carlisle, Pennsylvania on Friday evening, September 1, leaving them time the next morning to explore the Gettysburg battlefield before driving on to Philadelphia the same day. ML-J preached in the city on Sunday, September 3, and then at Westminster Seminary on the Monday and Tuesday.² A free morning made it possible for them to visit Neshaminy Creek – scene of the ministry of William Tennent and, in ML-J's words, 'One of the most idyllic spots I have ever seen'. On the Wednesday morning an early start took them to New York to be on board the 'Queen Mary' by 11 a.m.

In this crowded trip in the summer of 1967 I think there was nothing which ML-J personally enjoyed so much as the initial weeks of relaxation in New England. It was his longest visit to that part of the States, and he had the leisure to explore the parts of its history and literature which interested him most. He was fascinated by the new Beinecke Library at Yale, and especially by the room housing the Jonathan Edwards manuscripts where he was welcomed by two of the men responsible for the new Yale edition of Edwards' *Works*. He spent an afternoon with them in conversation and in examining the preacher's letters and sermon notes. No less memorable was a day spent at Stockbridge – the outpost among the Indians where Edwards went after his dismissal from Northampton. ('I always

¹*Knox Church, Toronto*, 1971, p. 122. It will be clear to the reader that ML-J was in the habit of preaching some of his sermons many times and regarded the practice as neither unbiblical nor unhelpful.
²It was at this time that he gave the address, 'What is Preaching?' See *Knowing the Times*, pp. 258–77.

remember that if Edwards could be ejected by his congregation anyone could!' he was to say at the 'At Home' in September.)

Another historical scene which he enjoyed was the town of Litchfield, Connecticut, where Lyman Beecher had once ministered, and he was impressed by the willingness of the Public Library in Litchfield to allow him to borrow the two-volume *Autobiography of Lyman Beecher.*[1] These, along with two rare volumes of Jonathan Dickinson (Edwards' son-in-law) loaned from the Library at Yale, provided his chief relaxation on this holiday. Lyman Beecher (father of Henry Ward Beecher) interested him for a number of reasons, but chiefly on account of his part in a turning point in American religious life. Having been brought up in the tradition of Edwards, Beecher became impressed with Finney and parted company with the convictions of Asahel Nettleton who was opposing the 'new measures' introduced into evangelism in the 1820's. What ML-J says on Beecher's *Autobiography* is relevant to his own biography:

But what interested me was this, that there I was able to read the details of this great controversy. It is one thing to know that there was a controversy and that there was a change; but I personally am greatly helped always by having the details, because we are always involved in details, and what one always wants when one is passing through some controversial period – such as you and I are living in – what one always wants to know is, how did our fathers face this kind of situation?[2]

Dr Lloyd-Jones saw Lyman Beecher as an evangelical who threw his weight on the wrong side at a critical juncture in history. Thoughts of the current situation in England were thus never far from his mind.

*   *   *

As usual, the beginning of another year's work at Westminster Chapel in September 1967 brought the arrival of a number of new students at the Chapel from various parts of the world. Joan Gibson, arriving from South Island, New Zealand, made her way there for the first time on October 1, 1967. The following week she wrote home:

[1]Edited by Barbara M. Cross, Harvard University Press, 1961.
[2]*The Annual Meeting of the Evangelical Library 1967*, p. 19.

The End of an Era

Last Sunday I did the double. Heard John Stott in the morning and the Doctor at night. I sat up in the balcony at Westminster Chapel and just imagined you thriving on it. There were all and sundry there – black, white, brown, old, young, mothers, fathers, kids and even a dog sitting up the front with his head on his paws! He is a guide dog for a young blind man who has been converted. The Doctor is small, wizened, glasses and wears a black gown which he pulls across and then clutches – but not for long because he then starts to wave his arms around. While I was there he dealt with, 'I am what I am by the grace of God'. 'A repetitive expositor,' according to the Principal! I was tickled pink and determined to go back.

Westminster Chapel became Joan Gibson's spiritual home, and many similar accounts of Sundays at Buckingham Gate occurred in her correspondence for as long as she was in London.

At the Puritan Conference for 1967 ML-J again broke new ground with an address on 'Sandemanianism'. It was one of his most influential lectures and dealt with the danger which arises from false or superficial teaching on the subject of faith and on assurance of salvation.

At the end of 1967 ML-J wrote his usual annual letter to the members, dated January 1, 1968. It included the following:

As far as we are concerned at Westminster Chapel, by the grace of God we have so much for which we can be truly thankful. I am more than ever conscious of a deep seriousness among us and an ever increasing desire to know God and to serve Him. This is something which many visitors notice and discuss with me when they come into my vestry at the close of a service. A letter recently from an American doctor serving in Vietnam testified to the fact that she had been more conscious of the presence of God while worshipping with us for several months than anywhere else, and that amidst the horrors of war she was helped and sustained by the memory of this.

Nothing can be more encouraging to any preacher than to feel that people come to the services, not out of habit or a sense of duty, but with a deep desire to worship God and to get to know more of Him through our Lord and Saviour. The sense of expectancy can actually be felt – and again visitors sense this.

As a direct result of this there is also the desire for the salvation of others. I have been told at times that certain critics have said of me, 'Oh! he just preaches to a group of people who agree with him'. The fallacies in that statement are staggering. The church after all is not a debating society, and these critics are the very people who are always talking about unity!

But, furthermore, the statement is a lie. Constantly I am being told not only of individual non-Christians who are attending on Sunday nights, but sometimes of even groups of such. But above all I have had the regular experience of welcoming such friends at the close of services, and hearing from their own lips of how they had been brought to a knowledge of salvation.

Thus I find myself greatly encouraged, and thank God for His goodness in calling me to minister to people who are so concerned about His glory and the extension of His Kingdom.

When one turns to the more general position however, the situation is very different. Here, the main impression is one of confusion, uncertainty, and divided opinions. This is true not only in this country but throughout the world. This is something that one expects in 'Christendom', but in the past it has not been true of those calling themselves evangelical. This is the new feature which is so disturbing. No longer can it be assumed that to be evangelical means to accept the authority of the Scriptures on matters of history, and on the creation of the world and man, and at the very lowest to be sceptical about the theory of evolution. In the same way there has been a recrudescence of denominationalism and an entirely new attitude towards Romanism.

It is, alas, a time of conflict and of trial, indeed a time of tragedy when old comrades in arms are now in different camps. It is not that one in any way questions the honesty or the sincerity of such friends. There is only one explanation and that is, 'an enemy hath done this'. Never has that enemy been more active or more subtle . . .

What the outcome of the present upheaval will be no one can tell. Our duty is to be faithful knowing that the final outcome is sure.

As Dr Lloyd-Jones entered upon the new year of ministry at Westminster Chapel in 1968 he had, as usual, no long-term preaching programme. He had been preaching in the Gospel of John on Sunday mornings since 1962 and his method was to stay on a passage for as long as it continued to supply him with fresh and relevant material. On the first Sunday morning (January 7), from the starting point of the Samaritan woman as a new person in Christ, he preached a sermon on the subject of how his hearers should examine themselves. His two main heads were:

(1) Self-examination with reference to the past, Is your knowledge of Christ the greatest thing that has happened to you? Is your greatest rejoicing in what He has done for you? Has this knowledge been increasing? (2) Self-examination as we look to the future, What is your greatest desire? How do you face the unseen possibilities (a) Immediate:

The End of an Era

disappointment, loss, illness, accident, sorrow? (b) Ultimate: death and eternity?

These questions say much about his own view of life. On the following Sunday morning he continued on the theme of the new experience of the Samaritan woman with respect to her witness to others. His main point, over several Sundays, was that her testimony was spontaneous, there was something within her which was urging and compelling. 'The idea of training people to do this is new and modern and really belongs to the cults.' 'The best workers are always the best Christians – best in knowledge and understanding, best in experience, best in life, those most filled with the Holy Spirit.' From the passage he demonstrated the reasons why witness is spontaneous and then went on to show that this is because of what the gospel does *in* Christians, 'what they are is more important than what they say'. In what were to be, unknown to him, his last two Sunday morning sermons in the pulpit of Westminster Chapel (February 18 and 25) his sermons were summaries of what he saw as the priorities in Christian character. A Christian is to be: serious (but not solemn or pompous); joyful (but not superficially jovial); possessed of inner peace (having an understanding of life, its meaning and object); having inner resources (not easily disturbed or shaken by what happens); reliable and dependable (not variable, changeable, moody); showing concern for others in sympathy, patience, understanding and gentleness.

He resumed Romans on Friday, January 12, 1968, taking up verses 15 and 16 of chapter 14 and, of course, there was the usual routine of other mid-week activities. The church meeting of January 18 was to prove his last such meeting. It dealt with normal matters of membership, including the deaths of a much-esteemed retired missionary, Phyllis Wright, and another lady, Martha Wright, who had been a member of the church since 1912. The members' meeting was followed by an address from a former member of the Chapel, Dr John Tester of the Edinburgh Medical Missionary Society (who had gone to Nazareth from Westminster in 1952).

In February 1968 his work was interrupted by a bout of influenza, and those who attended the Chapel on Sunday, February 11 had the unusual experience of not finding him in his pulpit. He was back for the next Friday night and, although somewhat struggling in health, there was no sign of it in the preaching. He was having much liberty in his Sunday evening evangelistic preaching. On the first Sunday evening of the year, January 7, he had preached on the passage in the Acts of the Apostles at chapter 8, verse 26, recording the conversion of the Ethiopian eunuch through the witness of Philip. The first words of verse 26 gave him his theme for the first sermon, 'And the angel of the Lord spake unto Philip, saying, Arise, and go . . .'. The world is not *man's* world – angels, unseen powers, a supernatural realm! 'Oh, what a message to start a new year with!' he told the congregation that night. 'How I thank God that I am not dependent upon what men are going to do in this coming year. There is God, and He knows all and He is illimitable in His power! The initiative is always with God and we never know how He will act.'

Look at this man Philip; he was a brilliant success as an evangelist in Samaria, many converts, great joy; these people need to be trained and built up. You would have thought, well, God will leave him there. No, no! God knows that there is this one man, this isolated solitary soul who is in desperate need and He takes Philip out of his success and prosperity, and sends him into a desert way to meet an individual soul . . .

The God who has made everything, who sustains everything, who owns everything, and who controls everything, is interested in you and concerned about you. This is the staggering thing.

The programme of God is not one of social or political improvement. It is individual, it is personal. It is a Gospel that takes hold of us individually and delivers us out of this present evil world, and translates us from the kingdom of darkness into the kingdom of God's dear Son. The Gospel that tells you tonight whoever you are and whatever you are, whatever your past may have been, how filled with failures and disgraces and shame, it does not matter, God is interested in you, and is able to redeem you.

And the marvellous unexpectedness of it all! You never know when it is going to happen. This Ethiopian eunuch was expecting nothing when it happened to him. There are people in this congregation tonight who were not Christians twelve months ago. They did not expect twelve months ago that this mighty thing was going to happen to them. Oh, my dear friend, the possibility is always there! The angels are around us, and God is over all, and He sees you and knows you. Do not listen to the pessimism, the hopelessness, and the despair of this materialistic age. Believe in this supernatural, miraculous, divine Gospel!

The next evening sermon dealt with the kind of man the Ethiopian eunuch evidently was – moral, religious, yet dissatisfied. All this was paralleled with the modern scene and it led to the application:

Have you got as far as this Ethiopian eunuch had got? Are you serious? Do you know there is a soul in you that is immortal? Have you realized your precarious position before the holy God before whom you will have to stand? Do you know anything about eternal torment and the damnation of hell? How are you living? Are you ready to die, ready to face God? . . .

On the following Sunday evenings the different parts of the passage were expounded in relation to the theme of what it means to become a Christian. His first two sermons had dealt with common stumbling blocks in the way of being converted, first, the failure to realise the supernatural realm and, second, the danger of being religious without being a Christian. For the third Sunday night (January 21) he took the fundamental problem indicated in the eunuch's acknowledged inability to understand the Scriptures (Acts 8:30–1): 'the Christian message is something that cannot be understood by the natural man'. To make the Christian message acceptable to unregenerate man, to take out the offensive and make it 'intelligible', is to deny it. The nature of Christian truth is such that it requires a rebirth in order to receive it for man by nature is a hater of God. The Gospel is a message which proclaims that the help man needs, God supplies. God sent Philip to the desert to preach to the eunuch:

Here is a man filled with the Spirit, he can teach, he can expound. God sends him. And then the Spirit works in the man himself and he is ready to listen to his teacher. And that is God's method, and that has been God's way throughout the running centuries. I would not dare stand in this pulpit unless I had been sent, unless I had been called. I do not expound my own theories and ideas; I simply hold before you and divide, as I am enabled by the Spirit of God, the words, the message of God. But it will mean nothing to you until you have become as a little child and realize your helplessness, your hopelessness, your ignorance and are ready to listen.

The main theme the following Sunday night was that Philip could speak with authority because Scripture is a revelation from God, containing good news from heaven:

I have no other authority as I stand in this pulpit. The authority of the cults is the authority of experience. They talk about experience, they recommend experience, that is what they have got to offer. That is not the case here. This is exposition of the truth and we have no other authority. My dear friends, let me put it as plainly and as simply as this: standing in this pulpit tonight on the 28th of January 1968 I am doing nothing different from what Philip did with the Ethiopian eunuch.

For the three Sunday nights in which he was in his pulpit in February, 1968, he preached the passage – Isaiah 53 – which Philip found the eunuch reading in his chariot. His 'heads' on February 4 were: (1) the death of Christ was not an accident, for it is the theme of Old Testament prophecy; (2) that death was the action of God himself, 'It pleased the Lord to bruise him; he hath put him to grief' (Isa 53:10). It was God's way of providing salvation.

On February 18 and 25 (which was to be the last Sunday night he ever stood in the Westminster Chapel pulpit) his subject was the depth and the profundity of the human problem which required the death of the Son of God before the lost could be saved. Men must know the horror of sin, and their own guilt, before they can understand the cross of Christ:

It is no use saying to people, 'Come to Jesus'. They do not come to Jesus: why not? They have never seen any need of Jesus.

Man is rebellious, lost, miserable, defenceless under the power of sin. And so he closed his Sunday ministry preaching the death of Jesus Christ as the only means by which man may be saved and reconciled to God.

The above gives no idea of the comprehensiveness of these sermons, each one different yet each containing a full statement of the gospel and delivered with an urgency, tenderness and unction which makes them live still in the memory of many these twenty years later.

The week following Sunday, February 25, he worked as usual, preaching in Bedford on the Tuesday. He was conscious of being unwell but put it down to the after-effects of his recent influenza. On the Friday he had interviews in his vestry at Westminster with people requiring help and advice, starting at 4.45, prior to the evening meeting at 6.30 p.m. It was to be the 372nd occasion of his preaching from Romans and he had come to the word 'peace' in the statement, 'For the kingdom of God is not meat and drink; but righteousness, and peace, and joy in the Holy Ghost'.

In his sermon that night, with reference to the divisions at Rome, he pointed out how too often professing Christians fail to enjoy peace in relation to others because of their own insecurity. People who are querulous and over-ready to be critical and to pass judgment upon others are people who, in the first place, are not at peace with themselves: 'Lacking yourself in peace and in rest, you are all on edge, and so you react, and react generally in the wrong way when you meet others . . . It is people who are uncertain about themselves who are generally most critical of others . . . The tragedy is that it leads not only to strife but to divisions and to schisms and to parties, and so the Christian church gives the impression that she is just a collection of warring groups and sects and divided personalities'.

This was a warning he had long given.[1] Certainly Christians must sometimes be involved in controversy, but 'their great characteristic is that they are peacemakers. Their Father is the God of peace and they are like their Father.' The last exhortation to his flock was, therefore, in the words of Paul, 'Let the peace of God rule in your hearts, to the which ye are also called in one body: and be ye thankful' (Col 3:15). The preacher himself did not realise the finality of these words. He concluded his twelve-and-a-half years in the exposition of Romans with the sentence, 'God willing, we will go on to consider the other great characteristic next time – "joy in the Holy Ghost".'

I am not sure at what point Dr Lloyd-Jones knew that he would not be able to preach on the following Sunday, March 3. He was probably hoping for some improvement in the abdominal discomfort from which he was suffering, but at 8 a.m. that Sunday morning Mrs Lloyd-Jones had to ring his assistant, Edwin King (who lived outside London at Chesham, where he supplied a church), indicating that he was needed at once for the Westminster pulpit.[2] It was becoming clear to ML-J that something was seriously wrong: the following Thursday, March 7, he was admitted to the Royal London Homoeopathic Hospital where he underwent major surgery the next day for an obstruction in the colon – a condition brought about by cancer.

[1] For example in *WR*, June, 1963, he says: 'The bigot thinks he is contending for the faith but he is not. He is a man who lacks balance, who lacks discipline, who does not know how to control his own spirit . . . I believe that ultimately the cause of all bigotry is a spirit of fear . . . a defect of character, a psychological condition . . .'
[2] Prior to this date ML-J's assistants in the sixties were George Hemming and Herbert M. Carson.

No one, outside his immediate family, knew the nature of his illness. The Christian press for the following week simply announced that he was ill and in hospital. In a note to Philip Hughes, on March 13, Bethan Lloyd-Jones said:

He is making good progress so far and pleasing the doctors. He cannot yet deal with any correspondence. He has been very ill. He sends his love and covets your prayers . . .

Many different fears and hopes were entertained. I recall having to go to the Chapel during the week of his operation. I was to take a wedding a few days later, which he had hoped to conduct, and preparation for this required a mid-week visit to the premises. With time to spare, I entered the vast church through the door behind the pulpit, the rows of empty pews facing me, and wandered down an aisle to the far end where I took a seat, alone, in the shadows beneath the encircling gallery. The silence was full of the memories of many years, of congregations assembling on warm summer evenings and in their wet shoes and overcoats in the depths of winter, of times of thunderous praise and others of great stillness when such hymns as

He loved me, and gave Himself for me

were sung at the administration of the Lord's Supper. Thousands had been here who knew something of what Moses knew when he was told 'the place whereon thou standest is holy ground'. But then my thoughts were interrupted as I observed another figure, tall although bent with age, entering the auditorium from the same direction that I had come and, not seeing me, she stopped beneath the pulpit and stood motionless looking up at its empty desk and closed Bible. It was Margaret Smith who had spent long years as a missionary in Peru. She was now, in her latter years, one of the brightest of the many single ladies whose lives contributed so much to the congregation and for whom Westminster was their true home. As she stood motionless, supposing herself to be entirely unobserved, nothing could have expressed more eloquently the feelings of multitudes. I think we both sensed that it was the end of an era.

I did not doubt that Margaret Smith was praying, and it was subsequently clear that the weeks which followed were a time of very widespread intercession. Many ministers wrote to give assurance of

20. *With Mr. and Mrs. John Bolten and Bethan at an IFES gathering in Schloss Mittersill.*

21. *39 Mount Park Crescent, Ealing. The family home from 1945 to 1965.*

22. *The exterior of Westminster Chapel.*

23. *The interior of Westminster Chapel from the pulpit.*

24. *In conversation with John Stott at the conclusion of the Evangelical Alliance meeting of October 18, 1966.*

25. *At John and Mari Jones' farm, Llanymawddy, 1968.*

26. *Graduation Day at Westminster Seminary, 1969.*

27. *With Cornelius Van Til at Westminster Seminary.*

28. *Aged 69, a photograph taken at the time of the delivery of his addresses on 'Preachers and Preaching' at Westminster Seminary.*

29. *At the British Homoeopathic Congress. Margery Blackie (Physician to the Queen) presents M. L.-J. to Her Majesty,*

30. *Mawddach, Wales, part of the scenery which M. L.-J. loved so much.*

31. *At 'Bwlch y Groes' near Llanymawddy, 1977* [see page 702].

32. *With Bethan, at the home of Professor Bobi Jones on his last visit to Aberystwyth, May 14, 1980* [see page 735].

33. *With the Catherwoods at Balsham, summer 1976.*

34. *Adam, Elizabeth and Rhiannon Desmond who spent many of the early years of their lives in the company of their grandfather.*

35. *The funeral cortège at Newcastle Emlyn, March 6, 1981.*

36. *The burial at Gelli Cemetery, Newcastle Emlyn.*

37. *Portrait photograph by Desmond Groves, 1970's.*

38. *Bethan Lloyd-Jones, July, 1987.*

39. *The congregation at Westminster Chapel for the memorial service, April 6, 1981.*

the prayer in their churches. One, writing from Carmarthen to Mrs Lloyd-Jones, said, 'We hope and pray like hundreds of others throughout Wales, that the operation will be successful'. Similar messages came from many parts of the Principality, including several from his former congregation at Port Talbot, where his old friend E. T. Rees reported, 'We are praying much for you these days'. England was not, however, far behind Wales. From Wiltshire, in the heart of English countryside, Pastor Harry Matthews wrote, 'The Lord hear the prayers of many thousands of his people, and give the "Doctor" back to us for a little while'. From Yorkshire, Suffolk ('a small group of us here are remembering you in prayer'), and many other quarters, news of prayer reached the Lloyd-Joneses. While letters revealed much personal concern and sympathy, there was another reason, often expressed, why many cried to God for his recovery. One writer, from Kent, said: 'With many thousands of humble, thankful people, I earnestly pray that God in His goodness and gracious mercy will restore him to us . . . sincere ambassadors of God's living Word are so few in this present age.' The Rev A. W. Rainsbury, whose own ministry in South Croydon was much valued, wrote: 'You will know that you are surrounded with the prayers of thousands of the Lord's people who owe so much to your leadership and need it more than ever today.'

This same intercession extended far beyond Britain. From Chicago, William Culbertson wrote of the prayer of ML-J's friends at Moody Bible Institute. From California, Wilbur Smith wrote to Mrs Lloyd-Jones on March 16: 'No letter could have brought news that would so go straight into my heart as yours, telling me of this serious illness of your beloved husband, and one of the dearest friends I will ever know. He is a giant, not to be measured with anyone else, in the present great battle of the Christian faith.' On April 8 Smith wrote to ML-J: 'What volumes of prayer ascend, every day, for your full recovery'. On hearing the same news at L'Abri, Switzerland, Francis Schaeffer immediately sent word to say: 'I, and we, will be praying for you. Very specially my prayer will be that Satan will have no victory and that your illness will not diminish what is so very much needed in the midst of our generation and which you are saying.'

Two missionaries, returning to South America by sea, wrote from RMS 'Aragon', 'approaching Rio de Janeiro', on March 27, to say that with thirteen other missionaries they had been meeting nightly and praying for ML-J ever since they had heard the news when they reached the Canary Islands.

Besides assuring him of their prayers, the only persons to offer ML-J advice at this critical time were friends who were fellow medicals. Once through his operation, he was advised to be sure not to prescribe his own treatment and not to plan on an early return to Westminster. C. Langton Hewer, a contemporary at Barts, wrote on March 22:

Having seen well over 70,000 operations in 50 years I am ashamed to say that I rather looked upon them as more or less normal incidents in life. I then had three major abdominal operations in three consecutive years and I discovered the difference between watching the proceedings from a stool and being the patient on the table . . . It takes much longer than one would think to get really fit again and while we are longing to hear you again from the pulpit, I do trust that you will not start too soon.

I would like to say how much my wife and I have appreciated your ministry and we join with thousands of others in praying for your rapid and complete recovery.

Cards and letters received by the Lloyd-Joneses at this time ran into the hundreds. Perhaps the most remarkable thing about this correspondence is its diversity. It came from correspondents in many lands and from many different backgrounds. From the elderly and the young, from the cultured and those little used to any form of correspondence.

When news spread that the operation had been successful and that he should be able to resume work by September there was great joy at Westminster Chapel. People began to speak of counting the weeks until his return, and one of his regular hearers wrote to say that he was 'the only preacher she could understand'. This he especially prized on account of the fact that its writer was only eleven years old! I think it must have touched him deeply for another reason: he knew that he would not be returning to Westminster. On the evening before his operation on March 8, seeing some apprehension in Bethan as they talked together, he assured her of his confidence that the operation would be successful. At the same time, he added, their lives would not be the same again for he believed this was God's answer to the question when his pastorate should be concluded. There would be other ministries but his work at Westminster Chapel was done. For several years he had struggled with this question and he now believed that his guidance was clear.

Early in April 1968 ML-J left hospital and, with Mrs Lloyd-Jones, went to convalesce at Hedingham Castle, the beautiful home of Musette Majendie in Essex. He returned to London before the end of April – before further convalescence at Balsham and in Yorkshire – and called a deacons' meeting on May 29. It was then that they heard of his decision to retire at the end of August, with no resumption of his ministry before then. And as he came to Westminster, without any recognition service, so he wished to leave. There would be no farewells, no speeches, no presentations. 'He talked to us for a little while,' writes Geoffrey Kirkby of that meeting, 'and I for one felt that we were experiencing all over again something of that which took place at Miletus when Paul said his farewells to the elders of the church at Ephesus, reminding them that he had not shunned to declare to them all the counsel of God. The Doctor then prayed with us but the emotion of the occasion was too much for him and he stopped and I believe someone else carried on. I am sure that we felt the same emotions stirring us as did the Ephesian elders and we would fain have fallen on his neck and kissed him.'

The next day, in another characteristic action, ML-J took up his pen to write to members of the church with the news which he wished each to receive personally from him. After thanking them for their prayers and saying that he would not be returning in September he went on:

I thank God that this decision is not based on considerations of health. My medical advisers assure me that I can regard myself as having had 'a complete surgical cure,' and I am thankful to say that I am conscious of returning and increasing strength daily, and am already looking forward to fulfilling my various preaching engagements in various parts of the country, as from the first week in September. In other words, I am simply retiring from the pastoral charge of Westminster Chapel and hope to continue with all my other interests and activities.

My illness has simply acted as a precipitating factor in what was becoming an increasing conviction that I should take this step. However, owing to the wonderful and affectionate bonds that have bound us together for so long, I simply could not bring myself to do it. The moment I realised that I had to undergo an operation, I felt that God was saying to me, 'This is the end of one ministry and the beginning of another.' I said that to my dear wife and colleague before the operation, and, ever since, this conviction has deepened and become more and more clear.

The considerations that had weighed with me were the following. I am already past the age at which most people retire today. I have completed 30 unbroken years in the ministry of Westminster and given the best years of my life to it. This has meant that I have refused invitations from various parts of the world to lecture at colleges and seminaries and to address conferences of ministers, etc., etc. But, and perhaps most important of all, it has meant that I have only been able to publish but little of what I have preached at Westminster. Great pressure has been brought to bear on me to publish more, and recently, increasing pressure to write some account of my spiritual pilgrimage and what it was that led me – over 41 years ago – to leave the medical profession and become a whole time preacher of 'the glorious gospel of the blessed God.'

It is because I am as certain that God has now called me to fulfil these tasks, as I was of His call 41 years ago, that I am taking this step and informing you of it.

As I said at the beginning, my feelings are mixed, inevitably so, and I cannot imagine what my life will be like without preaching three times each week at Westminster Chapel – apart from my summer vacation. But when God calls, He is to be obeyed in spite of all natural feelings.

I know that you dear people will understand. If you do not, then my ministry has been in vain. I must not begin to write about the past and of the blessed and happy times that by the grace of God we have been allowed to have together. I cannot imagine a happier ministerial lot than mine has been. No minister could wish to have a more faithful and loyal people. I shall ever thank God for you all and those who have 'gone before'.

*　　　　*　　　　*

There was no announcement for the press from Westminster, but it reflected the changing scene in Britain that his resignation drew little attention in the national press. *The Daily Telegraph* (June 11), under the erroneous heading, 'Isaiah in Three Years', noted the end of 'what must surely be London's longest preaching marathon' and spoke of ML-J as 'this Welsh Presbyterian' who 'sticks to the Bible and expects his listeners to have it in their hands for reference'. The writer went on to report, 'In one of his courses Dr Lloyd-Jones took three years to preach his way through the Book of Isaiah'.[1] In 'Ulster

[1] The statement about 'preaching through Isaiah' was pure fiction.

The End of an Era

letter from London', the *Belfast Telegraph* (June 7) told its readers that 'A great preacher steps down: By the retirement of Dr Martyn Lloyd-Jones from the pulpit of Westminster Chapel, London loses the last of its great preachers in the evangelical tradition . . .'. The *Western Mail* (June 3) expressed the same opinion:

Dr Martyn Lloyd-Jones's resignation, at the age of 68, from the pastorate of Westminster Chapel, London, marks the end of an era the like of which his Church is never likely to see again. For Dr Lloyd-Jones is not only the finest pulpit orator of his generation but the last of the great preachers in the true evangelical tradition, with an utter contempt for so-called secular Christianity.

The Christian press was also muted in its comment. *The Life of Faith* and *The Christian* wrote with the brevity of people taken by surprise. I surmise that the Editor of *The Evangelical Times* respected a direction from ML-J that there should be no comment but merely a statement of the fact. The non-evangelical religious press reflected both by its silence and sometimes by its comment the general change in the Christian scene. The *British Weekly* (June 13), in which news of Westminster Chapel was once so prominent, gave the announcement of ML-J's retirement in a short column under the heading 'Wales'. In another religious periodical, under the heading, 'The Wider Fellowship: Notes, news, opinion from Roman and Free Churches', the Rev Kenneth Slack wrote a paragraph on ML-J's 'remarkable ministry': 'It has been no mean feat to fill the windy vastnesses of that great auditorium with a very large congregation Sunday by Sunday for twenty-nine years . . . Dr Lloyd-Jones' ministry has not been in the main stream of Free Church life today, but he had a profound capacity as an expositor in the conservative tradition.' The longest comment of all came, curiously, in the *Methodist Recorder* (July 25) from the pen of the Rev A. E. Gould, a former Chairman of the Congregational Union of England and Wales. Under the heading, 'End of a marathon ministry', Gould spoke of the disappointment which ML-J's retirement was going to mean to many besides evangelicals:

Without any doubt, this has been one of the most influential Free Church ministries of our time . . . His expositions of Scripture in Friday evening Bible School have been like a mighty magnet throughout these

years, at a time when many influential voices have been trying to tell us
that the day of preaching was over . . .

The man's name has become a legend in his own lifetime. One has
heard often not only of visitors to London from all parts of the country,
and indeed of the English- (and Welsh-) speaking world, feeling that
their stay in the capital lacked its full blessing without a visit to
Westminster Chapel . . .

It would be wrong and misleading to pretend that the theological
emphases of this exceptionally gifted servant of Christ have always, or
usually, found a ready welcome in what the BBC has taught us to call the
'mainstream' Christian denominations. Some of us, while praising God
for the manifest blessing which He has bestowed and for the mighty use
He has made of Lloyd-Jones's outstanding gifts, could have wished for a
greater readiness to find points of agreement and fellowship in
emphasising the great, positive notes of the one glorious Gospel which
has been entrusted to us by the Head of the Church.

Sometimes there has been sadness or disappointment because theological differences have been overstressed, or what seemed unhelpful
criticism levelled at fellow-workers. But, at such a moment as this, we
are all at one in recognising the greatness of this inspired and inspiring
ministry. We are relieved to know that it is not coming to an end because
of continued ill health or because recent surgery has not achieved the
hoped and prayed for results; we are indeed assured that there has been
'a complete surgical cure', and for this we thank God.

Far more illuminating and valuable than this press comment is
the personal correspondence addressed both to the preacher and
his wife. For once the restraints of English reserve broke
down. Beresford Dean, deacon and church treasurer, and recently
widowed, wrote a long letter 'from a heart full of thankfulness to
God for you and for ever bringing me under your ministry . . . I have
just wanted you to know the feelings I have been unable to express before!' Another characteristic letter, from Edith Brown (one
of the faithful workers at the Chapel), began:

Our very dear Doctor and Mrs Lloyd-Jones
So many times have I tried to write this letter, but the remembrance
of why I have to write it came flooding in together with (and I am not
ashamed to admit this) the tears which blinded my eyes. I know now
what the Ephesians felt when they had to say farewell to Paul . . .

Yet the theme of these letters was not sadness. Both affection and thankfulness overflowed. Another letter may again serve as an example:

God has so blessed us through the years that we have been privileged in having you as our minister. How good is the God we adore! We thank Him for your wonderful recovery . . . My prayer, each day, has always been that God would bless our beloved minister and his dear wife – and my prayer will be the same until I die for you still belong to us. As for me, I love you and Mrs Lloyd-Jones better than anyone in this world . . .

In a few cases letters came from those who had been with him through the thirty years at the Chapel. One man, of eighty-three years, wrote of memories at the Chapel going back to the First World War and could recall that his attendance began in the year 1911. At the other extreme there were letters from those who had only recently found their way to Westminster. One lady wrote of her praise to God for the assurance of salvation given to her in the last month of his ministry. Some converted under his ministry told him of it now for the first time. A letter from a man in Switzerland read:

I feel it to be my duty to tell you that on the occasion of one of your Sunday evening sermons in 1954, I have been convicted of my sin and brought into the glorious light and joy of Christ's redeeming grace. I have not told you this before – please forgive me – but the Lord knows! He also knows the great numbers of young men and women from all over the world who have found *life* at Westminster Chapel . . .

A doctor in Sheffield wrote: 'I felt I would write on this particular date as it was on this day ten years ago that I was converted under your ministry at the Chapel . . . I have great cause to thank the Lord for your faithful ministry.' 'It was through Marilyn and Westminster Chapel,' wrote another, 'that I was led to the Lord.' A husband and wife wrote to say: 'We realize that there is only one foundation for true happiness and we are so thankful to God that He has shown us this through you'. 'I owe it you,' said a correspondent from the Channel Islands, 'that I am a Christian.'

One man testified to what the Chapel had meant to his whole family – to his mother, now deceased, to his nephew ('converted under your ministry at Westminster in 1960') and, more recently, to his brother and sister-in-law who had started to attend Westminster

the previous autumn and were now Christians: 'It is obvious for all
to see, they have a hunger for the things of God, His Word and
prayer, and have a job to believe that something so wonderful has
happened to them'.

There were multiplied testimonies from Christians of what they
had learned from his ministry: 'how to study the Scriptures'; 'how to
read'; 'that it is in the Lord our God that we must encourage
ourselves'; 'to love the First Chapter of 1 Corinthians'; 'something of
the wonderful love of Jesus Christ'; 'the sheer bigness and generous
affection of our Lord Jesus Christ'; 'a wider, fuller conception of
what Christianity can mean and a deep sense of the infinite love and
mercy of God and our Saviour Jesus Christ'.[1]

Others spoke more generally: 'You have been the means of leading
me into a richer and fuller Christian life'; 'your preaching and
prayers and personal help have wrought such a wonderful
transformation in my whole life'; 'I have been coming to Westminster Chapel now for about 15 years . . . how many many times I have
come out of the services feeling that I had been at the very gate of
heaven'; 'Many times I went home from the services just to get down
on my knees to praise the Lord for all the wonders of His grace, or
perhaps to seek Him in repentance'; 'As one who has received so
many blessings from your ministry at Westminster Chapel, I feel
constrained to tell you a little of what it has meant to me. Without
any doubt the greatest blessing has been the consciousness of the
Divine Presence. I can remember a number of occasions when my
faith was drooping and when I was full of doubts, I came to the
Chapel and then, under your preaching of the Word, God so dealt
with me that I found my doubts dissolving away and my faith
confirmed and strengthened. Very often it was not because you had
been dealing with the particular point with which my doubts were
concerned, but because all the spiritual realities became alive, and I
was so conscious of the presence of God, and that it was nothing less
than the Word of the living God which was being addressed to me,
that my doubts were just taken away – they seemed to be so utterly

[1] The appreciation of the love of God, so often expressed in these letters, belongs
to that same ethos in which the nature of sin and the power of the Holy Spirit are
also evident. Some while after ML-J's retirement a brief and anonymous
correspondent wrote: 'Daily I thank God that I have been able to attend
Westminster Chapel and to be taught by you about what really matters . . . I feel
it is wrong of me, but often I wish you were there to teach of the love of God
through Jesus Christ.'

foolish and illogical and positively sinful for me who had been redeemed by the Son of God.'

Sometimes comment was made on particular aspects of his life and ministry, with many references to help which he and Mrs Lloyd-Jones had given in private: 'I write out of a full heart to thank you for your faithful, loyal and fearless ministry'. 'Where *might* I have been now,' one woman asked in her letter to them both, 'if you had not been faithful?' Another expressed his thankfulness 'for your indifference to what men thought'. 'In spite of the greatness of the congregation, you have always dealt with us as though nothing is too much trouble for the individual soul.' 'I think that perhaps one of the greatest things I have valued at Westminster – apart from the great personal blessings that God has given me there – has been the fact that God has given me scores of people in need whom I had had the privilege of bringing to hear the gospel, knowing that they would indeed hear it at Westminster Chapel.'

Many ministers and Christian workers wrote to tell him or Mrs Lloyd-Jones what he meant to them. 'He is a father in Christ to so many of us,' one preacher wrote from Bermuda. A Suffolk pastor, telling ML-J how greatly he was being missed at the Westminster Fellowship, concluded, 'You are God's gift to many, not least to ministers who need a Pastor, and we are thankful for you'. A letter from a Methodist minister brought the reminder of the large numbers of students for the ministry who had received the most valuable part of their training at Westminster:

I have just seen the notice of your resignation as minister of Westminster Chapel. At such a time I feel that I must tell you what a very great help your ministry was to me and to several other theological students while we were studying for the Methodist ministry at Richmond College. Often, at the end of a week of lectures which sometimes left us wondering just what we could believe, we would go up to the Chapel, as we called it, and there we would receive food for our souls, and would catch a fresh vision of the power and relevance of the gospel we had been called to preach. We came to see that God was greater than we had ever imagined before, and that the Bible was indeed His Word to us, inspired and wonderful in all its teaching.

To have sat under your ministry as often as possible for a period of four years has been a privilege that I shall never forget for it has changed the entire course of my own ministry and the ministries of my friends who were at College at that time.

Dr Lloyd-Jones had always valued the friendship of the family of Campbell Morgan, whose youngest daughter, Mrs Ruth Shute, was born during her father's first ministry at the Chapel and who remained an active member. Through Mrs Shute, Morgan's sons in the States soon heard of ML-J's illness and then of his retirement from the pulpit. In a letter of June 7 Howard Moody Morgan (Minister of Chambers-Wylie Memorial United Presbyterian Church, Philadelphia) wrote:

As all the Morgans know and you, dear friend, know as well, you were Dad's first and only choice to be his Colleague at Westminster and also to succeed him when God called him into the House of Many Mansions! And it has been a wonderful ministry for these thirty years, I believe. The thousands who have been strengthened by your steadfast faith continually thank God for you and among them, believe me, I certainly count myself.

We conclude this chapter with part of a letter from Jim Packer:

Latimer House
131 Banbury Road
Oxford
26.9.68

Dear Dr Lloyd-Jones,
I should have written to you long since to say, first, how glad I am to know you have recovered so fully and, second, how I felt at the news that you were leaving Westminster Chapel. God gave you a truly momentous ministry there, and it gives one pause to think that it has ended. It is not given to many of us to change the course of things in the Christian world to the extent that you have been used to change it, nor to restore so much of its true value to so much of our debased Christian verbal coinage. I shall always be grateful myself for the understanding of the meaning of preaching which you gave me – not by talking about it, but by doing it – during the winter of 1948/9, when you peregrinated on Sunday evenings through Matthew 11. I was at Oak Hill, teaching, at that time, and was able to get in fairly regularly. I recall both my mystified fascination as to what you were at when you started in on verse 3 and my sense, by verse 30, that whereas I had never before grasped what preaching really was, I knew now. Incidentally, my sister, who was at Bedford at that time, thinks she became a Christian about verse 29! For me, your preaching

of the gospel from the gospels remains the finest thing of all in your pulpit ministry. This is the time to say thank-you, and I say it from my heart.

PART FOUR

WORKING FOR AN EVANGELICAL SUCCESSION

Dr Lloyd-Jones was carrying so much of the leadership of a large part of evangelical witness in 1968 that had all his work been ended suddenly with his illness in that year it is not easy to describe the sense of desolation which might have ensued. When John Doggett for the Evangelical Library spoke of him as 'our directing force, humanly speaking, our rudder' his words could equally well have been those of very many other agencies and churches. Instead, ML-J was given further years and, relieved of the great pressure of the responsibility for Westminster Chapel, he deliberately sought to reduce dependence upon himself as he gave first priority to encouraging and preparing others in the work which would continue when he was gone. The words 'Keep on!' were perhaps to be his characteristic exhortation to these men in the 1970's.

An 'Anniversary Charge' delivered to the students of Westminster Theological Seminary in the summer of 1969 epitomises what was now uppermost on his heart. He spoke of the need to stand for the message that Paul affirms in 1 Corinthians 15:1–4, and the Bulletin of Westminster Theological Seminary *(Second Quarter 1969) reports:*

'With particular urgency he stressed the repeated phrase, "according to the scriptures". He warned against the pride of academic achievement that makes men wiser than God, so that their minds are no longer in subjection to his Word.

'In a poignant moment, alluding to his own compulsion to continue in the struggle for the gospel, he quoted from Arnold's poem Sohrab and Rustum:

> But now in blood and battles was my youth
> And full of blood and battles is my age,
> And I shall never end this life of blood.

'He called to the young men to join him in that battle from which there can be no retirement until Christ comes.'

29

The Last Visit to America

At the time of Dr Lloyd-Jones' sudden and serious illness in March
1968 some were encouraged in praying for him by the memory of the
manner in which prayer was answered for another Welsh leader of an
earlier period. When the life of Thomas Charles of Bala was in danger
in November 1800, it was long to be remembered how an old man
pleaded that their minister might be spared. In earnest simplicity,
Edward Evans pressed his petition at a prayer meeting with the words,
'Fifteen, Lord; wilt Thou not give him to us for fifteen years? For my
brethren's sake this prayer is made . . .'. Charles did live, and for only
six weeks short of the time which was asked.[1]

Probably no one thought of such a time period with reference to
ML-J. When I saw him for the first time after his operation at Balsham,
in early June 1968, it seemed that he had suddenly become all his
sixty-eight years. Although in good spirits, the vigour and strength so
long associated with him were largely gone. I scarcely believed that he
could resume his engagements around the country in the first week of
September – preaching in Glasgow and Stirling – as he hoped to do.
Far less did I anticipate that I would be hearing him preach in Glasgow twelve years later. But the fact is that in June 1968 he was only
half-way through his convalescence. A complete recovery was to
follow. From Friday, March 1, 1968, the day when he preached to
his congregation at Westminster for the last time, another thirteen
years exactly were to be given him.

The main part of his active ministry for the future was clear to him as
he reflected further upon it in the quiet summer of 1968. As he wrote to
Philip Hughes on July 6:

What really drove me to retire from Westminster was not so much my
illness as the fact that I had been there for 30 years and that I have felt

[1] *The Life of Thomas Charles*, D. E. Jenkins, 1910, vol 2, p 243.

---

increasingly that I must put into book form more of the material that I have accumulated – for example, I am anxious to print what I have tried to do on the Epistle to the Romans among others.

In the letters he received from his congregation, and others, following his illness and resignation there was one subject often raised which he must have read with profound thankfulness. His people rose to the vision to which he had referred in his letter to them and, instead of complaining about what they were to lose, they believed that the world needed to *read* the truths which they had heard. At this point in time, twenty years later, that may seem obvious enough to us, but in 1968 there were many who thought ML-J's thought required a pulpit for its presentation. While they supposed that those who, with the aid of their memories, could put his voice to his written words would buy his books, they doubted whether he could ever be popular with others. There was, after all, no parallel in the twentieth century to support the idea that the publication of consecutive expository sermons could be successful, and what he had published thus far had not been without its critics. One reviewer, under the pseudonym of 'Evangelist', had, for instance, compared ML-J's sermons on *Spiritual Depression: Its Causes and Cure* with a new volume by the liberal Bishop James A. Pike, *A Time for Christian Candour*. He saw Dr Lloyd-Jones' book as a 'hefty volume' in which there was, he regretted, 'nothing intellectually adventurous, no theoretical ranging into new worlds, no destructive criticizing of long cherished creeds and habits'. 'It is rather dreary matter,' 'Evangelist' concluded, 'compared with the stimulating new thought of *A Time for Christian Candour* and belongs, it seems to me, to an old world which has for many of us long since disappeared.'[1]

Such opinions certainly did not disturb, or surprise, ML-J, but the faith of his people must have added strength to his resolution. In various ways the same thought was expressed in many letters which he received: 'that relief from your arduous labours at Westminster will enable you to be a sort of minister-at-large to the church of Christ throughout the world'; 'I am glad that many others should share the riches He has showered upon us through your expositions

---

[1] An 'American Bishop of Woolwich' (i.e. James Pike) in *The Methodist Recorder*, June 10, 1965. Yet Operation Mobilization was soon to distribute more than 300,000 copies of *Spiritual Depression*, apart from regular sales by its publishers on both sides of the Atlantic!

in the mighty power of the Spirit'; 'Maybe you have been called away from the limits of the pastorate for a special and greater work in these terrible days'.

Others spoke of what the *Westminster Record* and his books thus far published meant to them. One wrote of reading every issue of the *Record* since leaving the London Bible College in 1957, and said, 'It is impossible to compute how much these Bible expositions have meant to me over the years'. A missionary in Mombasa had been a reader of the monthly sermon since 1948 and was convinced, with respect to ML-J's illness, that the Lord of the harvest had arranged things for His Greater glory: '. . . We look to you as one whom the Lord has graciously empowered to be a strong leader as the enemy comes in like a flood.' From Fez, Morocco, a correspondent wrote to him: 'I want you to know that the *Westminster Record* and your books have been a very great blessing and help to us during the last ten years.' And from Japan another missionary wrote to the publishers of his *Spiritual Depression*: 'For a long time I have had a burden or a desire to see more of Dr Jones in print. I must be amongst thousands.'

From the United States came these words:

The *Westminster Record* has been so enriching. In these times we thirst for the exposition of truth and this little magazine has refreshed me and mine for years. I have one daughter but she is more than a thousand miles from us. She delights to read the *Record* because it impresses her with truths she hasn't been taught. Her husband is a belligerent unbeliever . . . She came to know the Lord after her children were born. Many others appreciate the *Record*. It is like feasting at the table of the King.

The same writer spoke of how she hoped to live to see the whole of his exposition of Ephesians in book form.

A member of his first congregation at Aberavon reported, 'I am following his studies in Ephesians in the *Westminster Record* and I cannot put into words the blessings, the instruction and the convictions I am receiving'. A reader in Southampton wrote to him: 'Through your written ministry the Lord has opened my eyes and heart and mind to such riches of His glory and grace.'

A plain-speaking Englishman from Devon, writing to ML-J before he had seen a copy of the letter of resignation from Westminster, summed it all up in these words:

Very sorry to learn you have had surgery. This was sad reading . . . Trust
you will or have made arrangements for the continued publication of your
sermons for many years to come. C. H. Spurgeon is read more and in
greater demand all over the world than he was in his life time. You are a
greater Bible expositor than he was. Remember our Saviour's words to
Peter, 'strengthen thy brethren'. You must do this by ensuring the
continued output of your sermons. Our prayers continue for you . . .

Parallel to ML-J's commitment to produce further books was his
determination to do everything possible to help the younger ministers.
The need of their churches took first place in his acceptance of future
engagements and, from September 1968, while continuing his usual
mid-week itinerant ministry, he was also free to preach on Saturdays
and Sundays. His arrangements for the autumn of 1968 had, of
course, been made before his illness, and some time was to pass before
it was realized that he was now available at weekends.

There was perhaps never an occasion which brought out more
clearly the bond between him and so many ministers than the meetings
of the Westminster Fraternal on October 9, 1968. For many there was
the excitement of seeing him for the first time since the last Fraternal he
had attended at the beginning of February and the joy of witnessing his
evident restoration to health. It was anticipated that he might give
some kind of address, which would put new life into us, and this he
certainly did. He announced no subject and began by apologizing for
'the interruption' in his attendance, though it had been 'beyond his
control'. Until his operation, he went on, he had known remarkable
health and would have found it difficult to visualize what illness would
mean. From the experience of the past months he said:

I think I know now 'the peace of God which passeth all understanding'.
Peace is a very real thing and I was given that in a way I shall never forget as
long as I live. Negatively, I have to confess, I wondered afterwards why
I did not feel as Paul, desiring to depart and to be with Christ. It wasn't
that I was craving to live, but looking back on it, there was a lack there. I
knew I was going to get well. It seems to me I should have known something of that other aspect, facing death in the spirit of expectation. I regard
it as a deficiency. Our relationship to the Lord should make it otherwise.

He then spoke solemnly of the folly of waiting for illness to happen
to us before we give it thought, rather we should always be preparing
for such a time. And one way to do that is to see that we love God with

all our strength while we are well, for when illness comes we shall have no strength and be 'so weak we cannot even read, not even the Scriptures'. Strength must be used now and reserves laid up for the day of trial.

Our danger is to be victims of our routine – you get carried on by the momentum of the work until suddenly pulled up as Edmund Burke was by the death of an opponent in an election at Bristol when he was brought to say, 'What shadows we are, what shadows we pursue'. We tend to exaggerate things which in the end are not vital, allowing ourselves to be moved overmuch. In the light of eternity we see things at their real value.

There is another thing to be said, and I am more concerned about this at present. The interruption of my ministry had a message for me. I was at Romans 14:17. I had dealt with 'righteousness', with 'peace' on March 1, and there I was stopped. I was not allowed to deal with 'joy in the Holy Ghost'. I have the feeling that this was not accidental. God intervened and I could suggest a reason why. I was able to deal with righteousness and peace (I had fleeting experiences of it), but the third thing is the profoundest of all. Why was I not allowed to deal with it? Because I knew something but not enough about it. 'I want you to speak with greater authority on this,' God said.

I think that one reason why Dr Lloyd-Jones gave us the confession of the last paragraph was that it provided a right starting point for his main theme. He had acknowledged his own measure of failure and thus put us in a position to search our own hearts before he proceeded to address *our* need.

Here is what I would put before you. For six months, until September, I did not preach at all. For four months I have had the most valuable experience of being a listener. My general impression is that most of our services are terribly depressing! I am amazed people still go to church; most who go are female and over the age of forty. The note missing is 'joy in the Holy Ghost'. There is nothing in these services to make a stranger feel that he is missing something by not being there. It is as though there is a weight upon us and the minister, feeling this, thinks he must be short. So the people come together in order to depart! Speaking generally, I think it is true to say this and there is little difference in this respect in evangelical churches.

It is a great thing to be a listener. You want something for your soul. You want help. I don't want a 'great sermon'. I want to feel the presence of the God I am worshipping and to know that I am considering some great and glorious subject. If I do get this I do not care how poor the sermon is.

I suggest to you that our greatest danger is the danger of professionalism. We do not stop sufficiently frequently to ask, What are we really doing? There is the danger of just facing a text and treating it as an end in itself with a strange detachment. It is all intellectual. Nor should our preaching be just emotional, or only to the conscience. Far too often it is one or other of these things. There is no life, no power! We of all people ought to have it. Joy and power are intimately related. One without the other is spurious.

He went on to take up a point which I do not think had been discussed at the Fraternal before. He was disturbed at the extent to which ministers were beginning to act as though giving 'a running commentary' on a passage was the same as *preaching*:

People say it is biblical. It is not. It is biblical to bring out a message. A mechanical explanation of the meaning of words, etc. is not preaching. Scripture has to be fused into a message, with point and power – a sermon has to be something that is moving and which sends people away glorying in God. We have got to bring a *message* and deliver it 'in demonstration of the Spirit and of power'. M'Cheyne did not just prepare sermons. He had the burden of the people on his soul and he came from God with a message. This was the glory of a man like C. H. Spurgeon. His sermons had form and thrust and made an impact. This whole notion of a *message* needs to be recaptured. The hardest part of a minister's work is the preparation of sermons. It is a trying process. There is an agony in it, an act of creation. That is why I feel so well at the moment, I do not prepare three sermons a week.

Such effective preaching is bound up with experience of the Holy Spirit. 'The main trouble of evangelicalism today, apart from its slipping away from truth, is its lack of power. What do our people know of "joy in the Holy Ghost"?'

From this point his address went on to the whole question of raising the standard of preaching and especially of gospel preaching – 'the most difficult of all – it is the preaching that costs, that brings an element of burden to the preacher'. There was need, he urged, of more reading but not for gramophone repetition in the pulpit. There had also to be more prayer, more use of history, more anecdotes ('I reacted too much against them') and more confidence: 'There is nobody hopeless in our congregations. All can grasp doctrines. But we have got to cook it well and make it attractive.' 'Use the best language, the best of everything.'

In conclusion, he said, he thanked God for giving him a pause and a period for self-examination. Without this 'joy in the Holy Ghost' the situation in the country was hopeless. 'But it is not hopeless. We must start with ourselves. Do I know anything of this fire and if not what am I doing in the pulpit?'

ML-J's concern to help preachers coincided with many requests to him for a series of addresses on preaching, and it was to be of lasting significance that another such request came at this point. He had already promised to visit Florida in the August of 1969 and Edmund Clowney now asked him to come to Westminster Theological Seminary to lecture on preaching in the Spring of 1969. To this he agreed, planning to leave Britain on April 8, 1969, and to use part of the summer in the States, after finishing at Westminster, to start preparation of his Romans sermons for publication.

In the meantime there were several other addresses to be given in the UK besides his itinerant preaching. On November 5, 1968, he spoke to the intimate circle which gathered for the Annual Meeting of the Evangelical Library. In his address he argued that the Library was needed more than ever and that it served a purpose of great importance – concentrating as it did on 'the great classical evangelical literature of all centuries'. 'I have resigned,' he said, 'from certain activities this year, but I have not resigned from this Evangelical Library.' He went on to recall what it had meant in his own life:

I will never forget my sense of joy and of rejoicing when, with the Reverend Eliseus Howells I visited Beddington thirty years ago. Nothing was so tantalizing to a young preacher, or any young student of these matters, than to read a book in which you find a reference to some unknown writer of some great book which greatly helped people in the past. You felt, 'Well, I would like to read that very much myself. If it helped him it would help me.' Then you were confronted by the question, 'Where can I get it?' I used to spend a great deal of my time burrowing in the secondhand book shops. Many of you here tonight are too young to remember Paternoster Row. Whenever I came to London from South Wales I spent most of my time in Paternoster Row climbing up ladders and hanging on by one hand while I was looking at a book round the corner somewhere. It was the only thing one could do. And then suddenly to find in this Library this great wealth! There they all were! Not only books on theology, and Puritan works, but biographies and books on hymnology, etc. . . . I imagine that during the thirty years I have borrowed more books from this Library, and used more books from this Library, than any other single individual; and I do thank God for it. It has been one of the greatest aids to me in my work and ministry, and what it has been it still is. So it is our desire that this work should continue and that it should increase.[1]

The following week he was in Liverpool for the closing Rally at the second major Conference of the British Evangelical Council when he spoke on, 'What is the Church?'. At the Puritan Conference in December, when the general subject was Calvinism and Arminianism, he spoke on 'William Williams and Welsh Calvinistic Methodism'. In March, 1969 (having already that year preached in Scotland, Wales and various towns in England), he gave three addresses. The first to an audience of junior doctors at the Royal Commonwealth Society, London, on 'The Making or Breaking of a Medical Registrar: A Study in Stress'; the second – again under the auspices of the Christian Medical Fellowship and at the same venue – on 'Will Hospital Replace the Church?'; the third at the Inter-Varsity Fellowship Conference at Swanwick when he was asked to speak with reference to the Fellowship's fiftieth anniversary.[2]

This Swanwick address, on March 30, 1969, was his last major address to an IVF Conference in Britain. The subject which he took illustrated how carefully he considered his hearers in preparing these addresses. He could, for instance, easily have given to the ministers at the Westminster Fraternal the address he gave on Preaching in Grand Rapids in 1967: instead he gave a new address, specifically suited to the men belonging to the fraternal. It was the same at Swanwick. The IVF anniversary was intended to be a time of thankfulness and he was thankful – 'There are many who owe the greatest thing in life, namely their salvation, under God to the work of the IVF'. 'But the best way to show our thanksgiving to God for the IVF,' he argued, 'is to make sure this work will go on.' He proceeded to remind the 500 students present of the origin of the IVF and how it came into being because of the great change within the Student Christian Movement:

[1] *Why The Evangelical Library must go on, An Urgent appeal*, delivered at the Annual Meeting on November 5, 1968, by Dr D. Martyn Lloyd-Jones.
[2] This was the anniversary of what Douglas Johnson calls 'the first Inter-varsity Conference' (December 1919) although the IVF did not formally come into being until 1928.

The Last Visit to America

'Men came to see that they were not to stay and try to win the Movement from the inside. They felt that the only way in which they could safeguard the gospel and the truth of God was to separate from the SCM.'

The decline of SCM (and the consequent beginning of the IVF) illustrated, he believed, the tendency for institutions to become the exact opposite of the purpose for which they were founded. The state of the Protestant denominations demonstrated the same truth. 'If the fathers and founders of these various denominations came back they would not believe their eyes.' He went on to ask, 'Is the IVF still in the position that it held at the beginning?'. If anyone thought it wrong to ask such a question they did not understand the very danger about which the New Testament has much to say. Individual Christians and churches may gradually slip away from the truth without being aware that any change whatsoever is taking place.

This led him to take up the case of the church in Corinth, as illustrated in 1 Corinthians. Here was an outstanding church which had fallen into decline and that on account of three things:

Carnality. A kind of antinomianism seemed to have entered in.

Intellectualism. There was a desire to be 'wise' and to forget the difference between 'the wisdom of this world' and 'the wisdom of God'.

An unbalanced spirituality. The whole church was being torn by this unhealthy interest in phenomena and, in particular, gifts, especially the gift of speaking in tongues.

Each of these points he dealt with in turn, and there can have been few who did not see their contemporary relevance. Then he proceeded to 'lessons': (1) The need to recognize that because a church or institution or movement was once right there is no guarantee that it continues to be right. (2) The danger of allowing secondary or third-rate matters to occupy the centre of attention, whether these matters concern questions of gifts, or of unfulfilled prophecy, or of the social and 'cultural' implications of the gospel. The Corinthian error is being repeated when such things are the centre of attention. (3) The vital importance of self examination.

ML-J believed that the prescription to meet these dangers was exactly what Paul gave to the church at Corinth in 1 Corinthians 15:1–4, where he says, in effect: 'Now there is only one treatment for all this. It is to come back to the things that are central and foundational. That is to say, to the Scriptures as divine revelation (God speaking to men, not man trying to arrive at a knowledge of God — the passing of 50 years, or of 5,000 years, makes not the slightest difference); the need of salvation (man fallen in Adam, and under the wrath of God) and God's redemption provided in Christ.' In this faith Christians must 'stand fast' and be constantly watchful — not only in behaviour but in their thinking and reading:

Be careful with whom you associate if you want to stand fast in the faith. You have got to avoid false teaching, to avoid error, to avoid wrong practice. The IVF deliberately separated itself from the SCM believing that that was the only way to safeguard this truth and to 'stand' in it. It is still the same. Fraternizing with those who deny the Gospel will never do us any good, indeed it will do us positive harm. 'Be not deceived: evil communications corrupt good manners' (1 Cor. 15:33). Let us be careful that in our desire to be considered intellectually respectable we do not expose ourselves to infections which can do us grievous harm in a spiritual sense. The Apostle has already said it all. There were people who called this colossus of a man, this genius — there were people who called him a 'fool'. He was quite content to be a fool for Christ's sake. If you are out for intellectual respectability you will soon get into trouble in your faith . . .

Believe the message, trust it utterly, absolutely, and look to the Holy Spirit of God to open the blind eyes and to give understanding to the spiritually dead.

*　　　　*　　　　*

On April 8, 1969, Dr and Mrs Lloyd-Jones left London for what was to be their longest and their last visit to the United States. Instead of the usual five or six days, the journey took precisely seven-and-a-half hours. It was their first trans-Atlantic flight. Leigh and Miriam Powell — young people who had been at Westminster — met them at Philadelphia airport and took them to a private home in Jenkintown where the Seminary had arranged convenient accommodation for them. The first few days were free, as was the first Sunday, April 13, when they attended Calvary Orthodox Presbyterian Church beside the Seminary in the morning, and in the evening the downtown church in Philadelphia where Campbell-Morgan had heard ML-J preach 32 years earlier.[1] The next day Dr Lloyd-Jones gave the first of his

[1]See vol. 1, p 330.

sixteen lectures on 'Preaching and Preachers', his class being scheduled to meet for an hour at 2 pm on Mondays, Tuesdays and Wednesdays. Attendance was either on a voluntary basis or it could be taken as an elective course with an examination at the end. Forty-four men took the elective and the lecturer – for the first and last time in his whole ministry – had to set and mark the examination paper!

It had also been arranged by the Seminary that Dr Lloyd-Jones would give a series of evening public addresses in the auditorium of the nearby Beaver College campus. The subject announced for the evening series was 'Biblical Renewal', a more respectable term – in reformed circles in the United States – than 'Revival', though it was in fact on the subject of revival that he preached at these meetings.

A letter home by Bethan Lloyd-Jones, written on April 17, gives a glimpse of a day in their first week. Her hostess (whose husband was an army chaplain in Vietnam) was a supply teacher, but free on this particular day:

Gloria and I went this morning an hour's run along one of these turnpike roads to a US Army base where she did her shopping for a month. We left your father to get his own coffee and lunch snack and returned about 2.45. It is open lecture tonight so we can go and we are having an early supper.

Most days ML-J maintained his old routine of morning study, chiefly the preparation of his class lectures for which he needed no reference books. He drew on the memory of his own experience and reading over many years. For the evening public addresses he took his material from his notes of his sermons at the Chapel on revival in 1959. Mrs Lloyd-Jones had also her own desk-work to do; her husband's sermons on Ephesians 2, as printed in the *Westminster Record*, needed some further revision before they could become his first published volume on Ephesians. Her practical problem, as she wrote home, was to know how much to cut out of each introduction, 'I cannot bother your father while he is working so hard'.

From Sunday, April 20, onwards ML-J was also preaching every weekend. On that date he was in another city church in Philadelphia for the morning service and 'a lecture' at 4 pm. Amidst various general news, Bethan wrote to Keith and Ann of these services:

I enjoyed my day enormously yesterday in the down-town church we were in. Your father was in excellent form, especially in the afternoon on 'Human wisdom and the wisdom of God'. The good congregation really listened. There was a Baptist minister and his wife sitting in front of me – late middle-age. He was from Newcastle-on-Tyne and she from Aberdeen. She had to take her glasses off, for she was unashamedly weeping. She turned to me at the end and said: 'That is an experience I shall never forget. I can't tell you what it has meant to me.'

I felt there was great freedom and power.

There was also, however, time for relaxation, including evenings with Faculty members, with Philip Hughes and his wife (now living just outside Philadelphia) and with several people who had once attended Westminster Chapel. Among the latter was Mary-Carson Kuschke, whose parents they now met and her brother, the Rev. Arthur Kuschke, the Librarian at Westminster Seminary, with whom ML-J at once found so much in common. Another kindred spirit with whom he became acquainted was Dr G. Hall Todd of Arch Street Presbyterian Church. Todd and the Kuschkes were their guides to sight-seeing in the historic parts of Philadelphia.

Amidst all the stimulus and enjoyment of this company, and the different surroundings, the Lloyd-Joneses suddenly received very grievous and unexpected news. The Rev. John B. E. Thomas had been the minister of Bethlehem Presbyterian Church, Sandfields (Dr Lloyd-Jones' first charge) since leaving College in 1953. One of the best-known leaders of the Evangelical Movement of Wales, he was often in touch with ML-J and frequently at such events in London as the Puritan Conference. John Thomas died on April 25, 1969 at the age of forty-one after an illness of only twenty-four hours. ML-J immediately wrote to his widow:

> at 519A Walnut St
> Jenkintown
> Pa, 19046
> April 26, 1969

Dear Eluned

I shall never forget what I felt last night when Elizabeth told me the shattering news of the passing of your dear one. Bethan and I still cannot realize that it is true. It seems quite impossible for he appeared to be unusually well when I was with you a month ago.

There is so much that I would like to say and could say. Perhaps the greatest thing of all is that in my opinion he was of all the younger men in Wales the one whom we could not afford to lose. Ever since I first met him as a student I formed the highest opinion of him, his character, his ability and his leadership. He more than fulfilled this throughout the years and one looked forward to yet greater things in the years to come. It is a most grievous blow to the whole evangelical cause in Wales and to all of us who knew him and loved him. But God's ways are not our ways and He knows best, though we cannot understand.

All of us who knew you both well can realize what this means to you. You had continued to be lovers though married for years and you were so perfectly suited to each other.

Thank God you know to whom to turn and He will not fail you. All we can do is to continue praying for you. It grieves me much that I cannot be at the funeral to pay my tribute to him, but I am glad to think that he knew what I thought of him.

With loving and deepest sympathy,
Yours very sincerely,
D. M. Lloyd-Jones

The month of May 1969 was to prove his busiest. In addition to the Seminary work and Sunday engagements, he preached on Graduation Day at Northeastern College, Essex Fells; at a two-day conference for 'Reformed Laymen'; and at the General Assembly of the Orthodox Presbyterian Church. His last of six addresses on Revival was given on May 22, after which they left Philadelphia by train for Washington where he was to take Sunday services and four consecutive evening meetings the following week – a period which coincided with the hottest May weather in the capital since 1941. Nonetheless, with these meetings over, Bethan could write on May 30: 'We have had really wonderful meetings and I confess I am enjoying myself. Your Father is marvellously untired and looks well.' Later that same day, Friday, they left by car for Carlisle where they were to be the guests of Mr and Mrs Ernest C. Reisinger and of Grace Baptist Church. He already knew Reisinger (who was shortly to be the first American trustee of the Banner of Truth Trust), but it was his first stay in this historic country town and Bethan and he were to make several enduring friendships over the next week, including one with Pastor Walter J. Chantry and his wife, Joie. From Monday to Thursday a Conference was held at Grace Baptist Church, being made up chiefly of young people of Baptist persuasion who had recently come to the doctrines of grace. ML-J preached on the three evenings on 'Justification by Faith'. An incident on the first evening was to be long remembered. About the time the meeting commenced a terrific storm was building up and soon the thunder and lightning seemed to be right on top of the church, with unbelievable noise and drenching rain. This was not so unusual at the conclusion of a hot summer's day, but when ML-J was about three-quarters of the way through his address all power and lighting failed, leaving him, his desk and the entire gathering in darkness. Yet, while these conditions continued for some five minutes, ML-J proceeded without the slightest pause or reference to what was happening.

Leigh Powell has recorded another incident which occurred at one of the evening meetings this week:

A student-friend of mine who had a Ph.D. in mathematics from Temple University, Philadelphia, sat tensely on the edge of his seat, following as the preacher ascended the ladder of Paul's logic in Romans. This unemotional mathematician, stirred to the depths by the preaching which was climaxed and driven home by the singing of the final hymn – tore out the page from the hymnbook (inserting a $5.00 bill to pay for a new one!) and strode out into the night. Afterwards he told me that he had always thought the Gospel was like that, but that he had never heard it preached in that way before. 'As he was preaching,' he told me, 'I said, "Ah, yes, but" – and then he answered the but, until I had no buts left.'[1]

On the Thursday morning he gave a final address on 'The Responsibility of Evangelism'.

After what Mrs Lloyd-Jones describes as 'a very enjoyable week' at Carlisle, Bill and Louise Wenger drove them back to Philadelphia for some final engagements, including a farewell dinner with the Hugheses, an outing with Dr Todd and the Commencement at Westminster Seminary on June 11 when ML-J addressed the graduating students.

The next day brought a new stage in their visit as they became the guests of Mr and Mrs A. M. Kinney of Cincinnati. The Kinneys came to meet them at Philadelphia and they then spent two days together at 'The Greenbrier', a hotel at White Sulphur Springs, West Virginia, before proceeding to Cincinnati where ML-J was to be preaching on the Sunday. In the course of writing home about these days, Mrs Lloyd-Jones said:

Greenbrier is, in every conceivable way, a dream of unimaginable luxury. I really am not exaggerating. When Mr Kinney discovered that your

[1]'Dr D. Martyn Lloyd-Jones, A Personal Appreciation', in *The Gospel Witness*, Toronto, April 9, 1981, p 10.

father was by no means averse to golf he was overjoyed. The two of them disappeared at 10.30 am Friday and did not re-appear till 4.0. Wales held its own and tied with the US! Then they went to the 'spa' and had a *sulphur bath* and a hosing down with powerful hoses! And then a merciless massage. Your father turned up looking bronzed, healthy and untired and never had a moment's stiffness.

A. M. Kinney, eager to forward the preparation of ML-J's books in any way that he could, had obtained a private apartment for the Lloyd-Joneses' use in Cincinnati until August when they were to leave for Florida. It was here at 210^B The Regency, 2444 Madison Road, that ML-J started working on the transcripts of his expositions on Romans which he had brought with him. Though he preached every weekend except one (and once as far away as Ocean City on the Atlantic coast) the week days were largely free. In July he wrote to Fred and Elizabeth, at home:

You will be glad to know that I have started work on correcting my sermons on The Epistle to the Romans. I have already done 9! The work on Ephesians 2 is nearing completion. I am hoping to talk to various publishers at The Religious Books Exhibition which is to be held here the last week in this month.

After going to this exhibition (held in Cincinnati in 1969) and meeting various publishers, he made the decision on the volume on Ephesians which Mrs Lloyd-Jones reported when writing home on August 7:

He has now done more than half the Romans he brought with him – he is really getting on with them.[1] Did I tell you that he has handed Ephesians 2 over to Moody? That, of course, won't make any difference to who has it in England, he has only given them USA and Canadian rights.

There was time also for recreation which included one visit to the opera, watching fireworks on the 4th of July and a number of games of golf. 'Golf de luxe I call it,' Bethan commented, 'they don't walk a step, but they certainly enjoy themselves.' Another letter reported:

[1]This was the material covering Romans 3:20–4:25 which was to constitute the first volume to appear in his expositions of that Epistle.

'Mr. Kinney and your father had lunch with some minister and then went to play golf! He really loves it and I'm sure it's good for him.' His chief relaxation, as ever, was reading. A small part of that reading had an amusing aspect to it. He was feeling starved of British news in Philadelphia when Philip Hughes arrived with a number of back copies of *The Times*. These he fell upon eagerly, too grateful to say that he might have preferred to see the *Guardian* – once the leading non-Tory paper in Britain and still his daily newspaper at home. Yet the truth was that he had been having misgivings over his loyalty to the *Guardian* and now, with the latter unavailable, the big decision seems to have been made. Fred Catherwood, his son-in-law, was now the Director General of the National Economic Development Council, and after appreciating a report of that Council in the Business Supplement to *The Times*, ML-J sent word to Fred about his new allegiance. 'We get *The Times* a day or two late,' Mrs Lloyd-Jones wrote to Balsham from Cincinnati on August 7, 'but it keeps us in touch, and your father says that it is now a much better paper than *The Guardian* and he thinks he will change!'

As always, the reading he most enjoyed consisted of major volumes and frequently these were books long since forgotten by the Christian world at large. At the next annual meeting of the Evangelical Library he was to say, 'I really had a most enjoyable time in the United States, not in looking at scenery but going round libraries!'.[1] The theme of that address was the excitement to be found in a good library where one can look at books not to be found elsewhere. His major 'find' in the 'most excellent' library of Westminster Seminary was Charles Hodge's thick volume, *The Constitutional History of the Presbyterian Church in the United States of America*. At one point, however, Hodge dissatisfied him. He had very little to say about revival. But he put ML-J on the track of works of Jonathan Edwards' contemporary Jonathan Dickinson ('not equal to Edwards', in ML-J's words, 'but he came pretty near') which he had not seen in 1967 and also of Davidson's *History of Presbyterianism in Kentucky*. Dr Lloyd-Jones' hope was to find these works in the Library of Lane Seminary at Cincinnati, not knowing that both Seminary and Library had long since been removed to Chicago. Mr Kinney came to his rescue with the discovery that a complete catalogue of all the Lane Seminary books was available and he could have Dickinson's works sent from Chicago without delay!

[1] *The Annual Meeting of The Evangelical Library* 1969, p. 18.

The Davidson volume, which neither Westminster nor Lane could supply, ML-J was overjoyed to find among old books preserved in a Public Library in Cincinnati, and the same Library was able to show him volumes of *The Christian Observer*, a monthly magazine referred to by Davidson which had commenced publication in England around 1800, which he found 'most profitable reading'. When he wrote to me from Cincinnati on July 21 he was still reading the volume of Hodge loaned from Westminster by his friend Arthur Kuschke, but he said no more about his discoveries, apart from another large volume: 'I must not begin to tell you about the most useful and enjoyable reading I have been able to do. I have devoured most of Volume 5 of the complete works of Thornwell[1] with great interest, amongst several other things.'

A letter of Mrs Lloyd-Jones of August 12 spoke of excitement both in Ealing and in Cincinnati. In Ealing it was the news they had just received that Ann and Keith were expecting another baby. In Cincinnati it was a tornado which had passed within a mile of them, cutting a path of destruction a quarter of a mile wide. Still more sensational weather lay ahead. On Saturday, August 16, they left Cincinnati for Pensacola, Florida, where ML-J was to be one of the speakers at the Pensacola Theological Institute, organized by Dr Donald Graham and held in McIlwain Presbyterian Church. Begun in the early 1960's for ministers and students, the Pensacola Institute was becoming a popular family conference. The location of Pensacola (at that time a city of some 150,000) on the beautiful Gulf of Mexico was an added attraction. When the Lloyd-Joneses arrived by air to be met by Donald Patterson the minister of McIlwain, they commented on the fineness of the day, only to be told that the weather was, in fact, a matter of serious concern. A hurricane, 'Camille', was currently heading from the Gulf directly northwards and towards them. Mrs Lloyd-Jones wrote:

When we got into the town from the airport all the shopkeepers were boarding up their windows and sandbagging their doors. All the people holidaying on the beaches had to pack up and leave. The Conference had 100 or more families parked out in various bungalows and cottages on

[1] This was *The Life and Letters of James Henley Thornwell*, 1875. Volumes 1 to 4 consisted of his *Collected Writings*. The biography and *The Collected Writings* were reprinted by the Banner of Truth Trust in 1974 and the latter re-issued in 1987.

[615]

the beach. They all had to leave in a hurry and were parked out in various places. Everything you heard was hurricane and it was expected Sunday [evening]. It was hard to believe in view of blue skies and calm sunshine, but the TV interrupted itself every few minutes to give its distance away and to urge everybody to leave the shores.

The concern was justified. Six hundred lives had been lost in the worst of a number of hurricanes in the Pensacola area in 1926. A Saturday evening reception meeting was cancelled. The next morning, when there was an electricity failure at the church, it was so dark that two men with hurricane lamps had to stand behind ML-J to give him enough light to read the Scriptures. As Camille was expected Sunday evening, the second service, at which the Doctor preached again, was transferred to 3 pm. By the time this was concluded there was lashing rain and a howling gale in which it was virtually impossible to stand. When they alighted from the car which took them back to the San Carlos Hotel they were 'literally blown through the entrance door'. This was but the edge of the approaching hurricane which, at 8 pm, dramatically changed its course and struck the coast some eighty miles further west around Gulfport and Biloxi. In that region the tide rose thirty feet and over 160 lives were lost in the destruction. By 6 am on Monday the Pensacola weather had returned to normal – 'as hot as a Turkish Bath' – and there was very general thankfulness for their deliverance from what others had suffered.

At the outset of the Institute week it seemed that the Lloyd-Joneses might not know the proverbial Southern hospitality in full measure. Their room at the San Carlos was comfortable, with air-conditioning, but in other respects, Mrs Lloyd-Jones wrote, 'This hotel belongs to the same period as the Ark!' No meals were provided after 2 pm and, as ML-J could not eat the evening meal provided by the Institute at McIlwain Church before preaching at seven, the only prospect was sandwiches and coffee in the hotel bar – 'what a place for the preacher but there is literally nothing else'. Mrs Lloyd-Jones was wrong. Although very few at the Institute had met the British visitors before, Southern warmth soon prevailed over the initial reserve. As they flew back to Cincinnati on Monday, August 25, the family scribe put the record straight. After describing the various conference sessions, which they had both appreciated attending, she went on:

They deputed different people to take us out to supper after the service every night, and we had very entertaining times. Your father really had a good week of meetings – twice on each Sunday and every night at 7.0, bar Saturday. I thought that last Friday night and both yesterday were outstanding. The people were transfixed and very appreciative – I think he must have autographed a thousand books! These Southerners are very nice and warm-hearted people.

Dr Lloyd-Jones thought so too and said, at the last session of the Institute, how much they had enjoyed the fellowship of the week. Once again they left many new friends behind them on their departure. Recalling this conference fifteen years later, Donald Graham its organizer, wrote:

The coming of Dr Lloyd-Jones was a challenge as our own auditorium seated, packed, held only 450. For his evening meetings we secured the First Baptist Church, a beautiful new edifice seating 1,800, including its very large balcony. Obviously, we were introducing Dr Lloyd-Jones to a southern constituency which in Pensacola itself knew nothing of his fame and would be known chiefly to ministers attending and this through his writings.

Nonetheless this particular Institute had a much larger attendance and over 900 made a full-looking crowd on the main floor of the auditorium. His ministry sought out a number of themes rather than restricting to a series and was of the greatest blessing. But, I tell you, if I had known the treasure God had planted in this earthen vessel, I would have gone over this country and sought people to hear him from every nook and corner. A great man of God came our way only once and the largest part of the city heeded not.

The gracious manner with which Dr Lloyd-Jones mingled with our people is a lovely memory. To dine with him was a privilege. He did not dominate conversation but contributed warmly. At the time, I recall, he was anticipating the publication of his Romans series and he commented rather earnestly that he felt that he had insights which needed to be shared. Then, it was delightful how he complimented the entire institute by attending, along with Mrs Lloyd-Jones, the morning classes under other members of the faculty, finally sitting with them for the Question Hour at the end of the morning. While we have been privileged to have some of the best-known preachers and professors of the Reformed family from around the world, I doubt that any has made the profound impression upon us all that came under this good man's Spirit-anointed and highly incisive ministry.

After Pensacola there was a final week with the Kinneys, which included more golf, a television discussion with an R.C. 'Father' and a Jewish Rabbi, and a Sunday night service at a huge Methodist church. The first Sunday of September Dr Lloyd-Jones preached at the church in Ocean City, where he had been five weeks earlier, and these were to be his last services in the United States. After a final night with the Hugheses in Philadelphia, they flew overnight Tuesday, September 9, back to London.

* * *

There was, of course, in 1969 no 'At Home' at Westminster Chapel, but at the first Westminster ministers' fraternal after his return on October 5 he gave some account of this his longest visit to the States. The five months had made a number of impressions on him. He had been in many churches and talked with many people. He thought the country had passed its peak in church attendances and that there was also now some reaction against the mass evangelism crusades. A Graham crusade in New York in June had been televised and re-broadcast over 300 stations in August at a cost of nearly a million dollars a night. This had led to criticism on financial grounds. What had concerned him more as he watched two of these broadcasts was the marked slide towards an atmosphere of entertainment in the meetings. In 1957 the place given to music in services had disturbed him but now, with hand clapping, applause and cheering, he believed there had been a further deterioration.

Another factor affecting evangelism, ML-J noted, was an entrance of doubt in a number of quarters concerning the appeal for would-be converts to commit themselves by a public response. He said how after a morning service when he preached in a Baptist Temple – reputedly the fourth largest church in the USA – an appeal had been given which lasted for 25 minutes! 'Better men are all querying this,' he believed, 'and a reaction is coming in against it.'

He gave a general description of the Presbyterian Church in the North and the South before speaking more particularly of the history of Westminster Theological Seminary and the new denomination formed by Machen. After Machen's death in January 1937 that denomination had split in two – the Orthodox Presbyterian Church and the Bible Presbyterian Church, with the latter dividing yet again. But they were agreed on all basic doctrines. The danger for people concerned with doctrine was to lose a sense of proportion and to put details before the big general issues. He believed he had seen something of this in the General Assembly of the Orthodox Presbyterian Church, where two days were given to the question of Sabbath observance and the alleged difference between Calvin and the Puritans on that point. In the US situation, in general, there was a tendency for men to care more about what divided them rather than what should hold them together.

With the retirement of John Murray at the end of 1966, the death of Edward J. Young in 1968 and the advancing years of other members of the first faculty, Westminster Seminary was clearly facing a period of change. ML-J had found a consciousness of the need to produce preachers, but there were several influences in the Reformed scene which militated against preaching. One of these influences was the idea that all who go to Reformed churches are Christians, so all they need, it was thought, is instruction. There was not enough evangelism. Preaching had become lecturing; it was too intellectual. Preachers did not 'get at the people'; there was little 'application'; so the people were never humbled. Many did not know about repentance except as a doctrine. In orthodox, Reformed congregations he found a hardness and a superficiality. They were no more ready to listen to a long sermon than the broader Presbyterian and Baptist churches, in fact, he often received a better hearing in the latter churches.

Another injurious influence among the Reformed he traced to the teaching of Herman Dooyeweerd of Holland, 'in many ways the greatest living philosopher'. Out of his teaching a school had grown up whose great message is the implementation of the cultural mandate of Genesis 1:27, with the aim of bringing the world in every respect under 'the Lordship of Christ'. Those of this view criticized evangelicals for being too concerned about personal salvation. The Christian is to go out and capture every realm: schools, politics, economics, trade unions – all are to be made Christian. He regarded Francis Schaeffer as a popularizer of this kind of thought but without taking it to an extreme. At its extreme the effect of the movement was anti-church and anti-preaching. Its priority was the need to change society and culture.

He believed that the tendency of Westminster Seminary (where he had spent 'six very happy weeks') to be over-concerned with the intellectual had an important lesson:

I want to say a word in defence of the Orthodox Presbyterian Church and Westminster Seminary. In the 1920's the liberal movement possessed great power and made inroads everywhere in the Presbyterian Church. These conservative men were driven into a defensive position, so when they came to form a seminary the uppermost idea was the defence of the Faith, to establish a bulwark of orthodoxy. The fundamentalist was also defending the faith, but in an unintelligent way. It had to be done in an intelligent manner, with more scholarship and more learning . . . it was almost inevitable that a lack of balance should occur, and a lack of vitality and power in the propagation of the gospel. We must not allow the situation we are in to determine what we are and become. We should be masters of the situation, not victims of it. We can all easily be jockeyed into a false position by circumstances and by other people. We must be firmly in control, with our position controlled by the New Testament. This was the great lesson I learned in five months in America.

There can be no question about the long-term benefit to others which came from ML-J's 1969 visit to the United States. Had it not been for the invitation of Edmund Clowney to deliver lectures on preaching to the students at Westminster Seminary, there would have been no volume on *Preaching and Preachers*, for the book, published in 1971, was basically the lectures. These he did not write, rather he spoke, as usual, from a skeleton outline of notes and the text of the book was simply an edited transcript of what was tape recorded at the time. The truth is that he was so wedded to the spoken word that he would never have sat down and *written* a book on preaching. It was the six weeks at Westminster which thus produced what was to be, in some respects, his most important volume.

The Christian Herald (November 20, 1971) called *Preaching and Preachers* 'a very great book' and accurately forecast its reception with the words, 'It will please many, anger some, challenge all'. Hostile criticism generally focused on two points, the first being that the book represented a view of preaching which simply failed to come to terms with the modern world. Thus James Good wrote in *The Irish Times* (February 5, 1972):

Congregations have got the message back to us in the clearest terms that they will tolerate us for a maximum of ten minutes or so, and any attempt to preach in the grand manner is met by a psychological switch-off not a whit less effective than the electrical one on the television set . . .

The Last Visit to America

Dr Lloyd-Jones is so convinced that he is possessed of the Spirit that on one occasion, being allotted fifteen minutes to preach on a broadcast service, he kept going for another thirty. One wonders why some radio technician hadn't enough spirit to switch him off. What one must question, however, is this: is our age ever going to accept monologue again? Does it not seem that our generation is demanding, and insisting on having, the right of talk-back? From the theological point of view, it does not seem any more difficult to me for the Spirit to be operative in dialogue than in monologue, and the resurgence of Pentecostalism, particularly in the Catholic Church, is a clear reminder to us that we have over-emphasized the distinction between the *ecclesia docens* and the *ecclesia discens* – between the teaching church and the taught church. One way communication may well have been sufficient in the past. Nowadays there is feed-back, and right of reply, and letters to the editor: must the preacher be the sole exception to this general trend?

Others, however, who were not themselves committed to Dr Lloyd-Jones' beliefs were ready to concede that his case for the primacy of preaching needed to be heard. Donald Tytler of Birmingham Cathedral wrote:

Dr Lloyd-Jones' book expresses in its length and style the author's conviction that forty-five minutes is not a moment too long for a sermon at the present day. He is a fanatic about preaching . . . Yet, however repellent his narrow-mindedness, however ponderous his occasional touches of humour, however antique his preaching heroes, this survivor from eighteenth-century revivalist evangelicalism has much to say that we sophisticated twentieth-century radicals and moderates need to hear.
 The old man gets better and better as he tramples onward with face sternly set towards the heavenly Jerusalem; having evacuated most of his hates in chapter 1, he proceeds to affirm the life-saving task of the preacher with deep insight into the spiritual qualities that the preacher needs and excellent practical advice on the skills he must deploy. No one who has read his book will ever again preach light-heartedly.[1]

Another reviewer in *The Times Literary Supplement* (January 28, 1972) made the same point:

These lectures set an alarmingly high standard. But they ought to shame the next generation of ministers from being content, as too many parsons now are, with folksy chats about anything rather than God.

[1]*Theology*, Nov. 1976, pp. 375–76.

Others agreed. Donald Coggan, Archbishop of York, wrote: 'There may not be much that is new. But there are emphases which sorely need to be made, and they are made and underlined with power.'[1] Support came even from the Roman Catholic press. Father Ronald Potter OP, in a review entitled, 'Why the pulpit is vital', judged the book to be 'a weighty indictment of much that is going on in some religious circles today'. 'From every page of this work,' said the same reviewer, 'there stands out that life-long care and trouble taken over preaching. This in itself is a lesson to all would-be preachers.'[2]

That Lloyd-Jones, despite the strong criticism from some quarters, could appeal to a considerable cross-section of reviewers tells us something that deserves comment. Michael Harper, in an editorial in *Renewal*, noted: 'For those of us engaged in controversy with other Christians this book shows that it is possible to hold to the strongest possible beliefs and yet still to be gracious and warm-hearted towards others from whom we would differ. Of personal animosity and petty-mindedness there is not a trace in this book.'

The second point of criticism had to do with Dr Lloyd-Jones himself. In this work he deliberately drew on his own experience and in some passages it comes near to autobiography. For a number of reviewers this gave the book no small part of its appeal. John Stott, noting this point, wrote: 'The book is a very human document and will help to introduce Dr Lloyd-Jones to readers who do not know him personally.'[3] Others, however, took offence at the dogmatism. The fact is that the book is so stamped with the qualities identified with his life and preaching that it was bound to divide people. 'This is a robust *confessio fidei*,' said *The Times Literary Supplement*, '– the real thing with all the rough edges.' James Good, looking at the same picture, believed 'Dr Lloyd-Jones is self-opinionated and arrogant throughout'. Dr Howard Williams, Central Baptist Church, London, pays compliment to 'the wisdom and power' of the book, but he does not hide his fear that the author was suffering from delusions of grandeur:

The publishers have presented this book in Bible-black with gold lettering on the cover. This reveals a rare sense of propriety. Dr Lloyd-

[1] *The Expository Times*, March, 1972.
[2] *The Universe*, December 24, 1971.
[3] 'Privilege of Preaching', *Church of England Newspaper*, Dec. 3, 1971.

Jones's camp followers will accept it as holy writ . . .

The contents page is pedestrian and the style is unpolished, put into print just as it was spoken. This makes the book, like Dr Lloyd-Jones's sermons, longer than mortal men would consider wise. Unlike his sermons there are a good many personal stories in the book and some of them make him a little less forbidding.

The book is written with supreme arrogance. There is nothing mean about this. He is magnificent in his assurance, like Moses descending from the mountain and scattering all novelty seekers as they prance around the Golden Calf or allow themselves to be deceived by the beguiling ways of Baal . . .

I find that Lloyd-Jones, when he is positive, says so many things which stimulate and encourage, as we have a right to expect from a man who has fulfilled such a splendid ministry. His weakness lies in his silly strictures on other ministers and especially his lust for dabbling in ecclesiastical politics as though he had some divine right to manipulate the church by personal edicts from Sinai.[1]

John Stott, in the review already quoted, saw it quite differently:

Though he is sometimes dogmatic, at other times he is flexible ('there are no absolute rules in this matter') and at all times he is humble ('my only title to give such advice is that I am a great sinner who has fought this battle for so many years').

In a book of 325 pages it is remarkable that so many reviewers seized with approval upon one thought: 'What is the chief end of preaching? I like to think it is this. It is to give men and women a sense of God and His presence.'[2] The sentence exemplifies ML-J's uppermost concerns with respect to the pulpit. 'There have been other books on preaching,' wrote the Editor of *Evangelical Action*. 'Most of them are interesting, but very often they deal with trivia. This book deals with the main things.'[3] Most evangelical reviews placed a high significance on *Preaching and Preachers*. In Graham Harrison's opinion, the book 'is arguably the most useful that Dr Lloyd-Jones has ever published.'[4] Another preacher, D. Koerner, considered it 'the most absorbing I've read in years', and Eric

[1]*Methodist Recorder*, Nov. 25, 1971, Supplement, pp. iii–iv.
[2]*Preaching*, p 97.
[3]W. R. McEwen, in *Evangelical Action* (Melbourne), Feb. 1972.
[4]*Evangelical Magazine of Wales*, Dec. 1971–Jan. 1972, p. 2.

Alexander confessed that he 'kept his wife awake late into the night on one occasion, reading to her some of the Doctor's quite magnificent anecdotes!'.[1] The latter incident is a reminder that the book has a general appeal. As one British reviewer remarked, 'there is much in it for the non-preacher',[2] a view borne out by at least one eminent non-ministerial reviewer. Lester de Koster, in Grand Rapids, described it to his readers as 'exciting stuff on what ought to be an exciting subject'.[3]

I do not mean in these pages to enter upon the subsequent history of the congregation of Westminster Chapel but there is one passage relevant to it in *Preaching and Preachers* which should not be missed in any discussion of that subject. ML-J points out that the influence of the Spirit of God in preaching is not solely through the Word to the people but it is also *from* the people to the preacher: 'the preacher while speaking should in a sense be deriving something from his congregation. There are those present in the congregation who are spiritually-minded people, and filled with the Spirit, and they make their contribution to the occasion. There is always an element of exchange in true preaching.'[4] Certainly at Westminster a congregation was raised up which included many who were no mere listeners. They hungered for the Word of God and to know the presence of God, and the existence of that hunger – hidden though it now is by the passage of time – has to be seen as closely connected to the sermons to which it gave rise. In a church which prospers spiritually the bond between pastor and people is always very close and a little of what that bond meant to ML-J is revealed in these poignant sentences:

I know of nothing comparable to the feeling one has as one walks up the steps of one's pulpit with a fresh sermon on a Sunday morning or a Sunday evening, especially when you feel that you have a message from God and are longing to give it to the people. This is something that one cannot describe. Repeating your best sermon elsewhere never quite gives

---

[1]*Christian Graduate*, June 1972, p. 50. In his review Alexander observes: 'It has been said wisely that great books on preaching must come from great preachers. In Dr Martyn Lloyd-Jones, God has given to the church one of the greatest preachers of this century.'
[2]Philip H. Hacking, *TSF Bulletin*, spring 1973, p. 23.
[3]'On Taking Heart Again', *Banner*, June 2, 1972.
[4]*Preaching*, p. 84. See also *Knowing the Times*, p. 273, 'There is a unity between preacher and hearers and there is a transaction backwards and forwards'.

you that. That is why I am such an advocate of a regular and a longish ministry in the same place. That is something, I fear, I shall never know again having retired from the pastoral ministry. But there is nothing to equal that.[1]

When Dr Lloyd-Jones was so suddenly laid aside in February 1968 the Rev. Edwin King, his assistant who did not normally conduct Sunday services at the Chapel, was faced with the duty of taking all the services – Fridays and Sundays – over the following five weeks. To the surprise of some this occasioned no change in the size of the congregation. On this point, King writes:

As one with limited gifts called upon to stand in his pulpit in an emergency, I can testify to the greatness of the congregation. No man could take the Doctor's place, anymore than they could Spurgeon's; but I found that if you were yourself, your doctrine was sound, and you adhered to the Scriptures then the congregation welcomed you as it were with open arms. It was a fearful sight to behold, and one stood in fear and trembling, but once the nerves had been overcome, then it was difficult to stop praying and preaching. I was aware that I was facing a unique congregation, one that God had drawn together over the years that the Doctor might exercise the gifts God had given him, and when it was all over I knew I would never see the like again. Because it was a great congregation, when in time it failed to receive what it had grown accustomed to, it broke up, to the strengthening of churches all over the land. But it was a very loving congregation, and a true reflection of the pulpit which had served it with such whole-hearted devotion. The Chapel has often been dismissed as nothing more than a preaching centre, yet nothing was further from the truth.[2]

In King's view, with which I concur, the post-1968 difficulties at Westminster Chapel came not from the people but from a weakness in the leadership. Not since the 1920's had the church to face the

---

[1]*Preaching*, p. 297.
[2]Letter to the author, March 6, 1981. Edwin King continued to preach frequently at the Chapel and notes that the numbers in attendance were still much what they had long been when he did so for the last time on June 1, 1969. It should be added that people from Westminster Chapel were scattered not only 'all over the land' but all over the world as I have often been reminded in Australia and New Zealand. A good part of the congregation was always young and temporary – a fact which explains why those who were church members probably constituted no more than a third of the numbers in attendance.

question of calling a new minister[1] and the deacons had now to face a task for which they were inadequately prepared. Dr and Mrs Lloyd-Jones continued to be members after his resignation but he endeavoured to remain removed from all decision-making in the Chapel's affairs. If he was in church on Sundays (which was rare on account of engagements elsewhere) he came in during the first hymn, sat at the back and left before the benediction. This cannot have been easy for him especially as he felt his own failure to give more time to training the deacons in the exercise of leadership. The omission was partly a time problem. In his own words, as he reflected on later events, 'It was quicker to do things myself'. But if he is to be criticized on that account let it be in the context of his massive labours.

[1]The resettlement of Campbell Morgan, and then of ML-J in the 1930's, had both occurred after they had come to help the existing ministry (in the first instance that of Hubert L. Simpson and in the second that of Morgan himself).

We have had to replace our original copies of Studies in the Sermon on the Mount *several times and have bought seven copies of the two volume set over the years. All around New Guinea are friends of ours reading Martyn Lloyd-Jones. I have read every one of your books many many times. I was absolutely gripped anew by* God's Way of Reconciliation. *In the last three years I have had such a sense of the reality of the Holy Spirit and your sermons have enhanced and encouraged this in the most marvellous way.*

MARGARET AND FRANK SMITH,
Australian missionary
doctors, April 6, 1980, in a letter to ML-J.

I sat at the feet of Dr Martyn Lloyd-Jones as I relished his teaching in his book on Romans, *chapter 5. This is theology in the field; theology related to life and its conflicts . . . I have completed an arrangement which provides for a copy of D. M. Lloyd-Jones'* Daily Readings *to be sent to every fishing-boat in Scalpay.*

The Diary of James Morrison, *of North Uist in the Scottish Hebrides, ed.* G. N. M. COLLINS, 1984, p 82

30

A World Pulpit

As we have already seen, Dr Lloyd-Jones saw his retirement from Westminster Chapel as the beginning of 'a new ministry'. In the event, viewed simply in terms of his weekly engagements, much of his time was to be spent as it had been before 1968. In the period 1969–1976 his diaries show that he was virtually as busy preaching in different parts of the country as he had been in the previous forty years and these engagements now included weekends away from home as well as weekdays. Similarly, he continued to preside at most of the meetings with which he had long been associated, including all those of the Evangelical Library, the Westminster Fellowship, the Puritan (Westminster) Conference, and the ministers conferences of the Evangelical Movement of Wales. When such meetings were held at Westminster Chapel, ML-J was always in his old vestry for additional hours, talking with men who were looking for personal help. If the numbers who saw him in the vestry slowly decreased in the 1970's it was, in part, because ministers had discovered that he was more ready to speak with them on the phone at home than he had been previously.

But retirement from Westminster had brought a major change. The burden of having to practise a very strict economy of time throughout ten months of each year was lifted and there was now an element of leisure such as he had rarely enjoyed before. Chief among those to benefit from his larger opportunities for relaxation were his grandchildren whose number was completed with the birth of Adam Martyn Desmond on May 18, 1971. At that date the Catherwood children, Christopher, Bethan Jane and Jonathan were sixteen, twelve and nine, and the Desmond girls, Elizabeth and Rhiannon, were three and one respectively. It was remarkable how children were at ease in ML-J's presence and the six grandchildren knew that in a special way. From infancy they lived near him (the Desmonds in an apartment in the same house) and were used to wandering in and out of his presence at will. For his part, 'Dadcu' (a variation on *Tadcu*, the Welsh for Grandpa) entered into all their interests with enthusiasm. If he was at home and free when such programmes as 'the Waltons' or 'The Little House on the Prairie' were on the television, they much preferred to have him watch with them. Whatever appealed to them, or concerned them, had his immediate attention whether it was the finer points of wrestling, problems at school, or a game of croquet on the lawns at Balsham. Remembering his own experiences at that age, he believed that teenage years possessed difficulties which merited much sympathy and understanding from adults. Certainly those of his grandchildren who reached that stage before his death knew that as did no one else, and he was never dismissive of their problems. Lady Catherwood has recalled how their younger son, Jonathan, became enamoured with the ideas of transcendental meditation at the age of fifteen and, ignorant of the danger, briefly became an advocate of the books which offered the message to the world. His grandfather listened carefully to him and then asked to borrow the book on which Jonathan set particular value, *The Third Eye* by Lobsang Rampa. This he read from cover to cover while on a train journey to a preaching engagement and later went through his conclusions, positive and negative, with Jonathan.[1]

The enjoyment of the grandchildren also figured largely in the decisions on joint family holidays. The attraction of the sports centre at Aviemore, for example, took the Catherwoods to that area of the Scottish Highlands on two occasions in the 1970's, while the beaches of Cornwall and of the Isle of Wight drew the younger Desmonds. Dr and Mrs Lloyd-Jones entered fully into these and other holidays.

In connection with the freedom which young people felt in approaching ML-J, an incident is worthy of record at this point. In May 1973, the day before he was to preach at a mid-week service at Burgess Hill, he received a phone call from sixteen-year-old Juliet Richings whose parents had brought her to Westminster Chapel from her childhood. She was the girl who five years earlier had written him to say that she hoped he would soon be back at Westminster Chapel 'because he was the only preacher she could

---

[1] *Martyn Lloyd-Jones: Chosen By God*, p. 150. Elizabeth's title changed in January 1971 when her husband was knighted for his service as Director-General of the National Economic Development Council.

understand'! The phone call was to ask permission to tape- record his sermon at Burgess Hill the next day and – making bold – to ask him if he had decided on the subject for his sermon. 'I haven't completely decided,' he replied, 'why do you ask?' Juliet's reply was that she had heard him preach on Paul's words to Felix in Acts 24 some years earlier and she hoped he might preach that sermon again so that she could play the recording to some friends! This unexpected information produced a pause at ML-J's end of the phone and then the comment, 'I won't promise anything but I will think about it'. The outcome we give in Juliet's own words:

The following evening I sat in the front row with my portable tape recorder and when it came to the reading the minister of the church stood up and announced the reading – from Acts 24. I quickly looked at Dr Lloyd-Jones who gave me a slight smile and a nod. After the service was over I went to thank him for his memorable sermon on 'righteousness, temperance and judgment to come' but before I could speak he eagerly said to me, 'Was that the one?'

There were many similar instances which would have surprised those who supposed that ML-J's ministry could have little appeal to young people. A London youngster who heard him for the first time in the 1970's was overheard to say, 'This old boy has got it!' After one service in the north of England at this same period, Dr Lloyd-Jones was surprised to see a phalanx of Teddy boys advancing down the aisle towards him as though to make trouble. But they had come rather with the question, 'Why did you stop, Sir?'

*   *   *

Before we turn to the main difference in Dr Lloyd-Jones' post-Westminster ministry, reference needs to be made to his temporary connection with English television in 1970. Far from being in a hurry to speak on either radio or television he had declined opportunities to speak on the former when the British Broadcasting Corporation imposed unacceptable limitations.[1] He was not prepared to turn sermons into sermonettes and accordingly it was only in Wales – where BBC Wales were willing to broadcast full-length sermons –

[1]See *Preaching*, p. 248.

that he was heard preaching on the radio in Britain. His effectiveness in broadcasting had early been recognized in Wales[1] and appearances on Welsh television followed at the beginning of the 1960's. He may have been on English television only once or twice before January 6, 1970, when he spoke on the ecumenical movement and other subjects in the programme 'Viewpoint'. Later that same month, on January 25, he was interviewed again by BBC television in a programme entitled 'All Things Considered'. In this programme he debated the meaning of the conversion of Saul of Tarsus and of conversion in general with Magnus Magnusson. No, ML-J insisted, Saul's Damascus road experience could not be explained in terms of epilepsy or anything of that kind. All true conversions are the work of the Spirit of God and they are not to be confused with 'decisions'. In response to Magnusson's question, 'Why are there so few conversions?', he replied bluntly, 'Ultimately, this is the will of God'. At the same time, he went on to say, there is a certain 'periodicity' observable in the numbers of converts. There are periods of revival when far larger numbers become Christians than was being seen at the present time.

There was something unusually arresting about these television interviews and comment was widespread. Writing in the March issue of *Dedication*, its editor reported that a junior BBC executive had told him, 'Dr Lloyd-Jones speaks with divine authority, we hope to have him taking part again in our programmes'.

This hope was soon fulfilled with ML-J appearing in a programme entitled 'Fact or Fantasy' screened on April 12, 1970. This time he was one of a panel of four with the main subject for discussion being whether religious conversion was essentially the same type of experience as 'falling in love'. Two members of the panel – a psychiatrist and a marriage guidance counsellor – argued that both experiences were to be understood in the same way and that 'the religious element' in conversion did not change its basic nature. Thus, they believed, adolescents were most likely both to fall in love and to be converted. Not until these assertions were well aired did ML-J argue that the two things were entirely distinct. Age makes no difference to conversion, as he illustrated from the case of a 77 year old man. Further, unlike 'falling in love', there is no sexual

[1] J. C. Griffiths, writing in *The Western Mail* in the 1930's observed: 'Few of our preachers have yet mastered this exacting new medium of expression'. First among the exceptions whom he names as 'masters of the microphone' was ML-J.

factor in conversion, and whereas romantic experience tends to fade with time what happens to a person in true conversion both lasts and grows. The day after this programme a viewer from Derby wrote to BBC television:

I have never before written to the BBC but I was so impressed with the programme last evening that I feel I just have to commend you for it. I could have listened all night.

May I particularly say how helpful I found the comments of the elderly minister. Why haven't we seen him on TV before? He seemed so sincere, so understanding, so sure of his ground and yet so humble. Quite unlike many of the religious experts who always seem so keen to make an impression. Please may we see much more of this man on TV?

This writer had clearly missed the fact that the programme had been Dr Lloyd-Jones' third television appearance in a few months. In a lengthy review of the April 12 programme, A. Morgan Derham commented humorously in the *Life of Faith* on April 18, 1970: 'We shall soon have the liberals protesting that the BBC is favouring the evangelicals! Once again the BBC-tv Sunday evening religious programme included Dr. D. Martyn Lloyd-Jones. . .'.

If the opportunity to preach on television was not given to ML-J his participation in debate with an interviewer or panel was the next best thing to it. The ease with which ML-J handled these situations may possibly have contributed to his promotion to another role in an historical film. Oliver Hunkin, a BBC television producer, had noted that 1970 commemorated the bicentenary of the death of George Whitefield and sought ML-J's help in the preparation of a twenty-minute programme. In June ML-J spent a couple of days with Hunkin and his film crew in London, Bristol and Gloucestershire. In the scenes connected with Whitefield's ministry which they shot ML-J was the narrator and spoke 'live' to the cameras as he stood on a grave top in Islington churchyard and in similar places. With the title 'The Awakener' the film was shown in colour on September 30, 1970. But although ML-J had been perfectly happy to speak on Whitefield without any script, he was not entirely at ease in the unfamiliar role of the professional commentator who has to talk direct to the cameras with no one else in view. The Whitefield film scarcely conveyed the inspiration usually felt by people when they had been with ML-J at some historic location in church history. If the experience gave ML-J any misgivings over his criticism of training ministers to speak on television he never said so.[1] The studied techniques of the professional he always tended to despise.

Dr Lloyd-Jones' invitations to speak on English television seemed to end almost as suddenly as they had begun. His last appearance of which we have any record was in the BBC 1 programme 'The Open Persuaders', shown on December 5, 1972. His interviewer was the well-known Joan Bakewell who had familiarized herself with some of his writings and, as the discussion showed, was particularly interested in his convictions on man in sin. After giving him time to state what was wrong with the modern view of man their exchange continued:

Joan Bakewell: This point of view is obviously held with great conviction by you, but I would have thought it brought you into conflict not only with people who do not subscribe to the Christian religion but with many other Christians, too?

ML-J: Of course it does. I'm sorry about this. This is something I deeply regret, but this isn't the first time, you know, that minorities have been right. We don't decide this kind of question by counting heads . . .

Bakewell: But what I would suggest is that whereas they would tolerate your point of view as a rather different and divergent view of Christianity, you are unprepared to tolerate their view as a possible version of the truth. Is that right?

ML-J: I am, of course I am, and I say 'of course' quite deliberately for this reason: Christianity is a very exclusive and dogmatic faith . . . If a man asserts his own point of view, the result of his own thinking, in this intolerant manner, well, he is a boor and he is not to be tolerated. But when you are given truth which you claim is truth from God then you have no right to be anything but intolerant. When I find people insinuating their own theories and ideas and using the name of Christ I have to protest. This is dishonest apart from anything else, in my opinion.

Joan Bakewell: But, none the less, it's a highly regarded Christian virtue these days to be both charitable and tolerant to people of different views from oneself. Do you disapprove of that?

ML-J: Well again, and for the same reason, I'm bound to . . .

and he went on to speak of the uniqueness of Christ and of the biblical revelation. His interviewer then returned to his earlier point

[1]But though such criticism had occurred in his lectures at Westminster Seminary in 1969 it did not appear in their published form.

that a sense of sin is necessary in order to be saved and, remarking that sin was not of any immediate concern to many people, she asked how this point of view could possibly prevail in these circumstances. It certainly could, ML-J concluded. The modern indifference was caused by ignorance. Let people hear the truth about themselves, let them hear the ten commandments, and then they would be ready to listen to the message of the New Testament 'which I maintain is only represented by the evangelical standpoint'.[1]

Dr Lloyd-Jones had much liberty in speaking on this programme but it had a sad side to it. In a continuation of the discussion with Joan Bakewell after the filming had concluded she confessed that this was a kind of Christianity which she had never met before. All the clerics whom she had previously interviewed had been concerned to assure her that she was a Christian. ML-J was the first to tell her what she knew was the truth about herself.

It would be intriguing to know why this programme – the best of all he had done – brought his television work to an end. Perhaps the reason lay simply in that very fact. Morgan Derham's half-humorous prophecy about 'liberals protesting' may well have come true. Whatever the reason, the end of invitations to appear on television certainly did not trouble ML-J who was convinced that, next to the pulpit, it was *books* which could most effectively spread the Christian faith.

This brings us to what was the new feature in his later ministry. The main change in his post-1968 timetable was that much of the time which he had formerly given to Westminster Chapel now went into the editing of the accumulated manuscripts of his Westminster ministry. For the rest of his life a major part of his working hours in private – including the long summer days at Balsham – went into the preparation of this material for the press. When one reviewer wrote, 'It is an apparently easy transition for his preaching to be reduced to print' he was quite wrong. The process was lengthy and involved several stages. First, ML-J would edit and revise the transcription of his sermons taken down from tape recordings by his secretarial assistant, Mrs Elizabeth Burney.[2]

[1] The text of this interview was published in the *Evangelical Magazine of Wales*, Feb–March, 1973, pp. 8–11.
[2] Elizabeth Burney became a member of Westminster Chapel in November 1948. Her great work in transcribing tapes went on through the 1970's. She died in January 1981.

The changes were so numerous that the MS then had to be retyped. The retyped version was then passed on to S. M. Houghton who would note corrections he judged necessary and suggest further possible improvements in the interests of clarity. This was so detailed that it entailed a second reading of the entire manuscript by ML-J who made the final decision on Mr Houghton's proposed emendations. He found the whole process arduous work – more tiring, he would sometimes say, than the initial preparation of the sermons at the time he had preached them. Paperwork for ML-J lacked the stimulus which he found in preaching, and the need for more 'stimuli' was his chief acknowledgement of his advancing years. 'Getting going' in the mornings became harder than it used to be and he would sometimes stir himself by putting on a cassette of rousing music before beginning a day's work on his manuscripts! Brief summaries of his doings to Philip Hughes would contain such sentences as the following, 'I have had a very busy time preaching in various parts of the country and trying at the same time to correct MSS, but I am feeling well' (Dec 15, 1972). The desk work was, however, by no means all drudgery. There were times when he became 'lost' afresh in the truths before him and the work then became 'most exhilarating'. The dozen years following his 'retirement' became the most important of his life in terms of the output of his books.

As he faced this editorial work there were, at the outset, certain difficulties to be resolved. First, there was the sheer amount of material in manuscript form from which choice had to be made. Following the Second World War various hearers had taken his sermons down in shorthand and then typed them up. With the advent of the use of tape recorders at the Chapel in 1953–54 there was no longer need for these shorthand copies, but the work of transcribing from the tape recordings was constantly done by Mrs Burney. Many hundreds of unrevised manuscript copies of sermons thus existed by 1968, of which, for reasons already noted, comparatively few had appeared in print. He did not hesitate in choosing to put his Romans sermons first for publication in book form, to be followed by those on Ephesians.

Less immediately clear to him was what should be the *size* of the series to be published on these two New Testament books. Consecutive volumes of expository sermons were virtually an unknown literary genre in the mid-twentieth century prior to his *Studies in the*

A World Pulpit

Sermon on the Mount and while the latter had demonstrated the existence of a market there was no proof that the market could stand half a dozen volumes on Ephesians and, perhaps, twice that number on Romans. The opinion was still common among those in the publishing world that his style was not the best for the printed page and many continued to think that the appeal of his books would be largely confined to those who had heard him and who could match the voice to the words.

ML-J hesitated and came down on the side of caution. Although he was uncomfortable with the recognition that he would not be following the apostolic sequence, he had decided, as already noted, to begin the publication of his Romans sermons in chapter three of that Epistle as the first of possibly four volumes with the title 'The Heart of Romans'. These would cover Romans chapters 3 to 7, or perhaps to chapter 8, which was the section of the Epistle which he regarded as possessing special contemporary importance in its treatment of the doctrines of salvation and sanctification. In the case of Ephesians, he also decided against any announcement of a full series and simply commenced with a volume, *God's Way of Reconciliation*, which could stand alone as an exposition of chapter two.

The next question to be settled was his choice of publisher. His prolonged stay in the States in 1969 gave him the opportunity, as we have seen, to talk with American publishers who would handle the North American market but he thought hard on who would print for Britain and the rest of the English-speaking world. His earlier policy in Britain had been to spread his titles among various publishing houses. He had not confined himself to the most conservative of his publishers, the IVF. Now, however, with the ecumenical question a critical issue he was more concerned to aid those agencies likely to be most dependable in the years of confusion which lay ahead. It was this consideration, principally, which led him to give the publishing of his *magnum opus* on Romans to the Banner of Truth Trust in 1969, and his volume on Ephesians chapter two to the Evangelical Press.[1]

ML-J laid down a few ground rules for the Banner of Truth Trust as he made this organization, henceforth, his principal publisher. Mr S. M. Houghton would assist ML-J as a copy editor, but the

[1]'I have seen amazing changes in publishing houses . . . The publishing houses which stood for the evangelical faith have moved and wandered . . . in this country and in the United States of America'. ML-J, *Annual Meeting of the Evangelical Library 1968*, p. 9.

publisher's part in any revision of the original would be strictly limited to the literary and if manuscript sermons were excluded from publication – as occasionally they were – this would be entirely at his decision. On one initial point, however, our representations were heeded. His proposed title, 'The Heart of Romans', would have amounted to an announcement that the publication of the whole series was not envisaged and we did not wish to accept any such limitation. The title was dropped and instead the first Romans volume simply carried the sub-title, 'An Exposition of Chapters 3.20–4.25, Atonement and Justification'.

The appearance of this volume on Romans late in 1970 quickly established two things. It was eminently readable and many people were eager for more. A reviewer in *Christianity Today* (Oct 8, 1971) wrote: 'This is no average book. Nor will you read it indifferently. It is the kind of book that will grip your mind and heart . . . it has been a long time since I have read a book I enjoyed so thoroughly as this.' W. J. Grier in *The Evangelical Presbyterian* (Jan 1971) described it as 'glorious exposition' and, referring to those 'who wondered if he should not have continued his fruitful ministry at the centre of the great Metropolis,' he observed, 'If there was any doubt about the wisdom of that decision, it vanishes when one reads the first volume on Romans from his pen which has just been issued'. W. H. T. Richards, the Editor of *Dedication*, wrote of how refreshed he was after spending most of his spare time over the Christmas holiday in reading it and, like Mr Grier, he saw the part which such books had to play in the wider purposes of God: 'If and when revival comes, we need to be in a position to teach vital truths so as to consolidate the work of the Holy Spirit' (Jan 1971).

Private correspondence echoed the same sentiments. A pastor in Romania wrote to Roger Weil in England on March 4, 1971: 'I am very grateful to you for the book concerning the Epistle of the Apostle Paul to the Romans. What a marvellous book!' From Yugoslavia, Simo Ralevic wrote to ML-J:

20 June 1975

My very dear brother and teacher in the Lord,

I just can't start to write this piece of paper. Purpose of writing is to express my great thanks to you for your precious books I received from Banner. I am a minister of the Gospel in the south part of Yugoslavia since 1965. For the first time I came in England 1967. My dear friend

Roger T. Weil took me to Westminster Chapel and you were preaching a sermon just for me. You preached from Acts 7 on the stoning Stephen. It was for me a mount of transfiguration. After that I got all your printed books. In my church I have gone through the *Sermon on the Mount.* Now I preach on *Romans!* I preached Ephesians 2. I never understood so clear Justification by Faith as now with the help of your books . . . I pray to God to give you good health that you may help with your writing to thousands. My English is so poor to express my thanks to you for saving me from the false teachings which we have in our country also.

It would be great if you go to the end of Romans and the whole Ephesian letter, and many more.

For the six years 1970–75 Dr Lloyd-Jones concentrated on the preparation of Romans for the press with a new volume in the series appearing every year. They followed, in sequence, from the exposition of chapters three and four. Chapter five – upon which he needed 370 pages – he regarded 'the key chapter of this great Epistle – absolutely essential to any true understanding of chapters 6–8'. In his Preface to the volume on chapter six he included the following fragment of autobiography:

One Sunday evening at the close of a service at Westminster Chapel, somewhere about 1943, a certain well-known preacher came into my vestry and said to me: 'When are you going to preach a series of expository sermons on the Epistle to the Romans?' I answered immediately: 'When I have really understood chapter 6.'
Like many others I had struggled with this chapter for several years, and had read, not only the well-known commentaries, but also many sermons and addresses on it. But none had satisfied me . . . In 1954, while preaching a series of sermons on Spiritual Depression, and studying this chapter again, I suddenly felt that I had arrived at a satisfactory understanding, and preached three sermons on Sunday mornings giving what I now regarded as the true exposition of the main argument of the chapter . . .
Personally, I found my new understanding of it to be one of the most liberating experiences in my Christian life. I trust that this may be repeated in the lives of others.

After the publication of the sixth in these Romans volumes, subtitled, *Exposition of Chapter 8:17–39, The Final Perseverance of the Saints*, there was to be a major delay in the series. This last volume with 457 pages was the largest thus far and the American publishers, apprehensive of what chapters 9 to 11 would come to if they matched this scale, urged ML-J to give serious consideration to the possibility of an abridgement of his material on the next three chapters so as to contain their exposition within one volume. Confident of the ability of Sinclair B. Ferguson, who was then working for the Banner of Truth Trust, ML-J agreed to the suggestion that Ferguson should attempt such an abridgement. But when it was at length done, and done as well as anyone could do it, he remained unconvinced that this was the right way to continue the series. In the event, no further volumes were to appear until after his death.[1]

The main reason why the Romans series stood still after 1975 was that his attention was now being given to his work on Ephesians. In 1973 he had decided to go forward with further volumes on Ephesians and to publish these, also, through the Trust. Accordingly the Banner of Truth Trust published *Life in the Spirit, An Exposition of Ephesians 5:18 to 6:9* in 1974 and the preacher's Preface expressed the hope 'that it will eventually take its place, in due course, as one volume in a series on this great Epistle'. Subsequent volumes were published by the Trust in 1976, 1977, 1978, 1979 and 1980, which also reprinted the volume on chapter two, *God's Way of Reconciliation*, first published in the United Kingdom by the Evangelical Press in 1972. Only one volume remained to complete the whole Ephesians series and this was issued in 1982, the year after his death.

In terms of literary output the 1970's were thus, unquestionably, the most important decade of his life.

At the same time as his books expounded Scripture they also dispelled a number of fallacies. One of these was the idea that expository volumes of this type could scarcely have any point of contact with non-Christians or even with many church-goers. William Neil concluded a review of ML-J on Ephesians chapter 2 with the words, 'This is preaching for the "twice-born" and as such it is admirable, but one feels it would not make much impact on the intelligent sixth-former or the puzzled middle-of-the-road Christian looking for answers to the problems of day-to-day living in a

[1] *Romans, Exposition of Chapter 1, The Gospel of God*, 1985; and *Romans, Exposition of Chapters 2–3:19, The Righteous Judgment of God*, 1988. Manuscripts exist of all the unpublished sermons down to the breaking-off point, Romans 14:17, and further volumes are anticipated.

bewildering world'.[1] Again, there is a similar implication in the otherwise favourable words of a review by Howard Marshall: 'Some aspects of the Calvinistic understanding of Scripture are less convincing than others . . . But any who are tempted to think that preaching is a dying art should take note of this book, and observe that even if preaching no longer attracts the outsider it is still vital for the upbuilding of the "insider".'[2] Yet the fact is that 'outsiders' were reached by the books as they had been by the original sermons. Not a few owed their conversion to his writings. An Annual Report of the London City Mission records how a woman left her husband and her children only to return later when 'she had been converted through reading a sermon of Dr Martyn Lloyd-Jones'.[3] A prisoner in Wormwood Scrubs, London, wrote to say how a copy of *Romans, Atonement and Justification,* loaned to him by a visitor, had been used to open his eyes and bring him to repentance.[4] A student at Reading University heard Dr William Sargant lecture on 'The Mechanism of Brainwashing and Conversion' and then, being convicted by the truth in reading ML-J's reply to Sargant, became a Christian.[5] A Scottish emigrant to Durban, South Africa, found herself 'a failure in every way'. 'Unhappiness and loneliness drove me deep into the pit,' she later confessed to the author. In that state of mind she was loaned one of the Lloyd-Jones volumes which brought her to understand how someone with 'absolutely nothing' could be reconciled to God. 'For the first time in my life I wept with *joy.*'

Another conversion, which affected several lives, occurred in the Midlands of England. A man had been a member of the Watchtower movement for 18 years when he suffered from an illness which was followed by depression. As he later wrote:

Down I went, spiritually shaken to pieces, devoid of faith and convinced I was eternally lost. The next year or more was a spiritual nightmare. I despaired of ever getting out of the dark pit and thought I would never see light. One afternoon my doctor gave me a gift, a book

[1]*Scottish Journal of Theology,* vol. 28, no. 2, 1975, p. 195.
[2]*The Expository Times,* June 1972, p. 282.
[3]*From Darkness to Light,* Annual Report, 1984, p. 37.
[4]When staying in the home of a prison visitor in Wellington, New Zealand, I heard of how ML-J's books had been used to help men in prison.
[5]This ML-J booklet, entitled *Conversions: Psychological and Spiritual,* IVP, 1959, is reprinted in *Knowing the Times.*

entitled, *An Exposition of Romans, 3:20–4:25*, by Dr D. M. Lloyd-
Jones. I decided I might as well read it . . .[1]

A few years later in a letter of November 27, 1973 he told ML-J
some of the results of that reading:

Your book has lit a fire that has spread far wider than myself. About
three weeks ago my wife and I were disfellowshipped from the local
congregation of Jehovah's Witnesses, this is the ultimate punishment
that can be handed out, to a 'backsliding' Witness. We are now free and
feel every day the work of grace within us. I can never express the joy we
feel and the peace of mind. Your book came to me about two-and-a-half
years ago. I thought it strange that a man not of my faith should give me
such a book. Now looking back I see so well the providence of God in the
matter. It was only a few weeks later that I sat down one evening to read
a few pages and arose a changed man. In your writings you stressed the
true state of man before God and I saw myself for what I was. Over the
next few months a great change began to come upon me . . . Now I can
tell you that the Lord has opened the eyes of two more souls and one of
these is my dear wife.

Another erroneous impression which the circulation of the ML-J
volumes dispelled was the belief that it was those who had heard him
preach who would be the principal readers of his books. For only
those readers, it was said, could add from memory the factors
missing in cold print. This opinion – thoroughly disproved in the
1970's – illustrates how not all his hearers understood his *theology*.
They should have known that the apprehension of truth in personal
experience owes its presence to something other than human
instrumentality. It is the work of God to make the truth effective to
anyone, anywhere. A correspondent in the West Indies understood it
correctly when she wrote to ML-J: 'In your first volume of Romans
you made mention of the fact that theology has no appeal until the
Spirit has started to deal with one. And oh, the glorious way in which
the Spirit has been dealing with me! My prayer life, my worship, my
daily living all took on a new dimension.'
Nothing is more striking in the letters which came to Dr Lloyd-
Jones from readers than the testimony to the spiritual power which
came to them *with* the truths which they read. Instead of 'dull

[1]This story and that of others who left the Jehovah's Witnesses is given in the
Evangelical Times, May 1974.

sermons' they found that theological preaching is the true way to assurance, strength and joy, regardless of age or nationality. A man browsing in a public library at Stoke-on-Trent picked up a volume by ML-J of whom he had never heard and wrote to the Banner of Truth Trust to ask where he could obtain more. One reader of the books wrote to testify to how he had been delivered from the fear of death; another – an Anglican vicar – to say that their message had kept him from suicide. A lady wrote from Georgia, 'I am filled with thanksgiving that I have found your books . . . May you cast a shadow throughout the world'. An American tourist on a cruise in the Black Sea discovered *Studies in the Sermon on the Mount* in the ship's library and was so impressed that, on returning home, he bought fourteen copies to give to his fellow elders. He could later write to ML-J: 'The response in our church has been quite remarkable'.

A Christian in Melbourne, Australia, had long struggled over assurance of salvation when he came across ML-J's rejection of the 'take it by faith' teaching: 'It was like a beam of sunshine in a dark room that had been shut up for years'. Twenty-eight-year-old Jorge Sanchez in Argentina read a booklet by ML-J in Spanish and determined to learn English so that he could read more. Of the booklet he later wrote, 'It caused me such an impact that I could never be the same as before'. With his English improved, he got into the Romans volumes and wrote again to the author: 'The last days I have been studying the first part of Romans 8 and I was thinking, how is it possible that a sermon given in 1960 can change a life in 1979? But it is possible! And thanks to the Lord for it.' Sanchez also wrote what many others only *felt*, 'I love you very deeply and I would like to give you a strong embrace for all that you have done for me'.

Any indication that it was one type of person or one age group which benefited most from the books is totally absent from the correspondence which came in. One letter came from a ninety-year-old man in Yorkshire, thanking him for 'a most encouraging exposition' of assurance; and the next from a young Irishman of Roman Catholic background in Dublin, writing to say: 'Your series on Romans was an absolute revelation to me . . . I have often asked myself the question, "what did I know before I read your books?" The answer I give myself, "I don't think you knew anything at all".' From a different part of Southern Ireland another former Roman Catholic who had become a Christian in 1972 wrote:

Before I was saved I never read anything but comics, I had no interest
in learning. Since I got saved I cannot learn enough – of the Bible,
that is. There are many getting saved in the South of Ireland, all from
R.C. backgrounds. In a day when wolves abound, when books are
everywhere, when everyone's opinion matters and the Bible doesn't,
our cry is, Lord lead us into the *truths* of your Word, stablish our feet
in your Word! That cry has been answered. At a time when I was in a
fog as to what to believe, your sermons brought light and certainty to
my soul. But this is only one testimony among many. We do not have
big Christian bookshops or secondhand book shops where you can
pick up books on the Puritans and those great teachers of years gone
by. But we find they are all contained in those sermons on Romans
and Ephesians.

In a sense you have become part of this fellowship here through your
teachings. The flock under your care has increased. We praise God for
the ministry he has given you . . . May I say on behalf of myself and
other Christians who read your works, Don't leave us to the wolves.
Publish more of your works on Romans, Ephesians and on other parts
of the Bible . . .

In December 1976 ML-J received a letter which I believe must
have moved him deeply. It was from the widow of the Rev. Charles
Hilton Day who had died the previous year. Mr Day had known
lonely and difficult ministries during his years of service in the
English Presbyterian Church. Fellowship with Dr Lloyd-Jones at
occasional conferences and, more particularly, through his books
had often refreshed him, and never more so than in the four years of
illness which marked the close of his life. In these years, when he
was not in hospital, he and his wife read many of the Romans and
Ephesians volumes together, chapter by chapter in the evenings.
Speaking of the time when he had returned home after a final
period in hospital, Mrs Joy Day writes:

We did not realize we had only ten days left together here. We resumed
our evening reading and these times together increased in preciousness.
On the Saturday evening after a distressing day I suggested that
perhaps he would like something a little lighter. I didn't think he was
able to take in a serious book and I was just anxious to read him to
sleep – 'No,' he said, 'it must be the Doctor'. I read the chapter from
Ephesians, Life in the Spirit on Christ as the husband of His church
right through, hoping my beloved was sleeping, but as I finished he just
raised his head and said, 'That was very deep wasn't it?'. It was deep

and glorious! We settled him at 9.30 p.m. and the Lord took him home to glory in his sleep a few hours later.

Many who wrote to ML-J (as Simo Ralevic in Yugoslavia already quoted above) told of how they were able to repeat what they had learned in preaching and speaking to others. 'The understanding that has come to me,' wrote a reader of the *Romans* volumes in Dubai, 'was not intended for me alone', and he went on to speak of how the books were being passed round. A missionary in the Dominican Republic reported: 'Very few authors get to me like you do . . . I want you to know that many people in the Dominican Republic are being blest by your books as I teach what I learn from them in the Spanish language . . .'. A psychiatrist in Toronto, witnessing the help which many had received from *Spiritual Depression* and the *Romans* series, wrote to say, 'I felt that it was time for me to sincerely express my gratitude both on my own behalf and on behalf of *many* many patients who have been brought from a dreadful state of emotional disturbance and even catastrophe back to real health and happiness'.

A thirty-eight-year-old leader of a Bible class in Alabama wrote of the effect of the *Sermon on the Mount* in his class and confessed: 'I emulate your style, I plagiarize your content (with acknowledgement however), I'm sort of a miniature Lloyd-Jones. How successful you are in a suburban upper middle class Episcopal church in Birmingham! When I started there were about 15 faithful. For the last class I taught we had over 50 – thanks in no small measure to your writings . . .'.

The refrain in so many of these letters was the same. It was not praise for the preacher or his style but thankfulness to God for the life- changing power of the truth. In the words of a correspondent in Texas, 'God so opened up His sovereign grace to me through reading your books'; and of a College student in Georgia, 'You have opened my eyes to many of the great doctrines of Scripture'.

*   *   *

All this is not to say that there was no criticism of the Lloyd-Jones titles. There was, and yet considering the hundreds of reviews which his books were given it was surprisingly muted. Many reviewers probably thought, with Dr Leslie Newman, that 'the critic will find the onus of proof resting on himself'. The preaching style drew

frequent comment. Some considered it too expansive and repetitious. Yet, at the same time, it was usually recognized that the
sermonic form had much to do with the readability: 'Many sermons
lose something when they are imprisoned in print, but these
messages appear to retain all their vigor, freshness and clarity even
on the printed page.'¹ *The Presbyterian Journal* (Jan 8, 1975),
reviewing the fourth volume in the Romans series, said, 'Dr Lloyd-
Jones has become widely known in Reformed circles for his
eminently readable style'.

Sometimes reviewers noticeably disagreed among themselves over
the point they raised for criticism. His expository method, for
instance, was at times criticized for the alleged allowance of
'digression' from the passage under consideration. Others, however,
noted these same passages as possessing particular value in the
opening up of Scripture as a whole: 'We have become used to Dr
Lloyd-Jones' method of digression,' wrote Keith Warren in the
Trowel and Sword (Australia, August 1972), 'but what thrilling
excursions they become: always along the safe track of the Bible!' In
ML-J's own view he was doing no more than is warranted by the
principle of interpreting Scripture by Scripture.²

There was, similarly, disagreement among reviewers over the
amount of 'application' relevant to the present day in the Lloyd-
Jones sermons. While one reviewer believed 'the presentation is
contemporary in the best sense', and that ML-J dealt with current
errors and objections, others were critical because major matters of
social or political interest seemed to be left to one side: the preacher,
it was said, did not sufficiently address the implications of Christianity to 'society at large'. William Neil, already quoted, complained
that 'economic problems' were touched on rarely and, he continued,
'one misses any concern with social and international problems'.
Assessments of this criticism will clearly depend on an individual's
view of the preacher's calling. If the first business of the preacher is to
deliver a message to the people *before him*, and to see that they know
the power of the world to come, he will not have much to say on such
circumstances in the world as are likely to change from one decade to
the next. Had ML-J said what some thought he ought to have said,

¹Curtis Vaughan in *Southwestern Journal of Theology*, June 18, 1960.
²For those unconvinced of the true unity of Scripture this amounted to 'starting
with a theological framework and solving all scriptural problems by appealing to
that framework'.

then a good deal of his preaching in the 1950's would have already been out-of-date by the time it was published twenty years later. The public mood in England in the fifties, with a fear of Communism bringing such interests as pacifism and CND to the fore, was very different from the mood of the seventies.

The truth is that topical sermons on the social or political application of Christianity do not remain relevant from one generation to the next. More than that, they cannot even accomplish such changes in society as can the preaching which deals directly with the individual. Dr Lloyd-Jones' standpoint here was close to that of W. G. T. Shedd who, speaking of the Puritan view of the pulpit, wrote:

That unearthly sermonizing, so abstracted from all the temporal and secular interests of man, so rigorously confined to human guilt and human redemption – that preaching which, upon the face of it, does not seem even to recognize that man has any relations to this little ball of earth, which takes him off the planet entirely, and contemplates him simply as a sinner in the presence of God – was, nevertheless, by indirection, one of the most fertile causes of the progress of England and America. Subtract it as one of the forces of English history and the career of the Anglo-Saxon race would be like that of Italy and Spain.[1]

A few reviews of ML-J's books were themselves the starting point of controversies. In Britain the weekly evangelical paper, *The Life of Faith*, had for long been the representative organ for the 'Keswick' teaching on sanctification. The Rev. H. F. Stevenson, its Editor, gave praise to the volumes on Romans despite the criticism that teaching received. Even when *Romans, Exposition of Chapter 7:1–8:4* appeared (which rejected the standard Keswick view that the speaker at the end of Romans 7 is a defeated believer in need of sanctification) Stevenson concluded a review of May 11, 1974: 'Whether one agrees with his thesis or not, it is plain that all who preach or speak on Romans, and all speakers at Keswick especially, should give this book very thorough reading and attention.' But the subject could not be left there. Returning to it in the issue of June 8, 1974, Stevenson revealed that his review had been badly received by a number of the paper's traditional readers: 'My recent note on the latest volume in Dr D. Martyn Lloyd-Jones' *magnum opus* . . . has evoked a larger

[1] *Homiletics and Pastoral Theology*, pp. 217–18.

readers' reaction correspondence than any topic for months past . . . There is apparently some misunderstanding as to my views: one correspondent goes so far as to say, "It is a pity you must be so supine – where do you stand on Romans 7?".' The answer, Stevenson went on to assure his correspondents, was that 'the defeated Christian' interpretation remained his own view as well as that of the Keswick Convention.

Sharper controversy followed, this time on the other side of the Atlantic. *Moody Monthly* had been one of the first journals in the States to give prominence to Dr Lloyd-Jones' ministry. But a magazine which equated the prophetic teaching of dispensationalism with classical Christianity could not be other than uneasy with some emphases in ML-J's ministry.[1] The October 1980 issue carried a short but warm commendation of his Ephesians volume, *The Unsearchable Riches of Christ* ('If you've grown weak on shallow teaching and fuzzy application, this work will provide strength . . . and courage'). A year later, however, another review of the same book carried a different view and at some length. ML-J's so-called 'polemic' against dispensationalism was highlighted and then, after criticism of his 'extravagant expressions and tiresome questions', the reviewer actually concluded by querying whether the book taught the 'universalist heresy' and whether it was orthodox on the deity of Christ.[2] Evangelical leaders who read *Moody Monthly*, including men of dispensational persuasion, were aghast at this smear treatment and under the heading 'Lloyd-Jones Heretical?' the journal opened the columns of its December issue to protests. These included a lengthy letter from Darrel Amundsen, Professor of Classics at Western Washington University. He believed that even if the reviewer 'is woefully ignorant of Lloyd-Jones' well deserved international reputation as a stalwart defender of the evangelical faith, and as an expositor of impeccable orthodoxy, there is no excuse for his being ignorant of the contents of the book he reviews'. The Editor of *Moody Monthly* apologized for the

---

[1] *Moody Monthly*, May 1960, noted that Lloyd-Jones rejected dispensationalism and regarded the Sermon on the Mount as specifically for Christians. Nonetheless, the reviewer of his *Studies in the Sermon on the Mount* described it as 'the most enlightening and edifying work on the subject' which he had seen.
[2] The critique of Dispensationalism in *The Unsearchable Riches of Christ* only extended to four out of over three hundred pages. The more serious criticism on content was wholly without foundation.

A World Pulpit

'unfortunate editorial comment' of its reviewer and affirmed that 'Dr Lloyd-Jones' exegetical and evangelistic contributions to the Church are profound'. It had not been the intention of *Moody Monthly* to question his orthodoxy.

A general criticism of ML-J which is expressed in some reviews has to do with his 'dogmatism' and, more particularly, with the alleged 'negative' aspects of his preaching. In a lengthy review of his booklet, *From Puritanism to Nonconformity*, The Annual Lecture of the Evangelical Library for 1962, Bertrand J. Coggle wrote in *The Methodist Recorder* (Nov 1, 1962):

It is indeed strange that he should say, 'my interest is not controversial', and then go on to castigate the Chairman of the Congregational Union for views which, he says, are typical of the members of the Free Churches today . . . Dr Lloyd-Jones evidently dislikes the frank admission by so many Free Church scholars that we hold today a different attitude to the nature of the inspiration of the Bible, from that held in 1662.

Verlyn D. Verbrugge, reviewing the Ephesians volume entitled *Christian Unity* in the *Calvin Theological Journal* (April 1983), complained of 'a severe negativism which pervades the book on anything other than staunch sixteenth-century Protestantism'. He was disturbed by the preacher's reference to the 'heresy of Roman Catholicism' and by the way in which 'he also blasts away at branches of Protestantism: liberal Christianity . . . and even Christianity which organizes evangelistic campaigns'.

The first review of the Romans series to appear in the *Church of England Newspaper* voiced the same censure. James D .G. Dunn wrote:

His stern unyielding dogmatism is rather off-putting; and too frequent over-simplifications seem to betoken a mind anxious to press the diversity of the New Testament gospel within a single dogmatic mould . . . In his often fiery polemic one detects something of the old anti-scholarship bias of an older generation of evangelicals (e.g., pp 87, 121); although anyone who calls C. H. Dodd 'arrogant' betrays more than a little of the same fault himself . . . Those who enjoy sermons in defence of strict orthodoxy will find much to relish. But for an exposition of Romans which does rather more justice to the sophistication of the New Testament faith others are better advised to

[649]

refer to the commentaries of Barrett, Bruce and perhaps even, dare I say, Dodd.[1]

'As years went by,' Christopher Catherwood has written, 'Martyn Lloyd-Jones . . . acquired an unfortunate, negative image in the eyes of many.'[2]

The explanation of this is bound to be one of the main areas of controversy in any interpretation of Dr Lloyd-Jones' life. In his own mind the issue came down to differing attitudes to Scripture. He saw that the elements of warning and of opposition to error were essential parts of any true commitment to the Bible and, therefore, believed that the 'disapproval of polemics in the Christian Church is a very serious matter'. Accordingly he expected no approval from those who accepted the prevailing attitude which put 'love' first and treated arguments over doctrine as unchristian. It was that very attitude, he believed, which was responsible for the removal of the note of authority from the pulpit: the charge of 'dogmatism' and the dislike of reproof and correction were criticisms of Scripture itself.[3]

One of the main characteristics of ML-J's ministry was thus both an offence to those who were supporters of the spirit of the modern pulpit and an inspiration to those who believed that a return to authority in preaching was a great need. The latter were profoundly thankful for the very thing with which the first group found fault:

Dr Lloyd-Jones has a penetrating – and courageous – diagnosis of the present situation . . . This is an age of appeasement, not in the political and international sense but in the realm of Christian affairs and of the Church. Winston Churchill is now acclaimed and almost idolized; in the thirties he was severely criticized as an impossible person because he knew what he believed, he believed it and he caused disturbance by criticizing the policy of appeasement. So it is today. Strong men who stand by their principles are today regarded as being difficult, self-assertive and non-co-operative.[4]

[1] April 8, 1971. It should be said that subsequent reviews of the Romans volumes in the same paper by J. I. Packer were entirely different in tone and warm in commendation (*Church of England Newspaper*, Feb 16, 1973 and May 3, 1974).
[2] *Five Evangelical Leaders*, Hodder & Stoughton, 1984, p. 89.
[3] See *Romans*, vol. 3, pp. 113–14.
[4] *The Evangelical Christian* (Canada), July 1961.

This writer puts his finger on the real reason for Dr Lloyd-Jones' alleged 'negative image'. How widespread that image became is impossible to assess. It was undoubtedly at its strongest in England in the 1970's where ML-J was blamed for dividing evangelicalism. Even so, the sale of his books went far beyond almost all expectations. In their first decade of publication the Romans and Ephesians series exceeded a million copies and the sale continues. I say 'almost all expectations' because there were some who correctly anticipated the extent of the future demand for his books. One of these was Dr L. Walker of Knutsford, Cheshire, who wrote to ML-J in 1968:

I am very pleased to hear that you are giving up the pastorate at Westminster to give more time to writing.

Through your faithful and outstanding pulpit ministry you have reached thousands. But through your writings you will reach millions both at present and in the future and a long future at that.

I look forward each month to the arrival of the *Westminster Record*. I am also a regular reader of Spurgeon and I see in your writings the same enduring qualities that I find in his. Spurgeon's work is never 'dated' because he was a man of the Word and so are you. There is a keen demand for Spurgeon's books in the secondhand shops. Often enquiries meet with the reply, 'Sorry, we had some last week but his stuff soon goes'. I am sure that in years to come they will be saying the same of yours.

The letters from which I have quoted in this chapter I did not see in ML-J's lifetime. He would make no more than an occasional passing reference to correspondence received and the mounting sales figures did not, in themselves, mean a great deal to him. What he prized was to hear of how God had used His Word to redirect lives and especially when that change was reported – as it often was – by those in the Christian ministry. And if there were ministers for whom he had a special concern and sympathy they were the men who had been at Westminster Chapel as students. As he saw new convictions born in a whole generation of these younger men, he understood very well what difficult and lonely days probably lay before them. Of course he urged them to exercise all patience and prudence in their future ministries, yet he knew that the principles which they had come to love could not be other than disruptive in the contemporary religious scene.

Leigh Powell was one of the many who came from this younger

generation to find serious problems upon settling into the work of the gospel ministry. From Canada Powell wrote to ML-J to express thoughts which the latter must have heard many times though the monastery metaphor was novel:

On our return to Canada we came to appreciate even more fully what one friend had said long ago: 'Westminster Chapel is a monastery!' He meant, of course, that one had a very restricted understanding of the general evangelical situation if one's experience were restricted to the Chapel as mine was!

Leigh Powell went on to describe how even though he was careful to avoid the use of such labels as 'Calvinism' or 'limited atonement' he soon encountered 'an ever mounting barrage of opposition . . . the real issue was not Calvinistic doctrine *per se* but whether Christians met together for entertainment or for worship'.

If the influence of Westminster Chapel's pulpit was powerful in the 1950's, it was also more limited in its range. Twenty years later, although ML-J's work at Westminster was done, that pulpit had become a world pulpit as the books gave light and assurance to the multiplying numbers among the nations who were coming to love the doctrines of grace. They also gave new strength to some who had wavered and in this connection ML-J received few letters which made him more thankful than one from a Baptist pastor in Pietermaritzburg, South Africa, dated August 1, 1977. Looking back across the sixteen hard years since he and his wife had left Westminster Chapel, Gordon Miller wrote:

During the years 1958 to 1961, as a student at London Bible College I simultaneously sat under your ministry at Westminster Chapel; with great benefit to my soul. I think I learnt more of practical Christianity at the latter school than the former.

Unfortunately, when I returned to Rhodesia and experienced the peculiar hazards of the Christian Ministry, I was drawn into the vortex of the 'Deeper-Life Movement' and adopted the new-evangelical approach to evangelism and holiness. Although I still made frequent excursions into *The Sermon on the Mount, Authority*, and *Spiritual Depression – Its Causes and Cure* – alas, I seemed to suffer from a kind of Schizophrenia between my inner convictions and my behaviour.

After twelve years I could stand it no longer, I resigned the high calling and began work as a manager of a very large Construction Company in

South Africa – much to the disgust of my colleagues. These three years enabled me to re-evaluate my priorities and objectively survey the current evangelical scene. *Preaching and Preachers* came hot from the press at that time, pursued by your expositions on Romans and *God's Way of Reconciliation*. But they were all 'a very big pill to swallow', for at this stage yours was very much a small voice crying in the wilderness – too strongly against the tide of much evangelical thinking; and yet its call was so clear – so certain. Its relevance so demanding. Thank God for the plea for a return to the Puritans and the Reformers.

This letter is an attempt to simply say 'Thank you'. Thank you so much. I thank God for your light shining so far into the dark world of 'Christendom'. May the Lord spare you many more years. Your words will speak when, alas, evangelicalism has foundered on the rocks of subjectivism. Then many more will rise up together with my wife Sheila and I to call you *blessed*.

We are living in evil days and never was the exhortation to 'watch' more needed, it seems to me, than at the present time. If I understand the situation at all, the whole evangelical outlook is fighting for its very life at this moment.

ML-J

in a sermon on 1 Corinthians 16:13–14,
at the Memorial Service for W. T. H. Richards,
November 1, 1974

God's Word will never pass away, but looking back to the Old Testament and since the time of Christ, with tears we must say that because of lack of fortitude and faithfulness on the part of God's people, God's Word has many times been allowed to be bent, to conform to the surrounding, passing, changing culture of that moment rather than to stand as the inerrant Word of God judging the form of the world spirit and the surrounding culture of that moment. In the name of the Lord Jesus Christ, may our children and grandchildren not say that such can be said about us.

It is hard to imagine how far things have gone in just a few years.

FRANCIS A. SCHAEFFER
The Great Evangelical Disaster, 1984, pp. 65,69

31

Understanding the 1970's

Without question the most descriptive word for English evangelicalism in the 1970's was 'confusion' and my purpose in this chapter is to give Dr Lloyd-Jones' analysis of how that condition came about. Of the main cause he had no doubt. It was the result of the cumulative effect of a weakening of doctrinal convictions. In the 1950's and 60's we have seen him warning that if evangelicalism allowed itself to be regarded as one possible 'interpretation' of Christianity, with those of opposing views being equally entitled to the same claim, then the true meaning of 'evangelical' would be lost. If an evangelical, who is defined as one who believes the New Testament gospel (*euangelion*) is to regard as Christians those denying that gospel, then the whole point of the word is bound to be lost. We have noted how ML-J regarded the Anglican evangelical leadership, who had announced their policy at Keele, as those primarily responsible for this change. At Keele there was no alteration in the content of evangelical doctrine; the change (forced by the desire to be treated as brethren in dialogue) was rather 'in the way the doctrine was held'. It was now said to be no longer held 'narrowly' and 'exclusively'. That meant that no lines were to be drawn between those who receive the Bible as the Word of God and those who do not. Anglican evangelicalism had to co-exist with ecumenism and accept, in the words of Donald Coggan's biographer, an 'increased convergence of views'.[1] Thus while in theory

---

[1] *Donald Coggan*, Margaret Pawley, p. 163. Coggan believed, said Pawley, that 'it was important to maintain a right proportion between traditionalism and liberalism and to retain the advantages of both' (p. 93). Prior to Keele, we are told, Coggan was 'regarded with something near suspicion by the Evangelical wing of the Church of England' (p. 161), but thereafter it was different. 'The attitudes which found their culmination at the National Evangelical Anglican Congresses of Keele (1967) and Nottingham (1977), he began to express earlier, when the going was hard' (p. 80). That Dr Coggan had ceased to be a conservative evangelical is very clear in his work, *Convictions*, 1975.

and in abstract the doctrinal position of the Anglican evangelical leaders remained what it had been, in practice an impetus was given to a long-term realignment and a far-reaching change.

This new direction is documented in a whole series of publications, the first of which was *Growing into Union: Proposals for Forming a United Church in England*, published by SPCK in May 1970. Written by four Anglican clergy who had all been involved in recent ecumenical discussions, what made the book of special significance was that here two professing Anglo-Catholics, E. L. Mascall and G. D. Leonard (then Bishop of Willesden), were co-authors with two evangelicals, C. O. Buchanan and J. I. Packer. The four men gave their proposals how *both* views not only could but *must* be contained within a future united Church. Their professed intention was to attempt to demonstrate the truth of the words of Michael Ramsey, quoted prominently at the outset: ' "Catholicism" and "Evangelicalism" are not two separate things which the Church of England must hold together by a great feat of compromise.' The four authors of this new alignment professed themselves to be ready 'for the misunderstanding of those who have been close to us hitherto', but they did not intend to go back to 'traditional stances':

Rather we pledged ourselves to stay together, to work together, and not at any stage to settle for a way through [to a future union] which would satisfy one "side" whilst hurting the other . . . We now present our work as those who are still definitely and confessedly Catholics and Evangelicals . . . But equally we are not what we were . . . We are determined that no wedge should be driven between us . . . [1]

Accordingly, *Growing into Union* was written as one piece of work, with each author owning responsibility for the whole. The book includes such statements as these:

It is a legitimate criticism of a great deal of post-Reformation theology, both Catholic and Protestant, that it has tended to interpret both the Scripture and the other documents of the Church in a very wooden way (pp. 31–2).

Both Scripture and Tradition must be seen as deriving from Christ and as confronting men with him (p. 34).

Tradition . . . is the handing on to each Christian of the riches of the Father's house to which he became entitled by his baptism (p. 34).

[1] *Growing into Union*, pp. 17–19.

Scripture keeps the Church true to its historical roots as nothing else, except perhaps the Eucharist, can (p. 36).

The bishop must be seen to be what he is in the liturgical life of the Church, the sacramental expression of the headship of Christ (p. 79).[1] Just as sin is corporate, so is its counterpart, faith . . . The gospel makes us one in the Second Adam by baptism (pp. 57–8). Only the children of communicants would qualify for baptism. They would then be eligible for admission to communion with their parents (p. 66). If we really believe in episcopacy as part of the skeleton of the Church from which the presbyterate and diaconate derive, then what matters is to get the episcopate right (p. 80).

The publication of this book, with no subsequent disavowal from the other leaders of the Anglican evangelical party, brought a final end to Dr Lloyd-Jones' public co-operation with the leaders of that party. More particularly, and more painfully, it terminated his work with Dr Packer. Supported by the three other Nonconformist members of the Puritan Conference Committee, he wrote to Packer indicating that the annual Conference must be considered as having met for the last time. No public statement, he believed, was necessary: there would simply be no Puritan Conference at Westminster Chapel in December 1970 as there had been for the last twenty years.[2] It needed no public statement, however, for news of this decision spread quickly. It was widely discussed at the Westminster Fraternal and elsewhere, and the outcome was that *Growing into Union* became the ground for a whole series of partings. Although the Bible Rallies held in many parts of the country since the early 1960's were organized generally (if not entirely) by Nonconformist evangelicals, Jim Packer had hitherto been a welcome speaker at a number of them and was the chairman of the council which organized the one held regularly in the Cotswolds. His connection

---

[1]As the book elevates Christ above Scripture, if the question were asked how this Christ is to be further known, the answer would seem to be related to this and other statements concerning 'the ministry' (i.e. episcopal) as 'the sacramental expression of the continuing headship of Christ over his church' (p. 84).
[2]At the prompting of members of the Westminster Ministers' Fraternal a committee was formed in 1971 and ML-J was asked if he would be chairman for a conference which would continue the work of the Puritan Conference. He agreed and the first Westminster Conference met in December 1971. Apart from the change of name, and the absence of an annual paper by Dr Packer, it was to all intents and purposes the old conference resumed.

with these, with the *Evangelical Magazine*, and with the Evangelical Movement of Wales, were now severed.[1]

But this sad disruption of evangelical co-operation put no brake upon the new policy of broader ecumenical relationships. Subsequent writing from Anglican evangelical leaders in the 1970's all followed the example of Keele and of *Growing into Union*. The book *Evangelicals Today*, 1973, a symposium by a team of Anglican evangelicals, criticized 'traditional evangelicalism' for such things as the way it dealt with the question, What is a Christian?, and for its policy of encouraging attendance at 'only strictly evangelical churches'. 'Evangelicals,' it affirmed, 'recognize other Anglicans as fellow Christians however critical they are of Evangelicalism.'[2]

In 1976 *Christian Believing* was published by the SPCK. This was the joint work of the Church of England's Commission on Christian Doctrine, the chairman of which was Professor Maurice Wiles, Regius Professor of Divinity at Oxford. Wiles' radical disbelief was already well known. Reviewing his book *The Remaking of Christian Doctrine*, *The Times* said that it was an 'endorsement for those . . . who have turned their backs on church-made dogma . . . His theology hinges on the acceptance of uncertainty.' The uncertainty included the deity of Christ (which belief Wiles did not consider to be necessary) and even the very existence of God. 'Professor Wiles' theology gives Christianity the benefit of the doubt, but it also makes that doubt respectable.'[3]

Christian Believing, of which J. I. Packer was a signatory, made full allowance for the co-existence of such views as those of Wiles within the Church of England. Michael Green was another evangelical signatory to *Christian Believing*. In his book *The Truth of God Incarnate* Green answered Wiles' *The Myth of God Incarnate* and yet the Preface to *Christian Believing* describes both men as 'followers of a common Lord'.

In April 1977 the second National Evangelical Anglican Congress met at Nottingham. Its lengthy report *The Nottingham Statement* was as silent on discipline as it was on the 39 Articles (to which

---

[1]See Appendix 4 below.

[2]*Evangelicals Today*, ed. John C. King, pp. 9–11, 164, 169. The same attitude was now adopted towards *all* Roman Catholics, thus Julian Charley (spokesman for Anglican evangelicals at the Evangelical Alliance Congress of 1966) wrote, 'We should affirm our acceptance of Roman Catholics in principle as our fellow Christians' (*I believe in the Church*, David Watson, 1978, p. 351).

[3]'Respectable doubt about the divinity of Christ', *The Times*, August 26, 1974.

'general consent' was now no longer required of the clergy in the Church of England[1]). The 'attempt to gather a "pure" church' was summarily dismissed as 'impossible'. The tone was one of benevolence towards all – to non-Anglican evangelicals ('We repent of the . . . insensitivity on our part'); to charismatics ('Rejoicing in the grace and gifts of God that "charismatic" and "non-charismatic" evangelicals find in each other') and to the Roman Catholic Church ('We shall encourage every kind of co-operation that may bring the goal of full communion nearer')[2]. In writing to invite Archbishop Coggan to speak at the Congress, its Secretary had assured him, in Margaret Pawley's words, 'that most Evangelicals were anxious that they should not appear to be entrenching themselves as a party'.[3] Such an assurance was scarcely necessary. Little more than a week after speaking at Nottingham, Coggan was in Rome, urging co-operation in 'evangelism' and in 'the Sacrament of Unity', while John Stott was to go to Venice to be a part of the Evangelical–Roman Catholic Dialogue on Mission.[4]

While all this readiness to accept the Christianity of those holding very different beliefs was not intended to diminish the importance of any doctrine, that was the inevitable result as ML-J had long forewarned. Evangelicals within the Church of England, hitherto uncritical of the Keele policy, began themselves to speak of an 'identity crisis' and one Nottingham delegate put the question in words quoted in the *Church of England Newspaper*: 'How can we know where we are going if we do not know what we are? What is an evangelical? Tell us, somebody, please.'

If some were beginning to be dismayed, there were others who considered the very asking of this question to be a relic of a mindset which ought to have passed away. They showed no regret over the word 'evangelicalism' being emptied of its former meaning. This was clearly the attitude of Archbishops Coggan and Blanch, both appointed in 1974 and said to be 'evangelicals'. Interviewed in the *Church of England Newspaper*, Stuart Blanch said: 'I think I

[1]The change came into effect on September 1, 1975. Henceforth the Articles were only to be regarded 'as one of the historic formularies through which the Church of England has borne witness to Christian truth'.
[2]*The Nottingham Statement*, 1977, pp. 40, 41, 76, 45.
[3]*Donald Coggan*, p. 224.
[4]See *Donald Coggan*, pp. 225–30, and *The Evangelical–Roman Catholic Dialogue on Mission, 1977–1984*, ed. Basil Meeking and John Stott, 1986.

agree that it is significant that there should be two evangelical Archbishops but I no longer find this distinction in the slightest bit meaningful.'

* * *

The change in Anglican evangelicalism was the first major influence of the 1970's which, in ML-J's thought, was contributing to the growing indifference to the place of doctrine in true Christianity. But we must now turn to a second equally powerful influence among evangelicals. The charismatic movement, whose beginnings in the years 1963–64 we have noted above, had become a major force in English evangelicalism, and the disparagement of doctrine which ML-J had noted in David du Plessis was now a feature of the movement as a whole. The priority of 'gifts' and 'experiences' was established wherever its influence prevailed. This was the case both with those who believed in the renewal of the old denominations from within and – sometimes to a lesser extent – with those committed to a new unity outside all the old structures. Speaking of this second group ('the restorationists'), Andrew Walker refers to the years 1970 to 1974 as 'heady days of great excitement and discovery'.[1] Part of their 'discovery' was the contemporary existence of 'apostles and prophets'. 'This means,' says one of the best known restorationist writers, 'that *men* – rather than particular doctrines or structures – must become prominent again.'[2] The work of these same men was also believed to point the way to 'true Christian unity'. 'It will be a *unified* church . . . No isms or denominations for "all our isms will be wasms"!'[3]

Anglican evangelicals in dialogue within ecumenism weakened their emphasis on the fundamental truths of the gospel because the rules of the discussion required all participants to be regarded as fellow Christians. For a different reason the charismatic programme similarly put no emphasis upon the need for a recovery of the

---

[1] *Restoring the Kingdom, The Radical Christianity of the House Church Movement*, 1985, p. 50.
[2] *Church Adrift*, David Matthew, 1985, p. 220. A revival of apostles had, of course, occurred earlier in the century in one branch of Pentecostalism: 'There is a church known at the present time as the Apostolic Church. They claim to have apostles and prophets among them. We could easily show that they are not scriptural' (ML-J on Romans, March 18, 1966).
[3] *Ibid*, p. 228.

meaning of conversion. Conversion, it seemed to be assumed, was common enough: the great need of the churches was to experience a transforming change from the adoption of other interests – from tongues, prophecy and healing to dance and drama. Teaching fell into the background and encouragement was inevitably given to the whole trend towards doctrinal indifferentism. ML-J made special reference to this development among evangelicals of charismatic views as early as 1966 when preaching from Romans 12 on Friday evenings at Westminster Chapel:

This is one of the great problems facing all of us as evangelical Christians at the present time, because there are evangelical people who are talking like this now: they say that doctrine does not matter. What matters is that a man has got the Spirit and the rest does not matter. A man may receive the Spirit in all His fullness and continue as a Roman Catholic . . . In other words, they say that you can have this true unity in spite of profound disagreement concerning vital and essential doctrine . . .[1]

Again, in a further sermon in the same series, he said:

Certain people tell us that bishops and even cardinals in the Roman Catholic Church have been baptized with the Spirit recently and are speaking in tongues and so on. But if you say to them, Does this mean therefore that they no longer believe in the Assumption of Mary and the Immaculate Conception? Do they no longer believe in Transubstantiation and all those other additions which are not scriptural at all and which, indeed, are contrary to Scripture? Do they therefore renounce these errors of Roman Catholicism? The answer they give is: 'Oh no, no! not at all; it does not make any difference, and what does it matter? The great thing is that they are now speaking in tongues or that they are prophesying.' Apparently it does not matter that they should be holding these grievous errors.[2]

In the years that followed, as ML-J kept abreast of events and studied the charismatic literature, his concern deepened. At the IFES Conference of 1971, in the course of dealing with the various influences which were encouraging a vague, nebulous, ecumenical-type thinking, he said:

[1]January 28, 1966.
[2]February 25, 1966.

There is a factor which to me is a very serious one at the present time and that is what is known as the charismatic movement. Now I am sure that you are all familiar with this. This is a phenomenon that has been confronting us for the last fifteen years or so. And it is very remarkable. It began in America and it has spread to many countries, most countries probably by now.

The teaching of this movement is that nothing matters but 'the baptism of the Spirit'. Sometimes they may put it in terms of speaking in tongues, but at any rate they put it in general in terms of 'the baptism of the Spirit'. Nothing matters but this! . . . You can believe Roman Catholic doctrine or be Methodist or be without any doctrine at all if you like; it does not matter. The great thing is that you have this experience. And so they have their conferences and their congresses in which they all meet together, and virtually they are proclaiming that doctrine does not matter at all.[1]

The question of the gift of 'prophecy' is particularly relevant to what we are here considering. On this gift it has sometimes been thought that there was some agreement between charismatic views and ML-J's own. He certainly believed that prophesying could be a contemporary gift and even said, 'I think I know just a little about this. I think I know something of what it is to be preaching or teaching and suddenly to find myself prophesying.' But he was not talking about the prophetic office through which infallible revelation is given to the church. He was referring to something broader which has to do with the inspiring of a speaker to exhort, comfort and warn with God-given directness, making manifest 'the secrets of the heart' (1 Cor. 14:25).[2] Such speaking may well overlap with preaching, enabling the preacher to declare more than he had actually prepared. The remarkable gift of exhortation possessed by such a man as Howell Harris he viewed in that way.

However, far from giving ML-J sympathy towards what was now being popularized, this understanding of 'prophesying' was actually a major factor in convincing him of its wrongness. Because, he

[1]From three addresses on 'What is an Evangelical?' See *Knowing the Times*, pp. 312–14.
[2]See sermon on Romans 12:6, Feb 18, 1966. Also *Ephesians*, vol. 2, pp. 441–42; vol. 4, pp. 183–86; *Romans*, vol. 1, pp. 46–49 and p. 77; *Puritans*, p. 295; and *Knowing the Times*, p. 276. It is interesting to note that John Owen agreed with him on 'prophesying' in Romans 12 but not in 1 Corinthians (*Works*, vol. 4, p. 452, pp. 469–70). ML-J's view on the nature of the prophesying in Corinth was different in 1966 from his view given in *Ephesians*, vol. 2, pp. 441–42 (preached in 1956).

argued, the 'prophesying' which has to be distinguished from the prophetic office has always to be *judged* by Scripture, or 'according to the proportion of faith' (as he interpreted Romans 12:6). This was precisely what the modern movement was failing to do. Paul required every utterance to be tested by the 'body of teaching and doctrine that has been given to us by God through the apostles and prophets'. 'It is a very wrong and a very dangerous teaching that puts prophecy over against Scripture. It is even worse when it puts it above the Scripture.'

When a man utters a prophecy in the church he must be certain, says the Apostle, that it in no way contravenes, or does not fit into this body of truth . . . Now let me show you how important all this is at the present time. Any teaching which tends to speak a little disparagingly about doctrine or about theology or teaching is wrong; it contradicts the direct command of the Apostle. He says that 'prophecy must be uttered according to the proportion of faith', so if you dismiss and deride the only standard by which you can apply that test, you are contradicting the very thing that the Apostle lays down.

We must always be very careful not to base our position, our teaching, upon a prophetic utterance. Prophetic utterance is only of value as it directs attention to this 'faith' that has already been given. What prophetic utterance does is to bring out some particular aspect or facet and to emphasize it because it may be the thing that is needed supremely at that present time, but it never lays down doctrine.[1]

The charismatic movement with its readiness to say, 'Listen to the Spirit speaking today' instead of, 'Listen to the timeless Word of God', and its tendency to substitute Christian experience for faith in biblical truth, was inevitably a powerful contributing factor to the undermining of doctrinal Christianity.

Because every revival in history has been marked by the recovery of the great truths of sin, redemption and regeneration it has

[1]He treats this at length in his Romans 12:6 sermon of Feb 25, 1966 in which he says, 'I am in trouble with so much I am hearing at the present time'. As an example of the peril of treating prophesying as a revelation of new truth he instanced the teaching of the secret rapture of the saints which originated in a 'prophetic utterance' in Edward Irving's church in 1831. He also warned against messages which gave authoritative guidance to individuals which could not be tested by Scripture and he quoted with approval the words of Donald Gee that spiritual gifts are not to 'take on the directive character in private or church affairs. That is where trouble begins'.

prompted strong opposition from nominal Christianity. The charismatic movement, however, was marked by another kind of result
altogether, namely, the achievement of unity among professing
Christians of many different backgrounds and irrespective of their
continuing differences in belief. In Peter Hocken's words, there has
been an outpouring of 'ecumenical grace' so that people 'holding
together apparent opposites in the one mystery of Christ' can be
one.[1] Speaking of the phenomenon of unity achieved where charismatic influence prevails, René Laurentin regards it as 'truly astonishing' and observes that the forces separating Catholic and Protestant
'are not operative today'.[2]

Dr Lloyd-Jones believed there was nothing 'astonishing' about this
new unity at all. It is truth which brings confrontation. When
evangelicals are willing to play down the distinctive, unacceptable
emphases of biblical Christianity the disappearance of opposition
should be no surprise. 'Doctrine divides' had long been the slogan of
ecumenism. The so-called unifying force of the charismatic movement, and the ability to remove old barriers, had its origin in the
willingness of du Plessis and others to adopt the non-doctrinal
approach. So it was not the recovery of fundamental biblical truths
which the movement heralded. Its emphasis was not on the *content* of
the gospel message at all, it was rather upon external 'signs' and 'gifts'
and experiences. Instead of the 'exclusiveness' and 'dogmatism' of the
old evangelicalism which had looked for unity in belief, this was an
experience-orientated movement with full liberty to interpret the
'experience of the Spirit' according to the different religious traditions
of the participants. The old fixed positions – the 'wooden' approach

---

[1]*One Lord, One Spirit, One Body*, Peter Hocken, 1987, p. 99. Hocken's
argument is that since signs and experiences prove God to be the author of the
charismatic movement 'we have to seek out the mind of the Lord, if we are to
grasp the meaning and purpose of the movement' (p. 44). God's mind is given to
us in contemporary prophecy and Hocken directs us to give special attention to
the prophecy of Smith Wigglesworth to David du Plessis in 1936: 'There is a
revival coming that at present the world knows nothing about . . . When you see
what God does in this revival you will then have to admit that all that you have
seen previously is a mere nothing in comparison with what is to come. It will
eclipse anything that has been known in history' (*Streams of Renewal*, p. 19).
From Hocken's standpoint, submission 'to the Holy Spirit present in the
churches and their traditions' is clearly not to be identified with submission to
Scripture. 'Revelation in the Spirit,' he says, is 'one of the hallmarks of this
[charismatic] renewal' (*One Lord, One Spirit, One Body*, p. 89).
[2]*Catholic Pentecostalism*, 1977, pp. 145–46.

(as it was now called) of both Roman Catholics and Protestants to the Bible and to church history – could now be bypassed. Both Catholic and Protestant, it now came to be said, were in equal need of help. In the words of Michael Harper: 'Both of those major traditions run the risk of being "imprisoned" – either in historic forms and practices (the Catholics) or in doctrinal chains (the Protestants) . . . Both need to be liberated'. His standpoint, he confessed, was 'not the old rigid doctrinaire approach of the past, but the spirit of ecumenism'.[1] David Watson's approach seems to have been very similar. In Harper's view, 'David's ministry helped forward proper ecumenism more than perhaps anyone else's in Britain during that time'.[2]

We have noted earlier that when the charismatic movement began in the Church of England it was opposed by John Stott and by the party of evangelical Anglican leaders who organized the Keele Congress. Ten years later that opposition had disappeared and both sides came to see one another as partners in a common cause. *The Nottingham Statement* declared: 'We see a particular ecumenical significance in the charismatic movement, especially in its strong witness to the primacy of God . . . In various ways we are indebted to the charismatic movement in our own spiritual insights and priorities . . .'[3] The one thing which could have prevented such a truce, namely, a determination to withstand the doctrinal drift, was missing from both sides. In a decade when the general religious scene cried out for men who would oppose compromise and speak with no uncertain sound of the fundamental issues of Scripture, the majority of both charismatic and non-charismatic evangelical Anglicans were preoccupied with other concerns. Both were disinclined to make any doctrine a matter of division.

*   *   *

When major changes occur in the history of the church such as the

[1] *Heritage of Freedom*, Michael Harper with twelve other contributors, 1984, p. 96, and *Evangelical Times*, Sept 1974, p. 10.
[2] *David Watson, a portrait by his friends*, ed. Edward England, 1985, pp. 57–8.
[3] *The Nottingham Statement*, 1977, pp. 41–42. That the Fountain Trust under Harper (leading 'charismatic renewal' in the Church of England) always adopted the ecumenism of du Plessis is very clear. Mervyn Stockwood, Bishop of Southwark, and not known for his encouragement of biblical ministry among his clergy, was apparently an early supporter (*Streams of Renewal*, Hocken, p. 126). A Fountain Trust Conference at Guildford in 1971 included three Roman Catholic speakers.

doctrinal slide in England of the 1960's and 70's there are always major reasons. In ML-J's view two things principally explained why this occurred as it did.

First, it happened because of the degree to which the spirit and attitudes of the world had penetrated the church. It was no accident that evangelicalism began to favour openness and to repudiate 'exclusiveness' at the very period when the prevailing climate of opinion was against dogmatism in every field of knowledge: even science had lost its one-time near infallibility. The contemporary mood was against all absolutes. Almost all beliefs in society at large had become of only 'relative' value, none could be said to be definitely right or wrong. Religion was acceptable in terms of human experience, not in terms of any revelation from heaven. 'Experience', not truth, was now central. Describing the general situation as he saw it in 1971, Dr Lloyd-Jones said:

There is a very obvious reaction at the present time against intellectualism . . . This is found among the students in America, and increasingly in this country. Reason is being distrusted and set on one side. Following D. H. Lawrence many are saying that our troubles are due to the fact that we have over-developed our cerebrum. We must listen more to our 'blood' and go back to nature. And so turning against intellectualism, and deliberately espousing the creed of irrationality, they yield themselves to the desire for 'experience', and place sensation above understanding. What matters is feeling and enjoyment; not thought. Pure thought leads nowhere.[1]

Instead of seeing the danger, evangelicals accommodated themselves to the change as though it could serve the interests of their own cause. The popular culture was openly appealed to for justification of major change in the life and witness of the church. The old 'written culture', it was said, was dying. There had to be a new appeal to the eye and to the senses: 'It is surely the job of this generation of Evangelicals to recreate the dramatic and poetic means of passing on guidance in the spiritual, ethical and social life of man.'[2] The leading role in the introduction of this change was taken by David Watson of York who saw 'the potential for marvellous communication' in

[1]*The State of the Nation*, BEC Address, 1971, p. 16.
[2]*Evangelicals Today*, p. 101.

music, dance and drama. 'The reason why I travel with a team,' he later wrote, 'gifted as they are in the performing arts, is that they are able to communicate the Gospel much more effectively than I could with mere words.' He criticized 'much western Christianity' for concentrating 'almost exclusively upon the mind'. 'Most churches rely heavily on the spoken or written word for communication and then wonder why so few people find the Christian faith to be relevant.'[1]

There were many variations in this new emphasis. In the groups where tongues-speaking was prominent the anti-intellectual approach disarmed any criticism of the widespread use of 'language' which no one understood. Hocken represents a common view in regarding 'baptism with the Spirit' as of divine origin because its reception bypassed the mind: 'Not being first mediated through human understanding, it involves a directness of encounter with the living God'.[2]

This same influence not only switched attention from preaching to 'sharing', it came to justify a massive change in what was now considered warranted in the singing and music of services and evangelistic meetings. Worship was 'liberated'. It was plausibly proposed that sound, rhythm and the form of lyrics be brought closer to what was popular in the everyday world. The early development of this change drew some critical comment in the Christian press. 'Countryman' wrote of how the Filey Christian Convention in 1967 had become 'Swinging Filey', 'with a Sunday afternoon sacred concert; a fresh beat to the music and a drum-roll in the middle of "Praise my soul, the King of heaven".'[3] At the Evangelical Alliance Assembly meetings in London the following year, the platform was given one evening to the youth who presented the 'Why Generation'. Commenting on this event, Tim and Doreen Buckley, instructors in music at the London Bible College, wrote in *The Life of Faith* of the impression gained by friends who had attended: 'The programme was intended to show how to communicate in the '60's, but the decibels of sheer noise made it impossible to distinguish either the tune or the words of the first three items. If this is '68 communicat-

[1] David Watson, *I believe in the Church*, 1978, and *You Are My God*, 1983, where these themes are pursued at length. For ML-J's opposition to this see his address on 'Preaching' in *Puritans*, p. 373.
[2] *One Lord, One Spirit, One Body*, 1987, p. 44.
[3] *English Churchman*, October 13, 1967.

ing, our friends, who are not "squares", were not communicated to . . ."[1]

But criticisms such as these were few and far between and the 1970's saw changes in the content and conduct of public worship on a scale scarcely imaginable a few years earlier. ML-J traced this same change to the effect of a popular culture which wants 'sensation' and feeling and is against stress 'on the intellect and the understanding'. Speaking on one occasion of how this spirit 'militates very much against the kind of thing for which we stand in the Evangelical Library' he went on:

In this country the form which it takes, perhaps most of all, is what is known as the charismatic movement . . . The emphasis is upon experience and feeling, and a type of service with much singing, but not the singing of the kind of hymns that are to be found in the Evangelical Library, nor the hymns written by the men whose biographies are in the Evangelical Library! They have their own hymns and choruses . . .[2]

Making a similar point about the way in which Christians were being influenced by the spirit of the world, he said at another Library meeting:

The days in which we live are characteristic of superficiality, the cry is for entertainment and endless meetings, music, drama, dancing, etc., but a solid life and witness cannot be built up that way.[3]

Few voices were to be heard in support of ML-J's contention that the drift within evangelicalism was following the mood of the age but two testimonies from a few years later are worthy of note. In the opinion of Francis Schaeffer: 'A significant section of what is called evangelicalism has allowed itself to be infiltrated by the general world view or viewpoint of our day.'[4] What he called 'The Great Evangelical Disaster' was the acceptance of the mentality of

[1]The same writers urged readers to obtain the WR for October 1968 which contained ML-J's sermon, 'Melody and Harmony' on Ephesians 5:19 (preached in 1959); it 'leaves one in no doubt as to where this preacher stands as regards modern trends in music'.
[2]The Evangelical Library Bulletin, Spring 1978, pp. 9–10.
[3]Ibid, Spring 1975, p. 6.
[4]The Great Evangelical Disaster, 1984, p. 51.

accommodation: 'in the most basic sense, the evangelical establishment has become deeply worldly'.[1]

A second testimony comes from a less expected source. Dr Carl Henry was Editor of *Christianity Today* and a leading figure in the Billy Graham organization during the period when that organization was commonly regarded as the epitome of the new evangelical strength. ML-J, as we have seen, spoke alone in that period when he expressed to fellow ministers his conviction that the Graham programme was actually weakening historic evangelicalism. Carl Henry's book *Confessions of a Theologian* is a revealing book in this connexion. Henry saw the image building and the concern for influence with non-evangelicals at close quarters and came at last to the conclusion that 'the evangelical movement looks stronger than in fact it is'.[2] 'While evangelicals seek to penetrate the culture, the culture simultaneously makes disconcerting inroads into evangelical life.'[3] The truth, as he wrote in 1986, was that evangelicalism was no longer definite about its own message:

> The term evangelical during the past fifteen years has become ambiguous through deliberate distortion by critics and needless confusion invited by some of the movement's own leaders ... Many evangelicals now measure growth mainly in terms of numbers; distinctions of doctrine and practice are subordinated in a broad welcome for charismatic, Catholic, traditional and other varieties of evangelicals. Theological differences are minimized by evangelical publishers and publications reaching for mass circulation, by evangelists luring capacity audiences and even by evangelism festivals seeking the largest possible involvement. Church growth seminars have even embraced 'miracle-growth' churches that claim to raise the dead and to reproduce all other apostolic gifts. Numerical bigness has become an infectious epidemic.[4]

This brings us to Dr Lloyd-Jones' second reason for the drift in evangelicalism. The compromise with worldly standards of thought had occurred because of the basic spiritual weakness within the evangelical churches themselves. In other words, it was ultimately

[1] *Ibid*, p. 142. 'What is the use,' he asks, 'of evangelicalism seeming to get larger and larger if sufficient numbers of those under the name evangelical no longer hold to that which makes evangelicalism evangelical?'
[2] *Confessions of a Theologian*, 1986, p. 390.
[3] *Ibid*, p. 388. See also Marsden, *Reforming Fundamentalism*, p. 275.
[4] *Confessions of a Theologian*, p. 387.

the old problem upon which we have heard him speak repeatedly in these pages. 'Evangelism' and 'influence' had become ends in themselves instead of being seen as the results of the church being true to her calling: the acceptance of expediency and compromise could only mean that prayer, confidence in Scripture and dependence upon the power of the Holy Spirit were no longer the great priorities. Evangelicals had ceased to say 'that, if we are faithful, the Holy Spirit has promised to honour us and our testimony, however small our numbers and however despised by "the wise and prudent"'.[1]

Carl Henry's book gives indisputable evidence on this point. It confirms that the overall policy of the Graham organization (closely parallel to the policy taken up by Anglican evangelicals at Keele) was to attain 'prestige' and influence for evangelicals.[2] To do this there had to be a successful image and that would not be possible, it was believed, unless every effort was made to avoid a division with those who did not believe the Bible. Henry speaks of the church's credibility being 'compromised by an evaporation of discipline' and regrets that Graham did not call evangelicals to 'a long, hard look at their need of more comprehensive unity and at the neglected issue of evangelical ecclesiology'. But Graham could not do this because it 'would have seriously complicated relationships of his crusades to ecumenically oriented churches, since he exacted their endorsement as the price of city-wide meetings'.[3] The Graham organization, for precisely the same reason as the Anglican evangelicals, was unready to 'forfeit dialogue with the ecumenical leaders and churches'.[4] It feared a loss of influence. So it also said one thing and did another. The Berlin Congress of 1966, says Henry, 'exposed the speculative philosophy that underlay pluralistic ecumenism' but, simultaneously, the Graham Crusades were *committed* to such ecumenism. The direction was set long before the American Festival on Evangelism of 1981, where the participants, writes Henry, included everyone from 'partisans of traditional papal Catholicism' and '150

[1]*Puritans*, p. 147.
[2]In the years when 'the new evangelicalism' was first being heard, Edward Carnell of Fuller Seminary wrote to Henry: 'I want to command the attention of Tillich and Bennett; then I shall be in a better place to be of service to the evangelicals. We need prestige desperately.' Marsden's book, *op. cit.*, details the effects which this priority came to have in the history of Fuller Seminary, where Dr Graham was a prominent member of the board of trustees.
[3]*Confessions of a Theologian*, p. 384.
[4]*Ibid*, p. 293.

Protestant denominations' to 'charismatics and establishment conservatives'. In a major understatement, he concludes, the Festival 'did little to clarify the identity of evangelicalism'.[1]

I have given this space to the general scene in the 1970's because without this background there can be no understanding of ML-J's own ministry in the last decade of his life. The way in which he addressed himself to these conditions will be the subject of the next chapter.

[1] *Ibid*, p. 351.

REJOICE IN THE LORD ALWAYS AND AGAIN I SAY REJOICE

The Christian is meant to be a rejoicing person
The repetition here. What is stated everywhere in the New Testament. It is a command. Not miserable or carrying a great burden.
All Christians are meant to rejoice
Not some. Not temperament. Not works or mystics.
The nature of the rejoicing
Not outward. Not forced. Not psychological. Not bright and breezy. Not in ourselves or what we are. Not in what we do or our gifts (Luke 10:20, 1 Cor. 1:30).
Inward and true.
'Always' – whatever the circumstances and whatever our mood, state or condition.
Paul and Silas (Acts 16:25). 'Rejoicing in tribulation'.
Only explanation is that it is 'in the Lord'
My status in Him – can never be changed.
Rejoice in Him – in spite of me or what I may do (Rom. 8:1)
Rejoice in Him – in spite of what may be happening to me (Rom. 5:3)
Rejoice in Him – in spite of what I may feel ('I dare not trust the sweetest frame, But wholly lean on Jesus' Name').
My knowledge that He will keep me.
My knowledge of the glory that He is preparing for me (John 14:1).
The way to be like this
Meditate on these things.
Baptism of the Spirit.
Why we should obey the command
1. Our own happiness.
2. Our witness and testimony – early Christians, Wesley and the Moravians.

ML-J

Skeleton sermon notes jotted down in the late 1970's (until 1978 ML-J continued regularly to draft new sermons in this way).

32

'Rejoice in the Lord Always'

From the background of the general trend in evangelicalism in the 1970's we now turn to the priorities which claimed Dr Lloyd-Jones' own attention at this same period. Amidst the increasing confusion his own policy was clear. There is one general characteristic of his work in these years which must first be mentioned. In terms of its sheer amount there was no reduction noticeable until after 1976, yet its scope was deliberately narrowed. He ceased to move in all the wider circles as he had once done. This was, in part, a consequence of the controversies of the 1960's but, more especially, it was the result of his own choice. His assessment of the situation no longer led him to look for a broad influence. Instead he aimed to concentrate on the strengthening of those churches and agencies which shared some common commitment in the existing conflict. He was not turning his back upon others, rather he was convinced that the way for the whole situation ultimately to be improved was for a minority to stand fast and, in so doing, to prepare the way to brighter days. By the grace of God, 'the remnant' principle of Judges chapter 7 would be vindicated again.

It was in this conviction that ML-J had willingly accepted the possibility of reduced numbers after both the Westminster Fellowship and the Puritan Conference had been reconstituted. I believe he also had the same thing in view when, after 1971, he concentrated all his new publications in the United Kingdom into the hands of the Banner of Truth Trust. The distribution of that publishing house might not be as broad as some of the better known religious publishers, but he had the assurance that its testimony would not add to the existing confusion by the publication of all kinds of views and opinions. When the Trust moved its headquarters to Edinburgh in 1972 he was one of the first to visit the new premises and wrote on the first page of the Visitors' Book:

D M Lloyd-Jones, London, on the occasion of the commemoration of the 4th Centenary of the death of the great John Knox. God bless this house and premises and use them to propagate the Truth for which John Knox stood and fought and prevailed. November 14th, 1972.

For the same reason as he was attached to the Banner of Truth Trust, the Evangelical Library continued to have his regular attention and wholehearted support. It is remarkable how many of the original team which had carried on the work since the 1940's were still active at the beginning of the 1970's. Geoffrey Williams, in his Librarian's Report for 1971, could speak of himself as feeling 'fitter at 85 than when I was 18'. Nor was he the oldest. Mr W. Gurden, in his nineties, remained 'a most energetic and valued helper of the Library', especially in the packing and despatch of books! But a few years were to see a great change. In 1971 Marjorie Denby, at 81, had to give up after more than a quarter-of-a-century as Mr Williams' secretary. It was a role in which she 'usually worked six days a week'.[1] Her successor, Mrs M. Urwin, was another esteemed Christian from Westminster Chapel who had already been helping since 1953. She also had to retire in 1975. Geoffrey Williams, assisted by a colleague, soldiered on until 1974 and in April of the following year a small band of us assembled for his funeral at the old parish church of Fishbourn, near Chichester, where ML-J took the service. We all felt the passing of one to whom we owed so much. Speaking of their friendship, ML-J was to say:

I look back with great joy over the many years of our fellowship and co-operation in this work. In recent years I have missed his frequent telephone calls, which occasionally came at a not too convenient moment. They generally had reference to news about some treasured volumes for sale which he felt we should purchase, or they were requests for my opinion on certain books or persons. Whatever my immediate reaction to such calls, when I was perhaps struggling with some difficult text on which I proposed to preach, I was always so impressed by his keenness and enthusiasm that he was soon forgiven. His lively interest continued unabated almost to the end to the amazement of all of us who knew him.[2]

[1] *The Evangelical Library Bulletin*, Spring 1972, p. 6. Marjorie Denby died on August 8, 1974 and there is a tribute to her in the *Bulletin* of Winter, 1974.
[2] 'Tribute to Mr Geoffrey Williams', *The Evangelical Library Bulletin*, Autumn 1975. See also ML-J's Closing Address in the *Bulletin* for Spring 1975.

In the main work of the Inter-Varsity Fellowship, which, in 1975, became the Universities and Colleges Christian Fellowship (UCCF), ML-J's influence had decreased by the 1970's. A new generation of evangelical students were on the scene who scarcely knew him and could not imagine the force he had long been among their predecessors.[1] The truth was that his stand on ecumenism in the 1960's had received a mixed reception from the senior advisers of the Fellowship. Though ML-J offered no public criticism of those in the Fellowship who took a different view on the ecumenical issue, he spoke of the inconsistency of older men 'fraternizing with those who deny the Gospel' while supporting a student movement which disallowed that practice for the younger age group. His 1969 IVF Conference address, already referred to above, was never published and one can only think that the brake on publication may have been the same as that which had operated in the case of that at the London Bible College of 1958. There were some within the IVF, and especially among those professionally involved in university theology, who clearly believed that a 'scholarly', non-partisan approach to that subject could win the influence which an earlier generation had failed to achieve. For those of that outlook ML-J was negative and pessimistic.

While ML-J still gave valued counsel to Dr Oliver Barclay, the General Secretary of the IVF and UCCF from 1964 to 1980, his most significant influence was in the medical side of the work, in the Christian Medical Fellowship. Here the long-standing association with Douglas Johnson still obtained, for though DJ had laid down the General Secretaryship of the IVF in 1964, he was still very active in CMF. It was the CMF which remained least affected by the incipient doctrinal weakening now present in some other parts of the student work. Four of the addresses in ML-J's book *Healing and Medicine* were given under the auspices of the CMF in the 1970's and others, unrecorded, were given in the same period – the last at a Study Group Dinner on November 23, 1978.

In passing, it should be said that Dr Lloyd-Jones' addresses to medicals in the 1970's show the extent to which he remained abreast of current thought in the medical world. The books to which he referred were not those written ten or fifteen years earlier. He was

[1]This was particularly so among Anglican students, one of whom, hearing ML-J at the Oxford Christian Union in the 1970's, commented to his grandson, 'Christopher, your grandfather wasn't at all bad!'.

particularly interested in the greater attention being given to the
'psychosomatic', and to the whole complex relationship between
body and spirit and the influence of the latter upon the former. He
welcomed the new considerations on health and disease which were
gaining currency and replacing the former neglect of the psychic
aspect. 'We have been too materialistic and mechanistic in our
outlook,' he said to fellow doctors in 1971. 'The changed outlook in
medicine in this respect is really quite astounding.' Such discoveries
as the DNA and RNA were giving rise to a new humility in scientific
circles, 'there is so much more in the cosmos than the scientist
dogmatically assumed in the past'.[1]

ML-J considered that this change had an important bearing on two
subjects much debated among evangelicals in the 1970's, miraculous
healing and demonic influence. On the question of healing his own
views underwent no major change. 'God's customary way of dealing
with disease is through means and methods – through the therapeutic
abilities He has given to men and the drugs that He has put in such
profusion in nature.'[2] That it was always God's will to heal, or that
physical healing was provided for in the atonement and intended to be
a regular part of the church's ministry, he emphatically denied. But
this was not all. He did believe in miraculous healing as a sovereign
action of God.[3] He also came to consider that the area of the effect of
the spirit upon the body was a much larger one than had been generally
recognized by evangelicals. (He was, in that connection, sympathetic
with the view that cancer may not be simply a local disease but a
general condition in a person brought on, perhaps, by shock,
disappointment or something mentally or emotionally traumatic).

While his addresses from the 1970's show his concern for balance
on this subject, with warnings against being swayed merely by
apparent phenomena, they also underline his fear of the attitude
which would dogmatically exclude any expectation of the power of
God to be demonstrated in healing.

With regard to the second subject, demonic influence, ML-J also
thought that much current evangelical thought needed serious
revision. Demonic activity is not to be confined to the New
Testament era, and for medicals to attempt to treat the demonic
influence by ordinary means was a disastrous mistake. Speaking to

[1] See *The Supernatural in Medicine*, CMF, 1971, pp. 9–14.
[2] *Healing and Medicine*, p. 106.
[3] *Ibid*, pp. 105–6. Further on this subject see Appendix 2 below.

Christian doctors in 1971 he says, 'We have underestimated tragically, as evangelicals, the power of evil spirits'.[1] Demonic activity, he believed, was on the increase in Britain, a fact to be expected on account of the general decline in godliness. The growth of drug addiction was not unrelated: 'Drug taking knocks out the higher centres of control and the ability to discriminate, and leaves the victims a prey to the influence of the evil forces round about us.'[2]

There were several instances at this period of cases where ML-J was used to deliver fellow ministers from the unrecognized symptoms of satanic attacks, one of which we shall mention. At the opening of Emmanuel Chapel, a new building for the congregation of the Rev. Graham Harrison at Newport, South Wales, in November 1977, ML-J was sharing the services with the Rev. Vernon Higham of Cardiff. The former had preached on the Saturday afternoon and Higham was due to preach in the evening. For several years the Cardiff minister had suffered from an asthmatic condition, sometimes so acute that it had almost resulted in his death. During the tea interval before the evening service this complaint was so evident that it appeared very doubtful if the sufferer could preach as planned. In the vestry ML-J prayed for his friend, not specifically for 'healing' but for his whole life and ministry. There and then the trouble disappeared.

✻   ✻   ✻

We turn now to the area which received the greatest amount of his time and concern in these latter years, namely, the encouragement and guidance of ministers whose witness would continue when he was gone. Without the care of a particular congregation, he was now more than ever the helper of others. He was constantly available to men individually to give advice by interview, phone or letter and allowed nothing to interfere with his chairmanship of such meetings as the monthly Westminster Fellowship and the annual (and occasional day) Ministers' Conferences of the Evangelical Movement of Wales. One of his greatest desires in this connection remained the longing to see these men more closely bound together in a unity of churches. The difficulties in the way of that wider unity were immense. Evangelical thought had been conditioned for so long

[1] *The Supernatural in Medicine*, p. 23.
[2] *Healing and Medicine*, p. 156.

both by existing denominational affiliations and by the 'spiritual unity' emphasis which left so much control to the non-church organizations and societies. Given the breakdown of the denominations, with their incapacity to exercise any discipline, and the disarray of the evangelical organizations, 'the problem ahead,' as he said in the Westminster Fraternal on April 5, 1971, was 'how there should be control without denominationalism'. This difficulty was increased by the failure of the superficial optimism with which many had greeted the work of the British Evangelical Council. Before the end of the 1960's doubts were surfacing among BEC supporters and there were signs – later to be fulfilled – that a number of participating churches were going to revert to giving their main interest to their own more restricted groupings. The *English Churchman*, hitherto sympathetic, in its issue of November 7, 1969, wrote: 'The BEC is not a Church body, and apart from the closer fellowship there appear to be very few, if any, signs of brethren in the evangelical nonconformist denominations working towards visible church unity at the local level.' But ML-J never slackened in urging the larger need though in private he often mourned the lack of 'big men' with the vision to see it.

He often returned to the subject of unity at ministerial gatherings and warned that though great difficulties were inevitable at this 'turning-point in history' they had to be addressed. To do nothing, or to begin to treat the hope of any greater unity as impossible, was to fail to grasp the nature of the situation. He wanted a minimum of organization between churches yet enough to ensure co-operation and the maintenance of discipline over fundamentals. Evangelicals had too long acted as individualists – at their personal whims starting new movements, new publications and new conferences – with no attempt to act in a church way:

People have set themselves up and almost become movements in themselves. Evangelicals have done this. Wealthy men even set up churches . . . There is sheer indiscipline. Perhaps most serious of all, these movements have got into a controlling position over the local church. At the end of the 1930's and in the 1940's the IVF was controlling the doctrine of the evangelical churches.

Recently other movements have been becoming more aggressive . . . We have to work out the implications of all this. It was only part of our idea to separate ourselves from ecumenism. I am not sure that we are clear about this, and our people are not. Facing it will lead to a tremendous upheaval. I am not sure you can persuade your people to face this without some great movement of the Spirit. All this work done by movements should be done under the church or under a fellowship of churches. I do not mean the FIEC. I mean something more like the BEC. There needs to be control which is church based but not a 'denomination'. The church must sanction everything which happens. Student work should be under the church . . .

Can we modify the position in our evangelical churches or does the implementation of our principles necessitate a fresh start? I say this with fear and trembling. We are already small in numbers and will be smaller if these things are implemented.[1]

It was a sorrow to him that the BEC seemed to lack leaders to rise to the challenge of a movement towards a greater unity and initial hopes receded.[2] He continued to give major help to the BEC and yet, by declining to attend and speak at every annual conference, he deliberately stepped back from the leading role which some had wanted him to take. For the annual BEC two-day Conference in the 1970's he spoke in 1970, 1971, 1973, 1977 and 1979.[3]

But if ML-J did not believe he was called to lead in what had to be a new era ahead he constantly sought to lay down principles which would be of service to others at a later day. I will list five of these:

First was the importance of taking a whole view, in every situation the main thing should always be put before details. He warned of the danger that a multiplicity of subjects and problems could distract from the great issue of the gospel itself. Above all else, the nature of evangelical Christianity must be kept at the centre of attention. With some variations in content, he spoke repeatedly on 'What is an Evangelical?' and his three addresses on that subject at the IFES Conference of 1971 at Schloss Mittersill in Austria are probably the most

[1]The Westminster Fellowship, April 5, 1971.
[2]The reasons for this go beyond the scope of this biography. They must include the fact that the member churches from Scotland and Ireland were not well placed to understand the crucial church problems in *England* and that the principal English influence in the BEC, the FIEC, was unready to see their structure merged into something larger. 'The hopes for a much larger type of FIEC under the BEC umbrella are passing,' noted the Council of the FIEC in 1976, and they went on to express the belief that, as far as England was concerned, 'the future of evangelical unity at this time still remains with the FIEC and we see no reason whatsoever to remove ourselves from that position' (reported in the *Evangelical Times*, June 1976). See also the words of the Rev. David Mingard, for 25 years the General Secretary of the FIEC, in 'The Man in the Hot Seat', *Fellowship*, the magazine of the FIEC, May/June 1988).
[3]Illness prevented him speaking in 1976.

important of all those which he gave in the 1970's.[1] Evangelicalism, he never tired of arguing, is not one of several possible interpretations of the Christian faith: it is the essence of the only message of salvation which God has given to men. To the point of how largely this governed his own practice in the 1970's we shall return later.

*   *   *

Second, the negative should never be allowed to displace the positive. This principle implies no criticism of the negative. As we know, he believed that much of the existing confusion had arisen because ministers had declined to be forthright in opposing the wrong and the erroneous. But it is possible for the negative and the denunciatory to begin to take the chief place in a man's thinking and message, and when that happens the result is never profitable.

ML-J's concern over this can be well illustrated from an event in 1970. Tension was high at that time between evangelicals within the main denominations condoning participation in the ecumenical movement and those, led largely by ML-J, who took the opposing view. The division was apparent for all to see in the autumn of 1970 when both the BEC and the Evangelical Alliance separately commemorated the 350th anniversary of the sailing of 'The Mayflower'. Lloyd-Jones and Charles J. Woodbridge spoke at a meeting at Westminster Chapel in October and Billy Graham spoke for the Evangelical Alliance at the Royal Albert Hall in November.[2] The Westminster Fraternal met earlier on the same day as the Westminster Chapel commemoration of the Pilgrim Fathers. The morning session proved to be an extraordinary meeting and it underlined something very basic in ML-J's approach to the subject we are now discussing.

Dr Woodbridge, the speaker at the morning session of this Fraternal, was a stranger from the United States and his subject was 'the new evangelicalism'. The subject was not a new one, for Marcellus Kik had already spoken on the beginnings of that movement in the States when visiting the Fraternal some years earlier. What was new was the force and the seeming belligerence with which our guest delivered his address. He cared not, he told us

---

[1]This was the last occasion when he was outside the UK.
[2]Dr Graham, said the *Evangelical Times* report (December 1970), gave 'a fine challenge to the ills of our modern world . . . He stressed that the pilgrims were committed to great principles, but gave no hint as to what these principles were.'

bluntly at the outset, whom he might offend. No less than five different parties, he confided, had advised him what he should or should not say to us, but of all such advice he meant to take not the slightest notice. The 'new evangelicalism' was 'a shift against militancy'. With such a shift, he meant us to understand, he had not a shred of sympathy. He did not come to us, or to anyone else, looking for acceptance. His position was, 'Whatsoever the Lord saith unto me that will I speak.'

While there was something refreshing about this boldness, there was an element in it which many knew that ML-J would never allow to pass without comment, and when this veteran Boanerges at length concluded all interest fastened on how the Doctor intended to cope with such a situation. Woodbridge was both a guest and a minister ordained as far back as 1927. He had never met ML-J before and seemed to have some doubts over where he stood with regard to the new evangelicalism.

When Dr Lloyd-Jones rose from his chair to speak, directing his words primarily to the visitor, he said:

One is always ready for the unexpected. I knew what you would say but not how . . . You and I have arrived at the same position in different ways. On the general position we are agreed. The difference between us concerns *how* we bring men to that position.

ML-J went on to illustrate what he meant by reference to Paul's method of approaching men as outlined by the apostle in 1 Corinthians 9:19–22. If men are to be gained for the truth then the manner in which we seek to influence them must be controlled by wisdom. We should not, therefore, adopt the same approach for every situation. 'I would have thought it bad teaching,' he said, 'to speak as though this country was the same as America. I say that in love. Some men are antagonized rather than attracted . . . I do not disagree with what is said but with the presentation. We rejoice in God's servant and in his clear understanding . . . I also was ordained forty-three years ago. I, like you, am a foreigner in this country [England]. One of the greatest struggles of my life has been to realize the different character of nations. We need to pay attention to this in order that the message may have the maximum effect.'

At this point the visiting speaker rose to his feet and, interrupting him, addressed his audience:

You men do some thinking, be honest! If I have antagonized you I want
you to let me know – tell me – raise your hand if I antagonized you.

British reserve and the surprise of seeing the chairman thus
challenged combined to produce a shocked silence. The whole
assembly was speechless. Then, as though to ease the tension,
someone began to say, 'No one was antagonized . . .', but ML-J was
not pleased with this help from the floor. He waved the would-be
helper to be silent and resumed speaking himself:

No, there is no question of anyone being antagonized. We are all
concerned about the same thing. All I am contending for . . .

At that point my attempt to continue note-taking had to give way
to the desire to watch what was happening! I do not doubt that what
he went on to say was that we must be wise in seeking an objective,
and wise in the presentation of our case.

The most remarkable thing of all on this memorable day was the
transformation in Charles Woodbridge when he reappeared after a
lunch-time period spent with ML-J. The latter had clearly succeeded
where five earlier 'advisers' had patently failed. Our guest was now
so pacified and good-humoured as he answered questions in the
afternoon discussions that it required some effort to believe that this
was the same man. ML-J's combination of winsomeness *and* strong
conviction had thoroughly disarmed him.

In retrospect this incident has an amusing aspect to it but it was not
so at the time. Had the speaker been younger, and one of ourselves,
ML-J would have corrected him a good deal more strongly at the
morning session. He obviously believed that the visitor had too much
relish for controversy and was too little aware of the danger of a hard
spirit. If negative statements have to be delivered, boldness is not the
only prerequisite, there has also to be tenderness and compassion. If
we have true concern for those who may differ from us, or even
oppose us, he would urge, then we will never stop at the negative.
The atmosphere of controversy is a dangerous one. Those who 'contend for the faith', he would say, must *also* be much in prayer in the
Holy Ghost and they must keep themselves 'in the love of God'
(Jude 21). Zeal for God and His glory has to include love for people
as well as love of the truth.

Illustrations of this same principle can be seen in many of ML-J's addresses, one of the notable examples being in his BEC address of November 9, 1977. By that date many of the downward steps by evangelicals listed in the last chapter had taken place and this led him to speak more openly than he had ever done before on what he saw as the failure of the Anglican evangelical leadership. Announcing as his theme the text, 'Let the saints be joyful in glory: let them sing aloud upon their beds. Let the high praises of God be in their mouth, and a twoedged sword in their hand' (Psalm 149:5–6), he took the two duties there commanded, 'singing and fighting'. 'I am compelled,' he said, 'to start with a sword and to remind you that we are in a fight.' This was not new, he went on. There had long been the necessity for contention with liberalism and unbelief in the churches as all evangelicals had once recognized:

Until about ten years ago we were engaged in this fight alongside other evangelicals in the mixed denominations. But now the situation has taken a very sad and a very tragic turn and this is something I deeply regret to have to say. Whatever you may think of me I am not a natural fighter, I am a man of peace. My greatest defect is that I am too patient with people, so I would much prefer not to be saying this kind of thing. But we are here to face facts because the times are evil, the circumstances are desperate. When I spoke in 1966 I was aware of certain trends and of certain tendencies, but in my wildest moments I never imagined that things would take place which have actually come to pass during these past ten years – almost incredible.

He went on to mention several things contributing to the current failure of evangelicalism to enter into combat with error, the chief of which, he had no doubt, was the 'definite shift in the whole position of Anglican evangelicalism'. This he demonstrated at length from the series of proofs which we have given above and then he anticipated the question:

Someone may say to me, Are not these Anglican Evangelicals still preaching the gospel? The answer is that they are, of course they are, but it seems to me that it is entirely nullified and negatived by the fact that in this Commission on Christian Doctrine, and in other places, they are acknowledging that the liberal, modernist – almost infidel – attitude to Scripture is a possible point of view. So what they say on the one hand is negatived by what they say on the other hand . . . If they say that they are ready to co-operate with the Roman Catholics, and their view of salvation, they are denying what they are uttering on one hand with their mouths, so the gospel is being compromised.

We are fighting a battle for the Church, a true conception of the Christian Church. We are not interested in positions and power; we are not prepared to recognize all who 'call' themselves as 'being' Christians. This is what these people are doing. They assume that if a man says I am a Christian and he belongs to a church, it does not matter what he believes, it does not matter what he denies, if he regards himself as a Christian then they regard him as a Christian. They say that it is wrong to say that any man is not a Christian if he says he is a Christian, irrespective of his belief.

It was only as he reached the second half of this address – the last polemical address, I believe, which he ever gave – that we were conscious of why he had reversed the order in which 'singing' and 'fighting' appeared in his text. Instinctively he wanted to deal with the positive last so that he could leave the privilege of singing 'the high praises of God' uppermost in the attention of all his hearers. The earlier and more negative part of his address cost him much to deliver. He would gladly have finished with all controversy long before he had reached the age of seventy-seven had the choice been left to him. The truth of what he had to say in his review of evangelicalism's disastrous failure in battle distressed him personally. Sorrow there was and had to be, yet, on his old principle of preaching to others what he had first preached to himself, he would not stop there.

We are fighters, yes, but we should not be depressed. Christian people! if we give the impression we are miserable, that we are mournful, that we are just negative critics, then we do not deserve to be noticed . . . Of course, we are persecuted, but you remember the words of our Lord: 'Blessed are ye when men shall revile you, and persecute you, and say all manner of evil against you falsely, for my sake. Rejoice,' he says, 'and be exceeding glad: for great is your reward in heaven.' We are blessed and we should be exceeding glad. What was the condition of the early church? How small they were in number, with everything against them and utterly insignificant. But we are told: 'They . . . did eat their meat with gladness and singleness of heart, Praising God' (Acts 2:46–47). And you remember even when they were threatened with extinction, when the apostles had almost been put to death, we are told, 'They departed from the presence of the council, rejoicing that they were counted worthy to suffer shame for his name' (Acts 5:41). Of Paul and Silas in the prison – arrested, backs scourged, beaten, feet fast in the stocks, everything against them – I read: 'And at midnight Paul and Silas prayed and sang praises unto God' (Acts 16:25). Are we doing this? Are we giving people the impression that because we have the truth of God, and take it as it is, that we are a rejoicing people? That is the way to attract people and it is something which we are commanded to do.

This is the greatest challenge that comes to us. We are standing for the truth, we are fighting for the truth, but are we rejoicing? Are we such people as these early Christians were that make people long to have what we have got? If we really believe what we read we must praise Him. We are not here to defend Him but to praise Him and to show that we have a knowledge of Him and not merely a knowledge 'about' Him. We are to praise Him, and His high praises should be on our lips because of what He has done in His Son. We must praise Him for whatever may be happening to us. We do not wait for a mood or a state, we do not wait for results; we praise Him for what He has done, and for the wonderful works of God. What are we? We are sons of God! We are the children of the living God! And the exhortation that comes to us is this,

> Children of the heavenly King
> As ye journey sweetly sing . . .

* * *

A third principle upon which ML-J acted at this period has already appeared in these pages and, as with the other principles we are here listing, it had long governed his practice: the possibility of the extraordinary work of God in revival should never lead us to neglect the truth that the Holy Spirit is always present to grant us sufficient aid for the performance of every duty. Christians are not responsible for the extraordinary but they are responsible for their personal obedience and for such reformation of the church as is required by the Word of God. Faith in the possibility of revival in the future, if it is true faith, will never lead to passivity in the present. In the 1960's he had criticized those who seemed to put all their emphasis upon reformation and very little on prayer for the outpouring of the Spirit. In the 1970's there was danger from another direction – from the hope some seemed to entertain of receiving experiences from heaven as an alternative to action which God requires of us.

This point came into one of his BEC conference addresses when his subject was Elijah's 'repairing of the altar of the Lord that was broken down' and the consequent giving of fire from heaven (1 Kings 18:30–40). Christians, as Elijah, must be ready to fight, to work and to pray: the altar must be repaired; truth must be restored. Such is the call to reformation and for these things we are responsible. But the fire of God must also be given! As a decade earlier he had criticized those who seemed to think that *their* work of reformation could restore the church, now there was criticism for some who thought '"Nothing matters except the fire – all we need is experience!" – no repairing of the altar, no trouble over false prophets – no insistence on the absolute necessity of the Word of God'.[1]

Both emphases, ML-J believed, were essential. To think of reformation alone leads to self-dependence; to look to revival alone, while failing to do what God commands, means unbelief, mysticism and spiritual paralysis. What has historically been known as 'illuminism' (the danger which comes to those whose temptation is to exclude everything but direct communication with God) was again on the scene in the 1970's and recognized by ML-J. In his copy of *Catholic Pentecostalism* by René Laurentin he has heavily pencil-marked the following words and written in a cryptic marginal note the name 'Evan Roberts':

Illuminism is characterized by a penchant for passivity, for the non-activity of the soul in the approach to God. It relies excessively on direct interventions of the Holy Spirit and tends to let man be moved rather than to have him freely direct his action by a mind under the influence of faith and its teaching.[2]

After ML-J's 1977 BEC Address from Psalm 149, from which we have already quoted, he mentioned to me that he had deliberately made no reference to revival because there was need to emphasize the duty that we are to 'rejoice in the Lord *always*'. The hope of revival was never to be seen as an alternative to present duty. This same subject also came up in an interview with his friend, Elwyn Davies which was published in *The Evangelical Magazine of Wales* (April/

[1] BEC Annual Conference, October 17, 1973.
[2] Laurentin, *op. cit.*, p. 134. Evan Roberts was a passionate but erratic leader in the 1904 revival in Wales. Sometimes people would travel long distances to hear him preach only to be disappointed by the news that 'the Spirit' had not given him any message or that 'the Spirit' forbade him.

May 1975). Was it true, asked Mr Davies, that he was disappointed in seeing no powerful revival in these years? ML-J replied:

I wonder whether the word 'disappointed' is the right word here. I *lament* the fact. And of course my great desire, not only during the last 25 years but also during the previous quarter century, was to see a great and powerful revival. I never suspected I was destined to remain for 40 years in the wilderness. I was confident that we would have seen a great revival before now. To that extent, perhaps, one can speak of disappointment. But in this world one learns to realize that we are entirely in the hands of God, and that we must be content with this, and acknowledge that revival in the last resort is a matter for His sovereign will.

Despite the general barrenness, the interviewer went on to ask, had not some things of real importance been happening which might prove to be preparatory to revival? Dr Lloyd-Jones agreed:

I would be prepared to say on the whole, judging by history, that reformation comes before an awakening or a revival. It need not be so, but I think that this is what we see quite clearly in the history of the Church over the centuries . . .
    It is important not to despise 'the day of small things'. A number of things have taken place. I believe that we can claim that a reformation, in the sense of gaining a clearer grasp of the great doctrines, *has* and *is* taking place. And if this is a preliminary to revival, well then, this time has not been lost. Now I think that the 1904–5 revival sheds some light on this. What was deficient in that revival – there is no doubt about it – was the fact that there was such a wide gap between the revival itself and the belief of the churches. You must have a basis on which to build. You must have something which is going to take hold of this great power in order to safeguard it and keep it for the future. Therefore, I would say that in these last years there has been a preparation and that it is going on at present . . .

*   *   *

A fourth principle has again often appeared in these pages. It has to do with the need for balance, moderation and self-examination in all matters of controversy. In the confused situation of the 1960's and 1970's the potential for increasing controversy abounded and ML-J constantly urged the need for care and discriminating distinctions. The two extremes of 'unrestrained laxity' and 'egotistical rigour' have both to be avoided. Error has to be distinguished from heresy and mistaken belief from false teaching. Professing Christians who *condone* serious error are not to be treated as those who only *suffer* it and who work for its removal in their denomination.

Distinctions of this kind certainly entered into ML-J's own assessments. He broke off all public co-operation with the Anglican evangelicals who, by their deliberate practice, accepted the Christian standing of fellow denominationalists whose beliefs might be fundamentally at variance with biblical and Protestant Christianity. His criticism of the policy followed by the Congresses at Keele and Nottingham was very definite and outspoken. But this was no blanket condemnation of all Anglican evangelicals. On the contrary, a number remained his close friends and he had no hesitation in speaking for them when he was invited. He could say in his BEC Conference address of 1977:

There are many good honest men in the Church of England who are filled with grief and with sorrow. They have expressed their disagreement, they have expressed their fears and I, for one, not only know a number of them, I am praying for them because they are men who want to serve God in a true and in a right way.

The contrast between his attitude to evangelicals engaged in ecumenism and his attitude towards those of Pentecostal or charismatic views is also significant. From 1964 he would occasionally meet with or speak for pastors of the older Pentecostal position who were as averse as he was to the movement towards doctrinal laxity. He was ready, in the interests of the wider unity of those holding to supernatural Christianity, to make no issue over points at which he personally considered these brethren to be confused. It would have been alien to his whole attitude to have attacked Pentecostal churches. With respect to the charismatic movement there was some difference for, as we have seen, he could speak strongly on the general tendency of that movement and he would not accept invitations to charismatic gatherings. Yet there was also a moderation here which puzzled some observers and the explanation lay in his assessment of the factors which had given the charismatic phenomenon its strength. Christians were adhering to it not because of policies deliberately drawn up by clergy (as in the case of the dominant Anglican evangelical programme), but rather because of general conditions at the grass roots among the churches. Under the one – sometimes misleading – label 'charismatic', a whole series of reactions was in progress – reactions against the aridity and spiritual deadness, against a weak 'one-man ministry', against dullness and formalism in public worship and against the former era when believers heard very little of the Holy Spirit or His gifts. At a time when spiritual conditions were generally low, and when the traditionalism which had held a number of denominations together had run its course, it was inevitable that the presentation of something new, with emphasis upon the love, the fellowship and the spiritual liberty which are so conspicuous in New Testament Christianity, would gather wide support. Whatever the amount of confusion, and often division, which the movement engendered, there was within it an element of true spiritual hunger and zeal.

It was therefore no part of ML-J's conception of his duty to engage in open opposition to all things which might be regarded as 'charismatic'. He rather followed his old policy of trying to educate and win those who might be supporting something for lack of the knowledge of anything better. He was therefore not sympathetic to a purely negative attitude to evangelicals who were being influenced by charismatic views. 'I believe there is a true element in what we are seeing today,' he would say. 'We hope they will recognize their fundamental unity with us.' And again: 'There is something right in the ferment today . . . There is clearly something wrong with things as they are among us . . . We must reject the idea that anything new is wrong.'[1] When the argument was urged at one Westminster fraternal (Dec. 1977) that the charismatic movement was only going to be a temporary phenomenon, he replied that such an opinion should increase our concern to help these brethren. 'If it is right that it is only temporary, there are going to be some tragedies left behind.'[2] In other

---

[1] Westminster Fellowship, 2 October 1978, quoted by Robert Horn in *Martyn Lloyd-Jones: Chosen by God*, pp. 29–30.

[2] This was actually ML-J's own belief. He had said the previous year at Bryntirion (February 19, 1976), 'I prophesy that the charismatic movement will soon be in trouble and will disintegrate'. He feared that its excesses were leading to a large repetition of the tragedy of Edward Irving but he also remembered that R. M. M'Cheyne called Irving 'a holy man in spite of all his delusions and errors'. While some were to object to the sub title of Arnold Dallimore's book, *The Life of Edward Irving*, The Fore-Runner of the Charismatic Movement, 1983, charismatic writers have themselves supported that designation – unaware, perhaps, of the sad conclusion to Irving's life and ministry.

words, here were fellow Christians in need of help and such help would not be received if it was given in a spirit of denunciation. We also serve others best when we remember what *we* ourselves are lacking in 'righteousness and peace and joy in the Holy Ghost'.

Some examples here should make ML-J's own position unmistakable. In 1968–69 he became involved in a difference between two professors in the Reformed Church of Australia living at Geelong, Victoria, John A. Schep and Klaas Runia. Professor Schep, aged seventy-one, opened a correspondence with ML-J in the autumn of 1968 with a report that a revival had started in his neighbourhood a few months earlier. In his replies Dr Lloyd-Jones was encouraging but expressed his concern at the emphasis which Schep seemed to be putting on 'gifts' and on speaking in tongues as proofs of revival. If the power of the Spirit was confused with tongues, he warned, the truth about the possibility of the baptism with the Spirit and revival itself would be liable to be rejected, 'That would be to me a tragedy and would tend to delay revival'.[1] To Stuart Fowler, a pastor in Melbourne, Schep passed on Lloyd-Jones' opinion 'that all cases of tongues-speaking he [ML-J] has met are psychological and that this is proved by the very fact that they claim to exercise this gift at will'.[2] Schep does not seem to have agreed. But time was to show that ML-J was right in fearing that Schep's thought had been influenced by the same identification of 'gifts' with revival as was being made elsewhere in the world. There was no awakening at Geelong. In due course the former professor of the Reformed College was to join the Pentecostal churches. While this controversy was still proceeding, however, ML-J was also in correspondence with Klaas Runia whose critical comments on Schep's booklet *Baptism in the Spirit According to Scripture* had been sent to him. From ML-J's reply of February 28, 1969, to one of Runia's letters we give these sentences:

What is so interesting to me once more is that I find myself in a position between you two.

[1]Letter of Feb. 28, 1969.
[2]Letter to Stuart Fowler, also written on Feb. 28, 1969. That Schep is correctly quoting ML-J is confirmed by words written by ML-J to his old friend, Gerald Golden on September 18, 1969: 'Most of what are claimed to be miracles by the Pentecostalists and others certainly do not belong to that category and can be explained psychologically or in other ways. I am also of the opinion that most, if not all, of the people claiming to speak in tongues at the present time are certainly under a psychological rather than a spiritual influence.'

I certainly feel that Prof. Schep has crossed the line into a form of Pentecostalism. He shows this in his emphasis on tongues and also in his urging people to seek this particular gift and, indeed, to claim it.

I still feel that you really do not allow for revival. You show this where you say, 'Read all the passages that speak of the Holy Spirit in the Church. It is always: "Become what you are", ALL of you.' If it is simply a question of 'Become what you are' and nothing more, then how can one pray for revival, and indeed how does one account for the revivals in the history of the church? . . .

Where you deal with Schep's chapter 4 and the distinction between different types of Christians, I feel that you are discounting entirely the difference between faith and the assurance of faith. It is possible for a believer to be lacking in assurance, so that at any rate you have unbelievers, believers, and believers with full assurance. Is not the whole argument of 1 John really concerned with this, and especially the specific statement of Chapter 5, verse 13? Note also the different types of Chapter 2 of that Epistle. I feel that if you are right then in the light of the New Testament picture of the Christian (as seen, e.g. in 1 Peter 1:8) that there are really very few Christians at all. What also of the argument in Gal. 4:15 about 'Where is the blessedness ye spake of', and also Chapter 5:7? What also of the arguments against 'grieving and quenching the Spirit'? There were clearly people who were guilty of this and who had therefore lost something which they once had, but still they are Christians. This is also surely the point running through the Letters to the Churches in Revelation 2 and 3 . . .

[Regarding] the final paragraph of your page 8: Surely the Confessions were concerned primarily with defining doctrine as over against the false teaching of Rome. It is for that reason that those of us who stress their importance are ever in danger of falling into a scholasticism lacking in life and power. As you will know, this has happened many times in history, and that is what seems to call for repeated revivals.

To sum up what I feel, I would say that Prof. Schep is failing to 'prove and to test the spirits', while your danger is to 'quench the Spirit'.

Please forgive me for having written in such a dogmatic manner. I have done so in the interests of brevity and I know that you will understand.

May I say once more that I hope you will be given grace to bear with one another and to avoid any precipitate action.

May God grant great grace unto us all at this time of terrible confusion.

As in the mid-1960's, ML-J was again seeking to bring men to distinguish between the older experimental view of full assurance and those later Pentecostal views which had only a superficial similarity. In this connexion he had drawn Schep's attention to the Puritans and Thomas Goodwin in particular but the Dutch professor failed to observe the point rightly noted by Henry I. Lederle: 'The fact that Goodwin's Spirit-baptism was an experience primarily of the assurance of salvation and that this cannot just be identified with two-stage Pentecostalism does not seem to have made any impact on Schep.'[1]

The same kind of moderation and balance as was revealed in ML-J's correspondence with Schep and Runia was very frequently in evidence in the ministers' meetings where he presided at Westminster and in Wales. Unlike others who seemed to be adjusting their criticism of charismatic beliefs as the movement attained to wider popularity ML-J continued to speak plainly. At a time when most of us were not even aware of it he warned of the general alteration to church life which the 'restorationist' side of the movement wished to introduce. Whereas the ecumenical movement had been largely concerned with the merging of church structures, there was now a new danger from an entirely different direction. In discussion at the Westminster Fraternal on July 1, 1974, he said:

There is a movement which is opposed to all these church structures. The desire for something new and living . . . the 'Jesus' movement, the new charismatic movement . . . There is little interest in what happens to the old structures. It is an anti-church movement with an impatience with the old structures and forms; there is a call for house-churches, a dislike of church buildings, a preference for smaller units, a criticism of preaching. The interest is in phenomena and experiences. The very existence of the church in the old form is at stake.

Dr Lloyd-Jones was not at all impressed by the call for the dismantling of the existing form of worship on the Lord's Day. As he pointed out in his Romans 12 sermons of 1966, the over-reaction of the Quakers to the distinction of clergy and laity had led them to the position of not recognizing any offices in the church at all. Church history, he went on, gave many examples of the consequences of this error. James Haldane in nineteenth-century Edinburgh, in place of the former preaching service, instituted a 'general meeting' on

[1] *Treasures Old and New: Interpretations of 'Spirit-Baptism' in the Charismatic Renewal Movement*, (Peabody, Mass.: Hendrickson), 1987, p. 95.

Sunday mornings at which 'anybody could get up'. 'He wrecked a great church; it came to nothing.' The Irvingite 'tragedy' was connected with the same mistakes.[1] The possession of gifts, he argued, does not qualify an individual for leading in public worship.[2] True 'participation' in worship depends upon the work of the Holy Spirit in the hearts of the worshippers.

Still more serious, in his view, was the fact that the revival said to be in existence in the charismatic movement lacked the primary marks of such sovereign movements of the Spirit as had awakened the church in times past. As he said at the Welsh Ministers' Conference in June 1977:

1. Revivals always have common features and therefore we can test what is being talked about at the present time. The trouble with the charismatic movement is that there is virtually no talk at all of the Spirit 'coming down'. It is more something *they* do or receive: they talk now about 'renewal' not revival.
2. The tendency of the modern movement is to lead people to seek experiences. True revivals humble men before God and emphasize the person of Christ. If all the talk is about experiences and gifts it does not conform to the classic instances of revival. And the true *always* leads to evangelistic concern and outreach.

Nonetheless, along with these and other similar words there were many warnings of another kind, often directed to those of his colleagues in the ministry who appeared far too satisfied with existing conditions and whose churches were in little danger of excitement or excess. There *was* need for change. In too many congregations all was left to one man and anything like the 'experience meetings' of the eighteenth century had disappeared. There was a general lack of full assurance, of the consciousness of God among the people and hence an absence of joy, rejoicing and true praise. There was too much formality and too little freedom. For this state of affairs he saw the preachers themselves as chiefly to blame. Sermons were lacking in exhortation as though preachers thought their one business was to convey information. Unction and authority were too often missing. 'It is a great grief to me to hear true

[1] March 18, 1966.
[2] If it did, he argued, women might be preachers or teachers, contrary to Scripture (Feb. 18, 1966).

words coming out of a pulpit that lacks authority'. Still more fundamental, the evidence of a consuming passion for the lost and perishing was too rarely to be seen: 'The Apostle Paul reminds the elders of the church at Ephesus of how he preached "with tears". And Whitefield used to preach with tears. When have you and I last preached with tears? What do we know, to use the phrase of Whitefield, about preaching a "felt Christ"?'[1] On another occasion he said the same thing in a different form in these words:

The present state of things is a reflection of a defect in the preachers; it is great preaching that produces great believers and great listeners and congregations who rejoice. I heard of a preacher only the other Sunday. In the act of preaching he stopped and asked the congregation: 'Why are you not shouting?' The man did not realize he was condemning himself. When a man preaches under the influence of the Holy Spirit he does not ask people to shout – he tries to hinder them from doing so! The congregation is stirred by great preaching.

Issues raised by the charismatic movement were thus not to be dealt with simply by criticism of the errors in theology and practice of those who recognized the need for change. A deeper analysis was needed. The upsurge of discontent which was in the movement was related to real deficiencies in the churches and the situation would not be remedied by simple opposition to the new ideas. Self examination and self criticism were equally needed.

At times (and more so after his death) it was alleged that Dr Lloyd-Jones' attitude to the charismatic movement was ambiguous, or even that he had sympathy for beliefs distinctively pentecostal or charismatic. Such criticism he saw as a total misunderstanding, and he was astonished when in the autumn of 1979 the *Monthly Record of the Free Church of Scotland* carried an article which, along with much thankfulness for his ministry in general, suggested that he encouraged ministers to be 'theoretically pentecostal'.[2] 'Theoretical', the writer explained, because the Welshmen who followed him also copied his example in making no actual changes in their conduct of public worship along the lines of the beliefs they were supposed to favour. Speaking to me about this article on October 24, 1979 ML-J

---

[1] See *Puritans*, pp. 189, 292.
[2] 'Wales Greets Scotland', *Monthly Record of the Free Church of Scotland*, Nov. 1979, p. 217.

was indignant: 'I was against Pentecostalism and still am. My doctrine of the baptism of the Spirit is that it gives full assurance. I have never been satisfied with any speaking in tongues that I have heard. He [the author of the article] is saying that my ministry [i.e. practice] is a contradiction of my teaching. It is very unfair to put the label pentecostal on me.'

*   *   *

I will close this chapter with a brief reference to a fifth and last principle upon which ML-J's own ministry was based: he believed that there has to be both the consciousness of the speedy approach of the end of time – the nearness of the coming judgment and glory – *and* of the duty of one generation of Christians to anticipate and prepare for the needs of the next. He held these two truths, content that the New Testament found no contradiction between them. 'The end of all things is at hand' (1 Peter 4:7), has to be balanced with, 'The end is not yet' (Matt. 24:6). Both entered largely into his whole outlook. For all men, and for civilization itself, eternity is imminent, and yet he was strongly critical of any Christian leader who showed little concern for the course of the church after his death – an attitude which he sometimes represented by the words of King Hezekiah, 'Is it not good if peace and truth be in my days'. Like C. H. Spurgeon, he believed in living for the next age as well as for his own and it was this, as much as anything else, which put any thought of retirement out of his head. Heaven was before him but he still thought of the long term for the church militant and that is why a chief part of his time in the 1970's went into the preparation of books and into the encouragement of the men who would be continuing the battle when he had gone. Part of his dislike of paperbacks, it could also be said, was his belief that their publishers were thinking only of the present. Books ought to be made to last!

ML-J had a profound sense of the providence of God in history and refused to give way to the pessimism which the scale of the contemporary problems was calculated to induce. 'Do not waste too much of your time in worrying about the future of the Christian Church,' was his counsel to younger men.

For me it was an incalculably enriching relationship. To be wholly forthcoming, genial, warmhearted, confidential, sympathetic, and supportive to ministerial colleagues of all ages was part of the Doctor's greatness. It was, I think, a combined expression of his Presbyterian clericalism, based on the parity of all clergy, plus his feeling as a physician for the common dignity of all who have charge of others' welfare, plus the expansive informality of the Welsh family head. It was an attitude that left countless ministers feeling like a million dollars – significant in their calling, purposeful about it, and invigorated for it. The Doctor's magnetic blend of clarity, certainty, common sense, and confidence in God made him a marvelous encourager, as well as a great molder of minds. He was a pastor of pastors par excellence. *He would have hated to be called a bishop, but no one ever fulfilled towards clergy a more truly episcopal ministry.*

JAMES I. PACKER
*Chosen Vessels: Portraits of
Ten Outstanding Christian Men,* p. 110

33

A Pastor of Pastors

It has been noted that Dr Lloyd-Jones' first principle was that the main thing should always be put before everything else. For ministers, without question, that meant the preaching of the gospel along with private preparation for that work. Men learned this from him in gatherings of pastors where he would repeatedly come back to it. They learned it still more from his example. In these later years we have seen him engaged in controversy but important though the issues were it would be entirely wrong to give the reader any impression that they now occupied a chief place in his thought and in the organization of his time. The truth is that he remained as busy in itinerant preaching as he had been forty years earlier and the serious differences affecting the contemporary Christian scene which were discussed elsewhere were never the substance of his preaching. While he still prepared new sermons, the content of earlier years was unchanged: the pulpit exists to herald the message of sin, salvation and the nearness of eternity. This same priority also affected the long hours he now put into the preparation of material for publication. Had the pursuit of existing controversies been his aim then he would have given priority to getting some of his major conference and fraternal addresses into public circulation: instead the appearance of his expositions of Romans and Ephesians in permanent form was deliberately put first.

From 1972 I had the opportunity of seeing in a new way what ML-J's itinerant ministry meant in parts of the United Kingdom 400 and more miles distant from London. In that year we moved to Edinburgh and, strange though it may seem, we were to see a good deal more of him in our home there than we ever did in London. Less than a month after our removal to the North we were on holiday in the Scottish Highlands and able to be at the little church at Rothiemurchus beneath the Cairngorm Mountains where he was preaching. A small congregation, chiefly of holiday-makers, heard a wonderfully simple yet compelling sermon from the words of 1 Corinthians 15:3–4, 'For I delivered unto you first of all that which I also received . . .'. He was supplying that Church of Scotland pulpit while on holiday. Three months later, on November 13, 1972, a very cold day with a light fall of snow overnight, he was back in Scotland to speak at an interdenominational meeting marking the 400th anniversary of the death of John Knox in Edinburgh. As though in keeping with the historic theme, the service was held in the Assembly Rooms built in George Street in 1787. From the text, 'Where is the Lord God of Elijah?' (2 Kings 2:14), he gave one of his greatest addresses. From Edinburgh he proceeded to Glasgow and Dundee for three nights of services which had been arranged by the Scottish Evangelistic Council. As usual he stayed with his old friend, Alick Murdoch of Giffnock who, at eighty-four years of age, retained much of his native vigour.

The next year, 1973, ML-J was back in Edinburgh for a weekend of services at Charlotte Baptist Chapel in early October and, six months later, for a similar weekend at Free St Columba's (of which congregation I was then a member). At his first service at St Columba's on Saturday, April 20, he preached a compelling sermon from 2 Corinthians 5:17 on the theme that the Christian shows he is a 'new creature' chiefly by the spirit of his *mind*, i.e. by what he thinks about himself, about the world and about Christ. On that Saturday evening he did not sleep well and, unusually, complained in the morning of abdominal pain which he later put down to the weather, 'You know I don't like the Spring'.

There was another side to his disturbed sleep which he never told me of but which I heard subsequently from the Rev. John MacLeod of Gairloch, who had planned to be in Edinburgh to attend the St Columba services that weekend. The two men were of similar spirit and MacLeod drank in such preaching, but in his sleep that Saturday night ML-J dreamed that he talked with the minister of Gairloch and received the candid opinion that it was time to stop this preaching about the country for he was evidently past it! Such a thought had certainly not remotely occurred to the real John MacLeod, next to whom I happened to be sitting when the Doctor preached a glorious gospel sermon on the Sunday morning from Hebrews 10:19–22. At the conclusion of that sermon we were called to prayer, but as we stood for prayer, instead of bowing his head, I was surprised to see

A *Pastor of Pastors*

Mr MacLeod lean his considerable weight towards me before exclaiming with delight, 'The *fire* has fallen!'.
    At the end of the day's preaching many of us must have had similar
questions in our minds. How was it that preaching as simple as this
should be so rare? And why did the pulpit not more commonly bring
the *consciousness* of eternity to those who hear? I wrote the
following note that Sunday evening:

The Doctor was comparatively quiet in the pulpit – not the 'lion', with
perspiration troubling his forehead, and not almost 'dancing' as he used
to do – yet absolutely convincing, the argument compelling attention
and assisted still by some 'action', especially this evening. Two emphases
were very clear and strong, Jesus Christ is God and He was punished for
our sins.

    If Dr Lloyd-Jones did have any thought of giving up his long
distance travelling (nearly always by rail to Scotland, never by plane)
he rejected it as a temptation and was absolutely committed to the
continuance of his itinerant evangelistic ministry as long as he had
strength. Thus he was back in Scotland in November of that same
year, 1974, and in the same month of 1975, for meetings in major
cities arranged by the Scottish Evangelistic Council.
    If these preaching journeys were spread all over the British Isles
their greatest frequency was without doubt in Wales. His engagements diary for 1974, for example, shows that he was in the
Principality in seven months of the year (sometimes for separate
visits within the same month). In 1975 there were only six months
out of the twelve months of the year when he was not to be found in
Wales for one preaching engagement or another and the percentage
remained the same as late as 1978. It was in Wales that he made the
one exception to his rule, by this date, that residential conferences
were now too tiring for him. For many evangelical ministers the
Evangelical Movement of Wales' two-day Ministers' Conference in
Bala every June was the high spot of the year and not least because
ML-J was always there.[1] The venue was Bryn-y-groes, amidst lawns
and trees, overlooking the beautiful Bala Lake. Originally built as a
family home, it had all the air of a family as men crowded its rooms

[1]He also, it should be said, usually spoke at least once a year at a day conference
organized by the Evangelical Movement at Bryntirion, their headquarters near
Cardiff.

[699]

and 'the Doctor' presided in the spirit of love so reminiscent of what is written of the Apostle John in old age.

One of my unforgettable memories is of the 1974 Bala Conference. It began at 5 pm on Monday, June 24 with an address on Bible Translations. Then after an evening meal ML-J chaired a discussion on the subject. He seemed both tired and old – not surprisingly, perhaps, as he had preached several times in the preceding days. But when he led a further discussion, the next evening, the change was remarkable. He was obviously refreshed and spoke as though he were several years younger. The subject was prayer and he presided, sitting in a chair in the crowded front parlour of the house – with its low ceiling and little white-framed windows looking out on the sunshine of the early evening. Discussion finally gave way to his own impromptu address, delivered with much authority and fervour, on our need of a great 'sense of God'. Prayer had declined because the belief that we could truly know and enjoy God had declined. Our chief failure as ministers was the failure to bring people into the presence of God. Our conviction that 'God deals familiarly with men' was too weak. 'The two greatest meetings in my life were both prayer meetings. I would not have missed them for the world.' All this and much more he said seated and, just when it seemed that his flow of speech and spirit must be concluded because anything else would have to be an anticlimax, he rose to his feet and, moving behind his seat as though it were a pulpit desk, continued without any interruption and still more forcefully and rousingly for a further ten minutes! While books and tapes may give some idea of what ML-J was as a preacher, no such helps exist to give a real impression of what he was as an 'exhorter' on such unrecorded occasions as these.

The following day he concluded the Conference with a sermon on 'Quench not the Spirit' (1 Thess. 5:19). After an introduction on the need for balance, he proceeded to deal with current ways in which the Spirit could be grieved and quenched. I can give only the outline:

Doctrinal: (i) Any theology which would restrict the unusual and exceptional work of the Spirit to the apostolic age. (ii) The belief that a Christian has received everything at regeneration and only needs to 'surrender' to what he has – with no expectation of the direct witness of the Spirit with our spirit. (iii) Intellectualism. The ultimate sin is pride of intellect. (iv) Undue emphasis upon the will. Arminianism always tends to quench the Spirit by decisionism (Finney) and the Keswick teaching, 'Take it by faith. Don't worry about your feelings.' (v) Fear of excess.

We have been guilty of grieving the Spirit in over-reacting to Pentecostalism. (vi) Interpreting Scripture by the measure of our own experience, instead of submitting to Scripture. *Practical*: (i) Trusting to prepared sermons rather than to the Holy Spirit. (ii) Over-formality in public worship. (iii) Trusting in techniques and methods. (iv) Attempting to work up emotions (Pentecostals are more guilty here – they clap, shout, repeat, etc.). It is the Spirit who can produce emotion and give a sense of joy and elevation which cannot be put into words. (v) Failure to pray for the Spirit.

He concluded by warning against giving way to young people who want Sunday services thrown open. That is wrong. The emphasis (in 1 Thess. 5:19–21) is on balance: 'Prove all things', by the Word, therefore by preaching and teaching. Let week-night meetings be open. 'The tragedy of the hour is that gifts are too prominent and great preaching is absent.'

After tea on that Wednesday afternoon we drove into Bala, as he was eager to show me where the old 'green' was where the great open-air services of the past took place 150 years earlier. We had some difficulty in finding a shop open where he could buy a daily paper – 'Are you concerned to keep up with the soccer results from the World Cup matches [then being played in Germany]?' I enquired light-heartedly. He smiled and surprised me by saying that he had recently watched the whole game between Scotland and Brazil on television!

At Bala ML-J was only fourteen miles away from his 'home' in North Wales, Brynuchaf, the hill farm of John and Mari Jones, where he and Bethan had stayed so often since he had driven past its gate with Mari in 1949. Mrs Lloyd-Jones usually stayed there while the Ministers' Conference was meeting. And so, a newspaper secured and the location of the 'green' identified, we then took the romantic mountain road from Llanuwchllyn – towards Dinas Mawddwy – the same route that Thomas Charles walked in all weathers from Bala when serving the curacy of Llanymawddwy in the 1780's. The light was fading by the time we reached the top of Bwlch y Groes (The Pass of the Cross) – an ascent of which it was once said: 'There are few better tests on the lungs and muscles and beast today than the climbing of that hill; and as for automobiles – if we have some idea of what defeated forces and lost tempers, together with the consequent retracing of many miles of a country road, mean to men bent on speed, the rest may be inferred.'[1]

[1] *The Life of Thomas Charles*, D. E. Jenkins, 1910, vol. 1, p. 466.

At the conclusion of the same Conference three years later, in 1977, we took the same road and stopped at the head of the pass, where a cross stood in ancient times, to admire the view and for me to take the photograph contained in this volume. ML-J – though he assumed a slightly 'disapproving' look for that photograph – was in his element in those majestic surroundings. In his thoughts he had 'walked' that road innumerable times with the Calvinistic Methodist preachers for whom it was once a main route from North to South.

Among the memorable services at which ML-J preached in Wales in these years were those in his former church at Sandfields, Aberavon, on Sunday, February 6, 1977 – exactly fifty years after his first Sunday as minister of that congregation. 'The Doctor' was joyfully welcomed by the people, not a few of whom had been converted under his ministry, and it added to his pleasure that his old friend and former Secretary of the church, E. T. Rees, was still to be found in his pew listening as eagerly as he had done half a century earlier. At the morning service he preached from Acts 26:28, 29 and from Paul's witness to Agrippa he drew out the principles needed for our witness today. In the course of these he said, 'During my time spent in this church, the main work of evangelism was done, not by myself preaching from this pulpit, but it was carried out by the life and daily witness of those who had been converted . . . The early Christians knew what they believed. When Christians know what they are, by the grace of God, they can and do influence people and their society.' The text for the evening was 1 Corinthians 2:2, the same text from which he had preached on his first visit to Sandfields on November 28, 1926.

ML-J's last visit to the Ministers' Conference at Bala was in June 1978 when he spoke on 'The Place of Phenomena in Revival'. It was a subject in which he had long been interested and the new excitement over 'phenomena' among evangelicals on both sides of the Atlantic was making clear thinking essential. The Bible records unusual phenomena (e.g. Daniel 10:7; Acts 26:13–14; 2 Cor. 12:4) and that similar things may occur, especially in the early days of a revival, he did not doubt. A revival is itself a phenomenon and God may employ the unusual to call attention to the spiritual realm in a manner similar to His use of miracles in the Gospels. Yet the existence of phenomena in themselves proves nothing. They are not necessarily a manifestation of divine power. His address, with copious illustrations from church history, was only an exposition of what he had said in essence when preaching on Revival in 1959 when he had warned: 'Phenomena should not be sought, they should not be encouraged, they should not be boasted . . . Anybody who tries to work up phenomena is a tool of the Devil, and is putting himself into the position of the psychic and the psychological'.[1]

*   *   *

Throughout the 1970's, except when ill, Dr Lloyd-Jones continued to preside at the meetings of the Westminster Fellowship, with the subject for each meeting usually being decided, as in earlier years, by a question posed by anyone at the outset. The questions dealt with included: 'Are our churches in a grievous condition?' 'How do we respond to the spread of house-groups?' 'Is it sufficient to be positive or must we be negative also?' 'What are the hindrances to greater unity?' 'Why are we not experiencing greater blessing?' 'What is the meaning of "the letter killeth . . ." (2 Cor. 3:6)?' 'How are individuals in spiritual trouble distinguished from cases of physical, mental or even demonic affliction?'

One great value of such discussions was, as noted earlier, that ML-J as chairman always controlled them. All were welcome to speak, but it had to be to the point: such digressions as make discussions aimless and unprofitable were not allowed. There had to be continuity of thought or argument from one speaker to another. In maintaining this direction ML-J began to be impeded at this date by a measure of deafness, though for a while the fact that he sometimes had problems in hearing was well hidden. When a speaker was on his feet, perhaps at the back of the room, whose words he could not catch, he would at times turn promptly to John Caiger, sitting beside him at the front and ask, 'Mr Caiger can you hear?' Then, before John Caiger had any time to reply, the inaudible speaker would be advised that he needed to raise his voice! Occasionally one suspected that this was also the explanation why a speaker was receiving more liberty than he deserved instead of being

---

[1] *Revival*, pp. 146–47. Dr Lloyd-Jones would not have appreciated the misuse of his words in *When the Spirit Comes with Power*, John White, IVP (USA) and Hodder & Stoughton, 1988. One of the main purposes of White's work is to justify the very kind of sensation-seeking ministry which ML-J warned against. No sources are given for the author's many quotations from ML-J. They seem to come exclusively from the years 1964–65.

halted by a swift repartee from the chairman. Yet there were still valuable discussions, as an extract from the afternoon of March 7, 1977 will illustrate. The subject was depression among ministers, how it is to be avoided and how are men to assess their own temperaments? As usual, in the early stages of the discussion, ML-J said little but allowed men to voice their opinions:

GOLDING.   The question is, how do we maintain our mental and physical well-being or we shall be more prone to depression?
BENNETT.   We need hobbies and friends separate from our ministerial work.
ALDRIDGE   Doesn't this tend to be a problem in independency, we look upon each other as competitors . . . ?
ML-J.   W-e-ll . . . [*The word drawn out in this manner was a sure sign he did not agree. Nonetheless, the next speaker gave support to Aldridge.*]
JAMES.   We are landed in positions of loneliness . . . men are battling on their own, with a lack of fellowship.
ML-J   This has nothing to do with independency at all. Fellowship, of course, is good. That is why we come here. We will take that for granted.

This brought a pause before the next speaker opened another line of thought:

JENKINS.   There is a danger in a pastor looking for relief apart from his local church. We must not accept a 'them' and 'us' approach as though we are different from our Christian people. We do not recognize sufficiently the devices of Satan to undermine the work.
BASSETT.   'Know yourself' needs to be our rule. The condition in which we get up in the morning can so easily condition the way we preach, etc. We should not get into a situation in which we are so under pressure that we cannot recognize this. We also need to broaden our reading. Jogging is very helpful and physical exercise is essential. Days off must be taken.
MATHIESON.   I left off golf when I was converted and don't need exercise, [*adding as final proof*], I am now eighty-six! [*Laughter.*]
SMITH.   We need elders to support us.
ANOTHER.   Since I have had an eldership it has taken more out of me!

Another change at this point when another speaker, recalling having heard how the Doctor spent his holidays, begged leave to disagree with him. He immediately faced a question:

A Pastor of Pastors

ML-J   What do *you* take on holiday with you?

RESPONDENT.   I take my Bible and a whodunnit book!

ML-J[*immediately*].   Is *one* enough for you? [*Laughter.*] You are making a mistake. On holidays you have time. My big difficulty was always to have to find time to read consecutively through a big book. If I did read a whodunnit book it would have been in my normal routine but big books need consecutive time – but perhaps people don't read big books now? We all agree about not becoming exclusively immersed in our work. The mind needs a rest and relaxation. Take physical exercise but remember that the muscular-type Christianity for some people is quite fatal. You have got to be careful here. Compton Mackenzie, when asked how he explained his good health, would say, 'I never run if I can walk, never walk if I can stand, never stand if I can sit . . .' I understand that perfectly! People are born in a certain way . . . How can we know ourselves? 'The heart is deceitful . . . who can know it?' [*Jer. 17:9*]. It is difficult to be honest with oneself. We want to be on good terms with ourselves. But this temptation is not the ultimate problem. We are more free of professionalism than any body of men I have come across. There used to be so much of it. I saw it often when I first went into the ministry . . .

Sleep is very important. If you feel sleepy, sleep! What merit is there in not sleeping? It is much wiser to sleep for twenty minutes in an afternoon than to nod, half-awake. Some men can go on four hours a night. Napoleon was one, and I knew a great surgeon here in London who also could do that.

I cannot remember ever sitting down to consider my temperament.

MURRAY.   You did not need to!

ML-J.   No, I am saying, a man should not do it . . . I remember a man preaching on the theme that a man's strength could be his greatest weakness. Absalom's hair was his downfall [2 *Sam. 14:26; 18:19*]. Moses' meekness failed. His theme was 'the danger of our strength'. If we start analysing ourselves and to begin to say, 'This is my strength', it may become your weakness.

I can assure you that depression in the ministry is *not* a problem of temperament. Men of every conceivable temperament get this trouble – the feeling that everything is on top of us. The one possible exception is the phlegmatic type who is not concerned about anything. He is so bucolic, ox-like, that he is not likely to feel a call to the ministry! Men in the ministry are sensitive men. I have met few others. The way to approach this problem is not along lines of temperament – that is incidental.

The big thing is not to *start* with the problem. Start with the question, what is your calling? Why are you in the ministry? What is the object of the ministry? Is the church mine? Why am I troubled? Am I concerned about my reputation? Why am I hurt? . . . Our reactions are too often due to a wrong view of our calling. Remember Paul: 'With me it is a very small thing that I should be judged of you, or of man's judgment: yea, *I judge not mine own self*' [*1 Cor. 4:3*]. I have found this to be the answer so many times. Paul had to go through it all. In Corinth men were praised more than Paul who were not worthy to shine his boots. Paul's concept of the ministry lay in his calling to be faithful. We should not make it a personal issue.

Isolate, then, the fact of your calling. Get that right. The antagonism we encounter is generally against the calling and most of our problems arise because we get immersed in day-to-day problems and forget *what we are*. 'Should such a man as I flee?' [*Neh. 6:11*]. Nehemiah was talking about his calling. That is the way to look at it. Certain things then become unthinkable and you will not hand in your resignation.

It is not your church or my church. It is the chosen people of God we serve. We must beware lest we offend the generation of God's people [*Psa. 73:15*]. The devil can come in to tempt us but it isn't always the devil. We have got to see it all in the right perspective. Let us remember who we are. We haven't entered a profession. We are servants of the living God!

Occasionally in these later years, instead of depending upon a spontaneous question, addresses might be given by one or even two speakers. This happened on March 8, 1978 when two members of the fellowship spoke on the advantages of training church members in the Evangelism Explosion methods of Dr Kennedy of Fort Lauderdale, Florida. ML-J listened patiently and then surprised a number by the strength of the criticism he offered. He was not satisfied to hear the course commended by Calvinists ('Many Calvinists today behave and act like Arminians'). What he wanted to know was the biblical evidence for the special training of ordinary members of churches. 'It is certainly not in Acts 8:4.' He objected to people being made to feel unhappy because they were not doing this, but his main concern was over how the Kennedy method stopped short in diagnosis. 'We all agree that people are not acting as witnesses as they should but instead of asking, Why are things as they are, we are being given a patent, cut-and-dried remedy which says we must train the people.' The first need was for change at a deeper level and the danger of this proposal was the same as the danger in large organized evangelism: 'Eyes are being taken off the ultimate need of spiritual awakening. Anything that prevents people from realizing that the only answer is revival is dangerous.' Referring to his own experience at Sandfields he said:

Conversions came slowly, then the converts were known and they talked. I never trained a single convert how to approach others but they did so . . . If our people cannot explain the way of salvation to unconverted men we are deplorably bad preachers . . .

Two days before Ebenezer Morris died two young preachers visited him to whom he said, 'If you two will live long enough you will see a time when no one will come to the Society meeting. At such a time do not try to drag unconverted people into the church but wait on the Lord and seek Him. Don't repeat the error of Abraham and Sarah (Gen. 16:1–3). Wait on God's promise instead of going after the flesh.'

While ML-J thus continued to lead ministers' meetings and to preach in large gatherings in such places as Glasgow and Cardiff, Manchester and Newcastle upon Tyne, his frequent visits to small, often struggling, congregations were equal in importance in his estimation. There was never a circle of pastors who were specifically known as 'his men'. He would have deplored such a term. But there were many in all parts of Britain whose call and commitment to the Christian ministry owed more than they could say to his teaching and example. These men had often settled in congregations which had seen long years of decline and neglect, and as they viewed the existing conditions they often felt like repeating the words of Nehemiah's helpers in Jerusalem, 'There is much rubbish'. It needed no small resolution to believe in a remedy which could promise no quick success and which was so out of accord with popular views. And although, overall, there had been a very considerable increase of men in the ministry committed to biblical preaching, their numbers were generally few in any one location. Some who had entered heartily into the enthusiasm of the doctrinal recovery of the late 1950's and early 1960's wavered when they did not see the results which they had expected to see in their churches. It was one thing to read the biographies of Whitefield and Spurgeon and another to remain faithful to the older principles when newer ideas were constantly claiming great blessing. Many men went through the experience of Gordon Miller of South Africa, mentioned above,[1] and

¹See pp. 652–53.

some never recovered their first commitment. Others hung on and faced the slow, uphill work of re-establishing congregations where the people would learn to see the Word of God and prayer as foundational to all true spiritual prosperity. No doubt this new generation of younger ministers were often themselves responsible for failures and imprudences but, like ML-J, they were also the subject of hostile caricatures. Speaking of London preachers, P. W. Greenslade offered this view of ML-J in 1965: 'If the lecture room atmosphere is no distraction to you, then you can still be stirred by the sprightly Doctor's aggressive mixture of exposition and polemic.' For a better pulpit model Greenslade advised attendance at the City Temple, a place 'where budding preachers go to worship'.[1] In later years others kept their invective for ML-J's 'followers'. Gerald Coates believed that when Dr Martyn Lloyd-Jones broke with a mixed evangelicalism 'he could have had no idea that this withdrawal would produce tunnel-minded Reformed theologians, incredibly boring fundamentalists and Calvinistic leaders fearful of anything subjective – including the work of the Holy Spirit'.[2] In what seems to be a division of blame between ML-J and these same pastors, James Packer, writing in 1985, thought that 'the 15 years of separatist drum-beating does appear in retrospect as something of a scorched-earth era in English evangelical life when much that was of value was destroyed'.[3] ML-J saw it entirely differently. In many churches it was a period of new beginnings, a period when the main effort of many men was going into the rebuilding of local congregations.

ML-J's concern and affection for the ministers who were working in this way was unbounded and his visits to hundreds of congregations and manses gave renewed hope and unforgettable encouragement. Even more than the help of having him in their pulpit was the long-term strength gained from being able, perhaps late into the night, to speak to him of how various problems should be approached and dealt with. In such visits there was no question of ML-J giving mere sentimental support. The closer men were to him the plainer he could be and he had not the slightest tolerance or sympathy for anything in the nature of self-pity or unbelief. On one occasion at the Westminster Fellowship, when the subject for

[1] 'Student World', in *Spurgeon's College Record*, June 1965.
[2] *Divided We Stand*, (Eastbourne: Kingsway), 1987, p.40.
[3] *Martyn Lloyd-Jones: Chosen by God*, p. 56.

discussion was, 'Why are we not experiencing greater blessing?', he said with vehemence: 'We are never promised automatic blessing. Look at the sufferings of the men involved in 1662! Get rid of the idea, "If I do this, God will give the blessing". God knows when to give blessing and when not to. We are not fit to have it. He couldn't trust us to have it. There is the sovereignty of God in this.'

As always his main personal counsel to pastors was of their need to be *spiritual* men. But there was also some adjustment in emphasis in the 1970's. There was now greater need than ten years earlier for asserting that true preaching *must* be doctrinal. Some had misused his strictures on 'dead orthodoxy' in the early 1960's to strengthen their prejudice against the necessity of theology. Later, while still warning against holding any truth only in the mind, he urged that the truth itself is *never* dead and it is only a strong hold upon the truth which can lead to great preaching: 'The more powerful Calvinism is the more likely you are to have a genuine revival and reawakening. It follows of necessity from the doctrine . . . I regard the term "dead Calvinism" as a contradiction in terms. I say that a dead Calvinism is impossible and that if your Calvinism appears to be dead it is not Calvinism . . .'[1]

Speaking of the weakening of a once great congregation which we had all known, ML-J put it down to doctrinal weakness in the pulpit. Anyone who thought that his own doctrinal commitment was less strong in his later years simply did not know him. On the contrary, the energy of his insistence that we younger men should not relax our convictions sometimes took us by surprise. I recall in this connexion his criticism of the reprint of Alexander Stewart's volume on Elisha by the publications committee of the Free Church of Scotland. The book was orthodox but he was dissatisfied. Fine language was no substitute for strong theology. He likewise thought that W. C. Burns' *Revival Sermons*, republished by the Banner of Truth Trust, was weak in doctrinal content. When Warren W. Wiersbe saw ML-J for the last time in London the two men spoke of authors and when the American preacher expressed his appreciation of the published sermons of George H. Morrison of Glasgow, ML-J replied, 'No doctrine – no doctrine! Only poetry! No substance!'. In this respect, as in others, what he said at a Christian Medical Fellowship meeting in 1978 was true, 'I am the man that I was'.

[1] *Puritans*, pp. 210–11.

Related to this doctrinal concern was his belief that even the ministers to whom he was closest were being affected by a decline in serious reading. A fresh, relevant ministry has to be maintained by constant reading. 'Our men are not reading enough,' he said to me with regret in December 1977, and he urged me to get hold of Wilfred Ward's two-volume *Life of Cardinal Newman* which he had recently finished. The breadth of his reading was astonishing and, apart from novelists, he had a lively interest in contemporary authors. He would often say that whereas younger ministers must read for food he now found that he read more for its stimulus: books were a tonic and their effect should always be to sharpen our reading of the Bible itself. Urging the words of Paul, 'Give attendance to reading', he said at the Bala Conference of 1976: 'Most of the great men of God have been great readers. Daniel Rowland was always reading and in the study . . . As I get older I read more than ever but the type of reading has changed. When one is young it is one's duty to read theology to get a framework for your preaching. But you do not go on doing that. You keep abreast . . . You also read false teaching . . .'

One of the factors to which he attributed the decline of reading was the growing popularity among Christians of tapes and cassette-recordings. He believed that for purposes of learning and meditation a book was a great deal more valuable than a recording of a sermon or address. Tapes, he insisted, must not be allowed to replace books.

There was certainly no reduction in the amount and the breadth of his own reading. Years earlier he had, on one occasion at Westminster Chapel, astonished the diaconate who knew a little of the reading he got through. The occasion was a deacons' meeting at which an architect was present for discussion on the renovation of the building. The visitor brought with him a model, which he had painted himself, of what the Chapel would look like after the redecoration of the interior which he proposed. When the meeting was over and the model was being further admired the architect confessed, 'When I retire I hope to go in for painting'. 'When I retire,' said ML-J, 'I hope to be able to *read*!' Perhaps he was now able to read more of the larger books which in earlier years he had reserved for the long vacations. He certainly made more visits to the library of Sion College: 'I find that Library increasingly useful,' he wrote to Philip Hughes in 1975, 'and shall ever be grateful to you for introducing me to it.' Jim Packer once met him in the late sixties 'carrying back to Sion College library W. H. C. Frend's heavy tome, *The Donatist Church*'. Once in the 1970's when I called to see him at Balsham I found him buried in the second volume of M. Schmidt's *John Wesley, A Theological Biography* (1966). At the point at which I interrupted him he was reflecting on a note which had arrested him on page 250 and which he proceeded to read aloud. The subject of the note was the temperament of John Wesley and Count Zinzendorf as observed by a Moravian contemporary, R. Viney. Viney disliked the appearance of pride in both men and was tempted to think that it was the 'choleric' type of personality which both possessed that pushed them 'to do and seek after great and high things'. Instead, however, of turning from both men in these early years of the evangelical revival in England, the Moravian came to see the overruling of God in this question of temperaments and wrote:

True he [Wesley] is of a choleric complexion and so is the Count, they are bold, they seem to take much upon them; but perhaps they are fitter for the Lord's purpose than others. A melancholic person tho he is suspicious of himself and so appears humble, yet he has no courage sufficient to carry on a great work, for should he but come into a melancholy fit he presently lets fall his hands, yea perhaps runs quite away. The phlegmatic has not understanding nor seldom honesty enough to screen him from the world's laying notorious faults to his charge, neither is he active. The sanguine are active enough and have understanding, but then he is fickle and unstable, fond of new things. So that the choleric seem to have been chiefly made use of in great undertakings and seem the fittest, but they are men, and what is peculiar of them (viz.) pride or haughtiness often appears, but they generally effect the things they begin, and the Lord does not make use of angels to preach or act visibly among men, so perhaps these sort are the best among men for such undertakings . . .[1]

With this whole quote ML-J seemed to be in hearty agreement and he went on to say how Owen Thomas, in his biography of John Jones of Talsarn (unhappily, never translated from Welsh into English), quoted Daniel Rowland's daughter speaking of her father as a choleric type – active, quick, hasty, perhaps short-tempered. 'These are the

[1]Viney is, of course, using the four-fold division in temperaments or 'humours': melancholic (i.e. prone to introspection and depression); phlegmatic (cool, calm, sluggish); sanguine (hopeful, habitually expectant); and choleric.

men,' he agreed, 'who achieve more than others.' I refer to this partly because it is not without relevance to his own temperament.

It was ML-J's concern for the ministry not only of the present but of the future which finally brought him in the mid 1970's to the conviction that a new theological college had to be started. Thoughts of such a step had been occasionally discussed for approaching twenty years. All along he had warned of the danger of men being accepted for ministerial training whose gifts were untested and who were then put through a system of training in which achievement was assessed by the standards set by the theological faculties of the Universities. Certainly men's minds needed to be sharpened by hard study, and he regarded a 'trained mind' as essential for the ministry, but he entertained some doubt whether *any* theological college was needed: after all, preachers are born not made. The practical needs of the situation, however, finally convinced him that something had to be done. He therefore chaired the meetings of a sponsoring committee, five of which had taken place by September 1976, and with a faculty of four ministers 'the London Theological Seminary' opened at Hendon Lane, Finchley, on October 6, 1977, when he 'preached' an inaugural address.[1] This was a statement of the purpose for which the Seminary had come into being. It was not intended to be 'a mere modification of the present system and the present position'. There had to be a fresh start, a new approach based upon the New Testament itself. ML-J remained chairman of the board of LTS and for the remainder of his life the new work had his fullest support. The Rev. T. Omri Jenkins, a fellow member of the board, has spoken of the inspiration of ML-J's leadership in their early meetings and of how it reminded him afresh of A. W. Pink's definition of a prophet, 'God's man for evil days'. Certainly the united prayer with which the new Seminary was founded was that such men would be raised up for the years ahead.

*   *   *

I close this chapter with a mental picture I have of ML-J at the age of seventy-seven arriving at the end of a long journey to take services in Edinburgh. It is a picture which others could duplicate in countless instances. This particular occasion was late in the evening of

---

[1]See *Knowing the Times*, pp. 356–75. The faculty appointed were Andrew Davies, Philip Eveson, Graham Harrison and Hywel Jones.

April 25, 1977. His train, due from London at 8 pm, was over an hour late and on its arrival I was anticipating a somewhat weary traveller. Instead he approached the ticket barrier where I was standing with a firm and quick step and not in the least disturbed over the delay he had suffered. In the long stretch from Newcastle, he told me, he had been absorbed with a new sermon outline on 1 Timothy 3:15 and had scarcely noticed the time. His attention had been particularly fixed on the question why Paul used the *two* illustrations in describing the church as 'the pillar and *ground* of the truth'. I was too surprised to ask him for his answer to that question but I ought not to have been. Had his concern been for his own ease and comfort he would not have been there at all. Alongside the great things for which he lived the inconveniences of that evening were too incidental to deserve consideration.

Christian! dost thou hear them,
  How they speak thee fair?
'Always fast and vigil?
  Always watch and prayer?'
Christian! answer boldly,
  'While I breathe I pray';
Peace shall follow battle,
  Night shall end in day.

JOHN MASON NEALE
From one of ML-J's favourite hymns,
'Christian! dost thou see them . . .'

Dr. Bonar used to tell, with great solemnity, what was said to
him at the beginning of his ministry by an old friend and
minister: 'Remember, it is a remark of old and experienced
men, that very few men, and very few ministers, keep up to the
end the edge that was on their spirit at the first.'

MARJORY BONAR
Andrew A Bonar: Diary and Letters, 1894, p. 349

34

Keeping On[1]

When Dr Lloyd-Jones entered upon his eightieth year on December 20, 1978, his engagements diary for the following twelve months was nearly as full as usual. Most of these engagements he was to be unable to fulfil and the year 1979 virtually brought the close of his public ministry. In the course of an enthusiastic letter to his old friend Philip Hughes regarding the latter's forthcoming book on Lefèvre, the French reformer, ML-J wrote on May 1, 1979:

I have had a bad winter. I believe I had a virus infection on my lungs and afterward I had to go into hospital for a small operation. I have actually not preached since the first Sunday in February, but I am now beginning to make real progress . . . If only we have some fine weather, with good sunshine, I would soon be quite well.

This hope was not to be fulfilled and instead there were indications of a recurrence of the cancer. From the time of his major operation in 1968 until the autumn of 1976 – when an operation for the removal of his prostate gland had been necessary – he had been free of all indications of the disease. Now in 1979 there were disturbing symptoms and for the first time since 1969 he could not be present at the Bala Ministers' Conference in June.

Yet, saying nothing of his condition, ML-J reappeared in his usual chairman's seat at the Westminster Fellowship on July 2 and, though looking pale and aged, he led a valuable discussion on homosexuality which extended over the morning and afternoon sessions. It was typical of the freshness of his mind that on what he called 'the approach to the question' he differed from all the early contributors

[1]ML-J often closed a phone conversation to fellow ministers with the words, 'Well, keep on!'

to the discussion who believed that the Scriptures had to be the starting point for what was now being so frequently debated in public. ML-J surprised everyone by arguing that in the wider, public discussion we would get nowhere if we *began* by denouncing homosexuality from Scripture. The majority of people already rejected the Bible and, if they were to be won, a different starting point was necessary. Preparatory to introducing the Bible he advocated an appeal to 'nature' ('Doth not even nature itself teach you . . . ?', 1 Cor. 11:14), that is to say, to the physical and psychological *evidence* that male and female are essentially different. That female attracts male and that the production of families is dependent upon that attraction are facts of nature. Homosexual practice is patently abnormal and unnatural. This is not to deny that there are biological variations – there are 'masculine' women and 'effeminate' men – but these variations no more justify the practice of sin in an individual with homosexual tendencies than they do in the case of those whose physical constitution inclines them to be highly sexed or hot tempered. Biological factors do not put the homosexual in a special category with a peculiar problem. 'The practising of homosexuality is sin, in exactly the same way as any other sin is sin.'

In the afternoon, when his voice was weaker and huskier, he continued to argue for what he called this 'indirect' approach. Men such as Mervyn Stockwood were making an impression in the defence of homosexuality; they argued that the Bible has 'a pre-scientific' view of sex while *their* understanding was scientific. That claim needed to be exposed by a demonstration that their view of homosexuality was not the result of new knowledge. If orthodox Christians appeared simply to defend a moralistic position they would not get a hearing. There had to be concern and compassion for people. 'We have been too guilty of moralism instead of being more like our Lord.'

Besides the helpfulness of this whole day, ML-J's starting point was a reminder of his belief that there *is* a place for the use of reason and argument in the approach to non-Christians. Apologetics are not for the pulpit but they do have their own sphere of usefulness.

At this meeting of the fraternal on July 2, 1979 – the last before the usual summer break – ML-J mentioned how the rise in petrol prices was affecting the cost of travel and queried whether the men might prefer to have a bi-monthly meeting. One response was enough to end any discussion: 'Even if it means hitch-hiking,' said Selwyn Morgan of Reading, 'we will still come *monthly!*'

We did not realize how few more fraternals Dr Lloyd-Jones would be able to attend. It was partly that the fellowship so invigorated him that he always looked much better when we parted and that final impression remained with us more than the memory of the weakness which we had seen earlier in the day. Again, in the week following the fraternal of July 2, 1979, when John Marshall gave the lecture of the Evangelical Library on 'Thomas Scott and *The Force of Truth*' such was the vigour of ML-J's chairman's remarks that few can have supposed it was to be his last appearance at that annual occasion. He took the opportunity to urge the need for more reading *and* meditation. In his childhood, he said, they used to have 'TtC' literature, that is to say, books 'Told to Children'. 'There is too much TtC today! Slim paperbacks and short daily readings are not enough!'

After spending the most of the later summer of 1979 at Balsham, ML-J did take up some of his scheduled engagements in the autumn. His usual September meeting at Corsham was cancelled for the first time, but he fulfilled a fifty-first consecutive annual visit to Water Street Church, Carmarthen, where he preached twice. On October 11 he preached from Romans 1:14 at the opening of a third year in the life of the London Theological Seminary and in the three following weeks he preached eight times, including engagements in Cardiff, Llanelli and Manchester, where his visits to the Free Trade Hall were always keenly anticipated. Early in November the BEC Conference met in London and, for the last time, he preached at the final evening meeting, taking Matthew 22:15–22 for his text, with special reference to the command of verse 21, 'Render therefore unto Caesar the things which are Caesar's, and unto God the things that are God's'. The theme was chosen very deliberately. The Pharisees were not listening to Christ because of their preoccupation with lesser things – the payment of taxes and such like. Today there was the similar danger of those in the churches being taken up with lesser things – with questions concerning politics, economics and the structures of society; or questions about culture, art and literature. These were all perfectly legitimate interests in their right place, but that place was not in the centre:

Pay your dues to Caesar, but don't be obsessed with them. 'Render to Caesar . . . *and* to God the things that are God's.' Taxes – money – bring benefits but how limited, how passing and uncertain, they are! They give

[717]

no help on the question: how to die? The benefits of God are incomparable: He gave His only Son. Nothing I know is more glorious than the death of Christ for sinners. This makes a man independent of circumstances; it sees him through loss, through prison, through death.

That night, November 7, 1979, was Dr Lloyd-Jones' last time in the pulpit at Westminster Chapel and I think he knew it. He seemed to abandon any care to conserve his limited strength and preached with considerable animation and physical vigour. The following week he preached for the last time in South Wales at the induction of a new minister, the Rev. Brian Higham, at Llansamlet – a service marked by the known conversion of one individual.

When I saw him at his home in Ealing the following week (November 23, 1979) he was quieter than I had ever known him and he confessed to being somewhat weary. He had overtired himself, he thought, at a service in Guildford three nights earlier. He was also suffering from fibrositis and – as he later discovered – a temperature. For the first time he talked to me of his doubt whether his work could continue, but this in a calm and confident tone far removed from gloom. He had heard of a clinic in Florida with treatment which might be obtained to improve his condition and he had hopes of going there, perhaps at the end of December. If the treatment was successful then he would carry on his work, 'but if not', he paused slightly and I am not certain of the conclusion of the sentence. I believe he said, 'Well, I shall do what I can . . .'. It was his calm acceptance of *either* alternative which affected me and took my mind instantly to the 'But if not . . .' with which Shadrach, Meshach and Abednego faced life or death in Daniel chapter 3. In the event, he put aside any thought of a transatlantic journey for medical help. His last engagements in 1979 had been the Westminster Fellowship on December 3 when many noted 'a particular urgency and pathos about the Doctor' and the meeting of the Evangelical Library committee on December 4. He could not chair or attend the Westminster Conference which met, as usual, before Christmas. As he passed his eightieth birthday on December 20, 1979, for the first time since he had been in the ministry, he possessed an almost blank engagements diary for the year that lay ahead. He knew that public work was almost done.

*　　　*　　　*

As we have seen, ML-J seldom gave interviews to the press but one important exception took place at this time. On September 4, 1979, he had met with Dr Carl Henry in the vestry at Westminster Chapel and a considerable part of their discussion was published in *Christianity Today*, February 8, 1980. ML-J was not entirely happy with this interview. He scarcely knew Henry and must have felt the problem of conveying in a few sentences to an American readership answers to such questions as to why he was not involved in the Graham crusades or such evangelical institutions as the Keswick Convention. He was equally conscious of being out of step with the evangelical establishment (on both sides of the Atlantic) in its new concern to address economic, social and political issues. 'What do you think Christianity ought to say to the economic situation today?' asked Henry at one point and got the blunt response, 'I think the great message we must preach is God's judgment on men and on the world . . . The main function of politics, culture, and all these things is to restrain evil. They can never do an ultimately positive work.'

To the question, 'What great emphases do evangelicals too much neglect?', ML-J replied:

To me the missing note in modern evangelicalism is the matter of godliness, or what was once called spirituality . . . People are no longer humble; there is little fear of the Lord. Modern evangelicalism is very unlike the evangelicalism of the eighteenth century and of the Puritans . . . The genuine evangelicalism is that older evangelicalism.

Another part of the conversation was recorded as follows:

Question: What evangelical gains and losses are noteworthy in Anglican circles and in the Free Churches of Britain?
Answer: The main trouble at the moment is confusion.
Q: In the Free Churches as well as the Anglican Church?
A: Yes: particularly among the Anglicans, but among the others as well.
Q: Why so?
A: Because the technical linguistic and ecclesiastical 'experts' have wrested control from the theologians. Concessions have been made to so-called scholarship, and there has been a slide toward a liberal view of the Scriptures and of particular doctrines. James Barr's *Fundamentalism* correctly represents some of this country's prominent Evangelicals as having

quietly and subtly crossed the line by concessions to higher criticism.

Given the questions, and the way they were put, the amount of negative comment in the responses was inevitable. Had ML-J been able to see his interviewer's volume *Confessions of a Theologian*, which was published seven years later, I think he might have been surprised and, certainly, encouraged by some of Dr Henry's own reservations over contemporary American evangelicalism. ML-J's deep concern for people was not prominent in this interview as it appeared in print and it is perhaps a pity that the *Christianity Today* editors chose to delete a passage in the original typescript which brought out the tenderness of his spirit. The passage concerned his father. After asking about his father's work, Carl Henry had continued:

Q.   Was he a Christian?

Long silence. Dr Lloyd-Jones faltered for words, tried to hold back tears then sobbed.

Q.   You wish you knew?
A.   [Broken voice] My father was the best natural man I've ever known, the kindest character and one of the most honest men I've ever met. I doubt he ever heard the Gospel. He reacted against sham piety and was critical of religiosity. Not knowing the Gospel, he somehow became a follower of R. J. Campbell's 'new theology' that spread in the period between 1901 and World War I. God knows he was better than many so-called Christians. On his deathbed he said to me (and he knew he was dying): 'My father told me, when he was dying, "Whatever else you do in life, be kind to the poor" and I want to say the same to you. God will help you to do that.' My father had a sense of social and political righteousness and concern for the betterment of people but he never heard an evangelical redemptive message. I myself hadn't heard it from the pulpit, and came to know it privately . . .[1]

[1] ML-J allowed this passage to stand in his own revision of the typescript of their recorded interview. Considerations of space doubtless contributed to the decision of *Christianity Today* to omit a number of paragraphs from the original transcript.

This emotion was a revelation of natural affection. But it was more. It showed how deeply he felt about the danger of a conversionless Christianity. He could never forget what he had seen in his own life and family of non-evangelical religion.

⁎   ⁎   ⁎

At this later stage in Dr Lloyd-Jones' life it might be supposed that conflict and controversy were now all behind him. They were not. One of these controversies concerned a complex discussion on the doctrine of justification which was dividing a theological seminary in the United States. It concerned such questions as, Is there a first justification for the believer 'without works' and an ultimate 'justification' in which works are an essential part? At the appeal of trustees of the seminary, ML-J read a large body of written material and from a hospital bed in February 1980 he dictated a statement expressing his conviction that the finality of justification by faith alone would be compromised if the teaching which had appeared in the seminary was allowed to continue. Most men in ML-J's state of health would have begged to be excused from what was a distressing difference between colleagues but, characteristically, that was not ML-J's attitude. As he had said to me on another occasion, 'One of the main weaknesses in the current scene is that men will not fight issues, they back out'.

The particular issue to which I have just referred was concluded by the termination of the professor concerned. Another controversy was more painful for ML-J, not least because it was a great deal closer to him and he was to die without seeing any resolution. It concerned the nature of saving faith and of assurance and had specific relevance to issues relating to Antinomianism which Ernest Kevan had raised in 1963–64. The Rev. Robert T. Kendall had been befriended by ML-J on his coming from the United States to undertake a doctorate at Oxford in 1973. His adherence to Reformed and Puritan theology was already known through articles by him in the *Evangelical Magazine* several years earlier.[1] At the 1974 Westminster Conference Kendall gave a paper on 'The Teaching of William Perkins and his Followers'. Through the years of the Puritan and Westminster Conference there had been no bar upon any speaker offering

---

[1] *Evangelical Magazine*, Issues 44–46 (1967), 50 (1968).

criticism of aspects of Reformed theology and, of course, variations
within that theology were often discussed and debated. There was,
therefore, no general concern when this new speaker in 1974 offered
his opinion that 'legalism often lurked in those who are commonly
called "Puritans"' because Puritan leaders taught Christians to put 'a
strong emphasis upon works as the supreme source of assurance'.[1]
ML-J believed that 'legalism' was always a danger for the orthodox
and he was willing to give a hearing to any viewpoint that professed to
have discovered it in otherwise good men. But when Kendall gave the
Annual Lecture of The Evangelical Library for 1976, entitled 'The
Influence of Calvin and Calvinism upon the American Heritage' his
criticism of the Puritans was both broader and more severe. He now
argued that 'legalism pervaded both English and American puritanism', that New England Puritans erroneously taught that men must be
'prepared' for conversion, that they treated faith as an 'act of will' (in
the same way as an Arminian 'appeals to man's will to make a decision
for Christ') and made good works the basis of assurance. In short,
'they stressed works more than grace and godliness more than God.' A
further address, 'John Cotton – First English Calvinist?', carried more
of the same thing in the Westminster Conference for 1976.

Only gradually did it begin to appear what was precisely at issue.
Kendall was arguing that the Puritans, instead of representing the
pure evangelicalism of the Reformation era, had gone back to
'works' and one of the 'proofs', so he alleged, was their view of faith.
Instead of believing (as he claimed Calvin held) that 'assurance, full
assurance, is of the essence of faith',[2] they erred in introducing the
evidence of *experience* as a means both to further assurance and as a
test of the reality of faith. This, he said, was 'legalism' for it taught
people to examine themselves instead of simply believing on Christ
alone. According to Kendall there was no need to test the genuine-
ness of the profession of anyone who says 'I believe Jesus died for me'
because Christ *has* died indiscriminately for all. And as this teaching
of universal redemption, he now thought, was also John Calvin's
teaching, the conclusion to be reached was that what had been
handed down from the Puritans as Calvinism was, in truth, 'a
misapprehension of Calvin's thought, not to mention misleading'.

In so far as this was an issue of historical theology concerning what

[1] *Living the Christian Life*, The Westminster Conference 1974, pp. 54–55.
[2] *The Influence of Calvin and Calvinism upon the American Heritage*, 1976,
p. 8.

Calvin did or did not believe, ML-J was against any public controversy. Although he personally believed firmly in a definite not a universal atonement, the last thing he wanted was disunity among men who otherwise appeared to hold Calvinistic beliefs in common. His initial hope was that R. T. Kendall, who became minister of Westminster Chapel in 1977, would soon pass from the issue which had occupied his doctoral studies at Oxford and settle down to a regular routine of biblical exposition. It was not to be.

What first brought ML-J into open disagreement was the conviction that the nature of evangelism itself would be changed if these views were taken seriously. To set aside the need for conviction of sin prior to conversion, and to call it 'preparationism', was fundamentally at variance with what he believed about true evangelistic preaching. There is a work of God in the unconverted preparatory to their seeing their need of faith in Christ. Sinners need to be 'awakened', not in order to be qualified for salvation, nor to 'prepare themselves' (a thing Puritans were wrongly accused of believing) but because it is God's general method to bring men to faith by first causing them to know their need of Christ.[1] So when the well known Puritan preacher John Preston was blamed for 'preparationism' at the 1978 Westminster Conference, and it was further suggested that John Bunyan was needlessly kept in the slough of despond by inadequate teaching at the time of his conversion, ML-J was forthright in expressing his disagreement. It was not enough, he affirmed, simply to tell men to believe in Christ:

I entirely disagree with that. It fathers easy believism and decisionism. Bunyan went through that agony not because of 'preparationist' preaching, *perhaps* partly, but I would say that was not his problem at all. It was *Scripture* which convicted him[2] . . . Look at the difference between Nettleton and Finney. Nettleton tended to leave people under conviction. Finney did the exact opposite. I would defend Nettleton without any hesitation at all. When people came to me under conviction I would not brush it aside. It is no use telling them, 'It's all right'. They have got to see it from Scripture. It may take time. I am never unhappy about people whose conversion took a long time, in fact I am happier

---

[1]Dr John Duncan summarizes this truth very well in saying: 'God needs to do a great deal *to* sinners in order to turn them; but God is requiring nothing *of* sinners but that they return.' *Recollections of John Duncan*, A. Moody Stuart, 1872, p. 219. See also John Owen's *Works*, vol. 2, p. 228ff.
[2]Further on this see *Sermon on the Mount*, vol. 2, pp. 247–48.

with them. I do believe in the possibility of instantaneous conversion but we must not standardize. There are great variations . . It is not enough that a man says, 'Yes, I believe'. The *whole* man is involved in conversion. Jesus preached *regeneration* to Nicodemus. The preaching of regeneration shows the need for justification. The lack of experience among our hearers is due to the lack of the preaching of regeneration.

He went on to instance the evangelistic effect of William M'Culloch's series of sermons on regeneration at Cambuslang in 1742 and to deplore the neglect of the subject at the present time. '*Hearts* have to be touched and where the heart is not touched we must be *concerned* about people.' The first need of such persons is not to be urged to 'believe'. They may respond, but a decision to 'believe' without *evidence* of a changed heart is no basis for thinking that anyone has become a Christian.

The Westminster Conference at which he said this on December 13, 1978 was, as already indicated, his last. But, with the publication in 1979 of R. T. Kendall's thesis, *Calvin and English Calvinism to 1649* (for which he was awarded Oxford's degree of Doctor of Philosophy) the controversy continued and ML-J followed it closely in private. He reread Calvin and took up the writings of Thomas Hooker (now alleged to be one of the foremost Puritan 'legalists'). ML-J became convinced that the case against Hooker was false[1] and that differences between Calvin and the Puritans were differences in emphasis, not substance. They could be readily explained in terms of legitimate development and the changed pastoral circumstances in which the Puritans were often preaching. Early in 1981 he read a critical review by Paul Helm of Dr Kendall's published thesis and in conversation on February 5, 1981, he expressed his warm approval and the hope that it would have a wide circulation.[2]

[1] In this I think he was aided by his discovery in a London bookshop of *Thomas Hooker, Writings in England and Holland, 1626–1633*, Harvard Theological Studies xxviii, Harvard University Press, 1975. The opinion he expressed on Hooker in 1976 was thus not his final one. Hooker's position on so-called 'preparationism' was, in fact, the same as both John Cotton's and Jonathan Edwards' (see *Puritans*, p. 350).
[2] Helm's review was an offprint of an article to be published in the *Scottish Journal of Theology* in April 1981. It was subsequently expanded into a book, *Calvin and the Calvinists*, Banner of Truth, 1982. The charge that the Puritans were legalists was, of course, not new. As Dr Kevan observed, 'The reason why Puritanism is decried by many modern writers is that they themselves are Antinomians in some sort' (*The Grace of Law*, 1964, p. 260).

Keeping On

This sad controversy is far too relevant to Dr Lloyd-Jones' biography to be excluded from these pages. We have seen that no small part of his ministry had been connected with the recovery of the works of the Puritans. It had also been the great work of the Evangelical Library. Certainly the Puritans were not to be regarded as above criticism but this attack was centred on the point where their reputation was strongest, on their work as 'physicians of the soul' and as masters in experimental divinity. If it was true that they were wrong *there* then the main reason for reading them today was gone. The recovery of their writings had been little more than a mistake.

Further, Dr Lloyd-Jones' own reputation as a teacher and leader was clearly involved in any assessment of these allegations. The substance of Dr Kendall's case had already been levelled against ML-J by Dr Micklem of Oxford in the columns of the *British Weekly* in 1953. Barthian theology, with its universalism and its desire to use the name of Calvin, had long claimed that what people usually thought of as 'Calvinism' was not Calvinism at all but a seventeenth-century aberration. So Micklem designated Lloyd-Jones' beliefs as 'the tenets of scholastic Calvinism'. Dr Kendall did not choose to apply his criticism of the Puritans to ML-J himself but it was clearly only a matter of time before others would do so. Clive Rawlins, biographer of William Barclay, passes off ML-J's warning of the Scottish liberal theologian on the ground that the critic was the 'doyen of traditional Calvinism south of the border'. Rawlins goes on to say: 'I emphasize that it was from the ranks of *traditional* (i.e. English) Calvinism that Willie received complaints. He did not live to see the fruit of R. T. Kendall's doctoral researches'.[1] Politely but nonetheless definitely, and on the basis of Kendall's charges, Michael A. Eaton has proceeded to correct ML-J on such things as 'Sandemanianism' and 'preparationism'. He blames ML-J – just as Kendall blames the Puritans – for teaching which 'is surely the highway to acute introspection' and 'a legalistic approach to the gospel'.[2] It is 'introspective and preparationist Calvinist orthodoxy' as 'imbibed from the Perkins tradition'.[3]

ML-J was beyond any regard for his own reputation in these last years of his life. He felt the immensity and gravity of the approaching judgment of God. But he was concerned for the preservation of the

[1] *William Barclay*, pp. 651, 776. See above, p. 443.
[2] *Baptism with the Spirit, The Teaching of Dr Martyn Lloyd-Jones*, pp. 244, 247.
[3] *Ibid.*, pp. 215, 245.

truths of Scripture and, on that ground, earnest in prayer that these errors should not succeed. To call preaching for conviction of sin 'preparationism' was to subvert New Testament evangelism. And to hold that 'full assurance' necessarily belongs to saving faith has devastating practical consequences. If it were true then it would follow: (1) that anyone lacking 'full assurance' has to be treated as not being a Christian at all; (2) that all converts can be told that their assurance is complete, contrary to the New Testament directions to converts to press on to fuller assurance (Hebrews 6:11; 2 Peter 1:5–10; 1 John 1:4); and (3) that if faith *means* full assurance then the many warnings of Scripture on the need to observe that true faith is always accompanied by holiness of life become needless.[1]

Removed though ML-J largely was from all public ministry by the end of 1979 there was no slackening in his vigilance and his conversations on the above subject were among the most solemn that I ever had with him.

[1]Dr Kendall was making the basis of salvation, namely the death of Christ, the exclusive basis of the believer's assurance. But the salvation of the Christian *includes* Christ's work *in* the believer and that work provides evidence of salvation which is distinct from what Christ has done *for* the believer. This evidence does not mean that sanctification is to be seen as the foundation of assurance but the Spirit uses the evidence of *experience* to strengthen and confirm assurance (see 1 John 2:3; 3:14 etc.). Antinomianism would exclude any consideration of inward grace in order to assurance and after ML-J's death Kendall was to go to the length of asserting that ungodly 'believers' will be saved and to say that those excluded by the Apostle Paul on moral grounds from 'any inheritance in the kingdom of Christ and of God' are not to be regarded as people who are lost (*Once Saved, Always Saved*, 1983, pp. 95–96). ML-J approved the Puritan and Westminster Confession position on assurance (*Romans*, vol. 7, pp. 247, 324; *Joy Unspeakable*, p. 40, etc.) and warned strongly against any assurance which lessened the necessity for obedience: 'If your so-called grace which you say you have received, does not make you keep the law, you have not received grace' (*Sermon on the Mount*, vol. 1, pp. 197, 208). See also *Ephesians*, vol. 5, pp. 151, 344–53, where he specifically answers the charge that to make holiness of life necessary to salvation 'is going back to justification by works'. The Puritans rejected the law as a basis of salvation but held to it as a rule of life; they did not seek holiness by the law but believed that Christian holiness is *expressed* through obedience to the law and commandments of God. In the words of William Fenner, 'Good works are a good sign of faith but a rotten basis for faith'.

'By faith Jacob when he was a dying . . . worshipped'.

Hebrews 11:21

Oh! for that peace, beyond all understanding
   Peace, heavenly peace, bought by eternal pain,
That my frail soul, beneath life's cruel pounding
   At rest at Jesu's cross may still remain.

Oh! give the peace, that in the stormiest fight
   Can never tire and still is amply blest,
So that my soul in midst of blackest night
   Can rest on God, my heavenly Father's breast.

Grant me the peace that leads to sweet endeavour
   In heavenly work, in disappointment's hour,
Without a fear, but resting in the favour
   Of God's love, despite the storm's great power.

Oh! for the peace, that like that river flowing
   Through heaven's city and the trees of life
Peace after war, to heavenward pilgrims going
   Beyond the vale, to joy and end of strife.

ML-J

Translation of Welsh hymn by H. ELVET LEWIS
Evangelical Library Bulletin, spring 1969

35

'Dying . . . He Worshipped'

After our meeting to which I have referred on November 23, 1979, when Dr Lloyd-Jones spoke of his thoughts of a visit to Florida for cancer treatment, although we spoke on the phone I did not see him again until I was back in Ealing on March 3, 1980. It was a lovely day in early Spring and I found him sitting in his favourite armchair in the sitting room, dressed in one of his normal dark grey suits but with thinness and weakness giving a marked change to his appearance.

When ML-J had spoken to Carl Henry the previous September he had expressed the intention of employing such time as he had left mainly in writing. The preparation of his Ephesians series was nearing completion but while he anticipated further volumes on Romans they were not his priority. Rather, as he said to Dr Henry, 'I am now ready to commence a spiritual autobiography'. This was a project about which he had often spoken yet in the ensuing autumn and winter of 1979–80 finally decided that he would not do it. Instead he gave me a far greater responsibility than he had ever done before. While I had kept notes for some time for a possible biography we had never actually discussed it seriously. Only at this stage did he commit himself to give me all the help he could in the setting down of a record which, as he charged me, should be for God's glory only.

A new dimension thus came into our conversations from this period and I arrived on March 3 with various questions ranging from, 'Why was Llangeitho also called Capel Gwynfil?' to, 'Who was the author of the anonymous attack on him in the *British Weekly* in 1953?' At this and at other times we talked not so much of any one period in his life as of the main turning points and the key factors.

I never asked him why he had laid aside the thought of an autobiography. I think there was an instinct against it in his make-up – the same instinct that had long led him to disapprove of any would-be biographer. There was also an instinct in his theology against it. I find this confirmed by a jotting which he made at this period. It remained his habit to write down a few special quotations which impressed him in his reading. On the back of a letter belonging to the year 1979 he noted these words of Henry Cooke, the Ulster Presbyterian leader of the previous century: 'No man can be trusted with a full and honest development of his own character, thought and acts. There are secret springs and motives within him which he does not reveal – which, indeed, it would be folly to attempt to expose to the world's eye.'

I believe there could well have been a further factor in his decision not to work on an autobiography. It had to do with his final assessment of the right use of such time as remained to him. There were members of his family in special need of his support and encouragement; others, also, could still be helped by letters and phone calls. These activities, however, were now linked in his mind with a still greater duty. It came home to him with much conviction that time to prepare for death was very important: he needed such time and believed that its right use was now his chief work as a Christian. This subject came to the fore in an unforgettable way in our meeting on March 3, 1980. In the early part of the conversation, as we spoke from 10.45 a.m. until 12.30, he answered my queries and gave some valuable comments. But what was uppermost in his thoughts did not lie in the past at all. Nor had he anything more to say of transatlantic treatment and possible recovery. The big thing before him was that all Christians need a pause from the activities of life in order to prepare for heaven. Referring to words of Thomas Chalmers on this subject and also to his own present condition, he went on:

I am grateful to God that I have been given this time. I agree with Chalmers absolutely. We do not give enough time to death and to our going on. It is a very strange thing this: the *one* certainty, yet we do not think about it. We are too busy. We allow life and its circumstances so to occupy us that we do not stop and think . . . People say about sudden death, 'It is a wonderful way to go'. I have come to the conclusion that is quite wrong. I think the way we go out of this world is very important and this is my great desire now that I may perhaps be enabled to bear a greater testimony than ever before.

We need to fight to realize our individuality and how limited we are. The world is too much with us. We hold on to life so tenaciously – that is so wrong, so different from the New Testament! Even until last

November I wasn't conscious of my age. I felt it ridiculous to talk about it. When we feel well and active it is difficult to realize the end. I remember as a boy the number of deaths from tuberculosis, which was a scourge in Cardiganshire, and the number of child deaths from diphtheria. We were reminded of death much more often. With modern medicine people are now living to an older age . . .
    Chalmers' emphasis on preparation for death is right. You remember Tennent's rebuke to George Whitefield.[1] But I think Whitefield was right. He had such a knowledge of the coming glory that he desired to be there. That should be true of us all.

He then went on to refer to the account of the death of Roxana Beecher which he had read in her husband's autobiography while in Connecticut in 1967. The passage he recalled read: 'She told her husband that her views and anticipations of heaven had been so great that she could hardly sustain it, and if they had been increased she should have been overwhelmed. . . .'.[2] 'People who have had a real glimpse,' he affirmed, 'are like this. It has nothing to do with age at all. The hope of a sudden death is based upon the fear of death. But death is not something to slip past, it should be victorious. I am grateful, therefore, for this experience. Maybe this present trouble [referring to his physical condition] is to give me this insight. All my ministry I have used the words "short uncertain earthly life and pilgrimage". One of my first sermons was on "For here have we no continuing city . . ." and I remember the second half of that sermon, "but we *seek* one to come" (Heb. 13:4). In my youth we moved such a lot. There were just nine years at Llangeitho before we moved to London. My brother died in 1918, my father in 1922. When I entered the ministry I had not lived in any house beyond twelve years. Until Port Talbot it was constant movement and change. . . .'.
    He went on to recall that he had often preached that death is a tremendous thing – to go out of this world and to leave all that one has ever known behind – and his ministry, he confessed, had not been without instances of the power of that message. 'But,' he added with much feeling, 'I can see that it should have been even more emphasized. What is this brief span in the context of eternity!'
    All this, it must be understood, was not said with an air of sadness nor with the slightest degree of resignation to the inevitable. The

---

[1] *The Log College*, Archibald Alexander, 1968 Banner of Truth reprint, p. 125.
[2] *The Autobiography of Lyman Beecher*, 1961, vol. 1, p. 217.

negative and the morbid were entirely absent. His whole attitude was one of thankfulness and expectation, 'looking for and hasting unto the coming of the day of God' – and this as something which belongs to all Christians: 'People are so idiotic – they think of death only in terms of age. In 2 Corinthians 4:18 the emphasis is on "looking", "we *look* not at the things which are seen . . .". I am quite certain we are leaving out the experimental emphasis. Christianity is faith but it is not *only* faith.'

In the course of this conversation I spoke of the glorious death of a Christian known to me who had been like Bunyan's 'Mr Fearing' in his lifetime but passed on with unspeakable joy. To a brief account of this I added the comment, 'How wonderful it would have been if he had *lived* like that'. The Doctor responded at once and with a definite element of disapproval: 'But don't underestimate dying! *Death* [with great emphasis] is "the last enemy". Men may live well who do not die victoriously.'

In his prayer before we parted he asked for more of what he already knew, 'that we might rejoice in hope of the glory of God'. As I left him at the front door, and it closed behind me, his smiling face remained silhouetted through the glass in the sunshine until I was out of sight. It was no more than the usual way in which he parted with friends but as I returned to Scotland it seemed very possible that this would be my last view of him.

The next time we spoke was on the phone on March 13, 1980, when I asked his advice on an address I was seeking to prepare on 'Is Calvinistic Evangelistic Preaching Necessary?'. He took this up with enthusiasm and in a few sentences clarified the whole theme. Referring to the controversy at the theological seminary in the United States (of which we wrote in the last chapter) he pointed out how it had allegedly arisen out of a concern to correct the stress which modern evangelism put on justification. But the diagnosis was wrong. The superficiality of modern evangelism was not the result of an over-emphasis on justification, it was because it did not preach the law, the depth of sin and the holiness of God. The gospel was being preached in terms of the offer of a friend and a helper. *The* characteristic of Calvinistic evangelism is that the majesty and glory of God is put first, instead of some benefit provided for man. Such preaching does not treat sin merely as some kind of sickness but as an affront to God, as lawlessness, and its great concern is that men should see themselves in relation to the glory of God. Modern evangelism pays lip service to regeneration but it does not really believe in it. True Calvinistic preaching shows the complete helplessness of man and regards the humbling of man as the main part of its work. If that is left out, the true glory of salvation cannot begin to be measured.

These words were a summary of his own evangelistic preaching, and as he was speaking – he in London and I in Edinburgh – I did not believe we would ever see him in a pulpit again. He had not been anywhere in public since early December nor was he expected to be. It was, therefore, with some amazement that we heard he hoped to preach in Glasgow at a service marking the Jubilee of the Scottish Evangelistic Council on Friday, May 9, 1980. To the delight of his friends, Eddie and Nora Stobart in Carlisle, he rang them in April to propose that he and Bethan pay a visit en route to Scotland and to express his willingness to preach once at one of the smaller chapels near Carlisle on Sunday, May 4.

The reason for the latter suggestion was partly that, having not preached since the previous November, he was not certain that he would have the strength to address a large gathering in Glasgow. To preach in a less demanding situation beforehand would, he hoped, give the confirmation he needed before continuing the journey into Scotland. I do not doubt that he planned this last itinerary with the prayer that he would be enabled to preach for the last time in places and among people that he loved. The prayer was to be wonderfully answered at every point of this journey. Eddie Stobart exceeded his commission by arranging an inter-church service at the Methodist Central Hall, Carlisle, at 8.15 pm on Sunday, May 4, which was attended by some seven hundred people. 'It was a night to be remembered,' writes Mr Stobart. 'Showing obvious weakness of body he was strong in the Spirit leaving his congregation in no doubt what it meant to be a Christian. Though perspiring heavily and very tired he was willing to give counsel to those who wished to see him in the vestry after the meeting.'

The following Friday he was, as anticipated, in the pulpit of St Vincent Street Free Church, Glasgow and facing a crowded congregation. In a few personal words before he started to preach he confessed he was 'not a well man'. 'My friend, Mr Murdoch, persuaded me to come and I thank God He has given me the health and strength to be here.' He recalled how, when the Scottish Evangelistic Council had first approached him in November 1938 to preach for them, he had promised to come but that promise had been delayed by the War until the St Andrew's Hall meeting of 1942: 'I am sure all who were present at that meeting will not forget it. We all felt that God was with us. I have had the privilege of coming to Scotland ever since.'

But they were not assembled, he went on, to talk about the past The best way to celebrate a jubilee was to consider what the SEC was to do at the present time. The need of the hour, he believed, was for the prophetic note, to show what the Bible has to say to the present world situation. This brought him to his text, the twelve verses of Psalm 2, upon which he proceeded to preach for almost the whole of the following hour, beginning with the words, 'Why do the heathen rage, and the people imagine a vain thing . . .'.

I cannot attempt to describe the sermon. The tape is available[1] and should be heard by every reader of these pages. The frail, dying man was, in truth, an ambassador from heaven. Knowing the message he had to deliver, and the time he would need, I believe he tried to husband what strength he had but there was no holding back. The message took over the man and every last vestige of energy was poured out in both word and action. The divine wrath, of which the Psalm speaks, was to him a terrible, present reality and he asked the congregation:

Do you still believe in the wrath of God? There are people in England – evangelicals – who think modern man needs entertainment. There is a mania for singing, for drama, for mime. 'People cannot take preaching,' it is said, 'Give them singing. Teach them how to dance . . .'. In the name of God I say that is to do violence to Scripture. The church is not here to entertain. It is here to call people to 'be wise', to 'be instructed' (v 10). It is not just an appeal to 'come to Jesus' – they are to be 'instructed', taught. People are dying through lack of knowledge. We are not here to be popular, but to tell the naked truth: 'Serve the Lord with fear, rejoice with trembling . . .' (v. 11).

The final verse of the Psalm was alive with light and power as he pleaded, with failing voice, 'Kiss the Son, lest he be angry . . . Blessed are all they that put their trust in him'.

The service over, he sat pale and exhausted on the bottom steps of the pulpit while old friends gathered to greet him for the last time. The next morning, Saturday, Eddie Stobart drove Dr and Mrs

[1]From Ian M. Densham (see below, p. 797).

Lloyd-Jones south through central Scotland on the A74. He recalled later how alert ML-J was on that part of the journey and how often he commented on the beauty of the scenery. After lunch at the Stobart home in Carlisle, they were driven on a further 150 miles to the border of North Wales where John and Mari Jones met them and took them home to Brynuchaf. On the Sunday evening ML-J preached in the little chapel at Llanymawddwy and, after this final visit to a place so dear to him, they left for two mid-week services on May 14 in Aberystwyth. Some 400 were present for a Welsh service at 2.30 pm, including Christian girls from the local school who had asked permission to attend. ML-J preached on 'wrestling Jacob' (Gen. 32:24). 'Here,' he said, 'is the essence of Christian experience.' It is *personal*, 'During the recent months of illness I have had to consider how a man feels when he is left alone and can do nothing'. But, further, 'in our loneliness there is Another with us. Fellowship with God is the only worthwhile thing in life and it makes us new.'

In the evening some 800 people, including over 300 students and young people, crowded the Baker Street Congregational Church and ML-J preached again on Psalm 2. The sermon included one personal reference. He recalled coming to Aberystwyth in 1911 in a horse-drawn trap, with other children from his school in Llangeitho, to see King George V and Queen Mary lay the foundation stone of the National Library. They had reached their destination at 10.30 and had to wait until after 2 pm for the arrival of the King.

As in Glasgow, it was a very sobering sermon, preached, in the words of the Rev. Geoffrey Thomas (who led the service), 'with wonderful authority and simplicity'. At the end many came to greet him at the front. 'Slowly the crowd spilled out into the street and into a beautiful summer's evening but they did not go away. The children played and were introduced to Dr and Mrs Lloyd-Jones. Old friends conversed and there was a common feeling of joy and thankfulness.'

This concluded ML-J's last evangelistic itinerary and the next morning he saw Cardiganshire and Wales for the last time.

During May his condition deteriorated but there were still a handful of opportunities which he was eager to fulfil. One of these was the East Midlands Church Officers' Conference held at Shepshed, near Loughborough on the afternoon and evening of Saturday, May 24. His friend Paul Cook, the minister at Shepshed, drove him there from Balsham on the Saturday morning and the two men conversed cheerfully throughout. ML-J had been asked to speak in the afternoon session on 'The local church and extra-church movements'. 'Although obviously weakened by his prolonged illness,' says Mr Cook, 'he nevertheless gave a full and clear address on this subject and its relationship to the anarchy too often tolerated among evangelicals.'

There were many present that Saturday in Shepshed who would have valued some of his time in the interval before the evening session but he chose to spend it with Mrs Faith Cook at the manse. The reason was that, despite the cheerful conversation on the drive from Balsham, her husband was in the midst of a critical period of oppression of spirit which was seriously affecting his ministry. Faith Cook was bearing a heavy part of this trial and he wanted to have tea with her alone so that they could speak together about Paul's condition. When she asked him to say grace, writes Mrs Cook, 'he appeared to forget that he was giving thanks for the meal and instead engaged for about five minutes in the most moving prayer for the blessing of God to rest upon the home and all in it'. In the ensuing conversation, she proceeds, 'I was astonished at the accuracy and the certainty with which he spoke of the root of Paul's trouble.' ML-J regarded it as a temptation of Satan to silence a preacher's effective ministry. 'I suppose,' Faith Cook writes further, 'the best thing of all that he said to me was just as we parted. Realizing, of course, that we would never meet again on this earth, he grasped my hand warmly and simply said, "Remember the love of God". These words, perhaps more than any others, carried me through all the distress of the months that followed.'[1]

The evening session that day was a discussion and it was noted how 'alive' ML-J was with conviction and with evident enjoyment of the fellowship among men with whom he was so much at home. 'The Doctor was relaxed and very much his usual self during this session, showing great human understanding and patience as he dealt with the questioning, with occasional flashes of his brilliant wit.'

On April 28, 1980, he had chaired the Westminster Fellowship and he did so again on June 2, when the morning discussion was on the subject, 'What should we do in the light of the rapid spread of Islam, Catholicism and Communism?' and in the afternoon Josef Tson of Romania spoke. On the Wednesday of that first week in June ML-J preached at an anniversary of another friend, Derek Swann of

[1] Paul Cook was delivered from the attack which resembled what ML-J himself had experienced in 1949.

Ashford, Middlesex and then, in a final effort to help a younger minister and a former member of Westminster Chapel, he preached for Ray Gaydon at Barcombe in Sussex on Saturday, June 7. This was his last sermon.

The next Tuesday, June 10, he had to return to hospital for a check on his worsening condition. There were by this time regular hospital visits for periods varying from a day to a week and generally for chemotherapy treatment. His last meeting in public was to be at the Westminster fraternal on July 7. What stood out chiefly in the memory of one who was there was the Doctor's closing prayer 'when he was especially earnest and very moving as he commended us all to the Lord'.

At this time when weakness and nausea were becoming so much a part of daily life, his spirit was bright with gratitude. 'God's great kindness,' became his main theme. There was thankfulness for 'a long life and remarkable health', 'for Bethan', for all that was past (including in all seriousness, 'The best thing I ever did was to refuse to go on committees . . . I have known many men ruined by committees'). Speaking to me on the phone on June 27 he said: 'I have nothing but praise in my heart. I am more aware of the goodness of God than ever before and that I am

A debtor to mercy alone.

That line of Toplady's he often quoted and, if he had ever been asked to reduce his biography to one sentence I believe it is the one he would have chosen. It was in connection with the grace of God to him that he mentioned how moved he had been to read reviews of new biographies of two eminent Cambridge men, G. M. Trevelyan, Master of Trinity (whom he had met in 1941–42),[1] and J. D. Bernal, the eminent physicist. 'These reviews,' he said, 'turned out to be a tremendous blessing to me. Here in Trevelyan is human nature at its best and it came to me with such force: Why did God ever choose to look upon me? Why *me* in contrast with these men and the despair in which they died?'

When I next saw him on July 26, 1980 at his home in Ealing, he had waited for seven hours at the hospital the previous day without being admitted. But he was in wonderful spirits and remained

[1] See p. 68.

thankful for everything. 'I have no complaints,' he declared in reference to the experience of the previous day. His conversation flowed. He began by speaking of how God times the encouragements He sends to us and then went on to talk of the great importance of the command which Christ gave to His disciples on witnessing their first success, 'Notwithstanding in this rejoice not that the spirits are subject unto you; but rather rejoice, because your names are written in heaven'.[1] 'Bear that in mind,' he said solemnly. 'Our greatest danger is to live upon our activity. The ultimate test of a preacher is what he feels like when he cannot preach.' Our relationship to God is to be the supreme cause of joy. To lean upon our sermons or words of testimony from others is 'a real snare for all preachers'. 'We cannot lean on them'. He then went on to speak again of death and of how it was to be faced without fear. Two things were needed. First, face it as a fact. We must all die. Second, Christians are able to be unafraid because God gives assurance that they will not be left alone and the company they possess at their departure will include that of angels, he affirmed, quoting Luke 16:22, 'the beggar died, and was carried by the angels into Abraham's bosom'. Adding, 'I believe in this ministry of angels, I think more and more of it':[2]

Our greatest trouble is that we really don't believe the Bible and exactly what it says. We think we know it but do we really appropriate it and actually believe it is true *for us*? That is Christianity to me. 'Our short, uncertain life' is the most difficult thing to realize. We do not put the emphasis as the New Testament does. We are not meant to despise this life but we are certainly meant to keep it in proportion – 'our light affliction, which is but for a moment' (2 Cor. 4:17). We have to take these statements *literally*. They are facts, not merely ideas. That is what I feel you people have got to emphasize more and more. . . .

From these and similar words it was evident that he was still preaching to himself ('more and more I can see that ministers *must* preach to themselves', he said in passing). Another subject upon which he clearly enjoyed meditating was the way in which some of the Christian men and women whom he had known had died. Spurgeon once said: 'If I may die as I have seen some of our church members die, I court the grand occasion. I would not wish to escape

---

[1]Luke 10:20. He also recalled that this was the text from which he had preached at the Induction of John Thomas in Sandfields in 1953.
[2]See vol. 1, p. 247.

death by some by-road if I may sing as they sang.' ML-J felt the same. He vividly remembered, for instance, the home-going of William Thomas, one of the early converts at Sandfields. When dying from double pneumonia, Thomas suddenly threw his arms upwards and with radiant smile left this world exulting in the clear recognition of his Saviour.

His prayer before we parted on July 26 was mainly praise for God's exceeding goodness and care – 'the hairs of our head are numbered' – and petition, 'Shed abroad Thy love in our hearts that we may rejoice'. Such words as, 'Have pity on Thy church', and pleas for colleagues in the work of the ministry were also rarely absent from these short prayers at the conclusion of conversations. 'Now I can pray for you men,' he told me as I left, 'and am doing so. People say to me it must be very trying for you not to be able to preach – No! Not at all! I was not living upon preaching.'

To his old friend Philip Hughes, ML-J wrote on September 20, 1980:

You will be sorry to hear that my health has not been at all good this summer; I have not been able to preach or to do anything else since the beginning of June. I have to go into hospital every three weeks for a few days' special treatment and it tends to leave me somewhat weak. However, I thank God for His great kindness and mercy to me over these long years and for the privilege of being able to do some work in His glorious kingdom. I am happy to be in His gracious hands and to be content with His will whatever it may be.

We met again in October and November 1980 for lengthy conversations on the biography. I was now beginning to produce some draft chapters which he was ready to go over but the main thing for me was to have down on tape his understanding of the more crucial areas of his life and ministry with which I knew I would have to deal. This was the more necessary for those years in which his thought had been unfamiliar to me.

As he looked back he was absolutely convinced that nothing of significance in his life had happened according to his own plans. Things *he* had thought to do, he said, such as going to the Theological College in Aberystwyth in 1925, and then serving permanently in Wales, had not happened, while his life had witnessed a succession of things of which he had never dreamed: 'I found myself living a kind of life I had never imagined for a moment.'

He had never intended to preach around the country, or to be a teacher of students or to publish any book. 'When I went to Sandfields if anyone had told me I was going to do what I have actually done I would have told them they were mad. My only thought was to be an evangelist in a local mission hall. There is only one explanation – the sovereignty of God! the guiding hand of God! It is an astonishment to me.'

We talked about the right framework and structure for the biography and after an interval of a few days he came back to me with this suggestion: 'I think I have got the key to it. From Sandfields, and for the rest of my life, I was confronted with a series of problems.' These, he explained, together with their answers, could well provide the divisions for a number of chapters. He went on to outline what he had in mind. There were the early problems such as the constant calls to preach away from his own church, his relationship to medicine when he was at Port Talbot, and the expectation of his denominational leaders that he would fit into the typical Welsh Presbyterian mould. Then there were the unexpected consequences of the study of Warfield (which put him into the role of a teacher), the problems of the War years at Westminster when the work seemed to have no future, the incompatibility between his convictions with those prevailing in English Nonconformity and – in many ways the greatest problem of all – his concern to be a helper to an evangelicalism whose traditions had diverged so much from the evangelicalism of the past. He reflected a great deal on this latter point. It was amongst evangelicals that he belonged more than anywhere else and yet, from the time of the invitation to be principal of the London Bible College to the Graham crusades and thereafter, he was constantly the outsider.

His divergence from the role which others expected of him would be, he knew, the crux issue in any biography. He posed the question, How did he arrive at the position which so often put him at odds with the religious current of his times? He knew that the answer could be treated in terms of his gifts, his individuality, even in terms of his 'Welshness', but any such treatment, in his view, would be directing attention away from the truth. He could only understand what had happened to him, as already said, in terms of divine providence. God had stopped him from going in ways he would otherwise have taken and constrained him to convictions for which the thought of taking any credit to himself was abhorrent. He was never more in earnest than when he said, 'I am such a sinner that God has always had to compel me to do things'. And again: 'My whole life experiences are proof of the sovereignty of God and His direct interference in the lives of men. I cannot help believing what I believe. I would be a madman to believe anything else.'

When he spoke, then, of his life in terms of problems and answers he was thinking entirely in this context. The hand that guided his life was not his own.

From October 1980 I never saw him rise again from his favourite chair. For the next four months this was where he quietly sat, still dressed in a suit, though it hung loosely on him as though no longer his own. I think it was towards the end of the year – on a final hospital visit – that he was told that the time remaining was short and he himself then took the decision to end any further treatment. Although he was progressively weaker, yet all his mental powers were unimpaired and, with scarcely an exception, his phenomenal memory remained. He had slowly lost interest in classical music but his love of good books was unabated and some of the books he enjoyed during the last year of his life must be mentioned. They included a biography of Philip Doddridge; *The Essays and Letters of Thomas Charles* ('definitely one of the most neglected of the spiritual leaders'); *Archbishop Grindal*, by Patrick Collinson; *The Works of Walter Craddock* (the Welsh Puritan); *The Diary of Kenneth MacRae* ('I am enjoying it tremendously'); *Drunk Before Dawn* by Shirley Lees; Calvin's *Letters* and John Owen on *The Glory of Christ*. Of Owen's classic, which he finished in December 1980, he said: 'It has done me great good and been a great blessing to my soul. I feel at times that he tends to go a bit too far. We are not saved by our love to Christ. At times he almost says, "Unless you are longing to be with Christ I doubt if you are a Christian". That is going too far. He was so concerned about glib *fideism* but God justifies the *ungodly . . .*'.

This comment was characteristic of his balance. He longed for more of the *felt* presence of Christ and yet always insisted that our feelings play no part in the basis of peace with God. In this connection I asked him one day if he agreed with Spurgeon's statement that strong faith can exist with little feeling or enjoyment. Emphatically he did, 'Feeling varies a lot. We are not the same from one day to the next.' And he proceeded to quote one of his favourite hymns:

My hope is built on nothing less
Than Jesus' blood and righteousness;
I dare not trust my sweetest frame

['They come and go,' he interjected]

But wholly lean on Jesus' Name,

On Christ, the solid Rock, I stand;
All other ground is sinking sand.

And then with reference to that hymn's last verse –

His oath, His Covenant and blood . . .

he exclaimed, 'Oh, its the Covenant . . '.

Hymns – Welsh and English – meant a great deal to him. I recall two others about which he spoke and which had often been sung at Sandfields (these were missing in *Congregational Praise*). They were, 'To-day Thy mercy calls us', and 'Come, ye disconsolate' with its beautiful closing line, 'Earth has no sorrows that heaven cannot heal'. It might be thought that at the end of such a life ML-J had no sorrows. He had, and they included painful disappointments with respect to men, once close to him, from whom he had expected better things. Yet he also knew, more deeply than he had ever done, that for the praying Christian there is peace in the midst of conflict. Peace is promised for *all* circumstances and its reality shone through his emaciated body and formed a main part of such testimony as he was enabled to give to others.

For one friend who was facing a difficult experience he urged the words, 'Be anxious for nothing', and went on, 'Your duty is to enjoy the peace of God – there is to be no anxiety'. To a younger minister who had been laid aside from his work by illness he wrote on December 4, 1980:

I cannot tell you what your letter of ten days ago did to me and meant to me. The very fact that in your present state of health you even thought of writing moved me deeply . . .

We have both been passing through new experiences and I am sure that you feel as I do that finally nothing matters but the fact that we are in God's hands. We and our works are nothing. It is His choosing us before the foundation of the world that matters and He will never leave us nor forsake us. More and more do I see that what we need is a simple child-like faith, just to believe His word and surrender ourselves to Him utterly.

The day after this he heard grievous news from a manse in Argyll, Scotland, the home of his friends John and Cynthia Murray. Their thirteen-year-old daughter, Lynda, had been seriously ill for many weeks and he and Bethan prayed often for her. The news was of Lynda's death and at once he wrote a letter to the sorrowing parents in his own hand. It included the words:

. . . There is no need for me to tell you what to do – you are fine Christians and you know. Nevertheless we are all 'in the body' and full of frailty and there is always the adversary who in his cowardice attacks us when we are tried. The one thing that really matters is that you should be utterly surrendered to our blessed Lord and completely resigned to His perfect will. Do not attempt to understand but believe, whatever you may feel, that 'all things work together for good to them that love God'.

During the past six months especially I have come to realize this truth with the result that I know more of 'the peace of God that passeth all understanding'. It is indeed beyond understanding but nevertheless real . . . Our prayer as a family is that you may be so conscious of being enfolded in the love of Christ that you may even rejoice.

ML-J was still able to see a few visitors who were close to him and one who came was the Rev. Vernon Higham of Cardiff. As he parted with this esteemed colleague of many years he asked him to pray that he might know an 'abundant entrance' into the everlasting kingdom. He longed to enter 'in full assurance of faith' – 'in the full sail of faith'. When Vernon was finally leaving the room, ML-J called him back for a last word. It was, 'Remember I am only a sinner saved by grace'.

One former divine says that God always gives to His people the degree of assurance that is appropriate to them. In Dr Lloyd-Jones' case it consisted at this time, and until his death, of quietness, calmness and profound peace. John Owen, who had passed the same way nearly three hundred years earlier and who also died in Ealing, says in one of his books:

Our minds in this world are not capable of such a degree of assurance in spiritual things as to free us from assaults to the contrary, and impressions of fear sometimes from those assaults: but there is such a degree attainable as is always victorious; which will give the soul peace at all times, and sometimes fill it with joy.[1]

[1]*Works*, vol. 22, p. 200.

Such was also ML-J's experience, with the peace deepening towards the end. But it was peace, he wanted to emphasize, *through believing*. All is done by Christ! On this subject he said to me when I was with him on January 19, 1981:

When you come to where I am, there is only one thing that matters, that is your relationship to Him and your knowledge of Him. Nothing else matters. All our righteousnesses are as filthy rags. Our best works are tainted. We are sinners saved by grace. We are debtors to mercy alone.

To this I replied that I used foolishly to think that there was something rather wrong about some of the old saints who, when dying, prayed the words that Jesus commended, 'God be merciful to me a sinner'. He proceeded:

So did I, but it's rubbish. That's where you will come to. I've been brought to that. Daniel Rowland said at the end, 'I am nothing but an old sinner saved by the grace of God'. I say exactly the same.

Then, after a pause, with profound emotion and broken voice,

God is very patient with us and very kind and He suffers our evil manners like He did with the children of Israel . . . The love of God!

His appearance in his last months combined the utmost gravity with more smiles than, it seemed to me, I ever remembered before; and his face often glistened, especially when he prayed. It so happened that I had been recently reading the words of Abraham Kuyper on Jacob, who, when the end drew near, 'strengthened himself and . . . worshipped'. Kuyper's exposition of Jacob's experience was remarkably parallel to that of this later servant of God. Commenting on the exercise of faith necessary for a dying believer, Kuyper wrote:

It must not be conceded that on his death-bed a man is permitted to let himself passively be overcome by his distress and by his weakness. In dying, the will, the courage and the elasticity of faith must still struggle against the weakness of the flesh. In this holy moment the spirit, not the flesh, must conquer. And this is what Jacob did. He strengthened himself in order that he might die in a godly manner . . . His mighty spirit shook itself awake. And so he glorified God in his dying.
  In dying Jacob worshipped.
  Dying he worshipped. In dying he felt impelled to offer unto his God the sacrifice of worship and adoration; to give Him praise,

thanksgiving and honor; to lose himself in the greatness and Majesty, in the grace and compassion of his God; and thus to offer Him the fruit of the lips, in a better fashion than he had ever been able to do in life. Such a solemn worship on one's death-bed is a summary of the worship which we have offered unto God in our life.[1]

True faith and worship are never merely individualistic and ML-J at this period – when he could see few outside his immediate family – remained full of interest in all that concerned the kingdom of God. He still dictated letters to his friend and helper, Miss Pamela Harris, which were sent to friends near and far. One such, dated January 22, 1981, went to the Rev. R. S. Miller, Professor of Church History in the Presbyterian Church of Australia at Melbourne, whom he had not seen for forty years. Miller had written a few weeks earlier 'as one of the many who owe you, under God, more than they can say'. ML-J replied:

Please forgive me for this delay in writing to thank you for your most kind letter received just before Christmas. I need not say that I deeply value your encouraging words about my volumes on Romans and Ephesians.

I well remember our meeting in Mrs André's home and have been interested in you and all you have done ever since.

Unfortunately, my health has not been too good during last year and I have not been able to preach or do anything else since the beginning of June. I will greatly value your prayers.

May God bless you and yours more and more in every respect.

In the course of a last letter to his old friend Philip Hughes on the same date, he said:

I thank God for all His bountiful goodness to me over the long years, and for all He has graciously allowed me and enabled me to do. My supreme desire now is to testify more than ever to the glory and the wonder of His grace. I shall greatly value your prayers that I be given strength to do so to His glory.

I am glad to say that God in a marvellous manner is granting Bethan most remarkable health and vigour. He is indeed a gracious God.

Letters of this kind continued into February 1981. Among the last was one dictated on February 11 to encourage a young minister and

[1]*To Be Near Unto God*, 1925 (1979, Baker, pp. 324–330).

another to John Caiger, the Secretary of the Westminster Fellowship, giving suggestions on the future leadership of the fraternal. That letter concluded:

Please convey my warmest love and greetings to all, and assure them of my daily prayers, both in their own churches and in the Fellowship. I believe the Fellowship is going to play a vital part in the coming years, and I am sure that God is going to bless it greatly and use it. I need not say that I have regarded it as one of the greatest privileges of my life to be actively concerned in it for so long, and I express my warm gratitude to all the men for their loyalty and loving patience with me.

Throughout these months his daily care was in the hands of his wife, supported by Ann (who was always close at hand) and Elizabeth. He would often refer with great thankfulness to Bethan and sometimes to the time fifty-five years earlier when, instead of marrying others – as he had feared possible! – she became his wife. As with every Christian husband, father and grandfather, he had not found it easy to contemplate leaving a much loved family but he now had assurance that all would be well for them and could say: 'When this illness came, because of my being the one who had made the decisions I was a bit troubled about Bethan and the children after I have gone and tended to worry as to what would happen to them. I have been delivered from it completely. I know that God can care for them very much better than I can and that no longer troubles me at all.'

He continued to give me help with this biography, though, as we spoke of things long past, he was more like an onlooker commenting on someone else's life rather than on his own. He was terribly weak and steadily losing ground. On the phone, on February 13, 1981, he thought he was 'better today', but confessed 'he had not had a very good week'. On February 19, his voice weak and husky, he spoke of being 'much the same'. It was our last conversation, for in the following week he gradually lost the strength and breath with which to speak and communication with the family had to continue by a nod of his head, by a look or sign and one or two very brief notes. Among his last audible words were those spoken to his consultant, Grant Williams, who visited him on February 24.[1] Mr Williams

---

[1]Mr Williams had known ML-J since 1952 when he became a member at Westminster Chapel.

wanted to give him some antibiotics. ML-J shook his head in disagreement. 'Well,' said his doctor, 'when the Lord's time comes, even though I fill you up to the top of your head with antibiotics, it won't make any difference.' His patient still shook his head. 'I want to make you comfortable, more comfortable,' Williams went on, 'it grieves me to see you sitting here "weary and worn and sad"' (quoting Bonar's well-known hymn). That was too much for ML-J. 'Not sad!' he declared, 'Not sad!' The truth was that he believed the work of dying was done and he was ready to go. 'Last night,' Grant Williams wrote to ML-J's local doctor on February 25, 'he refused to take any antibiotic, could hardly talk and I think will die very shortly. I think he is very lucid and knows exactly what he wants to do.'

At one point in these last few days when his speech had gone, as Elizabeth sat beside him he pointed her very definitely to the words of 2 Corinthians 4:16–18 which begin:

For which cause we faint not; but though our outward man perish, yet the inward man is renewed day by day. For our light affliction, which is but for a moment, worketh for us a far more exceeding and eternal weight of glory . . .

'When I asked him,' says Elizabeth, 'if that was his experience now, he nodded his head with great vigour.'

On Thursday evening, February 26, in a shaky hand, he wrote on a scrap of paper for Bethan and the family: 'Do not pray for healing. Do not hold me back from the glory.' The next day he was full of smiles for the little circle who gathered round him and by these, and gestures, he 'spoke' so clearly that one almost forgot the absence of his voice. By rolling one hand over another and pointing, he might request one of us, particularly, to speak, or, clasping his hands together, to pray. On Saturday, still in his sitting-room chair, he slept some hours and at other times appeared to be unconscious. At bed-time it was clear that he was unconscious and, with only Mrs Lloyd-Jones and Ann present, for the first time there was the problem of not knowing how to get him to the bedroom in the front of the house. This need was met by two kind ambulance men who responded willingly to Mrs Lloyd-Jones' call for help and put him to bed. There, a little while later, he came round and knew at once what was happening. To Bethan's enquiry whether he would like a cup of tea he nodded and, while she went to make it, Ann prayed with him. He then drank some of the tea as Bethan and Ann sat with him for about half an hour before sleeping. For over fifty years he had followed M'Cheyne's calendar for daily Bible readings, and one of those readings for the day just ended, February 28, was 1 Corinthians chapter 15. Perhaps the conclusion of that chapter, 'Thanks be to God, which giveth us the victory through our Lord Jesus Christ', or the words of Ann's prayer were in his consciousness as he fell quietly asleep. We cannot know for his next awakening was in 'the land of the blest'.

'As for me, I will behold thy face in righteousness: I shall be satisfied, when I awake, with thy likeness' (Psalm 17:15).

* * *

At lunch-time on Friday, March 6, 1981, the straggling Cardiganshire town of Newcastle Emlyn was alive with movement and people. It was a market day and not so dissimilar from the day, in the same place, where Martyn had first set eyes on Bethan. Now cattle trucks instead of horse-drawn carts almost blocked the narrow streets, along with farmers, jostling to reach the auction ring in their expectation of getting the best prices. For far higher reasons there were thousands of people elsewhere in Britain that day who wished they could have been there. Multitudes who would have attended a London funeral, or even a service in Cardiff, had no means of reaching that inaccessible part of West Wales – the district ML-J had loved in his boyhood and chosen for his burial.

In brighter times the whole of that Welsh town would have stood still to mark the passing of one of the nation's greatest sons. Yet, the numbers who did come for the funeral at 2 pm, perhaps nine hundred people, were enough to require the re-opening of the large, white-washed Bethel Calvinistic Methodist Chapel in a turning off the High Street. Through the morning the building – where Mrs Lloyd-Jones' grandfather had ministered for over fifty years – slowly filled until, an hour before the service was to begin, there was no room left on the ground floor.

The scene was unphotographed, but it will never be forgotten by those who were there. Through the narrow vertical windows, in the beige painted walls, light fell on the empty pulpit and the varnished pine pews. There was much to occupy the hearts of those who quietly waited and few can have lacked their personal reasons for a great sense of loss. Some present, including ninety-year-old Mr E. T. Rees, were fruits of Dr Lloyd-Jones' early ministry; there were widows who would never forget the kindness of his support; others whose callings in this world have been determined by his spiritual guidance; middle-aged folk who thought of how God had led them to Westminster Chapel in the days of youth;[1] one African of noble bearing – a lone representative of the thousands from the Continent who now read Dr Lloyd-Jones' books; and, above all, rows of ministers of the gospel from all parts of Wales – men who were proud to know that they had a special place in his heart.

The coffin was borne into the church by six of the closest male members of the family circle and placed inconspicuously in a side aisle beneath the pulpit. No great wave of emotion broke across the congregation as the fifty-minute service began with the singing of the hymn:

> Cyfamod hedd, cyfamod cadarn Duw . . .
> [The covenant of peace, the strong covenant of God . . .]

Peace seemed to possess the whole congregation and it deepened as the service progressed, led by Hywel R. Jones, Elwyn Davies, Graham Harrison and Vernon Higham who preached on 'an abundant entrance' from 2 Peter 1:11.

Then in the Gelli cemetery on the Cenarth road the greater part of the congregation shortly reassembled at the graveside for a further short service conducted by T. Omri Jenkins. The Chapel service at Bethel had closed with the triumphant singing (in Welsh) of David Charles' hymn:

> From heavenly Jerusalem's towers,
> The path through the desert they trace;
> And every affliction they suffered
> Redounds to the glory of grace.

On that hillside, in the beautiful, sheep-grazing valley of the Teifi with light rain falling, the coffin was lowered into the grave and

---

[1]One of these was Raymond Johnston who recorded the day in 'A very Welsh Farewell' published in *The Church of England Newspaper*, March 13, 1981.

upwards of five hundred Christians sang again the affirmation of the last verse of Charles' hymn:

> And we, from the wilds of the desert,
> Shall flee to the land of the blest,
> Life's tears shall be changed to rejoicing,
> Its labours and toil into rest:
> There we shall find refuge eternal,
> From sin, from affliction, from pain,
> And in the sweet love of the Saviour,
> A joy without end shall attain.

These four things were marked in him: viz. the strength and abundance of his natural gifts; – his great diligence in the use of them, night and day; – the very great extent to which he enjoyed the influence and power of the Holy Spirit in his own work; – and the immense blessing which the people received through him.

THOMAS CHARLES
ON WILLIAM WILLIAMS
The Life of Thomas Charles,
D. E. JENKINS, 1909, vol 2, p. 57

The best of men are only men at their very best. Patriarchs, prophets, and apostles, – martyrs, fathers, reformers, puritans, – all, all are sinners, who need a Saviour: holy, useful, honourable in their place, – but sinners after all.

J. C. RYLE,
Expository Thoughts on the Gospels: Matthew,
1856 (1986 reprint), p. 209

36

'The Best of Men . . .'

The impressions felt by those present at the burial of Dr Lloyd-Jones at Newcastle Emlyn on March 6, 1981 were necessarily different from those experienced at the thanksgiving service held at Westminster Chapel. A mourning family and a largely Welsh congregation now gave way on Monday, April 6 to a throng approaching 2,500. Before the service began at 6.30 p.m., the supply of hymn sheets printed for the occasion was already exhausted and there was standing room only left in the Chapel itself. Two hundred years earlier John Berridge described Whitefield's Tabernacle as 'that old bee hive which has filled many hives with her swarms'. In a measure the same had been true of Westminster Chapel and now, for one evening, the 'swarms' came back from near and far. 'It was a great, unrepeatable reunion for people from Westminster, the farthest corners of the British Isles and beyond,' *The Evangelical Times* reported, 'Many were excited to see long lost, once familiar faces and to exult in renewed fellowship'.

The Rev. John Caiger, Secretary of the Westminster Fellowship, opened the service with the words, 'We are gathered here tonight to give thanks to Almighty God for the life and ministry of His gifted and honoured servant' and there followed the singing of the hymn with which the former minister of the Chapel had resumed his work every September over many years:

> O God of Bethel! by whose hand
> Thy people still are fed . . .

'It was worth coming for the singing alone,' someone was heard to say afterwards.

Five speakers took up various aspects of Dr Lloyd-Jones' life and ministry. Dr Gaius Davies, himself a former Barts man, spoke of

'The Doctor as a Doctor'.[1] Dr Robin Wells spoke for the student world; the present writer for the world of Christian literature; Mr M. J. Micklewright for Westminster Chapel and the Rev. Omri Jenkins on the theme of ML-J as a preacher. These addresses were interspersed with other hymns before the proceedings were finally brought to a close by a sermon delivered 'with much acceptance and power' by the Rev. Peter Lewis of Nottingham from the words of Revelation 1:17, 18, 'And when I saw him I fell at his feet as dead . . .'. 'By the time the preacher had finished,' wrote Wesley Richards, 'it was a deep sense of God's presence and not that of His honoured servant that filled the Chapel.'

The thanksgiving concluded with the singing of 'Ten thousand times ten thousand' and 'a great and triumphant doxology' which 'thundered around the building'. John Doggett described it as 'an occasion some of us will never forget'.[2]

There was, however, a mixture of feelings in some of us over this service which brought to a final conclusion ML-J's connection with the building that had known his ministry through three decades. Thirteen years had gone since its pulpit had been his domain and the temporary regathering of so many who had benefited from that ministry was perhaps bound to produce a measure of artificial excitement. In the words of one observer, 'It was like a trip backwards in a time machine'. Yet, for all the volume of the singing, something of the element which had so marked the worship of God in former years seemed to be lacking. The past was gone and the preacher was right to take a text which made us look up and forward. There was also a problem in having five speakers and a sermon. While the arrangement was intended to give acknowledgement to the many-sidedness of ML-J's work, it was also an indication of the size of the difficulty which confronted the speakers.

These many years later I remain conscious of the same difficulty as I conclude these two volumes, and I shall comment briefly on why it should be so.

Dr Lloyd-Jones lived in several worlds at once. The thanksgiving service touched on the worlds of medicine, student work, literature, pastoral and pulpit ministry. The list could have been extended. But

---

[1]Reprinted in *Martyn Lloyd-Jones: Chosen by God*, pp. 60–74.
[2]'Man of God' in *Grace* magazine, May 1981. The other accounts of the thanksgiving from which I have quoted are in *The Evangelical Times*, May 1981, and *Dedication*, May/June 1981.

none of us knew him in *all* these spheres and as a result there is a tendency to assess his significance according to the viewpoint with which we are most familiar. Some think of him instinctively in terms of his Westminster ministry, others in terms of his books. There are those who regarded his work in student conferences, at home and abroad, as his greatest contribution, yet only, we suspect, because that was the area in which they happened to know him best. Evangelicals in Wales had their own unique assessment of his role and so had the Christian medical fraternity who, along with Welshmen, viewed him as one of their sons on loan to others. They believed that they benefited from him as others could scarcely do. Even such an observer of the broader scene as Douglas Johnson was surely being over-influenced by his closeness to the medical fraternity when he wrote, 'Perhaps where Dr Lloyd-Jones played his biggest role for the IVF was in the Christian Medical Fellowship'.

A variation in assessments arising from these differing standpoints was inevitably present in the thanksgiving service. Dr Gaius Davies said: 'First and foremost, he was a doctor of medicine. The great contribution he made to the church was because he was trained as a medical man, and because he remained to the end of his long life passionately interested in every aspect of medicine.' But Omri Jenkins, who had known ML-J in a different context from his childhood, began his address with a different proposition: 'Dr Lloyd-Jones was pre-eminently a preacher . . .'.[1]

In one sense all these different viewpoints are right, but discussion over how they should be combined to give a true overall assessment of the significance of ML-J's work will certainly not end with this biography. Furthermore, the difficulty of assessing Dr Lloyd-Jones is not due simply to the largeness of his work. That largeness is itself related to the complexity of his personal make-up and here also there are difficulties of interpretation. A certain unpredictable element in his nature has been mentioned in these pages – a feature which occasionally almost approached the contradictory. For example, he had great analytical powers and could be coolly logical and objective in his judgments. But he also acted from what was more like a lightning streak of intuition and from the same kind of 'impulse and uncanny insight' which was attributed to Churchill. Or again, he could be surprisingly influenced by his feelings and this sometimes led

---

[1] Jenkins' tribute was printed in *Dedication, op. cit.*

him to make over-generous allowance for individuals to whom he was attached. In big things he was normally resolute and determined in adhering to principles, in other things he was ready to be pragmatic and accommodating. Yet how he would distinguish the 'big' and the lesser could not invariably be anticipated by others in advance.

In temperament there can be little doubt that he belonged largely to the 'choleric' type mentioned earlier and that, alongside such Christian leaders as Count Zinzendorf, John Wesley and Daniel Rowland, he belonged to that group which is quick, active and energetic. Given the effects of the Fall, which has left every type of personality lopsided, this group has its own particular weaknesses. It can be too impatient, too vigorous, too prone to 'crack a nut with a sledgehammer'. ML-J recognized the danger. What he preached to others on the need to watch and control one's temperament he first preached to himself: 'The difference between the Christian and the non-Christian is that the former controls his temperament, while the latter is controlled by it.' Preaching from Philippians 4:5 in 1948, he urged the need for every Christian to be equable and self-controlled and gave the following illustration from John Morley's biography of the British Prime Minister, W. E. Gladstone. Gladstone's wife warned Morley in his preparation of the biography to remember that her husband

had two sides – one impetuous, impatient, irrestrainable, the other all self-control, able to dismiss all but the great central aim, able to put aside what is weakening or disturbing; that he achieved this self-mastery, and had succeeded in the struggle ever since he was three or four and twenty, first by the natural power of his character, and second by the incessant wrestling in prayer.

It was the same kind of interaction of different elements in ML-J which contributed to the complexity of his make-up and it seems to provide one of the reasons why he did not always act as people anticipated. He did not trust himself or his temperament and could say, 'The man who does not realise that he himself is his own biggest problem is a mere tyro!'.[1] To be slow and cautious was not his bent and, at times, it may well be that a concern to counteract his natural tendencies took him too far to the other side. We have, for instance, noted his confessing, at the age of seventy seven, 'My greatest defect is that I am too patient with people'. Yet impatience was the characteristic to which he was more prone by nature.

[1] For an important application of this point to Christian leadership see his *Ephesians*, vol. 4, p. 276.

To be included in the subject of the complexity of his make-up is the factor of race. 'He was,' writes his daughter, Elizabeth, 'a Welshman through and through.'[1] ML-J has himself offered an analysis of how national characteristics affect the religious life of Welsh Christians. He makes the point that the English character is simple compared with that of the Welshman, whose make-up involves 'a number of different levels which are not organically connected together'.[2] I will not attempt to relate this analysis to ML-J himself, except to point to one national characteristic which I believe did influence his ministry on the debit side: he possessed his fellow-countrymen's constitutional dislike of organisation. This goes far to explain why he could be a great leader and yet be so comparatively disinterested in plans and in management. It is an interesting fact that what he did for the wider work of the gospel was generally due to arrangements made by others into which he entered. Near the end of his life he went as far as saying that the Ministers' Fellowship meeting at Sandfields was the only new thing which he had ever begun! All organisations and all emphasis on methods he viewed with what he calls 'typical Welsh caution'. His words from which I am about to quote were not spoken in an autobiographical context but if we exclude the reference to laziness they are nonetheless self-revelatory. ML-J was a genuine South Walian:

The Welshman . . . tends to laugh at the excitement of the activist and the man who rushes to form organisations. The Welshman is amused at these things, apart from anything else . . . I think there is a slight difference here between North and South Wales. The North Walian is much more of a *pwyllgorwr*[3] than the South Walian. The South Walian's laziness, plus his genius, makes him despise committees. He is not concerned about carrying things out. The North Walian is much more interested in committees, in organisation and doing things. But even allowing for this, it is still true to say of the Welsh, Northmen included, that they are less subject to these things than the Englishman is . . .[4]

If this attitude kept ML-J from wasting energy on so many things

---

[1] *Martyn Lloyd-Jones: Chosen by God*, p. 157.
[2] *Crefydd a Nodweddion Cenedlaethol* ['Religion and National Characteristics'] three talks on the Welsh BBC, published in *Y Drysorfa*, vol. CXIII, 1943. Not currently available in English translation.
[3] 'Committee man'.
[4] *The Evangelical Magazine of Wales*, Aug-Sept 1969, p. 8.

which took up time in English evangelical circles, it also accounts for some of the omissions in his ministry. The Westminster Fellowship, for instance, suffered from the lack of any records of its discussions. In the course of the years there was too much repetition of the same subjects. Nothing existed to give to those who had missed earlier discussions. A much greater loss to his ministry, and to the church at large, was the fact that no one was ever appointed to see that his spoken material could be speedily prepared for publication. We have noted how Douglas Johnson lamented this failure over many years. The absence of a literary assistant had its most serious results in the 1960's when key addresses, which would have thrown much light on the confused controversy over ecumenism and evangelical unity, remained unpublished and unknown save to the relative few who heard them. The ministry of C. H. Spurgeon was enormously extended through the presence at his side of full-time literary assistants in whom he trusted. The absence of such men in ML-J's case was due, in part, to something in his own make-up.

We have also seen how the problem of turning the Westminster congregation into a true church fellowship concerned him, but its resolution was also hindered, to some degree, by the same lack of organization. In 1952, for instance, lists were prepared which placed all the members of the church in groups, depending on the location of their homes, in order to introduce 'a suitable system of visitation'. This scheme never came into effective operation. Worse, as Westminster Chapel had grown dependent over many years on a strong, single leader at the top, it was unprepared for the sudden vacancy in 1968. Dr Lloyd-Jones had considered, during the 1960's, a change to a shared ministry with perhaps two other men, but the organisation required by such a proposal was probably one factor which weighed against it. After 1968 he definitely regretted his failure to give more time to training the deacons in the exercise of leadership. This omission was partly a time problem, as he said, 'It was quicker to do things myself'. But the will to organise others was also lacking.

I must qualify this comment lest it be misunderstood. ML-J was not *against* planning and organisation. He was no mystical believer in things happening without hard work. On the contrary, he consistently opposed the attitude which spoke in terms of 'Let go and let God'. Therefore, with regard to sermon preparation he could say, 'The Spirit generally uses a man's best preparation'.[1] God's working

[1] *Ephesians*, vol. 8, p. 135.

does not dispense with our own. But he feared that in evangelical priorities *our* activities and plans were rated far too highly and this increased his constitutional caution. His position is well summarized in a conversation with Dr Gaius Davies, 'What I have always said is that we should have the minimum of organisation – the absolute minimum'.[1] His view of 'minimum', I am suggesting above, was sometimes at fault.

*   *   *

The three main factors which made Dr Lloyd-Jones what he was were, I believe, first, natural gifts; second, divine providence in the overruling of his life; and, third, the spiritual grace which shone in him as a Christian.

Of his natural gifts little more need be said. They were obviously with him from birth and his conversion and call to the ministry only changed their use. His mind was the greatest of his gifts, with its enormous capacity, clarity and energy 'sufficient to drive several turbines'. Whereas most men see issues in fragmented parts, ML-J could often see the whole; and he had the ability to state general principles in a manner which could put a mass of seemingly confusing details in their proper perspective. What his distinguished medical colleagues in the CMF Study Group wrote to him in 1968 might have been said by many others, 'We have been particularly grateful to you for so often cutting through our muddled thinking to give us a clear principle to serve as a guide line'.[2] The feature which ML-J particularly noted in Isaac Watts, 'greatness, and bigness and largeness', was no less marked in himself.[3]

[1] *The Evangelical Magazine of Wales*, Aug-Sept 1969, p. 8. What he feared in the contemporary scene is well stated by Francis Schaeffer: 'If we put activity, even good activity, at the centre rather than trusting God, then there may be the power of the world but we will lack the power of the Holy Spirit' (*No Little People*, 1979, p. 69).
[2] Letter signed by Jim Scorer and the ten other medicals of the Study Group, June 29, 1968.
[3] His words on Watts, spoken in 1968, are in *Puritans*, p. 203. One could wish he had developed a brief reference to Watts and himself made in a letter twenty years earlier to his daughter Elizabeth containing the following interesting sentences: 'I am due to lecture on behalf of the Evangelical Library tomorrow night on "Isaac Watts and the place of hymnody in church worship". The theme fascinates me very much and especially the second half. As to Watts I find myself far too much like him. Not as a poet (!) but as a type of mind.' (Nov 25, 1948). No record of this, the first of the annual Evangelical Library Lectures, appears to have survived.

As already noted, the size and clarity of his thought was matched by phenomenal powers of memory. One final example of the latter deserves inclusion here. When a book by Paul Ferris entitled *The House of Northcliffe* was published in 1971, several reviewers were particularly interested in the cause of Lord Northcliffe's death. Ferris was sceptical of the rumour that he died of syphilis yet unable to demonstrate the wrongness of that supposition. ML-J had special reason to be interested, for Northcliffe, chief co-proprietor of *The Times*, who died insane in 1922, had been a patient of Sir Thomas Horder. At that date ML-J was already assisting Horder and Horder's reputation was involved in the rumour that Northcliffe's condition was due to syphilis, for the eminent physician had named a very different cause, namely, bacterial endocarditis. Fifty years later in 1971 ML-J had no access to medical notes or records on the Northcliffe case but simply from memory he was able to put together a detailed letter published in *The Times* (Dec 10, 1971) showing that Horder's diagnosis was correct. When the syphilis rumour was repeated in 1980 another medical authority, Reginald Pound, advised future historians and biographers to take care to study the letter from D. M. Lloyd-Jones 'refuting that murky legend'.[1]

On the subject of divine providence in the overruling of ML-J's life I will restrict myself to a few main points.

First, the manner of his preparation for the Christian ministry, not through the normal channels and the approved denominational procedures but in a very different way, had life-long significance. Instead of coming from the lecture rooms of colleges dominated by the theorisings of liberal theology he entered upon his life-work from the exacting discipline of one of the finest medical schools in the world. The impression from his medical training was permanent and the quotation already given from Dr Gaius Davies is supported by ML-J himself. In giving the Welsh Oration to the British Medical Association gathering at Wrexham in October 1973 he could confess to his distinguished audience: 'For forty-six years I have been trying to shed medical thinking but I am a complete failure. I still have to approach every problem, whether it is theological or anything else, in this medical manner, and I start with the causes.'[2]

As will be obvious, it was this type of approach which led to ML-J's criticism of the modern church: she was trying to treat or eliminate the symptoms of her weakness without dealing with the

[1]*Times Literary Supplement*, May 16, 1980.
[2]*Healing and Medicine*, p. 118.

real cause. And, similarly, in her witness to the world she was too inclined to deal in 'mere palliatives' instead of the only message radical enough to meet the fundamental problem of man's alienation from God.[1] This type of diagnosis of the modern church was all the more surprising and unexpected because it was held as axiomatic that only the ignorant could expect to see a continuance of traditional doctrinal Christianity in the twentieth century.

The advance of education and the 'certainties' of science were supposedly making such a continuance impossible. It was superior knowledge, not a surrender to the superficial, which justified the changes in the churches. So it was confidently claimed. But here was a man coming from Barts, the citadel of science, and from the consulting rooms of Thomas Horder – one of the most brilliant rationalists of the age – prepared to preach that the modern problem was not intellectual at all; it was moral and spiritual! In another age, when the schools of the prophets failed in Israel, God took Amos from 'following the plough'. So, also, he took Martyn Lloyd-Jones and shaped him in a special mould for a special work.

If a second instance of providence in ML-J's early years is less obvious it is surely equally as important and still more pervasive in its influence upon his whole life. For over fifty-four years Bethan was to him the greatest of all earthly gifts. He never ceased to see the hand of God in the eventual fulfilment of the hopes he had long entertained of marrying the girl he had first admired as a young teenager in Newcastle Emlyn. Once committed to Martyn, and then, with his help, brought to assurance of salvation, Bethan gladly sacrificed the public career in medicine for which she was also qualified, for a higher purpose. 'My work,' as she was still saying in the 1970's, 'is to keep him in the pulpit.' The fact that he was able to undertake so much until the very close of his life was in great measure due to the wife God gave him. At the Memorial Service to Dr Campbell Morgan in 1945, ML-J quoted words on his late colleague's relationship with Mrs Morgan which echoed what he knew so well in his own experience: 'He could never have been the man he was were it not for the fact that he was always so certain, and happy, and sure of her sympathy and understanding.'[2] Lonely at times ML-J

[1]'It is dangerous to eliminate symptoms before the diagnosis has been assured. It is these symptoms which call attention to the presence and nature of the disease' (*Ibid.*, p. 114).
[2]*WR*, July 1945, p. 64.

certainly was, but Bethan was always at his side. Some loads she took off his mind by her practical gifts. She 'ran the home', as her grandson Christopher writes. Other things she shared and discussed with him. 'My grandfather,' says Christopher, 'esteemed her common sense very highly as well as her shrewdness.'[1]

At the close of his life I once asked ML-J what kind of woman he thought a minister's wife should be. His answer is relevant here:

What she needs above everything is wisdom, so that she does not create problems. And another thing is this, she should never have a special friend in the church. That is very important. Otherwise it will create division and jealousy. Her main business is to look after her husband – relieve him of worries about the home, about food, as far as she can about financial matters and, very important, not to keep on feeding him with the tittle tattle of the gossip of the church. She is to protect him and to help him.

Bethan Lloyd-Jones' work was done so quietly in the background that few had any conception of the extent to which he was dependent upon her. On his part their relationship was among those things which are too personal for public comment. But if Bethan had not outlived him, and had he ever paid a full tribute to her memory, we can be sure it would have contained all that he said of Mrs Morgan in 1945 and a great deal more: 'He could not have been what he was were it not for her . . . She was with him through all the long years; she willingly spared him for his larger work and never grudged his absences from her.'

It remains for us to give some consideration in conclusion to what Martyn Lloyd-Jones was as a Christian. This biography will have failed if it has not shown that it was eminent grace more than eminent natural gifts which made him what he was. The words of James Buchanan on Thomas Chalmers are equally true here. The secret of Chalmers' power as a preacher, said Buchanan, was often misunderstood, 'It lay far more in his deep convictions and heart-felt experience as a converted Christian man, than in his natural gifts as a man of genius'. The statement points to a universal principle which was once stated by Thomas Charles in the words, 'No solid, permanent work can be expected where the piety and spirituality of the instrument is low, whatever his gifts may be'.

Those who knew ML-J best would unite in saying that the first and deepest impression which he made upon them was as a living witness

[1] *Martyn Lloyd-Jones: Chosen by God*, p. 267.

to the realities of Christian experience. His life was of a nature which quietly and spontaneously impressed a sense of God upon us. Edmund Calamy describes a fellow Puritan as one whose 'life and conversation was a continual sermon'. This was no less true of ML-J. It was not because he always talked 'religiously' but because there was the evidence in him of things which lay deeper than words and without which his words would have had no force. Jack Walkey, one of Westminster Chapel's missionaries, spoke for thousands when, in the jungle of Amazonia, he wrote:.

Dr Lloyd-Jones' godly life I continually recall. I well remember when once on a forest journey how just the recollection of this left me with a great urge to seek a holy life and to pray for the same knowledge of God. It does so still today.[1]

Identical testimony comes from the fifteen-strong Executive Committee of the CMF who, on ML-J's retirement from Westminster in 1968, wrote to thank him for all he had meant to them: 'A full-scale attempt to put into words what you have meant to the CMF throughout its history would be daunting. We would, however, like first to refer to your personal example, which has emphasised in so unique a manner the importance and dignity of the Christian Ministry . . .'[2]

If ML-J's characteristics as a Christian were to be further analysed there can be no doubt that what should be put first was his consciousness of God. He believed – he knew – that God deals personally and individually with His people and that their highest privilege in time and eternity is to have communion with Him through His Son, Jesus Christ. For such fellowship with God he longed and one could not be in his presence without being soon reminded that in his scale of priorities all else was secondary.

To take time alone every day for the reading of Scripture and for prayer was foundational to his view of living as a Christian. Family prayer marked the close of every day and after his death Bethan Lloyd-Jones was to say that it was here that she experienced her greatest loss.

While ML-J drew a veil over his practice of prayer, we could all know something of it from its *effects*. In the *British Weekly* (Jan 20,

[1]Letter to the author, Jan 26, 1981.
[2]Letter dated June 29, 1968.

David Martyn Lloyd-Jones: Volume Two

1966) James Bremner, reviewing ML-J's *Faith on Trial*, gives us this perceptive statement:

> Some books of sermons move a preacher to an ephemeral admiration, others must send him back to his task wondering why his own preaching is not more like the sermons he has just read. This book falls into the second category; and the answer may well be that in the midst of our full and busy lives, we have not laid sufficient emphasis on the continual prayer and Bible study that have gone to the making of this book.

Another minister, Dr Alan Redpath, has spoken of how he was desperately ill and 'at a low ebb' in a Nursing Home in Edinburgh when Dr Lloyd-Jones unexpectedly visited him in October 1964. It was Redpath's conviction that the prayer in which ML-J 'besieged heaven' was the turning point in his recovery.[1] Recalling this in a letter which he wrote to ML-J in 1968, he said: 'I have marvelled at the grace of God and the anointing of the Spirit constantly maintained upon you over thirty years of ministry. This can only be the outcome of the building of a secret history with God in your own life which has been a tremendous challenge and example to hundreds of others, including myself, who would have fared better if we had followed it in such a disciplined way.'

For ML-J prayer was primarily fellowship with God: he abhorred any attitude which tended to represent it as a means of getting 'results'. His testimony was to God, not to 'prayer'. But one cannot truly draw near to God without being affected. In the words of John Flavel: 'Prayer begets and maintains holy courage and magnanimity in evil times. When all things about you tend to discouragement, it is your being with Jesus that makes you bold, Acts 4:13. He that uses to be before a great God will not be afraid to look such little things as men in the face.'[2]

A God-centred theology was not an addition to his personal life, it was central to it. If Calvinism means the joyful assurance that God is at the head of things, then he was a Calvinist with every fibre of his being. His jealousy for God's glory, his faith in God's promises and reverence for His Word, his sense of what sin deserves, his thankfulness, his hatred for all that is casual and flippant in holy things, his

[1]One account of this was given by H. F. Stevenson in the *Life of Faith*, July 29, 1965.
[2]*Works*, vol. 6, p. 65.

[764]

The Best of Men

seriousness, boldness in opposing promoters of error – all these features, and more, flowed from his knowing something of being in the presence of God.[1] It was this same awareness which in a marked measure delivered him from men-pleasing and enabled him to withstand loneliness and opposition. With much feeling he once said to me in the 1960's, 'I would have been dead long ago if I had depended upon men for encouragement'.

Invariably connected with a true consciousness of God is a life of love: 'he that dwelleth in love dwelleth in God and God in him' (1 John 4:16). To a marked degree love was the element in which ML-J lived and it was the leading impulse in his work. He loved the church, loved his people, loved all men. It was by the love in his preaching that hearers were most deeply affected. Indeed, in his view, the ultimate purpose of preaching to non-Christians is to persuade them to believe in the love of God to sinners, and the ultimate purpose of preaching to Christians is that they may be brought closer to the practice and the enjoyment of the First Commandment, 'Thou shalt love the Lord thy God with all thy heart, and with all thy soul, and with all thy mind, and with all thy strength'. To preach anything less is to fail:

The more I study this New Testament, and live this Christian life, the more convinced I am, indeed the more certain I am, that our fundamental difficulty, our fundamental lack, is lack of a love of God; it is not our knowledge so much that is defective, it is our love of God and our greatest object and endeavour should be to know Him better and to love Him more truly.[2]

This burden led him to preach much on the privileges of believers

[1]For a valuable delineation of the effect of true Calvinism on personal life see *Puritans*, pp. 211–213. The strength of his conviction that Scripture should never be listened to without reverence and full attention entered into a subject I have not dealt with in this book: his very cautious attitude to the use of cassette tapes. He could not understand how anyone could listen to a sermon on cassette while being half employed in doing something else. On the spirit of a Christian he once said: 'The Christian is serious, but not solemn; grave, but never cold or prohibitive; his joy is a holy joy; his happiness a serious happiness.' I believe also that his personal calm, which was a direct result of his spirituality, contributed in no small measure to the health he so long enjoyed: 'We are meant,' he said, 'to be at peace in the midst of great activity . . . that prevented me from being a worrier. I did not worry. I could go to bed and sleep soundly. I never had to take anything to help me to sleep.'
[2]Sermon on 1 John, October 9, 1949.

and entered largely into his conviction that Christians are most eminently useful in helping the world when their lives show what they enjoy. He would have heartily approved the words of B. M. Palmer, 'I have reached the conviction that the best way to reach the unregenerate is to show him what Christianity is able to do for the believer'.

Observers of his preaching have often commented on its 'warmth' and on his definition of preaching as 'theology coming through a man who is on fire'.[1] That fire was God-given love, the anointing which, as Charles Wesley knew, has to be sought from heaven:

> O Thou who camest from above
> The pure celestial fire to impart,
> Kindle a flame of *sacred love*
> On the mean altar of my heart!

When, in an address on 'What Is Preaching?' in the United States in 1967, ML-J confessed to the poverty of his preaching, his hearers laughed audibly, as though the speaker was guilty of false modesty.[2] The truth was that they were judging preaching by a standard different from his own. It was ML-J's conviction that the truth should be preached with seraphic love to God and men and it pained him to fall so far short. Philip Hughes provides an anecdote which illustrates this point:

I recall sitting with him in his hotel room in Oxford one night during a mission to the university at which he was the speaker. He had given in his own inimitable style a powerful presentation of the Gospel which had held the large student audience captive. As we spoke together afterwards, he said to me that he felt he had not been sufficiently animated by love.

ML-J prized many hymns but I think it is not without significance that the only verse I can still hear and see him singing is from Charles Wesley's 'O love divine, how sweet Thou art!' with its plea:

[1]*Preaching*, p. 97.
[2]His words, without the record of laughter, are given in *Knowing the Times*, p. 263. ML-J's conception of preaching was almost identical to that of J. H. Thornwell whom he resembled. See *Life and Letters of James Henley Thornwell*, B. M. Palmer, 1875 (Banner of Truth, 1974), pp. 315, 548–49.

The Best of Men

God only knows the love of God
O that it now were shed abroad
In this poor stony heart![1]

The prayer was heard to a far greater extent than ML-J himself realized, and it profoundly affected his ministry. His eloquence was that of a heart deeply moved. It came from within and gave him at times the appearance in the pulpit of 'a cataract of holy fire'.[2] This same love accounts for the catholicity of his spirit and for the appeal which his testimony has had in almost all sections of the Christian Church. It was preaching and teaching which belonged to the same ethos as that of the eighteenth-century evangelical leaders of whom it was said, 'Heedless, in a great degree, of denominational and sectarian attainments, their sole purpose was to bring sinners to Jesus Christ'.[3]

The same feature came out in ML-J's defence of the faith. Even those who could not agree with him could often see that he exemplified the distinction between 'contending' and 'contentiousness'. Where Christians disagreed with him or opposed him, he aimed to *win* them by consideration and friendship as well as by truth. Controversy born out of mere intellectual interest in doctrine, or still worse, by party spirit, he viewed as utterly unworthy of real Christians.

Gaius Davies has rightly pointed to words by Dr André Schlemmer on the French Reformed teacher Auguste Lecerf as illustrative of ML-J: 'Although there was something of the grand seigneur about his bearing, no one could have been more simple, more friendly or

[1]Since writing the above I have noticed how the Rev Herbert M. Carson, writing to ML-J on Feb 26, 1980, refers to the same memory: 'I still recall the fervour which was in your quotation of the hymn, "O love divine . . ."'
[2]The phrase was used of B. M. Palmer. Between Palmer and ML-J there also exists a striking resemblance with respect to both character and preaching. See *The Life and Letters of Benjamin Morgan Palmer*, T. C. Johnson, 1906, (Banner of Truth 1987), pp. 427–30, 653 ff. The same element is to be found in the Puritans. 'Love is a hot thing,' says John Preston, 'hot as fire' (*The Breast-Plate of Faith and Love*, 1634, (Edinburgh: Banner of Truth, 1979 reprint)). 'Love is the greatest thing in religion', said ML-J, quoting William Williams (*Puritans*, p. 187); 'The greatest characteristic of the greatest saints in all ages has always been their realization of God's love to them' (*Romans*, vol. 4, p. 104). See also his important words in *Ephesians*, vol. 3, p. 253 and *Preaching*, pp. 92–93.
[3]J. K. Foster in [A. C. H. Seymour], *Life and Times of Selina Countess of Huntingdon*, vol. 2, 1844, p. vii.

more finely comprehensive in his personal dealings. A terrible judge in regard to ideas, he was full of charity in regard to persons . . .'[1]

It was this same factor which explains how ML-J could frequently retain the friendship and esteem of those with whom he had strongly and publicly disagreed. They knew that his words expressed no hostility to their persons. Thus, after ML-J had forcefully answered the work of Dr William Sargant, *Battle for the Mind*, Sargant sent him copies of all his publications and signed his letters, 'Affectionately, Will'. The difference with John Stott was one of the most serious in his entire ministry but, again, Dr Stott's account of a visit which he paid to ML-J on December 19, 1978, reveals the other side:

On arrival, he could not have been more affable and welcoming. We sat in his roomy ground floor study, where he does his writing, and Mrs Lloyd-Jones brought us coffee and chocolate biscuits . . .

I told him that I had 2 main reasons for asking to call on him. First, because I had a strong admiration and affection for him ('I know, I know', he muttered) and was sorry we saw so little of one another. Secondly, in my travels people ask me how he is, and I have to say that I have not seen him lately. Worse, people say they have heard we are not on speaking terms with one another. 'Oh I know, it is absurd. People are very mischievous. They can't distinguish between principles and personalities.'

Discussion between the two men in the next hour and a quarter turned to the church issues which had divided them and, although it led to no resolution, Stott had no doubts over the sincerity of the older man's appeal: 'We ought to be together. If God spares me, and we could be together, I would say like Simeon, "Lord, now lettest Thou Thy servant depart in peace."'[2]

A similar example concerns the late Professor D. M. Mackay of the Department of Communication and Neuroscience at the University of Keele who, from the 1950's, became a well known spokesman for the IVF and for other evangelicals. But ML-J in the IVF Advisory Committee and elsewhere warned of the danger of Mackay's

---

[1] *Martyn Lloyd-Jones: Chosen by God*, pp. 73–74.
[2] I am indebted to Dr Stott for his notes of this meeting. The Evangelical Alliance was equally involved in the division of 1966–67 but Gordon Landreth, General Secretary of EA in 1981 also wrote, 'I have personally always had a very warm and friendly relationship with Dr Lloyd-Jones' (*Dedication*, May/June 1981, p. 19).

tendency to defend biblical truth in terms of scientific knowledge. When Mackay enquired why his position was under criticism ML-J replied in a personal letter stating his point. That it was received without any alienation resulting between them says much for the two men.[1]

*   *   *

Of course, Martyn Lloyd-Jones was not without weaknesses and faults, though such was his consistency of life that it is easier to surmise where he fought his personal battles rather than to state what they were. But he was fallible, and I will mention two points where this fallibility sometimes appeared. I believe he was speaking from self knowledge when he spoke on how a man's strength can be his greatest weakness: his own weaknesses lay very close to his main strengths.

For example, he was possessed of great wisdom – a fact which made him the unparalleled helper that he was in giving guidance to individuals; and the words, 'Be ye wise as serpents', were an injunction he often urged on young pastors. True wisdom includes insight into what to say, and what not to say. ML-J did not consider it a part of wisdom to reveal one's whole mind ('a fool uttereth all his mind' says Proverbs 29:11). He sought to discern what a particular individual needed to hear to help him at a given point in time and he took into account what he was ready to hear. In his shrewdness here he bore resemblance to Oliver Cromwell, one of his few English heroes. 'Whilst he was cautious of his own words,' said Sir William Waller of Cromwell, 'he made others talk until he had, as it were, sifted them.' It was this policy on Cromwell's part which made a man say to him on one occasion, 'Every man almost that talks with you is apt to think you of his opinion, my Lord, whatever he be'. He was even accused of being a 'dissembler'.[2]

[1]ML-J's letter of Dec 11, 1958 was kindly sent to me by Professor Mackay after the former's death, along with words of appreciation for his ministry and this fragment of biography: 'When I first started to attend Westminster Chapel on Sunday mornings (cycling gladly the 6 miles from Forest Hill!) in 1946–47, I was an Assistant Lecturer in Physics at King's College; and one of the folk I encouraged to go to hear him was R. V. G. Tasker.'
[2]These quotations are from Christopher Hill, *God's Englishman*, 1970, pp. 194–5. It is interesting to note a writer on Cromwell in the *Princeton Review*, 1867, p. 638, observing, 'In the neighbourhood of a man's strength lies the region of his weakness'.

The criticism which Cromwell drew on himself in this regard was criticism occasionally levelled at ML-J and it was not wholly without justification. I am inclined to think that the reverse side of his wisdom was a political kind of 'prudence' which could mislead people as to the real state of his own mind on a given issue. I recall, for instance, a highly strung man of confused views on the work of the Holy Spirit who believed that he had ML-J's support for a course of action which a number of us considered blameworthy. When the man had an interview with the Doctor which did not dispel his illusion, some of us protested to ML-J and got the response, 'I cannot help being a physician'. In other words, he judged that the condition of the man was such that to have said or done anything more would not have helped him. We were unconvinced. Another point of strength was his ability to present a case. For sheer force and brilliance in discussion and debate he was unrivalled. From childhood he loved to be a listener to – or, better still, a partaker in – a lively argument and, not without reason, his mother thought him to be the most suited of all her three sons for a legal career. Instead, his skill was to be seen in the pulpit and in the multitude of meetings which he chaired so uniquely. Stacey Woods has written of the evening discussions on spiritual subjects which ML-J chaired for ten memorable years in the four or five days of IFES Committee meetings convened in various places, 'In an extraordinary way Dr Lloyd-Jones stimulated all of us and after his resignation as Chairman, while we attempted to have similar seasons, they were never the same'.

Others could say the same but ML-J's love of debates would now and again carry him too far. 'He loved to win a point,' says Stacey Woods. 'He could hold tenaciously to an opinion when he might be wrong,' adds Douglas Johnson. In argument (I use the word in its best sense, for he was never ill-tempered) he knew how to debate an issue so that the strongest points of his case and the weakest of his 'opponent' would be foremost. He was not likely to concede where any weakness existed in his own position and to carry a point he could, at times, be guilty of exaggeration and even misrepresentation. He was scarcely ever indefinite or undecided.

The authority with which he spoke, which, as Packer says, made it 'hard not to treat him as an infallible oracle', did at times betray him into a dogmatism which was not well founded. Medical colleagues could complain of some of his generalisations, and so could historians. This weakness, though rare, is not entirely absent from

The Best of Men

his published expositions of Scripture. An instance of it occurs in his exposition of Romans 7:24 where he claims it is 'impossible' for a Christian to say, 'who shall deliver me from the body of this death?'. Yet he had himself for long used those words as a testimony of Christian experience![1]

This brief pointer to some of ML-J's limitations brings me, however, to possibly the most attractive of all aspects in his character as a Christian. He was a humble man. No one believed more firmly than he that 'in many things we all stumble' (James 3:2). A lesser man would have taken care to tidy up the occasional inconsistencies which came through from the pulpit on to the printed page but, in great measure, he was delivered from concern for his own reputation. 'Love seeketh not her own.' He was never angry at criticism. He did not claim any obedience from colleagues and subordinates and never, in our experience, crushed arguments which he knew were conscientious. While he had a great deal of 'presence', it was not that of 'the grand seigneur', Lecerf, whom he resembled in another respect, as already mentioned. Anything suggestive of self importance or 'dignity' was alien to his whole spirit.

Of the general directions which he gave me respecting this biography none were spoken more earnestly than those which had to do with the danger of exaggeration. 'Don't represent the state of Sandfields before I went there as worse than it was', he would say, and 'Don't make too much of Westminster Chapel'.

This humility was very different from the sort of modesty that can be acquired by education. Its source lay in his knowledge of God – knowledge which he regarded as poor and elementary yet which

---

[1]Compare his *Romans*, vol. 6, p. 255, with *Sermon on the Mount*, vol. 1, p. 57 and elsewhere. Those interested may wish to look at ML-J's whole treatment of Romans 7:25–8:5 as an example of some weakness in argument. He not only differs from his earlier statements (which in itself is no just cause for criticism) but he changes ground while in the course of expounding this passage. Before he came to detailed study of Romans 8:1–5 he assumed he was settled on the meaning and thought it important for his case on Romans 7:14–25 to argue that 8:1–5 has 'no natural connection' with the experience of the preceding verses. Romans 8:1–5 is *not*, he says, about the experience of the Spirit in the believer, but about the believer's standing in Christ (see *Romans*, vol. 6, pp. 265, 270, 282–83, etc.). He argues (p. 304) that Paul *begins* to deal with sanctification at verse 5 of Romans 8. Further examination, however, later took him to the very conclusion which he had earlier rejected (see pp. 348–55). This arose partly because of his mistaken view of the meaning of 'the law of sin and death' which he gives in advance of reaching those verses (p. 182).

amazed him at the grace which he saw. If he never said much about himself, he *lived* as one who was nothing but a saved sinner. His dying testimony to that truth revealed nothing surprising. The Christian life was *all* grace from first to last.[1] And he never forgot that although believers are children of God they are still *creatures* and ever to approach God as such.

Dr Lloyd-Jones' poor opinion of himself came through in many ways. Far from thinking he had the mastery of himself (in the manner claimed for Gladstone) he distrusted himself. 'He was conscious of his gift of eloquence,' says Philip Hughes, 'and even afraid of it.' He was thankful that God had kept him through most of his life in comparatively straitened financial circumstances because the lack of money puts a brake upon precipitate action in those who would be leaders. 'I thank God for that,' he could say, 'I never had any money so that I was never tempted to do things and just push them through.' He believed that God had mercifully put him into circumstances where he had to learn patience in working for the reformation of the church. People had to be won by gentleness, they had to be given time to learn. More than once he returned to this subject in our last conversations:

I must say I thank God He has given me the gift of patience. I realize that it is the gift of God because I think by nature I had an element of impulsiveness in me like my mother. My father – he couldn't suffer fools gladly and he would really cut people off. That element was in me but I feel God delivered me and gave me patience. I can say that to the glory of God.

I must here also balance an earlier comment on ML-J's seeming antipathy to organization and administration. In part, as I have said, that attitude was constitutional. But, in part, also, it had to do with his spirituality. So much of the activity which he saw in the contemporary religious scene had elements which suggested ambition and the love of power. 'Self-advertisement' and a lack of humility in the church he regarded as 'the greatest tragedy of all'.[2] That he had the gift to organize and control others I do not doubt. Had he wanted to start a new denomination he was probably the

[1]See his short testimony in *Spiritual Depression*, p. 132.
[2]*Ephesians*, vol. 4, p. 41.

only evangelical in Britain who could have done it effectively. But such a step would have been alien to his deepest spiritual instincts. 'Cease from man' was his text. As he said in his BEC address at Sunderland in 1970, 'We are not here to preach men, nor to stand on men, that is carnality'.

I scarcely ever recall ML-J drawing any parallel between his own ministry and that of any Christian figure of a past age. But one parallel which he did draw in conversation on February 5, 1981 is a striking illustration of what was uppermost in his heart. 'I feel in many ways,' he said, 'like Griffith Jones of Llanddowror.' The man to whom he hoped to possess a resemblance was a little-remembered figure, born in Carmarthenshire in 1683 and significant not so much for what he achieved as for what he did in preparing the way for others. Griffith Jones was 'the morning star' of the great awakening of the eighteenth century in Wales, the forerunner of the better-known men who were to follow. The comparison tells us a great deal. Dr Lloyd-Jones had yearned for something in his own day which, when he spoke these words, he knew he was not going to be permitted to see. But his mind was not on the question of how posterity would remember him, it was on the success of the gospel. I responded, 'As you have often said, God's calendar is not ours', but, only half-hearing me, he went on: 'I never thought it was going to take so long. I thought I was going to see great revival but I am not complaining. It wasn't God's time and this preparatory work had to be done.' If he could die believing that he had been permitted to do something to prepare the way for better men and greater days, that was enough.

* * *

Possibly the best summary of ML-J's work and character lies in a letter, never intended for publication, which Douglas Johnson wrote to him on June 8, 1968, on hearing the news of his retirement from Westminster Chapel. After expressing admiration for the copy of ML-J's letter of resignation – 'It is *God* honouring throughout' – Johnson went on:

Being myself such a poor steward of the Lord's interests I've never ventured to tell you what I really think of you and your ministry! But here goes.
In my opinion, the unique contribution you have made is not *simple*

(in itself) – it is a combination of race/gift/training and sites . . . The
Welsh background, intellectual grasp of theological differences and the
'ethos' of the Calvinistic-Methodist (Presbyterian) Church, wedded to
the practical applications and teaching methods of medicine, gave a
particular *matrix* to your intellectual and spiritual life, which was just
right for your own particular gifts. Then the Port Talbot–Aberavon
circumstances were ideal for the practical application of your growing
convictions and allowed almost a virgin soil for constructive action.
Westminster again was an excellent site (quite apart from its tradition
and situation in central London) because of its freedom from a lot of
denominational restrictions, jealousies and frustrations.

Your own particular gifts of theological discernment, theological
teaching, resistance to all but the central things which march hand in
hand with the dignity of the gospel were quite invaluable to IVF from
1936–1967. You *personally* have combined the true passion for the
gospel and Evangelicalism with intellectual perception of things that
differ. You have wedded an inspiring positive statement of the anatomy
of the Faith to the practical outworking of its true Physiology – just as
Wales (at its best) has succeeded in getting into a biblical proportional
relationship the Sovereign God of our Lord Jesus Christ, with the
practical activity of the Holy Spirit in the believer and the church. Apart
from the fact that names became party cries, Calvinistic Methodist is a
powerful (and may be the right) combination of Christian diversities.

I must not weary you – but quite apart from your services to every
department of IVF . . . I have much personally to thank you for. One of
the chief things is that, if it had not been for *you* I should have been very
lonely in the job of IVF Sec. As it grew, powerful forces of every kind
tried to take it over – only to have caused it to deviate to ecumenicalisms,
sectarianisms and no gospels, or American 'clap-trap'. There have been
many *good* men in senior leadership, but not strong intellectually and
theologically. They were broken reeds in a fight but I could always rely
on you to give a true verdict (biblically and theologically based) and
encouragement. Hundreds of times you said the reassuring words, called
attention to the right Scriptures and to the theological sources to deal
with multitudinous errors, little heresies – so easily becoming big
ones . . . Thank you for the hours and hours of time and nervous energy
freely given.

Whatever eternity may reveal of the effect of your actual ministry (and
public addresses all over the country, church anniversaries, 'big
meetings' and inductions, etc.), I myself would say that one of the most
valuable services to the country *as a whole* will prove to be the
encouraging and advising, in a number of forms, of young ministers. I do
not mean so much the Westminster Fellowship meetings, but *personal*
reassurances, personal advice, and advice on preaching to the young

newly ordained ministers in little difficult churches without much real fellowship. *This* attention to the candlesticks twinkling in the inhospitable country and dreary townships has been a truly important and, in influence, worthwhile action.

*　　　*　　　*

It is too early in point of time for any comprehensive assessment of Dr Lloyd-Jones' place in the church of the present century. He differed from most of his contemporaries in his conviction over the extent to which historic Christianity had been abandoned in the churches of the English-speaking world. His emphases were unusual because there were few beside him who were ready to give priority to the recovery of doctrinal Christianity, and few who were prepared to identify the Calvinism of the Reformers and Puritans with the Word of God and the gospel of Christ. But if he was out of step with his age he was certainly not original in the substance of his theology. In a discussion on Christianity and Wales he was once asked by a fellow countryman, 'Have we as a nation made any particular contribution to the church's understanding of the truth in the realm of theology?'. To which he replied, 'No, I would not say that we have', for he knew that the best theological and exegetical writings did not come from Wales.[1]

In his own case, he had aimed to do no more than he was exhorted to do in his early ministry: to 'put new clothes' on the old truths. But the remarkable thing is that he accomplished this at a time when so many of the old truths had fallen into utter disregard and were remembered only by handfuls of people in corners of the land.

That these truths in his day sprang into new life was surely connected with the way in which his life and ministry adhered so closely to the New Testament's own priorities. He lived for the gospel. 'They are the best ministers,' says the Puritan, William Fenner, 'that carry people unto heaven.' ML-J led many to heaven and by his personal example he gave a new impression to thousands of what Christianity ought to be. In a real sense he shares in the epitaph once given to some of the foremost Christian leaders of the eighteenth

[1]'We are not good research men, we are not sufficiently patient and painstaking. What we have done is to give *expression* to the truth once delivered to the saints. I think we have done so in the matter of preaching in an incomparable manner. It is in the expression of truth that we have excelled . . . This is our peculiar gift.' *The Evangelical Magazine of Wales*, Aug–Sept, 1969.

century: 'Men unfettered with worldly cares, and almost uncon-
nected with the world, these apostolic men lived alone, and were
striking emblems of primitive simplicity. Their manner of life carried
the mind many centuries back and set it down in the apostolic age.'[1]

Martyn Lloyd-Jones was used of God to interrupt what many
church leaders thought was the correct agenda for Christian
progress. In so doing he set in motion a train of events the full
consequences of which no one can yet know. Commenting on this,
John Doggett has written, 'In 1938 Dr Lloyd-Jones came to a city
and to a country in which the Reformed Faith of Calvin and the
Puritans, of Whitefield and Spurgeon, was almost extinct'.[2] John
Owen, in speaking of the gift of boldness in the faith, says, 'Ofttimes
the eminence of it in one single person has been the means to preserve
a whole church from coldness, backsliding, or sinful compliances
with the world'.[3] Something akin to that certainly happened in
England and beyond in the mid-twentieth century. As Jim Packer
wrote to ML-J in 1968, 'It is not given to many of us to change the
course of things in the Christian world to the extent that you have
been used to change it'.

In years to come Dr Lloyd-Jones will probably be remembered
chiefly on account of his books. They will go on being read when
much else from the present century has been forgotten. Yet they
should not be used *instead* of the commentaries and works of
theology which were often his own sources. Precise erudition and
exact exegesis were not his forte. Like Thomas Chalmers he was
more 'a great theologist' than he was a learned theologian.[4] He was a
populariser in the best sense of the word. His books will go on
showing that where the Bible is taught spiritually, it possesses
timeless relevance for by it God Himself speaks, directs and comforts
those whom He is bringing to glory.

Yet should Martyn Lloyd-Jones' lasting place in Christian history
become mainly associated with his books, we hope it will be
remembered that books were always secondary to him and that he

---

[1] *Life and Times of Selina Countess of Huntingdon*, vol. 2, 1844, p. 373.
[2] *Free Grace Record*, summer 1968, p. 482.
[3] *Works*, vol. 4, p. 462.
[4] I owe the phrase to John Duncan who applies it to Thomas Chalmers. 'Though
very inferior,' says Duncan, 'I took the liberty of differing with him sometimes
about doctrine . . . my doctrine about faith was better than his – but he went to
prayer and his faith was better than mine.' *Life of John Duncan*, David Brown,
1872, p. 484.

never set out to write them. He was a preacher. He believed in preaching which was unadorned, unstudied (so far as mere sentences were concerned) but alive, a union of truth and fire, and both humbling and uplifting to the sublime in its effects. With John Knox and his successors, he knew that the 'tongue and lively voice' are *the* chief means to which God has promised His power in the recovery of lost mankind: 'The Spirit of God maketh the reading, but especially the preaching of the Word, an effectual means of convincing and converting sinners, and of building them up in holiness and comfort, through faith, unto salvation.'[1] His prayer for revival was accordingly associated with the profound conviction that every great movement of the Spirit will be found to be bound up with the giving of men who *preach* 'with the Holy Ghost sent down from heaven'. In his lifetime he led many other men to the possession of that same vision and I think he would have had no higher wish for the usefulness of this record of his life.

Certainly for those who knew Martyn Lloyd-Jones as a pastor, when all has been said of what he was in other aspects of his life, the final memory will remain that of the slight yet commanding figure behind the pulpit desk, his face shining with light and his words summoning us to Christ and to heaven. While we have in these pages looked back with love and thankfulness, we know that the things described will never become only the things of years that are gone. Rather, as in the past, so in the future it will be said, 'How beautiful upon the mountains are the feet of him that bringeth good tidings, that publisheth peace; that bringeth good tidings of good, that publisheth salvation; that saith unto Zion, Thy God reigneth!' (Isa 52:7).

[1] *The Shorter Catechism*, Answer to Question 89.

APPENDICES

Appendix 1

A Personal Letter[1]

May 18th 1937   R.M.S. 'Berengaria'

My dear Bethan,
 The fact that I am writing to you from here on this particular date is
altogether wrong, and makes me feel very odd. As far as I can remember,
this is the first time, ever, that I have written to you for your birthday! I
hope that the ship-letter-telegram that I sent you this morning arrived
safely on your birthday morning. The authorities told me that there was
no doubt about it. I had endless pleasure and happiness in sending it, I
somehow felt I was in touch with you once more. In this awful distance
of separation a thing like that is a great help – but oh! what a poor
substitute.
 I cannot describe the various feelings I have experienced since I saw
you last on Waterloo station. And I had better not try to do so. Let me
say just this much – thinking of you gives me endless happiness, and I am
more certain than ever that there is no one in the world like you, nor even
approaching you – not in all the world. I don't know if I am losing my
reason, like that poor Mrs Jt in St Brides, but I often feel that you are
with me and that I could almost talk to you. I have, at times, tried to
imagine where you all three are, and what you are doing. I would give
the whole world if you could have been with me, but there, I must be
content to look forward to some four weeks today, when I shall D.V. be
back with you again, looking into your eyes and sitting beside you. I
think I shall be perfectly content just to be with you and Elizabeth and
Ann, just sitting with the three of you and doing nothing else. I have said
in my 'letter-telegram' that I am sending you all my love and here I am,
saying it once more. You shall give some bits of it to the two girls. I have

[1]This letter and a few others written on ML-J's second visit to North America
were rediscovered by Mrs Lloyd-Jones after volume 1 was printed and I am
grateful to her for the translation of those pages which were originally written in
Welsh. As Ann had been born only five months earlier, he had to make the 1937
crossing without Bethan – a thing he vowed never to do again! See vol. 1,
p. 327ff.

been thinking of eleven years ago tonight, when we went together to Covent Garden and then back to Dilys's. I thought, at that time, that I loved you, but I had to live with you for over ten years to know you properly and so to love you truly. I know that I am deficient in many things and must at times disappoint you. That really grieves me, and I am trying to improve. But believe me, if you could see my heart you would be amazed at how great is my love. I hope you know, indeed I know that you know, in spite of all my failings. I can do nothing but say again that from the human standpoint, I belong entirely to you.

Forgive me for writing in English from this point on. This pen is not too good, and it would be easier to tell a little of the voyage in English! I had thought of writing daily, but I found that to attempt to write tended to produce a feeling of nausea. Furthermore, the weather has been so good that I have literally carried out your injunctions about sitting out on the sun-deck. Then, at night, I was too tired and heavy to think, leave alone to write. I told you in the letter posted at Cherbourg about my new room and how comfortable it is. It has been excellent. You are absolutely right about being high up on a boat. It is a great advantage. I shall go for it always in future. This boat is certainly the best that I have travelled on. She is bright and roomy and also very steady. Above all, there is practically no vibration at all. It is a real pity that she is an old boat and is soon to be broken up. I have – naturally – been comparing and contrasting her with the 'Olympic'.[1] She is altogether better. I thought much of you as we drew into Cherbourg. This time we went right in and it was most interesting to watch the people landing. Cherbourg is now a perfect harbour, and the embarking arrangements are well-nigh perfect. I walked alone on deck after leaving – it was then 10.30 p.m. – and watched the lights of land gradually disappearing. Oh! that you had been with me! I slept perfectly that night, after committing you and Elizabeth and Ann and myself to the care of God. What I should have been like if I did not 'know' Him, I do not know. I was told that the clocks were *not* to be put back that night. Actually they were, at 11.30. That meant that I got up at 7.50 – ship time – instead of 8.50 as I had intended. I made a good breakfast. I started off with figs and prunes and cream, and have continued to do so each day!!! But I only take a poached egg after that. The food, by the way, is excellent and, again the best I have found, so far, at sea. Everyone makes the same comment. Apparently, it is partly due to the competition of the French and German lines. We took deck chairs and cushions on the sun-deck, and were fortunate in getting a good position. The weather was good and as I say, has continued to be good ever since apart from very short intervals of dullness or slight mist. We have had a fairly strong breeze – S.W. – most of the way, and last night it developed into a gale. However, it has not been cold at all, and we have kept out practically all the time.

I have already read two complete books and am now into the third.

[1] The ship on which they had first crossed the Atlantic together in 1932.

They are: *God the Creator, Introduction to the Psychology of Religion* and *Theism, Agnosticism and Atheism!*[1] I mention this that you may see that I have been reading the most difficult books that I brought with me.

That is how the days have been spent, you will be interested to hear that the average per day of the ship is 580 miles. The 'Olympic' average was about 550 wasn't it? I have often thought of the way in which you kept that chart of yours. Indeed, everything you did on the 'Olympic' seems to come back to me and a thousand times have I wanted to turn to you to make some comment or other. I spotted one waiter as a man that was on the 'Olympic' in a similar capacity!

The service on Sunday was quite good as these services go. A fair number attended. One of the musicians in the Cabin class is a man from Porth. I have had several chats with him. He said this to me: 'Since I have been doing this job for the last ten years, it has been my custom to collect the autographs of film stars for my daughter. When my wife heard that you were to be a passenger this time, she said: "Now then, get the autograph of my star this time"!' Apparently she follows me about the Rhondda.[2] He knew that I was to be on board through Cynolwyn Pugh.[3] He attends the church in New York when he can. I cannot think of any other details as regards the ship that would interest you. The most interesting thing that has happened has been the fact that Mel Trotter the American evangelist who has been over for the Moody Centenary meetings in England[4] – the man I wanted to hear that Friday when you were in the Samaritan,[5] also the man who was for five nights at Westminster Chapel – is on board. You may remember that mother had said in a letter that Campbell Morgan had told her that he was to be on the boat. [He and C.M. were old friends.] I took it for granted that he would be travelling First, but he is Tourist. Well, finding that he was here, I went to the Purser and asked if it could be arranged for Dr Trotter to speak at the Sunday morning service. After consultation with the Captain, it was decided that they had better adhere to their rule not to have any speaker, but they said that they would be very glad indeed to arrange for either Dr Trotter or myself to have a service in the afternoon in the Dining Room. On the strength of this I went to speak to Trotter and told him what I had done. He was much interested. We decided

[1]An interesting reference to his reading occurs in a later letter to Bethan of May 26 in which he reports on an address he had given at a Conference on Evangelism prior to the General Assembly of the Presbyterian Church in the USA: 'I told them quite plainly the reason for the state of the church today was the substitution of philosophy for Biblical Theology, and I worked that point out. I have never been so thankful for the consistent reading which has been my custom for the past ten years'.
[2]A reference to his many preaching visits to the Rhondda valley.
[3]Welsh minister in New York.
[4]D. L. Moody was born Feb 5, 1837.
[5]The hospital in which their daughter Ann was born.

eventually that we would hold a meeting in the lounge and moreover that he would speak on Moody. He insisted upon my being his Chairman and that I should also speak. A fair number turned up, and we had quite a good meeting. That night, Trotter told me that he was celebrating his 67th birthday that very day. He is a delightful man, and most interesting. He was once a hopeless drunkard, converted forty years ago. He had known C.M. for 37 years, and Hutton, Gipsy Smith, John McNeil, and indeed everyone else, very intimately. We have had many chats together daily, and I like him more and more. Actually he has just left my room here now (10.40 p.m.). He prayed very beautifully before leaving. He has encouraged me very much, and has given me much helpful information about the Presbyterian Church. He himself belongs to it. I wish I were to be somewhere near his home, which is Grand Rapids, Michigan. But it is too far away. I shall tell you more about him again. The Purser asked me to make the appeal for funds to the various Sailors Benevolent Institutions after tonight's Cinema! I suggested that he should ask Trotter and he did it very well indeed. Tell Elizabeth that I saw the Coronation film there.

You will be glad to hear that I have not been ill at all. It is not 12.0 midnight yet, but I think I can predict safely that I shall go through without any trouble. I have not missed a single meal and I have enjoyed my food. I did not take John Phillips's patent, neither have I taken anything else. But the passage has been exceptionally smooth and easy. The Immigration people are expected on board at 11.0 a.m. and we are due to land at 1.0 p.m. tomorrow. It will then be 6.0 p.m. your time. I will leave this at this point now, and add a word after landing tomorrow D.V. Good night my dearly beloved, and may Mel Trotter's prayer for you and the children, be answered abundantly.

19.5.'37. New York.

Well, we have arrived safely and are now comfortably settled with the Allisons. We actually put our feet on land again at 3.0 p.m. The weather was unfortunately bad – misty and raining, so that we scarcely saw anything at all until we got to the Statue of Liberty! – Not your weather! – Cynolwyn Pugh and Mr and Mrs Allison met us and brought us here in their car. They live in a beautiful district and it is a fine house. I am leaving for Pittsburgh, alone on Friday morning, and am going to stay with the Vicar of Aberavon's brother. The only other addition to the list of engagements I sent you, is that I am due to preach at Philadelphia on June 3rd. There will be no further additions at all. I am now going to send you a night-letter-telegram to say that we have arrived. I have thought, and thought, and thought about you today and of the fact that I am not with you on your birthday. But I shall try to make up for it all when I return! [Return to Welsh] It is a crying shame that you are not here with me, it tends to spoil everything. Well, all my love to you my dearly beloved, again, and a kiss each for our two darling daughters.

Ever yours, Martyn.

Appendix 2

Miraculous Healing

Dr Lloyd-Jones never spoke or wrote at length on this theme, in part because, as he says in his Preface to the British edition of Frost's *Miraculous Healing* (1951, reprinted 1972), 'Henry W. Frost has already dealt with the matter in what I regard as a final and conclusive manner'. From the time that he wrote that Preface and spoke on 'Healing: Miraculous and Psychotherapeutic' (summarized in the *Christian Graduate*, March 1951) to the end of his ministry there was no change in his convictions on this subject. With Frost, he knew no *class* of miraculous healers (such as the apostles); he did not believe in the continuation of Christ's 'nature miracles' (*Prove All Things*, pp. 85–86); and he warned strongly against the error of thinking that all sick Christians will be healed if they only 'believe' (*Romans*, vol. 7, pp. 275–76; *Life of Joy*, p. 231 etc.) Dr Gaius Davies has written:

I remember one surgeon who was totally taken up with the Churches' Council of Healing telling me, in the late '40's, that the healing movement would sweep through the evangelical churches were it not for the qualified opposition of one man – Dr Lloyd-Jones. We know that, in spite of his cautions, there has been a tremendous growth of healing ministries. When I see some of the casualties of a wrong emphasis on healing, I wish that the Christian and scientific rigour of Dr Lloyd-Jones' mind had prevailed in keeping the claims and the practices of the healing ministry within a more thoroughly Christian framework.[1]

While Dr Lloyd-Jones always urged that normal medical treatment is not to be ignored (*Ephesians*, vol. 8, p. 136), he also believed in the possibility of the direct intervention of God in healing. He drew attention to the miraculous element in his Preface to the life of Pastor Hsi the Chinese evangelist, published in 1949, though also noting that Hsi's 'attitude to this was essentially different from that of many individuals and movements in this country and the USA which make much of this subject'. God may sovereignly choose to heal in a supernatural manner, and in that connection Dr Lloyd-Jones did not rule out the *possibility* of the New Testament 'gifts of healing' recurring today. He also agreed

[1] *Martyn Lloyd-Jones: Chosen by God*, p. 67.

with Frost that sometimes God gives to Christians the faith to believe that they will be healed and he therefore considered the words of James 5:14–15 to remain relevant (*Healing and Medicine*, p. 105). As a short summary of his own beliefs he had a high regard for the booklet by James II. McConkey, *Prayer and Healing*, 1973 (Box 82808, Lincoln, Nebraska 68501).

There was a measure of difference between Dr Lloyd-Jones and other members of the Christian Medical Fellowship on this subject. The tendency of these colleagues, in his opinion, came too near to excluding any expectation of the supernatural or, at least, to excluding the possibility of *gifts* of healing on the grounds of Warfield's argument that being the 'accompaniments of apostleship' they ceased with the apostolic age. *A Memorandum on Faith Healing*, published 'for private circulation' by the CMF in 1956, argued for the cessation of such miraculous gifts but although the committee which produced this Memo was chaired by ML-J he did not accept that part of the argument. As he wrote to his friend Gerald Golden on September 18, 1969: 'I expressed my disagreement with the view put in the Christian Medical Fellowship publication at the time. I think it is quite without scriptural warrant to say that all these gifts ended with the apostles or the Apostolic Era. I believe there have been undoubted miracles since then. At the same time most of what are claimed to be miracles by the Pentecostalists and others certainly do not belong to that category and can be explained psychologically or in other ways.'

In passing it is important to note that the strength of B. B. Warfield's influence in UCCF and CMF circles was related to ML-J's advocacy of his writings. It was ML-J who had done most to re-introduce Warfield's writings in England with the testimony that for conservative evangelicals probably no works have 'proved to be of greater practical help and a greater stimulus' than those of 'the greatest exponent, expounder and defender of the classic Reformed faith in the 20th century' (Introduction to *Biblical Foundations*, IVF, 1958). This explains why ML-J in his addresses to CMF colleagues made such a point of disagreeing with the Princeton divine whose influence, in all other respects, he rejoiced to see extended.

The opinion, sometimes expressed, that in the 1970's ML-J drew nearer to pentecostalist or charismatic views on healing is entirely without foundation. What he did tend to emphasize more strongly in the 1970's was that the causes both of illnesses and of healings were more mysterious than had often been supposed. Sudden healings connected with the exercise of 'faith', or bestowed by people possessed with a natural 'gift of healing', he would emphasize, are no proof of any divine authentication. As he said in 1971: 'So many factors can produce cures. Not only Christian faith, but any kind of faith, faith in "charismatic" personalities, psychological factors, intense emotion, shock, the activity of evil spirits – any one of these factors can do it' (*Healing and Medicine*, pp. 101–2). He went on to point out the danger of accepting the teaching of any healer (Kathryn Kuhlman, Roman Catholics or whoever) because of their 'results'. Judgment of all teaching is to be reached from Scripture, never from impressions made by phenomena. Miraculous happenings, of themselves, validate nothing.

Not a few of the miraculous claims current in the 1960's and 70's were found to be grossly exaggerated. Kathryn Kuhlman's *I Believe in Miracles* (1963) continues to sell today despite the critical exposure which her work received in William Nolen's book, *Healing: A Doctor in Search of a Miracle*, 1974. In Michael Green's work, *I believe in the Holy Ghost*, Hodder and Stoughton, 1975, large outbreaks of healings affecting 'thousands' in Tanzania were reported but a doctor working for many years in the areas where these miracles had occurred wrote, 'I have not come across a single case of undoubted cure' (see the valuable CMF publication which pays tribute to ML-J, though disagreeing with him at some points, *Some Thoughts on Faith Healing*, Vincent Edmunds and Gordon Scorer, 1979).

A comment is necessary on the one book on medical subjects published under ML-J's name. As listed on p. 806 a number of ML-J's CMF addresses were published as individual items. These were gathered and published posthumously by the CMF in 1982 under the title *The Doctor Himself and the Human Condition* but with a heavy abridgement of some of the addresses. In the case of his address 'The Supernatural in Medicine', for instance, approximately a third of the original is missing and this seriously weakens his case at some important points, including his evaluation of Kuhlman. With the addition of his BMA address at Wrexham, and another CMF address of 1974, the abridged addresses were reprinted for the popular market with the new, and less accurate, title *Healing and Medicine* by Kingsway in 1987. The book, in fact, contains little on healing and the addresses, while full of interest, are limited in their value by the context in which they were originally given, namely to fellow medicals who were already well versed in Scripture and on occasions when scriptural principles could be taken up more fully in discussion. If ML-J had been preparing addresses for a world readership there would probably have been some considerable differences in his emphases. Some reviewers, forgetting this, have criticized the addresses for not being what they were never intended to be.

The student will find it profitable to compare ML-J's views with those of John Owen on extraordinary gifts (*Works*, vol. 4, p. 453ff). Owen believed that we do not have 'any undoubted testimony that any of those gifts which were truly *miraculous* were communicated unto any' after the apostolic age, yet, he says, 'It is not unlikely but that God might on some occasions, for a longer season, put forth his power in some miraculous operations; and so he yet may do and perhaps doth sometimes' (p. 475). ML-J could agree with the latter statement and yet also hold, as reported by his friend Graham Harrison, 'that he had *never personally* known of an authenticated case' of miraculous healing (*Evangelical Magazine of Wales*, April–May 1986, p. 19).

ML-J would have agreed with Owen's assertion that in the New Testament record no one could 'work miracles *when*, and *where*, and *how* they pleased' (p. 467). A special God-given faith was given immediately prior to the working of a miracle without which none was attempted and there was, therefore, never a failure. Modern 'healers' have thus already departed from the Scripture when they announce their healing services or missions days or weeks in advance.

On a still more fundamental point ML-J and Owen were also agreed. It is not surprising that in all his preaching ML-J says so little on the subject of healing because he had a much more important message before him. He knew that men are eager to get rid of their diseases and disabilities 'so that they can speedily take their place in society again'. But medicine 'can only prolong man's life for a few more years'. Christianity addresses man's ultimate need which is reconciliation with God so that he can face death and eternity with composure. 'Men,' writes Owen, 'may have their *bodies* cured by *miracles* when their *souls* are not cured by *grace*' (p. 464).

Appendix 3

Dr Lloyd-Jones' Churchmanship

As in other aspects of his thinking, ML-J's approach to denominational differences was influenced by his esteem for the Methodism of the 18th century. Whereas the 17th century had seen prolonged debates over the question of which form of church government is warranted by Scripture, the 18th century awakening gave attention to the primacy of the church's inner life which, once revived, found expression in ordered fellowships of Christians but without any nationwide uniformity. In general, less insistence was placed on the need for any one scriptural pattern in external arrangements and more freedom was left for different needs and circumstances. Thomas Scott, the Anglican evangelical, summarized the views of many 18th century men when he wrote in 1798, 'I believe all parties were wrong in many things last century'.[1]

In other words, 18th century evangelicals generally believed that the various denominational groups of the previous century had all laid greater claim to a divine warrant for their positions than could be clearly justified by Scripture. This was also ML-J's view. Speaking of church government he says: 'You cannot prove which of the various theories is right. You cannot prove that episcopacy is right or presbyterianism, or independency. I have my views, but I am saying that it is questionable whether it is right to divide over this.'[2]

In Wales Calvinistic Methodism became the Presbyterian Church of Wales more by spiritual evolution than by weight of biblical conviction. In the late 1920's when ML-J entered its ministry, denominationalism rather than Scripture was the key to its unity. ML-J retained respect for some aspects of Presbyterian church government and as late as 1962 could say that 'where foundations are sure, Presbyterianism is the best form of government'.[3] But in most Presbyterian denominations the foundations were not sure and it was all too common for an authoritarian control to be exercised against evangelical congregations. It has been said that 'officially' Dr Lloyd-Jones remained a Presbyterian but, though his name was never removed from the accredited list of Welsh Presbyterian ministers, this is not how he saw it. From the pulpit

[1] *Letters and Papers of Thomas Scott*, 1824, p. 221.
[2] Sermon on 'Division – True and False' in *WR*, July 1963, p. 107.
[3] *Dylanwadau* ['Influences: The Rev. Dr Martyn Lloyd-Jones talks to Aneirin Talfan'], BBC TV Wales, March 14, 1962. This programme was in Welsh.

of Westminster Chapel on January 14, 1966, he told his people, 'I used to belong to the Presbyterian Church of Wales'.

ML-J became both a Congregationalist minister and a Congregationalist or Independent in his judgment on church polity. This is clear in his addresses on the Church which he gave in November 1954 as part of his series of Friday night 'Lectures on Biblical Doctrines'. 'Churches,' he said then, 'are to be independent but ready to have fellowship with other churches of like minded believers.'[1] But while careful to deny the opinion that 'this question of church government does not matter at all', the subject entered very little into his ministry and never formed the substance of Sunday sermons. Nor was his Congregationalism identical with what was common among the independent churches. His view of the authority of the ministerial office was more akin to old-school Presbyterianism and considerably less government was exercised by the 'democratic' vote of church meetings at Westminster Chapel than would have been normal elsewhere. Yet, unlike the Presbyterians, he was unsympathetic to the idea of church government shared in by non-preaching elders.[2] A diaconate was enough.

His position was also original on the subject of the administration of baptism. Though serving all his ministry in churches belonging to denominations of paedo-baptist belief, he early abandoned the practice of infant baptism. Yet he did not become a Baptist because he did not believe in immersion. Two authors in particular swayed his judgment against immersion; one was Charles Hodge and the other B. B. Warfield in his article, 'The Archæology of the Mode of Baptism'.[3] As a result he was to say: 'I was quite convinced that the case for infant baptism could not be proved but equally convinced that the case for immersion could not be proved.' In practice, then, he dedicated the children of believers and baptized others by sprinkling upon their profession of faith. The questions which he put publicly to those he baptized were usually taken from the Heidelberg Catechism. His views on baptism almost never appeared in his public ministry,[4] partly, I suppose, because opposition

[1] In his view of the need for association between churches by synods or other such gatherings he was particularly interested in the literature of the churches of New England (for example, the material in Cotton Mather's *The Great Works of Christ in America*, 1853 reprint, vol. 2, pp. 271–76).
[2] He was critical of the enthusiasm which many of the younger reformed ministers showed in the 1960's for the re-introduction of elders as though it would be the panacea for the existing indiscipline: 'They talk about it, they write about it, and I am quite sure many of them dream about it' (Address at the 1969 IVF Conference, *Knowing the Times*, p. 286). He also opposed any consideration of the introduction of elders at Westminster Chapel.
[3] *Studies in Theology*, 1932, pp. 345–86.
[4] The only exception known to me was his Friday lecture on Baptism on November 26, 1954, in his series on Biblical Doctrines. Although differing from Bunyan on immersion ML-J was in agreement with Bunyan on the secondary importance of the ordinance (*Puritans*, p. 399ff.).

to infant baptism would have been contrary to the trust deeds of the churches he served but certainly because of his burden to emphasize the things which all evangelicals hold in common. He especially regretted that baptism had ever been made a point of denominational identity and was critical of Baptists in that regard.[1]

From the above it can be seen that ML-J was only being half-humorous when he would say on occasions, 'I belong to a denomination of one'. He was a Puritan in his concern for church purity and in his opposition to any system of government which subverts the spiritual nature of the church, but in other respects he belonged more closely to the 18th century. Fundamental truth and its power took very definite priority over all forms of organization. The latter must always be seen as subsidiary to the former and it was failure to see this, he believed, which so often accounted for evangelicals retaining an almost blind denominational loyalty.

'The Bible is not interested in external unity', he could say in the early 1950's,[2] but in answering ecumenism he later came to emphasize that, while evangelicals were right to give priority to spiritual unity, more was needed.

The breadth which ML-J advocated in the interests of wider unity should not be confused with an indifference to any scriptural issue. He did not say that secondary things were unimportant things. Nor was he ready to make an appearance of spirituality the one basis for unity. There had to be doctrinal tests and he was therefore uncritical of the Puritan exclusion of Quakers from the unity implemented in the 1650's. The Quakers were in dangerous error in putting their subjective 'Inner Light' in the place of the Word of God.[3]

In conclusion, what was said by George Offor of another eminent Christian could equally well have been said of ML-J:

It is impossible to identify the sect to which Bunyan belonged by reading his works. He rises above all sectarian bias in his earnest efforts to win souls to Christ, and to keep them in a heavenly frame of mind.[4]

[1] At this point, as well as at others, there is a distinct resemblance between ML-J and Robert Haldane. Haldane's biographer says that 'he altogether disapproved of any external ordinance being made a bond of union instead of faith in Christ and sound doctrine . . . "it was the preaching of sound doctrine which the Lord blessed, and not particular systems of church-government"' (*The Lives of R. Haldane and of J. A. Haldane*, Alexander Haldane, 1855, pp. 580–83).
[2] *Sanctified Through the Truth*, p. 25.
[3] On ML-J and the Quakers see *Puritans*, pp. 204, 235; *Ephesians*, vol. 7, p. 266; *Romans*, vol. 7, p. 307.
[4] *The Works of John Bunyan*, 1860, vol. 1, p. 43.

Appendix 4

Dr James Packer and Anglican Evangelicalism

As Dr Lloyd-Jones' parting with such Anglican evangelicals as J. I. Packer represented an important event in his life I will here give some further references for those who wish to look at the nature of the difference more closely. Dr Packer's defence of his position over against that of ML-J puts weight on his denial of the allegation: 'Evangelicals were guilty by association of all the evils currently found in their own denominations. No matter how vigorously one opposed these evils, and sought to change them, one was ruinously compromised by them' (*Martyn Lloyd-Jones, Chosen by God*, p. 45; *Chosen Vessels*, p. 112). But this allegation, attributed to ML-J, does not fairly represent his position. His breach with Dr Packer did not come after the latter declined to withdraw from the Church of England in 1966; it came on account of the end of opposition to Anglo-Catholicism expressed in *Growing into Union*, 1970. Packer's endorsement of the Keele policy of dialogue with ecumenism led him to an increasing defence of Anglican comprehensiveness, a comprehensiveness which came to be inclusive of liberals. He writes of the 'unlovely intellectual perfectionism' of those who did not expect 'new insights' from 'non-evangelical partners' (see *The Evangelical Anglican Identity Problem, An Analysis*, Latimer Studies, 1978, pp. 11, 31–32). In *A Kind of Noah's Ark*, Latimer Studies, 1981, he argues the benefit of 'accepting Anglicanism's present doctrinal plurality' (pp. 35–39): 'The risks of the procedure (unending pluralism, constant muddle, public vacillation and embarrassment) are high; however, its benefits (ripe convictions emerging from a long hard look at alternatives) make the risks worth taking.'

Dr Lloyd-Jones continued to work in public with Anglican evangelicals who did stand apart from the drift to ecumenism and never viewed these men as being in the same position as those who were actively supporting the change.

It has been suggested that ML-J's opposition to the Anglican evangelical policy represented by the Keele and Nottingham Congresses was too largely influenced by an innate Welsh opposition to the English Establishment. But it should be noted that Anglican evangelicals themselves, if less conspicuously, raised the same objection as ML-J to the new policy over ecumenism. Dr Philip Hughes, for example, in 1967,

[793]

considered the doctrinal statements of the Anglican–Methodist Unity Commission's Interim Statement (to which Packer was a signatory) as revealing 'vicious latitudinarianism'. To this Packer replied: 'Dr Hughes' supposition that they reflect an ungodly and hazardous "desire to *make room for* theological turmoil and opinions that are in conflict with one another" . . . shows only that he has misconceived the nature of these statements, and their purpose in the Report' (*The Churchman*, Autumn 1967). Three years later the same charge as Hughes made in 1967 was repeated by the Rev. David Samuel, an Anglican clergyman who had himself been an Anglo-Catholic. Samuel believed that *Growing into Union* showed how 'the new evangelicals' had 'succumbed to the popular clamour for pluralism in belief and practice'.[1] To Samuel's review Packer again responded that what he and his co-authors had written had been misunderstood. But in whatever way the repeated 'misunderstandings' are to be explained they can hardly be put down to Welsh or nonconformist prejudice.

One noticeable thing in Dr Packer's writings on these issues is his unreadiness to use scriptural terminology in describing error in the church. He goes no further than using such terms as 'well-meant misbelief' and 'intellectual besetting sin'. Yet, at the same time, in these same booklets, he is critical of the Nottingham Congress Statement ('cracks had to be papered over'), and in a later Latimer Study, *The Thirty-Nine Articles: Their Place and Use Today*, 1984, he writes of Anglican evangelicalism: 'I hope I am wrong to suspect that with this enhanced participation has come a lessening of theological seriousness; for if I am right then however evangelical numbers grow . . . evangelical thought will hardly be able to maintain its own integrity, let alone shape the future of the Church of England.'

Other Anglican evangelicals who supported the Keele policy have spoken similarly of the decline of doctrinal emphasis and interest within their ranks since the 1960's. The Rev. Michael Saward has described 'the disturbing legacy' of the 1960's and 1970's in these words:

A generation brought up on guitars, choruses, and home group discussions. Educated, as one of them put it to me, not to use words with precision because the image is dominant, not the word. Equipped not to handle doctrine but rather to 'share'. A compassionate, caring generation, suspicious of definition and labels, uneasy at, and sometimes incapable of, being asked to wrestle with sustained didactic exposition of theology. Excellent

[1] 'Evangelical Catholicity', *The Evangelical Magazine*, November 1972, p. 15. The same author's critical review of *Growing into Union* appeared in *The Evangelical Magazine*, November 1970, pp. 2–12. The April 1971 issue of the same journal contained 'A Reply to Some Criticisms' by Dr Packer (pp. 1–10) to which Samuel responded with 'What, Then, Does Dr Packer Mean?' (June 1971, pp. 2–6).

when it comes to providing religious music, drama, and art. Not so good when asked to preach and teach the Faith or to express it in writing.[1]

If this situation did not come about as a result of the very things against which ML-J warned a different explanation has yet to be recorded.

[2]*Evangelicals on the Move*, Mowbray, 1987, p. 92.

Appendix 5

Tapes

A large proportion of Dr Lloyd-Jones' preaching ministry at Westminster Chapel is now available on cassettes through the work of the Martyn Lloyd-Jones Recordings Trust, Crink House, Barcombe Mills, Lewes, East Sussex BN8 5BJ. Agents for this Trust overseas:

United States: Bible Study Cassettes, 1716 Spruce Street, Philadelphia, Pennsylvania 19103.

Australia: Koorong Books, 17–19 Rydedale Road, West Ryde, Australia 2114.

Many sermons preached elsewhere, and addresses (including his BEC addresses), are also available from the Rev Ian M. Densham, 15 Ayr Terrace, St Ives, TR26 1ED, UK, and in the United States from Mr George Calhoun, Box 422, Mount Olive, Mississippi 42302.

Catalogues or lists of material available may be obtained from all the above sources.

Appendix 6

Bibliography of D. Martyn Lloyd-Jones

For convenience material published to date (1989) is divided into seven sections. The divisions are not, however, to be taken strictly. While all his published Sunday evening sermons at Westminster Chapel are placed under the heading 'Sermons: Evangelistic', it should be understood that there was also exposition on Sunday evenings just as there was preaching of an evangelistic nature on Sunday mornings and on Friday nights (when the expositions of Romans were given).

Individual sermons published in the *Westminster Record* and elsewhere are not here included. It is hoped that a full index of his sermons preached at Westminster Chapel, with information on their availability in print or on tape, will be made available in due course. Transcriptions of a number of these sermons await publication.

There is a reason to think that translations of ML-J's works into other languages are more numerous than our records indicate and we would value further information.

As for publication dates I have generally given only the date of the first printing. For many titles continued demand has necessitated many reprintings. *From Fear to Faith*, for example, went through 14 printings during the period 1953–79, and *Authority* 11 printings between 1958 and 1976. These titles and almost all the books listed below remain in print today.

As this list of publications is so extensive I have marked a few titles with an asterisk as suggestions where a new reader of ML-J's works might most helpfully begin.

1. SERMONS: EXPOSITION

PSALMS

[Psalm 51] See below under Sermons: Evangelistic.

[Psalm 73] *Faith on Trial* [11 sermons, 1953–54], Inter-Varsity Fellowship, 1965; US edition, Eerdmans, 1965.
Reprinted with next item as *Faith Tried and Triumphant*, Inter-Varsity Press, 1987; US edition, Baker Book House, 1988.
Dutch, 1966 (Rev. G. A. Brucks); Japanese, 1972 (Seisho Tosho, Word of Life Press); Indian (English Language), 1974 (Gospel Literature Service); Spanish, 1977 (Ediciones Hebron); Portuguese, 1983 (Publicacoes Evangelicas Selecionadas); German, 1985 (Brunnen Verlag, Basel).

HABAKKUK

From Fear to Faith [6 sermons, 1950], Inter-Varsity Fellowship. See also above.
Afrikaans, 1958 (United Protestant Publishers); Finnish, 1964 (Paiva Publishing House); Vietnamese, 1965 (Alliance Gospel Book Store); Swedish, 1966 (Swedish Alliance Mission); Korean, 1971 (Korean Society for Reformed Faith and Action); Japanese, 1972 (Seisho Tosho, Word of Life Press); Hebrew, 1974 (Church of Scotland Lit. Dept., Tiberias); Danish, 1976 (Dansk Luthersk Forlag); Chinese, 1976 (Campus Evangelical Fellowship); Spanish, 1982 (Ediciones Hebron).

MATTHEW

[Chapter 5] * *Studies in the Sermon on the Mount* [30 sermons, 1950–51], vol. 1, Inter-Varsity Fellowship, 1960; US edition, Eerdmans, 1959.
[Chapters 6–7] * *Studies in the Sermon on the Mount* [30 sermons, 1951–52), vol. 2, Inter-Varsity Fellowship, 1960; US edition, Eerdmans, 1960.
[Chapters 5–7] *Studies in the Sermon on the Mount*, reprinted in 1 vol, Inter-Varsity Press, 1976; Eerdmans, 1971.
Japanese (vols. 1 & 2), 1970/72 (Seisho Tosho); Spanish (vols. 1 & 2), 1971/72 (Latin American Committee of Banner of Truth Trust (Cochabamba)); Korean (vol. 1), 1974/75 (Chang Soo Moon); Portuguese (vols. 1 & 2), 1984 (Editora Fiel Itda); Thai (chapters 3–13),

1985 (Kanok Bannasan (OMF)); Chinese (vols. 1 & 2), 1986/88 (Seed Press); Dutch (vols. 1 & 2), forthcoming (Uitgeverij J. J. Groen); Slovak, forthcoming (Kirkevne Nakladatelstvo).

JOHN

[Chapter 17] *Saved in Eternity* [13 sermons, 1952], Kingsway, 1988; US edition, Crossway Books, 1988.

[Chapter 17] *Safe in the World* [12 sermons, 1952–53], Kingsway, 1988; US edition, Crossway Books, 1988.

[Chapter 17] * *Sanctified through the Truth* [11 sermons, 1953], Kingsway, 1989; US edition, Crossway Books, 1989.

[Chapter 17] *Growing in the Spirit* [12 sermons, 1953], Kingsway, 1989; US edition, Crossway Books, 1989.

ROMANS

Banner of Truth Trust; US edition, Zondervan (here listed in sequence of volume numbers) (Further volumes await publication.)

Vol. 1 * *The Gospel of God (1:1–32)*, 1985; German, 1987 (Bibel & Gemeinde).

Vol. 2 *The Righteous Judgment of God (2:1–3:20)*, 1989.

Vol. 3 *Atonement and Justification (3:20–4:25)*, 1970.

Vol. 4 *Assurance (5:1–21)*, 1971.

Vol. 5 *The New Man (6:1–23)*, 1972.

Vol. 6 *The Law (7:1–8:4)*, 1973.

Vol. 7 *The Sons of God (8:5–17)*, 1974.

Vol. 8 *The Final Perseverance (8:17–39)*, 1975.

EPHESIANS

Banner of Truth Trust; US edition, Baker Book House (here listed in sequence of volume numbers).

Vol. 1 *God's Ultimate Purpose (1:1–23)*, 1978.

Vol. 2 *God's Way of Reconciliation (2:1–22)*, 1972 (Evangelical Press), 1979.

Vol. 3 *Unsearchable Riches of Christ (3:1–21)*, 1979.

Vol. 4 *Christian Unity (4:1–16)*, 1980.

Vol. 5 *Darkness and Light (4:17–5:17)*, 1982.

Vol. 6 *Life in the Spirit (5:18–6:9)*, 1974; Spanish, 1983 (TELL, Grand Rapids); Japanese, as 4 items (Inochi no Kotobasha), 1985–88.

Vol. 7 * *Christian Warfare (6:10–13)*, 1976; Japanese (Inochi no Kotobasha), 1982.

Vol. 8 *The Christian Soldier (6:10–20)*, 1977.

PHILIPPIANS

[Chapters 1–2] *The Life of Joy* [18 sermons, 1947–48], Hodder & Stoughton, 1989.

2 PETER

2 Peter [25 sermons, 1946–47], Banner of Truth, 1983; Korean, 1985; German, 1986 (Bibel & Gemeinde).

2. SERMONS: PARTICULAR SUBJECTS

ASSURANCE

* *Spiritual Depression: Its Causes and Cure* [21 sermons, 1954], Pickering & Inglis, 1965; US edition, Eerdmans, 1965.
Japanese, 1983 (Inochi no Kotobasha); Portuguese, 1987 (Publicacoes Evangelicas Selecionadas); Dutch, 1988 (De Banier); Danish (11 chapters only), 1987 (Credo Forlag).

BAPTISM WITH THE SPIRIT

Joy Unspeakable [16 sermons, 1964–65], Kingsway, 1984; US edition, Harold Shaw, 1985.
Prove All Things [8 sermons, 1965], Kingsway, 1985; US edition, Harold Shaw, 1985.

REVIVAL

Revival [24 sermons, 1959] Marshall Pickering, 1986; US edition, Crossway Books, 1987.

WAR

Why Does God Allow War? [5 sermons, 1939] Hodder and Stoughton, 1939; Evangelical Press of Wales, 1986.

GENERAL

The Miracle of Grace and Other Messages [individual sermons from the period of his early ministry at Westminster Chapel, taken from *WR*] Baker Book House, 1986.

3. SERMONS: EVANGELISTIC

Evangelistic Sermons at Aberavon [21 sermons from ML-J's first pastorate, published from his fully written manuscripts], Banner of Truth Trust, 1983; Portuguese, 1989 (Publicacoes Evangelicas Selecionadas).

Out of the Depths [4 sermons on Psalm 51, 1949], Evangelical Press of Wales, 1987.

The Cross: God's Way of Salvation [9 Sunday evening sermons, 1963], Kingsway, 1986; US edition, Crossway Books, 1986.

I Am Not Ashamed: Advice to Timothy [11 Sunday evening sermons, 1964], Hodder & Stoughton; US edition, Baker Book House, 1986.

4. GENERAL ADDRESSES: PUBLISHED IN BOOK FORM

The Plight of Man and the Power of God [4 addresses in Edinburgh, 1941, plus 1 sermon], Hodder & Stoughton, 1942; Abingdon-Cokesbury Press, 1943; Pickering & Inglis, 1945; Baker Book House, 1982.

Crefydd Heddiw ac Yfory [Radio addresses, published in English in *Knowing the Times*, 1989, with the exception of 3 on 'Religion and National Characteristics'], Llyfrau'r Dryw, Llandybïe, Wales, 1947.

Truth Unchanged, Unchanging [5 addresses at Wheaton College, 1947], James Clarke, 1951; US edition, Fleming H. Revell, 1950; reprinted by Evangelical Press, 1969; Evangelical Press of Wales, 1989; Portuguese, 1976 (Editora FIEL).

Authority [3 addresses in Canada, 1957]; IVF, US edition, IVP, 1958; Banner of Truth Trust, 1984.
Portuguese, 1961 (Life Publishers International); Italian, 1962 (Edizioni GBU); Finnish, 1965 (Finnish Evangelical Lutheran Student Movement); Japanese, 1966 (Kirisutasha Gakusei Kai); Danish, 1971 (Lohses Forlag); Welsh, 1971 (Evangelical Movement of Wales); Chinese, 1976 (Christian Communications Ltd); Korean, 1979 (Word of Life Press); German, 1984 (Verlag Der Francke-Buchhandlung); Dutch, 1987 (De Banier).

* *Preaching and Preachers* [16 addresses at Westminster Theological Seminary, 1969], Hodder & Stoughton, 1971; US edition, Zondervan, 1972; Portuguese, 1984 (Editora FIEL).

The Puritans: Their Origins and Successors [19 addresses at the Puritan and Westminster Conferences, 1959–78], Banner of Truth Trust, 1987. The contents of this vol., originally published separately, are: Revival: An Historical and Theological Survey; Knowledge – False and True; Summing-Up: Knowing and Doing; Puritan Perplexities – Some Lessons from 1640–1662; John Owen on Schism; John Calvin and George Whitefield; 'Ecclesiola in Ecclesia'; Henry Jacob and the First Congregational Church; 'Sandemanianism'; William Williams and Welsh Calvinistic Methodism; Can We Learn From History?; Puritanism and Its Origins; John Knox – The Founder of Puritanism; Howell Harris and Revival; Living the Christian Life – New Developments in the 18th and 19th-Century Teaching; The Christian and the State in Revolutionary Times: The French Revolution and After; Jonathan Edwards and the Crucial Importance of Revival; Preaching; John Bunyan: Church Union.

* *Knowing the Times*, Banner of Truth Trust, 1989.

This volume contains:

(a) Reprints of major addresses already published:
The Presentation of the Gospel, 1942; *Religion Today and Tomorrow* (from Welsh), 1947; *John Calvin* (from Welsh), 1947; *Maintaining the Evangelical Faith Today*, 1952; *Conversions: Psychological and Spiritual*, 1959; *The Basis of Christian Unity*, 1962 (Japanese, 1967; Portuguese, n.d.; German, 1986); *The Weapons of Our Warfare*, 1964; *The Centenary of Westminster Chapel*, 1965; *A Protestant Evangelical College*, 1977.

(b) Unpublished addresses:
A Policy Appropriate to Biblical Faith (1954); Remembering the Reformation (1960); How Can We See a Return to the Bible? (1961); 'Consider Your Ways': The Outline of a New Strategy (1963); Evangelical Unity: An Appeal (1966); What Is Preaching? (1967); How to Safeguard the Future (1969); What Is an Evangelical? (1971).

5. GENERAL ADDRESSES: INDIVIDUAL PUBLISHED ITEMS

Proclaiming Eternal Verities, Bible Testimony Fellowship, 1936, (contains ML-J's address given at the Albert Hall, London, 1935.
'There Is But One!', Drummond Tract Depot, 1942 (contains ML-J's address, 'The Bible and Today', given at St Andrew's Hall, Glasgow, May 5, 1942).
Christ Our Sanctification, IVF, 1948 (first published in *Christ Our Freedom: the report of the Fourth International Conference of Evangelical Students*, Cambridge, 1939).
Tribute to Dr G. Campbell Morgan, WR, July 1945.
The Wider Evangelism: The Uniqueness of the Gospel, address given

[804]

during the Universal Week of Prayer, January 1946, World's Evangelical Alliance.

'The Position of Evangelicals in their Churches', WR, April/May 1948.

Address for the Evangelical Alliance during the Universal Week of Prayer, Jan 1948, *Evangelical Christendom: Organ of the World's Evangelical Alliance*, Jan–March 1948.

The Place of Law in the Divine Economy, Lawyers' Christian Fellowship, 1952.

The Annual Meeting of the Evangelical Library, 1955: Address by the President, Dr D. Martyn Lloyd-Jones and Report by the Founder and Librarian, Geoffrey Williams.

[The first of a series of informal addresses delivered at the annual meeting and published by the Evangelical Library, London. Others were published for 1956, 1959, 1960–69 and, thereafter, his usually briefer remarks at the annual meeting appeared in the *Evangelical Library Bulletin*, the last in no. 56, spring 1976.]

'Beware that Thou Forget Not', a message given at the Dedication Service of the IVF new office building, Sept. 1961, *Christian Graduate*, March 1962.

1662–1962: From Puritanism to Nonconformity: The Annual Lecture of the Evangelical Library, London, 1962.

Luther and His Message for Today [address at the conference of the British Evangelical Council, Nov. 1967], Evangelical Press, for the British Evangelical Council, 1968.

What Is the Church? [BEC Address 1968], British Evangelical Council and Evangelical Press, 1969.

The State of the Nation [BEC conference address 1971], British Evangelical Council and Evangelical Press, 1971. [It is anticipated that this item and the two preceding ones will be reprinted in one volume along with all the ML-J addresses delivered under the auspices of the BEC presently unpublished.]

The address given by Dr D. M. Lloyd-Jones at a service of thanksgiving for the life of David George Aufrère Leggett, Wimbourne Minster, 1979.

6. ADDRESSES ON CHRISTIANITY, SCIENCE AND MEDICINE

'An Experimental Study of Malignant Endocarditis', in C. B. Perry, *Bacterial Endocarditis*, 1936.

'The Christian View of the Universe'. Notes of an address at the Conference of Research Scientists, *Christian Graduate*, Dec. 1948.

'Christ and the Unconscious Mind'. Discussion and Summing up by ML-J, *Christian Graduate*, Sept. 1949.

'Healing: Miraculous and Psychotherapeutic'. Notes of a discussion conducted by ML-J, *Christian Graduate*, March 1951.

The Approach to Truth: Scientific and Religious, Tyndale Press for the Christian Medical Fellowship, 1963.

The Doctor Himself and the Human Condition, CMF, 1982; see next item.

Healing and Medicine, Kingsway, 1987; US edition, *Healing and the Scriptures*, Oliver Nelson, 1987.

Contains everything from *The Doctor Himself*, which was made up of addresses originally published as individual items by the CMF, namely: 'The Doctor Himself' (*In the Service of Medicine: Occasional Newsletter of CMF*, Feb. 1954); 'Fullest Care' (originally 'Medicine and "the Whole Man"', *In the Service of Medicine*, March 1957); 'The Christian and the State – with Reference to Medicine', 1957; *Will Hospital Replace the Church?*, 1969; 'The Making or Breaking of a Medical Registrar: A Study of Stress', 1969; *The Supernatural in Medicine*, 1971; The Doctor as Counsellor, 1972; On Treating the Whole Man, 1972.

Some of this material has been abridged from its original form. There is also an appendix containing Douglas Johnson's notes of an address by ML-J on 'The Moral Law', 1959.

To the above material there is added 'Medicine in Modern Society' (Welsh Oration for the BMA, 1973) and 'Body, Mind and Spirit' (Rendle Short Memorial Lecture, 1974).

7. REVIEWS

A. T. Schofield, *Christian Sanity*, (Marshall, Morgan & Scott), *Yr Efenglydd*, Jan. 1929.

D. R. Davies, *On to Orthodoxy*, (Hodder & Stoughton), *Christian World, Oct. 13, 1939*.

Emil Brunner, *Man in Revolt: A Christian Anthropology*, (Lutterworth Press), *Inter-Varsity*, Lent Term, 1940.

Jacob T. Hoogstra, ed., *The Sovereignty of God*, (Zondervan), *Inter-Varsity*, Michaelmas Term, 1941.

T. C. Hammond, *Fading Light*, (Marshall, Morgan & Scott), *Inter-Varsity*, Lent Term, 1942.

C. S. Lewis, *The Screwtape Letters*, *Inter-Varsity*, summer 1942.

Franz Hildebrandt, *The Man Is the Message*, (Lutterworth Press), *Inter-Varsity*, spring 1945.

B. B. Warfield, *Biblical and Theological Studies*, (Presbyterian & Reformed Publishing House), *Inter-Varsity*, summer 1952.

Cornelius Van Til, *Christianity and Barthianism*, (Presbyterian and Reformed Publishing Co), *Westminster Theological Journal*, vol. 27, Nov. 1964, pp. 52–55.

8. FOREWORDS

G. N. M. Collins, *Donald Maclean*, Lindsay & Co, 1944.

Philip E. Hughes, *Revive Us Again*, Marshall, Morgan & Scott, 1947.

Duncan Blair, *The Beginning of Wisdom*, Inter-Varsity Fellowship, n.d. [1945?].

Mrs Howard Taylor, *Pastor Hsi*, CIM, 1949.

E. J. Poole-Connor, *Evangelicalism in England*, FIEC, 1951.

Henry W. Frost, *Miraculous Healing*, Marshall, Morgan & Scott, 1951.

J. C. Ryle, *Holiness: Its Nature, Hindrances, Difficulties and Roots*, James Clarke, 1952.

V. Edmunds and C. G. Scorer, ed., *Ideals in Medicine*, Tyndale Press for CMF.

Searching the Word: A Method for Personal Bible Study, Evangelical Press of Wales, 1958.

George Burrowes, *The Song of Solomon*, Banner of Truth Trust, 1958

George Whitefield, *Select Sermons*, Banner of Truth Trust, 1958.

Robert Haldane, *Exposition of the Epistle to the Romans*, Banner of Truth Trust, 1958.

B. B. Warfield, *Biblical Foundations*, Tyndale Press, 1958.

William Hendriksen, *Commentary on the Gospel of John*, Banner of Truth Trust, 1959.

Richard Bennett, *The Early Life of Howell Harris*, Banner of Truth Trust, 1962.

J. H. Alexander, *More Than Notion*, Fauconberg Press, 1964.

David Fountain, *Contender for the Faith: E J Poole-Connor 1872–1962*, Henry Walter, 1966.

John Wilmot, *Inspired Principles of Prophetic Interpretation*, Gospel Witness, Toronto, 1967.

John Fletcher, *Christ Manifested*, Christian Literature Crusade, 1968.

Eifion Evans, *The Welsh Revival of 1904*, Evangelical Movement of Wales and Evangelical Press, 1969.

Arnold Dallimore, *George Whitefield: The Life and Times of the Great Evangelist of the Eighteenth Century Revival*, vol. 1, Banner of Truth Trust, 1970.

Mari Jones, *Trwy Lygad y Bugail*, Evangelical Movement of Wales, 1970.

Mari Jones, *In the Shadow of Aran* (English version of previous item). Evangelical Movement of Wales, 1972.

William Williams, *The Experience Meeting*, Evangelical Movement of Wales and Evangelical Press, 1973.

Peter Lewis, *The Genius of Puritanism*, Carey, 1975.

Thelma H. Jenkins, *John Bunyan's 'The Holy War'* – *A Version for Today*, Evangelical Press, 1976.

9. MISCELLANEOUS

'The Lordship of Christ' [an article], *Yr Efengylydd*, vol. 25, no. 1, Jan. 1933.

Translation of the hymn 'Rho im yr Hedd' (H. Elvet Lewis), in the *Evangelical Library Bulletin*, spring 1969.

'Know Thyself' [an article], *Spurgeon's College Magazine*, midsummer 1948.

'Y Fydd Efengylaidd' ['The Evangelical Faith', an article], *Y Cylchgrawn Efengylaidd*, vol. 1, no. 1, Nov.–Dec. 1948.

'Fy Nymuniad am 1950' ['My wish for 1950', an article], *Y Cylchgrawn Efengylaidd*, vol. 1, no. 8, Jan.–Apr. 1950.

Tribute to the Rev. Peter Hughes Griffiths in *Y Ganrif Gyntaf*, Eglwys Bresbyteraidd Cymru, Charing Cross Road, London, [1950].

A Letter to the Editor, the *British Weekly*, March 26, 1953.

'Yr Hyn a Gredaf' [Letter], *Barn*, no. 6, April 1963.

'Yr Hyn a Gredaf' [Letter], *Barn*, no. 8, June 1963.

'Os wyt Gymro . . . ' [Interview with Gaius Davies], *Y Cylchgrawn Efengylaidd*, vol. 6, 1964–65, vol. 7, 1965–66, (An English translation was published in the *Evangelical Magazine of Wales*, vol. 8, no. 4, Aug.–Sept. 1969.)

A *First Book of Daily Readings*, Epworth Press; US edition, Eerdmans, 1970; reprinted by Hodder & Stoughton, 1973; Portuguese, 1976 (Publicacoes Evangelicas Selecionadas).

'Martin Lloyd Jones' [Radio autobiography], *Y Llwybrau Gynt*, ed. Alun Oldfield-Davies, vol. 2, Gwasg Gomer, 1972.

'1950–75' [Interview with J. Elwyn Davies], *Y Cylchgrawn Efengylaidd*, vol. 15, no. 1, Jan.–Feb. 1975. (An English translation was published in the *Evangelical Magazine of Wales*, vol. 14, no. 2, April–May 1975 and the *Banner of Truth*, 141, June 1975.)

'Lloyd-Jones talks to Joan Bakewell' [Interview], *Evangelical Magazine of Wales*, vol. 12, no. 1, Feb.–March 1973.

'Truth Must Also Move the Heart' [Interview with Carl F. H. Henry],

Evangelical Magazine of Wales, vol. 19, no. 3, June–July 1980, reprinted from *Christianity Today*, Feb. 8, 1980.

Index

---

[1] In this Index I have included dates of some twentieth-century persons whose names occur more than once. Not all such dates have been accessible to me.

Index

Index

Index

Index

Index

Index

Index

Hebrides 477n
18th Century 129, 198, 344, 382n
1857–9 368–70, 380, 388, 566n
'1904' 203, 687
Rhondda Valley 204, 341, 519, 783
Rhyl 120
Richards, W. H. T. 638, 654
Richings, Juliet 630–1
Roberts, Evan 686
 Gwilym 246
Robinson, Godfrey 87
 John A. T. (Bishop of Woolwich) 439, 442, 504, 543
 W. C. 63
Rodwell, H. J. 454
Romaine, William 15
Roman Catholic/Catholicism/Church of Rome 72, 146, 173, 212, 229, 306, 334, 416, 440, 442, 444–46, 466, 470, 479, 515, 523–4, 528–9, 539–40, 542, 559, 578, 618, 622, 643–4, 649, 658n–9, 661, 665, 670, 684, 736, 787
Romania 638, 736
Rome 286, 440, 442, 466, 659
Rosapenna Hotel, Donegal 212, 275
Ross, Alex 63–4, 132
 James Paterson (Sir) 186
 Kenneth 315
Rothiemurchus 697
Rowe, Norah 100
Rowland, Daniel 242, 344, 710–11, 744, 756
Ruanda 236
Runia, Klaas 690, 692
Rupp, Gordon 448
Russell-Corsie (Mr) 420
Rutherford, Samuel 81, 264
Ryle, J. C. 53, 235–6, 327n, 345n, 556, 752
Ryley, J. 13–14, 17, 43n

Saillens, R. 358
St Andrews 276
Salvation Army 66, 126

Samuel, David 794
 Leith (1915–   ) 314, 315n, 317, 320, 529
Sanchez, Jorge 643
Sandemanianism 328n, 577
'Sandfields' (Bethlehem Presbyterian Church, Aberavon) 1, 52, 104, 204–5, 219, 248, 286, 372, 610, 702, 707, 738n–40, 742, 757, 771
Sandford, E. Noel T. 76
Sangster, W. E. (1900–60) 46, 59, 60, 189, 315n, 329
Sargant, William 641, 768
Saward, Michael 525n, 794
Sayers, Dorothy L. 131
Schaeffer, F. A. (1912–1984) 286, 585, 619, 654, 668, 759n
Schep, J. A. (Professor) 480n, 690–92
Schlemmer, André 767
Schmidt, M. 711
Schweitzer, Albert 296, 428, 444
Scofield, C. I. (1843–1921) 130, 235
Scorer, Gordon ('Jim') 759n, 787
Scotland, Church of 190, 315, 431, 438, 698
Scotsman, The 63
Scott, Thomas 717, 789
Scottish Evangelistic Council, 274–5, 518, 699, 733–4
Scripture Union (and CSSM) 89, 91, 189, 340
Scroggie, W. Graham 92–3, 109–10
Sebestyen 7
Second International Congress of Christian Physicians 519, 523
Secrett, A. G. (d. 1973) 101, 103, 134, 150, 209, 212, 248, 276, 279–80
Seddon, Herbert (Sir) 519
Sempangi, F. Kefa 395
Shedd, W. G. T. 259n, 647
Shepshed 735–6
Shields, T. T. 530
Short, A. Rendle (1880–1953) 6, 66, 69

MAJOR WORKS BY MARTYN LLOYD-JONES PUBLISHED BY THE BANNER OF TRUTH TRUST

ROMANS, 8 volumes (Zondervan in the United States)

'Dr Lloyd-Jones is a great biblical theologian but the reader will be impressed afresh by the strong experimental note in his theology.'
The Evangelical Quarterly

'It is solid fare that is presented, but with passion and fervour, with simplicity and clarity.'
The Expository Times

'The didactic style that proves so attractive in his pulpit utterances is equally effective in the written page.'
The Free Church of Scotland Monthly Record

'Over the years Dr Lloyd-Jones has given us many things but this [vol 4] is surely the best yet . . . Dr Lloyd-Jones' expository sermons on Romans are thorough, magisterial, warm-hearted, earnest and energetic.'
Church of England Newspaper

'It has been a long time since I have read a book I enjoyed so thoroughly as this [vol 3]. I anxiously await the rest of the series.'
Christianity Today

EPHESIANS, 8 volumes (Baker in the United States)

'Characteristically rich in insight, inspiration and interpretation, reflecting his long years of preaching and pastoral experience . . . Even in printed form these sermons reveal the authority of the man who preached them and the greater authority of his message.'
Church of England Newspaper

'Good old-fashioned theological preaching of this kind is a healthy antidote to the superficiality of many modern sermons.'
Scottish Journal of Theology

'If you have grown weak on shallow teaching and fuzzy application, this work will provide strength for the spiritual muscles and courage for the struggle.'
Moody Monthly

'A tremendous exposition and splendid pastoral application.'
Trowel and Sword

'Many thousands who did not share the advantage of the Westminster congregation will now have the privilege and joy of reading what they failed to hear.'
The Christian Herald

'Worthy of careful reading, study and meditation . . . Throughout there breathes a warm evangelical piety . . . Dr Lloyd-Jones' skill in setting forth some of the profoundest teachings of Paul in simple and striking language by way of word-studies, hymns and illustrations cannot easily be equalled.'   *Renewal*

KNOWING THE TIMES

One of the most important parts of Dr Lloyd-Jones' life had to do with conferences, fraternals and public gatherings where he was repeatedly asked to speak on biblical Christianity in its relationship to the present age. Many of these addresses had far reaching influence, yet of the seventeen included in this volume only six have previously been in print. This powerful book provides a penetrating analysis of twentieth century Christianity and at the same time gives vision for recovery and revival.

THE PURITANS: THEIR ORIGINS AND SUCCESSORS

'This book is hard to put down; it grips the reader and to it he will want to return again and again. None can read it without immense profit.'   *Evangelical Times*

EXPOSITORY SERMONS ON 2 PETER

'A masterly example of the kind of expository preaching in popular vein that can result in the building up of a congregation in the Christian faith.'   *Reformed Theological Review*
'A model for preaching and . . . a storehouse of spiritual benefit.'
                                                             Ministry

EVANGELISTIC SERMONS AT ABERAVON

'Early examples of that "logic-on-fire" which the author desired and commended to others. To me, their abiding value lies in the intense seriousness of the preacher. They are worlds apart from the triviality of so much evangelism today.'   Dick Lucas in *The Churchman*

OTHER TITLES BY IAIN H. MURRAY

D. MARTYN LLOYD-JONES: THE FIRST FORTY YEARS
Volume 1 of the authorised biography

'A very gripping narrative. A volume not to be missed.'
The Gospel Magazine

'One of the most significant biographies published in recent years. It will appeal to many both for the greatness of its subject and for its contemporaneity.'
Covenant Seminary Review

'A fascinating, well-written and spiritually powerful volume. There is much food for thought and fuel for prayer.'
Church of England Newspaper

'If D. Martyn Lloyd-Jones's life were a novel it would be panned by critics as too unrealistic. Because his life is a historical reality we are left to wonder at the providential energy that could have effected such an astonishing career . . . The book is an electrifying apologetic for the powerfully theologized pulpit emphases of the Reformers and the Puritans. Such an approach was in eclipse when Lloyd-Jones began his ministry. The renaissance of interest in Reformed theology is due in no small way to this man; he himself would attribute the resurgence to the sovereign grace of God.'
Christianity Today

'A fascinating book which one cannot put down until it is finished.'
Prophetic Witness

'Challenging and inspiring . . . This 381-page account of Dr Lloyd-Jones's early ministry offers much to everybody, because there was a man called by God from the cure of bodies to the salvation of souls.'
Life and Work

'Few books over recent years have stimulated me as much as this one.'
Grace Magazine

'Very profitable and exceedingly humbling. We warmly commend it.'
Gospel Standard

'Certain to be one of the major biographies of any Christian leader of the twentieth century.'
Sword and Trowel

'A well-rounded portrayal of an extraordinary man, feared by theological decadents and reviled by the conventional liberals. But wherever the doctrines of grace are revered . . . this biography will certainly be returned to time and time again.'
Book News, Welsh Books Council

'This reviewer found the priorities and emphases highlighted by this book challenging and convicting. To be true to them today would incur discipline, sacrifice and cost . . . They cut right across what many of us have come to accept in the Church.'

Prism, Scottish Baptist College

'This book is in reality a history of this century from a Christian standpoint and is as such a contribution of great value.' *Tivy-Side*

JONATHAN EDWARDS: A NEW BIOGRAPHY

'This volume, which gives evidence of devout scholarship, should replace most of the more recent offerings on Edwards and take a pre-eminent place along-side the others.'

Mid-America Journal of Theology

'Murray's splendid biography follows the pattern of Edwards' life, focussing on Edwards as a preacher, revivalist, and missionary. The author incorporates the latest findings on Edwards while offering his own interpretations. Murray is a reliable author . . . Surely Murray's fine biography will gain the audience it deserves.'

William and Mary Quarterly

'Murray has provided a most useful resource, an improved chronicle of Edwardean events. His homage to a great preacher and pastor is inspiring.' *The Christian Century*

'Murray attains a happy fusion of the story of Edwards' stormy life with astute clarification of writings which arose out of his pastoral experience . . . There are other biographies of Jonathan Edwards, but it is safe to say none more lovingly and perceptively fashioned.'

Christian Renewal

'Iain Murray's biography is a work of impressive competence and thoroughness and also candor which places in our hands an authentic portrait of a great Christian.' *Eternity*

'An inspiration not only for ministers but for all who care for the life of the church of God.' *Southwestern Journal of Theology*

'This biography of Jonathan Edwards is the one with which serious honest students of the man ought to begin.'

Calvin Theological Journal

'Murray provides a standard of excellence among Christian biographers. Edwards' life, especially as he presents it, offers a significant challenge to Christians. No one should come away from it without being challenged to a deeper commitment to Jesus Christ, a greater desire for prayer and wholeheartedness, and a stronger resolve to being a doer of the Word as well as a hearer.'

Moody Monthly

'This is my book of the year for which I have waited a lifetime . . . For long we have needed this masterly presentation of the authentic Edwards and his rich legacy to the Church.'

Australian Presbyterian Life

'Combining the piety and openness to the supernatural of Hopkins, Dwight and Gerstner with the engaging, anecdotal and analytic style of Winslow and Miller, Iain Murray, worthy successor to them all, deserves our hearty appreciation for the first full-length biography of Jonathan Edwards to appear in a generation.'

Journal of the Evangelical Theological Society